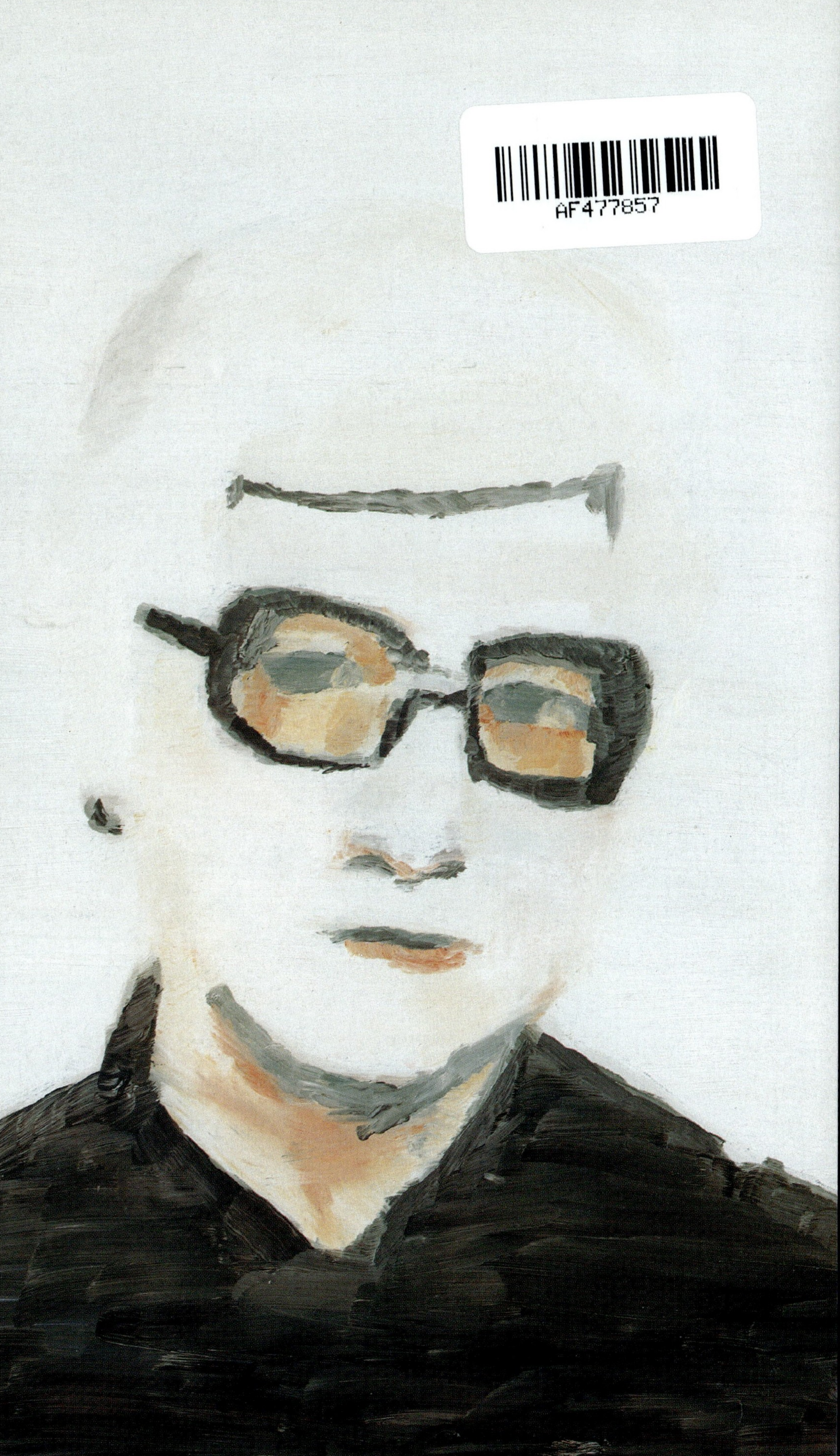

DIE PARKETT-REIHE MIT GEGENWARTSKÜNSTLERN / THE PARKETT SERIES WITH CONTEMPORARY ARTISTS

Book Series with contemporary artists in English and German, published three times a year. Each volume is created in collaboration with artists, who contribute an original work specially made for the readers of Parkett. The works are reproduced in the regular edition and available in a limited and signed Special Edition.

Buchreihe mit Gegenwartskünstlern in deutscher und englischer Sprache, erscheint dreimal im Jahr. Jeder Band entsteht mit Künstlern oder Künstlerinnen, die eigens für die Leser von Parkett einen Originalbeitrag gestalten. Diese Werke sind in der gesamten Auflage abgebildet und zusätzlich in einer limitierten und signierten Vorzugsausgabe erhältlich.

PARKETT NR. 61 ENTSTEHT IN COLLABORATION MIT • **BRIDGET RILEY, SARAH MORRIS, LIAM GILLICK, MATTHEW RITCHIE** • WILL BE COLLABORATING ON PARKETT NO. 61

JAHRESABONNEMENT (DREI NUMMERN) / ANNUAL SUBSCRIPTION (THREE ISSUES) SFR. 108.– (SCHWEIZ), DM 130,– (BRD), SFR. 118.– (ÜBRIGES EUROPA), US$ 80 (USA AND CANADA ONLY)

Zürichsee Druckereien AG (Stäfa)   Satz, Litho, Druck/Copy, Printing, Color Separations

PARKETT-VERLAG AG, ZÜRICH, DEZEMBER 2000   PRINTED IN SWITZERLAND   ISBN 3-907582-10-1   ISSN 0256-0917

HEFTRÜCKEN / SPINE 58–60: DAVE EGGERS

Cover, front page / Umschlag: The Sun as seen by the Solar & Heliospheric Observatory SOHO, May, 1998; used by DIANA THATER

in COMPOSITE SUN, 2000. (PHOTO: COMPOSITE IMAGE BY NASA/ESA)

Cover flap / Umschlagklappe: LUC TUYMANS, EMBROIDERY, 1999, oil on canvas, detail / Ausschnitt.

Inside cover page & flap / Innere Umschlagseite und Klappe: LUC TUYMANS, LEOPOLDVILLE, 2000, oil on canvas.

Page / Seite 1: LUC TUYMANS, PORTRAIT, 2000, oil on canvas. (ALL PHOTOS: FELIX TIRRY/ZENO X GALLERY)

Back cover / Rückseite: CHUCK CLOSE, EMMA, 2000, oil on canvas. (PHOTO: PACE/WILDENSTEIN GALLERY)

PARKETT   Zürich   New York   Frankfurt

Bice Curiger Chefredaktorin/Editor-in-Chief; **Jacqueline Burckhardt** Redaktorin/Senior Editor; **Cay Sophie Rabinowitz** Redaktorin USA/Editor US; **Susanne Schmidt** Textredaktion und Produktion/Editing and Production; **Trix Wetter · Hanna Koller** Graphik/Design; **Catherine Schelbert** Englisches Lektorat/Editorial Assistant for English; **Claudia Meneghini Nevzadi** Korrektorat/Proof Reading

Beatrice Fässler Vorzugsausgaben, Inserate/Special Editions, Advertising; **Brigitte Grüninger** Buchvertrieb, Administration/Distribution, Administration; **Mathias Arnold** Abonnemente/Subscriptions; **Ali Subotnick** Redaktionsassistenz, Vorzugsausgaben und Marketing USA/Assistant Editor, Editions and Marketing US; **Monika Condrea** Abonnemente USA/Subscriptions US; **Adrian Koerfer** Deutsche Verlagsvertretung/German Representative

Jacqueline Burckhardt – Bice Curiger – Dieter von Graffenried Herausgeber/Parkett Board; **Jacqueline Burckhardt – Bice Curiger – Dieter von Graffenried – Walter Keller – Peter Blum** Gründer/Founders

Dieter von Graffenried Verleger/Publisher

www.parkettart.com

PARKETT-VERLAG AG, QUELLENSTRASSE 27, CH-8031 ZURICH, TEL. 41-1-271 81 40, FAX 41-1-272 43 01
PARKETT, NEW YORK, 155 AV. OF THE AMERICAS, N.Y. 10013, PHONE (212) 673-2660, FAX (212) 271-0704
PARKETT-VERLAG AG, TANNENWALDALLEE 17, D-61348 BAD HOMBURG, FAX 06172-937 444

Kunst als Forschung

Als Chuck Close Ende der 60er Jahre einen über sechs Meter langen, liegenden weiblichen Akt in minuziöser Detailtreue malte und Gesichter, so gross und ausführlich, wie man das vorher nie gesehen hatte, war die Seherfahrung des Kunstpublikums herausgefordert. Rahmen sprengend wie vieles in dieser Zeit blieb die Kunst von Chuck Close jedoch der Malerei und ganz den klassischen Genres, Akt und Porträt, verpflichtet. Ein beharrliches Insistieren und ein Einmünden in einen langen Weg buchstäblich kleinteiligsten Vorwärtsschreitens – welch reiches Feld er in den folgenden Jahren damit erschlossen hat, lässt sich anhand dieses Bandes eindrücklich nachvollziehen. Dem Bild als Monument setzt Close dessen strukturelle Auflösung, ein Aufgehen im Raster und das spielerische Experiment gegenüber. Die Photographie bildet bei Chuck Close von Anfang an die Grundlage seiner malerischen Erkundungen. Jetzt hat er sich insbesondere der alten Technik der Daguerreotypie zugewandt (vgl. u.a. auch seine Edition für Parkett, S. 74).

Von der ganz alten zu den avanciertesten Phototechniken: Das Photo der Sonne auf dem Titelblatt stammt von SOHO, dem «Solar and Heliospheric Observatory» (ein Gemeinschaftsprojekt der NASA und ESA). Diana Thater hat es in ihrem Werk COMPOSITE SUN (2000) verwendet, und irgendwie erinnert das Bild an die «Jewels», jene kleinen Einzelteilchen der neueren Bilder von Chuck Close. Sie bilden das bunte «psychedelische» Geflecht, das man beim Zurücktreten langsam aus den Augen verliert –, um gleichsam im Gehirn die Ankunft und Komposition des übergeordneten Bildes beobachtend «abtasten» zu können.

Diana Thaters Videofilme und -Installationen greifen in den Raum und thematisieren Natur. Sie zielen auf das Bewusstsein und den Standpunkt der Kultur des Kunstpublikums. Da sie ohne Sound wie stille Bildereignisse inszeniert sind, ist ihnen die Nähe zur Malerei nachgesagt worden und eine Schönheit mit optimistischem Grundton.

In Luc Tuymans' Bilderwelt dagegen bricht immer wieder Düsternis ein. Es sind die Phantome des Wissens, die aus der Tiefe des geschichtlichen Raums ihre Wirkung tätigen. Auch Tuymans arbeitet mit Photos, mit vorgefundenen Images, die er in genau abwägenden malerischen Prozessen verändert.

Entstanden ist eine Parkett-Ausgabe mit Kunst, die unter dem Vorzeichen des Forschens steht und zuweilen Malerei entlang von physiologisch oder kulturell konditionierten Grenzen der Wahrnehmung definiert.

Das INSERT gestaltete Shirana Shahbazi, geboren 1973 in Teheran. Sie besuchte Kunstschulen in Deutschland und in der Schweiz; die hier gezeigten Photos stammen von ihren zahlreichen Besuchen im Iran.

Art as Research

When, at the end of the sixties, Chuck Close painted a reclining nude over 20 feet long in minutely detailed verisimilitude as well as faces of unprecedented size and exactitude, he challenged the visual practice of the art-viewing public. Although breaking out of the confines of convention as many others did at the time, Chuck Close still remained faithful to painting and the classical genres of the nude and portraiture. Stubborn insistence and a very long path traveled in literally the tiniest steps have staked out an exceptionally fertile land, as seen in the present volume. Close confronts the picture as monument with its structural dissolution, its de-composition and its treatment as playful experiment. Photographs have always been the starting point of his painterly excursions and have recently also become the substance of his art through forays into the venerable technique of the daguerreotype (also used in his edition for Parkett).

From one of photography's oldest techniques to its most advanced: The photograph of the sun on our cover comes from SOHO, the Solar and Heliospheric Observatory (a joint project of NASA and ESA). It appears in Diana Thater's work COMPOSITE SUN (2000) and somehow resembles the tiny particles, the "jewels," in Chuck Close's most recent paintings. These particles, in turn, form the colorful "psychedelic" weave that gradually fades on slowly moving away from the picture—in order to allow the observing, groping mind to make room for the arrival and composition of the larger image.

Diana Thater's video films and installations take possession of space for their exploration of nature. They target the art viewer's cultural standpoint and consciousness. Since they are silent pictorial events, staged without a soundtrack, they have been associated with the medium of painting and said to impart a beauty of optimistic undertones.

In contrast, twilight zones repeatedly encroach upon the work of Luc Tuymans, as he draws the phantoms of knowing out of the depths of historical space. He, too, works with photographs, with existing images, altered in precisely considered painterly processes.

The outcome is an edition of Parkett devoted to art that is informed with a spirit of investigation and at times defines painting along the borders of physiological or cultural conditioning.

Shirana Shahbazi's INSERT is composed of photographs taken during numerous visits to Iran. She was born in Teheran in 1973 and studied art in Germany and Switzerland.

Bice Curiger

4 REAL

GREG HILTY

Jeremy Deller and the Uses of Art

My remedy for drowsiness while driving—after doses of caffeine and loud music—is to pinch myself very hard on the arm or leg. Sometimes, after a long journey I have bruises. But I have never taken this technique a step further and opened the flesh on my arm with a razor blade to assert my core consciousness in face of the soporific or oppressive forces that surround me. Many people have. In Britain over the past decade "self-harming" has become, if not an epidemic, at least a significant indicator of social disaffection. Its practitioners are mainly teenagers, prematurely subject to a despair that compels them to turn the instinct for rebellion against their own bodies.

Richey Edwards was a rock star, guitarist for the Welsh band The Manic Street Preachers until he disappeared—inexplicably—several years ago. Richey's haunting beauty and the band's angry, engaged poetry made him an icon for many fans, even before a photograph was released that showed him displaying the forearm into which he had carved the words "4 REAL." Clare Rice, a fan of The Manics, wrote about the impact Richey had on her when she was at college: "Standing in front of him and looking into his eyes I felt happy for once, a connection. I didn't feel isolated. I felt among friends. I never knew until a while after that Richey cut himself and had so many troubles. This made the bond that I already felt to him stronger in my mind. I honestly thought I was the only person who felt like I did. I didn't want to kill myself I just wanted some kind of hope…" These words form part of a collection of tributes to the Manic Street Preachers gathered by British artist Jeremy Deller and presented as an artwork called THE USES OF LITERACY (1997). The title comes from a book of the same name published in 1957 by Richard Hoggart. Its author asserted that the "sensation with-

GREG HILTY is a writer and curator, and Director of Arts at London Arts.

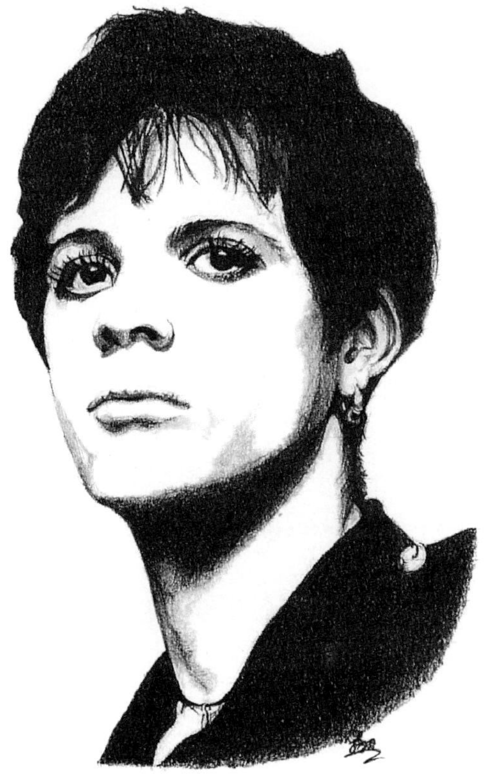

ing floral displays which people placed around Kensington Gardens in her memory. His title for the resulting photographic work, ADVANCED CAPITALISM (1997–present), distanced the image both from its celebrated subject and from his own personal relation to it. In another project, Deller was commissioned to create a series of billboard posters for an art program commemorating the Austrian presidency of the European Union. He combined contemporary photographic images of everyday epics—hysterical fans at a Boyzone concert in Sheffield, for example—and captions with a higher pedigree: in this case, Goethe's "Turbulent Bliss! Love you are this." The matches were disconcertingly apt. Deller's attention falls upon resonant phenomena that through their mass dissemination get woven into the fabric of everyday life. The coolness of his vision lets these phenomena declare their proper poetry, their underlying significance, away from the immediate noise that so often surrounds them and appears to overwhelm private experience and obliterate public discourse. The most telling example is probably Deller's best known work to date, ACID BRASS (1997). This piece was inspired by a train of thought derived from the social sciences, which recognized the profound if surprising political and social points of contact between the great northern English brass band tradition and Acid House music of the late eighties. The result, far from seeming dry or politically motivated, is an astonishing new hybrid musical genre.

Deller's choices of subject are curiously close to those of a very different artist, the late filmmaker Derek Jarman. Both share a love of the baroque and the demotic, the popular and the aesthetic. But Jarman, in his early films *Sebastian, Jubilee,* and *Caravaggio,* played on these camp dichotomies in a personal and highly romanticized way. Deller, having identified an interest in the same subject, rigorously objectifies it. For him, "art" is not the subjective frame into which the world's information finds meaning, it is closer to an objective context within which subjective meanings can find a serviceable rationale.

This surprising new role for art is epitomized in the ambitious project UNCONVENTION (1999) which Deller staged last winter in the cavernous setting of

out commitment" of popular culture was "surely likely to help render its consumers less capable of responding openly and responsibly to life." To collect the raw material for his work, Deller placed an ad in a rock journal, the *New Musical Express.* The many letters, poems, photographs, drawings, paintings, and collages he received could be seen as tragic flotsam of a culture where cultural authorities have abdicated responsibility and anything goes. Viewed with a more open mind, they could be seen collectively to represent a passionate affirmation of the power of thought and art to illuminate even desperate and lonely lives.

Jeremy Deller is drawn to sites of intense cultural expression and interface. He responds more to the mediation of extraordinary events than to the events themselves, perhaps because the former are revealing of deep-rooted structures while the latter are often indicative only of fate. After the death of Diana, Princess of Wales, Deller documented the astonish-

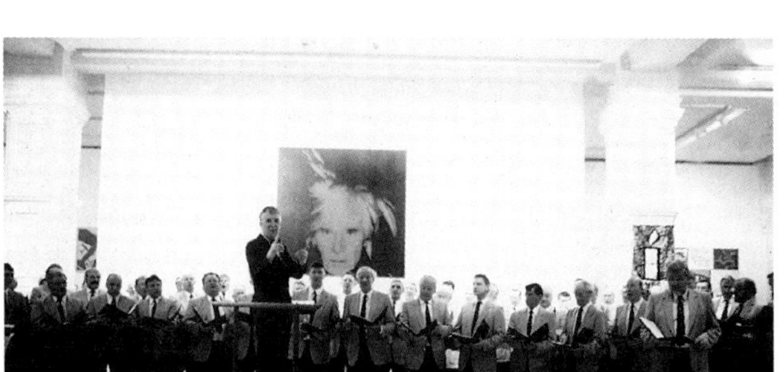

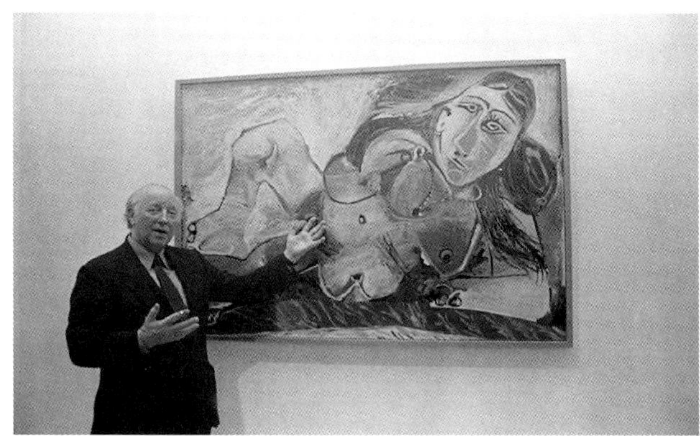

Cardiff's new Centre for Visual Arts. Revisiting his interest in The Manic Street Preachers, Deller effectively gave body to the political passions and cultural influences that had contributed to the band's distinctive vision. With the rigor and determination of a research scientist, he secured the loan of major works of art by Warhol, Picasso, Bacon, Pollock, and Munch, together with contemporary artists Martin Kippenberger and Jimmy Saville; he assembled photo-essays by Don McCullin and Robert Capa, alongside material documenting Welsh members of the International Brigade who fought and died in the Spanish Civil War; he gathered ephemera from the Situationist International and contemporaneous official photographs of the American war in Vietnam; and on the opening weekend, he invited Welsh and international organizations—including Amnesty International and the Campaign Against the Arms Trade, The National Eisteddfod and Gwent Tertiary College, art publishers and the publishers of fanzines devoted to the band—to set up stalls side by side in the center. One of the particular pleasures of the project was the way that surreal, but apt, juxtapositions arose from Deller's apparently neutral curatorial approach: a Welsh male voice choir singing "Jerusalem" beneath a Warhol self-portrait, or Arthur Scargill, legendary leader of the National Union of Mineworkers, declaiming next to a late Picasso nude. As in all his projects, Deller's own voice was to be heard only as the behind-the-scenes editor or coordinator of the voices of others, from fans to politicians, poets to environmental activists, and all kinds of artists. Deller's work has been called "democratic," which it clearly is in its inclusiveness. But his is a genuinely representative democratic approach, rather than a reductivist or homogenizing one. Writer and artist Matthew Higgs has described the event, "Each organization, each artwork, each document, each individual accorded an emotional equanimity, unburdened by the usual hierarchies, the usual distinctions—between 'high' and 'low' cultural artifacts—that art galleries so commonly reinforce."

Jeremy Deller's latest work—the most recent of a number of collaborations produced over the years with fellow London artist Alan Kane—is AN INTRODUCTION TO FOLK ARCHIVE (1999–2000), presented within the group exhibition "Intelligence" at Tate Britain in summer 2000. Although it is a collaboration, and more of an ongoing project than a defined "work," FOLK ARCHIVE shares an organizational premise with many of Deller's other initiatives: the idea of setting up a structure and letting others fill it, with considerable respect and openness of approach. The core of the archive was gathered during several months of travel across Britain by Deller and Kane, during which they either documented or collected manifestations of folk art ranging from small and highly individual physical creations—a small house constructed of kitchen sponges, customized mobile phones and cigarettes—to video records of community events which have occurred for hundreds of years—like the remarkable Crab Fair at Egremont. Some events, like the Wray Scarecrow Festival in which the inhabitants of this small town create and display in their front gardens scarecrows representing topical political or cultural figures, are in fact recent innovations although they exude an aura of tradition. The types of projects recorded fall into fairly clear categories, including those that in-

vert power or subvert values; those that lock into an established tradition but from a contemporary perspective; those that stake a personal claim to popular territory either by customizing objects or obsessively enacting rituals.

The FOLK ARCHIVE project acknowledges the similarities and reliance on longer-standing and more academic studies of the same territory—the work over thirty years of one Doc Rowe, in particular. It also makes explicit the idea that it represents a process of acknowledging rather than a formal program of archiving the vast range of "folk art": the Web site—www.folkarchive.co.uk—and P. O. Box are now the main sites of new additions to the archive, so the power to define the work resides with those who already have assumed the power to make it. What Deller and Kane achieve through the format and the context of this new project, and what Deller consistently demonstrates in his solo work, is a profound sense that the wider cultural web surrounding art and the positive responses of its audiences are not just context and commentary for art—they're the real thing itself.

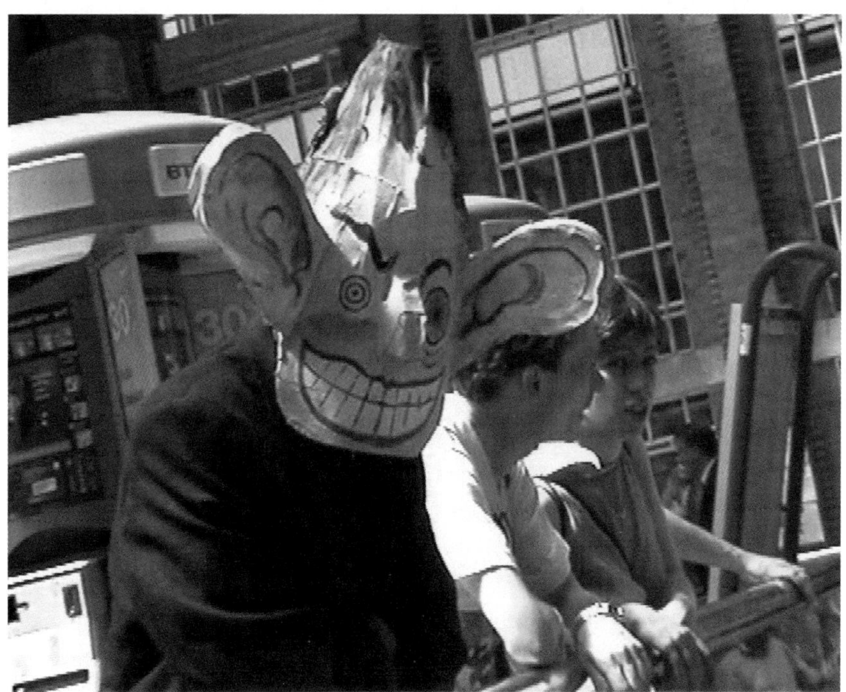

JEREMY DELLER & ALAN KANE, AN INTRODUCTION TO FOLK ARCHIVE (1999–2000), TONY BLAIR MASK, demonstrator in the City of London, Summer 1999 / EINFÜHRUNG INS VOLKSARCHIV, TONY-BLAIR-MASKE eines Londoner Demonstranten.

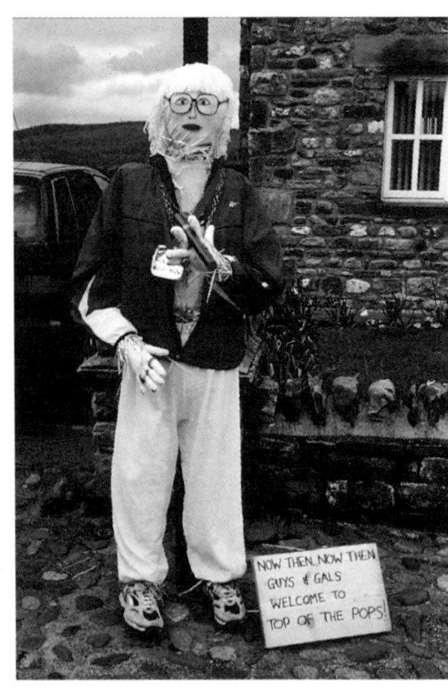

4 REAL

GREG HILTY

Jeremy Deller und die Anwendungen der Kunst

Einmal abgesehen von einer Menge Koffein und lauter Musik, besteht mein Mittel gegen das Einschlafen am Steuer darin, mich tüchtig in Arme oder Beine zu kneifen. Nach längeren Reisen habe ich manchmal blaue Flecken. Aber ich habe diese Technik nie so weit getrieben, dass ich mir am Arm mit der Rasierklinge eine Fleischwunde zugefügt hätte, nur um mich angesichts von bedrohlich einschläfernden, lähmenden Einflüssen meines vollen Bewusstseins zu versichern. Viele Leute tun das aber. In Grossbritannien ist Selbstverstümmelung wenn nicht zu einer Epidemie, so doch zu einem bedeutenden Indikator gesellschaftlichen Unbehagens geworden. Betroffen sind hauptsächlich Teenager, welche zu schnell einer Verzweiflung nachgeben, die sie dazu treibt, ihre instinktive Rebellion gegen den eigenen Körper zu richten.

Richey Edwards war ein Rockstar und Gitarrist der Walisischen Band *Manic Street Preachers*, bis er vor einigen Jahren auf unerklärliche Weise verschwand. Richeys berückende Schönheit und die zornig engagierten Liedtexte der Band hatten ihn für viele Fans zum Idol werden lassen, und zwar schon bevor jenes Photo im Umlauf war, auf welchem er seinen Unterarm mit den eingeritzten Worten «4 REAL» herzeigt.

GREG HILTY ist Publizist und Kurator und Director of Arts bei London Arts.

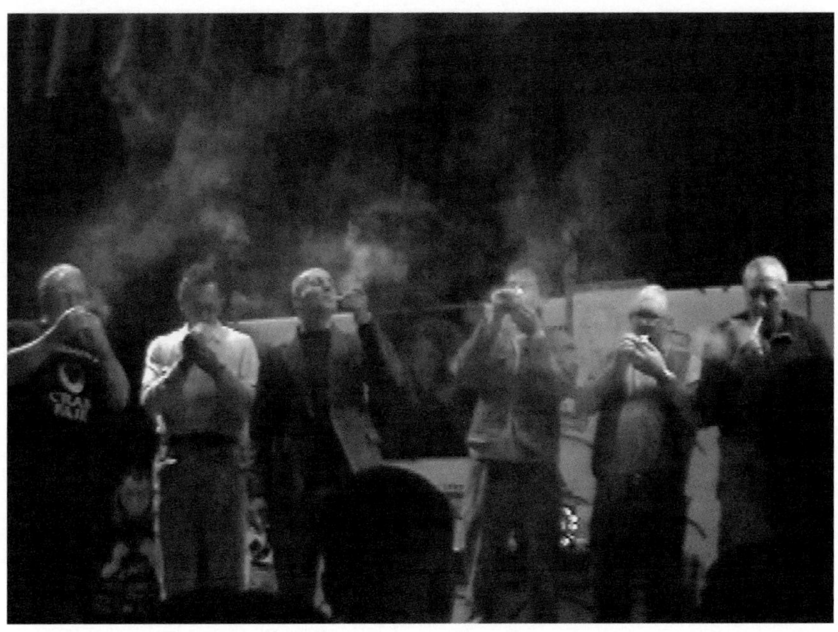

Page / Seite 22: THE WHITELEY FAMILY, JIMMY SAVILLE SCARECROW, 2000 / JIMMY-SAVILLE-VOGELSCHEUCHE.

JEREMY DELLER & ALAN KANE, AN INTRODUCTION TO FOLK ARCHIVE (1999–2000),
PIPE SMOKING COMPETITION, Egremont Crab Fair, Cumbria, 1999 /
EINFÜHRUNG INS VOLKSARCHIV, PFEIFENRAUCHWETTKAMPF, Krabbenmarkt Egremont.

Clare Rice, ein Fan der Band, beschreibt, welchen Eindruck Richey in ihrer College-Zeit auf sie gemacht hatte: «Als ich vor ihm stand und in seine Augen schaute, fühlte ich mich für einmal glücklich, da war eine Verbindung. Ich war nicht mehr einsam. Ich hatte das Gefühl unter Freunden zu sein. Ich erfuhr erst später davon, dass Richey sich diese Schnitte zufügte und so viele Probleme hatte. Dadurch fühlte ich mich ihm aber nur noch mehr verbunden, als ich es ohnehin schon war. Ich glaubte aufrichtig, die Einzige zu sein, die so fühlte. Ich wollte mich nicht umbringen, ich wollte nur ein bisschen Hoffnung...» Der Text gehört zu einer Sammlung von Texten rund um die *Manic Street Preachers*, die der britische Künstler Jeremy Deller gesammelt und als Kunstwerk unter dem Titel THE USES OF LITERACY (Die Anwendungen des Lesens und Schreibens, 1997) ausgestellt hat. Der Titel ist dem gleichnamigen Buch aus dem Jahr 1957 von Richard Hoggart entlehnt. Der Autor hielt darin fest,

dass die «unverbindliche Gefühlswelt» der Populärkultur ohne Zweifel die Fähigkeit ihrer Konsumenten einschränke, offen und verantwortungsbewusst mit dem Leben umzugehen. Um an das Rohmaterial für seine Arbeit zu kommen, schaltete Deller eine Anzeige im *New Musical Express*, einer Zeitschrift für Rockmusik. Die vielen Briefe, Gedichte, Photos, Zeichnungen, Gemälde und Collagen, die man ihm darauf zusandte, könnte man als trauriges Strandgut einer Kultur auffassen, in der die kulturellen Autoritäten jegliche Haftung ablehnen und deshalb alles möglich ist. Aus einem etwas weniger engherzigen Blickwinkel könnte man aber auch sagen, dass sie der kollektive Ausdruck und eine leidenschaftliche Bestätigung der Tatsache sind, dass das Denken und die Kunst auch in ein verzweifeltes und einsames Leben Licht zu bringen vermögen.

Jeremy Deller fühlt sich zu Orten intensiven kulturellen Ausdrucks und Austauschs hingezogen. Dabei beschäftigt er sich mehr mit der Vermittlung aussergewöhnlicher Ereignisse als mit den Ereignissen selbst, vielleicht weil die Erstere tief verwurzelte Strukturen sichtbar macht, während Letzteren oft nur ein Zufall zugrunde liegt. Nach dem Tod von Diana, Prinzessin von Wales, dokumentierte Deller das erstaunliche Blumenmeer aus Sträussen und Buketts, welche die Leute rund um Kensington Gardens zu ihrem Gedächtnis niederlegten. Der Titel der daraus entstandenen Photoarbeit, ADVANCED CAPITALISM (Fortgeschrittener Kapitalismus, 1997 bis heute), schuf eine Distanz zwischen dem Bild und seinem berühmten Gegenstand, aber auch zwischen dem Bild und des Künstlers persönlichem Verhältnis dazu. Im Rahmen eines anderen Projekts wurde Deller damit beauftragt, eine Serie von Grossplakaten für ein Kunstprogramm zu schaffen, das an die österreichische Präsidentschaft der Europäischen Union erinnern sollte. Er kombinierte Photos alltäglicher Begebenheiten – zum Beispiel hysterische Fans an einem Boyzone-Konzert in Sheffield – mit Bildlegenden höherer Art, in diesem Fall Goethes «Glück ohne Ruh, Liebe, bist du!». Die Paarungen waren geradezu verstörend gelungen. Dellers Aufmerksamkeit gilt bedeutsamen Erscheinungen, die durch ihre massenhafte Verbreitung ins Alltägliche Eingang finden. Sein kühler Blick macht die solchen Phänomenen eigene Poesie sichtbar, ihre verborgene Bedeutung jenseits des Lärms, der sie umgibt und jede persönliche Erfahrung zu überfahren sowie jede öffentliche Diskussion im Keim zu ersticken droht. Das deutlichste Beispiel ist wohl Dellers bisher

bekanntestes Werk, ACID BRASS (1997). Die Arbeit entsprang einem aus einer soziologischen Studie entliehenen Gedanken, der auf die tiefen, wenn auch überraschenden politischen und gesellschaftlichen Berührungspunkte zwischen der grossen Blechmusiktradition Nordenglands und der Acid-House-Musik der späten 80er Jahre hinweist. Daraus entstand alles andere als eine trockene oder vordergründig politisch motivierte Sache, sondern ein erstaunliches neues hybrides Musikgenre.

Dellers Themen kommen denen eines ganz anders gearteten Künstlers verblüffend nahe, nämlich denen des verstorbenen Filmemachers Derek Jarman. Beide verbindet die Liebe zum Barocken und Volksnahen, zum Populären und Ästhetischen. Aber Jarman spielte in seinen frühen Filmen, *Sebastian*, *Jubilee* und *Caravaggio*, mit diesen attraktiv-banalen Gegensatzpaaren auf sehr persönliche, stark romantisierende Weise. Deller jedoch objektiviert dasselbe Thema gnadenlos, sobald ihm sein Interesse dafür bewusst geworden ist. Für ihn ist Kunst kein subjektiver Rahmen, in welchem die Informationen der Welt zu ihrer Bedeutung finden, sondern eher ein objektiver Kontext, in dem subjektive Bedeutungen auf ihren rationalen Grund stossen können.

Ein Beispiel für diese erstaunliche neue Rolle der Kunst liefert das ehrgeizige Projekt UNCONVENTION (Unkonvention, 1999), das Deller letzten Winter vor der höhlenartigen Kulisse des neuen Centre for Visual Arts in Cardiff zeigte. Er kam darin nochmals auf sein Interesse an den *Manic Street Preachers* zurück

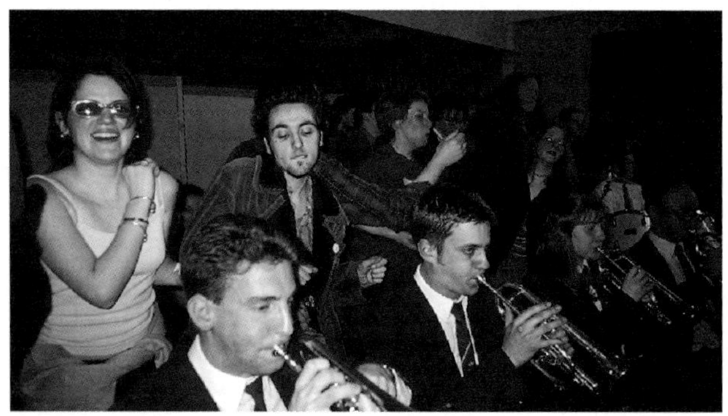

ACID BRASS PERFORMANCE, Cardiff, 1998.

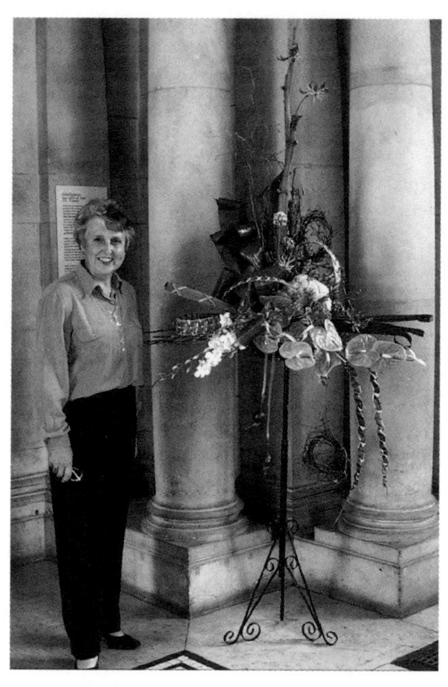

und stellte auf eindrückliche Weise die politischen und kulturellen Einflüsse dar, welche die spezifische Botschaft dieser Band prägten. Mit der Radikalität und Entschlossenheit eines Wissenschaftlers schaffte er es, wichtige Werke von Warhol, Picasso, Bacon, Pollock und Munch als Leihgaben zu erhalten, die er dann zusammen mit zeitgenössischen Künstlern wie Martin Kippenberger und Jimmy Saville zeigte; er kombinierte Photo-Essays von Don McCullin und Robert Capa mit Dokumentationsmaterial über walisische Mitglieder der Internationalen Brigade, die im Spanischen Bürgerkrieg gekämpft hatten und gefallen waren; er sammelte Drucksachen der Situationistischen Internationalen und zeitgenössische Photos aus dem Vietnamkrieg; und am Eröffnungswochenende lud er walisische und internationale Organisationen – darunter auch Amnesty International, die Liga gegen den Waffenhandel, The National Eisteddfod[1] und das Gwent Tertiary College, Kunstverlage sowie die Verleger der Fan-Magazine, die sich mit der Band beschäftigten – dazu ein, im Zentrum der Ausstellung Stände aufzustellen. Besonders schön an diesem Projekt war, wie sich aus Dellers scheinbar neutraler kuratorischer Haltung surreale, aber gelungene Gegenüberstellungen ergaben: Ein walisischer Männerchor singt unter einem Selbstporträt von Warhol «Jersualem», oder Arthur Scargill,

legendärer Führer der Minenarbeitergewerkschaft, hält eine Rede neben einem späten Frauenakt von Picasso. Wie in all seinen Projekten war Dellers eigene Stimme nur als Regisseur hinter der Bühne wahrnehmbar oder als Koordinator der Stimmen all der anderen, von den Fans über Politiker, Dichter, Umweltaktivisten bis zu allen möglichen Künstlern. Man hat Dellers Arbeit «demokratisch» genannt, was sie dank ihres offenen, integrierenden Charakters zweifellos ist. Aber sein Vorgehen entspricht einer zutiefst repräsentativ-demokratischen Haltung und hat nichts Simplifizierendes oder Gleichmacherisches. Der Schriftsteller und Künstler Matthew Higgs hat das Ereignis wie folgt beschrieben: «Jede Organisation, jedes Kunstwerk, jedes Dokument, jedes Individuum wird gleichmütig und neutral vorgestellt, frei von den üblichen Hierarchien und Unterscheidungen – etwa zwischen E- und U-Produkten –, die Kunstmuseen in der Regel streng beachten.»

Jeremy Dellers jüngste Arbeit, AN INTRODUCTION TO FOLK ARCHIVE (Einführung ins Volksarchiv, 1999–2000), ist zugleich die jüngste einer Reihe von Collaborationen mit seinem Londoner Künstlerkollegen Alan Kane und wurde im Rahmen der Gruppenausstellung «Intelligence» im Sommer 2000 in der Tate Britain Gallery gezeigt. Obwohl es sich um ein Gemeinschaftswerk handelt, das eher ein laufendes Projekt als ein begrenztes «Werk» ist, hat FOLK ARCHIVE eine organisatorische Voraussetzung mit vielen anderen von Dellers Unternehmungen gemeinsam: nämlich die Idee einen strukturellen Rahmen vorzugeben und ihn von anderen ausfüllen zu lassen sowie die dazu erforderliche respektvolle und offene Haltung. Das Kernstück des Archivs ist das Resultat monatelanger Reisen der beiden Künstler quer durch Grossbritannien. In dieser Zeit dokumentierten oder sammelten Deller und Kane Volkskunst, und zwar von kleinen, sehr individuellen und physisch greifbaren Dingen – ein kleines Haus aus Schwämmen, wie man sie zum Putzen in der Küche verwendet, individuell hergerichtete Mobiltelefone oder Zigarettenpäckchen – bis zu Videoaufnahmen von Gemeindeanlässen, die seit Jahrhunderten so stattfinden wie der bemerkenswerte Krabbenmarkt in Egremont. Einige Bräuche, wie das Wray Scarecrow Festival, wo die Einwohner des kleinen Städtchens Wray in ihren Vorgärten Vogelscheuchen aufstellen, die politische oder kulturelle Figuren und Themen darstellen, sind allerdings neueren Datums, obwohl sie sich einen traditionellen Anschein geben. Die Art der aufgenommenen Projekte lässt sich ziemlich klaren Kategorien zuordnen, einschliesslich derer, die Machtverhältnisse oder Werte umkehren; jener, die Teil einer alten Tradition sind, aber einen zeitgenössischen Bezug herstellen; jener, die einen persönlichen Anspruch auf populäres Kulturgut erheben, indem sie Gegenstände nach ihrem persönlichen Geschmack herrichten (customizing) oder begeistert Rituale befolgen.

Das FOLK ARCHIVE-Projekt gesteht die Ähnlichkeit mit schon länger bestehenden, wissenschaftlicheren Studien desselben Gebietes und seine Abhängigkeit von diesen ohne weiteres ein – insbesondere die Bezugnahme auf die mehr als 30-jährige Tätigkeit eines gewissen Doc Rowe. Es wird auch klargestellt, dass es sich eher um einen Anerkennungsprozess als um ein formelles Archivierungsprogramm des riesigen Gebietes der «Volkskunst» handelt. Die meisten Ergänzungen zum Archiv erfolgen heute über die Website – www.folkarchive.co.uk – und das Postfach, also liegt die Macht das Werk zu definieren ganz bei denen, die sich bereits angemasst haben es ins Leben zu rufen. Was Deller und Kane durch Format und Kontext dieses neuen Projekts erreichen und was Deller auch in seinen Einzelarbeiten immer wieder vorführt, ist das grundlegende Gefühl, dass das weiter gefasste Kulturnetz rund um die Kunst und die lebhafte Reaktion des Publikums auf dieses nicht bloss einen Kontext und Kommentar zur Kunst darstellen, nein: Sie sind die eigentliche Kunst.

(Übersetzung: Susanne Schmidt)

1) Organisiert das gleichnamige alljährliche, mit einem Wettbewerb verbundene Festival Walisischer Dichter und Musiker.

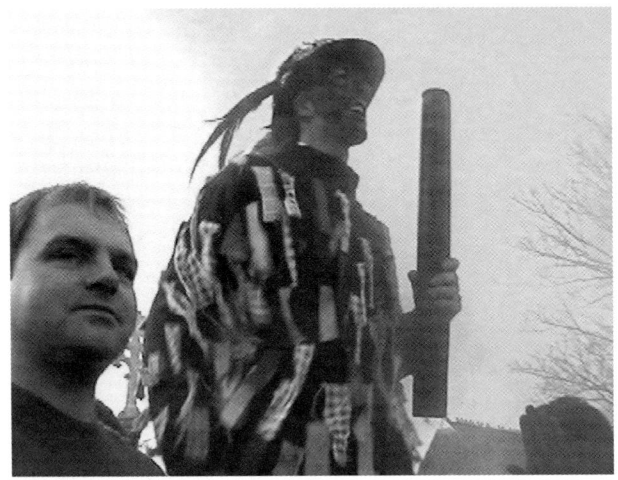

JEREMY DELLER & ALAN KANE, AN INTRODUCTION TO FOLK ARCHIVE (1999–2000), THE FOOL GIVING HIS SPEECH, The Haxey Hood, Haxey, South Yorkshire / EINFÜHRUNG INS VOLKSARCHIV, DER NARR HÄLT SEINE ANSPRACHE, Volksbrauch in Haxey, South Yorkshire.

Chuck Close

born 1940 in Monroe, Washington,
lives and works in Bridgehampton and New York.
geboren 1940 in Monroe, Washington,
lebt und arbeitet in Bridgehampton und New York.

Diana Thater

born 1962 in San Francisco, California,
lives and works in Los Angeles, California.
geboren 1962 in San Francisco, Kalifornien,
lebt und arbeitet in Los Angeles, Kalifornien.

Luc Tuymans

geboren 1952 in Mortsel, Belgien,
lebt und arbeitet in Antwerpen.
born 1952 in Mortsel, Belgium,
lives and works in Antwerp.

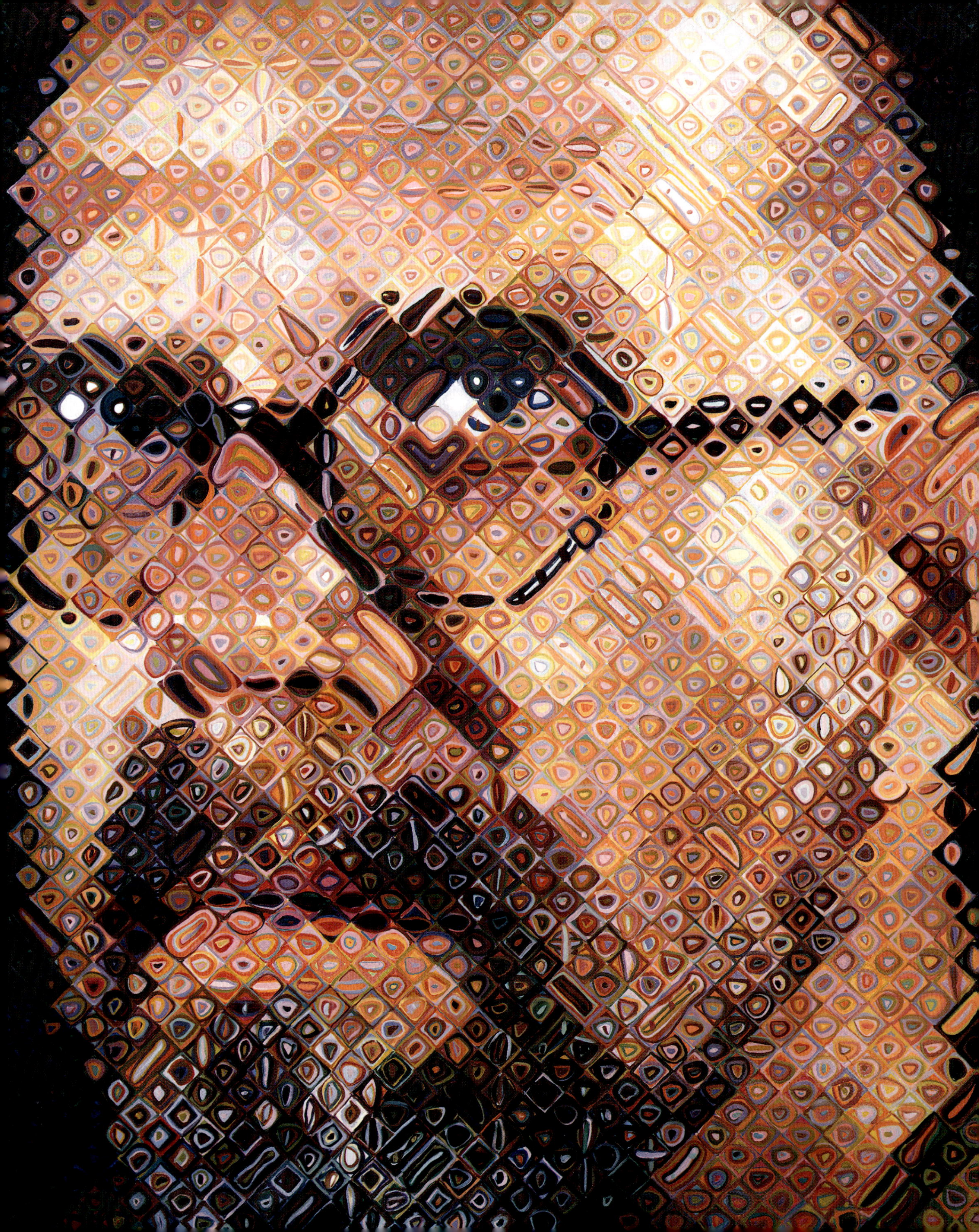

CHUCK CLOSE, SELF-PORTRAIT, 1997, oil on canvas, 102 x 84", work in progress / SELBSTPORTRÄT, Öl auf Leinwand, 259,1 x 213,4 cm, in unvollendetem Zustand. (PHOTO: ELLEN PAGE WILSON/PACE WILDENSTEIN GALLERY)

DISTANCES AND FACES OF THE MOON

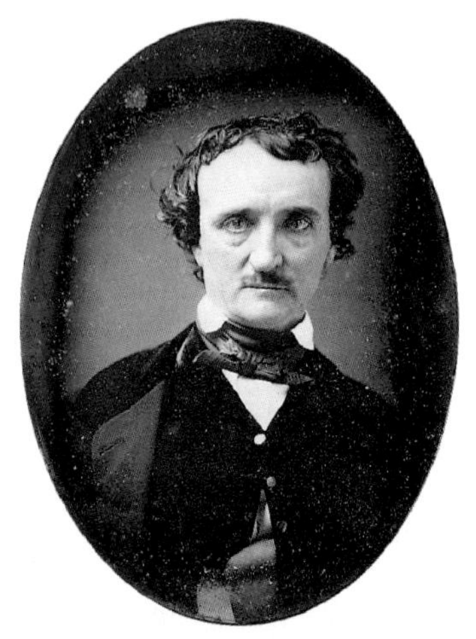

FRANCINE PROSE

In the issue of January 15, 1840, Edgar Allan Poe tried to make the readers of *Alexander's Weekly Messenger* somehow comprehend "the miraculous beauty" of an amazing new invention, the daguerreotype and what Poe called "photogenic drawing":

Perhaps, if we imagine the distinctness with which an object is reflected in a positively perfect mirror, we come as near the reality as by any other means. For, in truth, the daguerreotype plate is infinitely (we use the term advisedly), is infinitely more accurate in its representation than any painting by human hands. If we examine a work of ordinary art, by means of a powerful microscope, all traces of resemblance to nature will disappear—but the closest scrutiny of a photogenic drawing discloses only a more absolute truth, a more perfect identity of aspect with the thing represented.

FRANCINE PROSE is a writer who lives in New York. Her most recent novel is *Blue Angel* (Harper-Collins, 2000).

Chuck Close is not the first artist you might think of in conjunction with Edgar Allan Poe, but if you think just a minute more, you might wonder why you hadn't. The work of both men demonstrates a certain abiding interest in balancing on that high wire between the grotesque and the familiar, in the wonders and the mechanics of perception, in bizarre or radical technology, and in the physical and psychic spaces that separate us, one from the other. For poor Poe, it was often a nightmare space, a walled-in crypt, a room closing in, the hull of a ship, while for the more genial and expansive Close, it is more often the span across a room, or the more intimate distance that we think of as face-to-face.

So perhaps it's unsurprising that, a hundred and sixty years after he wrote his daguerreotype piece, Poe should have done such an excellent job of articulating at least some part of what Chuck Close is doing in his new photographic work, principally daguerreo-

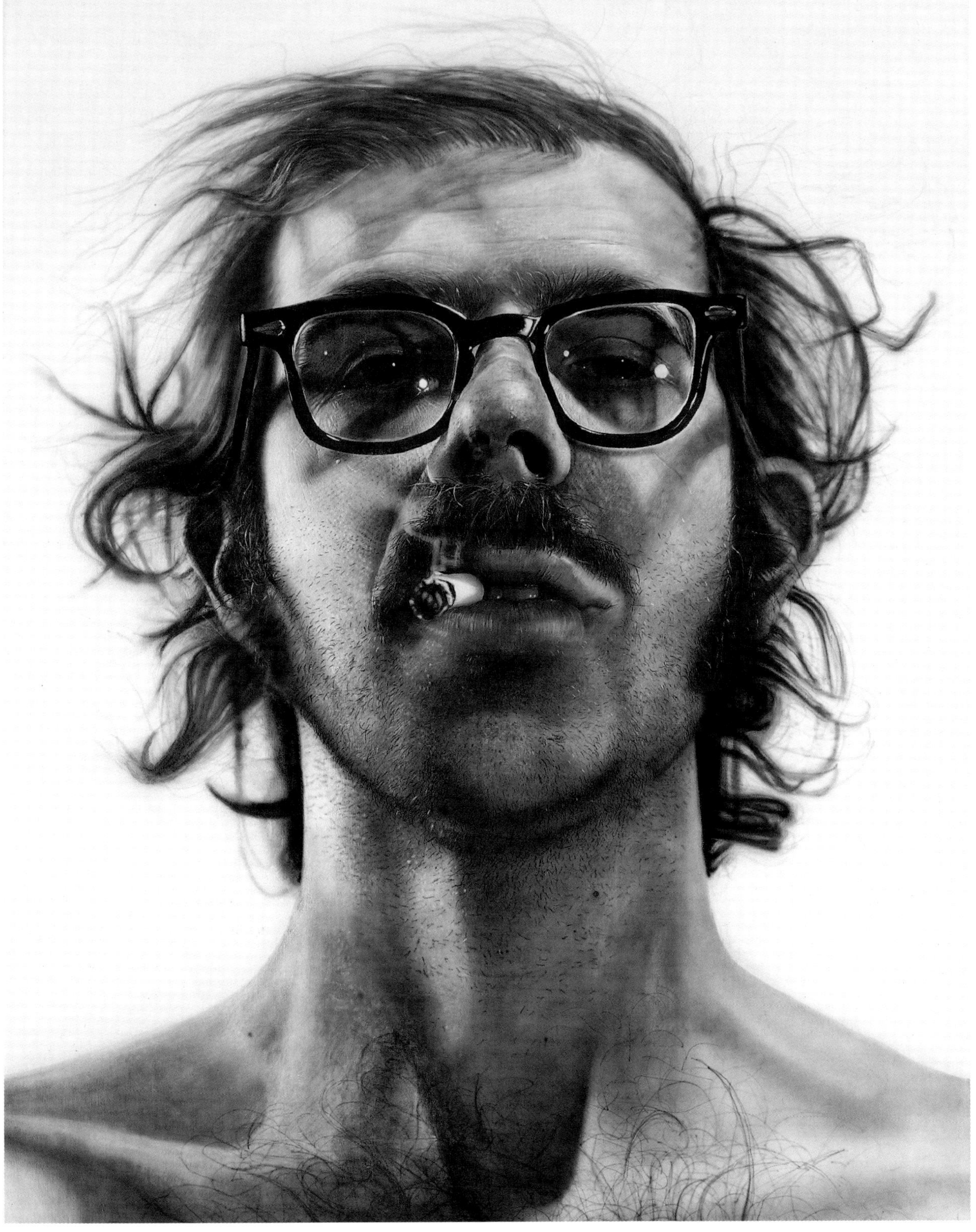

CHUCK CLOSE, BIG SELF-PORTRAIT, 1967–68, acrylic on canvas, 107½ x 83½" / GROSSES SELBSTPORTRÄT, Acryl auf Leinwand, 273,1 x 212,1 cm.

types and large ink-jet iris prints. Once more, as in his paintings, Close is exploring the distance at which the most "absolute truth" will be disclosed, the strategies of revealing a "more perfect identity of aspect."

If Poe believed that microscopic scrutiny would eliminate all resemblance to nature, he should have seen Close's more recent large painted portraits. No powerful microscope is required: stand two feet from the painting, and the huge recognizable face you'd seen from across the gallery turns into nursery-colored little worms and zillions of wacky painted squares like the results of some intelligence test for extraterrestrial preschoolers.

On first viewing, the daguerreotypes seem like the opposite of Close's recent paintings: small vs. large, intimate vs. public, a severely limited spectrum vs. that goofy generous rainbow. The paintings chase you further and further back if you want to see what they represent; the daguerreotypes draw you closer, and make you adjust your position until you are standing just exactly just so. Clearly, what the two modes of working have in common is the ability to make their viewers conscious of the split second at which an inchoate, vaguely familiar blur resolves into a more or less clear picture, and of the distance from the work needed to make this happen. Not counting those paintings done on revolving drums and sculptures done in the eye of a needle, the daguerreotype implies what is perhaps the most limited range of where you must stand in order to see the image and not the other aspects—the mirror, the blur—that the plate can offer. The lighting has to be near perfect, it helps if you wear black.

Meanwhile, Chuck Close raises the ante on the entire nineteenth century, when the daguerreotype portrait most commonly confined itself to representations of the face, most often wearing the gloomy mask that the face puts on when it is forced to remain motionless for longer than it wants. (Among the new works is a portrait of Close in which he looks simultaneously haunted and wise, like the faces in so many of Nadar's portraits of artists and writers.)

What ratchets everything up a notch, gives it a higher charge, is the fact that Close's focus—the lens—has moved downward from the head, aban-

doned those composed nineteenth-century faces, with every hair in place for the nude and unmistakably twenty first-century torso. The subjects represent an enormous range of body type, color, shape, age, etc. And it's a little startling (what would Poe have said?) that—given the narrow range of what our culture finds physically attractive or repulsive—most of these bodies (old, young, fat, thin, black, white) look good, and are pleasing and interesting to look at. The images are beautiful in ways that are difficult to quantify, to describe, and to predict.

Also they are wonderfully permissive in allowing us to contemplate the effect of time, not only the perpetually fascinating workings of the passing decades on the human body but the operation of history on our basic sense of perception. Many of these images deliver a particular shock generated by the fact that the daguerreotype establishes a set of nineteenth-century visual responses and psychological expectations, which are then subverted by the bodies Chuck Close has chosen—tattooed and pierced in ways that instantly return us to the utterly present moment. Though in some cases this process is not instant, given these daguerreotypes' propensity for using shadows to transform modern bodies into the wasp-waisted ideal of the Victorian era. The result is a series of small shocks, of perception followed by doubt followed by adjustment and correction: Could that really have been a navel ring we saw in that old-fashioned photo?

Like the daguerreotypes, the large-format ink-jet photographs effectively move the viewer, though what's being readjusted in this case is not our physical position so much as our psyche. The photographs of actors (Charles Durning, Stockard Channing, Julie Harris) provide the very opposite of the publicity shot, and again we are forced to pay attention to the speed and the mechanism by which we recognize—are still able to recognize—the human denuded of the familiar—in these cases, of the accustomed glamorous trappings. These are subjects who are used to projecting themselves, to taking on and projecting other selves. But in these extreme and unusual close-ups, what are they projecting? Are we right or wrong in supposing that they are revealing something close to their true selves in irreducible

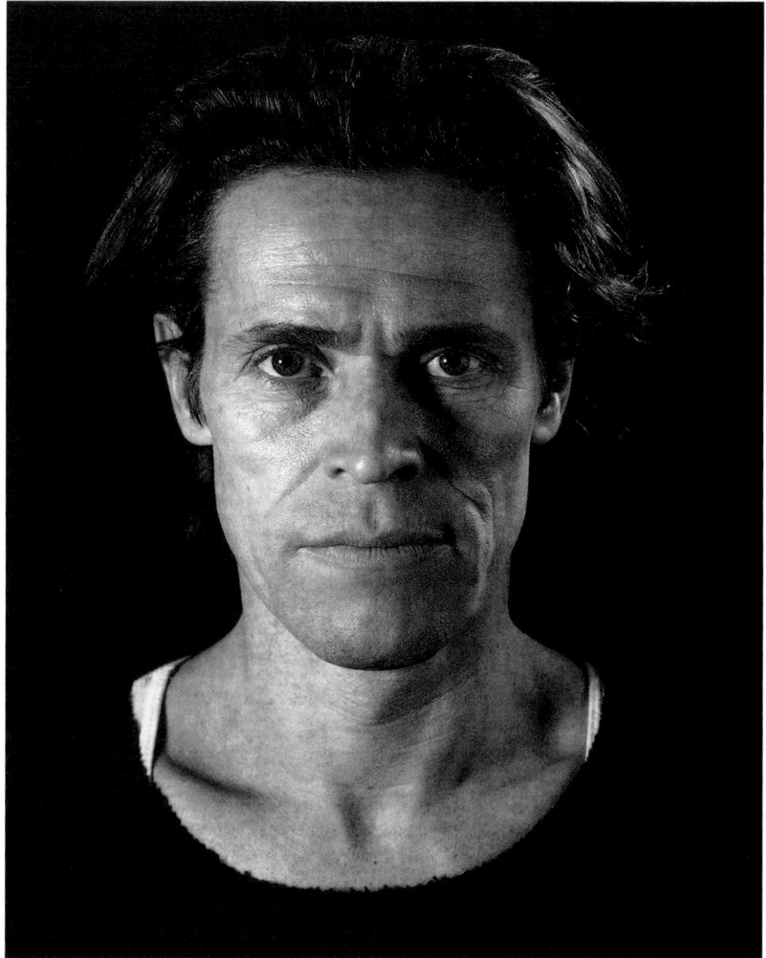

CHUCK CLOSE, WILLEM DAFOE, 1997, Polaroid, 24 x 20" / 61 x 50,8 cm.

and (again) unquantifiable ways? As unmediated presentations of at least some version of veritable truth, these continue Close's research into what happens when the viewer is confronted with the less-than-conventionally-beautiful body, the less-than-instantly-loveable face, and somehow the work insists that you love this face or that body, and think it's beautiful. And somehow it always works, somehow we always do.

In the last paragraph of his essay, Poe suggests that one use of the new invention will be to take soundings of the distances and the phases of the moon. The action of moonlight on the plates, or so he hopes, will facilitate the drawing of an accurate lunar chart. "The results of the invention cannot, even remotely, be seen—but all experience, in matters of philosophical discovery, teaches us that, in such discovery it is the unforeseen upon which we must calculate most largely. It is a theorem almost demonstrated, that the consequences of any new scientific invention will, at the present day exceed, by very much, the wildest expectation of the most imaginative."

And isn't that what art tries to do, to exceed the wildest expectation of the most imaginative and to calculate the unforeseen? These apparently paradoxical processes—the exceeding of excess and the dependence on the unknowable—are what transpire in the mirrors of Chuck Close's art, now more than ever that his use of photography (and all that it implies about observable and the real) brings us simultaneously closer and farther away from the essential mystery of the human body, the human face.

BEWEGUNGEN UND PHASEN DES MONDES

FRANCINE PROSE

In der Ausgabe vom 15. Januar 1840 versucht Edgar Allan Poe den Lesern von *Alexander's Weekly Messenger* die wunderbare Schönheit einer erstaunlichen Neuerfindung begreiflich zu machen; es handelt sich um die Daguerreotypie oder, wie Poe auch sagt, die «photogenische Zeichnung»:

Wenn wir uns die Deutlichkeit vorstellen, mit der ein Gegenstand in einem makellosen Spiegel reflektiert wird, kommen wir der Sache wohl so nah wie überhaupt möglich. Denn in Wahrheit ist die Daguerreotypie-Platte unendlich (und ich verwende diesen Ausdruck mit Vorbedacht), unendlich viel genauer in der Wiedergabe als jedes von Menschenhand gemalte Bild. Betrachten wir ein Werk herkömmlicher künstlerischer Technik unter einem starken Mikroskop, so verschwindet jede Spur von Ähnlichkeit mit der Natur – wogegen selbst die minuziöseste Prüfung einer photogenischen Zeichnung deren grössere Naturtreue und weitgehende Übereinstimmung des Bildes mit dem dargestellten Gegenstand erst recht zum Vorschein bringt.[1]

Chuck Close ist nicht der erste Künstler, der einem in Verbindung mit Edgar Allan Poe einfallen mag, überlegt man jedoch etwas länger, wird man sich alsbald fragen, warum man nicht früher an ihn dachte. Die Arbeit dieser beiden Männer zeugt von ihrem hartnäckigen Balanceakt auf dem Hochseil zwischen dem Grotesken und Vertrauten, zwischen wunderbaren und physikalischen Aspekten der Wahrnehmung, dem bizarr oder radikal anmutenden Einsatz technischer Mittel und schliesslich zwischen den physischen und psychischen Räumen, die uns voneinander trennen. Für den armen Poe war das oft ein albtraumhafter Ort, eine zugemauerte Krypta, ein sich allmählich verengender Raum, der Rumpf eines Schiffes, während es sich beim lebens-

FRANCINE PROSE ist Schriftstellerin und lebt in New York. Ihr jüngster Roman, *Blue Angel*, ist dieses Jahr bei Harper-Collins erschienen.

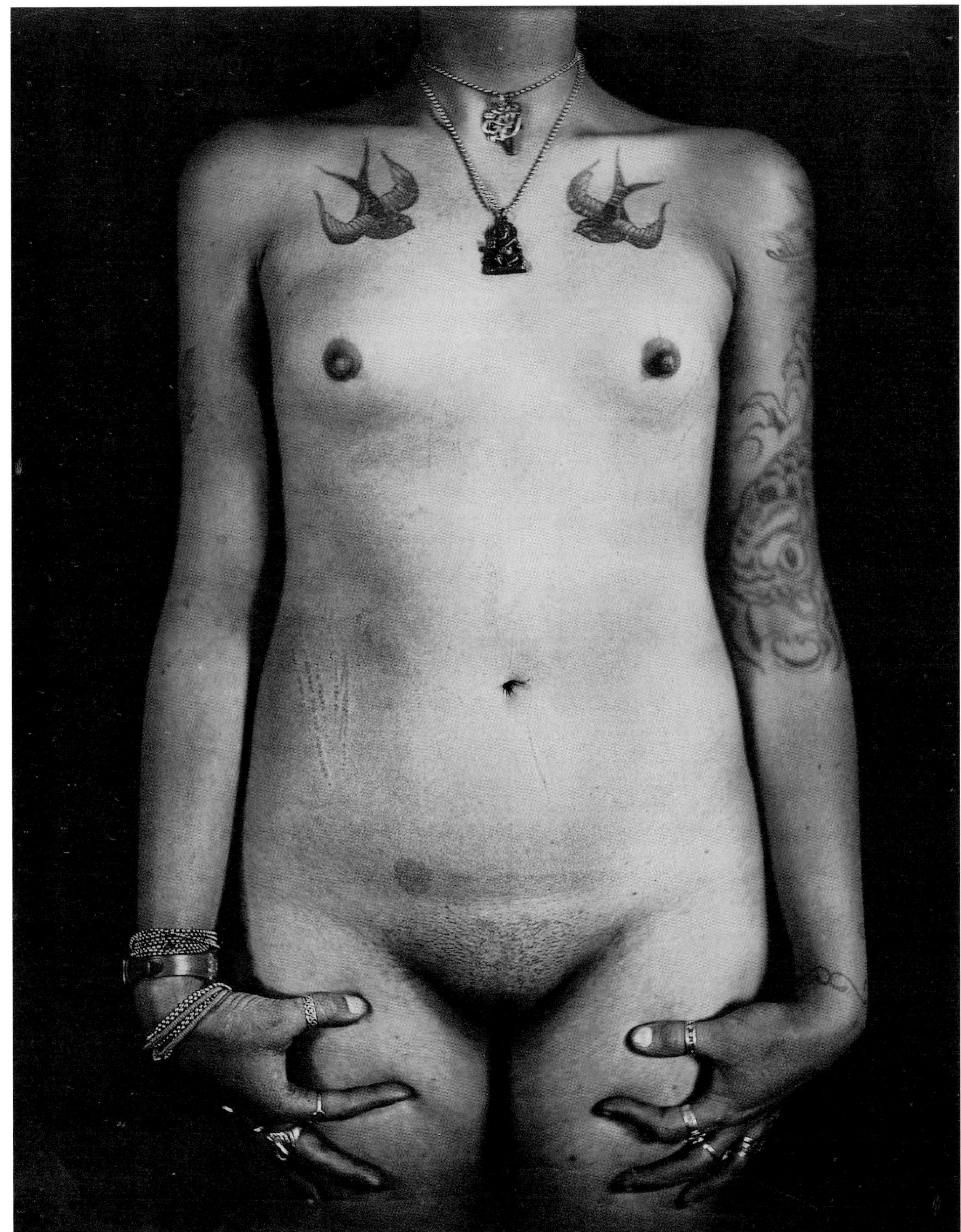

CHUCK CLOSE, TORSO (MA), 2000, daguerreotype, diptych, part 1, 8½ x 6½" / Daguerreotypie, Diptychon, Teil 1, 21,6 x 16,5 cm.

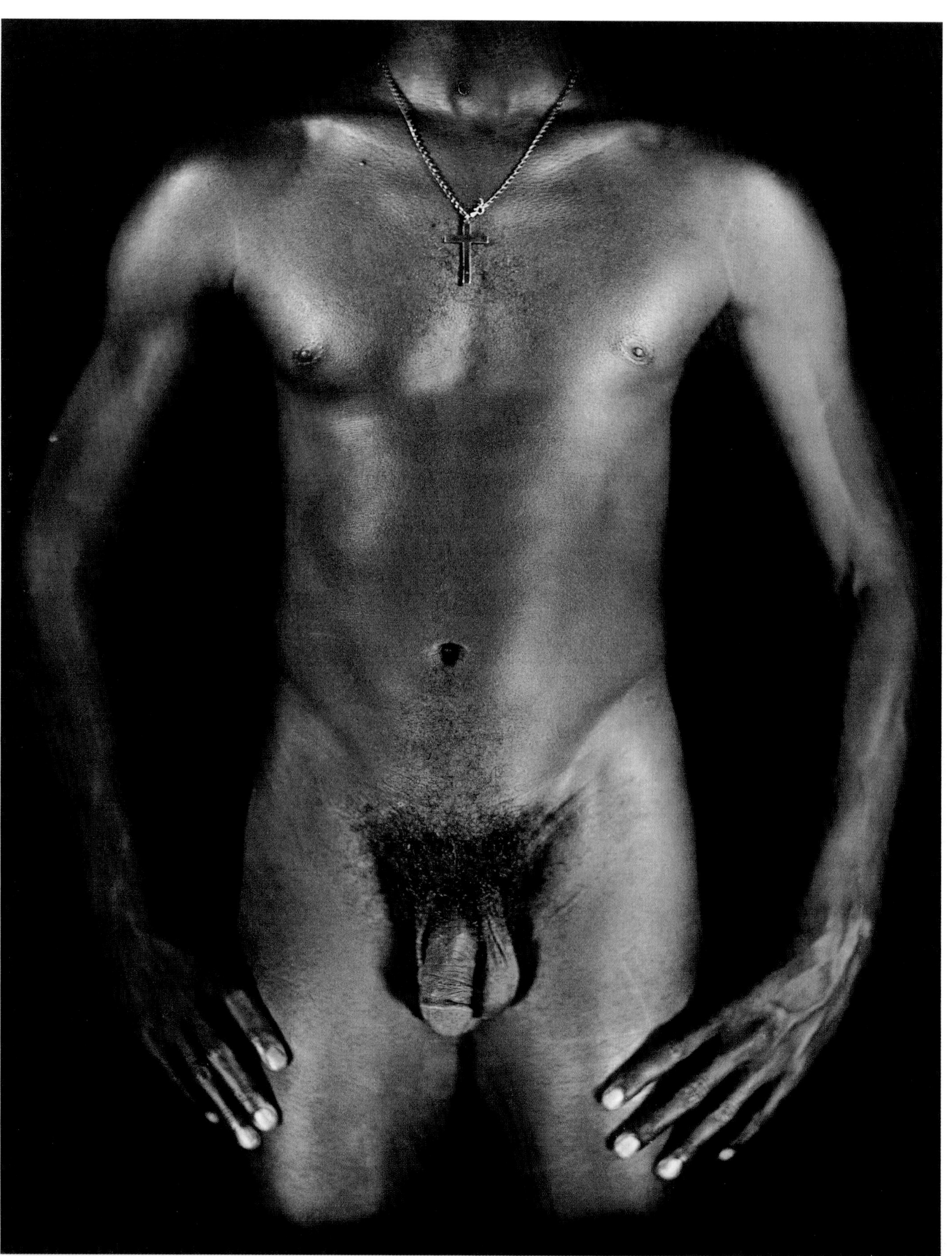

CHUCK CLOSE, TORSO (LH), 2000, daguerreotypes, diptych, 8½ x 6½" each / Daguerreotypien, Diptychon, je 21,6 x 16,5 cm.

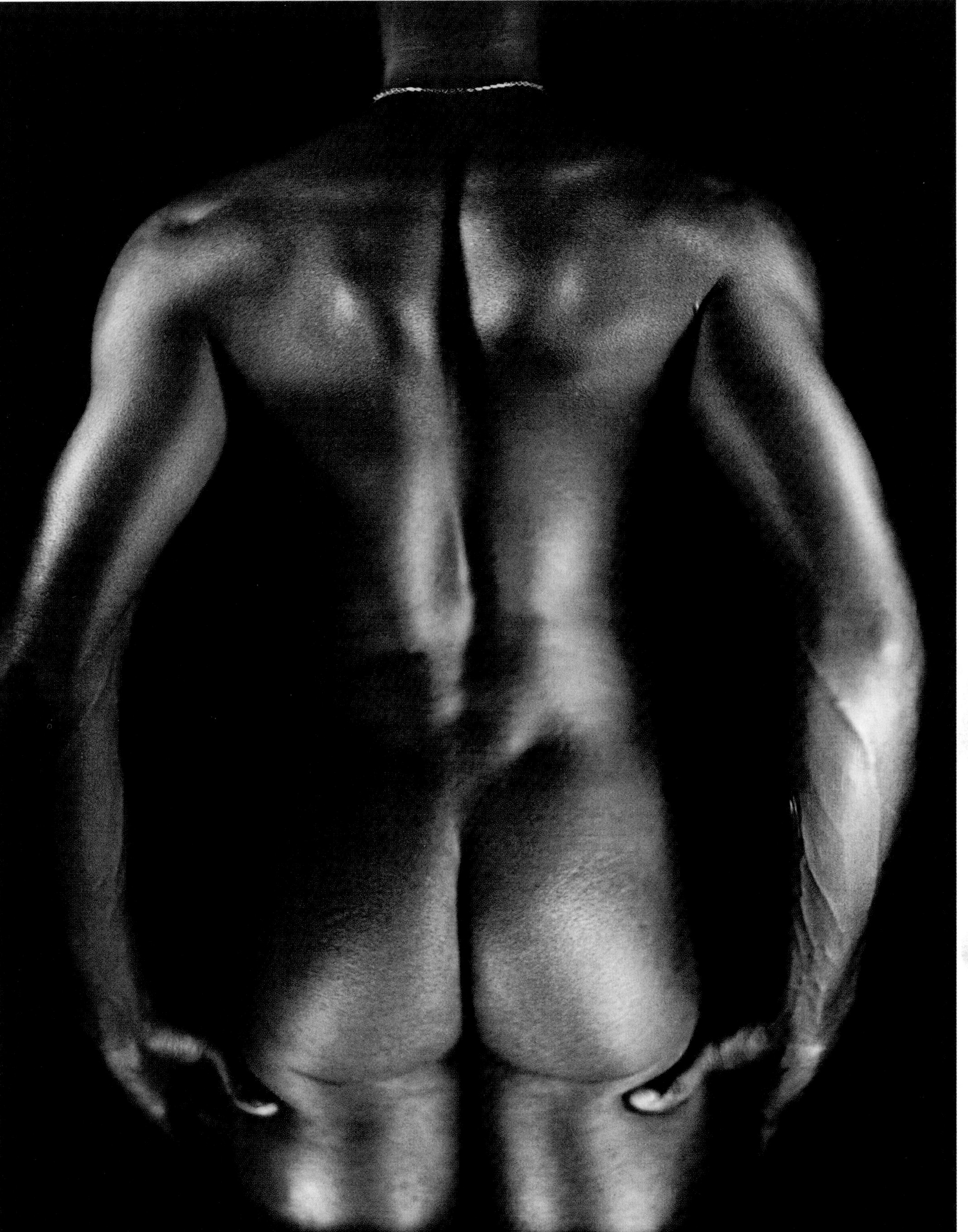

froheren und expansiveren Close eher um die Spannweite eines Raumes handelt oder um die intimere Distanz zwischen zwei Menschen.

Also ist es vielleicht gar nicht so überraschend, dass Poe noch hundertsechzig Jahre nach der Veröffentlichung seines Daguerreotypie-Artikels darin so präzise trifft, was Chuck Close wenigstens zum Teil in seinen neueren photographischen Arbeiten, zur Hauptsache Daguerreotypien und grosse Tintenstrahl-Iris-Prints, tut. Wie schon in seinen Gemälden untersucht Close einmal mehr die Distanz, in der die grösste «Naturtreue» sichtbar wird, sowie die Strategien zum Aufzeigen dieser «weitgehenden Übereinstimmung».

Wenn Poe glaubte, dass eine mikroskopische Prüfung jede Ähnlichkeit mit der Natur aufheben würde, so hätte er erst die jüngsten gemalten Grossporträts von Close sehen sollen! Es braucht gar kein starkes Mikroskop: Bereits sechzig Zentimeter von der Leinwand entfernt löst sich das grosse Gesicht, das von der anderen Seite des Galerieraumes deutlich zu erkennen war, in kindergartenbunte kleine Würmchen und zigmillionen stupide, ausgemalte Quadrate auf. Es sieht beinahe aus wie IQ-Testbogen für extraterrestrische Vorschulkinder.

Auf den ersten Blick scheinen die Daguerreotypien das genaue Gegenteil der neueren Gemälde von Close zu sein: klein statt gross, intim statt öffentlich, ein streng eingeschränktes Farbspektrum anstelle der lächerlichen Uferlosigkeit des Regenbogens. Die Gemälde treiben einen immer weiter weg, wenn man sehen will, was sie darstellen; die Daguerreotypien zwingen einen dagegen näher zu rücken und seine Stellung so lange zu korrigieren, bis sie genau, aber ganz genau richtig ist. Beiden Arbeitsweisen ist gemeinsam, dass sie die Betrachterinnen und Betrachter auf den Sekundenbruchteil aufmerksam zu machen vermögen, in welchem sich ein unstrukturiertes, vage vertrautes Flimmern zu einem mehr oder weniger deutlichen Bild fügt, sowie auf die Entfernung zum Werk, die nötig ist, damit dies geschieht. Einmal abgesehen von Bildern auf rotierenden Trommeln und von Skulpturen im Nadelöhrformat, schreiben Daguerreotypien vielleicht am genauesten vor, wo ein Betrachter stehen muss, um das Bild zu sehen und nicht irgendwelche

Nebeneffekte, die die Platte auch bietet, wie den Spiegeleffekt oder ein Flimmern. Die Beleuchtung muss nahezu perfekt sein und mit Vorteil trägt man schwarze Kleidung.

Inzwischen fordert Chuck Close das gesamte neunzehnte Jahrhundert heraus, dem es beim Daguerreotypie-Porträt meist um die Darstellung des Gesichtes ging, welches oft jenen traurigen maskenhaften Anblick bot, den ein Gesicht annimmt, wenn es länger bewegungslos bleiben muss, als ihm lieb ist. (Unter den neuen Arbeiten gibt es ein Porträt von Close, das gequält und abgeklärt zugleich wirkt, wie so viele der Künstler- und Schriftstellerporträts von Nadar.)

Der besondere zusätzliche Dreh, der dem Ganzen eine intensivere Bedeutung verleiht, ist jedoch die Tatsache, dass Close sein Augenmerk und seine Kameralinse vom Kopf weg weiter nach unten richtet; er hat die stillen Gesichter des neunzehnten Jahrhunderts, bei denen jedes Härchen am rechten Platz sass, zugunsten des nackten Torsos aufgegeben, der unverkennbar dem einundzwanzigsten Jahrhundert angehört. Die abgebildeten Personen bieten eine enorme Bandbreite an Körpertypen, Hautfarbe, Gestalt, Alter usw. Und angesichts der engen Massstäbe unserer Kultur in Sachen körperlicher Attraktivität ist es etwas verwirrend (was hätte Poe wohl dazu gesagt?), dass die meisten dieser Körper (alt, jung, dick, dünn, schwarz, weiss) gut aussehen und man sie gern und interessiert betrachtet. Die Bilder sind auf eine Weise schön, die sich schwer messen, beschreiben oder vorhersagen lässt.

Sie verfügen auch über eine wunderbare Freizügigkeit, indem sie uns erlauben die Wirkungen der Zeit zu betrachten, und zwar nicht nur die immer wieder faszinierenden Spuren der verstreichenden Jahrzehnte auf dem menschlichen Körper, sondern auch den Einfluss der Geschichte auf unsere Wahrnehmung. Viele dieser Bilder lösen einen besonderen Schock aus, weil die Daguerreotypie aus dem neunzehnten Jahrhundert stammende Sehweisen und psychologische Erwartungen weckt, die alsbald von den Körpern, die Close ausgewählt hat, unterlaufen werden: mit Tätowierungen und Piercings, die uns blitzschnell in die unmittelbare Gegenwart zurückholen. Obwohl dies in einigen Fällen etwas länger dauert, da die Daguerreotypien an sich schon dazu neigen, den modernen Körper dank Schatteneffekten ins Wespentaillenideal des viktorianischen Zeitalters zu verwandeln. Das Ergebnis ist eine Folge von kleinen Schocks, erste Eindrücke, gefolgt von Zweifeln, wiederum gefolgt von Wahrnehmungsanpassungen und -korrekturen: War das wirklich ein Nabelring, den wir in diesem altmodischen Photo gesehen haben?

Wie die Daguerreotypien üben auch die grossformatigen Tintenstrahldrucke von Photos eine grosse Wirkung auf den Betrachter aus, obwohl hier weniger sein physischer Standort in Frage gestellt wird als vielmehr seine Psyche. Die Photographien von Schauspielern (Charles Durning, Stockard Channing, Julie Harris) sind das genaue Gegenteil von Werbephotographien und einmal mehr werden wir dazu gezwungen, auf Geschwindigkeit und Art und Weise zu achten, in der wir den aller vertrauten Merkmale (hier: der gewohnten Starsymbole) entledigten Menschen erkennen bzw. immer noch zu erkennen vermögen. Die hier Dargestellten sind Leute, die es gewohnt sind, sowohl sich selbst darzustellen als auch ein anderes Selbst anzunehmen und darzustellen. Aber was stellen sie in diesen extremen und ungewöhnlichen Nahaufnahmen dar? Befinden wir uns im Irrtum oder gehen wir recht in der Annahme, dass sie uns auf nicht erschliessbare und (wiederum) nicht messbare Weise etwas zeigen, was ihrem eigenen Selbst nahe kommt? Mit diesen unvermittelten Darstellungen mindestens einer Version einer echten Wahrheit setzt Close seine Untersuchung der Frage fort, was geschieht, wenn der Betrachter dem Körper begegnet, der nicht ganz so schön ist, wie er sein müsste, oder dem Gesicht, das man nicht auf den ersten Blick mag, wobei das Werk

es darauf anlegt, dass man dieses Gesicht oder diesen Körper mag und schön findet. Und irgendwie klappt es jedesmal, irgendwie mögen wir es tatsächlich.

Im letzten Abschnitt des erwähnten Artikels meint Poe, dass ein Nutzen dieser neuen Erfindung das Festhalten der Bewegungen und Phasen des Mondes sein könnte. Die Spur des Mondlichts auf den Platten, so hofft er, würde die Aufzeichnung eines genauen Mondkalenders ermöglichen. «Die Folgen der Erfindung lassen sich noch nicht im Entferntesten abschätzen, aber alle unsere Erfahrungen im Zusammenhang mit philosophischen Entdeckungen lehren uns, dass es das Unvorhersehbare einer solchen Entdeckung ist, das wir in erster Linie in Betracht ziehen müssen. Es gilt als beinah bewiesener Lehrsatz, dass die Folgen jeder neuen Entdeckung eines Tages selbst die wildesten Spekulationen der einfallsreichsten Geister bei weitem übertreffen werden.»

Und ist das nicht, was die Kunst versucht, die wildesten Spekulationen der einfallsreichsten Geister zu übertreffen und mit dem Unvorhersehbaren zu rechnen? Diese scheinbar paradoxen Vorgänge – das Übertreffen der Übertreibung und die Abhängigkeit vom Unwissbaren – finden wir in der Kunst von Chuck Close widerspiegelt; und das gilt heute mehr denn je, da sein Umgang mit der Photographie (und allem, was diese über Beobachtbares und Wirkliches aussagt) uns dem eigentlichen Geheimnis des menschlichen Körpers, des menschlichen Antlitzes zugleich näher bringt und entrückt.

(Übersetzung: Susanne Schmidt)

---

1) Übersetzung aus dem Englischen durch die Redaktion. Der Artikel ist in keiner der deutschen Werkausgaben enthalten.

About Face

Chuck Close in Conversation with Elizabeth Peyton
October 3, 2000, New York City

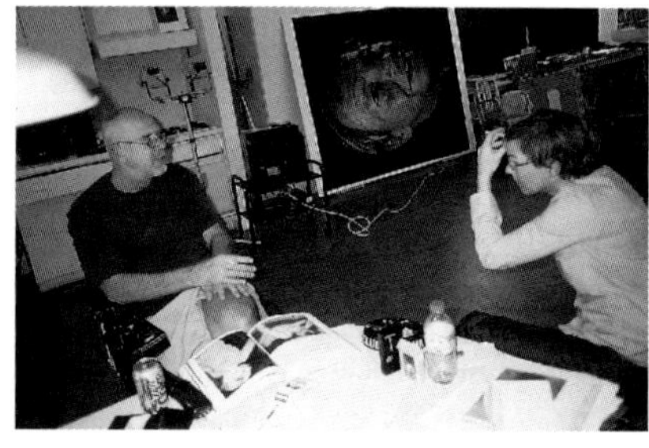

Elizabeth Peyton: In these photographs, you seem to like people's spots and wrinkles. Do you purposely choose media that highlight all their marks? Paint usually covers that up.

Chuck Close: When I started making nine-foot high paintings I was just going to paint big open areas with nothing much going on, which might have been a reaction to the way Warhol reduced everything to a few symbolic areas floating in a sea of silk-screened color. The other person making contemporary portraits then, Alex Katz, similarly had very open areas of flat paint with lips or eyes floating. I real-ized that the surface was also an indica-tor of what kind of life the person had led, and in a sense their humanity. You could see the hints of wear and tear: laugh lines and furrows. I was inter-ested in trying to make a painting as much as a portrait.

EP: It seems different than Lucian Freud who shows a lot of misery and ugliness in people. With you it doesn't seem miserable that Robert Rauschen-berg has age spots. It's his history, not a negative thing.

CC: Yeah, I think it's a sympathetic image even though it's gruesome in some details. I always say, if they don't like the paintings now, in ten or fifteen years they won't think it looks so bad.

EP: You can always look worse.

CC: I was committed to all-overness, to the whole rectangle which evolved into a way of working with dots and marks and funny shapes, areas that are not loaded psychologically.

EP: And before, when the grid wasn't visible, did you always think of the squares as abstract?

CC: Pretty much. I was not thinking about the whole image, rather I thought of each square as a building block or an increment. I think it comes from being learning disabled. I have Proso-pagnosia, which is forgetting faces.

EP: That's so strange. Do you really forget?

CC: Oh yeah, it's terrible. Someone walks into my studio, and I have to interview him or her to figure out why they're here. When I make someone flat I can remember that image. I have an almost photographic memory for flat things. Also, I'm really overwhel-med by the problem of the whole: by breaking it down into these little bite-size decisions, by not thinking about a face, just a chunk, I'm not worried about what it's going to end up as.

EP: That's a good idea. And when you

paint people, say CECILY (2000), are you thinking, "Oh, this is Cecily (Brown), she's young, she's great, etc." Or are you thinking purely visually?

CC: A little of both. It sort of drifts back and forth between the distribution of flat marks on the surface and what it warps into becoming—a nose or cheek or whatever… between the artificiality of color dirt on a flat surface and the reality in it. If there's too much distance, you're just copying shapes. I want to know who they are, but I do need arms-length distance.

EP: Do you ever lose interest in your subjects?

CC: There are a couple of people that I no longer feel kindly towards and that contaminates the way I feel about the paintings. But I've always been able to sustain it long enough to finish. I mean they're very much about whom the paintings are of and my feelings for them. And sometimes it's an excuse to get to know somebody, which is fun.

EP: Are you self-conscious about making someone more famous by painting them?

CC: I never really think about that. The very first paintings that I made were black and white, and I was looking for totally anonymous people. Warhol was doing superstars…

EP: So you were consciously thinking about Warhol?

CC: Yeah, I thought, "I'm going to pick the most everyday, anonymous people I know," so I painted Richard Serra and Nancy Graves and Philip Glass. They ended up getting famous, but in the late sixties they certainly weren't known outside of a very small circle.

EP: Were you friendly with Warhol?

CC: Yes. In fact I was going to paint him, and him me, as soon as he got out of the hospital. We talked just before he went in to get his operation and he never survived.

EP: Oh no…—It seems that you always just painted people head up. Where do the bodies go?

CC: Well I did a 22-foot long reclining nude in 1967; it was the last painting I did before my first portrait.

EP: Wow, it's huge! There are tan lines and…

CC: Yeah. And caesarean scars. Kiki Smith said it was the first body art.

EP: I saw this in the background of a photo of you and I was trying to figure

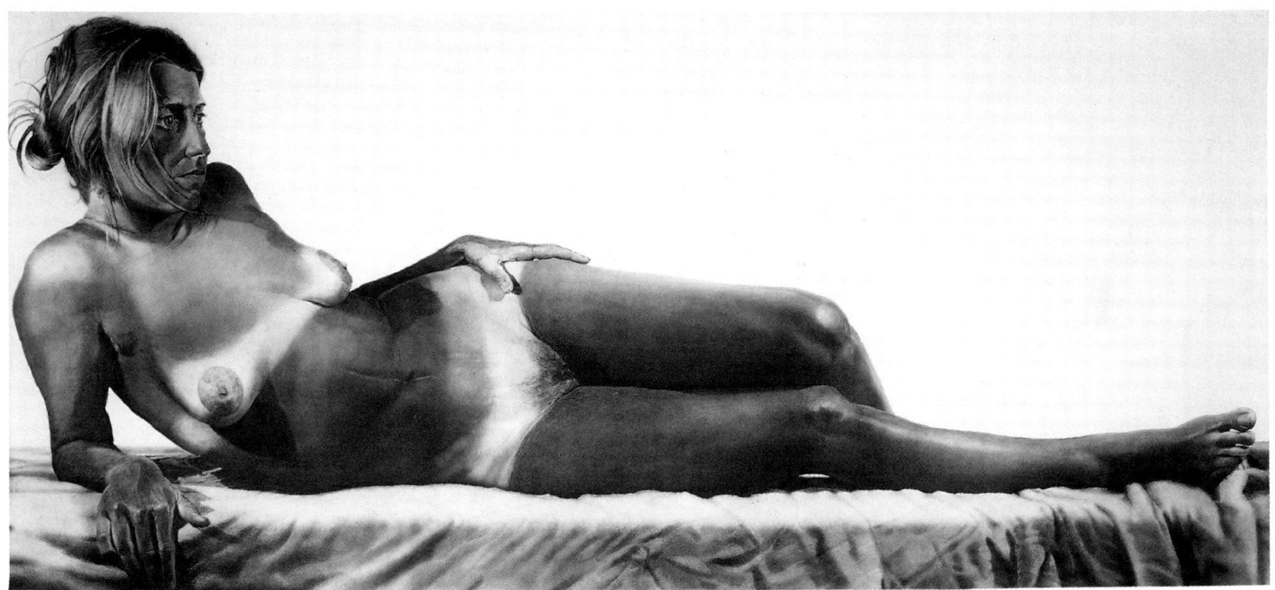

CHUCK CLOSE, BIG NUDE, 1967, oil on canvas, 117 x 253" / GROSSER AKT, Öl auf Leinwand, 297,2 x 642,6 cm.
(PHOTO: BILL JACOBSON / PACE WILDENSTEIN)

out who made that painting. That's amazing. In the conversation book you said something about not being able to look in the mirror in front of other people. But then you make these big self-portraits. When you do them do you think of yourself as another person?

CC: I think so. I don't look in the mirror very often. I never really liked the way I looked so I just sort of avoided it. I've certainly done a lot of self-portraits. One would assume that I really am in love with myself, based on the number of self-portraits I've painted.

EP: Is there a time of year where you suddenly feel it's time to do a self-portrait? Is it a cyclical thing?

CC: I usually do one self-portrait per show. If I'm going to do a warts-and-all version of somebody else in the kind of hard, glaring light that really shows everything, I try to turn the same light on myself. Then of course, you can watch me age and watch me lose my hair and then it's a history of eyeglasses.

EP: And fashion.

CC: How about the artist as fashion statement? It sort of started with the young Brits, but Cecily is often in these pieces which seem to feature what they're wearing as much as the paintings that happen to be behind them.

EP: I've done a bit of that myself.

CC: How about that?

EP: I don't know how interesting it actually is. You have to say well, if other people are interested in that... and there are a lot of fascinating people in magazines. I want to know what they're having for breakfast. I can understand wanting to see Cecily or John Currin looking great in a magazine. It's fun to do, but you can also get to a point when it's not helping you in the studio, because it takes time.

CC: Until recently, artists were always geeky and the idea that they would be grist for the fashion mills was just unthinkable. I see supermodels at openings and how glamorous it all is and I'm as infatuated and I love to read it as much as anybody, but it does seem like it's putting a tremendous pressure on people.

EP: Also earlier on you are recognizable to everybody.

CC: But thank god I wasn't being judged when handsomeness was a yardstick.

EP: Well it sort of seems like you've always been there. I couldn't not think about you. For me it's one of those things that made it okay. It was another reason that I didn't have to question what I was doing when teachers wanted to send me to the illustration department.

CC: I wanted to ask you about how you choose the people you paint, because some of the people you paint are just your friends and some...

EP: Yeah, some I don't know at all.

CC: Where do you get the images?

EP: From photographs, pretty much, because I don't like them to be around. I don't really go around choosing them, they're just in my life and I love them. It was a more conscious thing when I started painting people I knew because I spent so much time painting all of these pop musicians who really affected me. These people are in your lives, they're on the bus shelter ads, they're all around you, and they're just as real as your mom is. Then, suddenly I realized these people are down the street. They're my friends. They're these fantastic artists who are doing really valuable things, and I wanted to make a point of that. I think it's so important to have people like that in your life.

CC: Do you see a difference when you work from one of your own photographs as opposed to the published ones?

EP: It was harder at first, because they had already been edited and came through filtered and looking good. But now I've just been working with one person for about a year, it's amazing how much more you see.

CC: I recycle my favorites too. Philip Glass, I've been doing him for thirty-five years. I felt like I should at some point take his photograph and lift it into the rafters of my studio the way they retire a jersey in a sports arena.

EP: That picture is so sexy. Do you feel famous?

CC: Not particularly. A really interesting thing happened when I went into the wheelchair. I'm six-foot-three and I was always looking over the tops of people. So, when I got cut down to size, in a sense, something happened with the way people related to me. All of a sudden people began coming up to me to tell me that my work meant something to them. I do believe in making things for people. I was never interested in art as therapy. I go to therapy as therapy. I'm making these things because I really do believe that it's a language and that people are out there decoding it.

EP: Do you think a painting can change someone's life?

CC: Well, paintings have changed my life. I don't think art is a very good propagandizing tool or educational tool. We no longer fill churches with imagery to make people feel closer to their God. But art is my religion; it's the thing that matters to me. Of course, as an artist, you have to be arrogant enough to think that you have something to say that somebody else might

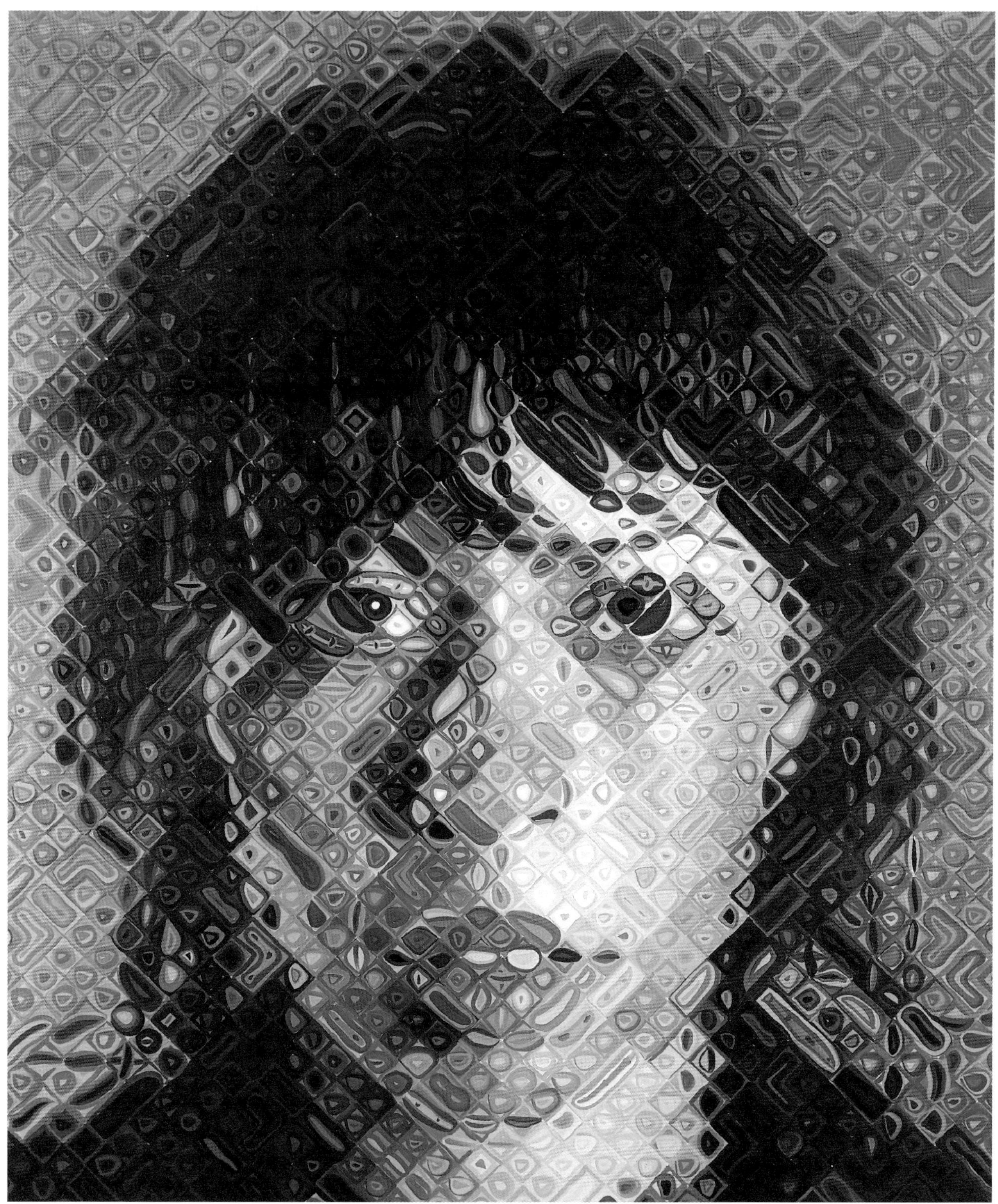

CHUCK CLOSE, CECILY, 2000, oil on canvas, 112 x 84" / Öl auf Leinwand, 284,5 x 213,4 cm.

want to hear. But artists are incredibly generous. The generosity is in exposing what's important to you. I think it can change your life. I never wanted to paint still lifes or landscapes because if I painted a rock, nobody but a geologist would know it. But we all have strong feelings about a face.

E P : Of anything in life, people probably are the most affected by other people. Even for them it can become something other than art, which is the freeing thing.

C C : I have such regrets, for instance, not painting my mother before she died. After a while you can't hear the voice of a person who has died and I wish for that level of intimacy with her image.

E P : Are you very aware of getting people at a certain point in their life? Let's say with Philip Glass he was just beginning. Or with Cecily, she's kind of at her early peak.

C C : I guess there's a kind of energy and excitement that you can see in their faces when they're beginning to put it all together and that personal vision is beginning to become clear. There is something very special about the beginnings of a career, a coalescing: it's an exciting time to be connected with someone.

E P : What's different right now as opposed to when you were coming up?

C C : When I was coming up, we were trying desperately to purge our work of all references to other artists. And today there is a very different attitude, the idea of raiding the cultural icebox. I feel a real connectedness to the scene today. I think it's a pretty tight time.

E P : I bet you see more than I do. I read in the New York Times that you told Al Gore not to paint? Was that just a joke or is he really a bad painter?

C C : I have no idea if he's a good or a bad painter. It was a joke, something to the affect that I thought we had a deal that he wouldn't make paintings and we wouldn't get into politics, but actually I think it helps that he has had that experience.

E P : Everyone seems sweeter if they paint, like Prince Charles.

C C : Yeah. I'm not sure it helped Eisenhower. Certainly Nixon didn't paint; we know that for sure. I don't think Ronald Reagan painted.

E P : You could see Gore having a need for that kind of peace.

C C : I once asked him a question at an event that he answered by talking about the "gestalt of a painting" and I thought, "A presidential candidate who even knows what the 'gestalt of a painting' is has my vote."

… I was just looking at your paintings. One of the things that I love about painting is how it's such a record of decisions. There it is just laid out for you. You find reasons for broken color and brush strokes and different ways to put down paint. One of the problems with criticism is that nobody describes paintings anymore, they assume that the reproduction is enough and no one describes what it feels like to be in front of a painting.

E P : That's true.

C C : I can imagine you thinking about the direction of the strokes and what you're doing. Clearly you must take pleasure in that kind of incident—the hand and the touch. It seems to me to be all about touch.

E P : When it's good, I love it. I don't really think that much while I'm doing it.

C C : I love Hals for instance, because you can see how he managed to make a hand out of four or five strokes. It is so much more than Rembrandt.

E P : That was great when you said, "I don't like Rembrandt."

C C : His paintings seem to be under a brown syrup. On the contrary, you can't decode a Vermeer. It's a miracle; it just looks like those things blew onto the canvas in a breeze. Who, in art history, turned you on?

E P : I like Velázquez, but Sargent's brushwork is just amazing, even in his boring portraits. And I was surprised that I liked the Ingres show, because he's one where you can't see anything, and it bugs me. Seeing where it came from helped to show that at one point he really was painting, he just got too good at it.

C C : What about ease? I think ease is an artist's greatest enemy.

E P : Except maybe if you're Alex Katz. But I know for me, it could get dangerous to really know what I was doing.

C C : You have to have a degree of resistance in there somehow.

E P : Yeah and sort of keep wanting more. But Alex Katz could make the same mouth forever and it would always be beautiful. But I know that he wants something else than I do, even in the surface, and he also has that Warhol thing of simplifying.

C C : Alex once complained to me that he was having a hard time with a painting because after three straight days it was really hard for him to sustain the energy. Talk about coming at it from a different point of view: I find it sustaining that I'm doing today what I did yesterday and tomorrow I'm doing what I did today and that I'm signing on to a long-term process. I find it really comforting, like knitting or crocheting…

Do you go for weeks without painting?

E P : Yeah, but not guiltlessly, although I like that uncomfortableness when I come back and I don't remember how I make an eye. It's kind of nice to do it again or to make it different. Are the photographs a place where you can get out other ideas?

CC: Yeah, and work quickly. Usually a series of eight or nine paintings takes three years to complete. So it's nice to be able to function differently. And then, one of the perks of being an artist is that you get to be around naked people.

EP: So, is t h a t what it's really about?

CC: Sure, you bet. And I throw in enough men to make it look like I'm not just interested in naked women. *(Laughter.)* And then I find myself really interested in bodies that are not perfect bodies. So, are you going to be doing aging rock stars?

EP: I guess they all get older with me.

CC: You have the "live hard, die young and leave a lot of beautiful memories" attitude within that culture as well.

EP: I've always thought about how they will never be like that again. There's a huge loss in that moment's passing. I wonder if I'll be painting wrinkles. They've gotten in there just by chance, by moving the brush the

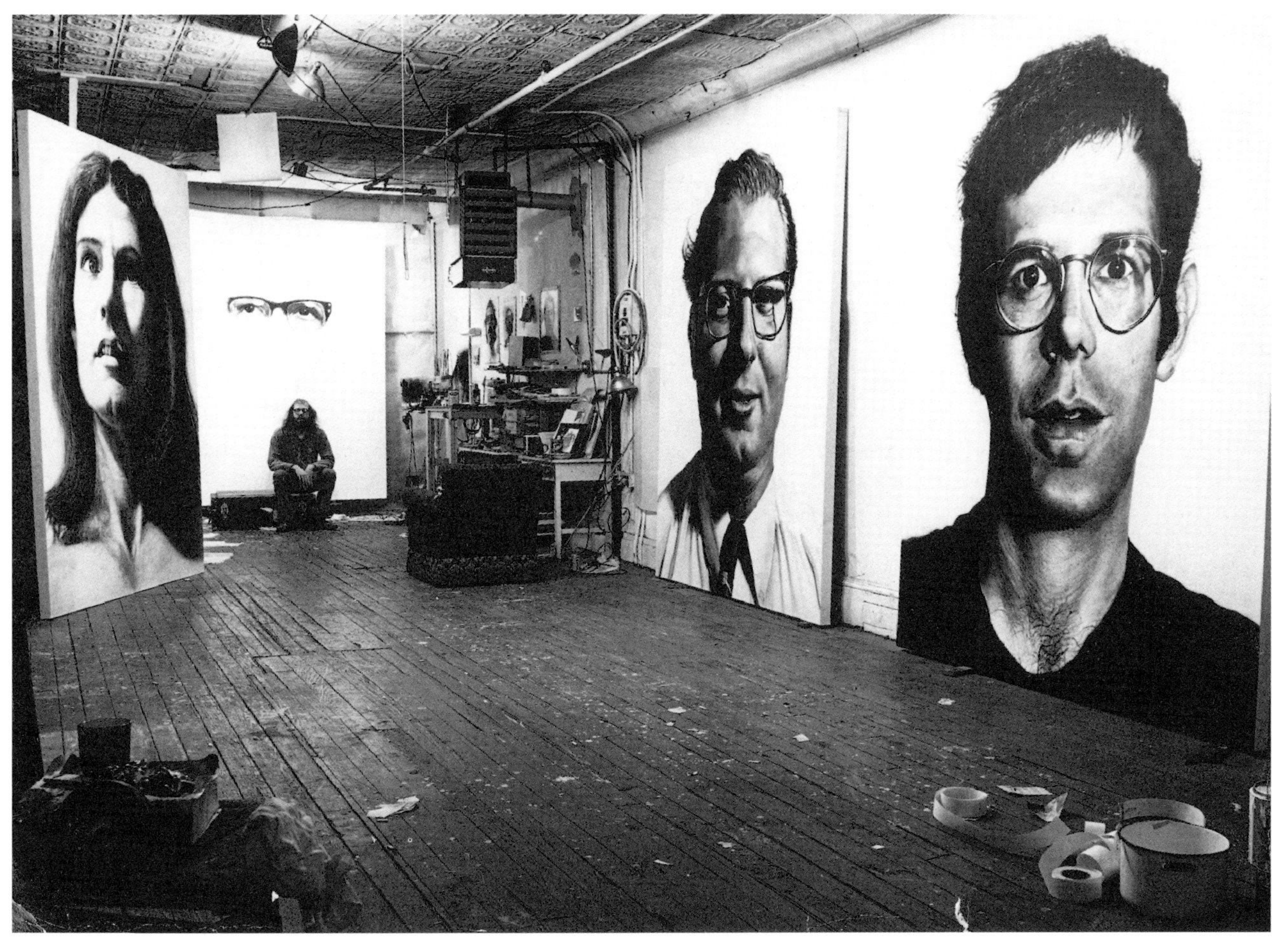

Chuck Close in his Greene Street studio in 1970 with paintings of NANCY, 1968, KEITH (unfinished), JOE, 1969, and BOB, 1969–70 /
Chuck Close mit Bildern im Atelier an der Greene Street, 1970. (PHOTO: WAYNE HOLLINGWORTH)

right way, but I don't think I know how to do it purposely or intentionally.

CC: How about the social scene? I am so aware of the role that the watering hole has played for my generation. I think we firmed up our ideas sitting in the bar with major forces like Robert Smithson or Richard Serra, people who were really tough on you. You had to defend yourself so much that a lot of things seemed to crystallize in the dialogue. They were showing you, at the same time, that they took you seriously and they cared whether or not you made another painting, even though they would like to convince you to make a different one. Is Gavin (Brown's bar) like that?

EP: In a way. But people are much more polite now. I've never seen anyone fight over art. But there is something about having to come face-to-face with people and also how much you find in common with people who do completely different things. I think you take that back to the studio. Most of my friends are conceptual artists, actually. I know very few painters. I guess it is a place where people hash things out: "Did you see this show? Did you read that review? What did you think of that?" It's probably the only place in my life where that goes on socially. But I think the art world is pretty much a rah-rah club. Everyone's pretty lenient and loving towards each other. There's no real ideologue of "You can't do that."

CC: Whether the art world is less competitive or more competitive it seems to me that you can't make art without any community.

EP: I think everybody's critical enough amongst one another, but on the face of it there's a kind of "Everything's okay" attitude. I do have moral problems with some work, you know I just think it's awful.

CC: Really, that's interesting, what's an immoral act that an artist could commit?

EP: It's something that's cynical or it's just intentioned after a career move, or if its motives are wrong, that makes me mad, or things that are really big and expensive that aren't really about anything.

CC: What about irony?

EP: I have a big problem with irony, actually. I know some people use it well. And often times I've thought of work as ironic that in the end turned out not to be.

CC: It can be a tyranny, irony. It's like you're never ever going to be serious about anything except for being ironic.

EP: Yeah, and it keeps something from being something in and of itself because it's dependent upon referring to something outside of itself for its meaning. And I still have this holy idea of the self-contained artwork that exists on its own.

CC: Well, I think that's part of the crux of intelligent criticism, that every-

thing you need to know and everything you need to judge the work is really right there in the work.

EP: Usually with other artists, I would only be critical of them if I really thought they were doing something wrong. But with taste issues, there's no reason to get upset. There are so many great artists everywhere, fascinating and beautiful and cute people, and then you look in those magazines and you feel like criticism isn't doing its job.

CC: People usually tune into an artist's career relatively late in the process when all of the issues seem to have been fixed. It is really much more interesting when there's still some confusion.

EP: Do you notice how similar people are to their bodies? Like the curve of their finger being the same as their nose. Do you look at those relationships?

CC: No, actually I hadn't noticed that, I better start looking.

EP: I love it when people are uniform like that. Their elbows are like their ears.

CC: Hmmm. I'll have to check that out. So will you let me photograph you?

EP: OK.

CC: Which do you want—the body or the head?

EP: Head! I'm not taking off my clothes. I've never asked anyone to take off their clothes.

CC: Really?

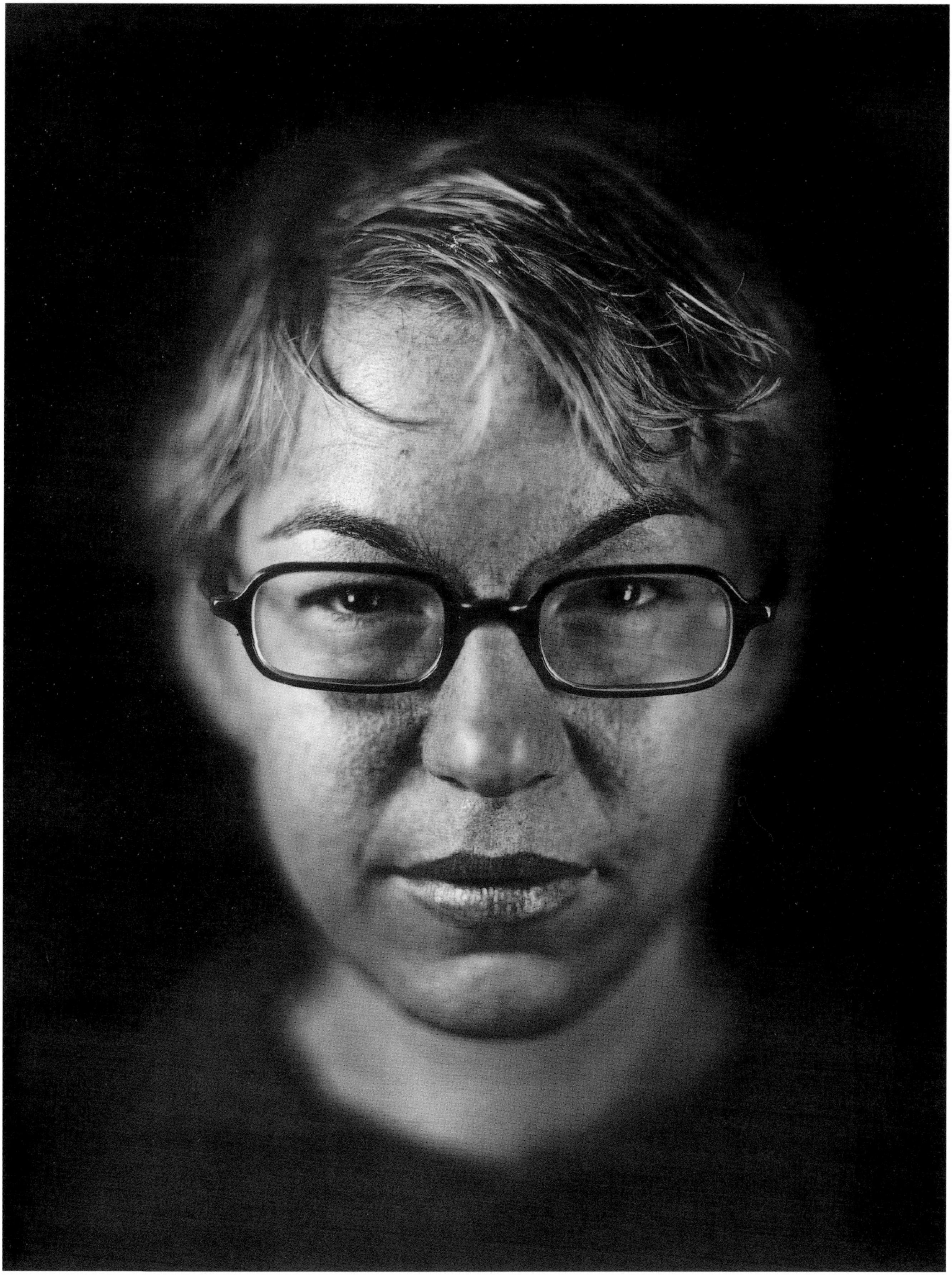

CHUCK CLOSE, ELIZABETH PEYTON, 2000, daguerreotype, 15½ x 12" / Daguerreotypie, 39,4 x 30,5 cm.

Von Gesichtern

Chuck Close im Gespräch mit Elizabeth Peyton 3. Oktober 2000, New York

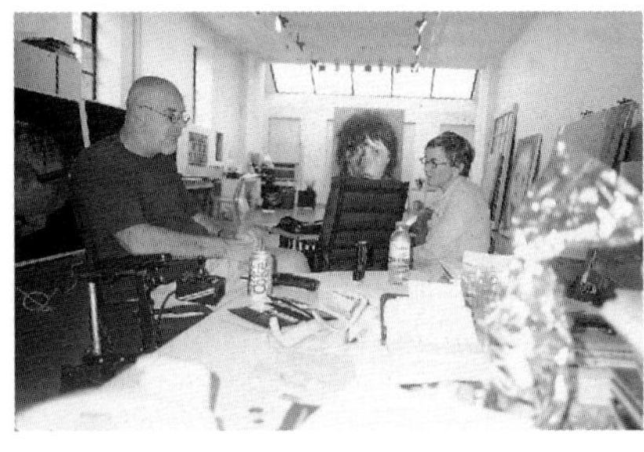

Elizabeth Peyton: Auf diesen Photographien scheint es, dass du die Hautflecken und Fältchen der Leute magst. Wählst du absichtlich ein Medium, das diese Spuren hervorhebt? Farbe lässt diese Dinge ja gewöhnlich verschwinden.

Chuck Close: Als ich mit den zwei Meter hohen Bildern begann, malte ich einfach grosse offene Flächen, auf denen nicht viel passierte, was eine Reaktion auf Warhol gewesen sein mag, der alles auf wenige bedeutsame Stellen in einem Meer von Siebdruckfarbe reduzierte. Der andere, der damals Porträts von Zeitgenossen machte, war Alex Katz, und auch der hatte weite offene, gleichmässig farbige Flächen und darin schwebende Lippen oder Augen. Mir wurde bewusst, dass die Beschaffenheit der Oberfläche auch ein Hinweis auf das Leben sein konnte, das jemand geführt hat, also gewissermassen ein Zeichen seiner Menschlichkeit. Man konnte Anzeichen überstandener Strapazen erkennen: Lach- und Kummerfalten. Ich wollte ein Bild malen, aber auch ein wirkliches Porträt.

E P: Es sieht anders aus als bei Lucian Freud, der das Elende und Hässliche der Leute zeigt. Bei dir ist es nicht so bestürzend, dass Robert Rauschenberg Altersflecken hat. Sie gehören zu seiner Lebensgeschichte und sind nichts Negatives.

CC: Ja, ich glaube, es ist ein freundliches Bild, auch wenn es in gewissen Details unbarmherzig ist. Ich sage mir immer, wenn sie das Bild heute nicht mögen, so werden sie es spätestens in zehn, fünfzehn Jahren gar nicht mehr so schlecht finden.

E P: Man kann ja immer noch schlechter aussehen.

CC: Mir war immer das gründliche Durcharbeiten des Ganzen wichtig, das ganze Rechteck. Das führte zu dieser Arbeit mit Punkten, Strichen und seltsamen Formen, zu Flächenteilen, die psychologisch völlig unbelastet sind.

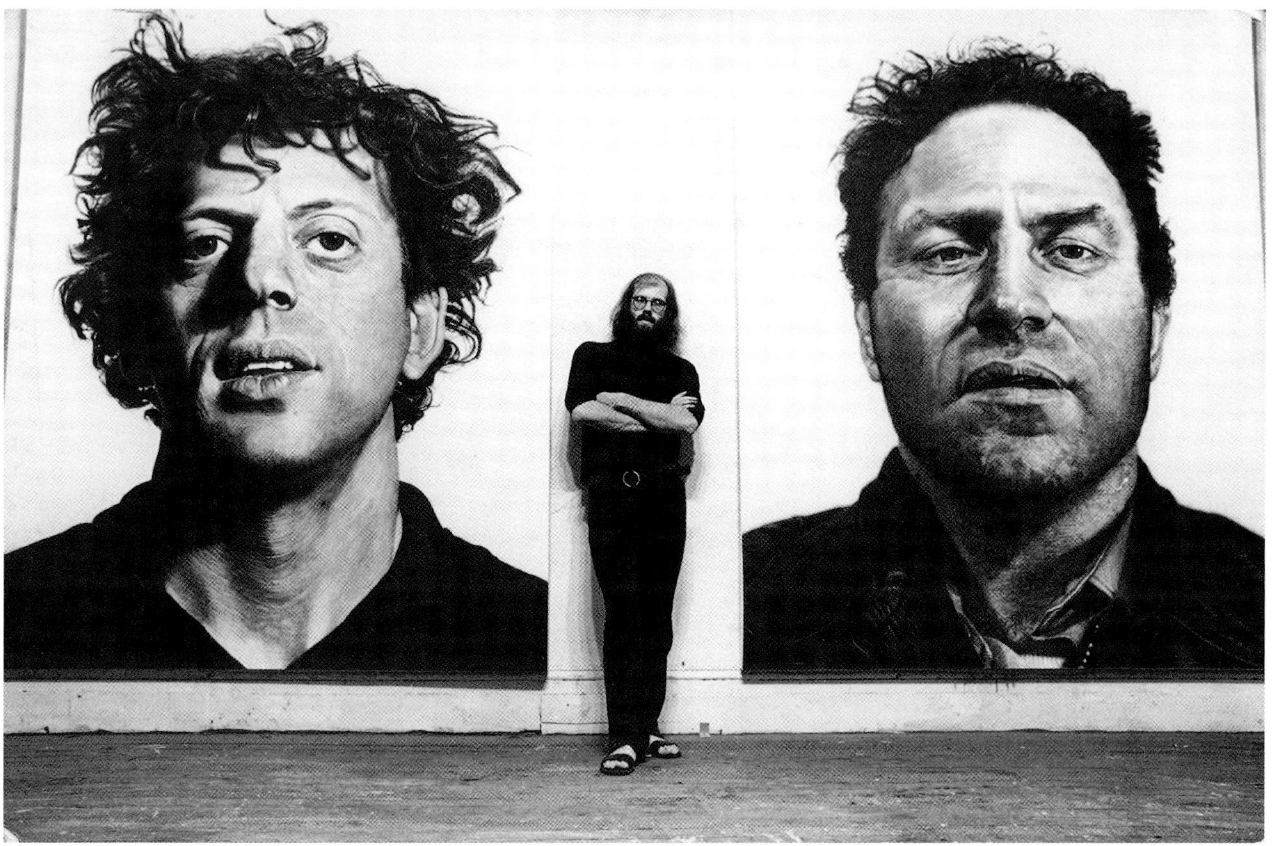

E P : Und vorher, als der Raster noch nicht sichtbar war, waren die Quadrate für dich schon immer etwas Abstraktes?

C C: Weitgehend schon. Ich machte mir weniger Gedanken über das ganze Bild als über jedes Quadrat als Baustein oder Beitrag zum Ganzen. Ich glaube, das kommt davon, dass ich lernbehindert bin. Ich leide unter Prosopagnosie, das heisst, ich kann mir keine Gesichter merken.

E P : Das ist ja merkwürdig. Vergisst du sie wirklich?

C C: Ja, es ist furchtbar. Leute kommen in mein Atelier und ich muss ihnen Fragen stellen, um herauszufinden, weshalb sie gekommen sind. Wenn ich jemanden zweidimensional male, kann ich mich an dieses Bild er-

innern. Ich habe ein beinah photographisches Gedächtnis für flache Dinge. Aber das Ganze ist für mich wirklich ein Problem und eine Überforderung: Wenn ich es jedoch in kleine Stücke unterteile und die Entscheidungen damit auch auf Bite-Grösse reduziere, wenn ich nicht mehr an ein Gesicht denke, sondern lediglich an irgendein Stück, mache ich mir keine Sorgen mehr, wie es herauskommen wird.

E P : Das ist eine gute Idee. Und wenn du Leute malst, wie CECILY (2000), denkst du dann: «Ah, das ist Cecily (Brown), sie ist jung, sie sieht toll aus usw.» Oder denkst du rein visuell?

C C: Beides. Es ist ein Hin und Her zwischen dem Verteilen der flachen Zeichen auf der Leinwand und was daraus werden soll – eine Nase, eine

Wange oder was auch immer…, zwischen der Künstlichkeit des Farbstaubs auf der flachen Leinwand und der Wirklichkeit, die auch drin steckt. Ist man zu weit weg, zeichnet man nur noch Formen nach. Ich will wissen, wer die Leute sind, aber ich brauche eine Armlänge Distanz.

E P : Verlierst du manchmal das Interesse für deine Modelle?

C C: Es gibt ein paar Leute, die ich nicht mehr so gut mag, und das beeinflusst meine Einstellung zu ihrem Bild. Aber ich konnte das Interesse immer so lange wach halten, bis ein Bild fertig war. Ich glaube, die Bilder handeln wirklich von den Leuten, die abgebildet sind und von meinen Gefühlen ihnen gegenüber. Aber manchmal ist es auch ein Vorwand, um jemanden kennen zu lernen, und das macht Spass.

E P : Denkst du manchmal daran, dass du jemanden mit einem Bild berühmt machen kannst?

C C : Darüber denke ich nicht wirklich nach. Meine ersten Bilder waren schwarzweiss und ich suchte mir völlig unbekannte Leute dafür aus. Warhol war spezialisiert auf Superstars…

E P : Also hast du dich bewusst mit Warhol auseinander gesetzt?

C C : Ja, ich dachte: «Ich nehme die alltäglichsten, unbekanntesten Leute, die ich kenne.» Und ich malte Richard Serra, Nancy Graves und Philip Glass. Sie wurden schliesslich berühmt, aber in den späten 60er Jahren waren sie ausserhalb eines sehr engen Kreises wirklich keinem bekannt.

E P : Hast du dich mit Warhol gut verstanden?

C C : Ja. Ich wollte ihn sogar malen und er mich, sobald er aus dem Spital gekommen wäre. Wir unterhielten uns darüber, kurz bevor er seine Operation machen liess, und dann hat er die nicht überlebt.

E P : Oh, nein… – Es macht ganz den Anschein, dass du die Leute immer vom Hals an aufwärts gemalt hast. Was ist mit den Körpern passiert?

C C : Nun, 1967 habe ich einen sechseinhalb Meter langen ruhenden Frauenakt gemalt; es war das letzte Bild vor meinem ersten Porträt.

E P : Wow, das ist riesengross! Man sieht, wo die Sonnenbräune aufhört…

C C : Ja, und eine Operationsnarbe.

Kiki Smith meinte, es sei das erste Beispiel von *Body Art*.

E P : Ich habe das Bild im Hintergrund eines Photos von dir gesehen und versuchte mir vorzustellen, wer das wohl gemalt hat. Das ist ja irre. Im *Conversation Book* sagtest du, du könntest nicht vor anderen Leuten in den Spiegel schauen. Aber dann machst du diese Riesenselbstporträts… Betrachtest du dich wie einen fremden Menschen, wenn du dein Porträt malst?

C C : Ich glaube schon. Ich schaue nicht oft in den Spiegel. Ich habe mein Aussehen nie wirklich gemocht, also habe ich das tunlichst vermieden. Aber ich habe eine Menge Selbstporträts gemacht. Aufgrund der Zahl meiner Selbstporträts könnte man geradezu meinen, ich sei in mich selbst verliebt.

E P : Gibt es eine Jahreszeit, wo du plötzlich das Gefühl hast, jetzt sei es Zeit für ein Selbstporträt? Und wiederholt sich das in bestimmten Abständen?

C C : Gewöhnlich mache ich ein Selbstporträt pro Ausstellung. Wenn ich ein Bild von jemand anderem mit jeder Warze, Pore usw. mache, in diesem harten, gleissenden Licht, das wirklich alles zum Vorschein bringt, versuche ich mich im selben Licht zu zeigen. Da kann man natürlich sehen, wie ich älter werde und immer weniger Haare habe, aber es ist auch eine Geschichte der Brillen.

E P : Und der Mode.

C C : Was hältst du vom Künstler als Modevermittler? Es begann mit den jungen Briten, aber Cecily taucht oft in solchen Beiträgen auf, in denen es offenbar genauso um die Kleider geht, welche die Leute tragen, wie um die Bilder, die hinter ihnen zu sehen sind.

E P : Ich habe auch solche Sachen gemacht.

C C : Was hältst du davon?

E P : Ich weiss nicht, wie interessant das wirklich ist. Man sagt sich, nun, wenn andere Leute sich dafür interessieren… und man stösst auf eine Menge faszinierender Leute in Zeitschriften. Man will wissen, wie sie frühstücken. Ich kann verstehen, dass man tolle Bilder von Cecily oder John Currin in einer Zeitschrift sehen will. Es macht auch Spass, das zu tun, aber man kann dabei an einen Punkt gelangen, wo es einen an der Arbeit hindert, weil es zeitaufwändig ist.

C C : Bis vor kurzem waren Künstler immer eher bizarre Erscheinungen und der Gedanke, dass sie im Modezirkus mitspielen würden, war unvorstellbar. An Vernissagen treffe ich auf Supermodels und den ganzen damit verbundenen Glamour, und ich bin so hingerissen und lese das so gern wie alle anderen, aber es scheint die Leute einem unerhörten Druck auszusetzen.

E P : Man wird auch früher von jedermann wiedererkannt.

C C : Aber Gott sei Dank war Schönheit zu meiner Zeit noch kein Massstab der Kritik.

E P : Für mich bist du irgendwie schon immer da gewesen. Ich kann dich gar nicht mehr wegdenken. Und das ist eines der Dinge, weshalb die Kunstszene in Ordnung war. Es war mit ein Grund, dass ich mich nicht verunsichern liess, als meine Lehrer mich in die Illustrationsabteilung schicken wollten.

C C : Ich wollte dich schon immer fragen, wie du die Leute auswählst, die du malst, denn einige dieser Leute sind einfach Freunde und andere…

E P : Ja, einige kenne ich überhaupt nicht.

C C : Woher nimmst du ihre Bilder?

E P : Von Photos, hauptsächlich, weil

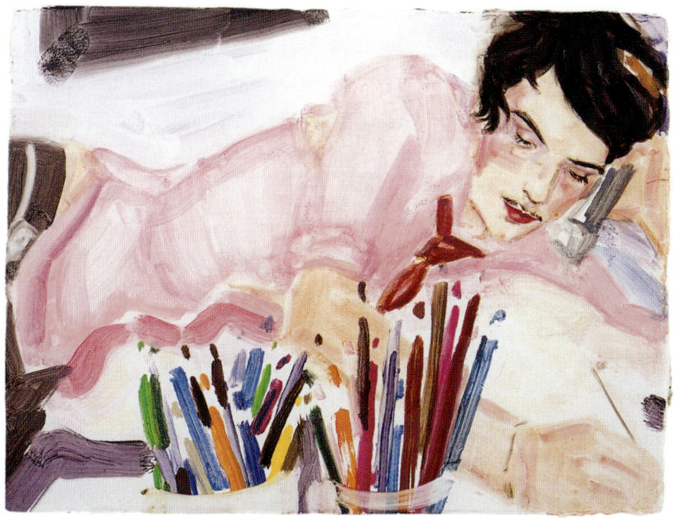

ELIZABETH PEYTON, SPENCER DRAWING, 1999, oil on MDF, 9¼ x 12" /
SPENCER BEIM ZEICHNEN, Öl auf MDF, 23,5 x 30,5 cm.
(PHOTO: GAVIN BROWN'S ENTERPRISE, N.Y.)

ich sie lieber nicht um mich haben will. Ich gehe nicht eigentlich hin und wähle sie aus, sie gehören einfach zu meinem Leben und ich mag sie. Das geschah bewusster, als ich mit dem Malen von Leuten, die ich kannte, anfing, weil ich damals viel Zeit damit verbrachte, all die Popmusiker zu malen, die mir wirklich etwas bedeuteten. Diese Leute gehören zu unserem Leben. Sie sind auf den Plakaten an der Bushaltestelle, sie sind überall, und sie sind so real wie Mütter. Dann wurde mir plötzlich bewusst, dass diese Leute ja um die Ecke wohnen. Es sind meine Freunde. Es sind tolle Künstler, die wirklich wertvolle Sachen machen, und das wollte ich auch kundtun. Ich glaube, es ist wichtig, in seinem Leben solche Leute um sich zu haben.

C C : Ist es anders, wenn du von einem selbst gemachten Photo ausgehst, im Gegensatz zu einem irgendwo veröffentlichten Bild?

E P : Es war zuerst schwieriger, weil die veröffentlichten Bilder schon bearbeitet waren und gut aussahen. Aber nun, nachdem ich ein ganzes Jahr mit einer Person gearbeitet habe, ist es ungeheuer, wieviel mehr man sieht.

C C : Ich rezykliere meine Lieblingsbilder auch. Philip Glass male ich seit fünfunddreissig Jahren. Ich habe schon gedacht, ich sollte sein Photo unerreichbar zwischen die Deckenbalken meines Ateliers hängen, so wie ein Sportler nach Spielende auch sein Leibchen abgibt.

E P : Dieses Bild ist so sexy. Fühlst du dich berühmt?

C C : Nicht besonders. Als ich in den Rollstuhl kam, geschah etwas Interessantes. Ich bin über eins neunzig und konnte immer über die Köpfe der Leute hinwegschauen. Nun war ich gewissermassen auf Normalgrösse zurückgestutzt und die Leute behandelten mich anders. Plötzlich kamen sie auf mich zu und sagten mir, dass ihnen meine Arbeit etwas bedeute. Ich glaube durchaus, dass man Dinge für andere Leute tut. Kunst als Therapie hat mich nie interessiert. Zur Therapie gehe ich in eine Therapie. Ich mache diese Dinge, weil ich glaube, dass es eine Form von Sprache ist und dass da draussen Leute sind, die sie entziffern können.

E P : Glaubst du, dass ein Bild ein Leben verändern kann?

C C : Nun, Bilder haben mein Leben verändert. Ich glaube nicht, dass die Kunst ein gutes Propaganda- oder Erziehungsmittel ist. Wir füllen die Kirchen nicht mehr mit Bildnissen, damit sich die Leute ihrem Gott näher fühlen. Aber Kunst ist meine Religion; sie ist das, worauf es mir ankommt. Natürlich muss man als Künstler so arrogant sein und glauben, dass man etwas zu sagen hat, was andere vielleicht hören möchten. Aber Künstler sind auch unglaublich grosszügig. Die Grosszügigkeit besteht darin, zu zeigen, was einem wichtig ist. Ich glaube, das kann ein Leben verändern. Ich wollte nie Stillleben malen oder Landschaften, denn wenn ich einen Felsen male, kann ihn nur ein Geologe wiedererkennen. Aber wir alle reagieren auf ein Gesicht.

E P : Die Menschen lassen sich wohl von nichts im Leben so sehr berühren wie von anderen Menschen. Auch für sie kann so ein Bild mehr sein als Kunst, und das ist das Befreiende daran.

C C : Ich bedaure zum Beispiel sehr, dass ich meine Mutter nicht gemalt

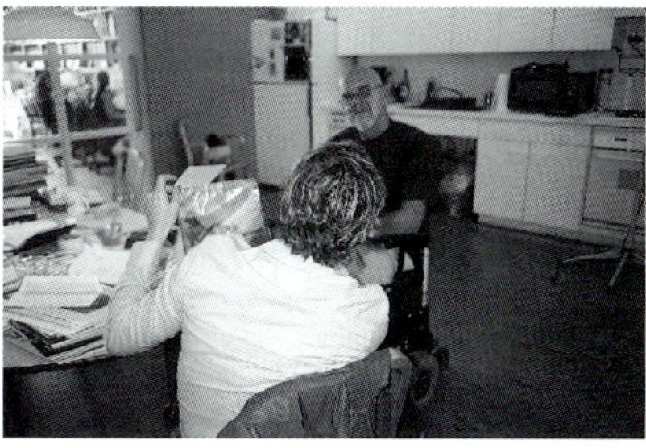

habe, bevor sie starb. Nach einer gewissen Zeit erinnert man sich nicht mehr an die Stimme eines Verstorbenen und ich würde gern diesen Grad von Vertrautheit über das Bild wieder herstellen können.

E P : Bist du dir jeweils bewusst, die Leute an einem bestimmten Punkt ihres Lebens festzuhalten? Philip Glass zum Beispiel stand ganz am Anfang. Oder bei Cecily, sie ist auf einem ersten Höhepunkt angelangt.

C C : Vermutlich ist eine gewisse Energie und Lebhaftigkeit in ihren Gesichtern zu erkennen, wenn sie gerade dabei sind, die Stücke ihres Puzzles zusammenzufügen und ihre persönliche Sicht der Dinge klarer wird. Da ist etwas Besonderes am Beginn einer Karriere, ein Zusammenkommen der Dinge: Es ist spannend, mit jemandem während dieser Zeit zu tun zu haben.

E P : Was ist heute anders im Vergleich zu deinen Anfängen?

C C : Als ich am Anfang stand, waren wir verzweifelt bemüht, alle Spuren und Einflüsse anderer Künstler aus unserer Arbeit zu tilgen. Heute ist die Haltung eine ganz andere, es geht eher darum, den kulturellen Vorratsschrank gründlich zu plündern. Ich fühle mich der Szene heute wirklich verbunden. Ich denke es ist eine ziemlich harte Zeit.

E P : Du bekommst sicher mehr davon mit als ich. In der *New York Times* habe ich gelesen, du hättest Al Gore vom Malen abgeraten. War das ein Witz oder malt er wirklich schlecht?

C C : Ich habe keine Ahnung, ob er gut oder schlecht malt. Es war ein Witz, etwa in der Richtung, ich hätte gedacht, wir hätten einen Pakt geschlossen, dass er nicht malen würde und wir dafür nicht in die Politik gingen. Tatsächlich denke ich, dass es gut ist, dass er über diese Erfahrung verfügt.

E P : Die Leute werden sympathischer, wenn sie malen, auch Prinz Charles.

C C : Ja. Ich bin nicht so sicher, ob es Eisenhower genützt hat. Nixon malte nicht, das ist sicher. Ich glaube auch nicht, dass Ronald Reagan malte.

E P : Man kann sich vorstellen, dass Gore diese Art der Ruhe braucht.

C C : Ich stellte ihm bei einer Veranstaltung einmal eine Frage, die er beantwortete, indem er von der «Gestalt» eines Bildes sprach, und ich dachte: «Ein Präsidentschaftskandidat, der weiss, was die ‹Gestalt› eines Bildes ist, der bekommt meine Stimme.»

… Ich habe mir eben deine Bilder angeschaut. Was mir am Malen unter anderem so gefällt, ist, dass es auch eine Art Aufzeichnung von Entscheidungen darstellt. Da liegt alles vor einem ausgebreitet. Man findet die Gründe für stumpfe Farben, Pinselstriche und verschiedene Arten des Farbauftrags. Eines der Probleme der Kunstkritik ist, dass keiner mehr ein Bild beschreibt, es wird angenommen, die Reproduktion genüge, und niemand sagt mehr, wie es ist, vor einem Bild zu stehen.

E P : Das stimmt.

C C : Ich kann mir vorstellen, wie du über die Richtung der Pinselstriche und darüber, was du tust, nachdenkst. Du hast offensichtlich Spass an diesem Moment – Hand und Pinselstrich. Es scheint sich alles um diesen Pinselstrich zu drehen.

E P : Wenn es läuft, geniesse ich es. Während der Arbeit denke ich aber nicht so viel darüber nach.

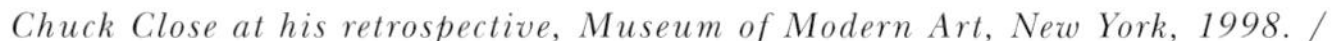

Chuck Close at his retrospective, Museum of Modern Art, New York, 1998. /

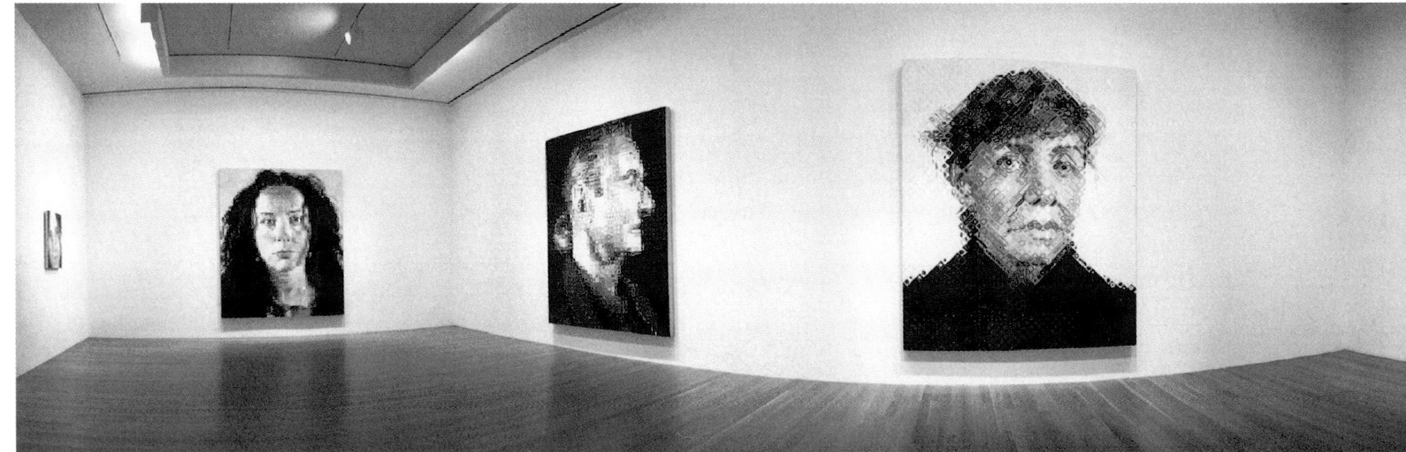

CC: Ich mag zum Beispiel Frans Hals, weil man genau sieht, wie er mit vier oder fünf Strichen eine Hand hinkriegt. Das ist so viel besser als Rembrandt.

EP: Das war ja vielleicht toll, als du sagtest: «Ich mag Rembrandt nicht.»

CC: Seine Bilder ertrinken in brauner Sauce. Auf der anderen Seite lässt sich Vermeer überhaupt nicht entschlüsseln. Es ist wie ein Wunder, als wären all diese Dinge von einer Brise auf die Leinwand geweht worden. Wer aus der Kunstgeschichte hat dich angeturnt?

EP: Ich mag Velázquez, aber auch Sargents Umgang mit dem Pinsel ist verblüffend, selbst in seinen langweiligen Porträts. Und ich war selbst überrascht, dass mir die Ingres-Ausstellung gefiel. Denn das ist einer, bei dem man gar nichts sieht, und das macht mich verrückt. Zu sehen, woher er kommt, zeigte immerhin, dass er an einem gewissen Punkt wirklich malte, er wurde dann einfach zu gut.

CC: Wie hast dus mit der Leichtigkeit? Ich glaube, das Leichte ist der grösste Feind des Künstlers.

EP: Ausser vielleicht, wenn du Alex Katz heisst. Was mich betrifft, so weiss ich, dass es gefährlich werden könnte, wenn ich wirklich weiss, was ich tue.

CC: Es muss irgendwie ein bestimmter Grad an Widerstand vorhanden sein.

EP: Ja, und ein immer noch mehr Wollen. Aber Alex Katz könnte immer wieder denselben Mund malen und er wäre immer schön. Aber Katz will etwas anderes als ich, auch was die Textur angeht, und er hat auch diesen Warholschen Hang zur Vereinfachung.

CC: Alex hat einmal bei mir geklagt, dass er Schwierigkeiten mit einem Bild habe, weil er nach drei Tagen am Stück die Energie zum Weitermachen beinah nicht mehr aufbringen könne. Wenn wir schon von verschiedenen Gesichtspunkten reden: Ich finde es hilfreich, dass ich heute dasselbe tue wie gestern, und morgen dasselbe wie heute und dass ich mich auf einen langwierigen Prozess einlasse. Das finde ich wirklich beruhigend wie stricken oder häkeln … Malst du manchmal auch wochenlang gar nicht?

EP: Ja, aber nicht ohne schlechtes Gewissen, obwohl ich diese Unsicherheit mag, wenn ich zurückkomme und nicht mehr weiss, wie ich ein Auge mache. Es ist irgendwie schön, es wieder zu tun und anders zu machen. Sind Photos etwas, woraus du neue Ideen entwickeln kannst?

CC: Ja, und wobei ich schnell arbeiten kann. Gewöhnlich brauche ich für eine Serie von acht oder neun Gemälden drei Jahre. Also ist es zur Abwechslung schön, anders voranzukommen. Und dann ist natürlich ein wesentlicher Reiz des Künstlerlebens, dass man sich unter nackten Leuten aufhalten kann.

EP: Ach, geht es im Wesentlichen darum?

CC: Aber gewiss. Und ich mische immer genügend Männer drunter, damit es nicht aussieht, als gehe es mir nur um nackte Frauen *(Lachen)*. Und dann interessiere ich mich plötzlich für Körper, die alles andere als perfekt sind. Und du, wirst du auch alternde Rockstars malen?

EP: Ich nehme an, sie werden mit mir zusammen älter werden.

CC: Nun, in dieser Kultur gibt es auch die «Lebe wild, stirb jung und hinterlasse eine Menge schöner Erinnerungen»-Variante.

Der Künstler in seiner Ausstellung, Chuck-Close-Retrospektive, Museum of Modern Art, New York, 1998. (PHOTO: KENNETH SNELSON)

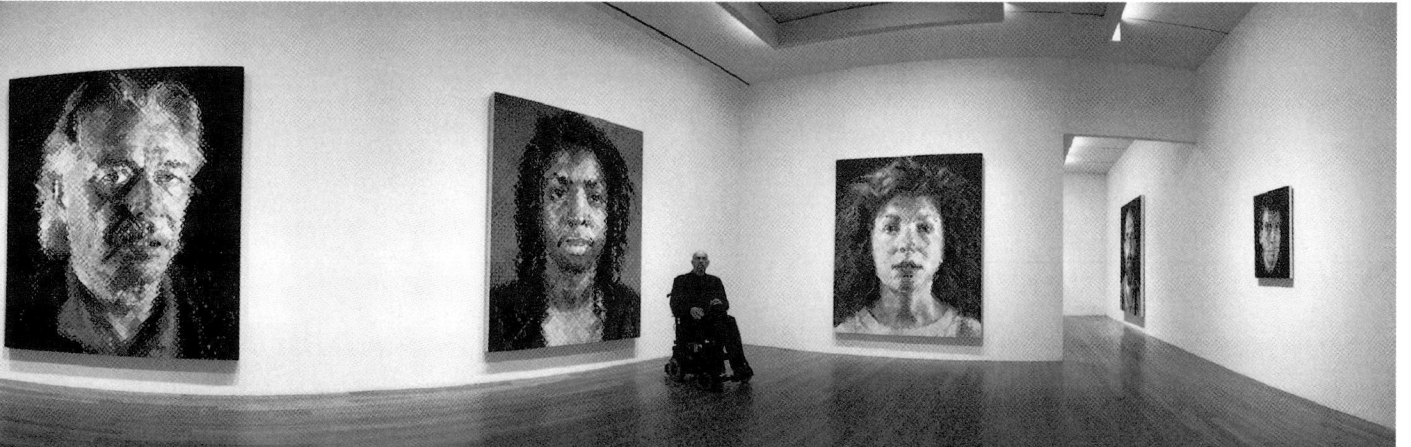

E P : Ich habe immer daran gedacht, dass sie nie mehr so sein werden, wie sie jetzt sind. Es liegt ein ungeheurer Verlust im Verstreichen dieses Augenblicks. Ich weiss nicht, ob ich Falten malen werde. Die, die da sind, sind zufällig reingeraten, weil ich den Pinsel gerade in die entsprechende Richtung zog, aber ich glaube, bewusst und mit Absicht kann ich das nicht.

C C : Mich lässt der Gedanke nicht los, wie wichtig das Umfeld war, das Wasserloch, an dem wir uns jeweils versammelten. Ich glaube, wir festigten unsere eigenen Ideen, wenn wir mit Grössen wie Robert Smithson oder Richard Serra in der Bar hockten. Diese Leute waren wirklich hart mit einem. Man musste sich so heftig verteidigen, dass sich im Gespräch eine Menge Dinge klärten. Gleichzeitig zeigten sie aber, dass sie uns ernst nahmen und dass es ihnen nicht egal war, ob man ein weiteres Bild malte oder nicht, auch wenn sie einen gern überzeugt hätten ein anderes Bild zu malen. Ist Gavin (Brown's Bar) auch so ein Ort?

E P : In gewisser Weise. Aber die Leute sind heute viel höflicher. Ich habe nie jemanden über Kunst streiten hören. Aber es ist etwas dran, den Leuten von Angesicht zu Angesicht zu begegnen und auch zu erfahren, wie viel man mit Leuten gemeinsam hat, die etwas ganz anderes machen. Man nimmt das mit zurück in sein Atelier. Die meisten meiner Freunde sind Konzeptkünstler. Ich kenne nur wenige Maler. Vermutlich ist es ein Ort, wo Menschen die Dinge auf die Reihe zu bringen versuchen. «Hast du diese Ausstellung gesehen? Jene Kritik gelesen? Was hältst du davon?» Und es ist wohl der einzige Ort

in meinem Leben, wo so was in Gesellschaft stattfindet. Aber ich halte die Kunstszene weitgehend für einen Hurra-Club. Man geht wohlwollend und liebenswürdig miteinander um. Es gibt keinen strengen Ideologen, der dir sagen würde: «Das kannst du nicht machen!»

C C : Egal, ob die Szene mehr oder weniger konkurrenzbetont ist, mir scheint, man kann keine Kunst machen ohne eine Gemeinschaft.

E P : Ich glaube, die Leute stehen einander schon ziemlich kritisch gegenüber, aber nach aussen zeigt man diese Alles-ist-okay-Haltung. Auch ich habe mit manchen Arbeiten meine moralischen Probleme. Ich halte sie einfach für grässlich.

C C : Ach ja, das ist ja interessant. Was für unmoralische Taten kann ein Künstler denn verüben?

E P : Etwas, was zynisch ist oder nur um der Karriere willen geschieht, oder aus falschen Motiven heraus, das ärgert mich. Oder Dinge, die nur gross und teuer sind, aber sonst gar nichts.

C C : Und wie hältst dus mit der Ironie?

E P : Ich habe tatsächlich ein Problem mit der Ironie. Ich weiss, dass manche sie klug einsetzen. Und wie oft habe ich Arbeiten für ironisch gehalten, die es dann am Ende gar nicht waren.

C C : Die Ironie kann tyrannisch sein. Derart, dass man nichts mehr ernst nehmen kann, ausser der eigenen Ironie.

E P : Ja, und sie verunmöglicht, dass eine Sache in und aus sich selbst etwas sein kann, weil immer ein äusserer Bezugspunkt da sein muss, damit Bedeutung entsteht. Und ich habe halt immer noch diese heilige Idee vom in sich geschlossenen, autonomen Kunstwerk.

C C : Ich glaube, das ist zum Teil auch die Schwierigkeit jeder intelligenten Kritik, dass alles, was man wissen muss, und alles, was man zu seiner Beurteilung braucht, schon im Kunstwerk selbst enthalten ist.

E P : Gewöhnlich kritisiere ich einen Künstler nur, wenn ich wirklich denke, dass er etwas falsch macht. Aber was den Geschmack angeht, gibt es keinen Grund sich aufzuregen. Es gibt so viele tolle Künstler überall, faszinierende, schöne und hinreissende Menschen, und dann schaut man sich diese Zeitschriften an und hat das Gefühl, die Kritik erfülle ihre Aufgabe nicht.

C C : Die Leute nehmen eine Künstlerkarriere gewöhnlich erst ernst, wenn sich alle wesentlichen Punkte geklärt haben. Dabei ist es viel interessanter, solange noch eine gewisse Verwirrung herrscht.

E P : Ist dir schon aufgefallen, wie sehr die Menschen ihren Körpern gleichen? Dass die Krümmung ihres Fingers die gleiche ist wie die ihrer Nase? Achtest du auf solche Beziehungen?

C C : Nein, das ist mir noch nie aufgefallen, ich muss wohl mal genauer hinschauen.

E P : Ich mag es, wenn Menschen auf diese Art uniform sind. Wenn die Ellbogen den Ohren gleichen.

C C : Hmm. Das muss ich nachprüfen. Darf ich dich photographieren?

E P : Klar doch.

C C : Was ist dir lieber: Körper oder Kopf?

E P : Kopf! Ich ziehe mich nicht aus. Ich habe auch noch nie von jemandem verlangt sich auszuziehen.

C C : Ach, tatsächlich?

(Übersetzung: Susanne Schmidt)

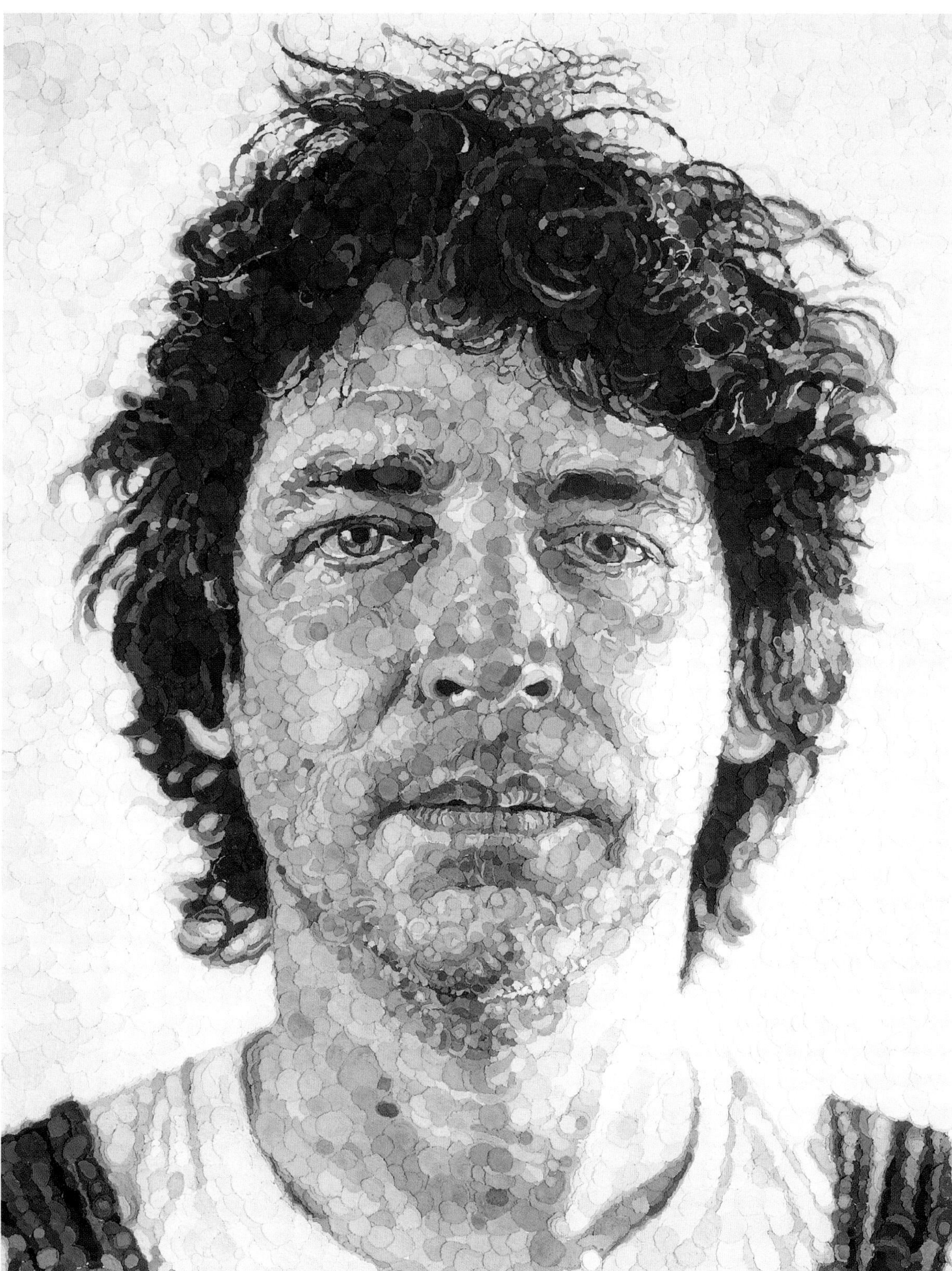

CHUCK CLOSE, JUD, 1982, pulp paper paper collage on canvas, 96 x 72" / Collage aus Papiermasse auf Leinwand, 243,8 x 182,9 cm.

RICHARD SHIFF

Raster + Vector = *Animation Squared*

Magic, an art of deception, was Chuck Close's first art, his childhood talent. Then he became a painter. I suppose his early student work was illusionistic, deceiving vision like magic. But Close must have realized (we all do) that the most ordinary appearance, the look of a friend's face, can be equally deceptive, that even everyday vision requires scrutiny. Where does this leave the representation of ordinary appearance? Does a picture of me become an interpretive problem for you? The conventions of representation are designed to normalize matters, converting deception into agreeable "truth." But just as likely, every successive pictorial practice adds to collective confusion. I often think of Close as our greatest investigator of the commonplace representations that guide our lives and secure our memories. Noth-

ing is more normal, nor more puzzling and magical, than a photograph of a familiar face, the type of portraiture that has been Close's content for more than thirty years.

Ours is a technocratic culture. Ever more sophisticated technologies—first mechanical, then electronic—register appearances, allowing one image to be verified or refined against the standard of another. Yet each technology has its own manner of representing. The differences indicate neither truth nor error nor improvement, but the fact that to shift from one mode of representation to another alters the apparent order of things. It would be wrong to accept as an absolute standard the imagery produced by any one medium, including the naked eye. The lenses of photography and film, their effects now enhanced by digital scanning, record visual events the eye sees, but with peculiar refinements and with details it doesn't detect. Whenever a new representational technology appears, we understand its prod-

RICHARD SHIFF is Effie Marie Cain Regents Chair in Art at the University of Texas at Austin, where he directs the Center for the Study of Modernism.

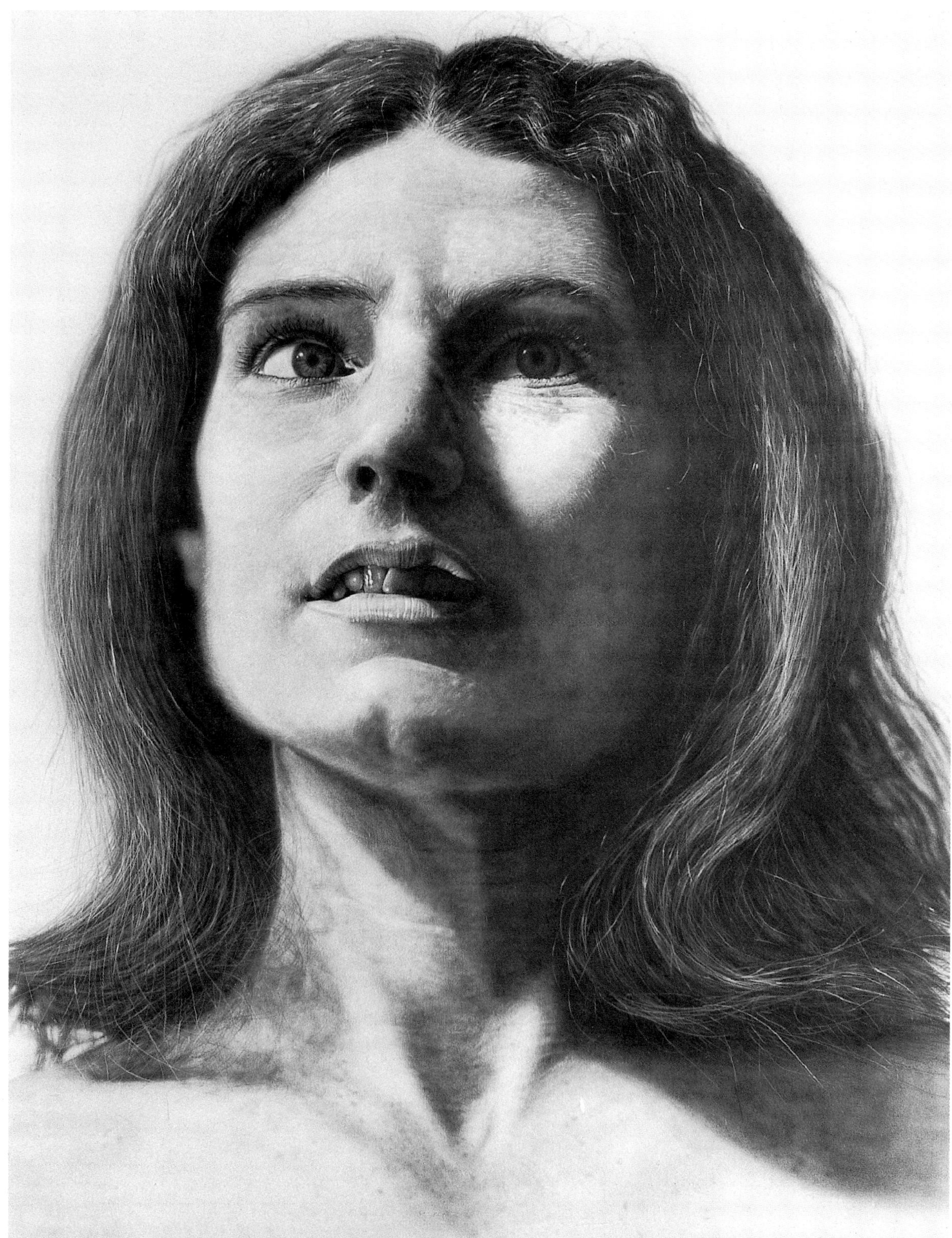

CHUCK CLOSE, NANCY, 1968, acrylic on canvas, 108⅜ x 82¼″ / Acryl auf Leinwand, 275,3 x 208,9 cm.

ucts by whatever links to earlier imagery can be discerned. Or forged, by an artist's pictorial invention.

An exploratory comparative method is the foundation of Close's painting. His model is not a living person but that person's appearance (often Close's own) viewed through the competing medium of photography. Close acts as both photographer and painter, mindful of how painting will respond to a photographic presence, as if he were adjudicating between two pictorial authorities, each with its own history and claims to a proper image. The interaction he stages stimulates both mediums to evolve. If photographic technology is automatic and remote, Close provides it with corporeal intimacy—not only a close-up intimacy with the model, but also with the artist's embodied vision, as he works his way through the image, reproducing by hand what originated in a mechanism, one he himself operated.

Although intimacy, accuracy, and the mechanics of vision—human mechanics as well as machine mechanics—are among Close's artistic interests, I don't think he has consciously sought to test technologies of representation against a putative human standard. He confines accounts of his motivation to modest, mundane concerns, as if to confess that his artistic magic is just a routine, a way of dealing with things he can't otherwise control. As a graduate student during the sixties, Close quickly mastered the gestural devices of Abstract Expressionism and indulged his talent in making new variations; this did nothing to challenge the "lazy and slobby and indecisive" person he claims he was.[1] Around 1967, he forced himself to shift to a rigorous photographic realism: "I found it incredibly liberating… to make very neat, precise paintings." (…) "I was trying to make my work look like photographs in order to get my hand out of there, because I had all of these habits that were associated with other people's work. I was trying to purge de Kooning…"[2]

Close's early photo-based portraits, such as NANCY (1968), were constituted entirely of black pigment against a white ground; this eliminated the de Kooning factor of willful color. The paint was thinned and applied with innumerable short puffs of an airbrush; this suppressed the de Kooning factor of expressionistic gesture. Close became his own per-

son, one he could respect, by denying himself familiar aesthetic pleasures of color and movement. Yet he's now quick to acknowledge the irony in much of his work of the eighties and nineties: the de Kooning he always loved gradually resurfaced in the garish rainbow of hues Close adapted to render flesh tones—intense pinks, bright oranges, acidic greens, lavenders. Did his art also return to something of de Kooning's animated movement?

Think of pictorial imagery in terms of two competing systems of description—the vector and the raster. Linear drawing, which establishes continuous contours and edges, is primarily a vector system: each stroke implies a directional movement the eye can follow, while what surrounds the stroke remains devoid of tone. With their fully colored surfaces, representational painting and (more obviously) photography are primarily raster systems: each distinguishable element of color or tone, each pixel, occupies a position on the organizing raster, a kind of invisible grid that maps a continuous field of illumination. A picture is virtually present even when the raster is blank, because the sum of pixel units is coextensive with the surface. Like light-sensitive photographic film, the pictorial raster merely awaits its activation, as if its differentiating tonalities were to be projected from within the surface as much as from without.

Appropriately, Close calls his early photo-based works "continuous tone" paintings; they look (he once told me) as if the filmy airbrushed image "moved in on a fog and fell into the painting." With this all-at-once quality, NANCY gives the stilled appearance of a photograph, but deceptively; for these two raster mediums diverge in a manner Close himself has articulated: "A photograph is complete in an instant, but a painting is incomplete until it is finished; with a painting, each thing you add changes what is already there."[3] The difference depends on successive actions of the hand, which, unlike fog or photochemistry, follow the vagaries of intuitive judgment. The artist adjusts and fine-tunes his elements in a play that approaches traditional composition, but at an unfamiliar level of resolution: hair by hair, pore by pore, mark by barely perceptible mark. This is why the images in Close's paintings are so

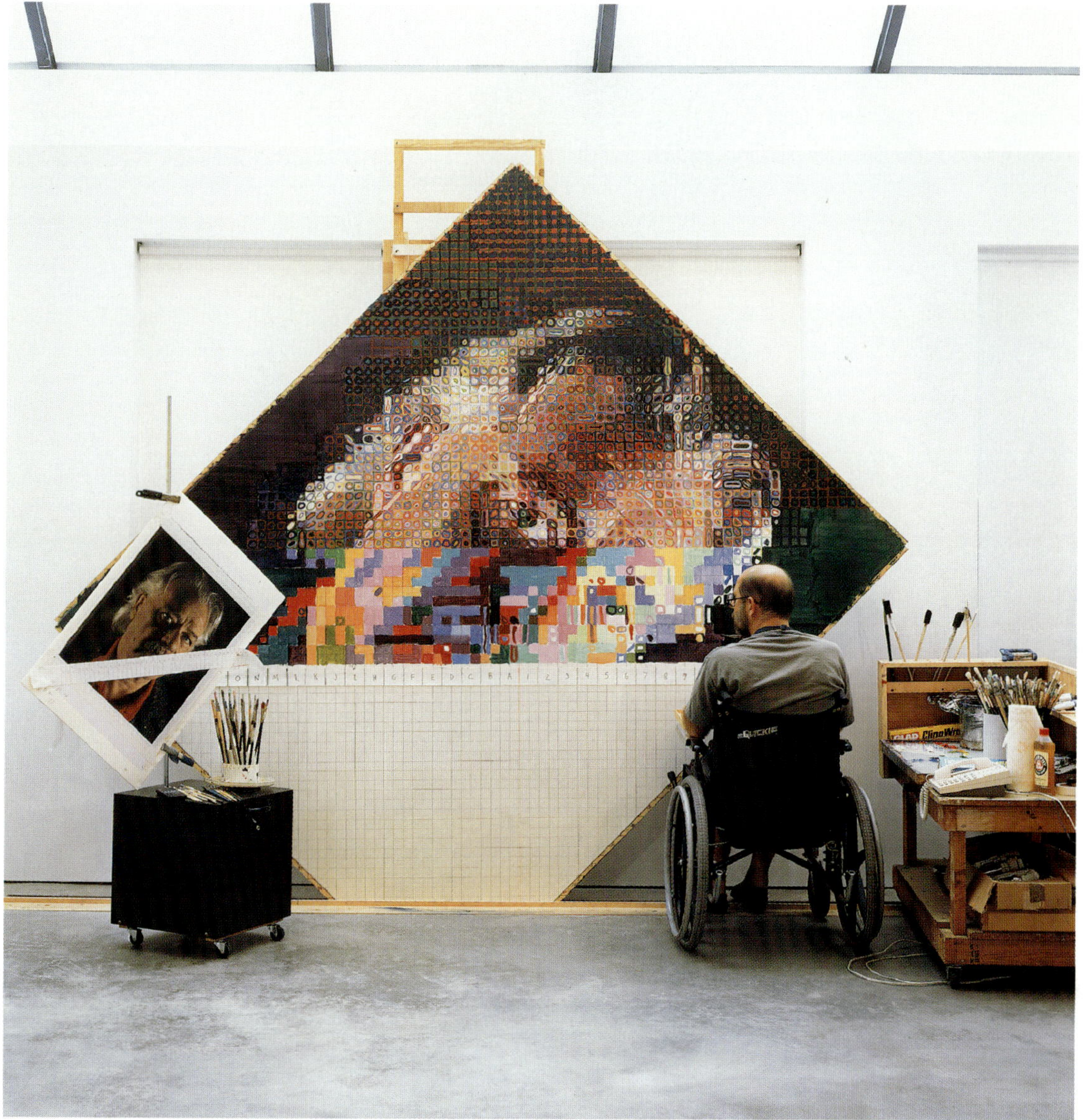

CHUCK CLOSE, JOHN, 1992, oil on canvas, 100 x 84", the artist with work in progress / Öl auf Leinwand, 254 x 213,4 cm, der Künstler während der Arbeit am Bild. (PHOTO: BILL JACOBSON)

arresting, beyond the wonder of their rigorous handwork. There's nothing "ordinary" about these appearances, which have been reconstructed from the photographic models with such subtle variation that you're more likely to notice sameness than difference. To the unwary, the differences remain subliminal: like the nuanced look on a face, eliciting response without consciousness; like the precise moment when a physiognomic feature becomes… paint. Is it magic?

During the eighties and nineties, the units of Close's grids increased in size relative to the overall dimensions of the format. This causes the viewer, even at a distance, to notice individual constituent marks, certain to see not only "the image made" but "the stuff that makes it." [4] While the earlier, smaller pixels held a single color mark, the larger ones now commonly include five or more contrasting colors. In many instances, the marks form concentric patterns that preserve raster-like directional neutrality. [5]

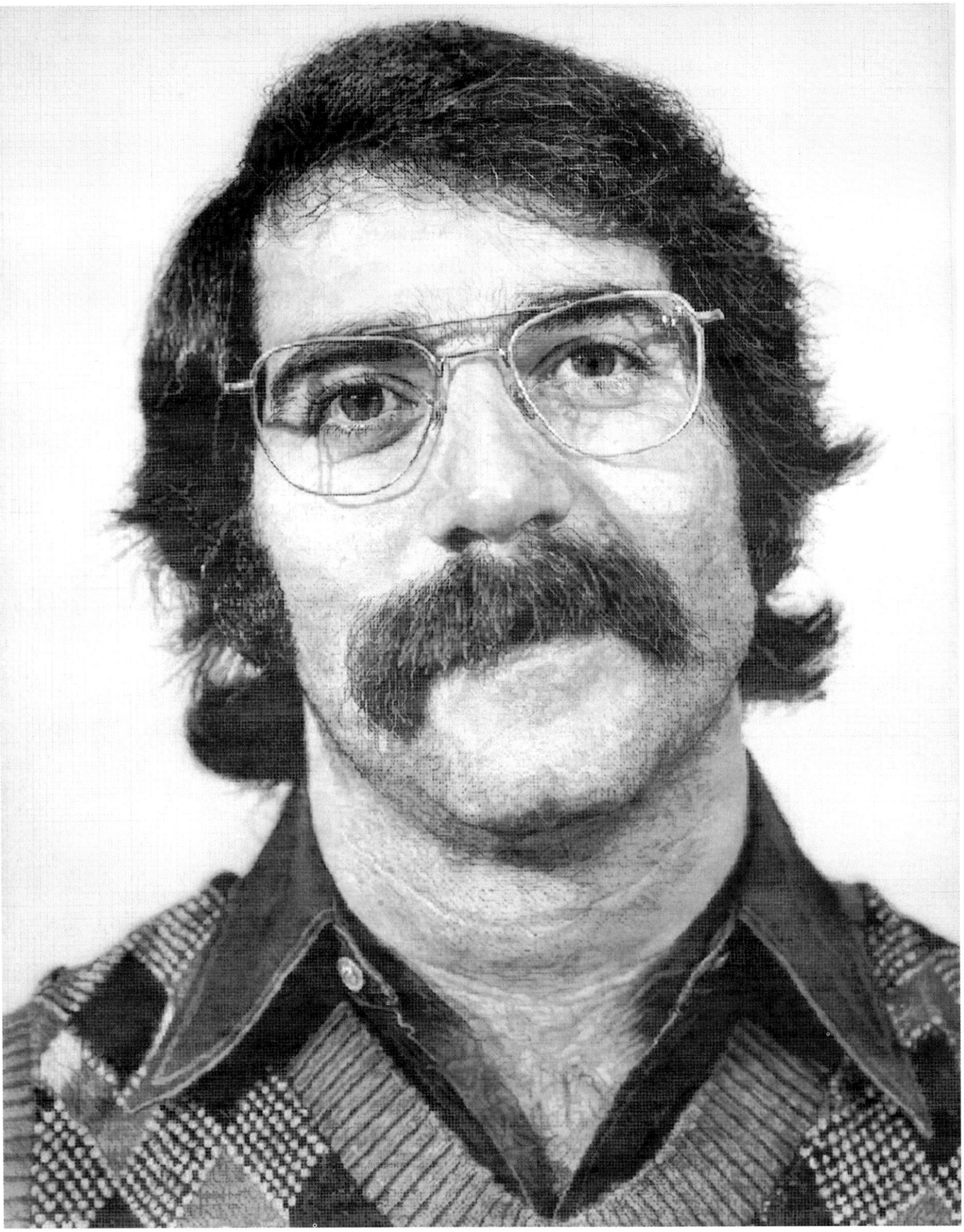

CHUCK CLOSE, ROBERT/104,072, 1973–74, ink and pencil on canvas with gesso, 108 x 84" / Tusche und Bleistift auf grundierter Leinwand, 274,3 x 213,4 cm.

(PHOTO: ELLEN PAGE WILSON)

A typical unit might hold a dot within two roughly circular loops, within two loosely configured squares, all within the squareness of the containing pixel.

When Close performs his pictorial translation, each grid unit of the photographic "maquette" is subdivided into four units on the much larger painting surface, facilitating work at the increased scale. It happens that a set of four symmetrical units is the smallest possible rectilinear raster, establishing a field in which up, down, left, and right assume equal value. Within this fundamentally neutral format, Close feels "liberated." He can choose any mark in any color to initiate a unit of the image, knowing that he can adjust its representational value with successive marks and through the play of adjacent units. Recall that the image created by conventional photography appears "in an instant," while painting develops through time. Close's painting mimics its photographic model successfully, but its temporality is unrelated to the photographic process. So the representational content of these distinct mediums is both different and the same. Close's art demonstrates how we (attempt to) regulate deceptive appearances through the play of incommensurable representational systems. One medium accentuates whatever "truth" there may be in the other (this is the sameness), while their differences appear ever more evident. If you, too, are "lazy and slobby and indecisive," Close offers an experience to make you a far more wary observer.

Not all of Close's pixels seem neutral with regard to a sense of direction or movement. Sometimes he stretches his loops across as many as four units in a row: see the right side of the chin in MAGGIE (1998–99), where such an extended form suggests the linear continuity of an edge and yet it doesn't, because the flesh-like tones are separated from the rest of the figure by darker colors indicating background. By averaging out such contrasts, the eye sees the edge of a face. This edge continues upward along the cheek, despite a serrated effect where light skin and dark ground seem interwoven, giving substance to the insubstantial raster. The grid units, which maintain their integrity, are straddling a pictorial edge, which maintains i t s integrity, but only virtually, as illusion. Now return to focus on the figure's

chin: the edge (virtual or real) may well vanish, replaced by the oblong, highlighted loop, a self-contained form with a length about nine inches. Here you experience the success and failure of representation in the near simultaneity of a photographic, painterly "instant."

At whatever moment you do follow a pictorial edge, Close's raster is generating a vector—or rather, its illusion. Yet, Close has actually vectored every pixel by inserting his little marks, each at least somewhat directional because his hand's movement remains evident. In certain instances, the directionality is quite pronounced. In MAGGIE, a slightly bowed vertical, confined to a single pixel, marks an edge between nostril and cheek, a physiognomic fragment otherwise blanched out by high illumination. Whether tracing a form in the photographic model or merely recording a hand's natural movement, every directional mark stretches and compresses, pulls and pushes the raster one way or another. Even within the nominally neutral background, nothing is still.

Every mark is itself a movement, animating "image" and "stuff" in their interaction, enhancing the life. I realize that in addition to de Kooning's color, Close has managed to regain de Kooning's organicism—radically transformed through an artistic discipline of comparative representational technology. I suppose Close would say he was just too "lazy and slobby and indecisive" to have let anything go.

1) Chuck Close, interviewed by Robert Storr, in: *Chuck Close*, ed. by Robert Storr, exh. cat. (New York: The Museum of Modern Art, 1998), p. 94.

2) Ibid., p. 95; Chuck Close, conversation with Roy Lichtenstein, 23 October 1995, in: *The Portraits Speak*, ed. by Joanne Kesten (New York: A.R.T. Press, 1997), p. 619.

3) Chuck Close, in: *Artist's Choice: Chuck Close*, ed. by Kirk Varnedoe, exh. cat. (New York: The Museum of Modern Art, 1991), p. 7. An "instant," of course, is not no time, but imperceptible time.

4) Chuck Close, interview by Brooks Adams, "Close Encountered," in: *Artforum*, vol. XXXVI, no. 8 (April 1998), p. 135.

5) Close often sets his grid diagonally, but, while working, rotates the photograph and painting so that the grid regains its normative orientation.

RICHARD SHIFF

Raster + Vektor = *Animation im Quadrat*

Zunächst war die Kunst von Chuck Close magisch, eine Kunst der Täuschung, eine Gabe, die ihm in die Wiege gelegt war. Dann wurde er Maler. Ich nehme an, seine ersten Arbeiten während des Studiums waren illusionistisch und führten das Auge genauso hinters Licht wie die Zauberkunst. Aber Close muss (wie wir alle) bemerkt haben, dass uns selbst die alltäglichste Erscheinung, etwa der Ausdruck im Gesicht eines Freundes, in die Irre führen kann und dass unser alltägliches Sehen der Überprüfung bedarf. Wird ein Bild von mir dir interpretatorische Rätsel aufgeben? Die Konventionen der bildlichen Darstellung sind dazu da, die Dinge «normal» erscheinen zu lassen, und machen aus der Täuschung eine annehmbare «Wahrheit». Aber es trifft auch zu, dass jede neue Abbildungstechnik zur kollektiven Verwirrung beiträgt. Ich halte Close für den bedeu-

tendsten Erforscher der gängigen Darstellungsweisen, die unser aller Leben und unsere Erinnerungen bestimmen. Nichts ist alltäglicher, aber auch nichts verwirrender und magischer als die Photographie eines vertrauten Gesichts und damit die Art von Porträt, mit der sich Close nun über dreissig Jahre lang auseinander gesetzt hat.

Unsere Kultur ist technokratisch. Mit immer raffinierteren technischen Mitteln – zunächst mechanischen, später elektronischen – werden Erscheinungen festgehalten, und damit können die verschiedenen Bilder in prüfender oder korrigierender Absicht miteinander verglichen werden. Dennoch hat jede Technik ihre eigenen Darstellungsformen. Die Unterschiede sind daher keine Zeichen von Wahrheit, Irrtum oder Fortschritt, sondern verweisen allein auf die Tatsache, dass der Übergang von einer Darstellungsweise zur anderen die scheinbare Ordnung der Dinge verändert. Es wäre falsch, die Bilder eines dieser Medien zum absoluten Massstab zu nehmen, das gilt auch für das unbewaffnete Auge. Die Linsen der

RICHARD SHIFF ist Inhaber des Effie-Marie-Cain-Lehrstuhls für Kunstwissenschaft an der Universität von Texas in Austin, wo er auch das Institut für Kunst der Moderne leitet.

Photographie und des Films, deren Wirkung durch die Technik des digitalen Scannens noch verfeinert wird, zeichnen visuelle Ereignisse auf, die das Auge sehen kann, liefern jedoch merkwürdige Feinheiten und Details mit, die das Auge allein nicht bemerkt. Und immer wenn eine neue Bildtechnologie auftaucht, verstehen wir deren Erzeugnisse dank Verbindungen zur bestehenden Bildsprache, die sich darin finden. Oder sich mit der Erfindungskraft eines Künstlers *herstellen* lassen.

Das Fundament der Malerei von Close ist das forschende Vergleichen. Sein Modell ist nicht eine lebende Person, sondern das Erscheinungsbild dieser Person (oft sein eigenes), und zwar im Blickwinkel des Konkurrenzmediums Photographie. Close spielt dabei beide Rollen, die des Photographen und die des Malers, wobei er immer im Blick hat, wie die Malerei auf das photographische Bild reagieren wird, als wäre er ein Vermittler zwischen zwei Bildautoritäten, die über ihre je eigene Geschichte und eigene Vorstellung vom richtigen Bild verfügen. Die Auseinandersetzung, die er so inszeniert, regt die Weiterentwicklung beider Medien an. Wo die Photographie automatisch und schwer fassbar ist, verleiht ihr Close körperliche Intimität – nicht nur durch die Nähe zum Modell, sondern auch zur greifbar werdenden Vision des Künstlers selbst, während er sich durch das Bild hindurcharbeitet und das Resultat eines technischen Prozesses, den er selbst ausgelöst hat, von Hand reproduziert.

Obwohl Intimität, Genauigkeit und die Technik des Sehens – sowohl die menschliche wie die maschinelle – Close künstlerisch interessieren, glaube ich nicht, dass er je bewusst versucht hat, die Repräsentationstechniken auf dem Hintergrund eines allgemein menschlichen Massstabs zu prüfen. In Aussagen über seine Beweggründe beschränkt er diese immer auf ganz alltägliche Fragestellungen, als wolle er sagen, dass seine Künstlermagie reine Routine sei, eine Art, sich mit Dingen auseinander zu setzen, über die er sonst keine Kontrolle hat. Als fortgeschrittener Student in den 60er Jahren hatte sich Close die Ausdrucksmittel des Abstrakten Expressionismus im Handumdrehen angeeignet und übte sich darin, neue Spielarten zu erfinden; aber das bildete eine ernsthafte Herausforderung für «den faulen, nach-

lässigen und unentschlossenen» Menschen, der er laut eigener Aussage damals war.[1] 1967 zwang er sich, zu einem rigorosen photographischen Realismus überzugehen: «Ich fand es unglaublich befreiend… ganz saubere, exakte Bilder zu machen.» (…) «Ich versuchte meine Arbeiten wie Photographien aussehen zu lassen, um freizukommen, denn ich hatte all die Gewohnheiten, die mit dem Werk anderer Leute verbunden waren. Ich versuchte de Kooning auszutreiben…»[2]

Die frühen, von Photos ausgehenden Porträts wie NANCY (1968) bestanden allein aus schwarzem Pigment auf weissem Grund; damit war de Koonings Farbigkeit gebannt. Die Farbe war verdünnt und wurde in unzähligen kurzen Airbrush-Pustern aufgesprüht; damit war auch de Koonings expressionistische Geste eliminiert. Close wurde er selbst, eine Person, die er achten konnte, indem er sich die vertrauten ästhetischen Freuden der Farbe und der Bewegung versagte. Aber heute gesteht er die ironische Komponente seines Werks der 80er und 90er Jahre sofort ein: de Kooning, den er immer gemocht hatte, tauchte allmählich wieder auf in den grellen Regenbogenfarben, die Close zur Wiedergabe von Hauttönen verwendete – intensive Pink-, helle Orange-, giftige Grün- und Violetttöne. Fand diese Kunst auch wieder etwas von de Koonings lebhafter Bewegung?

Stellen Sie sich die Bildsprache der Malerei als zwei konkurrierende Darstellungsprinzipien vor – Vektor versus Raster. Die lineare Zeichnung, die geschlossene Umrisse und Abgrenzungen erzeugt, ist in erster Linie ein vektorielles System: Jeder Strich ist mit einer gerichteten Bewegung verbunden, der das Auge folgen kann, während die Umgebung des Strichs ungetönt bleibt. Mit ihren vollfarbigen Flächen sind die figürliche Malerei und (noch offensichtlicher) die Photographie dagegen zur Hauptsache Rastersysteme: Jedes unterscheidbare Farb- oder Tonelement, jeder Pixel hat seine Stellung innerhalb des Ordnungsrasters, eine Art unsichtbares Gitter, welches das Kontinuum der Bildfläche unterteilt. Virtuell ist auch ein Bild vorhanden, wenn der Raster leer ist, weil die Summe der Pixeleinheiten mit der Fläche zusammenfällt. Wie ein lichtempfindlicher photographischer Film wartet der Bildraster auf

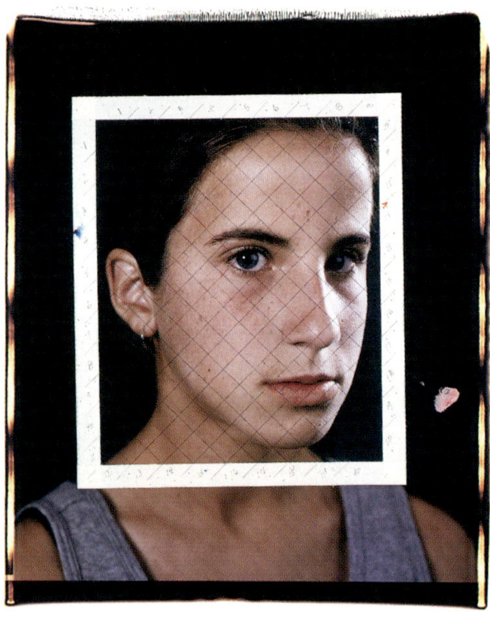

CHUCK CLOSE, MAQUETTE, no date, photograph on foamcore, 34 x 24½" / VORLAGE, undatiert, Photo auf Schaumstoffkernplatte, 86,4 x 62,2 cm. (PHOTO: ELLEN PAGE WILSON)

seine Aktivierung, als müsse die Projektion seiner Tonwerte ebenso von innerhalb wie von ausserhalb der Bildfläche erfolgen.

Close nennt seine frühen, von Photos ausgehenden Werke sehr passend eine Malerei des «kontinuierlichen Tons»; sie sehen aus (meinte er mir gegenüber einmal), als ob das filmartige Airbrushbild «in einen Nebel geraten und ins Bild gefallen» sei. Dank dieser Qualität der «Gleichzeitigkeit» vermittelt NANCY den Eindruck einer Photographie, doch das ist eine Täuschung; denn diese beiden Rastermedien unterscheiden sich auf eine Art, die Close einmal wie folgt umschrieben hat: «Ein Photo ist im Augenblick, in dem es entsteht, vollständig, aber ein Gemälde ist so lange unvollständig, bis es beendet ist; bei einem Bild verändert jedes Detail, das neu hinzukommt, das bereits Vorhandene.»[3] Es sind die aufeinander folgenden Handbewegungen, die die Differenz ausmachen, und diese gehorchen, anders als der Nebel oder photochemische Vorgänge, den Launen der Intuition. Der Künstler passt die einzelnen Elemente an und stimmt sie spielerisch aufeinander ab; dieser Prozess gleicht zwar der traditionellen Komposition,

erfolgt aber bei ungewöhnlich hoher Auflösung: Haar für Haar, Pore für Pore, Fleck für Fleck, hart an der Grenze des gerade noch Wahrnehmbaren. Deshalb fasziniert uns die Bildwiedergabe dieser Malerei derart, ganz abgesehen von der Verblüffung über die ungeheure handwerkliche Leistung. Diese Porträts, die anhand photographischer Vorlagen mit so subtilen Variationen rekonstruiert wurden, dass man eher auf die Ähnlichkeit als auf die Differenz achtet, sind alles andere als «alltäglich». Einem arglosen Betrachter werden die Unterschiede gar nicht auffallen: etwa die leicht veränderte Miene eines Gesichts, auf die wir unwillkürlich reagieren; oder der exakte Moment, wo ein Gesichtszug zu blosser Farbe gerinnt. Ist das Zauberei?

Im Laufe der 80er und 90er Jahre sind die Rastereinheiten im Verhältnis zum Bildformat grösser geworden. Das hat zur Folge, dass der Betrachter selbst aus der Ferne einzelne Bildbestandteile bemerkt und mit Sicherheit nicht nur das «entstandene Bild» erkennt, sondern auch «den Stoff, aus dem es gemacht ist».[4] Während die früheren, kleineren Pixel jeweils ein einziges Farbzeichen enthielten, finden wir bei den grösseren jetzt gewöhnlich fünf oder mehr miteinander kontrastierende Farben. Oft bilden die Zeichen konzentrische Muster, die die Richtungsneutralität des Rasters bewahren.[5] Eine typische Bildeinheit enthält etwa einen Punkt, umgeben von zwei mehr oder weniger kreisförmigen Schlingen, innerhalb von zwei ungefähren Quadraten, das Ganze wiederum innerhalb der Quadratform des jeweiligen Pixels.

Wenn Close seine Bildübertragung vornimmt, wird jede Rastereinheit der Photovorlage auf der viel grösseren Leinwandfläche in vier weitere Einheiten unterteilt, um die Arbeit im grösseren Massstab zu erleichtern. Zufällig ist eine Kombination aus vier symmetrischen Einheiten auch der kleinstmögliche rechtwinklige Flächenraster, bei dem ein Feld entsteht, in dem oben, unten, links und rechts gleichwertig sind. Im Rahmen dieses von Haus aus neutralen Formats fühlt Close sich «befreit». Er kann jedes beliebige Zeichen in jeder beliebigen Farbe wählen, wenn er eine Bildeinheit beginnt, weil er weiss, dass er deren Darstellungswert mit späteren Zeichen und durch das Zusammenspiel mit benach-

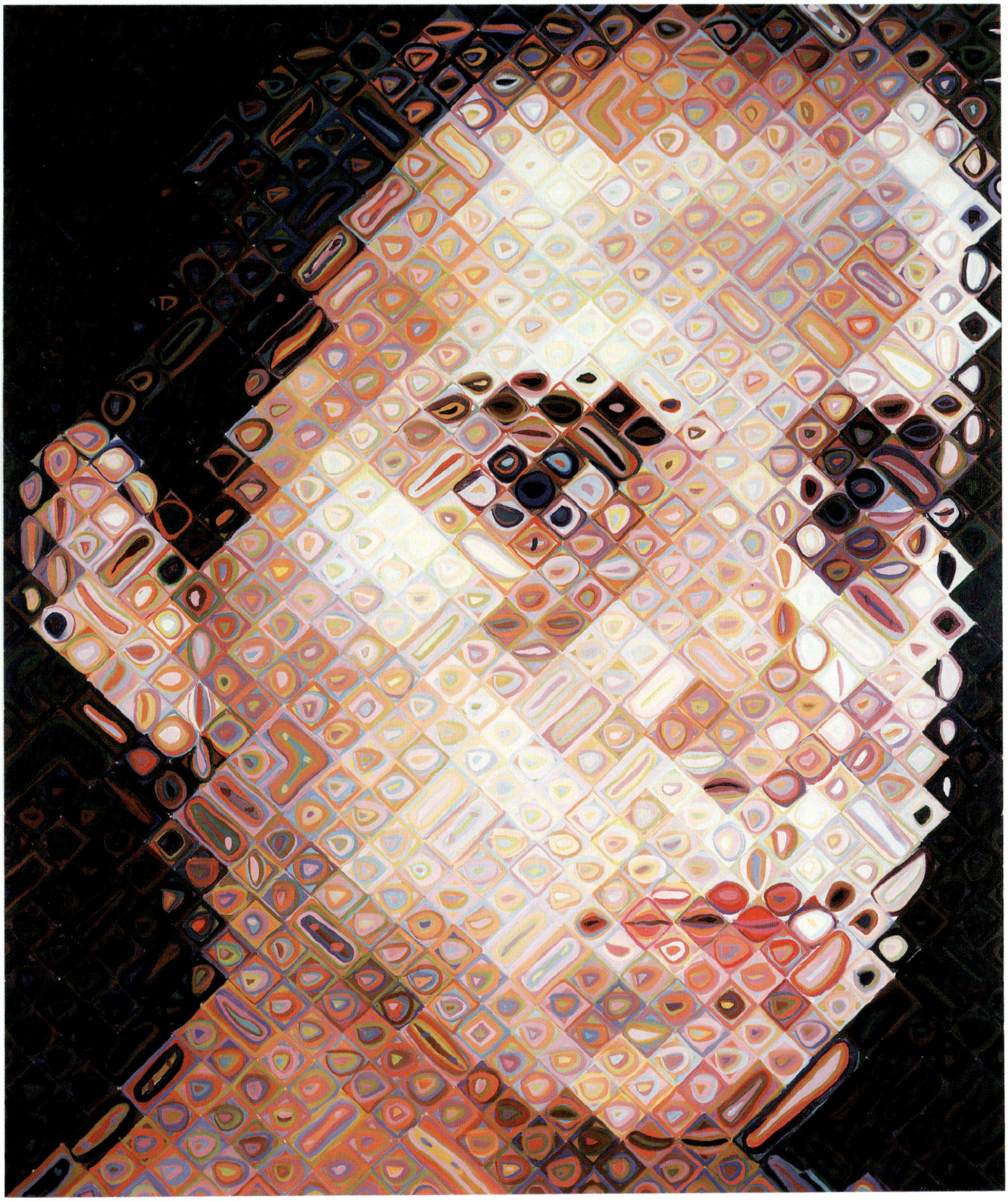

CHUCK CLOSE, MAGGIE, 1998–99, oil on canvas, 72 x 60" / Öl auf Leinwand, 182,9 x 152,4 cm. (PHOTO: ELLEN PAGE WILSON)

barten Einheiten korrigieren kann. Erinnern wir uns daran, dass das konventionelle photographische Bild «augenblicklich» erscheint, während das gemalte Bild sich im Lauf der Zeit entwickelt. Die Malerei von Close ahmt sein photographisches Vorbild erfolgreich nach, aber ihre Zeitlichkeit hat nichts mit dem photographischen Prozess gemein. Der dargestellte Inhalt dieser beiden so verschiedenen Medien ist verschieden und doch derselbe. Die Kunst von Close führt vor, wie wir trügerische Erscheinungen durch den Einsatz von nicht miteinander vereinbaren Systemen der Darstellung in den Griff zu bekommen versuchen. Jedes Medium unterstreicht die «Wahrheit», die im anderen Medium liegen mag (darin sind sie sich gleich), dabei treten ihre Unterschiede jedoch immer klarer zutage. Falls auch Sie «faul, nachlässig und unentschlossen» sind, bietet Ihnen Close eine Erfahrung, die Sie zu einem sehr viel misstrauischeren Beobachter machen dürfte.

Nicht alle Bildeinheiten bei Close erscheinen völlig richtungs- oder bewegungsneutral. Manchmal lässt er seine Schleifen über bis zu vier Einheiten nacheinander ausgreifen: etwa auf der rechten Kinnseite von MAGGIE (1998–99), wo so eine verlängerte Form an das fortlaufend Lineare einer Kante denken lässt, und dann doch wieder nicht, weil die hautartigen Farbtöne von der übrigen Figur durch dunklere Farben getrennt sind, die für den Hintergrund stehen. Wenn es diese Kontraste ausblendet, sieht das Auge die Kante eines Gesichts. Diese Kante führt aufwärts, der Wange entlang, trotz des Verzahnungseffekts, der entsteht, wo helle Haut und dunkler Hintergrund ineinander verwoben erscheinen und dadurch dem substanzlosen Raster Substanz verleihen. Die Rastereinheiten, die unversehrt bleiben, erstrecken sich über eine Kante im Bild, die ihrerseits unversehrt bleibt, aber nur virtuell, als optische Täuschung. Konzentrieren wir uns wieder auf das Kinn dieser Gestalt: die (virtuelle oder reale) Kante kann durchaus verschwinden, an ihre Stelle tritt die längliche, helle und deutliche Schleife, eine in sich selbst ruhende Form von gut zwanzig Zentimeter Länge. Hier lässt sich das Gelingen und Scheitern der bildlichen Darstellung beinah simultan, in ein und demselben photographisch-malerischen «Augenblick», erleben.

Wann immer man einen Umriss innerhalb des Bildes verfolgt, erzeugt der Raster einen Vektor – oder vielmehr die Illusion eines Vektors. Und tatsächlich hat Close jeder Bildeinheit durch das Einfügen der kleinen Zeichen auch vektoriellen Charakter verliehen, denn jedes dieser Zeichen verfügt über eine gewisse Ausrichtung, weil die Handbewegung des Künstlers sichtbar bleibt. In manchen Fällen ist diese Ausrichtung sogar sehr deutlich. In MAGGIE markiert eine leicht geschwungene Senkrechte, die auf einen einzigen Pixel beschränkt ist, die Grenze zwischen Nasenflügel und Wange, ein Gesichtsteil, der im Übrigen durch starke Lichtsetzung ganz ausgebleicht erscheint. Ob er einer Form der photographischen Vorlage folgt oder bloss die natürliche Handbewegung des Künstlers widerspiegelt: Jeder gerichtete Strich dehnt und komprimiert, zieht und presst den Raster in die eine oder andere Richtung. Selbst innerhalb des eigentlich neutralen Hintergrundes gibt es keine unbewegt ruhige Stelle.

Jedes einzelne Zeichen ist selbst schon eine Bewegung, die die Auseinandersetzung zwischen «Bild» und «Materie» belebt beziehungsweise deren Lebendigkeit unterstreicht. Wie mir scheint, ist es Close nicht nur gelungen, de Koonings Farbe zurückzugewinnen, sondern auch dessen organische Qualitäten – allerdings radikal verwandelt durch seine künstlerische Beherrschung der vergleichenden Darstellungstechnik. Ich nehme an, Close würde sagen, er sei einfach zu «faul, nachlässig und unentschlossen» gewesen, um irgendetwas wirklich sausen zu lassen.

(Übersetzung: Susanne Schmidt)

1) Chuck Close im Interview mit Robert Storr, in: *Chuck Close*, hrsg. v. Robert Storr, Ausstellungskatalog, The Museum of Modern Art, New York 1998, S. 94.
2) Close, ebenda, S. 95, sowie im Gespräch mit Roy Lichtenstein, 23. Oktober 1995, in: *The Portraits Speak*, hrsg. v. Joanne Kesten, A.R.T. Press, New York 1997, S. 619.
3) Chuck Close, in: *Artist's Choice: Chuck Close*, hrsg. v. Kirk Varnedoe, Ausstellungskatalog, The Museum of Modern Art, New York 1991, S. 7. Ein «Augenblick» ist natürlich nicht *überhaupt keine* Zeitspanne, aber eine nicht wahrnehmbare.
4) Chuck Close im Gespräch mit Brooks Adams, «Close Encountered», in: *Artforum*, Vol. XXXVI, Nr. 8, April 1998, S. 135.
5) Close legt seine Raster oft diagonal an, dreht dann aber bei der Arbeit Photographie und Bild so, dass alles wieder seine gewohnte Ordnung hat.

CHUCK CLOSE, MAGGIE, 1998–99, detail, oil on canvas / Ausschnitt, Öl auf Leinwand. (PHOTO: ELLEN PAGE WILSON)

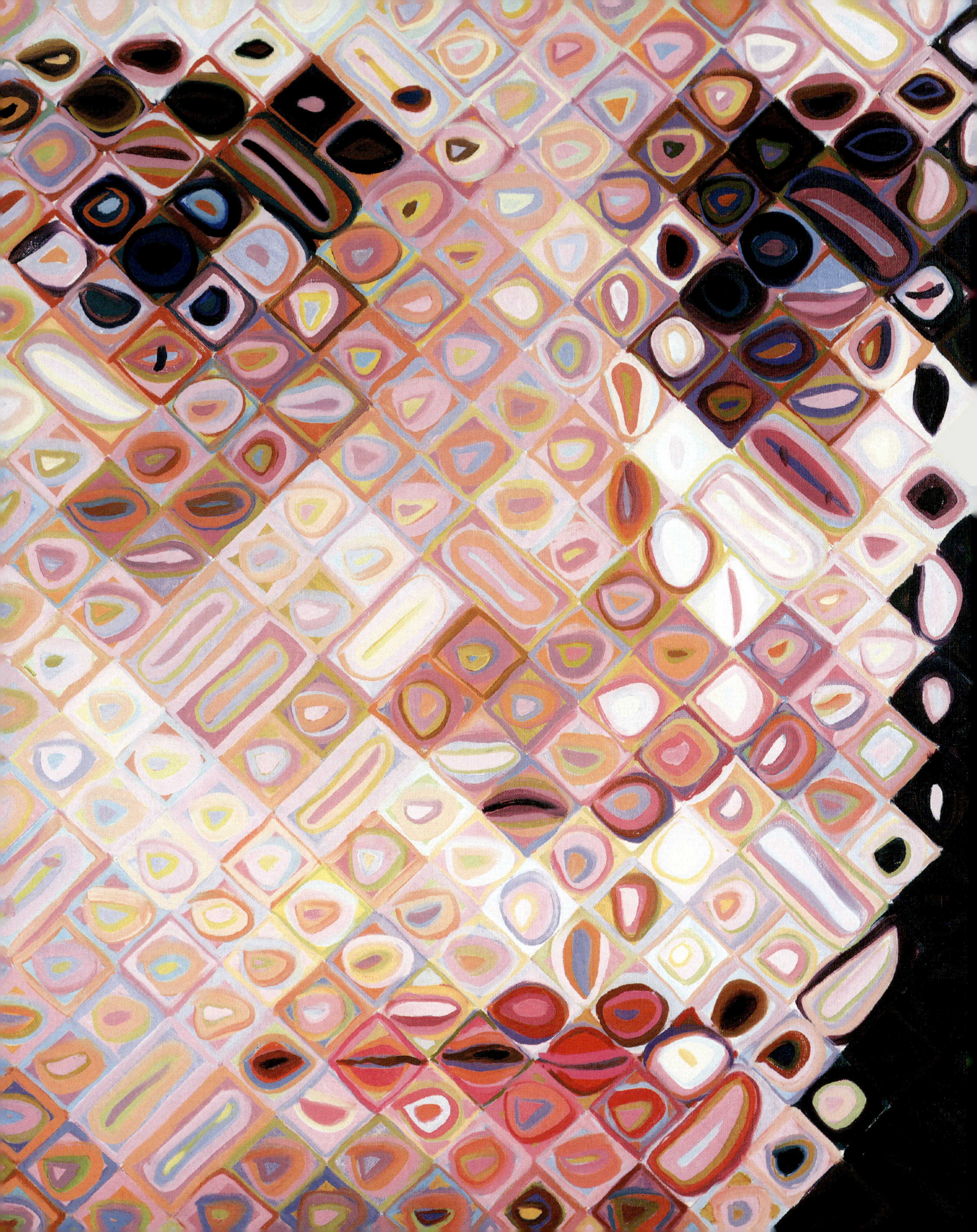

Putting English on the Stroke

Bice Curiger: From a European point of view I deeply admire the specifically American culture of painting. It's so rich and full of references covering a wide range: the former rules of Modernism, a host of old and new departures, artistic license, ruptures, and a pronounced visual directness. And against this background, there is also a very dynamic exchange between generations, which is not true in Europe. We just have an endless parade of individual positions.

Chuck Close: There's a lot of painting being done here. It seems to me that appropriation is still quite the modus operandi for some, which is really the influence of the eighties in some form or another. So kids keep raiding the cultural icebox and finding different models. I think there's an interest among a lot of younger artists in the object-status of painting, the fact that it actually is a thing: it's not like a flickering image on a video screen. Maybe it's because there's been so much installation art, so many videos, and the use of the computer and other technologies. A lot of people really do seem to be interested in pushing paint around again.

BC: Right. I think it is related to what you say about stopping the image and also wanting to make a mark by hand, painting with your hands, although of course there were machines earlier as well, like silk-screening. Interestingly, today the wish to handcraft something does not necessarily aim at an individual or personal statement, which was a factor for the Abstract Expressionists.

CC: When I was actually, physically making the paintings with my fingerprints, Rob Storr said something that I thought was nice. He described it as "using skin to make skin." It was almost as if I was caressing the faces of people I love. And I of course like the fact that I was making something that couldn't be forged by somebody else. I did it. And I couldn't deny it.

BC: That brings to mind the term "realism," the idea that you can take something from outside and just put it on a canvas. But today the relationship to the object is different from what it was in nineteenth century painting.

CC: My problem with realism is that I've always been equally interested in artificiality, so it's a reality/artificiality issue. It is always going to be the distribution of marks on a flat surface. And then there's the image that's made with them. But what I do like, or what I think has something to do with reality, is that no matter what art-historical

Chuck Close in Conversation with Bice Curiger

August 21, 2000, Bridgehampton, New York

baggage people bring with them when they look at one of my paintings, no matter how sophisticated they are, they share something with all viewers: an interest in the work through a life experience that comes from having looked at people, having looked at images of themselves in mirrors, having looked at photographs or magazines. When I was living in Rome a couple of years ago, people talked about my work in terms of Pointillism and other things I never thought made much sense. I was interested in looking at the mosaics in Ravenna, but when I got there, I was so disappointed. They were way up there, so far away, dark and glistening, that I thought, "What's the big deal?" But I loved the rows of Roman floor mosaics, especially because they're on the floor and the viewing distance is your height. They never stop being chunks of rock even though they warp into an image. For a while it's an image, and just when you're really intent on looking at an image, it goes back to being chunks of stone on the floor again. It's connected with the viewing distance and the size and the increment of the unit. And I thought, here they were, centuries ago, already dealing with that same notion of fracturing an image, breaking it down into incremental units that remain discrete in the end. And then managing to make clusters of them go together to build something that we relate to through a lived experience, or a person's face that couldn't be further away from stone. Flipping back and forth—that to me is a real kick.

BC: The whole thing gets much more complicated because of the way you work, with your canvas sitting on one corner at a diagonal which means that when you paint the face, it's at an angle.

CC: Well, two considerations are involved. First of all it gives me a little distance on what I'm doing, but mainly it's a practical decision. I don't want to paint uphill. So to be able to paint straight across with a diagonal grid, I just turn it on its corner. I'll then rotate the whole thing to another corner and finally I'll turn it right side up. It's like any way of working incrementally, like a novelist; it's almost like stream of consciousness the first time through. The second time I do major edits, moving things around, changing things, throwing out whole chunks. The third pass is fine-tuning, and then ultimately I start turning it right side up.

BC: When we did the catalogue for "Birth of the Cool" the designer used a detail, which she blew up. I think it was John Chamberlain's face, just a little part near the eyebrow. I looked at it and immediately recognized the painting. I thought, "This is incredible." It's so abstract and yet you can still remember the whole. I don't know John Chamberlain personally, so it's not just the recognition of the physiognomy...

CC: Each painting has its own vocabulary...

BC: I saw you a couple of years ago in your studio when you had just come back from Rome and you were talking about the light. How did that influence your painting?

CC: Well, the light in Rome was really nice and the academy has these huge skylights and windows. I used to paint entirely by artificial light. I figured they were going to be seen in artificial light, so I'm going to paint them that way. But the older I get, the more light I need. Now I need like klieg lights. And I can't work without natural light, which is the best thing about working out here (in Bridgehampton, NY). The light here is great because it's reflecting off the water. There's something about the light out here that is quite wonderful; it's not as warm as the light in Rome. My studio in the city has natural light, too, but when I drag the paintings back there, I can't believe what I can't see. Even though I have natural light and actually lots of other lights, it's just not the same. When I take them to the gallery, it's even worse, and I end up telling people, "Oh, you really should see this. If only you could see these two colors together. This is great, but you can't see it, I'm sorry."

BC: Do you work with a different palette in New York?

CC: Yes. Although I did start a painting in the city, which I brought out here to finish, and I don't think you can see a seam.

BC: So looking back at a certain moment in history, it was maybe eccentric to use all these traditional media, like copperplates and painting by hand. But what I find so wonderful is how your conceptual approach really works its way into the material.

CC: And sometimes you have to throw everything away to rediscover it. In the late sixties, no sculptor would use bronze or marble or anything like that. They had to find materials that didn't have someone's name already on them, like Serra using rubber or lead. Then gradually traditional materials came

back, but people had different reasons for using them. I make paintings with time-tested rabbit-skin glue and a white lead on top of it with the meshed oil paints and I'm using a palette, which I didn't use for years. But I had to find a way to get something else out of it. I had to get rid of all of the habits that were associated with it and purge all my gods, and then I was able to find my own reasons to use it.

BC: The first time I saw your paintings was at "documenta V" in 1972. Did you go to that show?

CC: No. I didn't.

BC: Seeing those paintings of yours, those huge faces and the hair… They had an incredible presence, and the meaning was as strong as the work itself.

CC: Thank you. I think it's hard to remember now that they were sort of shocking at the time. First of all painting was dead. And then if you were going to paint, you certainly weren't going to paint anything with a recognizable image. And if you were stupid enough to paint something with a recognizable image, portraiture as a genre was the lamest idea of all. So that had its appeal. I remember Clement Greenberg saying the only thing you can't do is paint a portrait. If he thinks you can't do it, there might be some room in there, some elbow room to mess around…

BC: But you can see it the other way around too. Being Swiss, in the sixties, we were discussing the Swiss writer Max Frisch who had written a book, *I'm not Stiller*. As the title says, the novel is all about identity and classifying people; as soon as you say something about a person, it's wrong, it's never the truth. Faced with the challenging immensity of your faces, you wonder: Who is that

really? What can you say about that person?

CC: Right. Well to me, the interesting thing was to watch people look at those early black and white paintings because they had a big, aggressive, confrontational, in-your-face attitude from a distance. But they were also like the little Lilliputians in *Gulliver's Travels* crawling all over the face of the giant, not even knowing what they are looking at because inevitably people were sucked up really close and I think, at that scale, the aggressive, confrontational aspect turns into something extremely intimate. Ordinarily we don't stand close enough to each other to see that level of information; we don't invade each other's space. So the only time you ever see that much detail on someone's face is if you're making love, the most intimate thing.

BC: If you're not farsighted.

CC: Right again! In any case, it's that combination of aggressive bigness and intimacy. Plus, of course, when you're up there you can see how they're made, which is part of what I enjoy too. I enjoy the syntax in the same way that you might when reading a novel. It's not just a narrative line, it's not just a story, but it's how these words trip off your tongue and the pleasure that you get in seeing how these words are pushed together and fashioned. There was a wonderful profile of the writer Don DeLillo in *The New Yorker* a few years ago, in which he said, if you think Hemingway is about the bullfights, you don't understand what makes Hemingway Hemingway. For Hemingway, the use of the word "the" is more important than the bullfights. Anybody can tell a story about bullfights; there's nothing particularly astonishing about them, but it's in the way he tells the

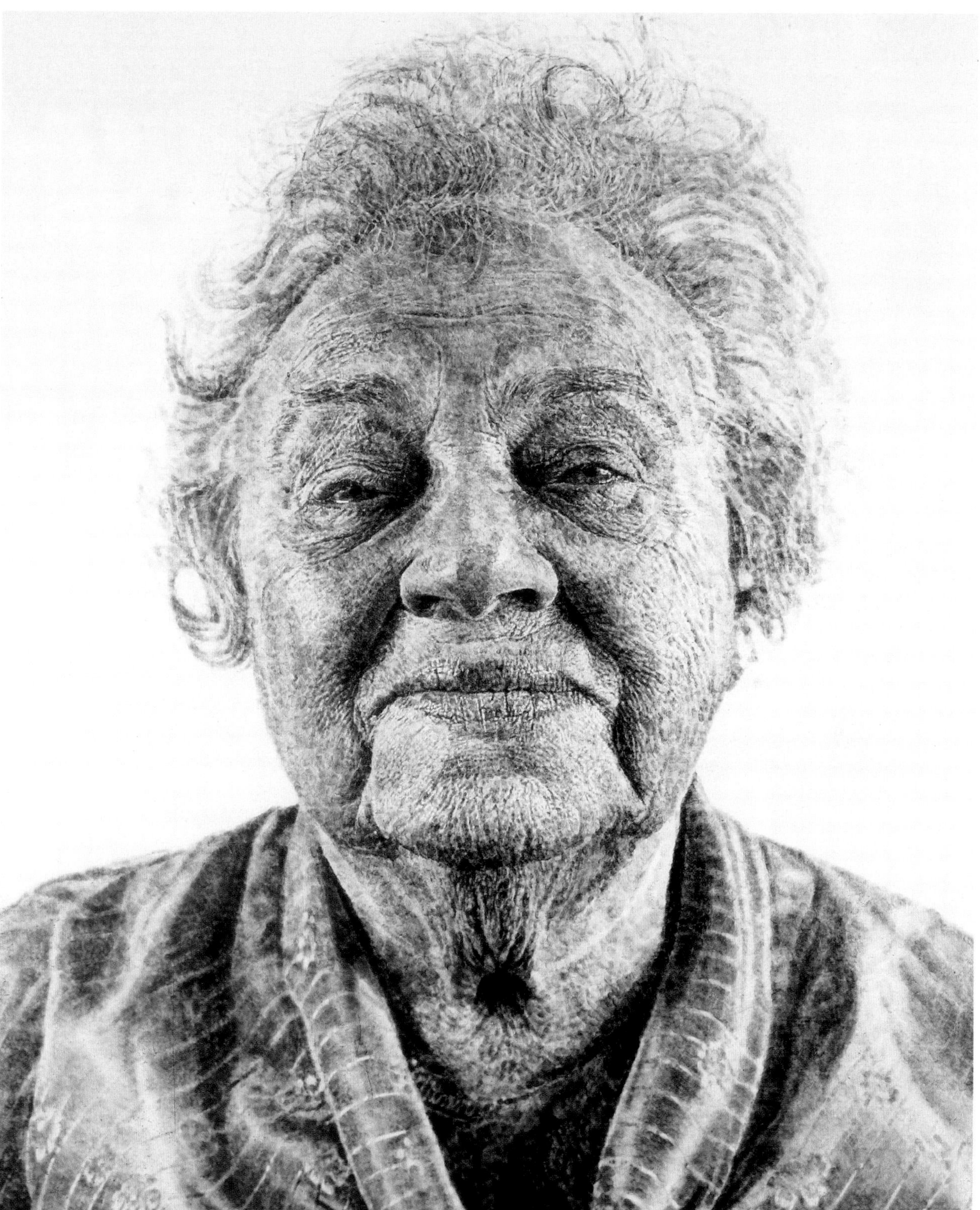

CHUCK CLOSE, FANNY / FINGERPAINTING, 1985, oil on canvas, 102 x 84″ / Öl auf Leinwand, 259 x 213 cm.

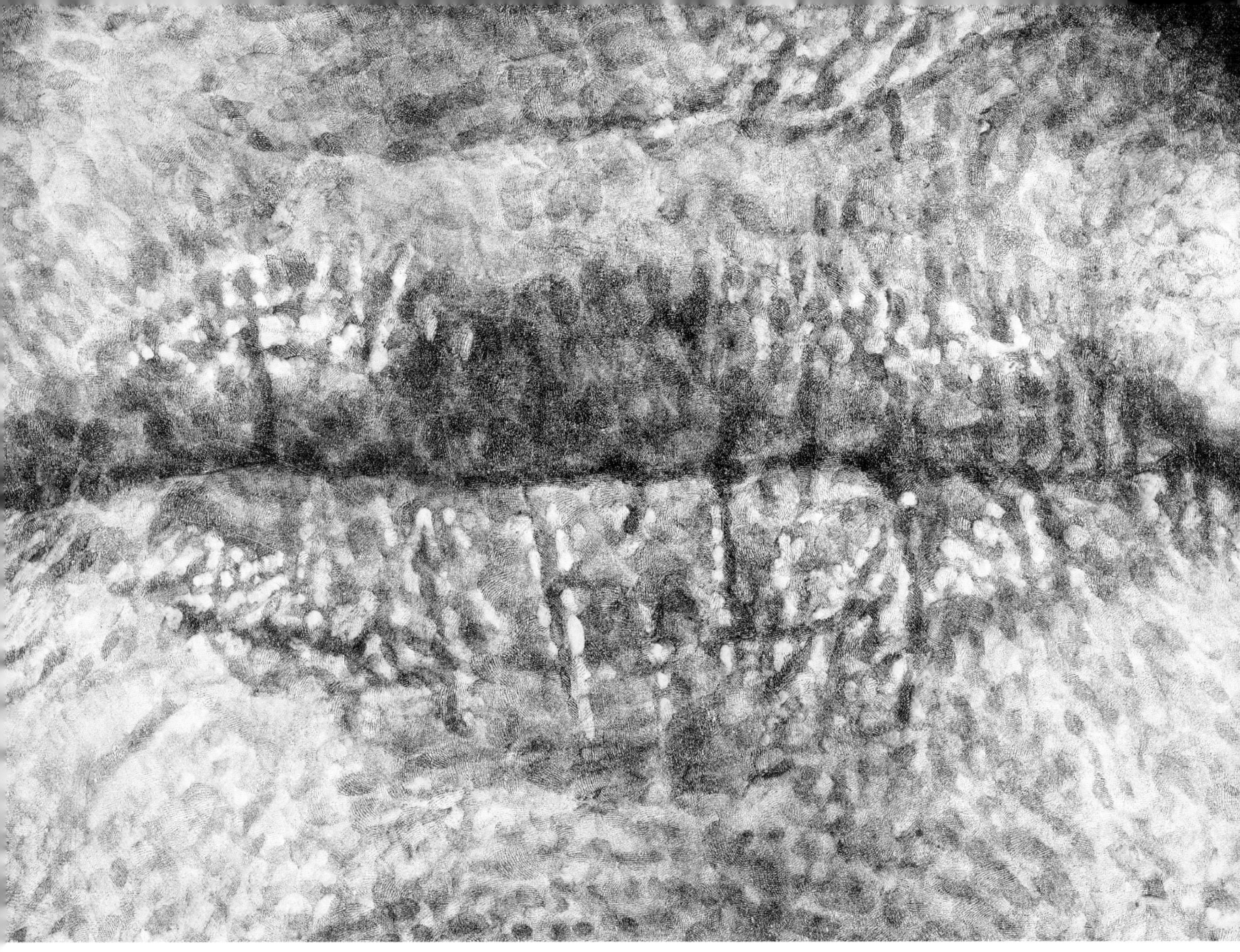

<CHUCK CLOSE, FANNY / FINGERPAINTING, 1985, detail, oil on canvas / Ausschnitt, Öl auf Leinwand.>

CHUCK CLOSE, FANNY / FINGERPAINTING, 1985, detail, oil on canvas / Ausschnitt, Öl auf Leinwand.

story—the incredible physicality of his words. And of course, the way they stack up to make images that tell the story. A great deal of pleasure and all of the style is rooted in those decisions.

BC: I can see this a little bit in your painting. I feel they're also like writing. They also start on the left...

CC: ...and move across.

BC: Yes, like a text with words and syl-lables and sounds that opens up into other dimensions.

CC: One critic, Adam Gopnik, com-pared the calligraphy of my paintings to the calligraphy of Brice Marden—we've been friends since 1961—and he was talking about the difference be-tween calligraphic marks that don't make an image and mine which do. But, for me, no matter how interesting the shape is, it has to be in the service of building an image.

BC: With these huge portraits, you think of Russian or Communist images or also billboards where there is no in-vention because there is such a clear source image that repeats itself over and over...

CC: Yes, the message is the image. Philip Glass (whom I painted around

1968) was married—a couple of wives ago—to a woman, a physician, and she came from Bulgaria or Romania or something like that. When her mother came over to visit for the first time, she took her to the Whitney Museum where my painting of Philip Glass was hanging. And her mother said, "Oh wow, Philip must be r e a l l y important." And she said, "Well, yes he's a very respected composer." And her mother said, "No, I mean r e a l l y important." Because for her anybody blown up that big would have to be somebody who was politically important like Lenin or Karl Marx.

BC: With your prints I was fascinated to read about how you work together with other people, rely on them, the give and take, being in control and losing control and then taking over again.

CC: I suppose it's because in the painting studio I'm such a control freak. I would never let anybody else ever do anything, but I was able to give up some of that control in the print shop. The first print that I made as a mature artist, I guess, was the mezzotint, which I picked because I didn't know how to make one and neither did the printers. I figured we could both figure it out together, because neither of us had the expertise. I didn't want to go someplace where they knew how to do something, but didn't have the permission to do it, while I had the idea, but didn't know how to execute it. I guess the first experience where a real true collaboration took place was when I went to Kyoto to make an Ukiyo-e style traditional Japanese woodblock. There, if you sign on to do it, you must buy into that system. It's a very stratified society. I worked with a guy who was a national treasure. So we don't tell him what to do. And then the guy beneath him,

who actually cut those blocks, he was on a different level. And so I would make the image in watercolor that we were going to work from, and he would start separating it and making decisions, and pretty soon it was his. And then I had to wrest control of it and bring it back and make it mine and then he would work on it some more and it was that tug of war which I found really interesting. But you cannot be direct with the Japanese; they don't ever say anything directly. That would be rude. The translator there was born in Kyoto, but had studied in California and had worked for a lot of American artists in California, so he spanned both worlds. For example I would say, "Tell them it's too green," and then he would go "dah, dah, dah, dah…" And finally I would say, "How long does it take to say it's too green?" And he would translate his answer back into English, "Well what I just said is: 'Chuck thinks it's perfect. He thinks you're a genius. It couldn't be any better. It could never be improved on. Everything is perfect. However, in the interest of intellectual curiosity, not that it would be any better than what you've just done, it might be interesting to see what it would be like, if you tried to make it a little less green.'" And that was necessary. So it was a really interesting process.

BC: And the response?

CC: He would nod and make it less green. But that got me used to the idea of true collaboration, where I didn't actually have to make any mark myself. Some artists are able to work with assistants or work as a team, but I don't know how they make decisions—Komar & Melamid or Gilbert & George or whatever. Who decides what? Which one does what? But this way of working

where someone can extend your ideas and then you decide which way you want to go, accepting some and rejecting others—it's really a wonderful kind of work.

BC: How were the works on paper made? Did you know about these possibilities at the time?

CC: Well, when I was on the board of governors at Skowhegan a papermaker, Joe Wilfer, came to the Skowhegan summer school to teach papermaking—and immediately got fired. He used to be called "The Prince of Pulp." He had moved his family, his two daughters and his wife, from Wisconsin to New York so he was desperate to make money and do something. Since I knew him through Skowhegan, he came to me and said, "Let's make some pulp paper." And I said, "Go away, leave me alone. I hate pulp paper. Why would I want to do that? Never in a million years. Sorry." Then he said, "Well, what's wrong with making paper?"— "Nothing," I said. "I don't want to do it." He said, "What's wrong with the paper pieces you've seen?" So I'd try to explain and he'd go away for a week, and then he'd come back and bring me a test. And I'd say, "You see, I was right, you can't do it." And he'd go, "Well, what's wrong with it?" And I'd explain some more and a week later he'd be back with another sample. He was the most creative problem solver I've ever seen, and slowly he got so close that I could actually imagine doing something with it. And then we were off, working together and it was great. We solved each other's problems. I worked with him for many years. Not just on that, the pulp paper, but all kinds of processes. It was really exciting. He would make anything into art. He'd make any mistake into a happy accident. And with every failure he'd find some way out. We had to carry these wet pulp things on their side to get them through the door and once they fell onto the floor and fractured into pieces. He said, "It looks like cracks in a Roman floor." So we just showed them, actually I don't remember where—he managed to make everything positive.

BC: It's like Duchamp's LARGE GLASS. You told me on the phone that you were doing daguerreotypes. What do they look like? And how do you make them?

CC: Exactly the same way as they were done in 1850. Nothing's changed. In some ways, photography has never improved. Everything that I love about photography was already there. And then of course, they're elusive. It requires active participation to see them, but the detail is phenomenal and the range of tones unbelievable. There's this warm patina to them and when solarized the highlights become bluish, making the other things warm too. They're really incredible; I really enjoy making them.

BC: How big are the prints?

CC: Not quite 8 by 10 inches, which is a large daguerreotype. It's a sheet of copper plated with pure silver and polished until it's like a mirror. After exposing it to the vapors of iodine and bromide gasses to make it sensitive to light, the plate goes into a film holder that's put into the back of a view camera. The plate is exposed to light and then the image is developed by subjecting it to the vapors of mercury, which is very dangerous. Then the process is stopped and the image is washed like a traditional photograph. Finally it's gilded by pouring gold chloride on top of it and heating it with a torch. That

really fixes the image. So, just like the Polaroids I make, you see each one before you make the next, which means that we, the sitter and I, have the opportunity to see what I've done. And we slowly move towards what we want. Instead of preconceiving what we want. That's why I've always liked Polaroid. It involves a dialogue from the very beginning. And the sitter is saying, "Oh god, not that one. Please don't do that one. Can't you do it again?" I, of course, keep absolute veto control, but I do try to accommodate the sitter. It's part of the dialogue.

BC: Listening to you, I realize what a long and intense process is involved in getting an image. Is that your main interest?

CC: The route taken, instead of where you're going, is always the most interesting because your experience will be so different if you take one route rather than another. And like I say, style is embedded in the process. Everything is a record of thought, a record of the decisions that you've made. That's why I think painting is so magical. And of course photography too. It transcends its physical reality. Yet at the same time a record of all of the decisions that you've made is embedded in it. So, it's a way to vicariously re-experience what the artist experienced. That may be what makes it so personal. People see how it got there as well as what got there. For me, that's the thrilling, magical part of it.

BC: I've watched people at your shows, completely astonished and trying to capture the moment when the image "falls apart" into all of these diamonds or magic stones. You see them going back and forth, playing with perception.

CC: Especially people who went through the drug culture… It's almost

like a psychedelic experience. I promise you a safe trip… For me all the fun lies in the act of painting. I don't think there's anything wrong with having somebody paint your work. Sol LeWitt is one of my best friends and he's certainly done quite nicely having other people do his painting, but it's part of what he does. For me though, the pleasure is so much part of the physicality. I let people do everything else in my life so that I can paint.

BC: Plus the fact that all of your decisions are so much part of how you think and what you've experienced. It would be almost impossible, I think, to train someone to do the work for you.

CC: Also, even if you could train someone to do it, all the things that occur to you while you're working would occur to them, too. But they wouldn't be able to act on anything because they would only be allowed to do what I had told them to do. But it's always the stuff that you bump into on the way that you hadn't anticipated that's…

BC: Like what, for instance?

CC: Well, you know, you're working away and you think, "That looks like something, I think I'll make it like a sock shape or a light bulb shape," or something like that. I wouldn't have started out saying, "I want to find some way to incorporate socks and light bulbs and whiskey bottles and donuts and hot dogs into my paintings." It grows out of the act of painting. Or with a color… In one square I might find the color I want by putting blue and purple and green and yellow together, but in the next square I might do it with green and violet and pink and orange. So I'm reacting to what I've already done. Similarly, when you're writing, you wouldn't end up using the same word twice in the same sentence. You want to make sure you tell the story, but you also want it to be rich and varied.

BC: I think you have about five lines or elements in a square in these paintings, so, as you described it, you probably have a pink row underneath and then you start making decisions and in turn reacting to them.

CC: Right.

BC: But you would know that somewhere here you must have a dark spot, though not necessarily in the center.

CC: No. There is no drawing other than the grid. When the paint is going on, I am doing two things. I am trying to arrive at the resultant color in that square in a kind of average. But also, if there's more than one thing in the square, like a dark line going through it, then I have to figure out how to do that, how to approximate that in a way that's not just symbolic. So then I swell or shrink the shapes and I run them together or I make them discrete things. It's not just making the stroke. In billiards or pool you call it "Putting English on the Stroke." You make the shot, but also the way you hit the ball causes other things to happen. So I'm putting some colors down, the English that I'm putting on the stroke allows it also to become something, the thing that's being portrayed.

BC: It's like a metaphor for what lots of painters have done before.

CC: If you look at Ingres or Velázquez or Frans Hals or any number of painters, you have this hard to hold relationship and you have strokes that become something and yet still stay strokes. You have a hand made of four or five or six strokes. So there's been that economy and the use of pictorial syntax, forever. I just lay mine out differently.

BC: And, of course, that reminds me of the term "all-over" which is very American.

CC: Oh yes. I was very conscious of making all-over paintings. Initially I was trying to figure out what made American painting, American painting in the sixties. And I thought, "Well it is this sense of all-overness, and the commitment to the entire rectangle. The idea that something that's in the left hand corner is just as important as something that's right in the middle— whether it's Pollock's ribbons of paint or Frank Stella's black-stripe paintings or Agnes Martin's grids." That seemed to me to be peculiarly American, along with the lack of hierarchy. And I wanted to impose that all-overness on top of something hierarchical. We think the eyes, the nose, and the mouth are the important parts. So how can I get away from that in a portrait? How can I say every piece of this painting is important? I was also very interested in what used to be called "women's work" like quilting, crocheting, and knitting—they're processes that you sign on to for a long time; you don't have to reinvent the wheel every day. Today you do what you did yesterday; tomorrow you do what you did today. You believe in the process and if you go with it, eventually you'll get somewhere. The wedding of those two thoughts—the sense of all-overness and the non-hierarchical image—is a way to work that I found personally liberating. Just like the reason that knitting or crocheting appealed to busy women on the prairie: they could pick it up and put it down; they could feed the baby, put the baby down, and knit a little bit. Then they'd put the knitting down and go weed the garden and come back in a little bit. The knitting

was also soothing and calming. And I was always a nervous wreck.

BC: Really?

CC: Oh yes, I'm a nervous wreck. I'm a slob, I'm lazy, and I'm impatient. All of which would seem to preclude me making the work that I make. What I did was find a way to work, which counteracted all of those things. You don't want to be held captive by your nature. You don't want your nature to dictate the only kind of art you can make. So by constructing a situation in which I could no longer behave that way, I was dealing with my nature... Maybe it's like the fact that the performing arts attract very shy people. For some reason, they want to get on the stage... And I know very undisciplined people who are writers and demand of themselves that they write so many words every day. I don't know anybody who makes compulsive paintings, who is truly compulsive in the sense of being driven and not being able not to do it. But a lot of us can behave compulsively even though we're not truly compulsive people. If you want a certain kind of thing, you've just got to stay there long enough to make it. If you're going to write a novel, it's going to take a certain length of time to put that many words together. So that's what you're signing up for.

BC: Sometimes art viewers, the art public, want to be able to get an image instantly. They go into a gallery or a museum and are impatient. But you can't understand a novel without reading it.

CC: And now we have virtual reality. Museums are offering their stuff online; you don't even have to go to the museum. I don't understand this. It's only the barest indication of the works.

BC: Yes, it's such a vague indication. That's why some people still paint.

CHUCK CLOSE, LYLE, 1999, oil on canvas, 102 x 84" / Öl auf Leinwand, 259,1 x 213,4 cm. (PHOTO: ELLEN PAGE WILSON)

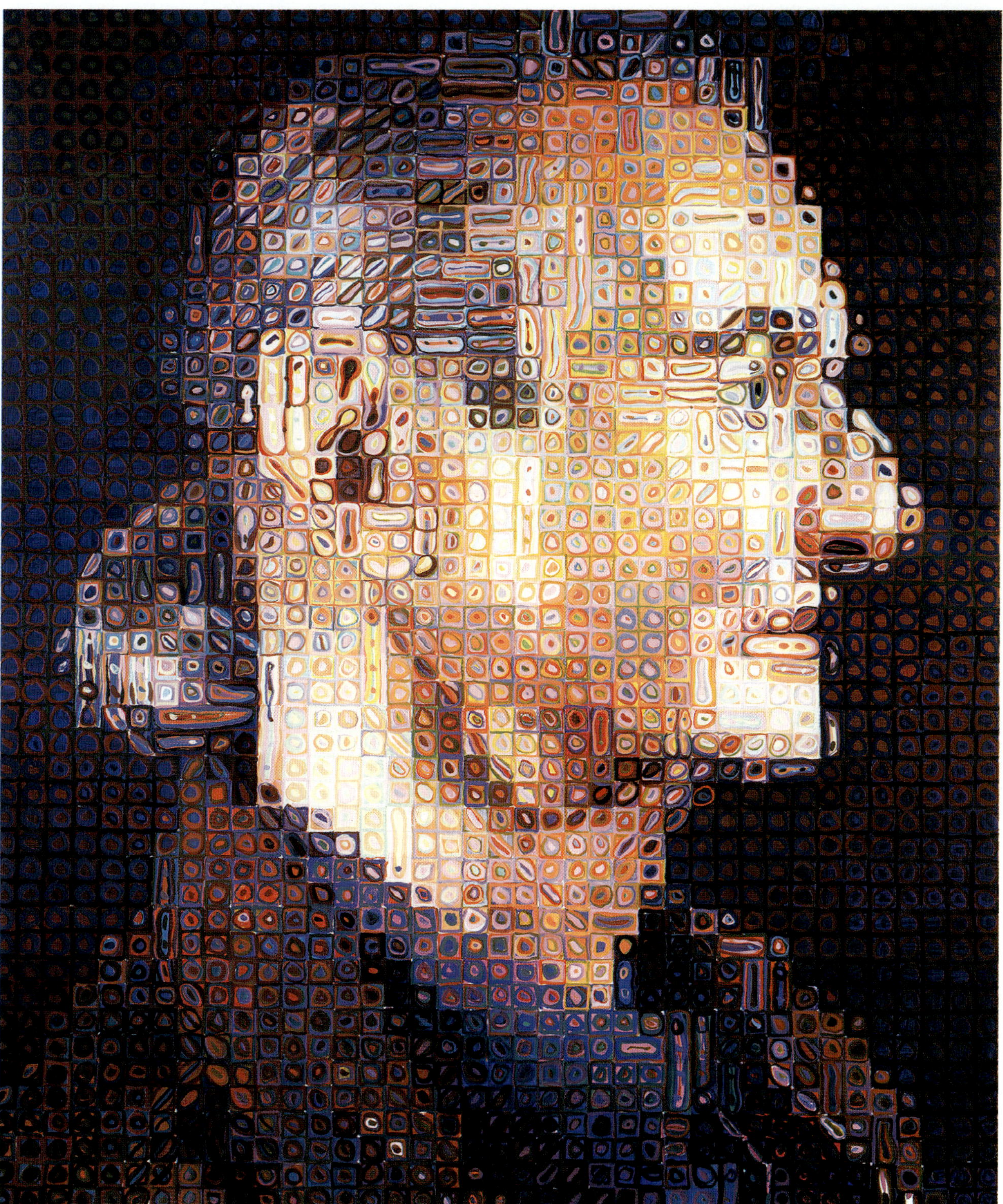

CHUCK CLOSE, ROY II, 1994, oil on canvas, 102 x 84" / Öl auf Leinwand, 259,1 x 213,4 cm. (PHOTO: ELLEN PAGE WILSON)

Mehr als nur Pinselstriche

Bice Curiger: Aus europäischer Sicht hege ich eine Verehrung für die spezifisch amerikanische Malkultur. Damit meine ich einen Reichtum, ein Bezugssystem aus den ehemaligen Regeln des Modernismus und vielen alten und neuen Abweichungen, Freiheiten, Brüchen und einem ausgeprägten Sinn für visuelle Direktheit. Vor diesem Hintergrund findet auch ein reger Austausch zwischen den Generationen statt, was in Europa nicht der Fall ist. Dort reiht sich Einzelposition an Einzelposition.

Chuck Close: Hier wird zurzeit sehr viel gemalt und mir fällt auf, dass Appropriation für einige immer noch ein Modus Operandi ist. Darin zeigt sich der Einfluss der 80er Jahre. Die Jungen plündern unentwegt die kulturellen Vorratskammern und finden immer wieder neue Modelle. Für viele junge Künstler ist der Objektcharakter der Malerei interessant, die Tatsache, dass etwas handfest da ist, etwas anderes als ein flimmerndes Videobild auf dem Monitor. Das ist wohl nur natürlich, nach so vielen Installationen, Videos, Computer-Arbeiten usw. Viele Leute scheinen gern wieder in Farbe herumwühlen zu wollen.

BC: Genau. Es geht um das Anhalten der Bilder und um das Von-Hand-Machen. Sie haben ja früher mit den Fingern gemalt, und gegenwärtig ist das Von-Hand-Machen nicht ein Vorgehen mit der Absicht, die eigene Individualität zu betonen, wie das noch bei den Abstrakten Expressionisten der Fall war, vielmehr geht es um die Spur der menschlichen Hand.

CC: Als ich wirklich direkt mit den Fingern gemalt habe, sagte Robert Storr, ich würde die Haut benutzen, um Haut zu machen. Das fand ich gut gesagt. Beinahe schien es, als würde ich die Gesichter von Leuten, die ich mag, streicheln. Zudem war ich froh, etwas zu tun, das von niemandem gefälscht werden konnte. Ich persönlich hatte es gemacht, und das liess sich nicht mehr verleugnen.

BC: Das bringt mich auf den Begriff «Realismus», auf die Vorstellung, man würde etwas von aussen auf die Leinwand bringen. Aber heute ist die Beziehung zum Objekt eine andere als in der Malerei des neunzehnten Jahrhunderts.

CC: Mein Problem mit dem Realismus liegt darin, dass ich gleichermassen an Künstlichkeit interessiert bin. Deshalb ist es eine Frage von Realismus/Künstlichkeit. Schliesslich wird es immer um Zeichen auf einer Fläche und um deren Verteilung gehen, um das Bild, das daraus entsteht. Was mir gefällt, und

Gespräch zwischen Chuck Close und Bice Curiger

vom 21. August 2000, Bridgehampton, New York

was mit der Realität zu tun hat, ist, dass mit welchen Voraussetzungen auch immer die Leute ein Bild von mir sehen, sie doch alle eines gemeinsam haben, nämlich das Interesse am Bild aus der eigenen Lebenserfahrung heraus, weil sie täglich Menschen betrachten und ein Bild von sich haben dank Spiegeln, Photographien oder Magazinen. Als ich vor einigen Jahren in Rom lebte, benutzten Leute in Bezug auf meine Arbeit den Begriff Pointillismus, was ich unsinnig fand. Mich interessierten aber die Mosaike von Ravenna, ich pilgerte hin, war dann jedoch unsagbar enttäuscht, dass die nur weit oben im Dunkel so eigenartig schimmerten. Ich dachte: «Warum so viel Aufhebens?» Was ich jedoch mochte, waren die einfachen römischen Bodenmosaike. Ihre Betrachtungsdistanz entspricht unserer Grösse, und es geht immer um

kleine Steinbrocken, auch wenn sich daraus ein Bild zusammensetzt. Für einen Augenblick ergibt sich ein Bild, aber wenn man es genau betrachten will, zerfällt es wieder zu einer Ansammlung von Steinchen auf dem Boden. Das hat nicht nur mit der Betrachtungsdistanz zu tun, sondern auch mit der Grösse und der Anzahl Teilchen. So dachte ich mir: «Komisch, da sind sie, hunderte von Jahren alt, und es geht genauso um die Vorstellung der Auflösung eines Bildes, um seine Aufgliederung in Einzelteile, die letztlich ganz unscheinbar sind. Komisch, wie sie sich zu etwas gruppieren, zu dem wir dank unserer Lebenserfahrung einen Bezug herstellen können. Aufregend, wie die Wahrnehmung hin und her kippt, das interessiert mich.»

BC: Bei Ihrem Arbeitsvorgang wird das Ganze noch um einiges komplexer,

weil Sie beim Malen die Leinwand diagonal auf eine Ecke stellen und drehen und folglich ein frontales Antlitz gekippt malen.

CC: Das hat zwei Gründe. Erstens gewinne ich dadurch etwas Distanz zu dem, was ich mache. Und zweitens gibt es einen praktischen Grund: Ich will nicht aufwärts malen, wenn ich ein diagonales Raster gewählt habe. Also drehe ich die Leinwand auf eine Ecke, um waagrecht zu arbeiten. Ich drehe die Arbeit immer wieder auf eine andere Ecke, bis ich sie zuletzt gerade vor mich hinstelle. So entsteht das Bild ganz allmählich wie bei einem Schriftsteller, zunächst in einer Art erstem Bewusstseinsstrom, dann allmählich in

verschiedenen Etappen der Bearbeitung bis zum Feinschliff.

BC: Als wir den Katalog für die Ausstellung «Birth of the Cool» machten, benutzte die Grafikerin ein vergrössertes Detail aus John Chamberlains Porträt, wirklich nur eine kleine Fläche neben der Augenbraue. Ich erkannte es sofort und dachte: «Das ist eigentlich unglaublich, es ist so abstrakt und trotzdem erinnert man sich sofort an das Ganze.» Ich kenne John Chamberlain nicht persönlich, also geht es offensichtlich nicht nur um die Wiedererkennung der Physiognomie.

CC: Jedes Bild hat seine eigene Sprache…

BC: Vor einigen Jahren in New York, als Sie eben aus Rom zurück waren, haben Sie mit mir über das Licht gesprochen, wie gross sein Einfluss auf Ihre Malerei sei…

CC: Das Licht in Rom war wirklich schön. Die amerikanische Akademie dort hat grosse Fenster und riesige Oberlichter. Früher malte ich immer bei künstlichem Licht, weil ich dachte, man sehe die Bilder nachher sowieso in diesem Licht. Jetzt brauche ich, je älter ich werde, umso mehr Licht, benutze eine Jupiterlampe und kann ohne Tageslicht gar nicht mehr arbeiten. Am liebsten arbeite ich in Bridgehampton, denn hier gibt es die Reflexion durch das Wasser. Das Licht ist wunderbar, nicht so warm wie in Rom. Auch mein Studio in der Stadt hat Tageslicht. Wenn ich aber meine Bilder in die Stadt schleppe, trau ich meinen Augen nicht. Obschon ich dort neben verschiedenen Lichtquellen auch natürliches Licht habe, ist es einfach anders. In der Galerie ist es noch schlimmer, und wenn dort die Leute kommen, sage ich: «Oh, wenn ihr es nur sehen könntet. Wenn ihr nur diese beiden Farben nebeneinander sehen könntet. Es ist grossartig, aber ihr könnt es nicht sehen. Tut mir leid.»

BC: Arbeiten Sie in der Stadt mit anderen Farben, einer anderen Palette?

CC: Ja schon. Aber wenn ich ein begonnenes Bild aus der Stadt hierher bringe, um es fertig zu malen, werden Sie darin keinen Bruch feststellen können.

BC: Auf einen bestimmten historischen Moment zurückschauend, denke

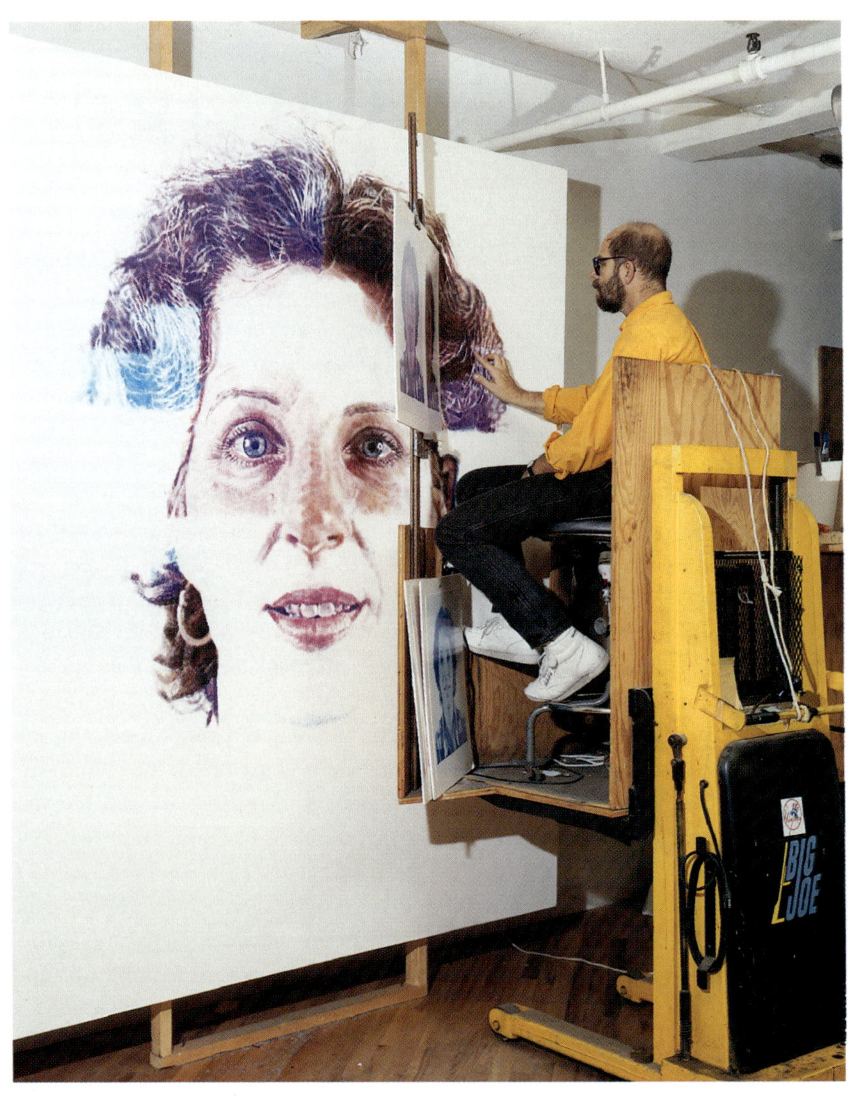

CHUCK CLOSE, LESLIE / FINGERPAINTING, 1985, oil based ink on canvas, 102 x 84", the artist with work in progress / Tusche auf Ölbasis auf Leinwand, 259,1 x 213,4 cm, in Arbeit. (PHOTO: DOUGLAS M. PARKER)

ich, war es wohl recht exzentrisch, diese traditionellen Medien zu benutzen, Kupferdruck, mit der Hand malen und all das. Wunderbar daran ist für mich, wie stark Ihr konzeptueller Ansatz bis ins Materielle hineinwirkt.

CC: Man muss halt manchmal alles über den Haufen werfen, um es wieder zu entdecken. Als ich in den späten 60er Jahren auftauchte, benutzte kein Bildhauer Bronze oder Marmor oder so was. Die suchten nach Materialien, die nicht schon mit einem Namen besetzt waren. Serra benutzte etwa Gummi oder Blei. Dann, ganz allmählich, kamen sie wieder auf die traditionellen Materialien. Sie hatten aber andere Gründe dafür. Ich male heute mit altbewährtem Hasenleim, Bleiweiss, feinster Ölfarbe und einer Palette, die ich jahrelang nicht benutzt habe. Zuerst musste ich alte Gewohnheiten ablegen und all meine Götter austreiben, um dann den Weg zurückzufinden und etwas Eigenes daraus zu machen.

BC: Ich sah Ihre Bilder erstmals 1972 an der «documenta V». Waren Sie damals selbst in Kassel?

CC: Nein, ich ging nicht hin.

BC: Diese Bilder damals, die riesigen Gesichter mit diesen Haaren…, sie hatten eine unglaubliche Präsenz, waren ungemein kraftvoll, und die Bedeutung dahinter war genauso stark wie die Arbeiten selbst.

CC: Danke. Man kann sich heute schon vorstellen, dass sie schockierend wirkten. Denn erstens war damals die Malerei tot. Zweitens, wenn schon Malerei, dann sicher keine erkennbare Darstellung. Und drittens war die Gattung Porträt wirklich die lahmste Idee, die man haben konnte. Darin lag für mich genau die Würze. Ich erinnere mich an Clement Greenbergs Äusserung, Port-

rät sei das Einzige, was man wirklich nicht malen könne. Und ich dachte, offensichtlich gibt es da einen Freiraum, wo man sich breit machen kann.

BC: Man kann es auch anders sehen. Als Schweizer in den 60er Jahren diskutierten wir Max Frisch und seinen Roman *Stiller*. Der erste Satz lautet: «Ich bin nicht Stiller.» Es ging also um Identität und darum, sich kein Bild von einem Menschen zu machen, denn sobald man etwas über eine Person sagt, ist es schon falsch. Vor deinen Bildern, diesen riesigen herausfordernden Gesichtern, fragte man sich auch: «Wer ist das denn wirklich? Was lässt sich über diese Person sagen?»

CC: Genau. Für mich war es interessant, die Leute zu beobachten, wie sie diese frühen Schwarzweissbilder anschauten, denn die hatten aus der Distanz eine ziemlich aggressive Präsenz, schauten einem frech ins Gesicht. Und aus der Nähe war es wie in *Gullivers Reisen*, wo die Liliputaner über das Gesicht des Riesen krabbeln ohne zu erkennen, was sie sehen. Ich glaube, es wirkte wie eine Kombination aus aggressiver Konfrontation und extremer Intimität. Wir stehen meistens nicht nah genug beieinander, um so viel Information voneinander zu erhalten. Wir dringen nicht in unseren gegenseitigen Raum ein. Der einzige Moment, in dem man je so viele Einzelheiten in einem Gesicht wahrnimmt, ist, wenn man Liebe macht, die intimste Sache…

BC: Falls man nicht weitsichtig ist.

CC: Ja… Wenn man nahe dran ist, sieht man, wie die Bilder gemacht sind, was ich auch immer gerne weiss. Ich mag die Syntax genauso, wie wenn ich ein Buch lese. Es geht nicht nur um den narrativen Text, um die Geschichte, sondern darum, wie diese Wörter auf der Zunge liegen, wie sie

zusammengefügt und geformt sind. Vor Jahren gab es ein wunderbares Porträt des Schriftstellers Don DeLillo im *New Yorker*. Darin sagte er, wer meine, es gehe bei Hemingway um Stierkampf, habe nicht begriffen, was Hemingway zu Hemingway mache. Denn bei ihm sei der Artikel «the» viel wichtiger als der Stierkampf. Jeder kann Stierkampfgeschichten erzählen und auch bei Hemingway erfährt man darüber nichts besonders Überraschendes. Es geht aber darum, wie die Geschichte erzählt ist, es geht um die unglaubliche Sinnlichkeit seiner Sprache; die Art, wie die Wörter sich zu Bildern auftürmen, die uns die Geschichte erzählen. Ein grosser Teil des Vergnügens und der ganze Stil gehen auf unzählige kleine Entscheidungen zurück.

BC: Ich sehe das auch in deinen Bildern. Ich empfinde sie ein wenig wie geschrieben. Sie beginnen auch oben links…

CC: …und schreiben sich fort…

BC: Ja, wie ein Text aus Wörtern, Silben, Lauten, die andere Dimensionen eröffnen.

CC: Der Kritiker Adam Gopnik verglich die Kalligraphie meiner Malerei mit jener meines Freundes Brice Marden, den ich seit 1961 kenne. Er sprach vom Unterschied zwischen kalligraphischen Zeichen, die kein Abbild ergeben, und solchen wie den meinen, die das tun. Aber wie interessant auch immer die Form sein mag, für mich muss sie im Dienst des ganzen Bildes stehen.

BC: Bei Ihren riesigen Porträts denkt man an russische oder kommunistische Porträts, an Propagandaplakate, für die es überhaupt keine Einfälle braucht, weil sie ein klares Vorbild haben, das endlos wiederholt wird.

CC: Ja, wo die Botschaft das Bild ist. Philip Glass (den ich um 1968 porträ-

tiert habe) war – einige Ehen früher –
mit einer Chirurgin verheiratet. Sie
stammte aus Bulgarien oder Rumä-
nien. Als ihre Mutter erstmals zu Be-
such kam, führte sie sie ins Whitney
Museum, wo mein Bild von ihrem
Mann hing. Vor dem Bild sagte die
Mutter: «Oh, Philip muss ein sehr
bedeutender Mann sein.» Die Frau
sagte: «Schon, er ist ein geachteter
Komponist.» Die Mutter antwortete:
«Oh, nein, wirklich bedeutend.»
Die Tochter verstand nicht, dass die
Mutter auf die politischen Porträts an-
spielte. Eine Person, die derart vergrös-
sert dargestellt wird, konnte für sie nur
jemand von grossem politischem Ge-
wicht sein.

BC: Bei Ihren Drucken faszinierte es
mich, über die Art der Zusammenarbeit zu lesen, wie Sie sich auf andere
verlassen, die Kontrolle behalten, diese
dann abgeben, um sie später wieder zu
übernehmen.

CC: Ja. Obschon ich im Atelier ein
Kontrollfreak bin und nie jemand anderen etwas tun lassen würde, gelang
es mir beim Drucker, diese Kontrolle
etwas abzugeben. Mein erster Druck als
reifer Künstler war ein Mezzotinto,
und der Grund, weshalb ich Mezzotinto wählte, war, dass weder ich noch
der Drucker wussten, wie man das genau macht. Wir mussten es gemeinsam
herausfinden. Ich wollte keinesfalls
irgendwo hingehen, wo sie wussten,
wie mans macht, es dann aber nicht
hätten tun dürfen, während ich etwas
hätte machen müssen ohne zu wissen
wie. Die erste Erfahrung einer echten
Zusammenarbeit hatte ich dann in
Kyoto, wo ich einen traditionellen
Holzschnitt machte, Genre Ukijo-E.
Dort ist die Gesellschaftsstruktur be-
kanntlich streng hierarchisch, und ich
arbeitete da mit einem Menschen, der

ein Nationaldenkmal war. Wir konnten
ihm nicht sagen, was er zu tun hatte…
Dann gab es noch einen zweiten, der
ihm unterstellt war, der schnitt die
Druckstöcke. Ich nahm das Aquarell,
das als Vorlage diente. Er begann die
Farben zu definieren und alles zu ent-
scheiden, bis die Sache plötzlich die
seine war. Also musste ich ihm die Kontrolle entreissen und es wieder zu meiner Sache machen. Darauf war er wieder dran, so gab es einen Kampf, hin
und her. Das fand ich interessant. Den
Japanern kann man nichts direkt
sagen, das wäre unhöflich. Ich hatte
einen Übersetzer aus Kyoto, der aber
in Kalifornien studiert und mit vielen
amerikanischen Künstlern gearbeitet
hatte. Er war also in beiden Welten zu-
hause. Als ich sagte, er solle bitte übersetzen, es sei mir zu grün, kam es zu
einem langen Blablabla, bis ich fragte:
«Wie lange dauert es eigentlich, zu sagen, es sei zu grün?» Er antwortete, er
habe ihm gesagt: «Chuck findet alles
perfekt. Er sagt, du seist ein Genie, es
könnte nicht besser sein, es ist wirklich
grossartig. Nicht, weil es besser wäre,
aber aus reiner Neugier würde er gern
sehen, wie es aussähe, wenn du es etwas
weniger grün machen würdest.»

BC: Und was geschah darauf?

CC: Er nickte und machte es weniger
grün. So konnte ich mich mit der
Idee einer echten Zusammenarbeit be-
freunden, bei der ich gar nicht selbst
Hand anlegen musste. Es gibt Künstler,
die mit Assistenten oder im Team arbeiten, aber ich verstehe nicht, wie Komar & Melamid, Gilbert & George oder
wer auch immer ihre Entscheidungen
treffen. Wer entscheidet, was zu tun ist?
Wer tut was? Hingegen finde ich den
Arbeitsprozess wunderbar, bei dem andere die eigenen Ideen weiterentwi-
ckeln und man gemeinsam entschei-

det, welche dieser Ideen weiterverfolgt
oder verworfen werden.

BC: Wie entstanden die Arbeiten auf
Papier? Kannten Sie all diese Möglichkeiten damals?

CC: Ich war im Vorstand von Skowhegan (Sommerschule für Malerei und
Skulptur in Maine) und einmal kam
der Papiermacher Joe Wilfer dorthin.
Man nannte ihn den «Prinzen vom Pa-
pierbrei». In Skowhegan schmiss man
ihn sofort raus. Er ging nach New York
und versuchte verzweifelt Geld zu ver-
dienen. Er kam zu mir und sagte: «Lass
uns was aus handgeschöpftem Papier
machen.» Und ich sagte: «Lass mich in
Ruhe, ich hasse das.» Und er: «Was ist
denn so schlimm daran?» – «Nichts,
ich will einfach nicht.» Er wieder: «Was
gefällt dir denn nicht an den Arbeiten,
die du gesehen hast?» Ich nannte ihm
einige Dinge. Nach einer Woche kam
er mit einem Muster und ich sagte:
«Siehst du, ich hatte Recht, es geht
nicht.» Doch er kam immer wieder und
wurde plötzlich zum kreativsten Prob-
lemlöser. So kam es zu einer jahre-
langen Zusammenarbeit. Jeden Fehler
verwandelte er in einen glücklichen
Zufall. Wir trugen die nassen Papier-
massen herum, unter jeder Türe mussten wir sie kippen, manchmal fielen sie
zu Boden und zerbrachen, und er
meinte: «Sieht aus wie Risse in römischen Böden.» So haben wir diese
dann irgendwo ausgestellt. Er konnte
einfach alles ins Positive drehen.

BC: Es ist wie DAS GROSSE GLAS von
Duchamp. Am Telefon sagten Sie, dass
Sie Daguerreotypien machen. Wie se-
hen die aus, und wie entstehen sie?

CC: Genau wie damals, um 1850.
Irgendwie steckt alles, was ich an der
Photographie mag, da drin. Es ist natürlich schwer, etwas darauf zu erkennen. Man muss sich anstrengen, um sie

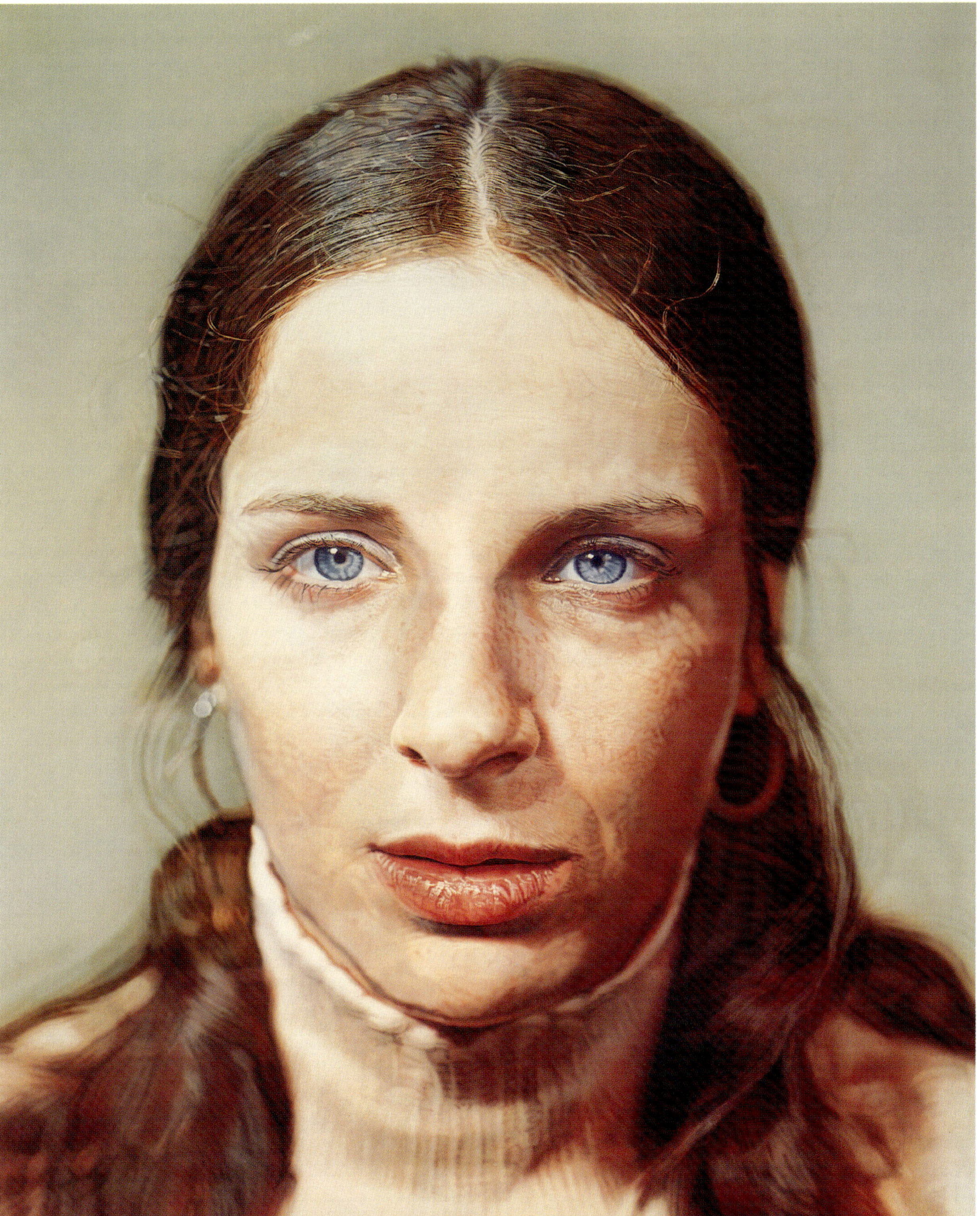

CHUCK CLOSE, LESLIE, 1973, watercolor on paper on canvas, 72½ x 57″ / Aquarell auf Papier auf Leinwand, 184,2 x 144,8 cm. (PHOTO: ELLEN PAGE WILSON)

zu sehen, aber die Details sind phänomenal und die Bandbreite an Tönen unglaublich. Sie haben diese warme Patina und solarisieren, so dass die Schlaglichter bläulich werden, während die anderen Partien warm bleiben.

BC: Wie gross ist so ein Abzug?

CC: Rund 20 x 25 Zentimeter, das ist gross für Daguerreotypien. Man stellt sie aus einer versilberten Kupferplatte her, die poliert wird, bis sie wirklich spiegelblank ist. Dann wird sie mit Jod- und Bromdämpfen lichtempfindlich gemacht. Schliesslich kommt sie in einen Filmhalter, den man hinten in eine Kamera steckt, und wird belichtet. Danach wird sie mit Quecksilberdampf behandelt, um das Bild zu entwickeln, was sehr gefährlich ist. Dann wird dieser Vorgang gestoppt und die Platte gewaschen wie bei der traditionellen Photographie. Zuletzt wird die Platte mit Goldchlorid vergoldet und kommt unter eine Lampe zur endgültigen Fixierung. Wie bei Polaroidaufnahmen sieht man jedes Bild, bevor man das nächste macht. So haben das Modell und ich die Möglichkeit zu sehen, was ich aufgenommen habe, und wir können langsam auf das zusteuern, was wir wollen, ohne alles vorauszuplanen. Das mag ich auch bei Polaroidaufnahmen. Es ermöglicht von Anfang an den Dialog. Das Modell kann sagen: «Nein, bitte nicht so. Kannst du nicht noch ein Bild machen?» Natürlich behalte ich mir das Vetorecht vor, aber ich versuche dem Modell entgegenzukommen. Das gehört zum Dialog.

BC: Wenn Sie das erzählen, wird deutlich, wie lange und intensiv der Prozess ist. Ihr Hauptinteresse gilt offenbar dem Entstehungsprozess…

CC: Der Weg ist immer viel interessanter als das Ziel, denn die Erfahrung ist stets eine andere, je nachdem, ob man diesen oder jenen Weg einschlägt. Der Stil bettet sich im Prozess ein. Alles wird zu einer Aufzeichnung der Gedanken, der Entscheidungen. Deshalb halte ich Malerei für etwas Magisches. Photographie ist natürlich auch extrem magisch, geradezu übersinnlich. Sie übertrifft die physische Realität und birgt trotzdem alle Entscheidungsschritte in sich. Sie bietet die Möglichkeit nachzuempfinden, was der Künstler erlebt hat. Das macht sie so persönlich. Die Leute können sehen, wie es dazu kam und was wohin führte.

BC: Ich habe gesehen, wie die Leute in Ihren Ausstellungen staunend den Punkt suchen, wo ein Bild «auseinander fällt», in all diese Diamanten oder magischen Steine. Man kann beobachten, wie das Gehirn beim Hin-und-her-Gehen arbeitet, und kann sehen, wie die Wahrnehmung spielt.

CC: Besonders Leute, die Drogenerfahrung haben. Es ist fast wie eine psychedelische Erfahrung, ein garantiert gefahrloser Trip…
Für mich liegt der Reiz im Akt des Malens. Ich habe nichts dagegen, wenn jemand seine Arbeiten von anderen ausführen lässt. Sol LeWitt, einer meiner besten Freunde, hat vollkommen Recht, wenn er das tut, das gehört zu seiner Arbeitsweise. Für mich jedoch liegt das Vergnügen im Physischen. Ich lasse die Leute alles andere für mich tun, damit ich malen kann.

BC: Bei Ihnen kommen alle Entscheidungen direkt aus dem Gehirn und aus der Erfahrung. Es ist wohl unmöglich, jemanden auszubilden, der das für Sie tut.

CC: Selbst wenn man einen ausbilden könnte, würde ihm doch nur das passieren, was mir während der Arbeit widerfährt, und damit wüsste er nichts anzufangen, weil er nur ausführen darf, was ich ihm sage. Es geht halt immer um Dinge, auf die ich während der Arbeit stosse und die man nicht voraussehen kann.

BC: Zum Beispiel?

CC: Wenn man am Arbeiten ist und sich sagt: «Da entwickelt sich was. Daraus will ich eine Art Socken- oder Birnenform oder so was machen.» Jedenfalls würde ich mich niemals hinsetzen und sagen: «Ich möchte einen Weg finden, wie ich Socken, Birnen, Whiskeyflaschen, Donuts und Hot Dogs in meine Malerei einbringen kann.» So etwas ergibt sich erst beim Malen. Oder nehmen wir eine Farbe. Vielleicht finde ich für ein Quadrat eine Farbe, die ich mag, wenn ich Blau, Violett, Grün und Gelb zusammenbringe. Im nächsten Feld will ich es dann ganz anders haben: mit Grün, Violett, Rosa und Orange. So reagiere ich auf das, was ich bereits gemacht habe. Es ist wie beim Schreiben, da verwendet man auch nicht zweimal dasselbe Wort im gleichen Satz. Man will zwar eine Geschichte erzählen, aber sie soll auch differenziert und abwechslungsreich sein.

BC: Bei dieser Malweise gibt es also etwa fünf Elemente in einem Feld. Wahrscheinlich haben Sie zuunterst eine rosa Reihe, dann beginnen Sie Entscheidungen zu fällen und reagieren darauf.

CC: Genau.

BC: Sie wissen dann aber auch, dass da irgendwo eine dunkle Stelle sein muss.

CC: Nein. Ausser dem Raster gibt es keine Zeichnung. Wenn ich aber die Farbe auftrage, mache ich zwei Dinge: Zum einen will ich auf eine resultierende Farbe in einem Feld kommen. Wenn es aber mehr als nur eine Sache in einem Feld gibt, etwa eine dunkle Linie, die durchläuft, muss ich herausfinden, wie ich das Problem löse, ohne es einfach symbolisch zu tun. Dann blase ich die Formen auf oder verkleinere sie, lasse sie zusammenlaufen oder zu unauffälligen Dingen werden. Es geht nicht nur um den Pinselstrich selbst. Im Billard oder Pool sagt man: «Putting English on the Stroke» (für einen spezifischen Effet-Stoss). Man macht einen Stoss, aber die Art und Weise, wie man den Ball trifft, bewirkt, dass noch anderes geschieht. Zwar setze ich ein paar Farben hin, aber erst der besondere Drall ermöglicht, dass daraus etwas wird, nämlich das, was letztlich das Porträt ausmacht.

BC: Das ist wie eine Metapher für etwas, was viele Maler zuvor getan haben.

CC: Ja, schauen Sie Ingres oder Velázquez oder Frans Hals oder sonst jemanden an, da sind diese Striche, die etwas darstellen und trotzdem einfache Striche bleiben. Da gibt es eine Hand, die aus fünf oder sechs Strichen besteht. Es gibt seit eh und je die Ökonomie und den Umgang mit einer malerischen Syntax. Meine ist nur etwas anders angelegt.

BC: Ja, da komme ich natürlich auf den Begriff *all-over*, der sehr amerikanisch ist.

CC: Oh ja. Ich war mir stets bewusst eine *All-over*-Malerei zu machen. Zuerst versuchte ich zu verstehen, was die amerikanische Malerei der 60er Jahre ausmachte. Ich dachte: «Nun, da ist dieser Sinn für *all-overness*, diese Verpflichtung gegenüber dem gesamten Rechteck, die Vorstellung, dass etwas in der rechten Ecke genauso wichtig ist wie etwas in der Mitte, sei es bei Pollocks Farbschnüren, Frank Stellas schwarzen

Streifen oder Agnes Martins Rasterbildern.» Das schien mir typisch amerikanisch zu sein, auch dieser Mangel an Hierarchie. Ich wollte Nicht-Hierarchisches mit Hierarchischem verbinden. Augen, Nase und Mund gelten gemeinhin als die wichtigen Teile eines Porträts und mir stellte sich die Frage: «Wie kann ich davon wegkommen und zum Ausdruck bringen, dass jeder Teil des Bildes gleich wichtig ist?» Dabei interessierten mich auch sogenannte «Frauenarbeiten» wie Steppen, Häkeln, Stricken – all die langwierigen Prozesse, denen man sich hingibt und dabei nicht jeden Tag das Rad neu erfinden muss. Man tut heute, was man gestern getan hat, und morgen, was man heute tut. Man hat Vertrauen in dieses Vorgehen und wenn man dranbleibt, wird man auch sein Ziel erreichen. Das ist eine Arbeitsmethode, die ich persönlich als befreiend empfinde. Genau wie die viel beschäftigten Siedlerfrauen, die strickten und häkelten, weil sie diese Arbeit jederzeit aufnehmen oder ablegen konnten. Sie konnten das Baby stillen, es hinlegen und ein bisschen stricken, dann die Strickarbeit wieder niederlegen und den Garten jäten, dann wieder zurückkommen. Stricken wirkt auch besänftigend und beruhigend. Und ich war nervlich ein Wrack.

BC: Wirklich?

CC: Oh ja. Ich bin nervlich ein Wrack. Ich bin nachlässig, faul und ungeduldig. Alles Voraussetzungen, die mich eigentlich hindern sollten zu tun, was ich jetzt tue. Aber schliesslich fand ich eine Arbeitsweise, die all das berücksichtigt. Irgendwie will man ja nicht der Gefangene seiner eigenen Natur

bleiben, man will sich nicht vom eigenen Charakter vorschreiben lassen, welche Art Kunst man zu machen imstande ist. Indem ich also eine Situation schuf, in der ich mich nicht mehr so undiszipliniert benehmen konnte, fand ich auch einen Weg mit meinem Charakter fertig zu werden. Deshalb zieht wohl auch die Performance-Kunst sehr scheue Menschen an. Die wollen auf die Bühne, obschon sie sehr scheu, introvertiert und was auch immer sind. Ich kenne sehr undisziplinierte Autoren, die sich zwingen, soundso viele Wörter am Tag zu schreiben. Ich kenne aber niemanden, der so aufwändige Bilder malt, der wirklich manisch wäre, also jemand, der einfach malen muss. Dennoch können sich viele unter uns wie Besessene verhalten. Denn will man etwas erreichen, muss man beharrlich sein. Schreibt man einen Roman, braucht man soundso lange, um soundso viele Wörter zusammenzufügen. Darauf muss man sich schon einlassen.

BC: Manchmal wollen Betrachter ein Bild sofort, auf den ersten Blick erfassen. Sie gehen in eine Galerie oder ein Museum und sind ungeduldig. Aber einen Roman kann man auch nicht verstehen ohne ihn erst einmal zu lesen.

CC: Und jetzt kommt noch die virtuelle Realität dazu. Museen bieten ihren Bestand online an, so dass man gar nicht mehr ins Museum gehen muss. Das verstehe ich nicht. Was soll man da von den Werken noch mitbekommen?

BC: Ja, das sind nur noch vage Hinweise. Deshalb malen einige Leute immer noch.

(Übersetzung: Jakobett)

Edition for Parkett   CHUCK CLOSE

Self-Portrait, 2000

Digital ink-jet print of a daguerreotype original on Crane Muséo paper.
Printed by Adamson Editions, Washington D.C.
22 x 17" (image size 15 $^1/_2$ x 12").
Edition of 70, signed and numbered.

Selbstporträt, 2000

Digitaler Ink-Jet-Print einer Daguerreotypie auf Crane-Muséo-Papier.
Gedruckt bei Adamson Editions, Washington D.C.
56 x 43,2 cm (Bild 39,4 x 30,5 cm).
Auflage: 70, signiert und nummeriert.

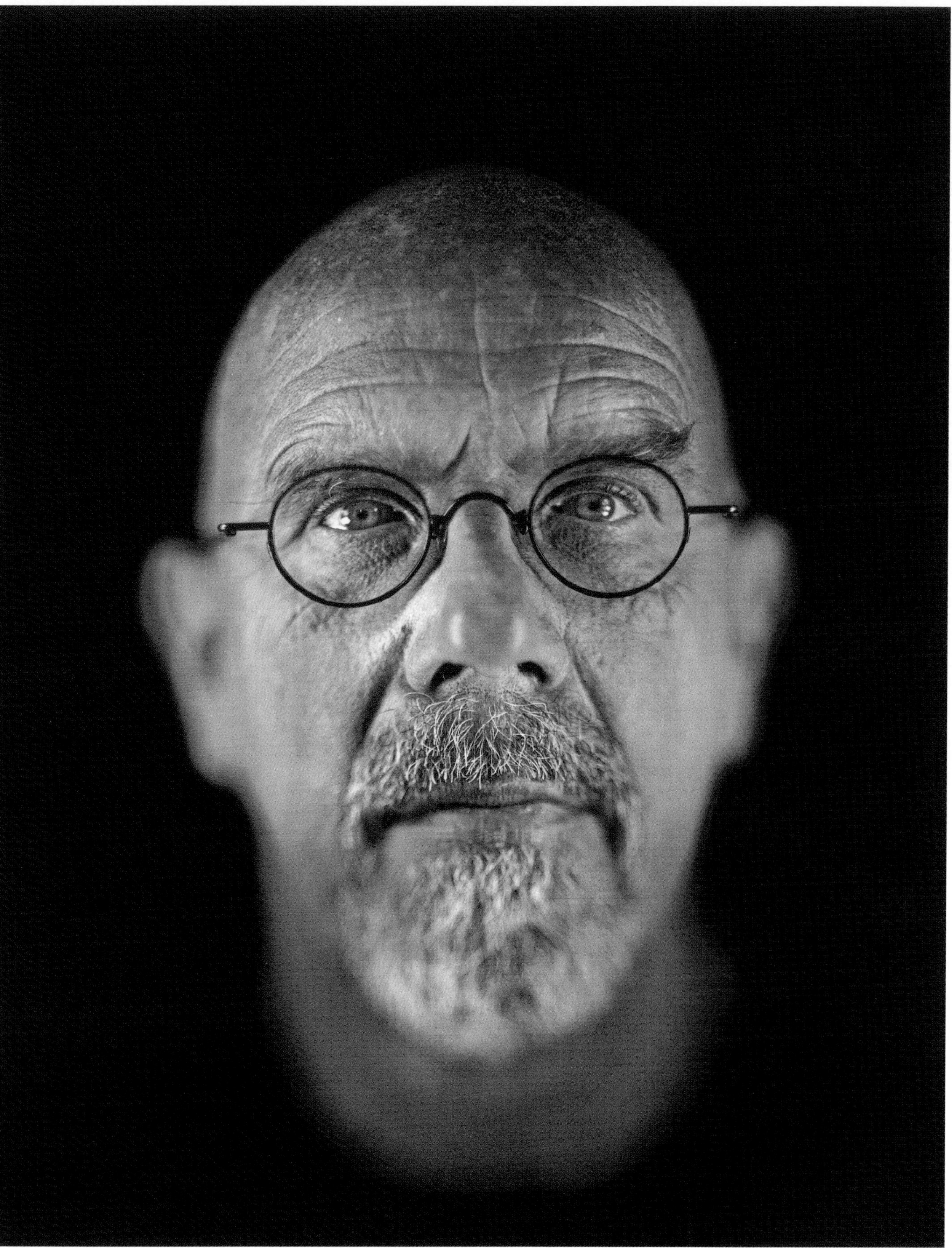

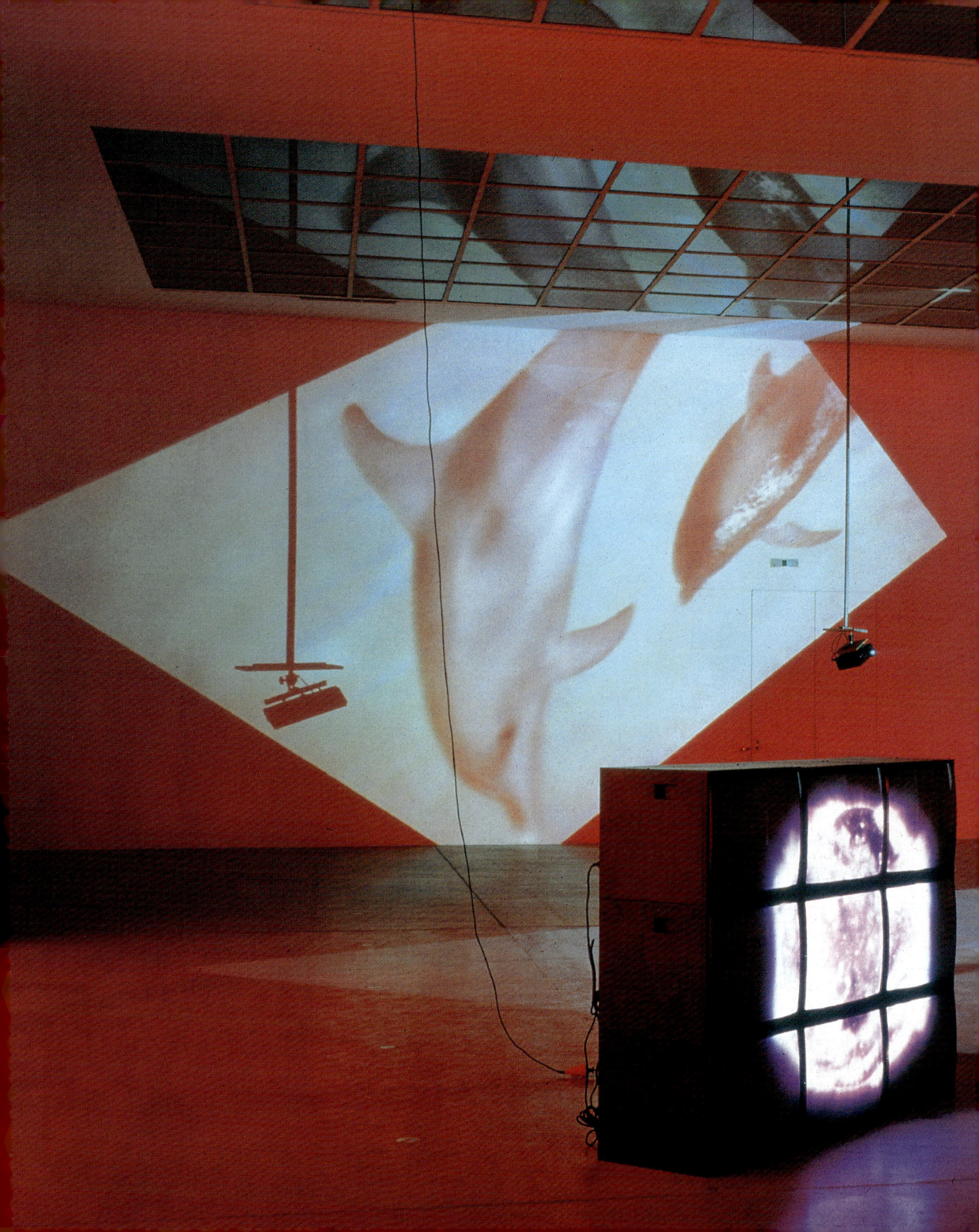

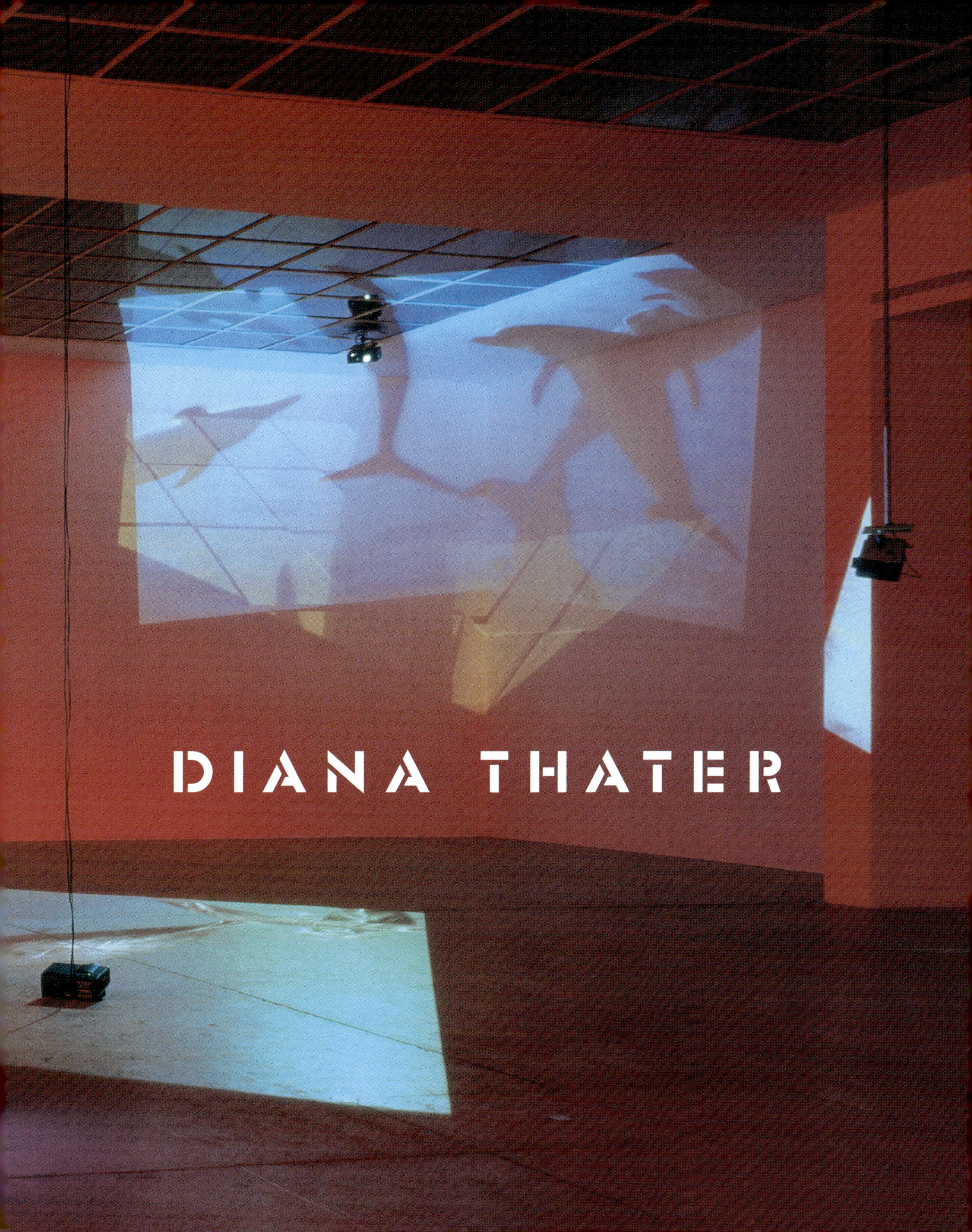
DIANA THATER

Page/Seite 76–77:
DIANA THATER, DELPHINE, 1999,
installation view, Vienna Secession, January 2000 /
Wiener Secession, Januar 2000.
(PHOTO: MARGHERITA SPILUTTINI)

SARA ARRHENIUS

Come Closer

On the Intimacy of Vision in the Art of Diana Thater

Images of animals have always been heavy with signification. The missing link, the short distance that separates us from animals, fills us with both curiosity and horror. When we put ourselves next to animals, the gap between nature and culture takes on a corporeal existence. We think that we are seeing humans as they were in pure nature, in the moment before taking the step into language and becoming

human. That is why our images of animals have never been about animals themselves. Animals and nature have had to serve as art's other, its raw materials, mute and faithful companions open to every projection. We could be content to describe—and it would still be saying a great deal—the way Diana Thater uses animals and nature in her work as a knowledgeable game with art and the history of photography. The references in her 1997 Münster Sculpture Project video installation BROKEN CIRCLE to the grand landscapes of Westerns could be seen as a twist on our contemporary production of the sublime. Or we could see—even though this may be fulfilling our duty to art history a little further than is necessary— the painterly qualities of the tamed zebra's skin in THE BEST ANIMALS ARE THE FLAT ANIMALS—THE

SARA ARRHENIUS is a critic and a writer based in Stockholm, Sweden. She is the editor of *NU: The Nordic Art Review* and a contributing writer for the Swedish daily newspaper *Dagens Nyheter*. She recently published her second book *En riktig kvinna* (A Real Women), which investigates the discourse of biology and gender in contemporary culture. She is presently editing an anthology on visual culture, gender, and psychoanalysis.

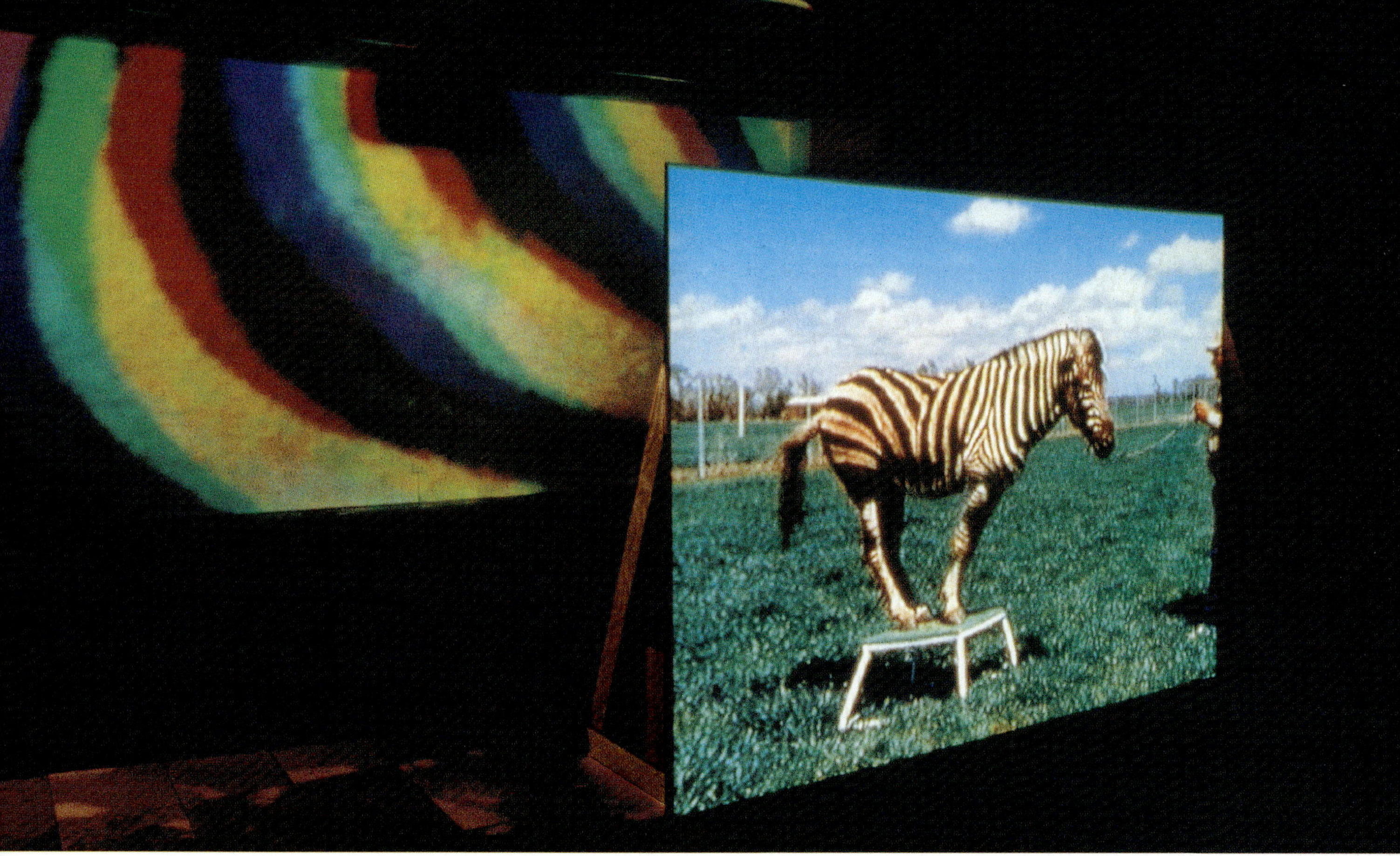

BEST SPACE IS THE DEEP SPACE (1998) as an abstract canvas. But Diana Thater goes beyond this. In her work, every interpretation leads to yet another possibility; there is always another story to listen to, another door to open. The tamed ape that the film team is carefully directing in the video installation ELECTRIC MIND (1996), the trained white stallion slowly dancing to the whip in THE BEST SPACE IS THE DEEP SPACE (1998), and, again, the sad, patient zebra that obediently forces itself onto a circus stool, all have the same insistent urgency as the symptom. They persist in coming back, they put themselves in the way and ask that we see and try to understand. But Diana Thater does not assign her menagerie any mythological dimensions or neat roles within a comforting cosmology. Such claims are given no room in

DIANA THATER, THE BEST ANIMALS ARE THE FLAT ANIMALS, 1998 (version 1), installation for LCD video projector, 2 three-lens video projectors, video monitor, 4 laser discs and players, window film, false wall (96 x 126"), and existing architecture at the MoMA, New York. / DIE BESTEN TIERE SIND DIE FLACHEN TIERE, Installation für LCD-Videoprojektor, 2 Dreilinsen-Video-projektoren, Videomonitor, 4 Laserdiscs und Abspielgeräte, Fenster-folie, falsche Wand (243,8 x 320 cm) und bestehende Räumlich-keiten.

the open, critical space that she constructs in her work. And it is also no coincidence that the animals that she shows are all trained. Because instead of remaining dumb as a way of signifying the real and the wild, they all play a role in our fantasy of nature as a pure point of origin.

The boundaries we mark out between animal and human, between nature and art, are not self-evident. That is why they are so charged. They are formulated within historical and cultural conditions where the body collides against science, knowledge against values, and the horror-struck inventiveness of the unconscious against the inevitability of matter. Human beings become human by marking out what separates them from animals. The creatures that transgress or contradict these boundaries are the monsters that both scare and fascinate us. They are the creatures that reappear as a running theme in the West's storehouse of images and narratives. The ape in ELECTRIC MIND, the screenplay that Diana Thater wrote based on a science fiction story by Pat Murphy, is exactly such a boundary creature. The chimpanzee's consciousness is really that of a young girl's. Her neurologist father has succeeded in making an electronic copy of his dead daughter's brain and her consciousness now lives on in the form of the ape. The touching and bizarre story of how Rachel finally receives recognition as a thinking—and legal—subject can of course be read as a critique of how we divide the world into a system of dichotomies (animal versus human, thinking versus feeling, body versus soul) and arrange these opposing pairs within a static hierarchy. The two monitors in the video installation named after the play flash the words "A mouse is a cat is a chimp is a girl." The monitors are surrounded by video projections that show how a chimpanzee is trained to become an animal actor in Hollywood. And Rachel's story is also the story of our increasing difficulty in maintaining the boundaries that have established our definitions of human consciousness and intelligent life. But Thater's attraction to these ambiguous border zones cannot be neatly summarized as cultural criticism. ELECTRIC MIND is also in its way a pastiche of a *bildungsroman* of development and change. Investigating the possibilities that change and metamorphosis harbor is a central theme in Thater's work, something that becomes even clearer in DELPHINE (1999). Here, Thater has constructed one of those fluid, changeable, and fluctuating structures so typical of her work. The viewer is enclosed within a room of video projections that show dolphins swimming in swirling waters. As always in Thater's work, the generation of the work and the act of looking are laid open—the dolphins are seen by the filming divers as a reflection of the viewer's own position. "I'd rather be a dolphin than a man," says Thater in an interview in the show's catalogue, and the work also seems motivated by a desire for transgressing boundaries, for approaching the unknown and experiencing other ways of being and experiencing the world. Literally and metaphorically, animals' dissimilarity stands for the unprejudiced examination of and relation to one's own ego and of the borders of one's consciousness.

If we begin to unfold and describe the different layers in Diana Thater's multi-faceted video pieces, it is remarkable how this examination and reformulation of boundaries occurs at every level of her work. Hers is not a transgressive logic resembling that of the carnival, that is to say, a temporary revaluation of hierarchies that in actuality serves to render visible

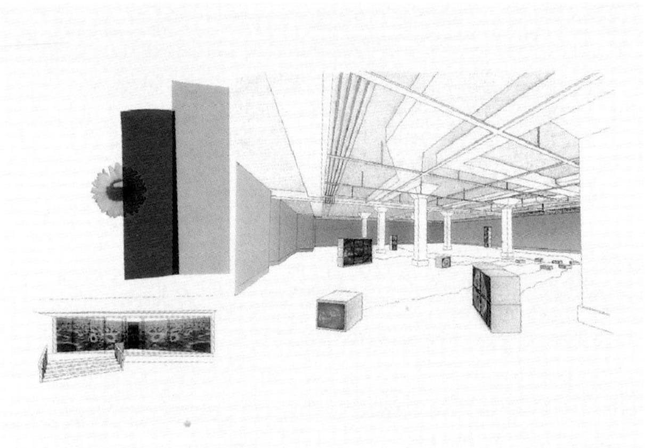

DIANA THATER, BROKEN CIRCLE, 2000,
installation sketch for Kunsthalle Tensta, Sweden,
December 2000, ink and collage on vellum, 24 x 36" /
AUFGEBROCHENER KREIS, Installationsskizze,
Tusche und Collage auf Zeichenpergament, 61 x 91,5 cm.

and affirm the ruling order. It is also not a question of the very thrill of transgression, the frisson we see in a mystic like Georges Bataille who has to assume the existence of a boundary so that the taboo can be broken. For Thater, it is more a question of trying to redefine and reconsider the boundaries and definitions on which our understanding of viewer and viewed, subject and object, and image and reality depend. Hence, the fascination with animal consciousness as different yet similar comes to function as a metaphor for a larger set of questions. DELPHINE breaks down vision and the distance between viewer and viewed by using the moving image throughout the room, rather than projecting it in front of the viewer like in a cinema. The image turns around corners and moves over the walls, floors, and ceiling. There is no clear distinction between image as image and image as architectural element, between the image's illusionistic space and the space in which the viewer finds him or herself. The images surround the viewer and create a new experience of space where the video's spatiality of light and time overlaps with the solid materiality of the room. In the same way, Thater breaks down the centrality of vision insofar as her video installations do not offer a linear narrative with a clear beginning or end. The installations offer an endless number of possible images and perspectives with no location offering a totalizing point of view and no viewer privileged in any way. There is no location in the room where I can stand in front of the work and consume it with my gaze. I am in the work and it becomes clear, to paraphrase Lacan, that the world looks at me as much as I look at it. I am in the image at the same time as I am in front of it. The dolphins swimming in the streaming, swirling water are looking at me as attentively as I am looking at them. Their gaze sees and shapes the world to the same degree as mine does.

Thater's works consistently reveal their own mode of production. The camera and the projector accomplish part of this task. In certain works, the video's primary colors are made visible by coloring the windows of the exhibition space. Her works investigate video's properties, its specific material conditions and its visual and spatial possibilities, and also account for their own means of production—the apparatus is not hidden to create illusion and to seduce. The works do not appear before the viewer as miracles fallen from the sky; they openly display themselves as composed of material and technique. However the apparatus does not create any sense of distance or alienation in the Brechtian sense. Rather, the visibility of the apparatus appears as an act of inclusion, a new sort of familiarity with the machinery whose role in the production of the image is no longer hidden. Finding ourselves in a symbiotic relationship with the apparatus we see better with the camera than without it. Thater's intimacy with the image and the screen makes projection a conscious artistic strategy in which the viewer can move within and along with the work. By "intimacy" I am not referring to any gender-specific associations of a soft femininity, but to a more general sense of proximity and to the erasure of the divisions that have structured our ways of seeing. Thater's sophisticated examination of the relation between the viewer, image, light, time, and architecture contributes to a decisive shift in the gaze and space of film viewing. The passive film viewer looking at the sparkling screen in a theater or standing before a spatially demarcated monitor has taken a final step into film history and has been replaced by another mode of vision. Unlike video installations prevalently produced throughout contemporary art's development, particularly in relation to film, Thater's works imagine a mobile viewer, moving through the room or through a series of rooms, flooded with moving images where no point can be marked as a beginning or an end, and no place can be designated as the center or the periphery. This is a mode of vision where the corporeality of the eye is recognized and the illusion of an all-seeing eye, capable of dominating the world, has been abandoned. But it is also the image that has become more corporeal, that has acquired spatial volume and presence. The line between image and viewer, between the space of reality and that of images, and between the solidity of architecture and the instability of the image has changed. We no longer stand in front of images whose surface quality has brought us to a standstill. We move toward the image and it takes one step toward us. Where this intimacy will lead remains to be seen.

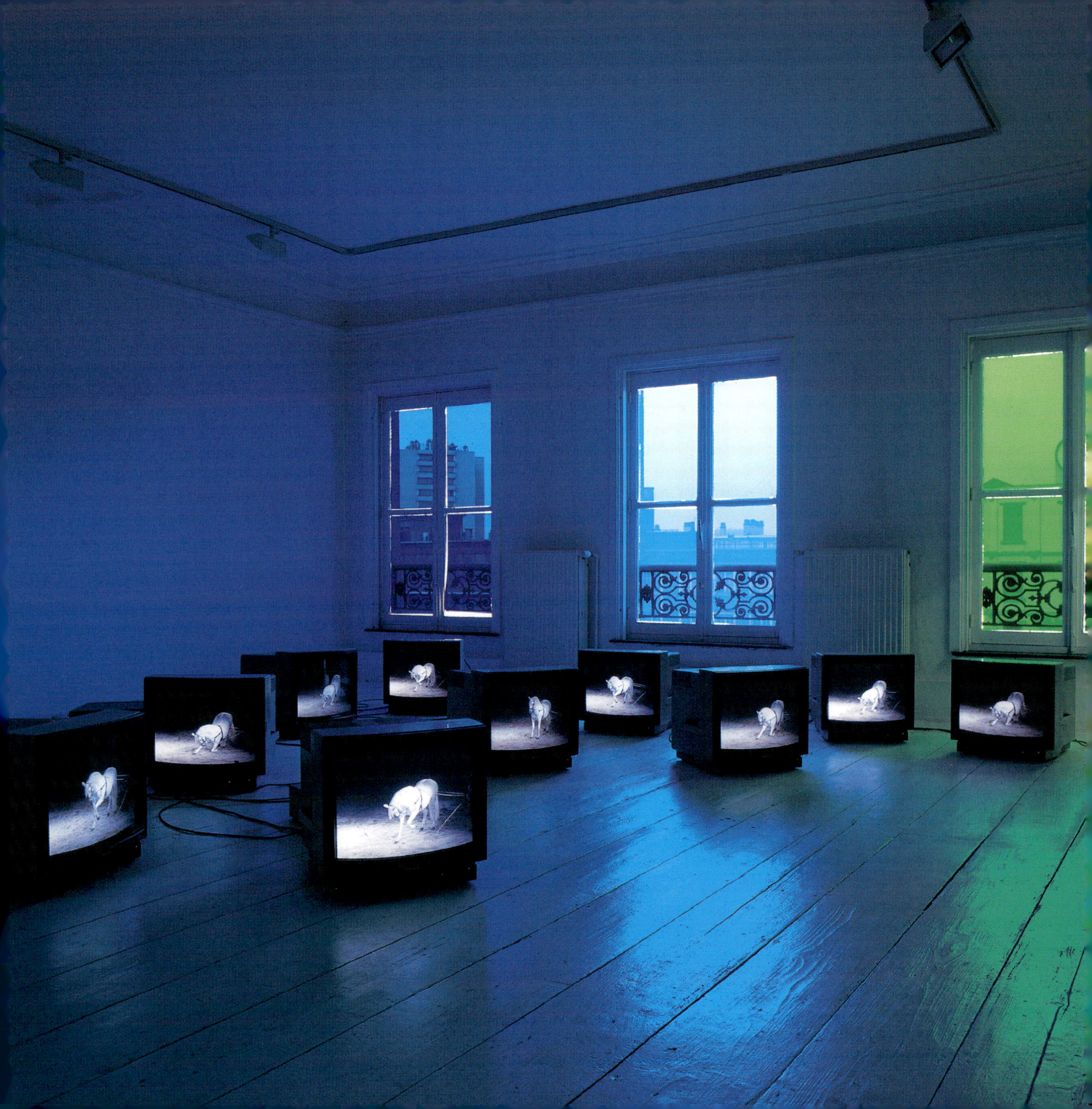

SARA ARRHENIUS

Komm näher

Die Intimität des Schauens in der Kunst von Diana Thater

Tierdarstellungen haben seit jeher besondere Bedeutung. Das fehlende Bindeglied und der nur geringe Abstand zwischen Mensch und Tier erfüllt uns mit ebenso viel Neugier wie Schrecken. Stellen wir uns neben das Tier, wird die Kluft zwischen Natur und Kultur geradezu körperlich greifbar. Es ist, als sähen wir den Menschen in seinem Naturzustand, un-

SARA ARRHENIUS arbeitet als Kritikerin und Publizistin in Stockholm. Sie ist die Herausgeberin von *NU: The Nordic Art Review* und schreibt regelmässig für die schwedische Tageszeitung *Dagens Nyheter*. Soeben ist ihr zweites Buch, *En riktig kvinna* (Eine richtige Frau), erschienen, eine Untersuchung des aktuellen Diskurses zum Thema Biologie und Geschlecht. In Vorbereitung ist ferner eine Anthologie über visuelle Kultur, Geschlecht und Psychoanalyse.

mittelbar vor dem Erwerb der Sprache, dem Schritt zur eigentlichen Menschwerdung. Aus diesem Grund stellen unsere Tierbilder nie einfach nur Tiere dar. Schon immer haben Tier und Natur die Rolle des Anderen gegenüber der Kunst gespielt, sie waren das Rohmaterial, stumme und treue Begleiter, die für Projektionen aller Art herhalten mussten. Wir könnten uns ohne weiteres darauf beschränken, zu beschreiben, wie Diana Thater Tiere und Natur in ihrem Werk einsetzt: in einem äusserst raffinierten und kompetenten Spiel mit der Kunst und der Geschichte der Photographie. So liessen sich die Bezüge zu den grandiosen Landschaften des Westernfilms in BROKEN CIRCLE (Gebrochener Kreis) – eine Video-Installation für «Skulptur. Projekte Münster, 1997» – als Anspielung auf unsere heutigen Bilder des Erhabenen verstehen. Oder wir könnten – gewissermassen in Übererfüllung unserer kunsthistorischen Pflicht – das Malerische des Zebrafells in THE BEST ANIMALS ARE THE FLAT ANIMALS – THE BEST SPACE IS THE DEEP SPACE (Die besten Tiere sind die flachen Tiere – der beste Raum ist der tiefe Raum, 1998) wie ein abstraktes Bild auffassen. Diana Thater geht jedoch noch weiter. Jede Interpretation ihres Werks eröffnet eine weitere Perspektive; da wird immer noch eine andere Geschichte erzählt, eine weitere Tür aufgestossen. Der zahme Affe in der Video-Installation ELECTRIC MIND (1996), den das Filmteam sorgsam herumdirigiert, der dressierte weisse Hengst in THE BEST SPACE IS THE DEEP SPACE (1998), der langsam nach der Peitsche tanzt, und das ebenso traurige wie geduldige Zebra, das sich gehorsam auf einen Zirkushocker quält – sie alle zeigen dieselbe seltsame Beharrlichkeit. Unbeirrt kehren sie immer wieder, stellen sich uns in den Weg und fordern uns auf hinzusehen, um zu verstehen. Aber Diana Thater verleiht ihrer Menagerie keine mythologische Dimension, und eine Geborgenheit bietende Kosmologie mit klar verteilten Rollen sucht man vergebens. In dem offenen, kritischen Raum ihrer Arbeiten haben derlei Ansprüche keinen Platz. Natürlich ist es auch kein Zufall, dass die Tiere, die sie zeigt, allesamt dressiert sind. Sie sind keine stummen Geschöpfe, die für das Echte und Wilde stehen, sondern jedes spielt seine Rolle in unserer Vorstellung von der Natur als reinem Ursprung.

Die Grenzen, die wir zwischen Mensch und Tier, Natur und Kunst ziehen, sind nicht selbstverständlich. Genau deshalb sind sie so bedeutungsvoll. Sie sind das Resultat einer historischen und kulturellen Situation konfliktträchtiger Spannungen zwischen Körper und Wissenschaft, Wissen und Werten, zwischen dem manchmal erschreckenden Einfallsreichtum des Unbewussten und der gnadenlosen Wirklichkeit. Der Mensch wird zum Menschen, indem er hervorhebt, was ihn vom Tier unterscheidet. Geschöpfe, die diese Grenzen überschreiten oder in Frage stellen, gelten als Monster und wirken auf uns ebenso erschreckend wie faszinierend. In den Bilderwelten und Geschichten des Westens sind sie allgegenwärtig. Ein solches Grenzwesen ist auch der Affe in ELECTRIC MIND. Es beruht auf einem Dreh-

buch, das Diana Thater nach einer Sciencefiction-erzählung von Pat Murphy verfasste. Das Bewusstsein des Schimpansen ist eigentlich das eines jungen Mädchens. Dessen Vater, einem Neurologen, ist es gelungen, eine elektronische Kopie vom Gehirn seiner toten Tochter zu machen, und nun lebt ihr Bewusstsein im Affen weiter. Die anrührende und bizarre Geschichte, wie Rachel schliesslich als denkende Person – auch juristisch – anerkannt wird, lässt sich natürlich auch als Kritik an unserer Aufteilung der Welt in Gegensatzpaare verstehen (Tier/Mensch, Denken/Gefühl, Körper/Geist: Diese Gegensätze fügen wir zu einer starren Ordnung. Auf den beiden Monitoren der nach dieser Geschichte betitelten Video-Installation erscheinen die Worte «A mouse is a cat is a chimp is a girl» (Eine Maus ist eine Katze ist ein Schimpanse ist ein Mädchen). Die Bildschirme sind umgeben von Video-Projektionen, die die Abrichtung eines Schimpansen zum Hollywood-Tierdarsteller zeigen. Rachels Geschichte ist auch die Geschichte unserer zunehmenden Schwierigkeiten, jene Grenzen aufrechtzuerhalten, mit deren Hilfe wir menschliches Bewusstsein und intelligentes Leben definieren. Doch Thaters Vorliebe für diese ambivalenten Grenzbereiche lässt sich nicht einfach unter dem Begriff Kulturkritik abhaken. ELECTRIC MIND ist in gewisser Weise auch eine Persiflage auf den Entwicklungsroman. Die Erforschung der Möglichkeiten von Wandel und Metamorphose ist ein zentrales Thema in Thaters Werk. Besonders deutlich wird dies in DELPHINE (1999). Hier begegnen wir einer jener fliessenden, veränderlichen und flüchtigen Strukturen, die für ihre Arbeit so bezeichnend sind. Der Betrachter steht im Raum, umgeben von Video-Projektionen, die in bewegtem Wasser umherschwimmende Delphine zeigen. Wie immer bei Diana Thater wird sowohl die Entstehung des Werks als auch der Akt des Betrachtens transparent gemacht – aus der Sicht der filmenden Taucher erscheinen die Delphine wie eine Reflexion des Betrachters und seiner Position. «Ich wäre lieber ein Delphin als ein Mensch», sagt Thater im Ausstellungskatalog. Und so scheint denn auch das ganze Werk geprägt vom Wunsch, Grenzen zu überschreiten, sich dem Unbekannten zu nähern, andere Daseinsformen zu erforschen und die Welt zu erfahren.

Sowohl im wörtlichen als auch im übertragenen Sinn steht die Andersartigkeit der Tiere für das unvoreingenommene kritische Verhältnis zum eigenen Ich und die Grenzen des eigenen Bewusstseins.

Hat man erst einmal begonnen, die verschiedenen Ebenen der vielschichtigen Arbeiten Thaters zu analysieren, stellt man staunend fest, dass die Überprüfung und Neuformulierung der Grenzen auf allen Ebenen des jeweiligen Werks stattfindet. Dabei geht es ihr nicht um jene Art von Grenzüberschreitung, wie wir sie beispielsweise im Karneval finden, also um eine vorübergehende Neubewertung von Hierarchien, die letztlich dazu dient, die herrschende Ordnung sichtbar zu machen und zu bestätigen. Es geht ihr auch nicht um den Kick der Überschreitung, jenen Schauder, welchem wir bei einem Mystiker wie Georges Bataille begegnen, der auf die Grenze angewiesen ist, um ein Tabu brechen zu können. Bei Thater geht es vielmehr um den Versuch, jene Grenzen und Definitionen zu hinterfragen und

neu zu bestimmen, auf denen unsere Auffassung von Betrachter und Gegenstand, Subjekt, Objekt, Bild und Wirklichkeit beruht. So wird die Anziehungskraft, die das Bewusstsein der Tiere – dieses Andere und uns doch Verwandte – für uns hat, zur Metapher für einen weiter reichenden Fragenkomplex. DELPHINE durchbricht unsere Sehgewohnheiten und die Distanz zwischen Betrachter und Gegenstand dadurch, dass das Bild sich durch den ganzen Raum bewegt und nicht wie im Kino frontal projiziert wird. Es biegt um Ecken und gleitet über Wände, Boden und Decke. Es gibt keine klare Unterscheidung zwischen dem Bild als Bild und dem Bild als architektonischem Element, zwischen dem Bildraum und dem Raum, in dem der Betrachter oder die Betrachterin sich befindet. Die Bilder umgeben die Besucher und schaffen eine neue Raumerfahrung: Die Räumlichkeit von Licht und Zeit des Videos vermischt sich mit der festen Materialität des Raums. Gleichzeitig durchbricht Thater aber auch den zentralperspek-

DIANA THATER, THE BEST ANIMALS ARE THE FLAT ANIMALS, 1998 (version 2), installation for LCD video projector, three-lens video projector, video monitor, 3 laser discs and players, window film, and existing architecture / DIE BESTEN TIERE SIND DIE FLACHEN TIERE, Installation für LCD-Videoprojektor, Dreilinsen-Videoprojektor, Videomonitor, je 3 Laserdiscs und Abspielgeräte, Fensterfolie und bestehende Räumlichkeiten. (PHOTO: FREDRIK NILSEN FOR MAK, L.A.)

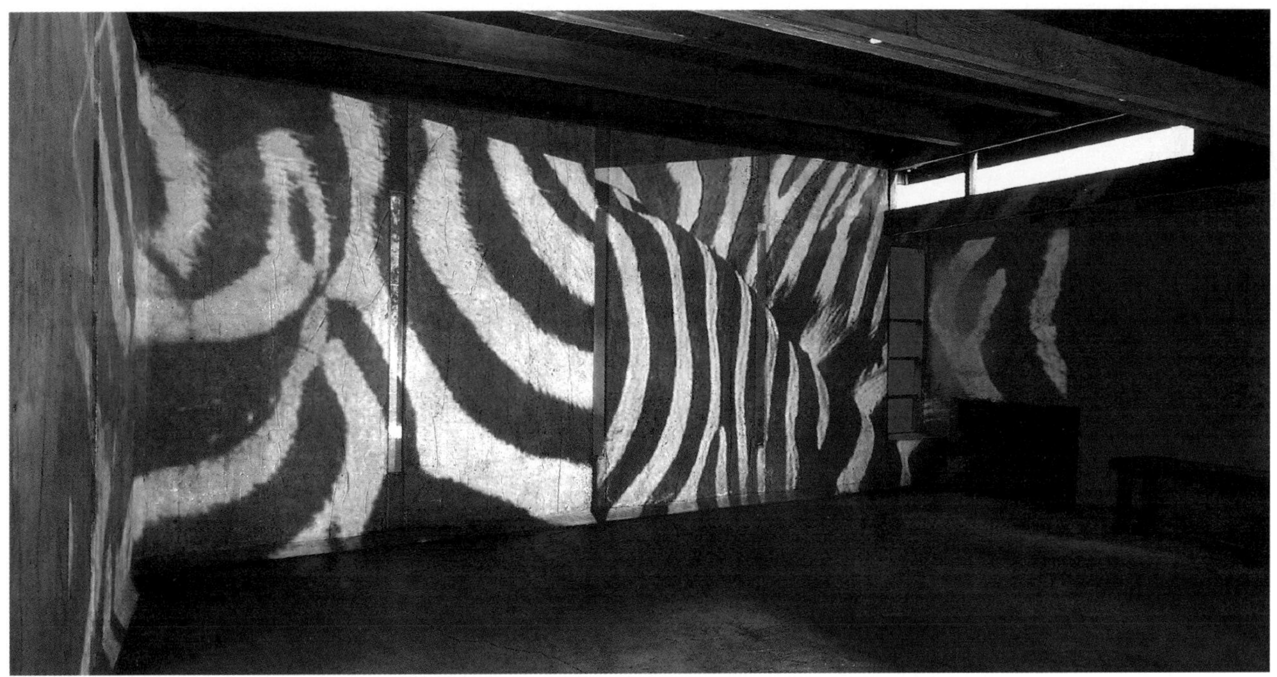

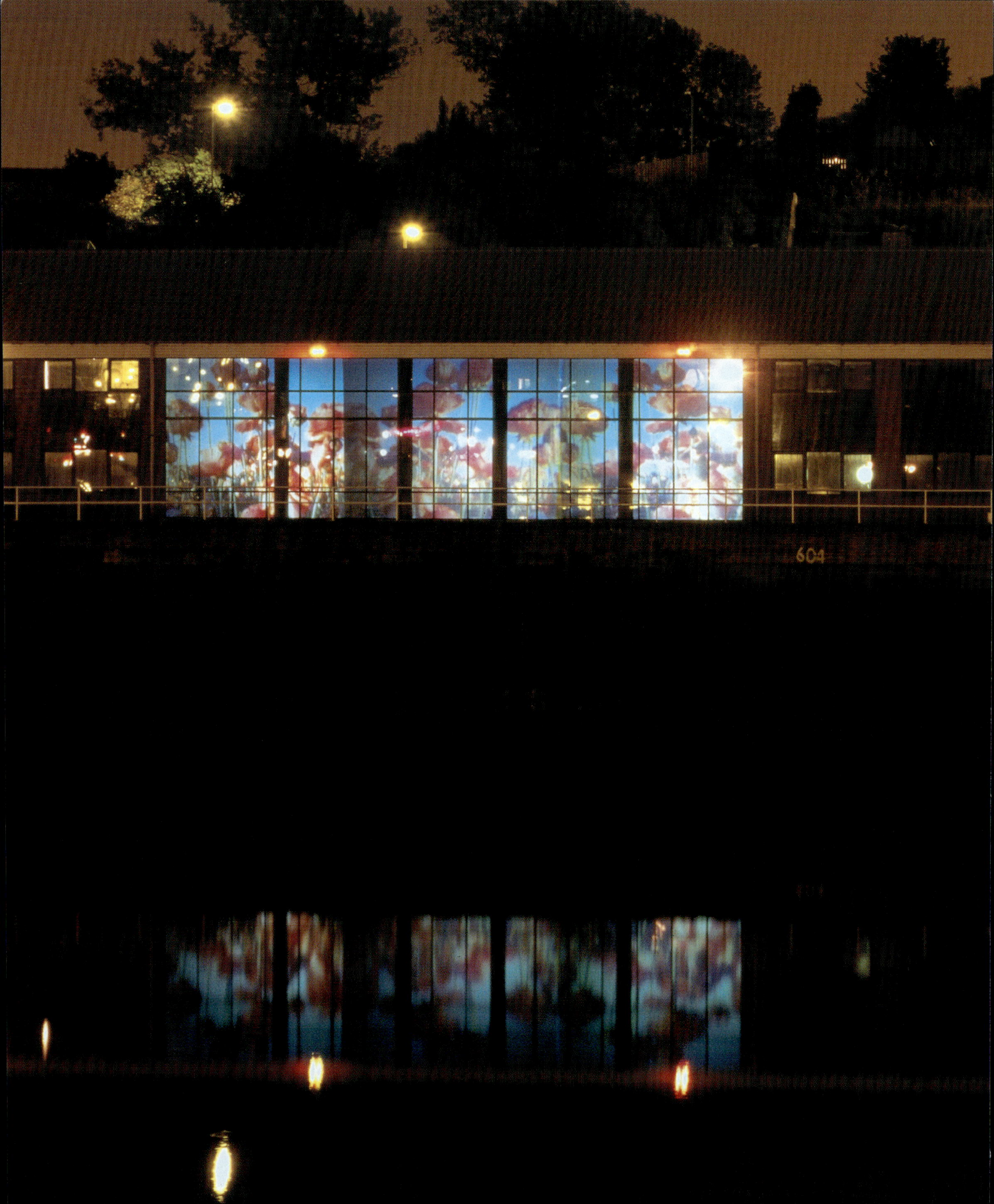

tivischen Blick, da es in ihren Video-Installationen keine lineare Erzählstruktur mit einem klaren An-fang oder Ende gibt. Sie bieten eine unendliche Zahl möglicher Bilder und Perspektiven an, und es gibt keinen Ort, von dem aus man einen umfassenden Überblick gewinnen könnte, kein Blickwinkel ist besser als ein anderer. Es gibt keinen Punkt im Raum, der einem erlauben würde, sich vor das Werk hinzustellen und es mit einem Blick zu erfassen. Ich befinde mich mitten im Werk drin, und es wird deut-lich, dass die Welt mich ebenso anschaut wie ich sie (um mit Lacan zu sprechen). Ich stehe vor dem Bild und bin zugleich mitten drin. Die im strömenden, wirbelnden Wasser hin und her schwimmenden Del-phine mustern mich genauso eingehend wie ich sie. Ihr Blick erfasst und formt die Welt so gut wie der meine.

Immer wieder offenbaren Thaters Arbeiten auch ihre eigene Entstehungsweise. Kamera und Projektor erfüllen einen Teil dieser Aufgabe. Manchmal werden die Grundfarben des Videos durch entsprechende Einfärbung der Fensterscheiben im Ausstellungs-raum augenfällig gemacht. Die Arbeiten untersu-chen die spezifischen Eigenschaften und materiellen Besonderheiten des Videofilms sowie seine visuellen und räumlichen Möglichkeiten, wobei sie immer auch ihrer eigenen Produktionsweise Tribut zollen: Nie sind die technischen Geräte zwecks Illusion oder Verführung versteckt. Das Resultat erscheint dem Betrachter nicht wie ein vom Himmel gefallenes Wunder. Vielmehr zeigt sich jedes Werk selbst un-verhohlen als das, was es ist: eine Komposition mit materiellen und technischen Mitteln. Und dennoch

erzeugt der Apparat keinerlei Distanz oder Verfrem-dung im Brecht'schen Sinn. Die Sichtbarkeit der Ge-räte bewirkt vielmehr eine Art Miteinbeziehung, eine neue Vertrautheit mit der Technik, deren Rolle bei der Herstellung des Bildes nicht länger verbor-gen bleibt. Wir befinden uns in einer symbiotischen Beziehung zur Technik und sehen schliesslich besser mit der Kamera als ohne. Thaters intime Vertraut-heit mit dem Bild und der Projektionsfläche macht aus der Projektion eine bewusste künstlerische Stra-tegie, dank der sich der Betrachter im und mit dem Werk bewegen kann. Mit «intim» meine ich übrigens keinerlei geschlechtsspezifische Anspielung auf wei-che Weiblichkeit, sondern eine Form von Nähe im weiteren Sinn sowie die Aufhebung der Unterteilun-gen, die unser Sehen geprägt haben. Thater stellt die Beziehung zwischen Betrachter, Bild, Licht, Zeit und Architektur ganz gezielt auf den Prüfstand und trägt damit entscheidend zu einer Veränderung des Blicks und der räumlichen Präsentation von Filmen bei. Der passive Filmbetrachter, der vor der leuchtenden Kinoleinwand sitzt oder vor einem räumlich von ihm getrennten Bildschirm steht, ist endgültig Filmge-schichte; stattdessen wird nun eine andere Form des Sehens wirksam. Anders als die Video-Installationen der zeitgenössischen Kunstproduktion, die vorwie-gend dem Film verpflichtet sind, verlangen Thaters Arbeiten einen mobilen Betrachter, der durch den Raum oder eine ganze Flucht von Räumen wandert, überströmt von bewegten Bildern ohne Anfang und Ende, ohne bestimmte Stellen, die man als Zentrum oder Peripherie bezeichnen könnte. Bei dieser Sicht-weise wird der Körperlichkeit des Auges Rechnung getragen und die Illusion des allumfassenden Blicks, der die Welt zu beherrschen vermag, über Bord ge-worfen. Doch auch das Bild selbst hat nun vermehrt körperlichen Charakter, es hat an Räumlichkeit und Präsenz gewonnen. Die Grenze zwischen Bild und Betrachter, zwischen realem Raum und Bildraum, zwischen fester Architektur und beweglichem Bild hat sich verschoben. Wir stehen jetzt nicht mehr vor Bildern, deren Oberflächencharakter uns zum Still-stand zwingt. Stattdessen bewegen wir uns auf das Bild zu und es kommt uns ein Stück entgegen. Wo-hin derlei Vertraulichkeit führt, werden wir sehen.

(Übersetzung: Nansen)

Die Erinnerung der Kunst an das Tier

REGINA HASLINGER

Im Wettrennen der Tiere aus *Alice im Wunderland* gewinnen alle – und alle bekommen einen Preis. Dieser glückliche Ausgang verdankt sich unter anderem dem runden Zuschnitt des *Caucus Race*, dem Dodo, der kluge Brachvogel, den Namen, aber keine Spielregeln gegeben hat. Die Spieler brauchten sich nur im Kreise aufzustellen und, statt nach eins, zwei, drei, loszurennen, sich ganz nach ihrem Gutdünken frei in alle Richtungen zu bewegen. Doch auch wenn Dodo am Ende lange in der Haltung des Denkers posierte, konnte es nur einen Schluss geben: dass alle gewonnen haben und dass es hier keinen Verlierer gibt. Alice, die Heldin der Geschichte, verstand wie üblich nichts von alledem, spielte aber fleissig ihren Part, der gefordert war, als alle ihr zuriefen: «Preise! Preise!»

Geschichten, wie sie nur im Märchen vorkommen oder im kindlichen Tagtraum, der noch nicht dem Primat der Vernunft unterliegt, zählen zu den bevorzugten Themen, die Diana Thater ihren Videoinstallationen zugrunde legt. Ihnen gemeinsam ist ein Motiv, das für die Künstlerin eine entscheidende Rolle spielt und doch in Besprechungen zu ihren Werken bisher noch nicht genügend gewürdigt worden ist: die lebensweltliche Nachbarschaft der Tiere zum Menschen. Im Unterschied zu den meisten literarischen Stoffen, auf die Diana Thater sich bezieht, geht es ihr bei der Darstellung tierischer Welten jedoch nicht um direkte affektive Reaktionen, sondern um die Entmystifizierung der Betrachtung. Dies äussert sich etwa darin, dass die Verwandlungen von Menschen in Tiere in den geschichtlichen oder literarischen Vorlagen buchstäblich als ein Übergehen von einem menschlichen Organ oder Körper in einen tierischen Körper zu verstehen sind (etwa im Roman *A Love for Rachel*, der Thaters ELECTRIC MIND aus dem Jahr 1996 inspirierte), während es in ihren Darstellungen um Austauschbeziehungen und Wechselwirkungen geht, die «nichts Jenseitiges» haben und «ganz und gar von dieser Welt» sind, wie die Künstlerin bemerkt. Um der Möglichkeit solcher Wirkung willen verzichtet Diana Thater auf illusionäre und narrative Elemente ebenso wie auf die traditionell-ganzheitliche Wiedergabe eines Gegenstands. Mit der Videoinstallation als raum- und bilderübergreifendem Medium ersetzt sie die naturgetreuen Abbildungskonzepte und traditionellen Sehweisen durch die Prinzipien der Konstruktion und Projektion, die den Gegenstand, den Betrachter und den Gestaltungsvorgang so aufeinander beziehen, dass sich eine komplexe, sich ständig verändernde Struktur ergibt:

…wir bewegen uns, zeichnen auf, projizieren, sehen und verändern dabei die Natur und Gestalt dessen, was

REGINA HASLINGER ist freie Kuratorin. Sie lebt in Karlsruhe und Wien. Ihre jüngste Ausstellung war «Herausforderung Tier. Von Beuys bis Kabakov» in der Städtischen Galerie Karlsruhe. Der Katalog ist bei Prestel (München 2000) erschienen.

wir sehen, durch unsere Bewegung und unser Sein und entdecken schliesslich, dass das Werk nicht Gegenstand, sondern Mittel der Betrachtung ist.[1]

In mehreren Interviews mit der Künstlerin wurde bereits auf diese Verlagerung des Akzents vom Inhalt auf die Form beziehungsweise den artifiziellen Eigensinn des Mediums hingewiesen, wodurch der Eindruck entsteht, dass die technischen Prozeduren zur Vergegenwärtigung des Gegenstands in den Vordergrund treten. Man kann diesen Vorgang als eine künstlerische Antwort auf die mediatisierte Welt interpretieren: In dem Mass, wie diese sich durch höhere Verfügbarkeit der Bilder und die Entwirklichung des Bildbezugs beschreiben lässt, drängen sich Darstellungsverfahren auf, die offen legen, dass dem «Subjekt» keine einheitliche Form oder Ansicht mehr unterstellt werden kann – «Subjekt» sowohl als Betrachter wie als Bildgegenstand verstanden. Die

DIANA THATER, ELECTRIC MIND, 1996, 6 video projectors, 2 video monitors, 8 laser discs and players, 1 sync generator, installation view at the Portland Art Museum, Nov–Jan, 1996 / ELEKTRISCHER GEIST, 6 Videoprojektoren, 2 Videomonitoren, je 8 Laserdiscs und Abspielgeräte, 1 Synchronisator. (PHOTO: FREDRIK NILSEN)

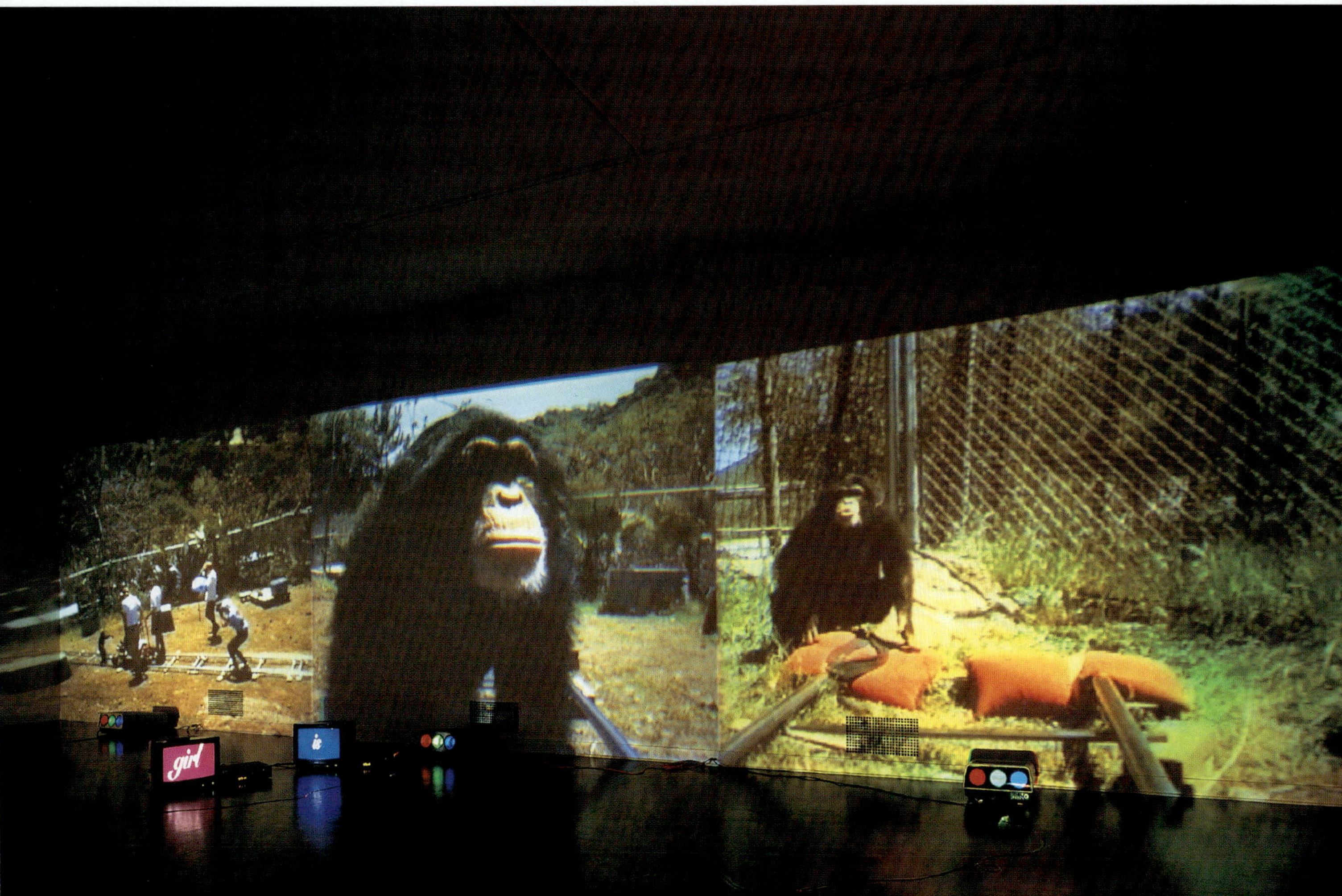

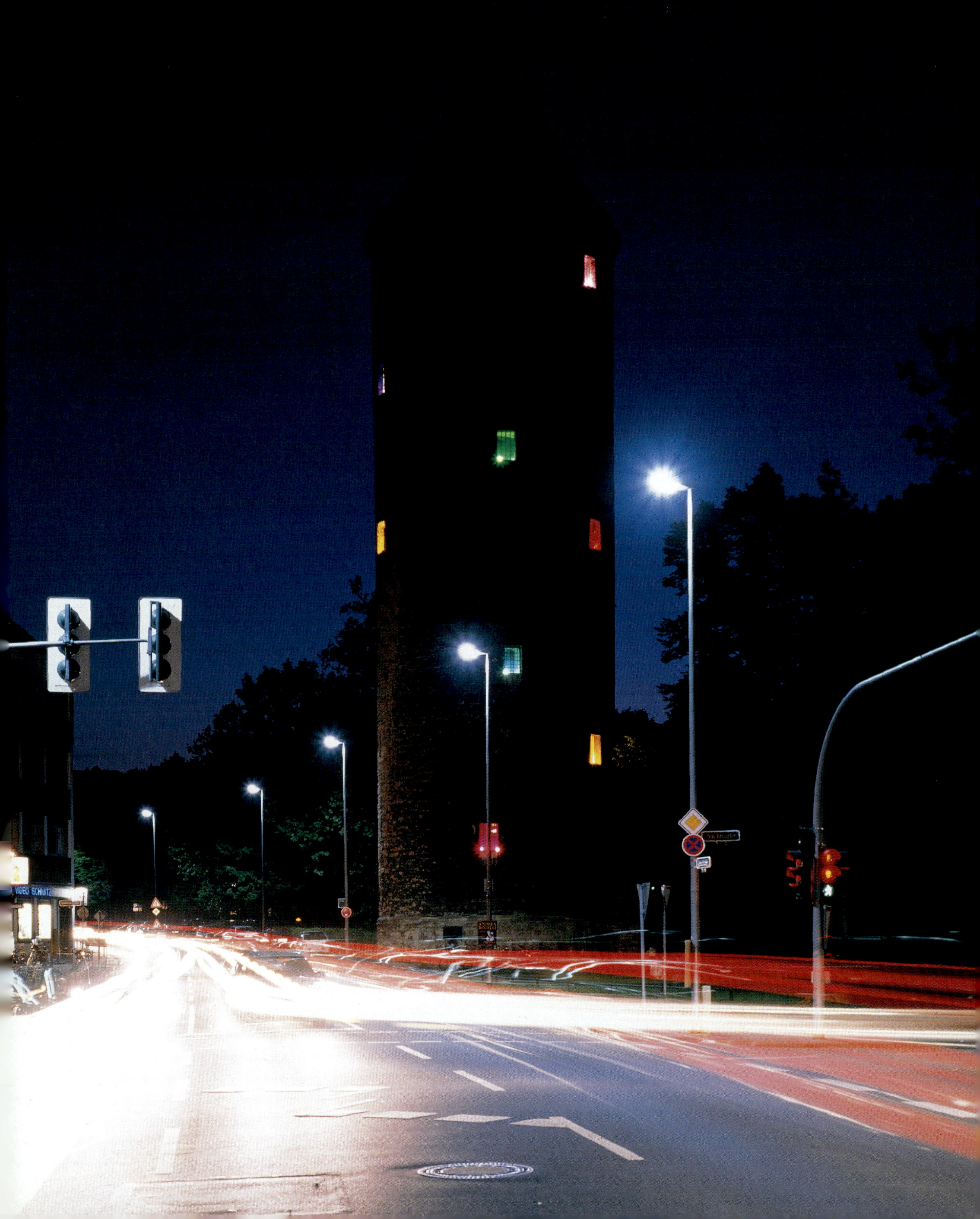

VIDEO SCHMITZ
Am Markt

Künstlerin erklärt diesen Sachverhalt mit folgendem Hinweis auf BROKEN CIRCLE (1997):

Es gibt also verschiedene Blickwinkel und aus jedem sieht man, wie sich die Pferdeherde teilt um der Kamera auszuweichen, aber jedesmal, wenn sie dazu ansetzt, wechselt der Blickwinkel und wir sehen eine leere Wiese, einige Kameraleute bei der Arbeit oder ein äsendes Pferd in der Ecke. Man ist immer weit weg vom eigentlichen «Schuss», schaut darauf zurück und merkt, dass es nicht so sein kann, wie es scheint.[2]

Die seit hundert Jahren entwickelten Prozeduren zur Vergegenwärtigung des Tieres in bildnerischen Werken und ästhetischen Aktionen sind für die Kunst an der Schwelle zum einundzwanzigsten Jahrhundert historisch geworden. Das heisst freilich nicht, dass diese Formen obsolet geworden wären. Sie stehen jetzt vielmehr als Folien für Variationen, Reinszenierungen und Verfremdungen zur Verfügung. In diesen Brechungen artikuliert sich das Bewusstsein künstlerischer Zeitgenossenschaft in einer technisch avancierten Zivilisation. In dieser Hinsicht macht der Fortschritt der Technisierung – etwa in den aktuellen *life sciences* – die direkte Anknüpfung an Programme wie die «Animalisierung der Kunst» bei Franz Marc oder an die therapeutisch-sozialreformerische Aktionskunst eines Beuys schwieriger und weniger plausibel. Ältere Formen von Einfühlungskunst – exemplarisch repräsentiert durch Marc – stellten den Versuch dar, das transzendente Reale oder «das grosse Leben» selbst ins Bild zu holen. Zeitgenössische Künstler gehen eher von der Erfahrung aus, dass das Reale dasjenige ist, was immer ausweicht. Dadurch hat sich der Anspruch auf «objektive Realität» des Ausdrucks zunehmend erledigt. Jedes Werk macht sich durch das Hineinnehmen unmittelbarer ausserkünstlerischer Dimensionen ästhetisch und ideologisch verdächtig, solange diese nicht mit der Frage nach Darstellungsform und Wahrnehmungsmodus verknüpft werden.

Während für Franz Marc die künstlerische Herausforderung noch im Anspruch lag, den Gegenstand so darzustellen, wie er «wirklich» ist, also nicht darin, «den Wald oder das Pferd (zu) malen, wie sie uns gefallen oder scheinen, sondern wie sie wirklich sind, wie sich der Wald oder das Pferd selbst fühlt, ihr absolutes Wesen, das hinter dem Schein lebt, den

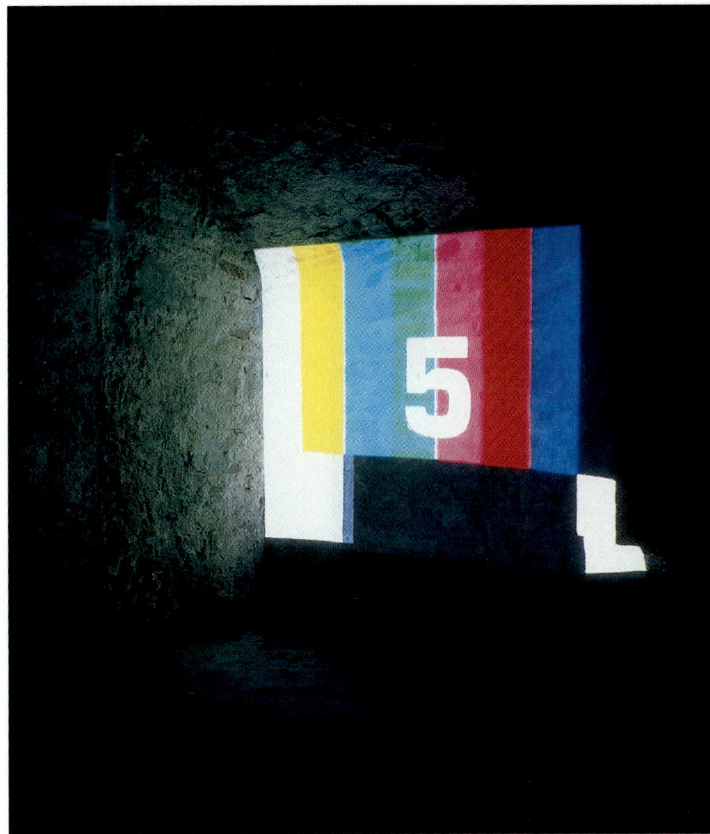

DIANA THATER, BROKEN CIRCLE, 1997, installation for 6 video projectors, 1 video monitor, 6 laser discs and players, 1 sync generator, window film, and existing architecture, exterior view of the Buddenturm, "Skulptur. Projekte Münster" (left), and interior view, first floor (above) / AUFGEBROCHENER KREIS, Installation für 6 Videoprojektoren, 1 Videomonitor, je 6 Laserdiscs und Abspielgeräte, 1 Synchronisator, Fensterfolie und bestehende Räumlichkeiten; Aussenansicht des Buddenturms in Münster (linke Seite) und Innenansicht im ersten Stock (oben).

wir sehen»[3], greift Diana Thater die «Wahrheit der Tiere» in erster Linie als Wahrnehmungs- und Darstellungsproblem auf. Weil die Wahrheit nur zwischen den Polen von Darstellung und Wahrnehmung – also zwei von Grund auf projektiven Prozessen – gefunden werden kann, versucht die Künstlerin den projektiven und konstruktiven Charakter der Bilder-Findung selbst ins Bewusstsein zu heben, wobei sich stets zwingend eine Mehrzahl von Anschauungspunkten und Darstellungsformen ergibt.

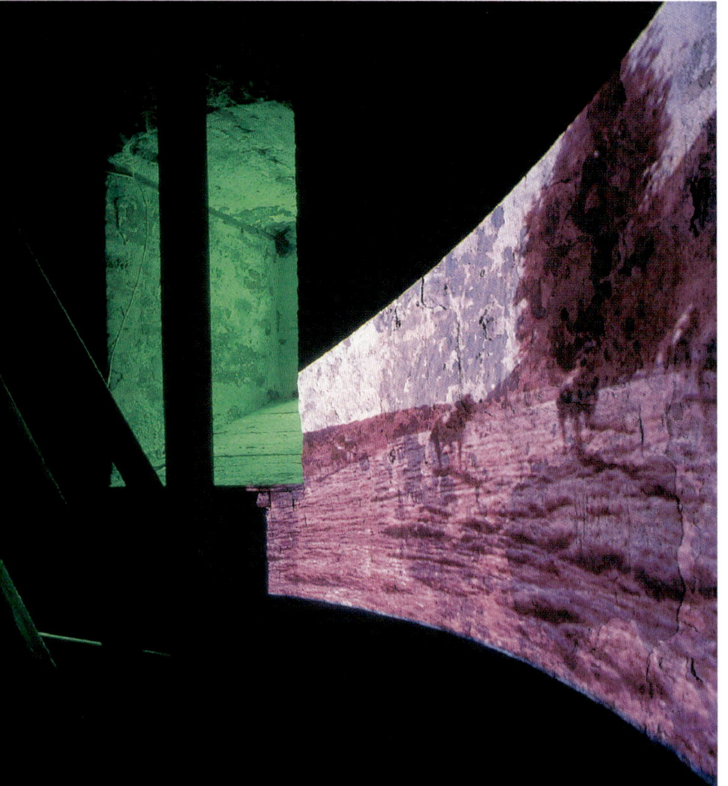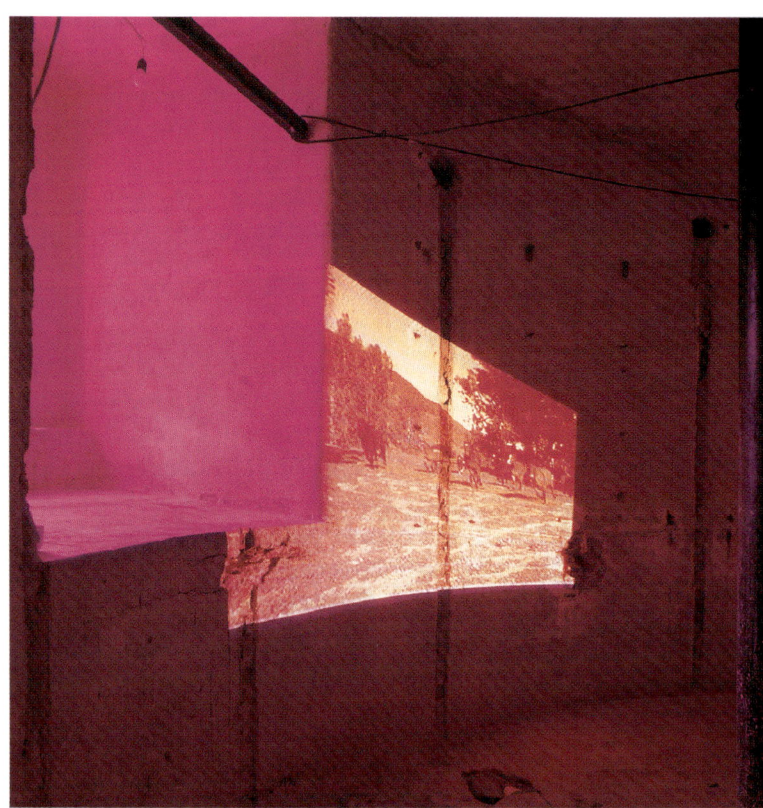

DIANA THATER, BROKEN CIRCLE, 1997, "Skulptur. Projekte Münster," Buddenturm, interior view, second floor /
AUFGEBROCHENER KREIS, Innenansicht, zweiter Stock.

Dass Kunst es in der Hauptsache mit sich selbst zu tun hat und kaum mit einer «ausserkünstlerischen Realität», ist inzwischen zu einer Selbstverständlichkeit geworden. Dies trifft auch für ein so manifest «externes» Sujet wie das des Tiers zu: Die Möglichkeiten seiner Repräsentation im Kunstwerk oder seiner Vergegenwärtigung in ihm werden durch die Orientierung der modernen Künste an ihrem artifiziellen Eigensinn stark eingeschränkt. An die Stelle des «Durchbruchs» zum Tier in seiner «eigentlichen Wahrheit und Wirklichkeit»; an die Stelle von Tier-Kultbildern, die im Dienste einer überhöhten

Gegenwart oder einer numinosen ästhetischen Gegenwelt stehen wollten, treten jetzt Darstellungsformen, die auf die immer schon wirksame bildlich-mediale Vermittlung der tierischen Präsenz reflektieren. Nichtsdestoweniger lassen sich auch Parallelen feststellen zwischen den beuysschen Kunstaktionen und den Videoinstallationen Diana Thaters. Knüpfte Beuys an vorkünstlerische Rituale der Wirklichkeitsauslegung an, die nicht weniger als eine Technik – eine schamanistische Kommunikation mit transzendenten Realitäten – bedeuteten, so wendet sich Thater an die Technik als Mittler zwischen verschie-

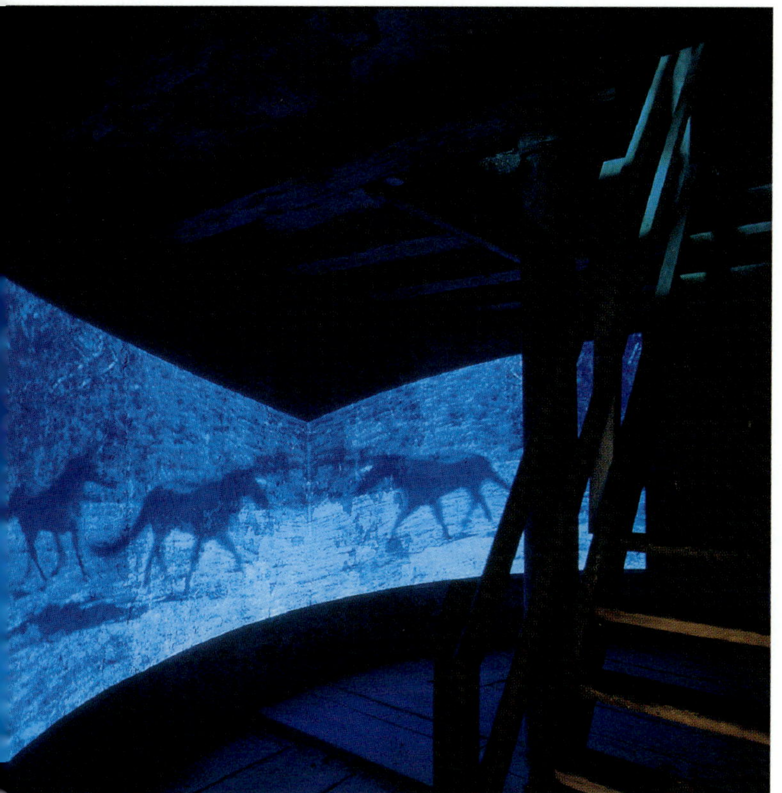 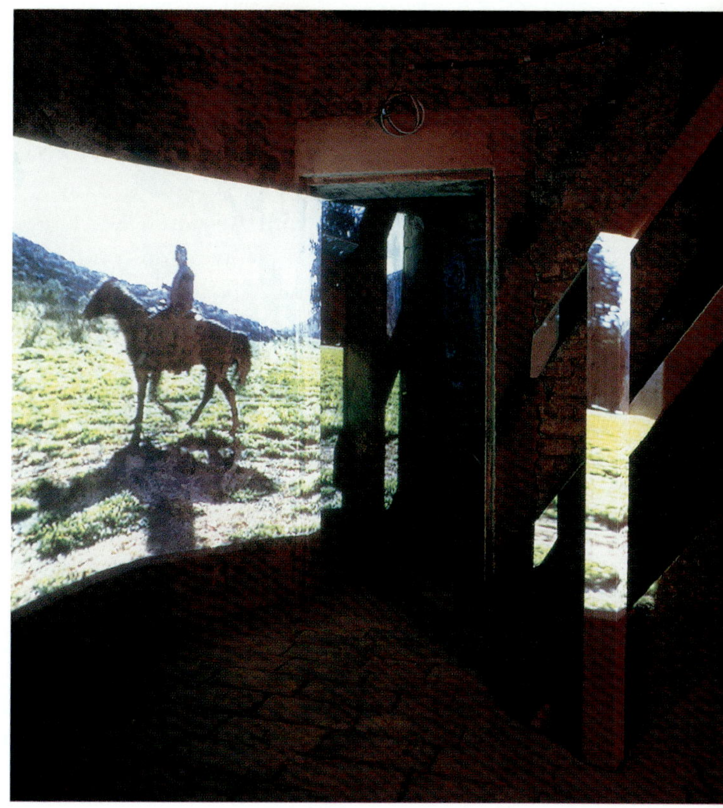

DIANA THATER, BROKEN CIRCLE, 1997, "Skulptur. Projekte Münster," Buddenturm, interior view, third and forth floors /
AUFGEBROCHENER KREIS, Innenansicht, dritter und vierter Stock.

denen Realitätsschichten. Trotz des hohen Stellenwerts, den sie dem Tier in ihrem Werk und Weltbild einräumt, versucht sie die technischen Potenziale des Mediums mit Hinweisen auf die prototechnische Intelligenz der animalischen Sphäre miteinander zu verbinden – sie zeigt auffallend viele Tiere, die als Amateurartisten auftreten und technische oder künstlerische Fertigkeiten zur Schau stellen.

Diana Thater begreift die moderne Technologie also genauso wenig als Antithese zur Natur wie Beuys, der technische Innovationen unter der Voraussetzung bejahte, dass menschliche Emanzipation von der Natur und Bewahrung des animalischen Erbes sich gegenseitig nicht ausschliessen. Statt Mensch und Tier durch fortschreitende Trennung voneinander zu entfremden, wie es dem Habitus der modernen Gesellschaft beim Umgang mit «Ressourcen» gleich welcher Art entspricht, versucht Thater zu zeigen, dass die Nachbarschaft zum Tier gerade unter modernen Bedingungen neu gestaltet werden kann. Die technischen Medien begreift sie als kreative Gestaltungsmittel, mit deren Hilfe Verwandlungen in Gang gesetzt werden können. Sie taugen besser zu kreativen und mehrdeutigen Neubeschreibungen des Wirklichen als der latent monologische, totalitäre Charakter der traditionellen metaphysischen Ordnung.

In der Art und Weise, wie Thater ihre Themen installiert und prozessual aufschliesst, spürt man das Aufkeimen einer neuen imaginativen Struktur, in welcher ein Wahrnehmen und Gestalten der Übergänge, der gegenseitigen Berührungen und Verwandlungen von Mensch und Tier möglich werden. Die Künstlerin bemerkt zu diesen transformativen Prozessen:

Mich interessiert die Überlagerung und der Austausch von Identitäten... Wenn ich diese Tiere mittels Video in den Kunstraum einführe, erhebt sich die Frage des Austauschs zwischen betrachtenden Subjekten und betrachteten Objekten.[4]

Die technische Apparatur, die bei Thater eine ähnlich tragende Funktion hat wie die «animistisch» aufgeladenen Objekte bei Beuys, erscheint immer mit Bezug zu konkreten Handlungsformen:

In der Installation werden Elemente der Umwelt, die wir gewöhnlich als Objekte wahrnehmen und betrachten, zu Subjekten, die uns anschauen. Genauso stehen auch die ganzen Videogeräte im Raum und man sieht, dass sie tatsächlich etwas machen.[5]

Es ist nicht zu übersehen, dass diese weitgehend unspektakulär ablaufenden interaktiven und transformativen Prozesse sich gegenüber ihren literarischen Ausgangspunkten sehr selbstständig verhalten. So bezieht sich Diana Thater etwa mit ihrer Videoinstallation ELECTRIC MIND (1996) auf Pat Murphys Sciencefictionroman *A Love for Rachel* – die Geschichte vom Tod eines Mädchens, dessen Vater eine computergenerierte Kopie des Gehirns seiner Tochter einem Schimpansenweibchen einpflanzt, um ihre Individualität in einem fremden Körper zu erhalten. In den

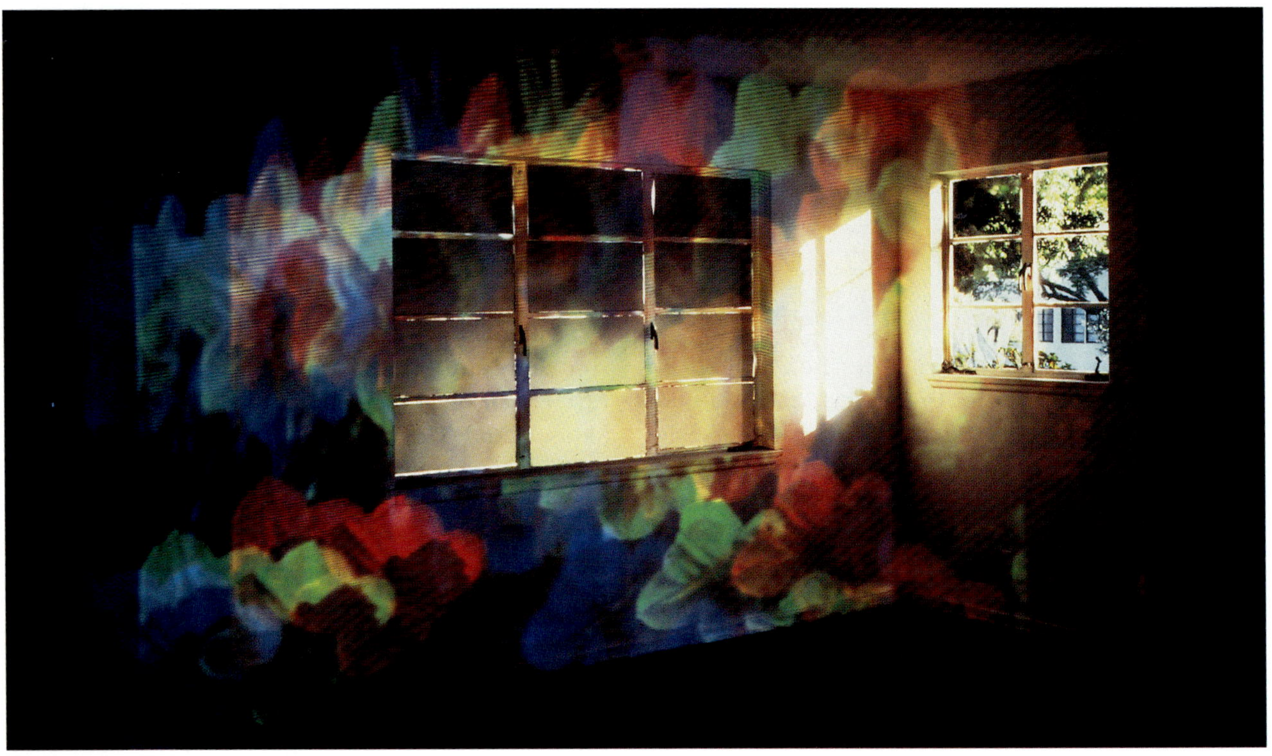

DIANA THATER, OO FIFI—FIVE DAYS IN CLAUDE MONET'S GARDEN, 1992, installation for 3 video projectors, 1 laser disc and player, film gels, and existing architecture at Shoshana Wayne, Santa Monica / OO FIFI – FÜNF TAGE IN CLAUDE MONETS GARTEN, Installation für 3 Videoprojektoren, 1 Laserdisc und Abspielgerät, Lichtfilter und bestehende Räumlichkeiten.

Bildern der Videoinstallation, die die Schimpansin in verschiedenen Szenen zeigen, lässt sich davon kaum etwas erahnen. Freilich ist in einer Vitrine eine Art Drehbuch ausgestellt, das den narrativen Hintergrund offen legt. Gezeigt wird in der Installation nicht das Drama als solches, sondern die mediale Praxis der Kameraleute, wie sie dem tierischen Protagonisten aus verschiedenen Perspektiven und Einstellungen folgen. Man wird explizit auf den medialen Produktionsprozess aufmerksam gemacht – eine ästhetische Strategie, die im Kontinuum der Kunst der Moderne angesiedelt ist, sofern diese auf dem Effekt der «medialen Aufrichtigkeit» (Boris Groys) basiert. Es gibt demnach keine Aufrichtigkeit gegenüber der «Sache» mehr, die nicht zuvor als Aufrichtigkeit gegenüber dem Medium erschiene.

In der Videoinstallation CAUCUS RACE (1998) wird ein Textausschnitt aus dem gleichnamigen Kapitel von *Alice im Wunderland* auf eine Wand projiziert. Wie ein Filmvorspann wird der Text in einzelne Worte zerlegt, die nacheinander auf der Bildfläche erscheinen. Sobald die letzten Worte projiziert werden, «Preise! Preise!», schalten sich abwechselnd vier Monitoren ein, die halbkreisförmig auf dem Boden gruppiert sind. Sie zeigen diverse Naturbilder: eine Giraffe, die direkt in die Kamera schaut; einen kleinen Orang-Utan, der auf einen Felsen klettert und wieder herunterfällt; zwei Nilpferde, die sich verspielt im Wasser tummeln; einen freien Himmel und Sonnenstrahlen in einer Baumkrone. Zum Schluss erscheint auf der zweiten Wand, gegenüber den Monitoren, eine Grossprojektion mit Blick in ein blaues Wasserbecken. Plötzlich springt ein Delphin aus dem Wasser, direkt auf die Kamera zu, und berührt diese mit seiner Nase. Dann wendet er sich ab und taucht wieder ins Wasser.

Im Unterschied zu ELECTRIC MIND, BROKEN CIRCLE oder CHINA (eine Videoarbeit, die zwei Wölfe – wiederum «Amateurdarsteller» – mit ihren Trainern auf dem Übungsgelände zeigt), gibt es in CAUCUS RACE keinen direkten Hinweis auf die Herkunft der Tiere. Es ist anzunehmen, dass es sich ebenfalls um gezähmte Tiere oder Zootiere handelt. Diese Option mag als indirekter Hinweis darauf gelten, dass die Gelegenheiten selten geworden sind, wilde Tiere in Originalsituationen oder traditionelle Haus- und Nutztiere in herkömmlichen Szenen zu erleben. Dennoch scheint Diana Thater darauf zu bestehen, dass die menschliche Fähigkeit, sich in die *conditio animalis* einzufühlen, nie wirklich ganz verloren geht. Das Schwinden der natürlichen Lebensräume der Tiere und die vielfältigen Bedrohungen, denen Tiere heute unterworfen sind, hat vielmehr eine sympathetische und moralische Hinwendung zu unseren Mitgeschöpfen begünstigt. Denn wenn nach dem Genesis-Mythos die Frage offen blieb, ob die Tiere an ihrem Ort verblieben oder auf irgendeine Weise an der Vertreibung des Menschen aus dem Paradies teilhatten, so drängt sich angesichts der heutigen Situation der Tiere die Frage auf, ob nicht diese Kreaturen hinsichtlich ihrer Vertreibung aus ursprünglichen Verhältnissen den Menschen noch übertreffen. Ein Bewusstsein von der schmerzlichen Seite des Tier-Mensch-Verhältnisses hat Beuys etwa in seiner Aktion I LIKE AMERICA—AMERICA LIKES ME (1974) als «Wunde» herausgestellt, die erst geheilt werden könnte, wenn «die Rechnung mit dem Kojoten» beglichen wäre, wobei dieses Tier für die gesamte amerikanische Realität vor der europäischen Eroberung steht. Im Gegensatz zu diesem quasi pantheistischen Ansatz, der in der religiösen Versöhnungsphilosophie und den idealistisch-lebensreformerischen Traditionen um 1900 gründet, zeugen Diana Thaters heitere und brillante Projektions- und Spiegelungsverfahren von den Möglichkeiten der zeitgenössischen Kunst, die Frage nach der Koexistenz von Tier und Mensch in einer etwas kühleren, gleichwohl verbindlichen Tonlage zu stellen. Sie geben der Einsicht Ausdruck, dass die Menschen gerade im Zeitalter des *artificial life* im tierischen Spiegel etwas von der sich immer wieder entziehenden Wahrheit über ihre eigene Kondition erfahren.

1) In: *Diana Thater. China*, The Renaissance Society at the University of Chicago, 1996, S. 15. (Übers. durch die Red.)
2) Aus einem Interview mit Douglas Fogle, in: *Flash Art International*, Januar/Februar 1998, S. 88.
3) Franz Marc, *Briefe, Aufzeichnungen und Aphorismen*, Bd. 1, Cassirer Verlag, Berlin 1920, S. 123.
4) *Flash Art International*, Januar/Februar 1998, S. 89.
5) Ebenda, S. 89.

Art Remembers the Animal

REGINA HASLINGER

Not only do all of the animals win the race in *Alice in Wonderland*, they all receive a prize as well. This happy conclusion is due in part to the circular course of the Caucus-race, as the wise Dodo calls it, though without specifying any rules for it. The players only have to form a circle of sorts and with no "one, two, three, and away," they are left to run in any direction they like. In the end, the Dodo thinks long and hard "with one finger pressed upon its forehead," but the conclusion is obvious: everyone has won, there are no losers. Alice, the heroine of this tale, is in the dark as usual but diligently plays the part assigned to her, when the animals all begin calling for "Prizes! Prizes!"

Stories of the kind that only appear in fairy tales or in children's daydreams, which are not yet governed by the primacy of reason, count among Diana Thater's preferred subject matter in her video installations. Common to all of them is a motif that plays a decisive role for the artist but has not yet received the attention it deserves in reviews of her work: the symbiotic cohabitation of animals with people. In contrast to most of the literary sources to which

Diana Thater refers, her representations of animal worlds do not target affective reactions but rather the demystification of our observations. This is expressed for example by the fact that the metamorphosis of humans into animals in works of history or literature quite literally involves the transformation of a human organ or body into an animal body (as in the novel by Pat Murphy, *A Love for Rachel*, which inspired Thater's ELECTRIC MIND, 1996), while the exchange and interchange in her representations are not the least otherworldly but "entirely of this world," as the artist says herself. For the sake of such effects, Diana Thater works without illusionary or narrative elements or the traditional total depiction of a subject. With the video installation as a visually and spatially overlapping medium, she replaces the true-to-nature concept of representation and traditional patterns of seeing with principles of construction and projection in which subject matter, beholder, and process are mutually related in such a way that a complex, constantly changing structure results:

…we move, record, project and see, changing the nature and configuration of what we see through our movement and our being and ultimately find ourselves not looking a t the work of art but w i t h it.[1]

This shift of emphasis from content to form, that is, to the artificial character of the medium has been pointed out in several interviews with the artist, underscoring the technical procedures entailed in representing the subject matter. This process might be

---

REGINA HASLINGER is a freelance curator who lives in Karlsruhe (Germany) and Vienna. Her most recent exhibition was "Herausforderung Tier. Von Beuys bis Kabakov" (The Animal as a Challenge. From Beuys to Kabakov), Städtische Galerie Karlsruhe. The catalogue was published by Prestel (Munich, 2000).

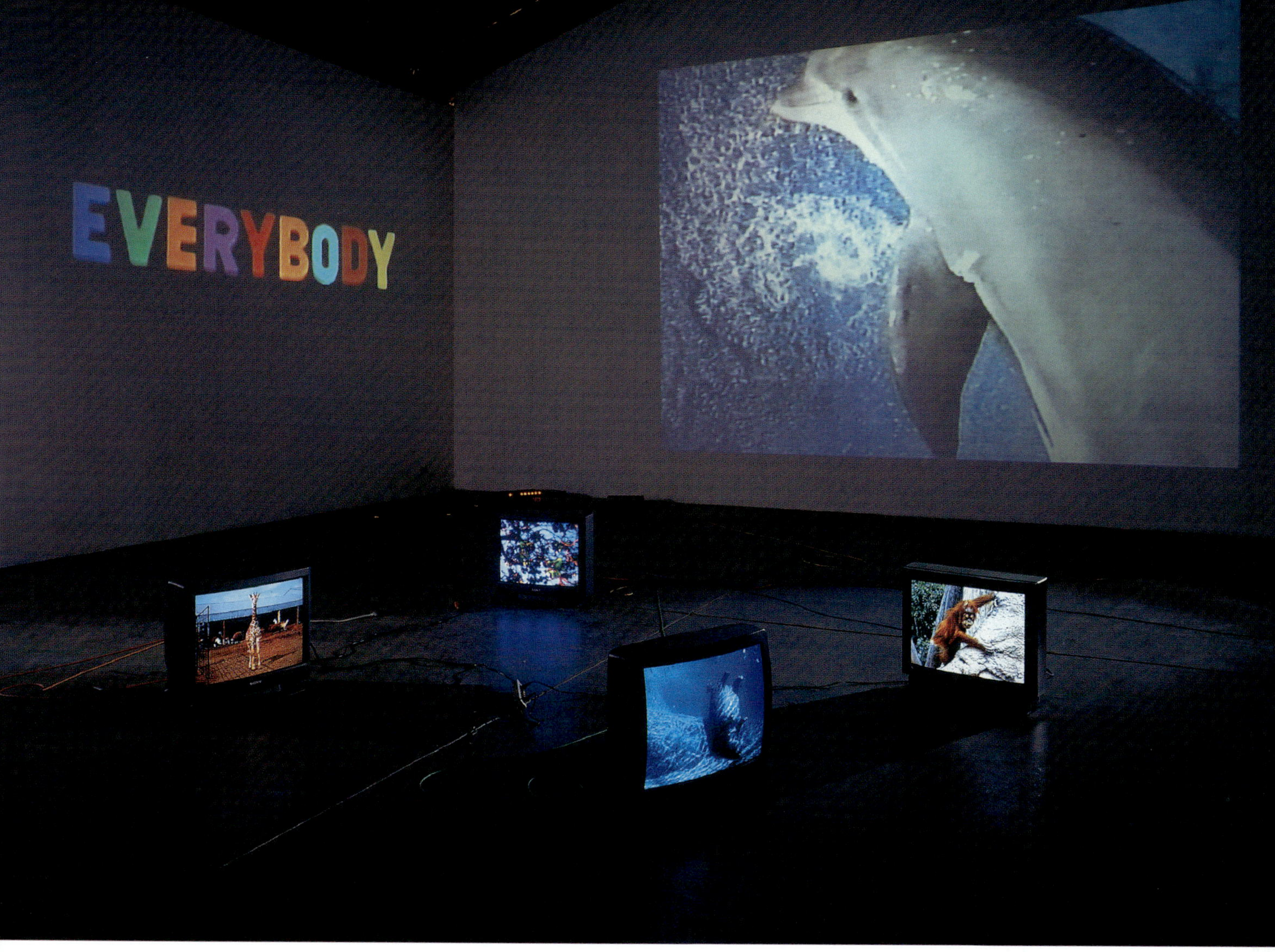

DIANA THATER, THE CAUCUS RACE, 1998, installation for 2 LCD video projectors, 4 video monitors, 6 laser discs and players, sync generator, window film, and existing architecture at Patrick Painter, Santa Monica / Installation für 2 LCD-Videoprojektoren, 4 Videomonitoren, je 6 Laserdiscs und Abspielgeräte, Synchronisator, Fensterfolie und bestehende Räumlichkeiten.

interpreted as an artistic response to a mediated world. To the extent that the mediated world may be described through the greater availability of images and the increasing unreality of the pictorial referent, procedures of representation now tend to focus on the fact that a uniform shape or view can no longer be imposed upon the "subject"—the "subject" being both the beholder and the subject matter of the picture. Speaking about BROKEN CIRCLE (1997), the artist explains:

…there are multiple points of view and from any point of view you see the herd of horses splitting around the cameras, but every time they are about to do this, we go off to another perspective where we see an empty field or camera people working or a horse in the corner eating grass. You're always distanced from "the shot" and you look back at it and realize that it can't be what it appears.[2]

For art in transition to the twenty-first century, the procedures developed over the past hundred years of rendering animals in pictorial works and aesthetic actions have become historical. It does not follow, though, that these forms have become obsolete. Rather, they provide an arsenal of material for variation, restaging and alienation. These breaks articulate an awareness of artistic contemporaneity in a technically advanced civilization. In this respect, technical advances, as in current life sciences, make the direct link to programs like Franz Marc's "Animalization of Art" or Beuys's therapeutic and social-reform-oriented action art more difficult and less plausible. Older forms of empathetic art, as exemplified by Marc's work, represented the attempt to capture transcendental reality or "the greatness of life" in pictures. Contemporary artists tend to work from the realization that the real is what always eludes us, so that the aim of expressing "objective reality" has ceased to prevail. The incorporation of immediate extra-artistic dimensions makes any work aesthetically and ideologically suspect unless related to investigating forms of representation and modes of perception.

For Franz Marc the challenge lay in representing the subject matter the way it "really" is and not in "painting a forest or a horse as we please or as they seem to appear, but rather the way they really are, the way the forest or the horse feel themselves, their absolute being that lives behind the appearances that we see."[3] Diana Thater, however, primarily addresses the "truth of animals" as an issue of perception and representation, for it is only between these two poles that the truth can be found. Moreover, as manifestly projecting processes, they dovetail with the artist's wish to reveal the projecting and constructing aspects of imagery, which necessarily entails a multiplicity of viewpoints and forms of representation.

It has long been obvious that art is largely self-referential and has little to do with "extra-artistic reality." This also applies to such an obviously manifestly "external" subject as the animal: its potential incorporation or representation in a work of art is substantially restricted by the idiosyncratic orientation of the modern arts towards the artificiality of their medium. Instead of a "breakthrough" that shows the animal in its "actual truth and reality," instead of cult pictures of animals that serve purposes of a sublime presence or a numinous aesthetic counter-world, forms of representation now explore the pictorial mediation of the animal presence. Even so, parallels can be observed between Beuys's art actions and Thater's video installations. While Beuys linked up with pre-artistic rituals of interpreting reality, also a manifest technique—the technique of shamanistic communication with transcendental realities—Thater turns to technology as a mediator between various layers of reality. Despite the profound importance of the animal in her work and her worldview, she seeks to combine the technical potential of the medium with indications of the proto-technical intelligence of the animal sphere. She shows a conspicuous number of animals as amateur performers of technical or artistic skills.

Diana Thater does not read modern technology as the antithesis of nature anymore than Beuys did, who affirmed technical innovation under the condition that human emancipation from nature and the preservation of our animal heritage did not rule each other out. Instead of estranging human and animal through progressive separation, as practiced by modern society in its treatment of "resources" of any kind, Thater tries to show that cohabitation with animals can in fact be reconfigured through modern conditions. She sees technical media as a creative tool which can add momentum to change and as a more effective means of finding new, creative and multiple means of describing reality than the latent, monologic and totalitarian character of the traditional metaphysical order.

The way in which Thater processes and installs her concerns signals the emergence of a new imaginative structure which allows a perception and articulation of borders, of mutual touch and transformations of people and animals. Regarding these transformational processes, the artist says:

I'm interested in the layering of identities on top of each other and in exchanges of identity… When I bring these animals into an art space via video it becomes a question of an exchange between viewing subjects and viewed objects.[4]

Technical equipment, which is as essential to Thater's work as "animistically" charged objects are for Beuys, always appears in connection with concrete forms of action:

*In the installation environment, things that we tradi-
tionally see as objects, which we look at, become subjects who
look at us. In the same way, all the video equipment is
present in the space and you see it actually making something.*[5)]

One cannot ignore the fact that these interactive
and transformational processes, which are unspec-
tacular for the most part, take a very independent
tack in relation to their literary sources. Thus as
mentioned, Thater refers to Murphy's science fiction
novel *A Love for Rachel* in her video installation ELEC-
TRIC MIND. The plot involves the death of a girl,
whose father transplanted a computer-generated
copy of his daughter's brain into a chimpanzee in order to preserve her individuality in a foreign body.
No hint is given of this background in the artist's
video installation, which shows pictures of the chimpanzee in different scenes. However, a kind of
screenplay on view in a display case does reveal the
narrative context. The installation does not show the
drama as such but rather the media practice of the
people behind the cameras as they follow the animal
protagonists from different angles and in different
takes. Our attention is explicitly drawn to the medial
process of production—an aesthetic strategy derived
from the continuum of modern art inasmuch as it is
based on the effect of "medial sincerity." According
to this term, coined by Boris Groys, we can no longer
treat "things" with sincerity without treating the
medium with sincerity as well.

In the video installation CAUCUS RACE (1998), an
excerpt from the eponymous chapter in *Alice in Wonderland* is projected onto the wall. The excerpt is
divided into single words that appear on screen con-
secutively like film credits. As soon as the final
words— "Prizes! Prizes!"—have come up, four monitors, placed on the floor in a semi-circle, alternately
start running. They show nature pictures: a giraffe
looking directly into the camera; a small orangutan
climbing onto a boulder and falling down again; two
hippopotami playfully splashing around in the water;
open skies and the sun shining into the top of a tree.
In the end, a large screen on a second wall opposite
the monitors shows a pool of blue water. Suddenly a
dolphin leaps out of the water directly at the camera
and touches it with its nose. It then turns away and
dives into the water again.

In contrast to ELECTRIC MIND, BROKEN CIRCLE,
or CHINA (a video piece that shows two wolves—amateur actors again—with their tamers on a training
field), CAUCUS RACE gives no indication of the location of the animals. One may assume that they are
tame animals or animals in a zoo. This option may in
turn be read as an indirect indication that it has become a rarity to see wild animals in their original
habitat or traditional pets and domestic animals in

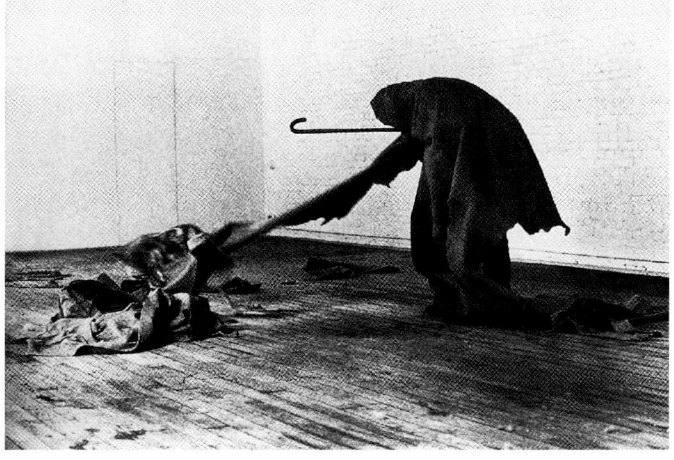

*JOSEPH BEUYS, COYOTE: I LIKE AMERI-
CA AND AMERICA LIKES ME, 1974, one-
week performance on the occasion of the
opening of the René Block Gallery, New York,
May 1974 / KOJOTE: ICH MAG AMERIKA
UND AMERIKA MAG MICH, einwöchige
Performance.
(PHOTO: CAROLINE TISDALL, FROM /
AUS: "JOSEPH BEUYS, COYOTE," SCHIRMER/
MOSEL, MÜNCHEN 1976/1980/1988)*

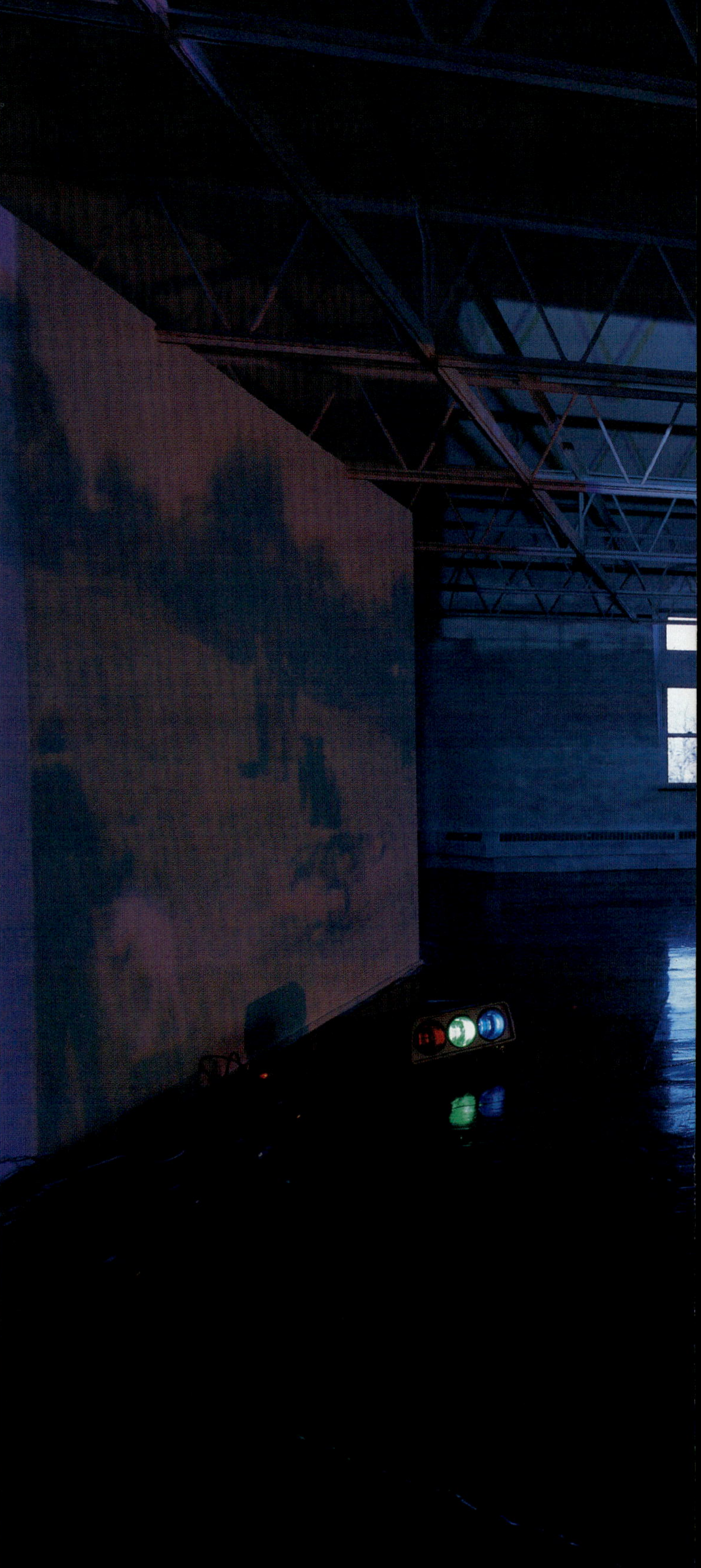

conventional scenes. Nonetheless, Diana Thater still seems to insist that the human ability to empathize with the *conditio animalis* can never atrophy entirely. The loss of animals' natural habitat and the untold threats that menace their lives have actually fostered a sympathizing and moral attitude towards our fellow creatures. The myth of *Genesis* does not tell us whether the animals remained in Paradise or whether they were also somehow involved in the expulsion of Adam and Eve, but given the animal conditions that prevail today one wonders whether they have indeed surpassed humankind regarding their expulsion from primal conditions. An awareness of the painful side of the relationship between human and animal is manifested in Beuys's I LIKE AMERICA—AMERICA LIKES ME (1974), in which he underscored the "wound" that cannot be healed until "accounts with the coyote" have been settled—whereby this animal stands for the reality of an entire continent prior to its conquest by Europeans. Unlike this quasi pantheist approach, based on the religious philosophy of reconciliation and idealistic traditions of reform around 1900, Diana Thater's serene and brilliant methods of projection and reflection testify to the potential of contemporary art to address the coexistence of humans and animals in somewhat cooler but still binding tones. They express the insight that especially in the age of artificial life, there is still something to be learned about the elusive truth of the human condition through the looking glass of animal life.

(Translation: Catherine Schelbert)

1) In: *Diana Thater. China.* The Renaissance Society at the University of Chicago, 1996, p. 15.
2) Quoted from an interview in: *Flash Art International*, Jan/Feb 1998, p. 88.
3) Franz Marc, *Briefe, Aufzeichnungen und Aphorismen*, vol. I (Berlin: Cassirer, 1920), p. 123.
4) Quoted from *Flash Art International*, Jan/Feb 1998, p. 89.
5) Ibid. p. 89.

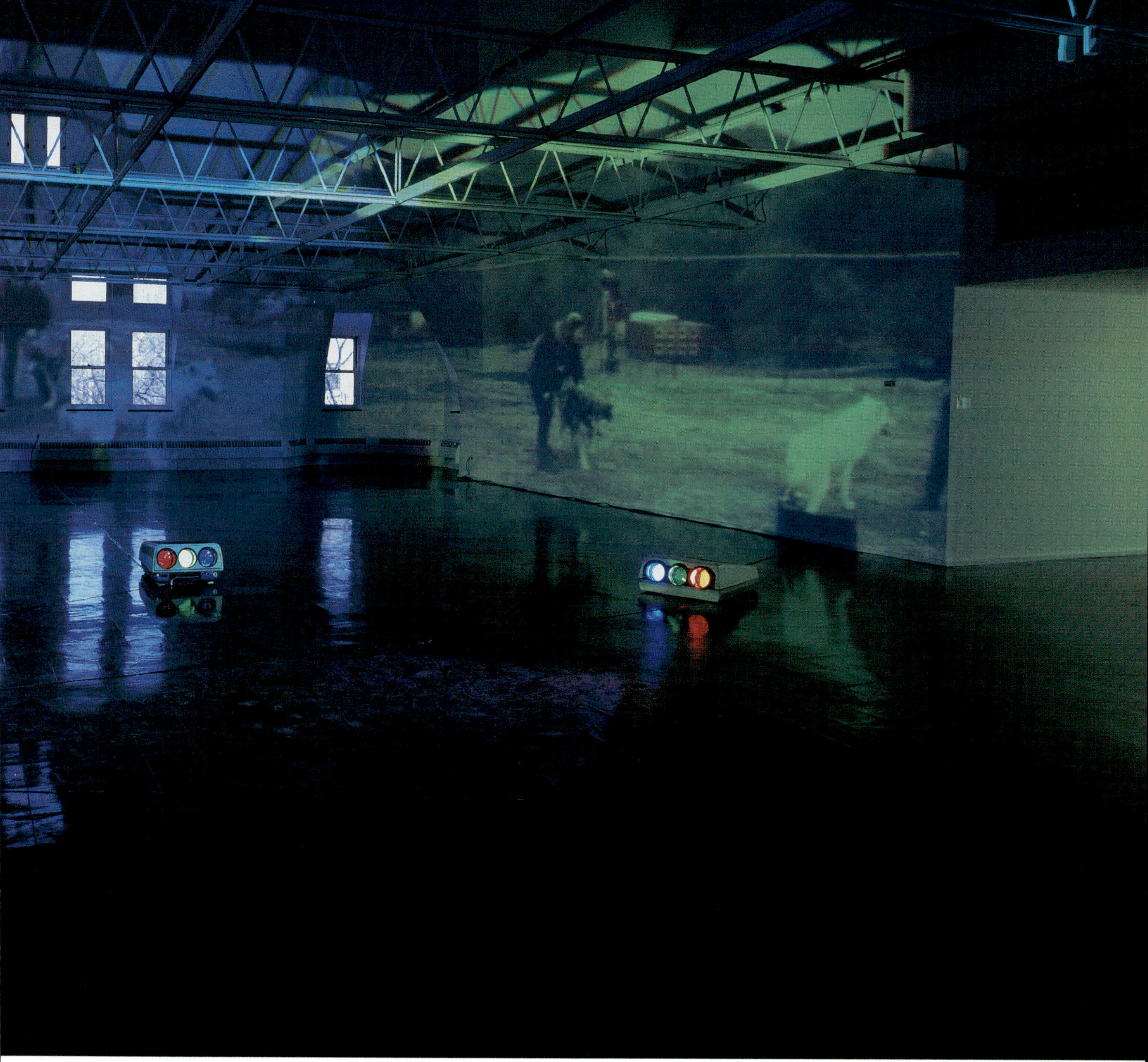

Water, Sun, and Thinking Bodies

JEREMY GILBERT-ROLFE

DELPHINE (1999)—the German for "dolphins," based on the Greek "delphinos"—was the title of an installation Diana Thater exhibited at the Vienna Secession last spring. The work used glamour to frame content found in nature. Thater colored the space with gels in a range of reds, from orange to magenta. Two nine-screen video "walls" each showed a continuous image of the sun, red on the one and magenta on the other. The sun was in the show as both the source of all energy, and as nature subdivided at will by technology, which can see both the spectrum (heat) and objects as the human eye cannot (for example, as an electronically encoded ball of exploding gas perceived as fluid).

The content framed by the dispersed redness of the gel and the video walls' composite images of the sun consisted of four video projections, each showing a sequence made up of both video and film shots in which dolphins playfully encounter film and video cameras and their human appendages. The exhibition space was divided into quadrants in one of which the projector was aimed at the ceiling, in an-

other at the floor, in the third at a point three quarters, and in the fourth at one quarter, of the distance between floor and ceiling.

Thater laid out the installation so as to reorient the building through first disorientating it, by replacing its architectural grid with an order (or perspective) that is neither its own nor incompatible with it. Neptune and Venus are both represented by the dolphin in art, but it is also the personification of water itself.[1] The museum was reoriented to a world without ground, where bodies move not on a surface but in a depth. This was a world made of figures not on a field, but within a body of water, not solids and voids but solids and a fluid mass that is itself a more tangible force than are the air or wind. Installation art is usually socio-anthropological or social-realist. Thater's installations relocate the institutional in relation to a content that, in being found in nature, comes from outside the historicist terms of reference to which we've become accustomed.

JEREMY GILBERT-ROLFE is a painter who also writes about art and related topics.

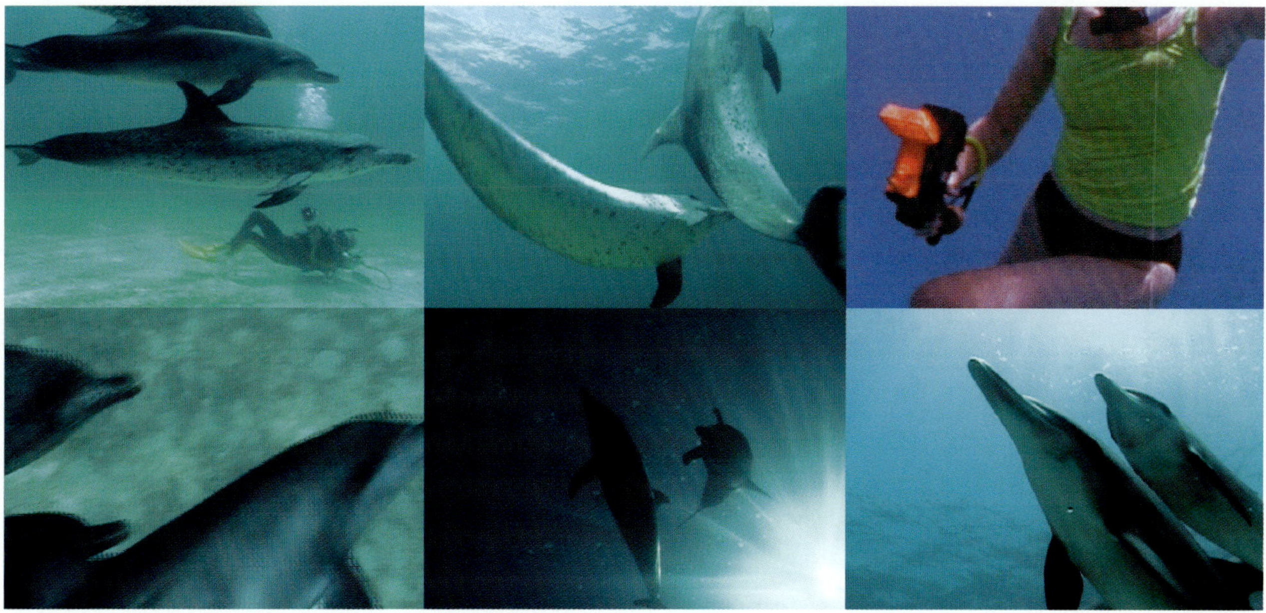

DIANA THATER, DELPHINE, 1999, video stills / Videostills.

In each of the four projections all film shots face down, and all video ones up, towards the surface of the sea and beyond it the sun. In each only the first shot isn't underwater, and traces the diver's entry into the water (and is therefore film) and each ends with shots that look up (and are therefore video). No projection has any kind of shot that the others don't, but no shot appears in more than one projection. All the shots are of divers and dolphins, either separately or together, sometimes in combination with the seabed (here entirely a property of film, since only film points down), and sometimes with fantastic rays of light from the sun (here entirely properties of video, since only video shots point up). Radiating through the sea rather than the sky, the rays remind one that the water is to dolphins as air is to us.

The dolphins can swim off and the image decomposes, or morselates, into a sea of pixels. At times shots are slowed down for the sake of revealing the grain of the video image. Thater seems to have been thinking about how real speed in the water is already experienced as slowed-down movement by perception conditioned by the movements of bodies on land and in the air. The slow movements of bodies moving through water are made even slower but, because video doesn't allow things to be heavy, the dolphins seem to become less rather than more massive when this happens. Video makes materiality the province of technology. Materiality is seen in the grain that shows up as the image slows down, while the same image robs very large animals of mass.

Thater says she chose the title DELPHINE because she likes the fact that "Delphine" is a woman's name that is also a plural noun. She named an earlier work CHINA (1995) for the same reason: "China" was the name of a female wolf at the center of the work and it can also be a woman's name, as well as being the name of the West's most obvious other, as the wolf is man's. She says that dolphins are "the ideal subject for my work which is... about this kind of living

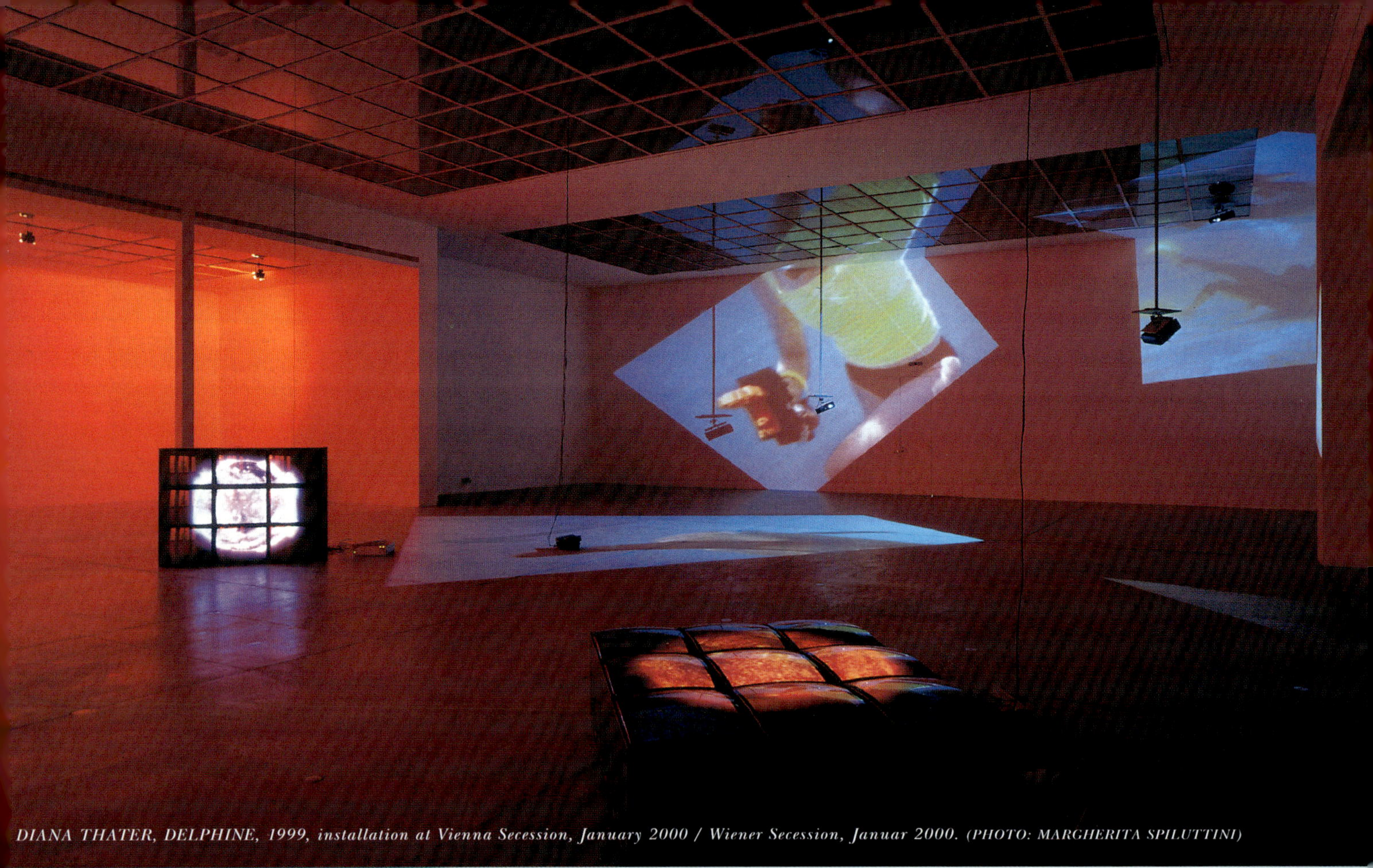

DIANA THATER, DELPHINE, 1999, installation at Vienna Secession, January 2000 / Wiener Secession, Januar 2000. (PHOTO: MARGHERITA SPILUTTINI)

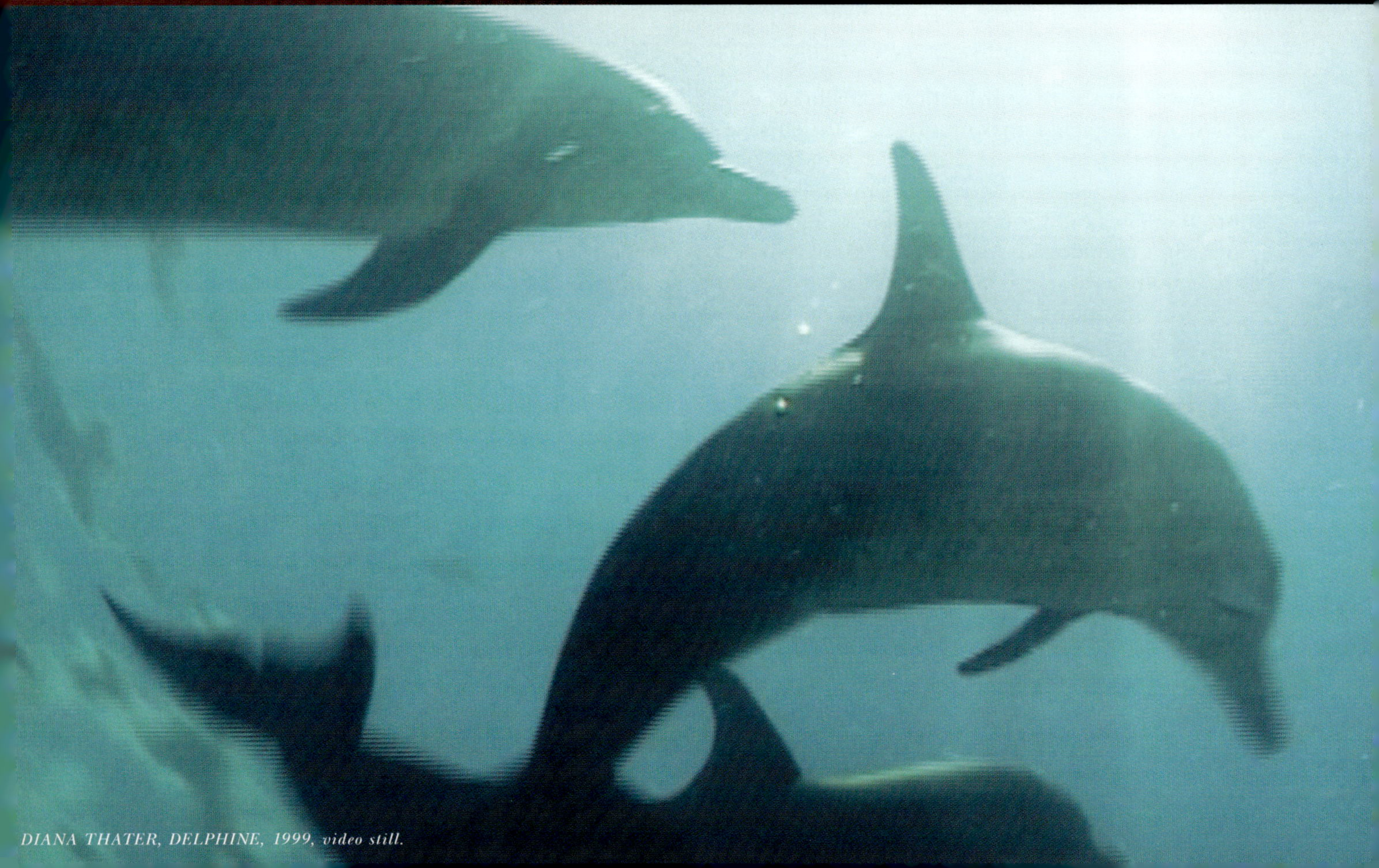

DIANA THATER, DELPHINE, 1999, video still.

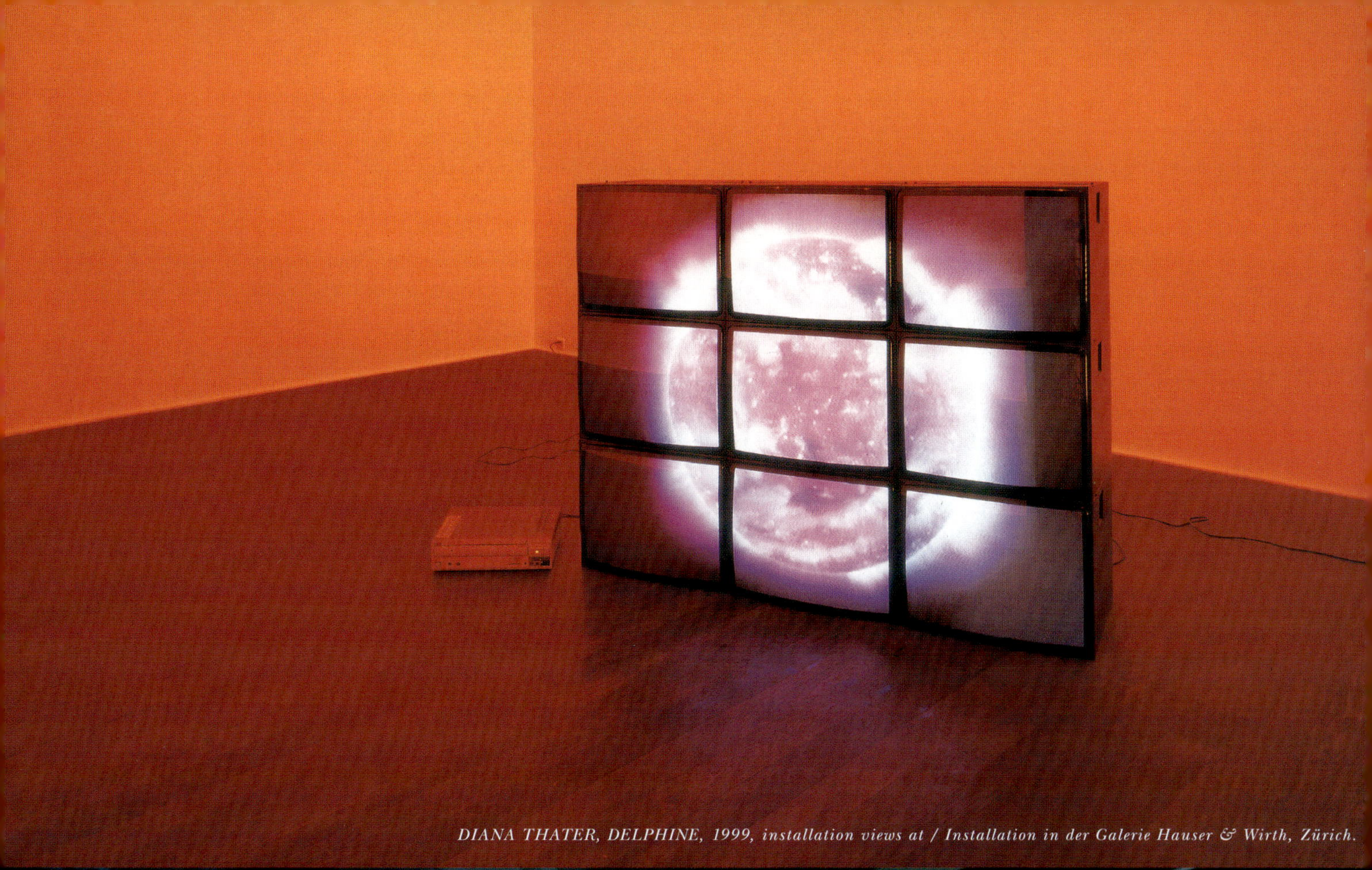

DIANA THATER, DELPHINE, 1999, installation views at / Installation in der Galerie Hauser & Wirth, Zürich.

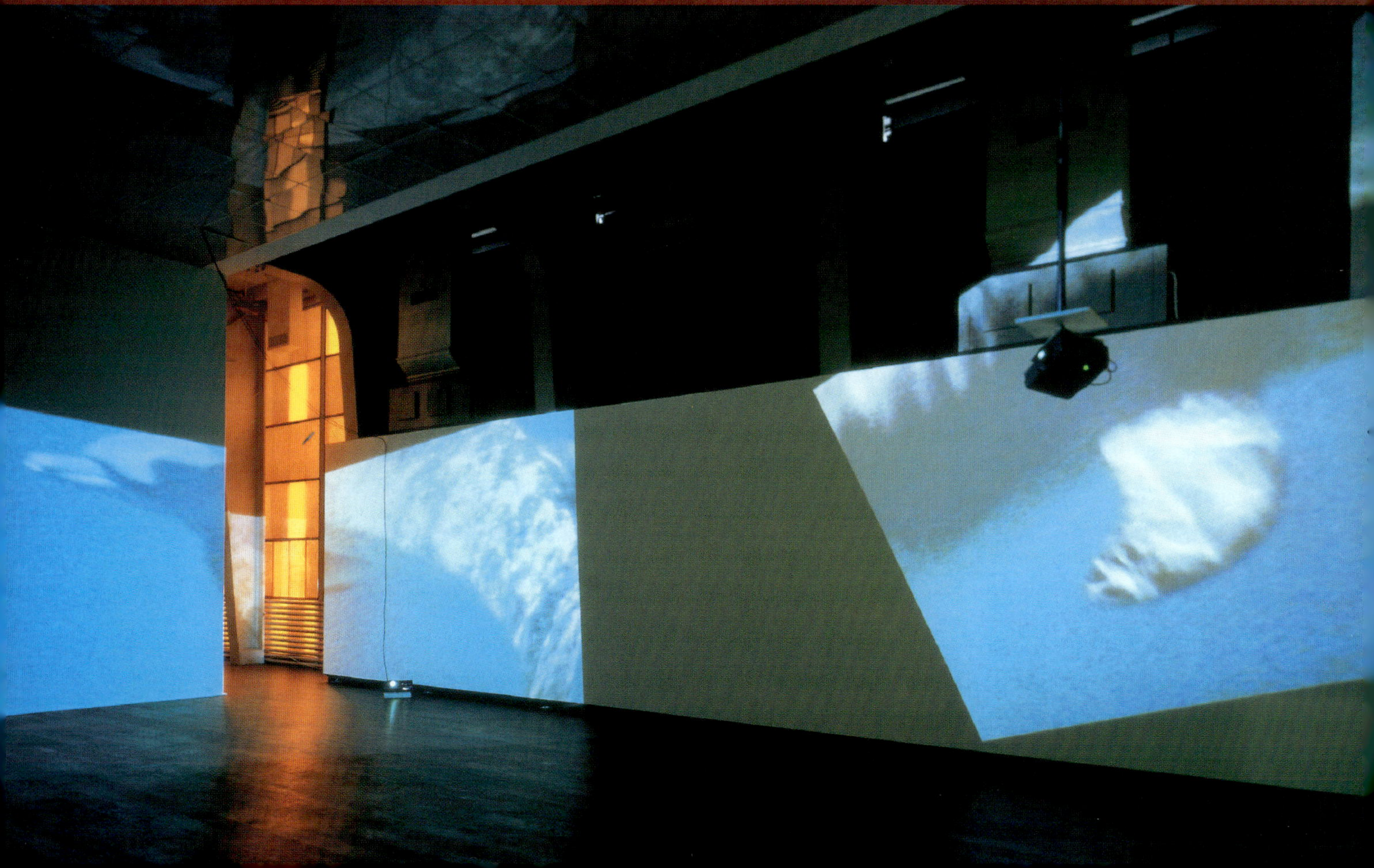

twice—seeing twice—of consciously being more than one."[2] If one were a dolphin, one would see the video camera twice: retinally, as we see it; but also as an X ray of itself provided by sonar visioning, which we don't have. DELPHINE proposes a parallel between two ways of seeing, one of which knows itself to be limited in comparison to the other. It was the movement in the cameras, invisible to the humans using them, which really got the dolphins' attention.

Thater has described underwater and outer space as the two conditions humans can enter but in which they can't survive. Dolphins have brains as big as humans do, but they live in an inhuman space. What is more, the dolphin brain is a different kind of brain which leads to different everyday requirements. A dolphin doesn't sleep as humans do, but turns off only half of its brain at a time. Dolphins are, then, never fully unconscious while, because of their sonar vision, they can't stand sound waves that bounce around. Unlike humans, they therefore can't tolerate enclosure. They don't like caves, the human's original refuge, and won't go into them. In making DELPHINE, Thater had the help of Richard O'Barry, who founded The Dolphin Project for the protection and promotion of dolphins' well-being after becoming disenchanted with what he had been trying to get them to do while serving in the US Navy, and subsequently when training dolphins for the television series *Flipper*. O'Barry compared a dolphin in an enclosed space to someone trapped in a hall of mirrors and never able to forget it. A dolphin's requirements are, then, the opposite of a human's, in that they can only be comfortable in an environment that seems to extend toward infinity, whereas even the hardiest human nomad likes to have a tent.

Thater's public career began with content that described a trajectory in which flowers (OO FIFI—FIVE DAYS IN CLAUDE MONET'S GARDEN, 1992) were succeeded by a field of moving elk (WYOMING ALOGON, 1994) but then proceeded to the wolf (CHINA). At that point the animal became defined as another consciousness than human. The elk were a field but the wolf was a subject (although the lone wolf is an anomaly, as are lone humans). However, where the wolf is an other with which man seems to have much in common, Thater finds dolphins' differences from humans more important than any discernible similarities between them.

The wolf is the human's other in an opposition defined in large part by the relationship to both of the dog, hated for its treachery by the one and loved for it by the other. Man's nightmare is a wolf-man, but the wolf's is a man-wolf which, says Thater, is not a nightmare but actually exists, and is the dog. Men and wolves have other things in common. Wolves, for example, are one of the few animals that adopt the abandoned offspring of other members of their species. Affinities such as these have led Thater to suggest that folk stories about boys turning into wolves and behaving as many men would like to behave are scary because they're believable in a way that the stories about princes turning into frogs are not—unless, perhaps, one is a prince. If wolves fear man because he has guns and fire, it is more than suggestive that man fears wolves despite having them.

In contrast, we do not fear dolphins nor do they fear us, and although she notes that dolphins care collectively for the newly born, Thater is more interested in their perception than their social life. Neither fear, nor hatred, nor familiarity joins us to dolphins, which are at once fearless, friendly, and strange in the sense that they see twice. While one may only film wolves from a distance, the dolphins came right up to the camera, almost ignoring the humans. They could see the camera's internal movement, and Thater invites one to compare the strangeness of their sonic perception to the technology contemporary humans use to record (and therefore think through) what they see. Watching DELPHINE reminds one of how film and video are prostheses which, in becoming crucial to what humans see, have come to determine how they see. We know that we do not see as cameras do, that the camera approximates human vision, but is quite unlike it because it attributes its own properties to what it records. The prosthesis has become a part of the human and/or the human a part of it. Thater considers, or seeks to present, the perception of animals in parallel with, or complementing, a human perception which may be described as either conditioned by technology (the camera-assisted human) or, and in my opinion more plausibly, as largely a product of it (the human wholly dependent on the idea of the photographic, i.e., as a post-human realization of itself). What is to be compared here is not the animal and the human as Kant might have conceived them, but the animal and the apparatus, and while the work's content may be projected on the wall, its subject is the viewer in the gallery.

Thater's work always recalls Kant's ideas about nature, the sublime, and beauty. Kathryn Kanjo has pointed out that "The Hudson River School painters" (whom Thater's rays of light in water instantly recall), "John Ford, and Mary Shelley all serve as influences on her work." Kanjo points to two instances in which Thater recalls the sublime as a concept of ungraspable extension found in the presence of nature or the natural (as in the Hudson River School or Ford's westerns, two versions of nature as a cultural promise) and as an uncontrollable terror unleashed through combining technology (in fact, electricity) and flesh. Like the cinematographic apparatus, or writing, *Frankenstein* is about the product of a concept escaping the latter's grasp, exceeding what imagined it, an idea with a mind of its own rather than the other way around. Significantly, Thater has said that Shelley's story becomes truly scary when it becomes apparent that Frankenstein has produced a monster that has its own dreams: no longer a mere mechanism, it has become a complete other, its possession of an unconscious indicating the presence of a consciousness.

In Kant the human subject is both product of nature and producer of nature as a concept, the latter guaranteeing autonomy. It is not at all clear that the contemporary subject can claim autonomy in a comparable relationship to the technology, which threatens to overwhelm nature. The contemporary subject is suspended between animal perception and a technological visualizing which has become inescapable and unconscious, as is evidenced by every dream in the twentieth century taking the form of a film. Thater has found an animal that is fascinated by the camera while itself naturally seeing twice, at will, and implicitly compares its comfortable movement between the retinal and the sonar with a human perception uncertainly caught between what are known

to be, but cannot be experienced as, two ways of seeing. While there must have been a brief period at the beginning of photography's history when the thrill of the photograph was that it was similar to but still different from how people usually saw, now it would be only through an immense effort that one could hope to be able to separate one's sense of sight from that of the camera. Totally lacking the dolphin's ability to see sonically (save through technology) the human is now also unable to see even visually without seeing an image as much technological as it is natural. If the human can only see the world as a photograph, it was very sensible of the dolphins to go for the cameras rather than the camera carriers. In DELPHINE one sees the animal and the technological in an engagement where the human is explicitly ancillary, at least as far as the dolphins are concerned, even though the camera always follows the diver and never the dolphin.

We see the whole thing in video (a certain kind of photographic image) substituting its own tactility (or lack of it) for that of the things it depicts. This leads to Thater's attitude to and use of beauty, the other side of the differential of which the sublime is one half. Her relationship to beauty is as uncomplicated as her reiteration of the sublime is complicated. It has to be. If this work didn't look good it would be impossible to look at because it would be another documentary about how dolphins are loveable but threatened, its presentation of their potential as a complement to human perception rendered illegible by its pathos. Thater has no intention of letting this happen, and she uses glamour (the secular form of the beautiful) to frame the dolphin projections so that we may instead see a creature that should be protected, but which is important for its potential as a model of ecstasy rather than as a symbol or symptom of doom.

Thater quotes Buck Henry, the screenwriter of the film *The Day of the Dolphin*, to invoke its superior sensitivity and capacity to communicate: "Imagine that every one of your senses has been heightened to a level that in a human might only be described as ecstatic… Imagine that you are able to carry on simultaneous conversations with two members of your species—one right next to you and the other several

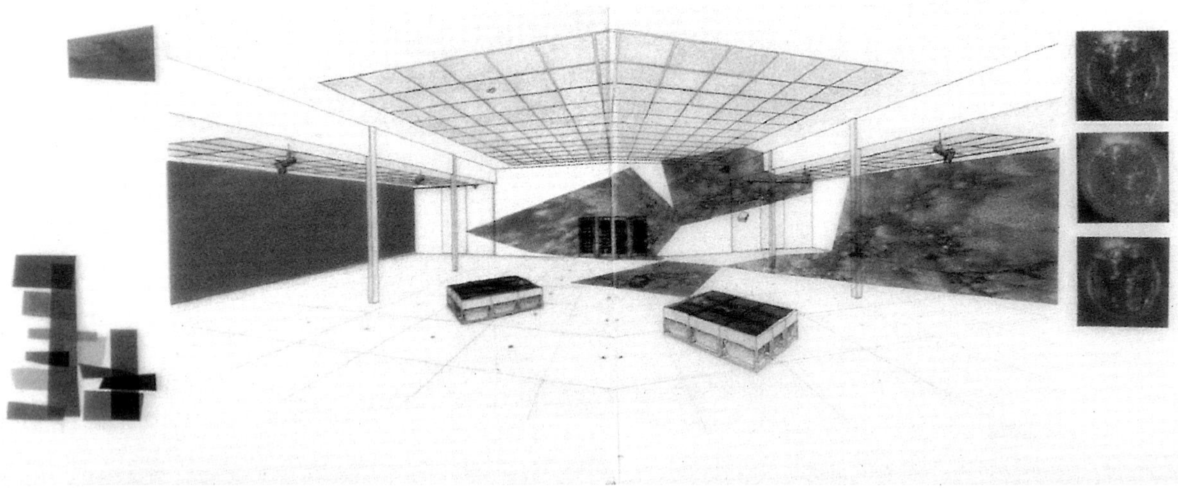

DIANA THATER, DELPHINE, 1999, video stills.

miles away…"[3] DELPHINE leads us to the thought that for humans the one is unattainable and the other banal, and neither is involuntary. For us, the first would be a body perpetually (as opposed to intermittently) open to aesthetic stimuli, while the telephone enables us to do a crude version of the second. DELPHINE is about the superiority of both nature and technology to the human: nature needs neither self-consciousness nor technology, but the human is made by them, the first precluding permanent ecstasy and the second crudely supplementing the shortcomings of the body. The work aligned the animal with the technological through glamour so as to incidentally ward off pathos while allowing us to contemplate nature within a context of (technologically) heightened sensibility. The red and magenta video suns frame the blue of the projections, where shots were chosen by matching them for color, the orange through magenta gels help to dissolve the solidity of the walls. A depth is projected on the floor, the bottom of the sea beneath the tiles. In Thater's work the question of beauty is one of indispensability, it is the only means through which she can approximate the condition described by Buck Henry. She wants the human subject standing in the gallery to be ecstatic, to experience contemplation as excitement. The extremely confident critic who said that beauty stops thought "like a stone wall" was perhaps not thinking clearly about either the truth of his assertion (which is that beauty must therefore be superior to "thought") or its reversibility (in fact "thought" has tended to define itself as that which can resist beauty).[4] Furthermore, in works of art, which are made out of thinking, beauty never stops thought because one is obliged to ask what it's doing there, and questions are thoughts. The answer is that it is there so that we can start elsewhere than the usual thoughts. DELPHINE frames nature with glamour so that dolphins could be present, naturally (as it were) through film or video, not as objects in a sea of (however well intentioned) discourse, but as subjects who could relate to the camera.

1) James Hall, *Dictionary of Subjects and Symbols in Art* (New York: Harper & Row, 1979), p. 105–106.
2) Diana Thater, E-mail to the author, July 29, 2000.
3) *Diana Thater: Delphine*, exh. cat. (Vienna: Vienna Secession, 2000), p. 21.
4) Ibid., p. 27. On this and related topics alluded to here, see also Jeremy Gilbert-Rolfe, *Beauty and the Contemporary Sublime* (New York: Allworth Press, 2000).

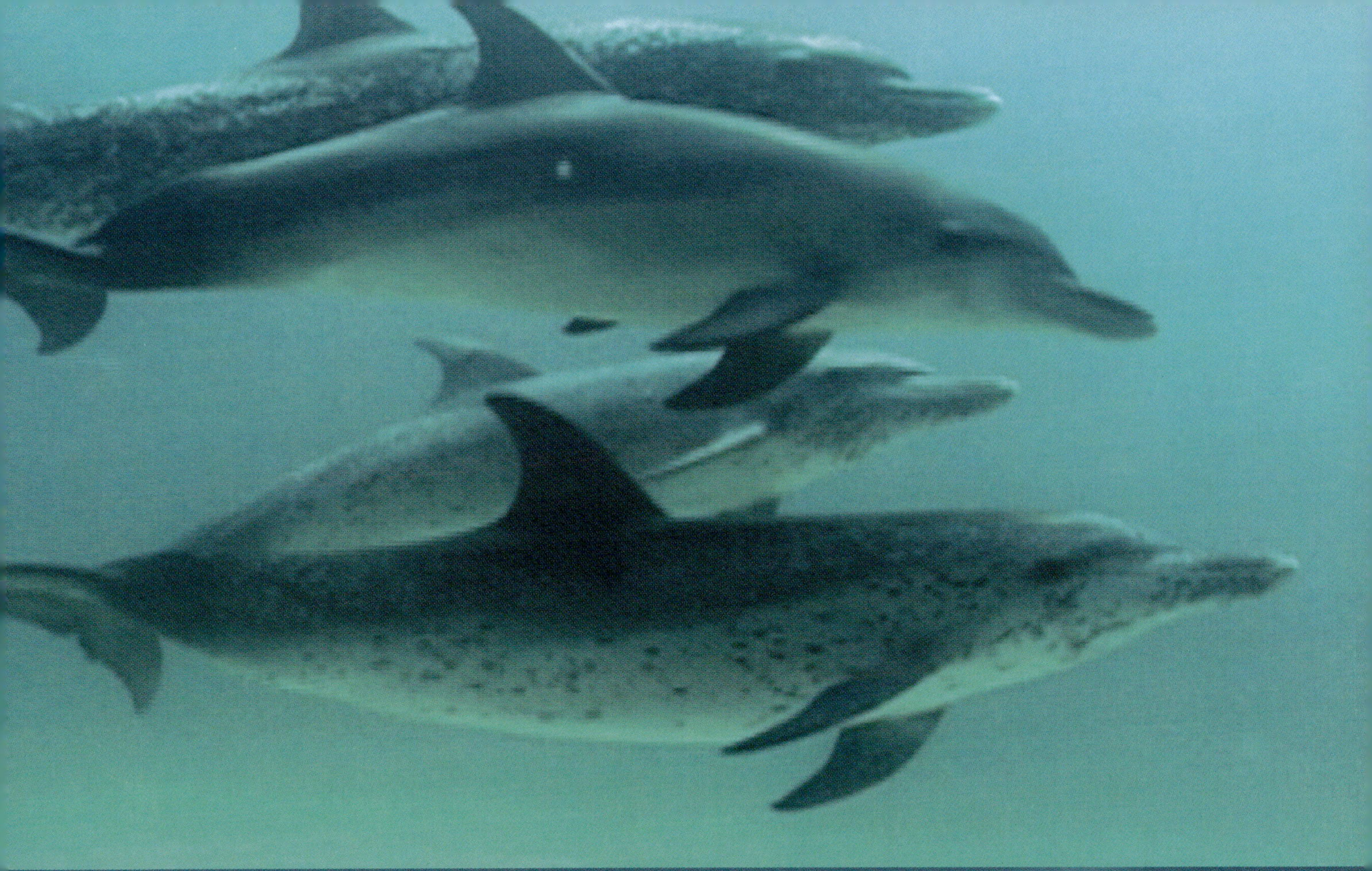

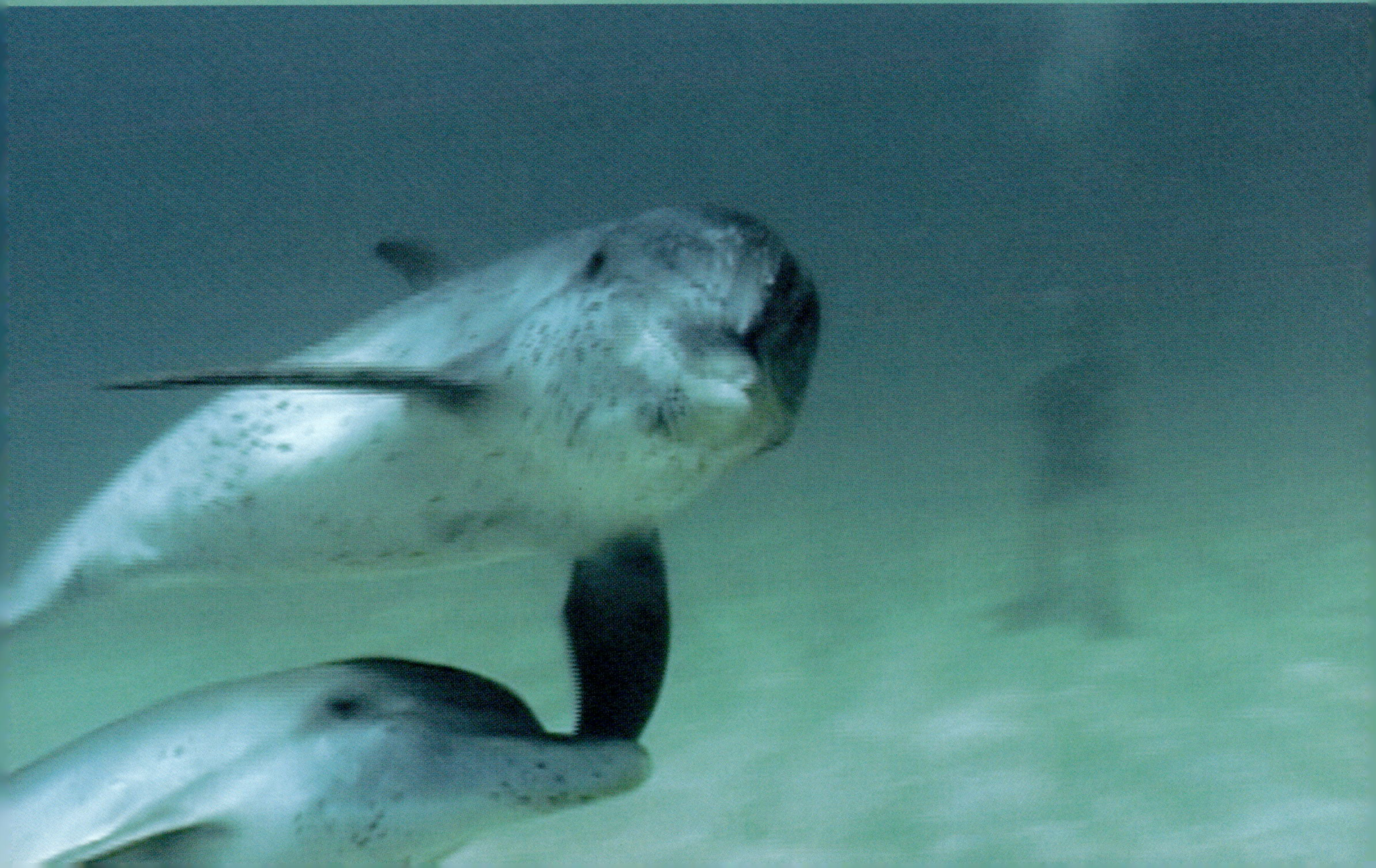

Wasser, Sonne und denkende Körper

JEREMY GILBERT-ROLFE

DELPHINE (2000) lautet der Titel der Installation von Diana Thater, die im Frühjahr in der Wiener Secession gezeigt wurde. Das Naturthema wurde mit viel Glamour inszeniert. Mit Lichtfilter-Folien in Rottönen von Orange bis Magenta brachte Thater Farbe in den Raum. Auf zwei Videowänden aus je neun Monitoren war die Sonne zu sehen – einmal in Rot, einmal in Magenta. Die Sonne war in der Ausstellung als Energiequelle schlechthin vertreten, aber auch als ein Stück technisch willkürlich zerlegbare Natur, insofern als die Technologie sowohl das Spektrum (Wärme) als auch Gegenstände sichtbar machen kann, die das menschliche Auge sonst nicht wahrzunehmen vermag (z. B. eine als Flüssigkeit wahrnehmbare, elektronische Umsetzung einer explodierenden, kugelförmigen Gaswolke).

JEREMY GILBERT-ROLFE ist Künstler und schreibt auch über Kunst und verwandte Themen.

Das von den Rottönen und Sonnenbildern umrahmte Herzstück der Installation bestand aus vier Videoprojektionen, die je eine Video- oder Filmsequenz zeigten, in der die Delphine mit den Kameras und ihren menschlichen Anhängseln verspielt Kontakt aufnehmen. Der Ausstellungsraum war in vier Teile unterteilt; in einem war der Projektor gegen die Decke gerichtet, im anderen auf den Fussboden, im dritten auf einen Punkt auf drei Viertel Raumhöhe und im letzten Quadranten auf einen Punkt auf ein Viertel Raumhöhe.

Die Installation gab dem Gebäude eine neue Orientierung, indem sie die gewohnte aufhob. Sie ersetzte sein architektonisches Grundraster durch eine Ordnung (oder Perspektive), die zwar nicht die seine, aber auch nicht mit ihm unvereinbar war. In der Kunst verkörpert der Delphin sowohl Neptun wie Venus, kann aber auch das Wasser selbst symbolisieren.[1] Das Museum wurde zu einer Welt ohne Boden, in der sich die Körper nicht auf einer Oberfläche, sondern in einem Tiefenraum bewegten. In dieser Welt bewegten sich die Figuren nicht auf einer Ebene, sondern im Wasser; sie bestand also nicht aus Festkörpern und Leerräumen, sondern aus Festkörpern und Flüssigkeit, einem Stoff, der greifbarer ist als Luft oder Wind. Installationskunst ist gewöhnlich sozialanthropologisch oder sozialrealistisch angelegt. Thaters Installationen jedoch positionieren den institutionellen Ausstellungsrahmen völlig neu durch ihr Thema, das aus der Natur stammt und somit ausserhalb des gewohnten historisierenden Bezugsrahmens angesiedelt ist.

Bei allen vier Projektionen sind die mit Filmkameras gemachten Aufnahmen nach unten auf den Meeresgrund gerichtet, die Aufnahmen mit Videokameras dagegen nach oben, in Richtung Wasseroberfläche und Sonne. Bei allen ist jeweils nur das erste Bild nicht unter Wasser aufgenommen und zeigt einen Taucher beim Eintauchen ins Wasser (deshalb die Filmkamera) und die letzten Einstellungen sind immer nach oben gerichtet (und daher unter Wasser mit der Videokamera gedreht). Die Art der Aufnahmen ist in allen Projektionen ähnlich, aber keine Einstellung erscheint in mehr als einer Projektion. Zu sehen sind immer Taucher und Delphine, entweder einzeln oder miteinander, manchmal mit einem Stück Meeresboden (aufgenommen mit der Filmkamera) und manchmal mit phantastisch anmutenden Sonnenstrahlen (Video). Die im Meerwasser glitzernden Strahlen erinnern uns daran, dass das Wasser für den Delphin ist, was die Luft für den Menschen.

Manchmal schwimmen die Delphine aus dem Bild, und dieses löst sich in ein Meer von Pixeln auf. Oder die Aufnahmen sind verlangsamt, so dass die Körnigkeit des Videobilds sichtbar wird. Thater scheint daran gedacht zu haben, dass die reale Geschwindigkeit im Wasser aufgrund unserer Bewegungserfahrungen an Land und in der Luft bereits als stark verlangsamt erlebt wird. Das Tempo der sich träge im Wasser bewegenden Körper ist hier noch zusätzlich gebremst; da aber ein Körper auf Video ohnehin nie schwer wirkt, erscheinen die Delphine nicht etwa wuchtiger, sondern eher leichter, als sie sind. Video macht Stofflichkeit zu einer technischen Angelegenheit. Sie kommt in der Körnigkeit zum Ausdruck, die durch die Verlangsamung des Bildes sichtbar wird, während dasselbe Bild den grossen Tieren zugleich ihre Massigkeit nimmt.

Wie Thater erklärt, hat sie den Titel DELPHINE gewählt, weil es ihr gefällt, dass «Delphine» auch ein weiblicher Name und ein Substantiv im Plural ist. Aus ähnlichen Gründen nannte sie ein 1995 entstandenes Werk CHINA: «China» war der Name der Wölfin, die im Mittelpunkt jenes Werks stand, und es kann ebenso eine Frau bezeichnen wie eine ganz «andere» Kultur aus der Perspektive des Westens, so, wie der Wolf auch das Andere des Menschen darstellt. Delphine, sagt sie, sind «das ideale Thema für meine Arbeit, in der es um (...) diese Art des doppelten Erlebens, des doppelten Sehens, geht – darum, bewusst mehr als eine Person zu sein».[2] Wären wir Delphine, so sähen wir die Videokamera zweifach: mit dem Auge, aber auch als eine Art durch Echolotung erzeugte Röntgenaufnahme. DELPHINE zieht eine Parallele zwischen zwei Arten des Sehens, von denen die eine weiss, dass sie im Vergleich zur anderen limitiert ist. Tatsächlich war es die für die Menschen unsichtbare Bewegung in den Kameras, welche die Aufmerksamkeit der Delphine erregte.

Thater hat die Unterwasserwelt und den Weltraum als Sphären bezeichnet, in die der Mensch eindringen, in denen er jedoch nicht überleben kann. Delphine haben ein Gehirn, das so gross ist wie das eines Menschen, aber sie leben in einer nicht menschlichen Umgebung. Zudem ist das Delphingehirn anders geartet und muss andere Anforderungen erfüllen. Ein Delphin schläft nicht wie ein Mensch, sondern schaltet jeweils nur die eine Gehirnhälfte ab. Delphine sind also nie völlig ohne Bewusstsein. Wegen ihres Sehvermögens mittels Echolotung ertragen sie keine abprallenden Schallwellen. Im Gegensatz zum Menschen halten sie es daher nicht in geschlossenen Räumen aus. Höhlen, des Menschen urtümlichste Zufluchtsstätten, mögen sie nicht und würden nie hineinschwimmen. Bei ihrer Arbeit an DELPHINE wurde Thater von Richard O'Barry unterstützt, dem Leiter des *Dolphin Project* zum Schutz der Delphine und zur Förderung ihres Wohlergehens. O'Barry, der früher für die US-Marine und die Fernsehserie *Flipper* Delphine dressierte, gründete das Projekt, weil ihm seine Arbeit suspekt geworden war. Er verglich einen Delphin in Gefangenschaft mit einem Menschen, der in ein Spiegelkabinett gesperrt ist und dies keine Sekunde vergessen kann. Die Bedürfnisse eines Delphins sind jenen des Menschen in dem Sinne genau entgegen-gesetzt, dass sie sich nur in einer Umgebung wohl fühlen, die sich ins Unendliche auszudehnen scheint, während selbst der verwegenste menschliche Nomade ganz gern in seinem Zelt weilt.

Thaters Ausstellungskarriere begann mit Inhalten, die eine interessante Entwicklung durchliefen. Auf Blumen (OO FIFI—FIVE DAYS IN CLAUDE MONET'S GARDEN / Fünf Tage in Claude Monets Garten, 1992) folgte eine Herde von Elchen (WYOMING ALOGON, 1994) und schliesslich ein Wolf (CHINA, 1995). An diesem Punkt wurde das Tier erstmals als nicht-menschliches, bewusstes Wesen definiert. Die Elche waren noch eine Herde, aber der Wolf war ein Subjekt (obschon der einsame Wolf genauso wie der menschliche Einzelgänger eine Anomalie darstellt). Doch während der Wolf ein Wesen ist, das viel mit dem Menschen gemein zu haben scheint, hält Thater im Fall des Delphins die Unterschiede zwischen ihm und dem Menschen für wichtiger als allfällig erkennbare Ähnlichkeiten.

Der Wolf ist das Andere des Menschen, und zwischen beiden herrscht ein Gegensatz, der sich vor allem aus ihrer Beziehung zum Hund ergibt, der wegen seines Verrats vom einen gehasst und vom anderen geliebt wird. Der Alptraum des Menschen ist ein Werwolf, doch jener des Wolfs ist ein Menschenwolf, der laut Thater kein Alptraum ist, sondern tatsächlich existiert, nämlich der Hund. Zwischen Mensch und Wolf gibt es andere Gemeinsamkeiten. So ist der Wolf eines der wenigen Tiere, die fremde, verwaiste Jungtiere adoptieren und aufziehen. Derartige Affinitäten liessen Thater zum Schluss kommen, dass Volkssagen über Knaben, die sich in Wölfe verwandeln und sich so verhalten, wie viele Menschen es gern tun würden, darum so unheimlich sind, weil sie in einer Weise glaubhaft sind, wie dies bei Geschichten über in Frösche verwandelte Prinzen nicht der Fall ist. Während Wölfe den Menschen fürchten, weil er Schusswaffen und Feuer besitzt, stimmt es schon eher nachdenklich, dass der Mensch trotz dieser Waffen vor Wölfen Angst hat.

Delphine fürchten wir dagegen nicht, und sie haben auch keine Angst vor uns. Und obschon Thater erwähnt, dass sich Delphine gemeinsam um ihre Neugeborenen kümmern, ist Thater mehr an ihrer Wahrnehmung als an ihrem Sozialverhalten interessiert.

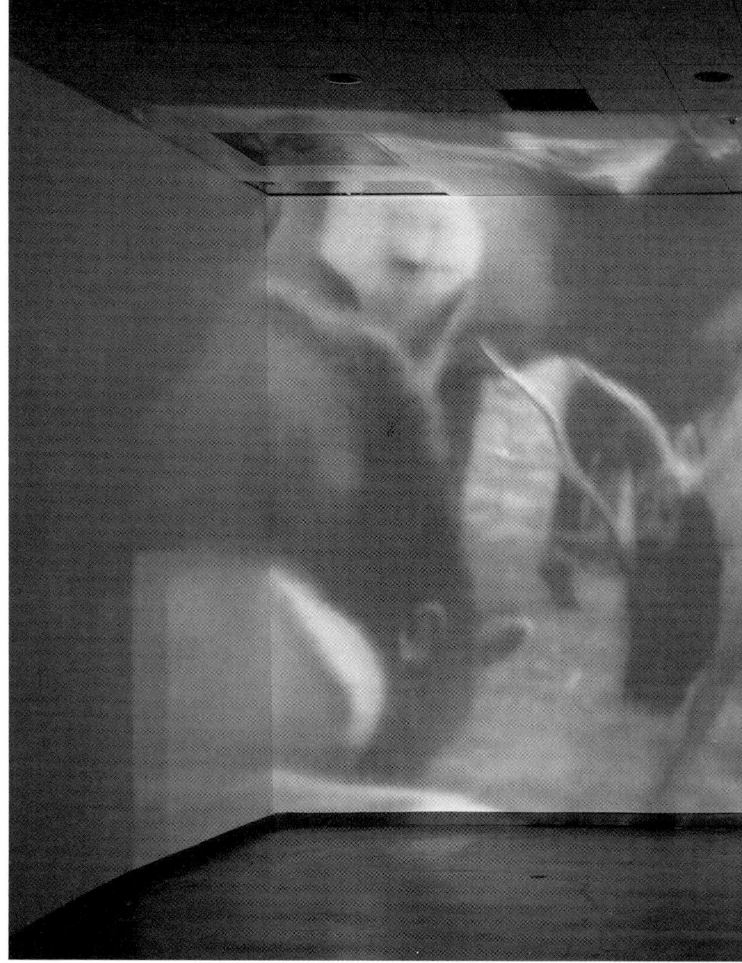

Weder Angst noch Hass noch Vertrautheit verbindet uns mit den Delphinen, die zugleich furchtlos, freundlich und – wegen ihrer doppelten Sehkraft – uns auch fremd sind. Während man Wölfe nur aus einer gewissen Distanz filmen kann, kamen die Delphine ganz dicht an die Kamera heran und beachteten die Menschen kaum. Sie konnten die Bewegung im Innern der Kamera «sehen», und Thater fordert uns auf, ihre Echolottechnik mit der Technik zu vergleichen, die der moderne Mensch benutzt, um Dinge aufzuzeichnen (und damit zu studieren). Beim Betrachten von DELPHINE werden wir daran erinnert, dass Film und Video Prothesen sind, die unser Sehen je länger, je mehr beeinflussen und mittlerweile schon bestimmen, w i e wir sehen. Wir wissen, dass wir anders sehen als eine Kamera, dass die Kamera der menschlichen Sehweise zwar nahe kommt, aber dennoch eine andere ist, weil sie dem, was sie aufzeichnet, ihren eigenen Stempel aufdrückt. Die Prothese ist ein Teil des Menschen

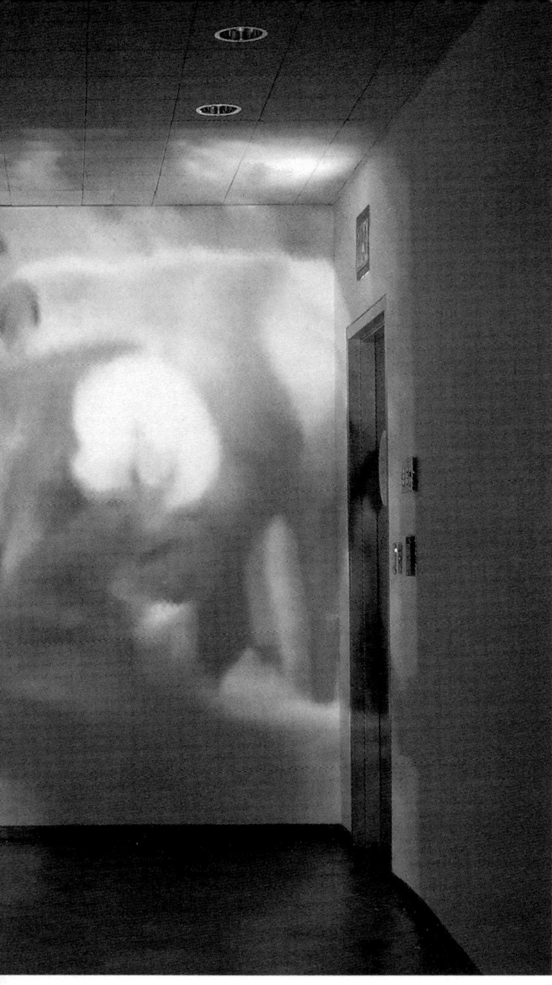

DIANA THATER, WYOMING ALOGON, 1994, 3 video projectors, 3 laser discs and players, sync generator, window film, and existing architecture at MoCA Los Angeles / 3 Videoprojektoren, je 3 Laserdiscs und Abspielgeräte, Synchronisator, Fensterfolie und bestehende Räumlichkeiten.

Thaters Schaffen beeinflusst hätten. Kanjo nennt zwei Beispiele, wo Thater das Erhabene sowohl als unfassbares Erweiterungserlebnis im Angesicht der Natur oder des Natürlichen zeigt (Natur als kulturelle Verheissung wie in der Hudson River School oder in John Fords Western) wie auch als unkontrollierbaren Terror, ausgelöst durch die Kombination von Technik (sprich: Elektrizität) und Fleisch. Wie beim Film oder beim Schreiben geht es in Shelleys *Frankenstein* um das Produkt eines Denkens, das über dieses hinauswächst und unkontrollierbar wird, ein Gedanke mit eigenem Willen und nicht umgekehrt. Bezeichnenderweise sagt Thater, dass Shelleys Roman erst dort so richtig gruselig wird, wo sich zeigt, dass Frankenstein ein Monster geschaffen hat, das eigene Träume hat: Nun ist es nicht mehr bloss ein mechanisches Geschöpf, sondern ein vollständiges Anderes, das offensichtlich mit einem Unbewussten ausgestattet ist und daher wohl auch ein Bewusstsein besitzt.

Bei Kant ist das menschliche Subjekt ein Produkt der Natur, das aber gleichzeitig auch eine Idee der Natur zu entwickeln vermag, was seine Autonomie garantiert. Es ist keineswegs sicher, dass das heutige Subjekt in einem ähnlich autonomen Verhältnis zur Technik steht, welche die Natur zu überwältigen droht. Das heutige Subjekt steht zwischen der tierischen Wahrnehmung und einer technologisch unterstützten Sehweise, die mittlerweile unentrinnbar und unbewusst ist, was die Tatsache beweist, dass im zwanzigsten Jahrhundert jeder Traum die Form eines Films annimmt. Thater hat hier ein Tier gefunden, das von der Kamera fasziniert ist und von Natur aus zweierlei Sehvermögen besitzt, die es beliebig einsetzen kann. Implizit vergleicht die Künstlerin den mühelosen Wechsel zwischen Auge und Echolotung mit der menschlichen Wahrnehmung, die unentschieden zwischen zwei Arten des Sehens schwankt, die zwar bekannt sind, aber nicht als solche erlebt werden. Während es in den Anfängen der Photographie eine kurze Periode gegeben haben muss, wo der Reiz einer Aufnahme in ihrer Ähnlichkeit (und doch auch Unterschiedlichkeit) mit der üblichen Wahrnehmung bestand, lässt sich heute das natürliche Sehvermögen nur noch mit äusserster Willensanstrengung von dem einer Kamera unterscheiden.

geworden oder der Mensch ein Teil der Prothese. Thater unternimmt eine Erkundung und Darstellung der tierischen Wahrnehmung, parallel oder als Ergänzung zur menschlichen Wahrnehmung, die entweder als von der Technik bestimmt oder – noch plausibler – überhaupt als ein Produkt der Technik zu verstehen ist (der völlig von der Idee der Photographie abhängige Mensch, quasi deren posthumane Selbstverwirklichung). Es handelt sich hier nicht um einen Vergleich zwischen Mensch und Tier im kantischen Sinne, sondern zwischen Tier und Maschine. Auch wenn der Inhalt der Arbeit an die Wand projiziert wird, ihr eigentliches Thema sind die Betrachterinnen und Betrachter.

Thaters Arbeiten erinnern stets an Kants Ideen der Natur, des Erhabenen und des Schönen. Kathryn Kanjo hat darauf hingewiesen, dass die Maler der *Hudson River School* (an die man sich durch die erwähnten Lichtstrahlen im Wasser unweigerlich erinnert fühlt), aber auch John Ford und Mary Shelley

Der Mensch, dem die natürliche Fähigkeit des Delphins, mittels Echolotung zu sehen, vollkommen abgeht, ist heute auch nicht mehr fähig, mit dem Auge etwas zu erkennen, das nicht mindestens ebenso technisch wie natürlich ist. Wenn also der Mensch die Welt nur als Photographie sehen kann, war es sehr vernünftig von den Delphinen, sich an die Kameras zu halten statt an die Kameraleute. In DELPHINE sehen wir ein Zusammenspiel von Tier und Technik, in welchem der Mensch klar zweitrangig ist, zumindest was die Delphine angeht, selbst wenn die Kamera stets dem Taucher und nie dem Delphin folgt.

Wir sehen das Ganze als Video (eine Art photographisches Bild), das seine eigene Taktilität (oder deren Fehlen) an die Stelle jener der abgebildeten Dinge setzt. Das führt zu Thaters besonderem Umgang mit Schönheit, der anderen Seite der Gleichung, deren eine Seite das Erhabene ausmacht. Thaters Verhältnis zum Schönen ist ebenso unkompliziert, wie ihre Wiederholung des Erhabenen kompliziert ist. Das muss so sein. Wäre dieses Werk nicht schön anzusehen, wäre es unmöglich, weil es einfach nur ein weiterer Dokumentarfilm über die ach so liebenswerten, bedrohten Delphine wäre, dessen Pathos die Darstellung ihrer Wahrnehmungsweise als mögliche Ergänzung der menschlichen unkenntlich machte. Thater hat nicht die Absicht dies zuzulassen und präsentiert die Delphin-Projektionen in einem glamourösen Rahmen (der säkularisierten Variante des Schönen), so dass wir ein Tier zu sehen bekommen, das tatsächlich schützenswert ist. Damit bleibt der Delphin das ekstatische Vorbild und wird nicht zum Symbol oder Symptom des Verhängnisses degradiert. Als Beweis für die aussergewöhnliche Sensibilität und Kommunikationsfähigkeit des Tiers zitiert Diana Thater den Drehbuchautor des Films *The Day of the Dolphin*, Buck Henry: «Stellen Sie sich vor, (...) jeder Ihrer Sinne ist auf eine Art und Weise geschärft, die man bei einem Menschen als ekstatisch bezeichnen würde… Stellen Sie sich vor, Sie wären in der Lage, mit zwei anderen Artgenossen gleichzeitig zu kommunizieren, einem gleich neben Ihnen und einem, der ein paar Kilometer entfernt ist.»[3] In DELPHINE geht es um die Überlegenheit von Natur und Technik gegenüber dem Menschen: Während die Natur weder auf ein Bewusstsein noch auf die Technik angewiesen ist, machen diese den Menschen erst aus, wobei Ersteres eine permanente Ekstase verhindert und das Zweite so gut als möglich die Unzulänglichkeiten des Körpers ausgleicht. Das Werk bringt das Tier durch die glamouröse Inszenierung mit der Technik in Verbindung, um jedes Pathos abzuwehren; dabei gibt es uns einen Einblick in die Natur in einem Kontext (dank technischer Mittel) erhöhter Sensibilität. Die roten und magentafarbenen Videosonnen umrahmen das Blau der Projektionen, deren Aufnahmen farblich aufeinander abgestimmt gezeigt werden, wobei das Orange gefiltert durch Magenta die Solidität der Wände auflöst. Auch auf den Boden wird Tiefe projiziert – der Meeresboden unter den Bodenplatten. In Thaters Werk ist Schönheit eine Notwendigkeit. Sie ist die einzige Möglichkeit, sich dem von Buck Henry geschilderten Zustand anzunähern. Sie möchte, dass der Museumsbesucher die Installation als etwas Aufregendes, ja Ekstatisches erlebt. Der reichlich kühne Kritiker, der schrieb, dass Schönheit das Denken blockiere, hat vermutlich nicht allzu gründlich nachgedacht über die Quintessenz seiner Behauptung (dass nämlich Schönheit dem Denken überlegen sei) oder deren Umkehrbarkeit (Denken definiert sich ja gewöhnlich als etwas, was der Schönheit widerstehen kann).[4] Ausserdem blockiert die Schönheit das Denken sicher nicht in Kunstwerken, die ja aus dem Denken entstehen und uns eben gerade zu Fragen im Zusammenhang mit dieser Schönheit veranlassen. Die Antwort lautet: Sie ist da, damit wir nicht mit den üblichen Gedanken beginnen müssen. DELPHINE stellt die Natur in einen glanzvollen Rahmen, damit die Delphine dank Film und Video (sozusagen) eine natürliche Präsenz erhalten, nicht als Objekte im Meer irgendeines (egal wie gut gemeinten) Diskurses, sondern als Subjekte, die mit der Kamera Kontakt aufnehmen konnten.

(Übersetzung: Irene Aeberli)

1) James Hall, *Dictionary of Subjects and Symbols in Art*, Harper & Row, New York 1979, S. 105–106.
2) Diana Thater in einem E-Mail an den Autor, 29.7.2000.
3) *Diana Thater, Delphine*, Wiener Secession, Wien 2000, S. 7.
4) Ebenda, S. 13. Vgl. dazu auch: Jeremy Gilbert-Rolfe, *Beauty and the Contemporary Sublime*, Allworth Press, New York 2000.

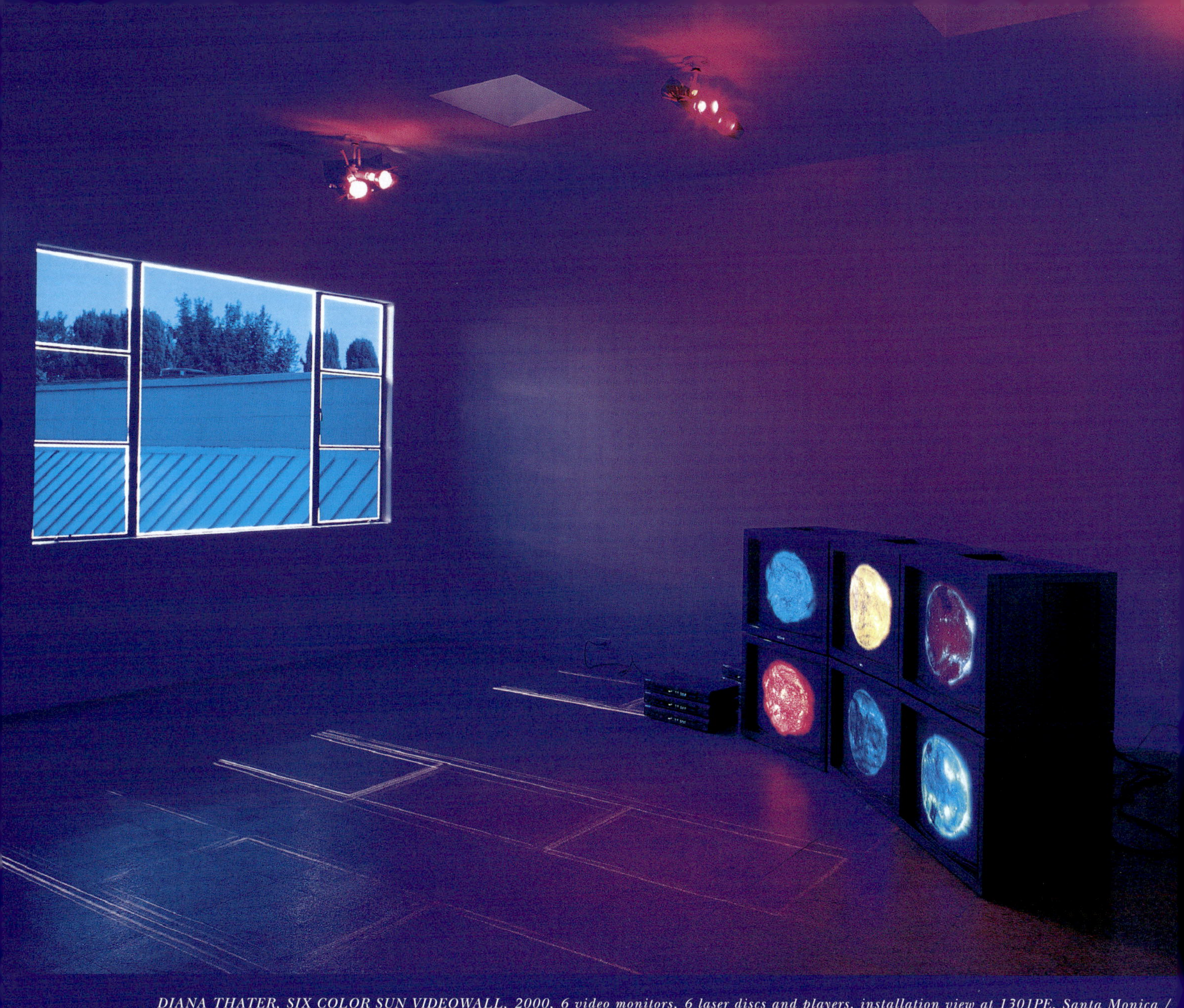

DIANA THATER, SIX COLOR SUN VIDEOWALL, 2000, 6 video monitors, 6 laser discs and players, installation view at 1301PE, Santa Monica / SECHSFARBIGE SONNENVIDEOWAND, 6 Videomonitoren, 6 Laserdiscs und Abspielgeräte.

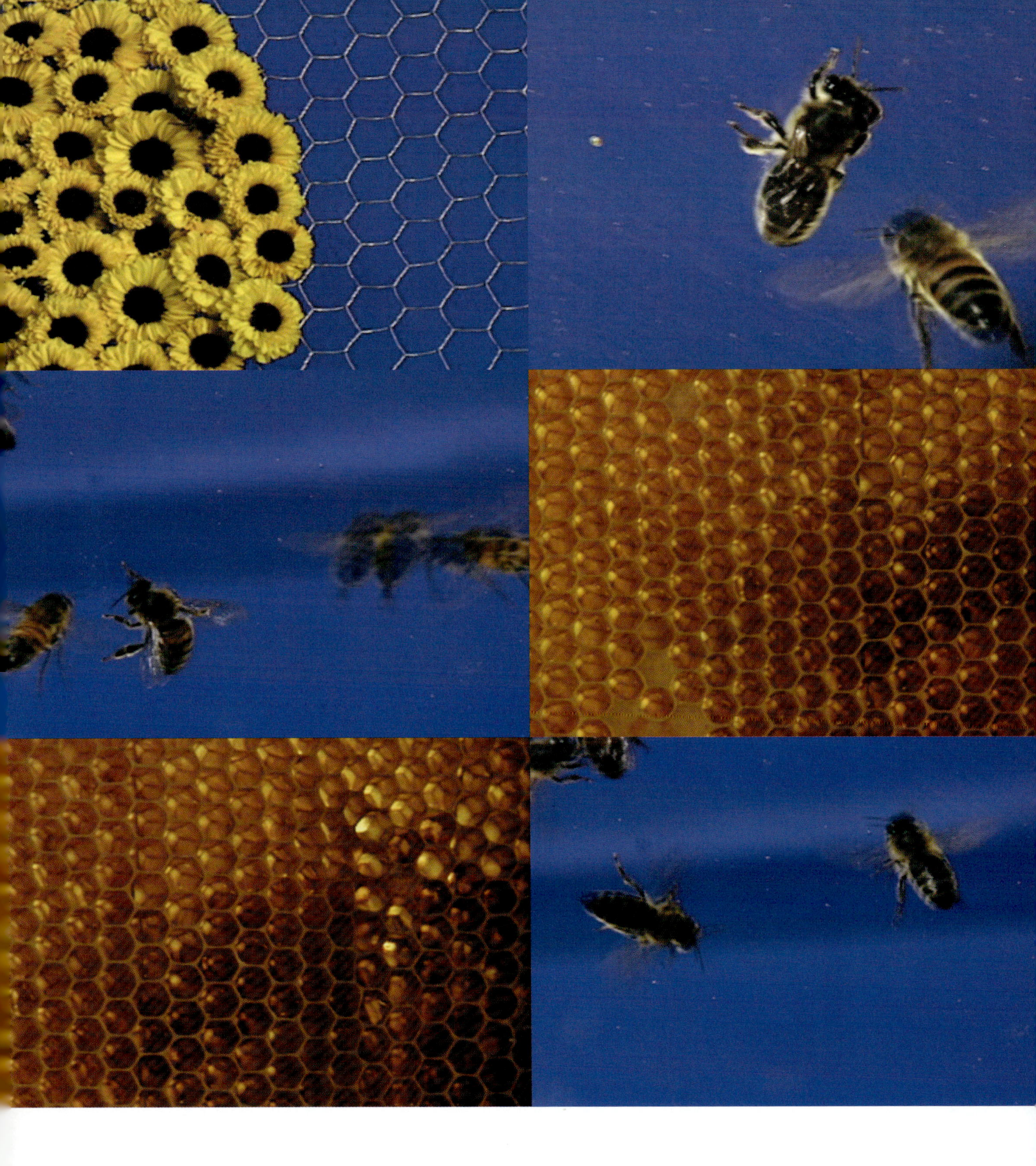

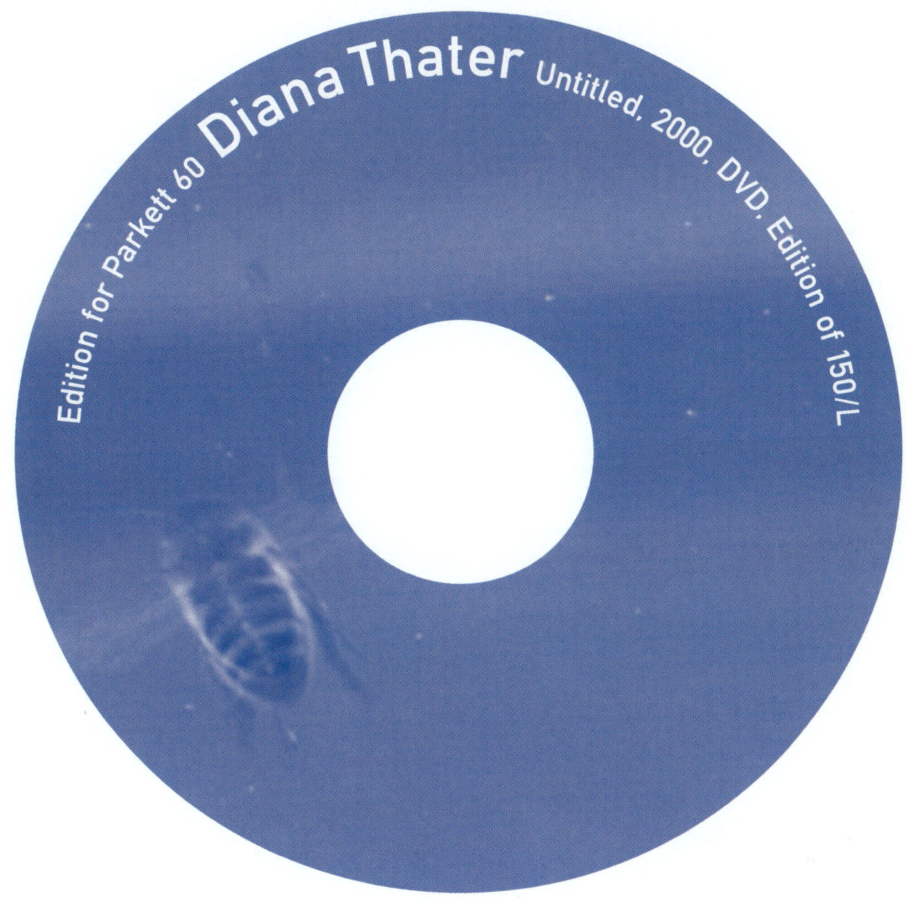

Edition for Parkett   DIANA THATER

Untitled, 2000
DVD (Digital Video Disc) with endless loop.
Edition of 150, signed and numbered.

Ohne Titel, 2000
DVD (Digital Video Disc), Endlos-Schlaufe.
Auflage: 150, signiert und nummeriert.

Luc Tuymans

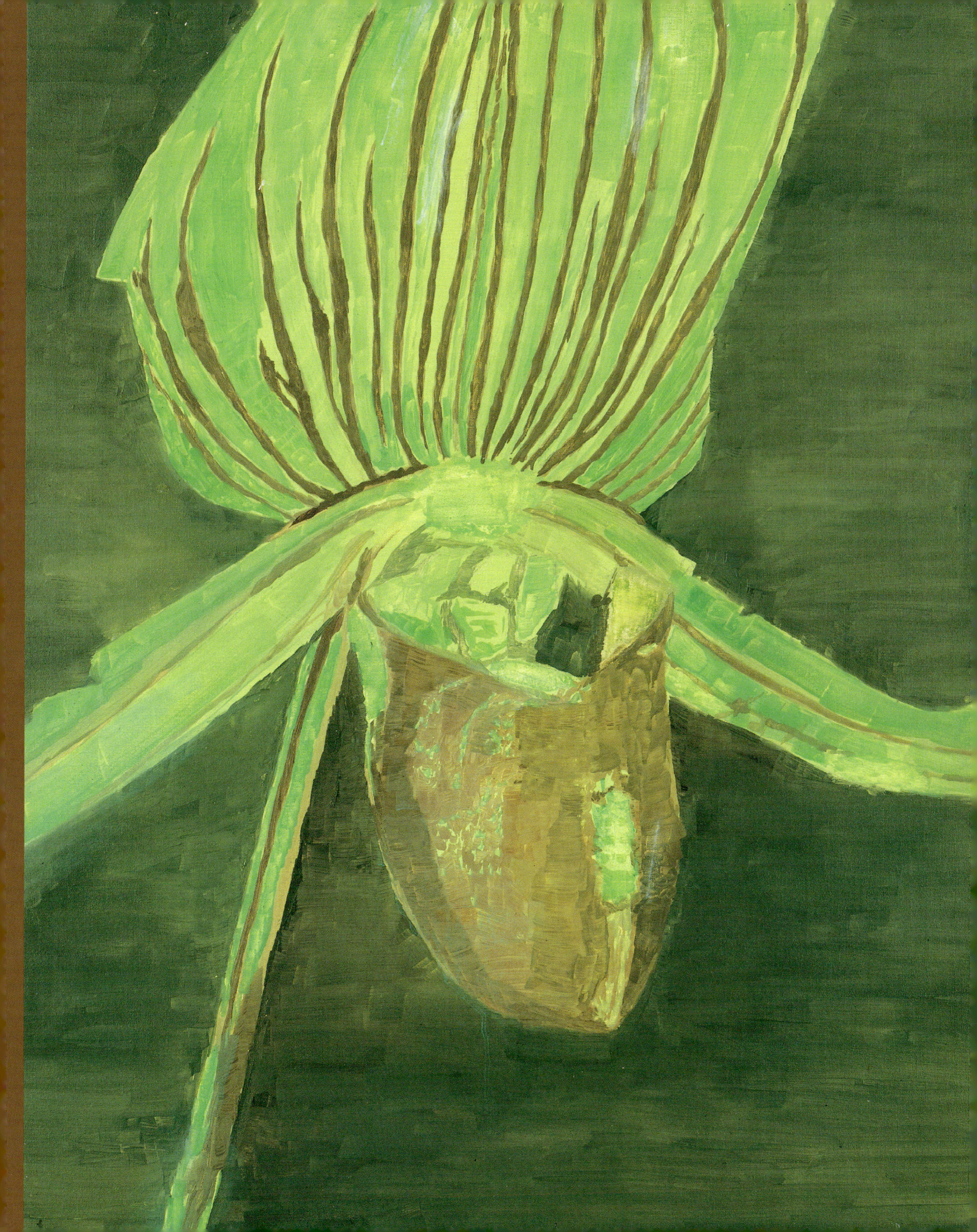

LAURA HOPTMAN

Ich bleibe… Als Bildchen, als Bildchen in eurer Pupille! [1]

Mirrorman

For almost every painting that Luc Tuymans has produced, a work on paper exists. Executed on old, irregular scraps with pen or pencil but more often with watercolor and gouache, these works follow the motifs of the paintings closely, but in extreme miniature. Because of this, it is commonly observed that the drawings are preparatory for his canvases.[2] This is no doubt true, but doesn't tell the entire story of the significance of the drawings themselves to the artist's entire project, nor of the connection between the drawn and the painted works. In addition to being, in Tuymans' words, a "basic plan" for a painting, each individual drawing is also a "picture in itself."[3] Like clues in a crime story, the drawings accrue to describe the artist's quietly terrifying narratives.

The Investigation

The classic detective story has two basic elements: the act of violence (usually murder), and the act of investigation.[4] The former is embodied by the corpse, the catalytic first piece of evidence and the distillation of the entire mystery. The latter is embodied by the detective, whose job it is to seek out the fragments of evidence and arrange them to create the story for which the corpse is the fitting conclusion. Tuymans' oeuvre is filled with allusive titles like PREMONITION, INTO THE NIGHT, and MISSING PERSON and a large percentage of his imagery—the barest outlines of shadows, fragments of figures isolated like amputated limbs, and faces bleached as if by the white beam of a police searchlight—could have been drawn from vintage examples of film noir. But Tuymans' work relates to detective fiction on a much deeper level. With his drawing project as a whole, Tuymans does not simply borrow the genre's imagery, but mimics the very elements of its structure.

For Tuymans, drawing is an exercise in information gathering, narratives constructed in the accumulation of images that reveal their meanings over time. Tuymans draws both from memory and directly from a motif (which in many cases is a photograph or

LAURA HOPTMAN is a curator of contemporary drawing at the Museum of Modern Art in New York.

film still),[5] and like the irrevocable fact of a corpse, once put down, "no correction is possible" to his images.[6] They remain untampered with even as they are translated into paint. A comparison between drawings and paintings of the same subject reveal only the most minute differences.

Once gathered, these images seem hermetically sealed from reality; hanging mute and unmoving in their airless environment, they are atemporal. In this, they set themselves apart from one of the givens of modern drawing. Numbered like exhibits in a crime lab, the tiny arms and hands in the drawing REPARATIONS (1989) float on the brown envelope that is their support, like specimens in formaldehyde.[7] Works like these do not reveal the thinking process of the artist as he crafts his composition. They are not about the act of seeing, but rather about "the limits of what is seen." Each drawing is a single, "dreadful fact" that in itself cannot reveal the entire story, but nonetheless embodies it, not a metaphor but a metonym; a piece of evidence that stands for (and leads to) the construction of the whole. [8]

Tuymans' strategy of presenting evidence varies. In the ongoing series entitled *The Heritage*, he juxtaposes cleanly rendered facsimiles of seemingly unrelated images: a bucket, a flag, two profiles with billed caps. Like a fingerprint, a lost glove or a body, the significance of each image is obscure until they are woven together by the investigator's hand. Gathered together, *The Heritage* drawings form a lexicon of nationalist symbols from which a story of mass pathology, intolerance, and violence can be inferred.

Although Tuymans has claimed that drawing "constitutes a different system of values," one that privileges reading over mere viewing,[9] many of his images oscillate between figuration and formlessness. Abstraction often cloaks an image, whose identity is revealed only by the title. Thus, the five brown squares set in perspective are revealed to be the maws of a gas chamber (GAS CHAMBER, 1986) and the two white disks sitting plumply on a gray background are two spinach tablets, examples of Nazi bio-engineering (DIE ZEIT 3/4, 1988). Abstraction serves Tuymans' purposes in two ways: first as a kind of code meant to shroud meaning, and secondly, and perhaps more importantly, as a method to separate the viewer and the object. Similar to the device of size, abstraction is used to achieve anonymity, the cold, dispassionate distance (what the artist has termed the "vacuum") that is the signature of all his works, even those with the most emotional content. Like a hero of Raymond Chandler or Dashiell Hammett, Tuymans goes about the collection of evidence coolly with the least emotional fuss, as if this mission to report on the unspeakable was just a job for a hardboiled gumshoe.

The Crime

Tuymans has called his transcription of drawings into paintings a practice in "authentic forgery,"[10] claiming that he hit upon this term after an ephiphanic experience as a young artist in which he realized that his first masterpiece shared too many affinities with the work of James Ensor. By acknowledging the impossibility of originality and the triumph of simulation, the notion of authentic forgery has inextricably linked Tuymans' work to a generation of conceptual artists that condemned painting to death by mockery for the double crime of hubris and obsolescence. As the critic Ulrich Loock has commented, "In Tuymans' work, a work of reproduction, the failure of painterly representation is overlaid with the acknowledgement of guilt—the fatal representation—in the disaster that the representation is incapable of picturing."[11] For what is he guilty? The idea of the "authentic forgery" can also be understood as an explanation for exactly the opposite impulse—the successful capture of the representational image. In the same interview in which he confesses to the crime of copying, Tuymans also declared, "Before I paint, the image already exists."[12] Given that in his practice the drawing of an image invariably precedes its painting, by this he means that the image already exists in the world even before the drawings, in a photo-

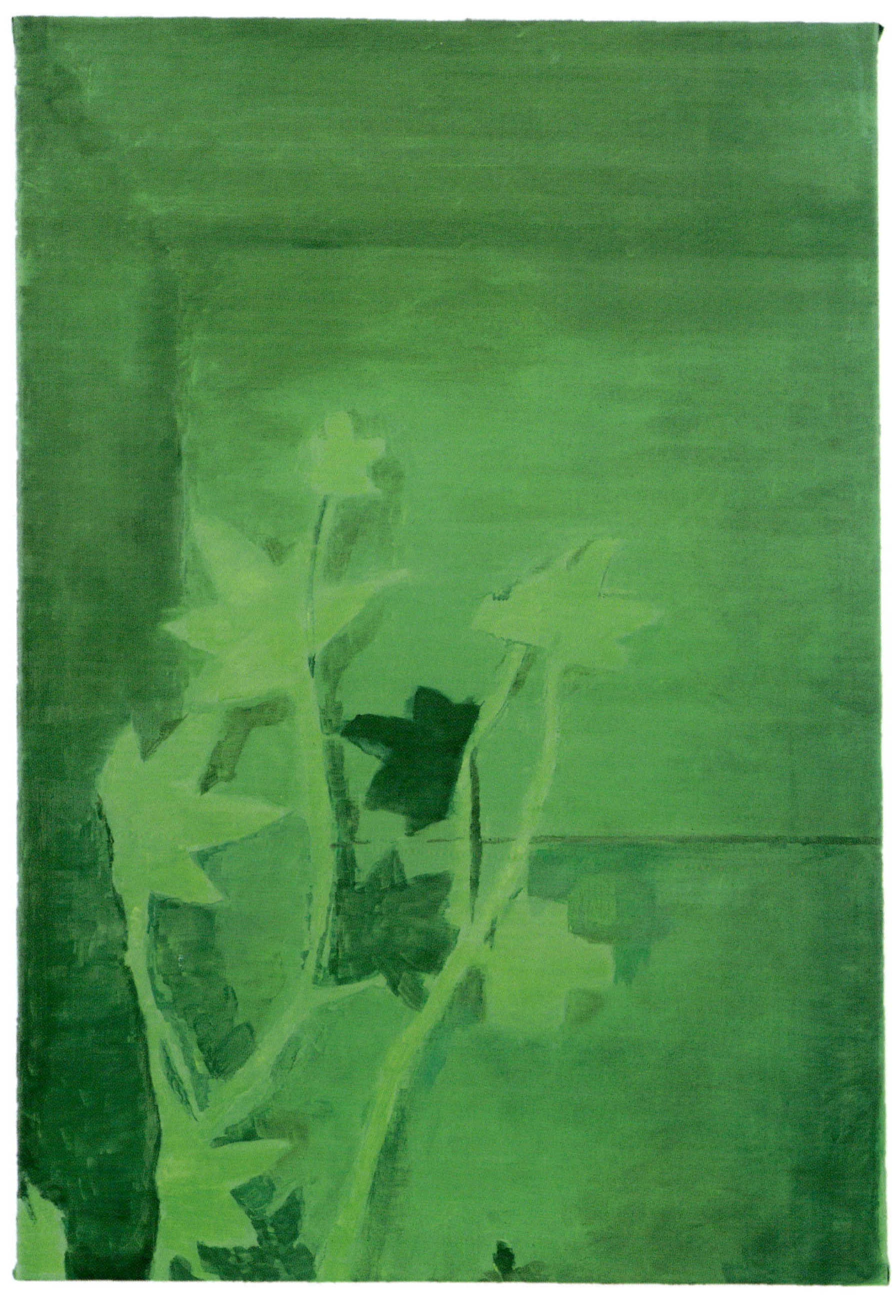

LUC TUYMANS, ILLEGITIMATE II, 1997, oil on canvas, 44$\frac{1}{2}$ x 30$\frac{1}{2}$" /
ILLEGITIM II, Öl auf Leinwand, 113,0 x 77,5 cm.
(PHOTO: FELIX TIRRY)

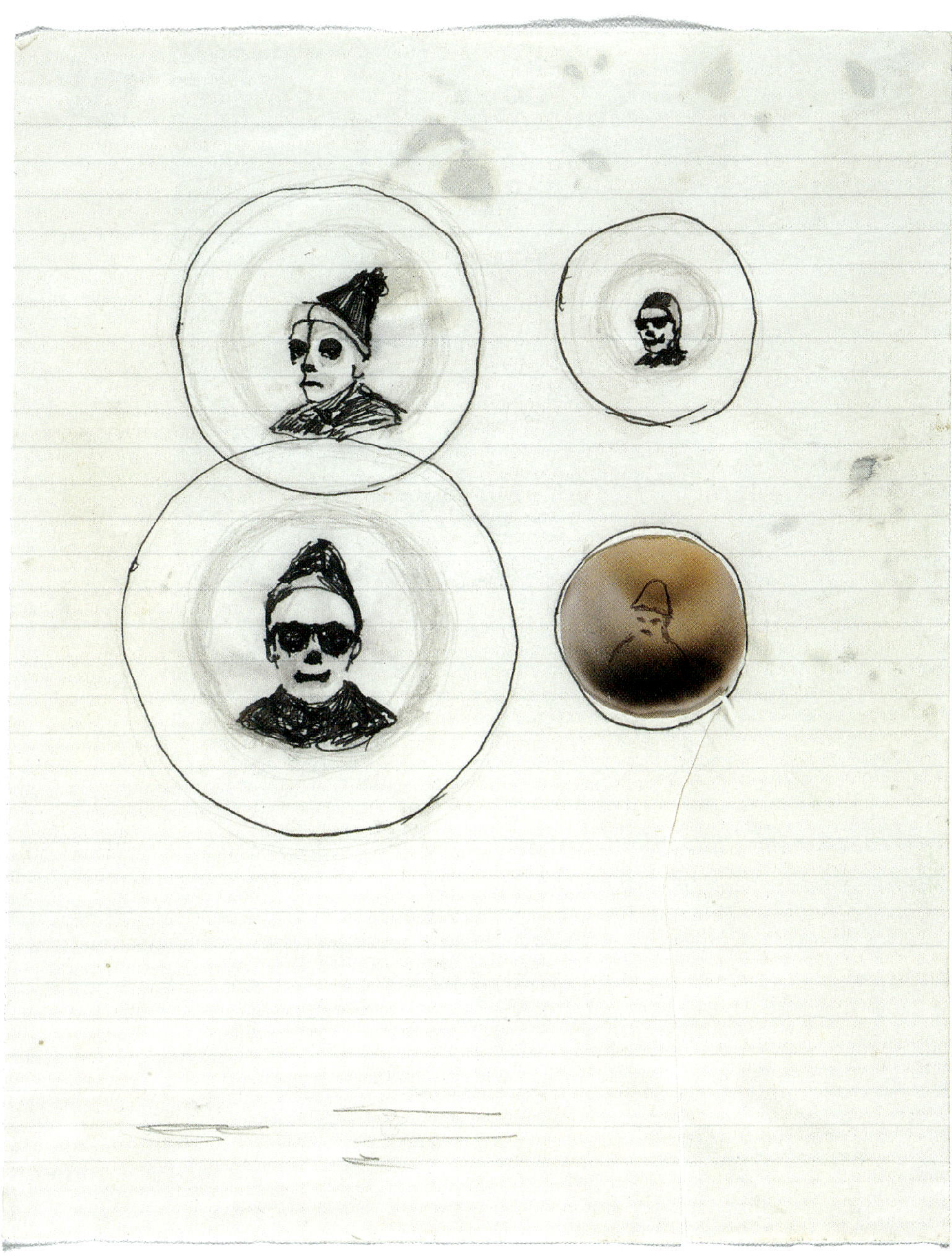

LUC TUYMANS, PREMONITION, 1994, collage, pencil and ink on lined paper on cardboard, 10⅝ x 8¼" / VORAHNUNG, Collage, Bleistift und Tinte auf liniertem Papier auf Karton, 27 x 21 cm. (PHOTO: PETER LAURI, BERN)

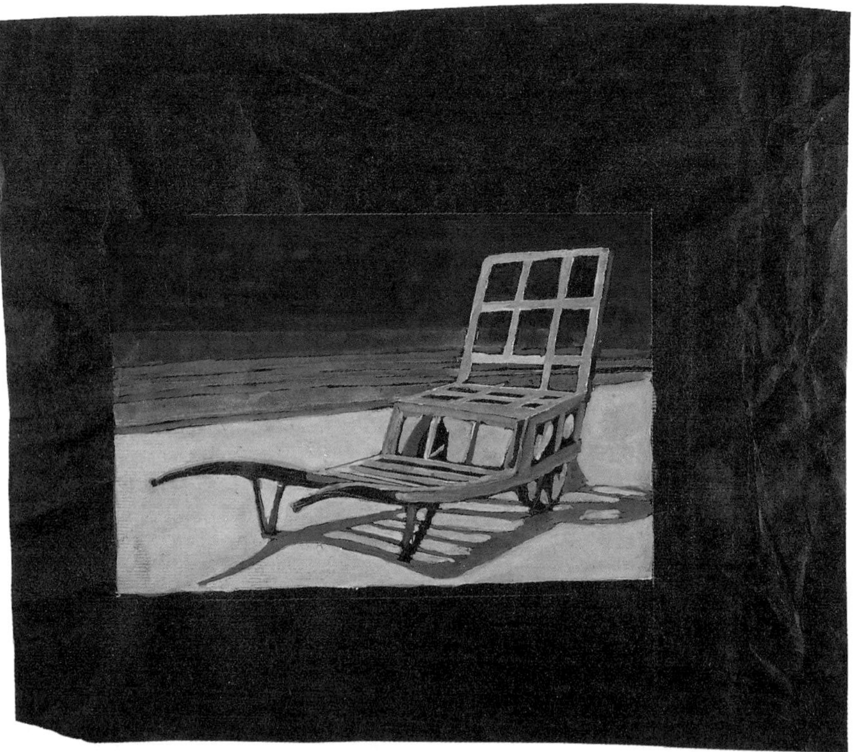

graph, or in observable reality. The drawings then, we are led to believe, are the first—the a u t h e n t i c attempt to perpetrate the forgery, that is the capture of reality.

This discussion of the primacy of drawings in terms of what Jean Baudrillard so long ago called "the precession of the simulacra" hints at another possibility; that the subject of Tuymans' paintings are the drawings they copy, that in every translation from drawing to painting, Tuymans attempts to "reconstruct the moment of drawing," the simultaneous moment of seeing and recording, as if the body were the lens of a camera. This hypothesis seems to be born out by the visual evidence of a painting like THE FLAG (1995), which is dominated by the motif of the Flemish flag painted in delicate grisaille. The only other marks on the picture are two curious, thickly painted black lines that form an L-shape in the left-hand corner of the painting. Following the vertical

and horizontal edge of the canvas, these lines seem to demarcate what one can read as the edge of a page. THE FLAG drawing from the same year does not include these lines. Rather, the motif of the Flemish flag is surrounded on three sides by a black border. Set slightly in perspective, it allows us to read the entire image, in depth, as a canvas on which a flag has been painted.

Forgery may be a crime, but is it serious enough to merit a mystery story, which according to the conventions of the genre needs a murder to justify it? If the paintings depict the drawings and the drawings are portraits of (albeit future) paintings, what has been done away with, through some clever sleight of hand, is the engendering image, the flag that once existed or does exist. The confession of forgery, then, is clearly a diversionary tactic, a red herring thrown out to cover the real crime of murdering the real.

The Culprit

The essence of a detective novel is good pitted against evil, innocence against guilt. These qualities are most often respectively embodied in the characters of the investigator—the good guy—and the perpetrator—the evil one. As the gatherer of evidence, the artist must naturally be compared with the investigator, but in some drawings—the snapshot details of MISSING PERSON (1993),[13] the peephole views of PREMONITION (1994)—the vantage point is less that of the investigator than of the perpetrator. Like Smurov, the anti-hero in Vladimir Nabokov's *The Eye*, who for an entire novel observes himself in the third person, Tuymans seems to be reporting on his own crimes. He stops short of a confession. In his rare self-portrait, Tuymans has obscured his identity, drawing himself from the knees down or dissolving the features of his face as if in a watery reflection. The artist even turns the mirror, a symbol of self-seeing, into one that connotes obscurity, an image lost or hidden.[14] Many of Tuymans' mirrors present empty landscapes or opaque pictures of surfaces that, like the drawings and paintings, reflect nothing but the state of reflection.

After unsuccessfully attempting to extinguish himself by suicide, Smurov notes happily that in the act of self-observation, he has actually managed to make his real self disappear. "I do not exist," Smurov concludes. "There exist but the thousands of mirrors that reflect me." Like Smurov, the identity of the culprit—Tuymans—can only be reflected in the myriad works of evidence that have been so carefully created, gathered, and arranged.

In one drawing, a mirror does reflect a figure. In an untitled diptych from 1990, three images are arranged on two yellowed, pocket-notebook pages each no more than four inches high. One page is mounted above the other like film stills. On the bottom page, a sharp-featured fellow is seen in profile. Wearing a trademark trench coat and fedora, made familiar by characters from Sam Spade to Dick Tracy, he could only be a private investigator. Behind and to the right of this figure surrounded by a rectangle that could be read as a doorway, a coffin—or a canvas, is a second figure, gaunt in outline, generic in feature and quickly drawn. He is the victim, the body that represents the act of violence that has already occurred, that has set the action in motion. On the sheet above, a third figure, faceless, is seen in cameo as if reflected in an oval mirror. This lurking image, one would assume, is the last indispensable element to the crime story, the culprit. Wearing a fedora that mimics the investigator, blank featured like the corpse, the reflection in the mirror is doubtlessly the artist himself, caught in the act of gathering evidence, caught in the act of murdering or being murdered. Caught, finally, in the act of drawing.

---

1) "I stay... as a little image, as a little image in your pupil." From Franz Werfel's play *Spiegelmensch (Mirrorman)*.

2) Tuymans has said that drawing used to be more autonomous and more recently is preparatory and exploratory. See for example Josef Helfenstein, "The drawing, raw material and basic plan of the work: An Interview with Luc Tuymans," in: *Premonition. Luc Tuymans' Zeichnungen* (Bern: Kunstmuseum, 1997), p. 35.

3) Ibid., p. 36.

4) David Lehman, *The Perfect Murder: A Study in Detection*, (Ann Arbor: The University of Michigan Press, 2000), p. xx. [sic!]

5) Tuymans interviewed by Helfenstein, op. cit., p. 36.

6) Ibid., p. 38.

7) "Every drawing or work of mine should create the effect of a vacuum," Tuymans has commented to Helfenstein, ibid., p. 55.

8) Ibid., pp. 15, 37, and 52.

9) Ibid., pp. 46–47.

10) Ibid., p. 47. On the experience that engendered the term, see the interview by Juan Vicente Aliaga, in: *Luc Tuymans* (London: Phaidon Press, 1996), p. 8.

11) Ulrich Loock, "On Layers of Sign-Relations in the Light of Mechanically Reproduced Pictures from Ten Years of Exhibitions," in: *Luc Tuymans* (London: Phaidon Press, 1996), p. 51.

12) Aliaga, interview with Luc Tuymans, in: op. cit., p. 12.

13) For who but the kidnapper would know the whereabouts of the figure that is pictured?

14) Loock, op. cit., p. 79.

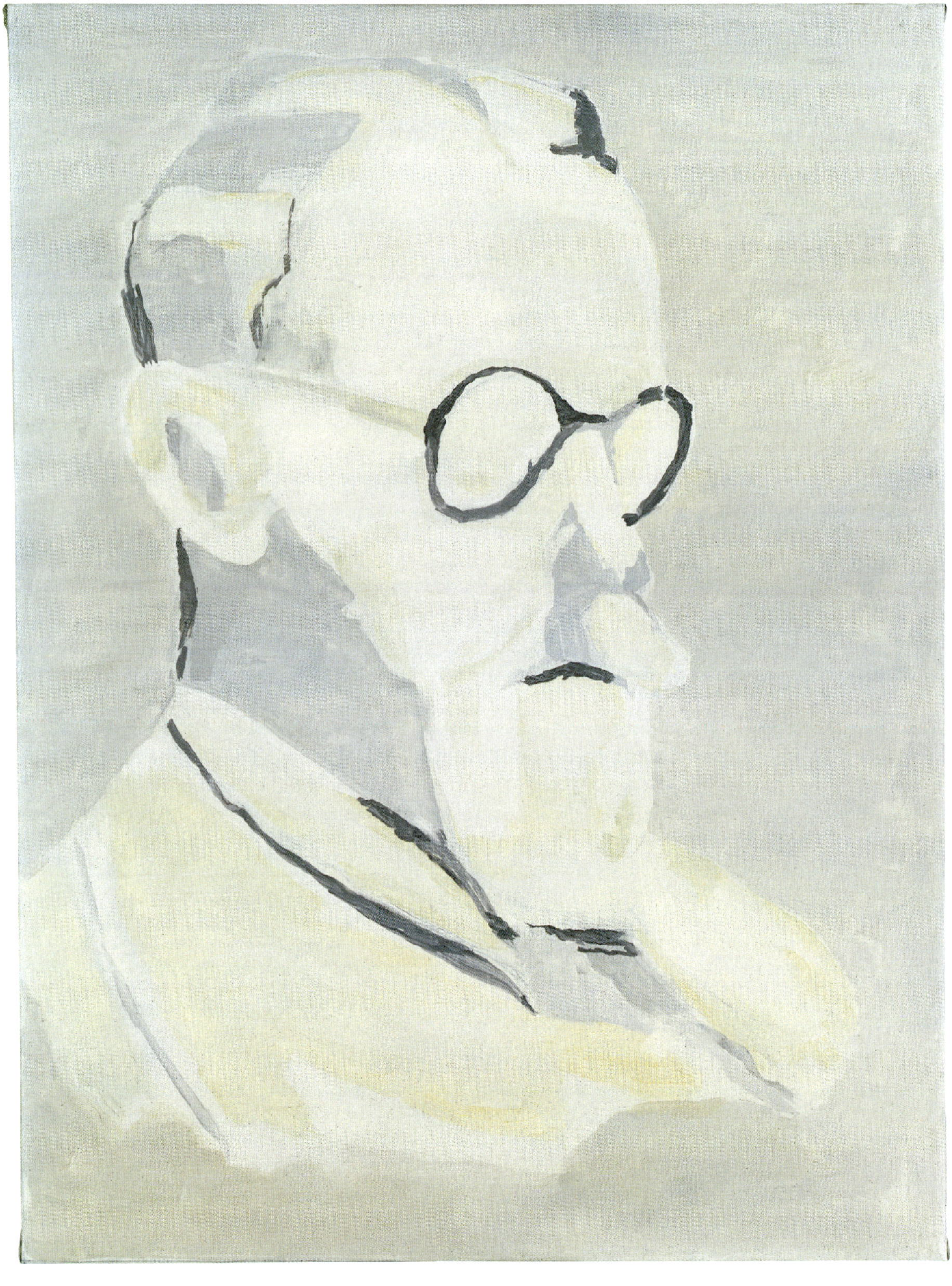

LUC TUYMANS, A FLEMISH INTELLECTUAL, 1995, oil on canvas, $35^{1}/_{4}$ x $25^{13}/_{16}$ " / EIN FLÄMISCHER INTELLEKTUELLER, Öl auf Leinwand, 89,5 x 65,5 cm. (PHOTO: FELIX TIRRY)

Ich bleibe… Als Bildchen, als Bildchen in eurer Pupille! [1]

Spiegelmensch

LAURA HOPTMAN

Zu beinah jedem Bild, das Luc Tuymans gemalt hat, gibt es eine Version auf Papier. Ausgeführt mit Tinten- oder Farbstift, meist aber mit Wasserfarbe und Gouache auf einem alten, schäbigen Blatt Papier, geben diese Arbeiten, wenn auch in extremer Verkleinerung, das jeweilige Bildmotiv sehr genau wieder. Deshalb sagt man allgemein, dass seine Zeichnungen der Vorbereitung der Bilder dienten. [2] Dies trifft zweifellos zu, enthüllt aber nicht die ganze Wahrheit über die Bedeutung der Zeichnungen für das Werk dieses Künstlers und auch nicht über die Verbindung zwischen seinem zeichnerischen und malerischen Werk. Laut Tuymans' eigenen Worten ist jede Zeichnung nicht nur «Vorzeichnung» für ein Bild, sondern ein «Grundriss» des jeweiligen Bildes. [3] Wie Indizien in einem Kriminalroman verraten uns die Zeichnungen schliesslich die wohl leisen, aber nicht minder schrecklichen Themen dieses Künstlers.

Die Untersuchung

Zu einer klassischen Detektivgeschichte gehören zwei Grundelemente: das Gewaltverbrechen (gewöhnlich ein Mord) und die Untersuchung des Verbrechens. [4] Ersteres wird durch die Leiche verkörpert, das alles in Gang setzende erste Beweismittel, das quasi die Lösung des ganzen kriminalistischen Rätsels in sich birgt. Letzteres, die Untersuchung, verkörpert der Detektiv, dessen Aufgabe es ist, Beweisstücke zu sammeln und so aneinander zu fügen, dass sich die Geschichte ergibt, die logisch mit dieser Leiche enden musste. Tuymans' Werk ist voll mit anspielungsreichen Titeln wie PREMONITION (Vorahnung), INTO THE NIGHT (In die Nacht) und MISSING PERSON (Vermisste Person), und viele seiner Bildelemente – kaum noch wahrnehmbare schattenhafte Umrisse, isolierte Fragmente von Gestalten, die wie amputierte Glieder wirken, und Gesichter, die so bleich aussehen, als stünden sie im grellen Suchstrahl eines Polizeischeinwerfers – könnten auch aus alten Kriminalfilmen stammen. Aber die Beziehung zum Kriminalroman ist wesentlich tiefer. In seinem gesamten zeichnerischen Werk verwendet Tuymans nicht nur die Bildsprache dieses Genres, sondern übernimmt auch seine spezifischen Strukturelemente.

Für Tuymans ist Zeichnen eine Übung im Sammeln von Informationen; Sinnzusammenhänge entstehen durch Bildergruppen, die ihre Bedeutung erst im Lauf der Zeit preisgeben. Tuymans zeichnet sowohl aus dem Gedächtnis als auch direkt vor dem Motiv (oft eine Photographie oder eine Standaufnahme aus einem Film). [5] Und so unwiderruflich wie der Leichenfund ist auch die Zeichnung, sobald sie auf Papier vorliegt, denn «es ist unmöglich, zu korri-

LAURA HOPTMAN ist Kuratorin für die zeitgenössische Zeichnung am Museum of Modern Art in New York.

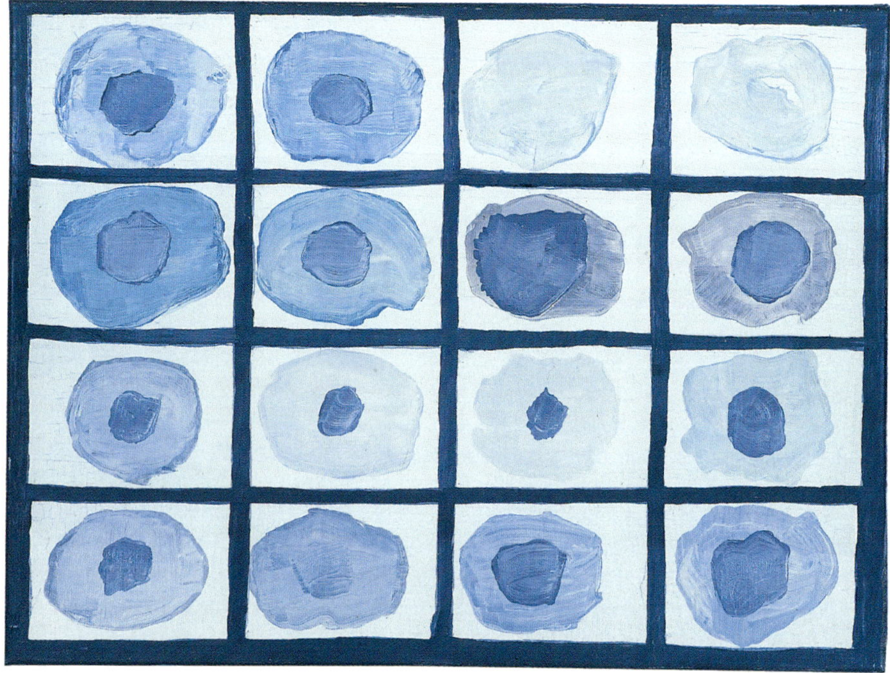

gieren».[6] Sie bleibt unangetastet, selbst bei der Umsetzung in Farbe. Beim Vergleich zwischen Zeichnung und gemaltem Bild desselben Gegenstandes zeigen sich nur minimale Unterschiede.

Sind sie erst einmal zustande gekommen, erscheinen diese Bilder wie von der Realität hermetisch abgeriegelt; still und stumm hängen sie in ihrer luftleeren Umgebung, der Zeit enthoben. In diesem Punkt unterscheiden sie sich grundsätzlich von anderen modernen Zeichnungen. Nummeriert wie Fundstücke im Laboratorium der Kriminalpolizei schwimmen die winzigen Arme und Hände in REPARATIONS (Wiedergutmachungen, 1989) auf dem braunen Briefumschlag wie in Formaldehyd eingelegte Musterexemplare.[7] Arbeiten wie diese verraten nichts vom Denkprozess des Künstlers während

der Arbeit. Es geht darin nicht um den Akt des Sehens, sondern eher um «die Grenzen des Sichtbaren». Jede Zeichnung ist eine einmalige «schreckliche Tatsache», die die ganze Geschichte allein nicht zu erschliessen vermag, diese aber trotzdem verkörpert. Sie ist nicht Metapher, sondern Metonymie – eine Spur, die für die Konstruktion des Ganzen steht und zu dieser führt.[8]

Tuymans' Methode der Präsentation von Hinweisen ist nicht immer gleich. In der noch nicht abgeschlossenen Serie *The Heritage* (Das Erbe) stellt er saubere Faksimilewiedergaben von Bildern nebeneinander, die scheinbar nichts miteinander zu tun haben: ein Kessel, eine Fahne, zwei Profile mit Schirmmützen. Wie bei einem Fingerabdruck, einem verlorenen Handschuh oder einer Leiche bleibt die

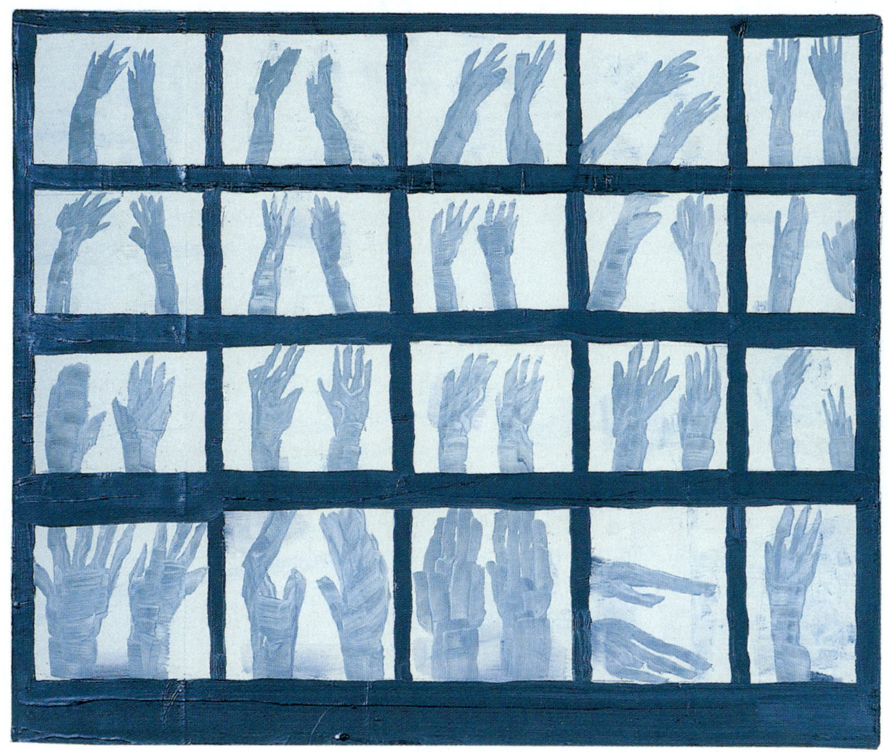

LUC TUYMANS, THE REPARATION (2/2), 1989,
oil on canvas, 15 x 17¾ /
DIE WIEDERGUTMACHUNG (2/2), Öl auf Leinwand, 38 x 45 cm.
(PHOTOS: RONALD STOOPS)

Bedeutung jedes Bildes unklar, bis es dem Ermittler gelingt, einen Zusammenhang herzustellen. Als Ganzes betrachtet ergeben die Zeichnungen aus *The Heritage* ein Lexikon nationalistischer Symbole, das auf eine Geschichte der Massenhysterie, Intoleranz und Gewalt schliessen lässt.

Auch wenn Tuymans behauptet, dass die Zeichnung «ein anderes Wertsystem» darstellt, in dem das Lesen über dem blossen Schauen steht,[9] schillern viele seiner Bilder zwischen Figürlichkeit und Gestaltlosigkeit. Oft ist ein Bild durch Abstraktion getarnt und erst der Titel verrät, worum es sich handelt. So erweisen sich die fünf braunen, perspektivisch angeordneten Quadrate als Schlünde einer Gaskammer (GASKAMMER, 1986) und die zwei weissen Scheiben auf grauem Hintergrund sind Spinat-

Tabletten, Beispiele nazistischen Bio-Engineerings (DIE ZEIT 3/4, 1988). Die Abstraktion dient Tuymans in zweifacher Hinsicht: erstens als eine Art Verschlüsselungscode und zweitens – wohl wichtiger – als Mittel zur Trennung von Betrachter und Objekt. Ähnlich wie die Grösse dient auch die Abstraktion dazu, eine gewisse Anonymität herzustellen, die kalte, leidenschaftslose Distanz (der Künstler umschreibt das mit «Vakuum»), die alle seine Werke kennzeichnet, selbst jene mit höchst emotionalem Gehalt. Wie ein Held von Raymond Chandler oder Dashiell Hammett macht sich Tuymans cool und ohne Gefühlsduselei an seine Bestandesaufnahme, als sei die Aufgabe über das Unaussprechliche zu berichten genau der richtige Auftrag für einen hartgesottenen Schnüffler.

Das Verbrechen

Das Umsetzen seiner Zeichnungen in Malerei hat Tuymans als eine Übung «authentischen Fälschens»[10] bezeichnet, wobei er behauptet, auf diesen Ausdruck als junger Künstler gekommen zu sein, als es ihm wie Schuppen von den Augen fiel, dass sein erstes gelungenes Selbstporträt zu viel Ähnlichkeit mit einem ebensolchen von James Ensor aufwies. Indem dieser Begriff der authentischen Fälschung der Unmöglichkeit von Originalität und dem Triumph der Nachahmung Rechnung trägt, rückt er Tuymans' Werk in die Nähe einer ganzen Generation von Konzeptkünstlern, die die Malerei dem Tod durch Lächerlichkeit preisgaben und sie für ihre Hybris und ihr Überholtsein gleich doppelt verurteilten. Wie Ulrich Loock bemerkte: «In Tuymans' Werk, einem reproduktiven Werk, wird das Scheitern der malerischen Darstellung von einem Schuldgeständnis überlagert – der fatalen Darstellung – inmitten des Verhängnisses, welches keine Darstellung abzubilden vermag.»[11] Aber wessen ist er schuldig? Die Idee der «authentischen Fälschung» lässt sich auch als Erklärung für den genau entgegengesetzten Impuls verstehen: das erfolgreiche Festhalten der bildlichen Darstellung. Im gleichen Interview, in dem er sich des Kopierens für schuldig erklärt, sagte Tuymans auch: «Das Bild existiert schon, bevor ich male.»[12] In Anbetracht der Tatsache, dass bei seiner Arbeitsweise die Zeichnung dem gemalten Bild immer vorausgeht, meint er damit, dass das Bild schon v o r den Zeichnungen existiert, in Form einer Photographie oder als beobachtbare Wirklichkeit. Die Zeichnungen sind also, so müssen wir annehmen, der erste und a u t h e n t i s c h e Schritt zur Fälschung, das heisst zum Festhalten der Wirklichkeit.

Diese Diskussion um den Vorrang der Zeichnungen im Kontext dessen, was Jean Baudrillard vor langer Zeit «das Vorausgehen der Simulakren» nannte, deutet eine weitere Möglichkeit an, dass nämlich der eigentliche Gegenstand von Tuymans' Bildern die Zeichnungen sind, nach denen sie entstehen, und dass Tuymans in jeder Übersetzung von der Zeichnung zum Bild den Moment des Zeichnens zu rekonstruieren versucht, jenen simultanen Moment des Sehens und Festhaltens, als wäre der Körper ein Kameraobjektiv. Diese These scheint von einem Gemälde wie THE FLAG (Die Fahne, 1995) gestützt zu werden; das Bild wird beherrscht von dem in feinster Grisaille-Manier gemalten Motiv der flämischen Fahne. Die einzigen anderen Zeichen auf dem Bild sind in der linken Ecke zwei merkwürdige, dicke schwarze Linien, die ein L bilden. Dem vertikalen und horizontalen Rand des Bildes entlang verlaufend scheinen diese Linien etwas zu bezeichnen, was man als den Rand einer Buchseite interpretieren könnte. In der entsprechenden Zeichnung aus demselben Jahr finden sich diese Linien nicht, sondern das Motiv der flämischen Fahne ist auf drei Seiten durch einen schwarzen Rand begrenzt. Durch die leichte Andeutung einer Perspektive wirkt das ganze Bild dreidimensional wie eine Leinwand, auf der eine Fahne gemalt ist.

Nun mag Fälschung zwar ein Verbrechen sein, aber ist es schwerwiegend genug für einen Kriminalroman, in welchem gewöhnlich mindestens ein Mord vorliegen muss? Wenn die Bilder die Zeichnungen wiedergeben und die Zeichnungen Porträts von (zukünftigen) Bildern sind, wurde durch einen geschickten Handstreich das ursprüngliche Bild beseitigt, die reale Fahne, die einst existierte oder noch existiert. Das Eingeständnis der Fälschung ist also nichts als ein Ablenkungsmanöver, eine falsche Fährte, gelegt, um das wahre Verbrechen zu verbergen: die Ermordung der Realität.

Der Täter

Das Wesen des Kriminalromans ist der Gegensatz von Gut und Böse, von Unschuld und Schuld. Diese Eigenschaften werden meistens von den Gegenspielern des Romans verkörpert, dem (guten) Detektiv

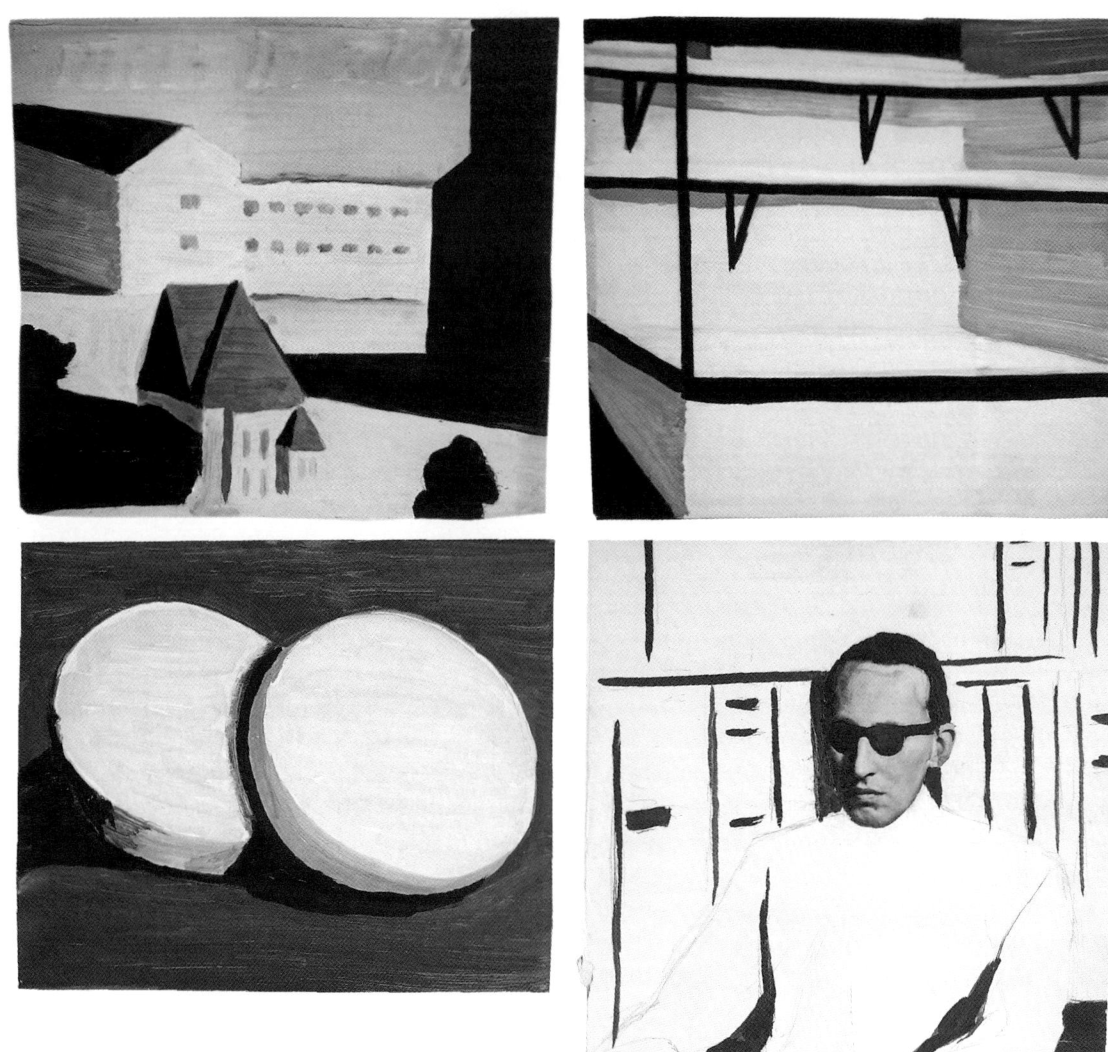

Top / Oben: LUC TUYMANS, TIME (1/4), 1988, oil on cardboard,
11⅞ x 15¾" / DIE ZEIT (1/4), 1988, Öl auf Karton, 30 x 40 cm;
TIME (2/4), 1988, oil on cardboard, 15⅜ x 15¾" / DIE ZEIT (2/4),
Öl auf Leinwand, 39 x 40 cm.
Bottom / Unten: TIME (3/4), 1988, oil on cardboard,
14⁹⁄₁₆ x 15¾" / DIE ZEIT (3/4), Öl auf Karton, 37 x 40 cm;
TIME (4/4), 1988, photo collage and oil on cardboard, 16⅛ x 15¾" /
DIE ZEIT (4/4), Photocollage und Öl auf Karton, 41 x 40 cm.
(PHOTOS: FRANK DEMAEGD / ZENO X GALLERY, ANTWERPEN)

und dem (bösen) Verbrecher. Als derjenige, der auf Spurensuche geht, ist der Künstler natürlich mit dem Detektiv zu vergleichen, aber in einigen Zeichnungen – etwa in den Schnappschussdetails von MISSING PERSON (1993)[13] oder der Schlüssellochperspektive in PREMONITION (1994) – scheint der Blickwinkel eher der des Verbrechers zu sein als jener des Detektivs. Wie Smurow, der Antiheld in Vladimir Nabokovs Roman *Der Späher*, der sich selbst den ganzen Roman hindurch in der dritten Person beobachtet, scheint Tuymans hier über seine eigenen Verbrechen zu berichten. Fehlt nur noch, dass er ein Geständnis ablegt. In seinen raren Selbstporträts verwischt Tuymans seine Identität, indem er sich von den Knien abwärts malt oder seine Gesichtszüge in den Spiegelungen einer Wasseroberfläche auflöst. Der Künstler verkehrt sogar den Spiegel, Symbol der Selbsterkenntnis, zu einem Symbol der Unkenntlichkeit, des verloren gegangenen oder verborgenen Bildes.[14] Viele von Tuymans' Spiegeln zeigen leere Landschaften oder nebelhafte Bilder von Flächen, die wie die Zeichnungen und Bilder nichts reflektieren als den Zustand der Reflexion.

Nachdem er sich erfolglos durch Selbstmord auszulöschen versucht hat, hält Smurow glücklich fest, dass es ihm durch den Akt der Selbstbeobachtung dennoch gelungen ist, sein reales Selbst verschwinden zu lassen: «Denn es gibt mich nicht: Es gibt nur die Tausende von Spiegeln, die mich reflektieren.»[15] Wie im Fall von Smurow spiegelt sich die Identität des Schuldigen – Tuymans – lediglich in den unzähligen Beweisstücken, die er so sorgfältig geschaffen, gesammelt und geordnet hat.

In einer der Zeichnungen reflektiert ein Spiegel eine Gestalt. In einem Diptychon ohne Titel aus dem Jahr 1990 finden sich drei Bilder auf zwei vergilbten Notizbuchseiten, die nicht mehr als zehn Zentimeter hoch sind. Eine Seite ist oberhalb der anderen montiert wie zwei aufeinander folgende Bilder auf einem Filmstreifen. Auf der unteren Seite sieht man einen Typen mit scharfen Gesichtszügen im Profil. Mit dem typischen Regenmantel und breitkrempigen Filzhut, den man von Figuren wie Sam Spade oder Dick Tracy kennt, kann es sich nur um einen Privatdetektiv handeln. Hinter und etwas rechts von dieser Gestalt, umgeben von einem Rechteck, das eine Tür, einen Sarg oder eine Leinwand andeuten könnte, befindet sich eine zweite Gestalt, knapp umrissen, mit unbestimmten Zügen, nur eben mal so hingeworfen. Es ist das Opfer, die Leiche, die für den Gewaltakt steht, der bereits stattgefunden und die Handlung in Gang gesetzt hat. Auf dem Blatt darüber ist eine dritte, gesichtslose Gestalt zu sehen, eine gerahmte Silhouette oder eine Reflexion in einem ovalen Spiegel. Dieses unheimliche Bild, muss man annehmen, ist das dritte unverzichtbare Element des Kriminalromans: der Täter. Das Spiegelbild mit seinem den Detektiv nachäffenden Filzhut und ebenso blassen Gesichtszügen wie das Opfer stellt ohne Zweifel den Künstler selbst dar: ertappt beim Sammeln von Beweisen, ertappt beim Morden oder Umgebrachtwerden. Und schliesslich: ertappt beim Zeichnen.

(Übersetzung: Susanne Schmidt)

1) Franz Werfel, *Spiegelmensch*, Kurt Wolff Verlag, München 1920, S. 189.

2) Tuymans selbst sagt, dass die Zeichnung früher autonomer war und in letzter Zeit mehr der Vorbereitung und Abklärung diene. Vgl. etwa Josef Helfenstein, «Die Zeichnung, Rohmaterial und Grundriss für das Werk: Ein Gespräch mit Luc Tuymans», in: *Premonition. Luc Tuymans' Zeichnungen*, Kunstmuseum Bern, 1997, S. 11.

3) Ebenda, S. 12–13.

4) David Lehman, *The Perfect Murder: A Study in Detection* The University of Michigan Press, Ann Arbor 2000, S. xx. [sic!]

5) Tuymans in: Helfenstein, «Interview», op. cit., S. 12.

6) Ebenda, S. 15.

7) «Jede Zeichnung oder jedes Werk von mir sollte ein Vakuum bewirken», Tuymans gegenüber Helfenstein, ebenda, S. 33.

8) Ebenda, diverse Stellen.

9) Ebenda, S. 23.

10) Ebenda, S. 24. Zum Erlebnis, das ihn auf diesen Ausdruck brachte, vgl. das Interview mit Juan Vicente Aliaga, in: *Luc Tuymans*, Phaidon Press, London 1996, S. 8.

11) Ulrich Loock, «On Layers of Sign-Relations in the Light of Mechanically Reproduced Pictures from Ten Years of Exhibitions», in: *Luc Tuymans*, op. cit., S. 51 (Übers. aus dem Englischen).

12) Aliaga, «Interview», ebenda, S. 12.

13) Denn wer, wenn nicht der Kidnapper, kann wissen, wo die abgebildete Person sich aufhält?

14) Loock, op. cit., S. 79.

15) Vladimir Nabokov, *Der Späher*, übers. v. Dieter E. Zimmer, in: Nabokov, *Gesammelte Werke*, Bd. 2, Rowohlt, Reinbek bei Hamburg 1992, S. 422.

LUC TUYMANS, THE FLAG, 1995, oil on canvas, 54⅜ x 30⅝₁₆" / DIE FAHNE, Öl auf Leinwand, 138 x 77 cm. (PHOTO: FELIX TIRRY)

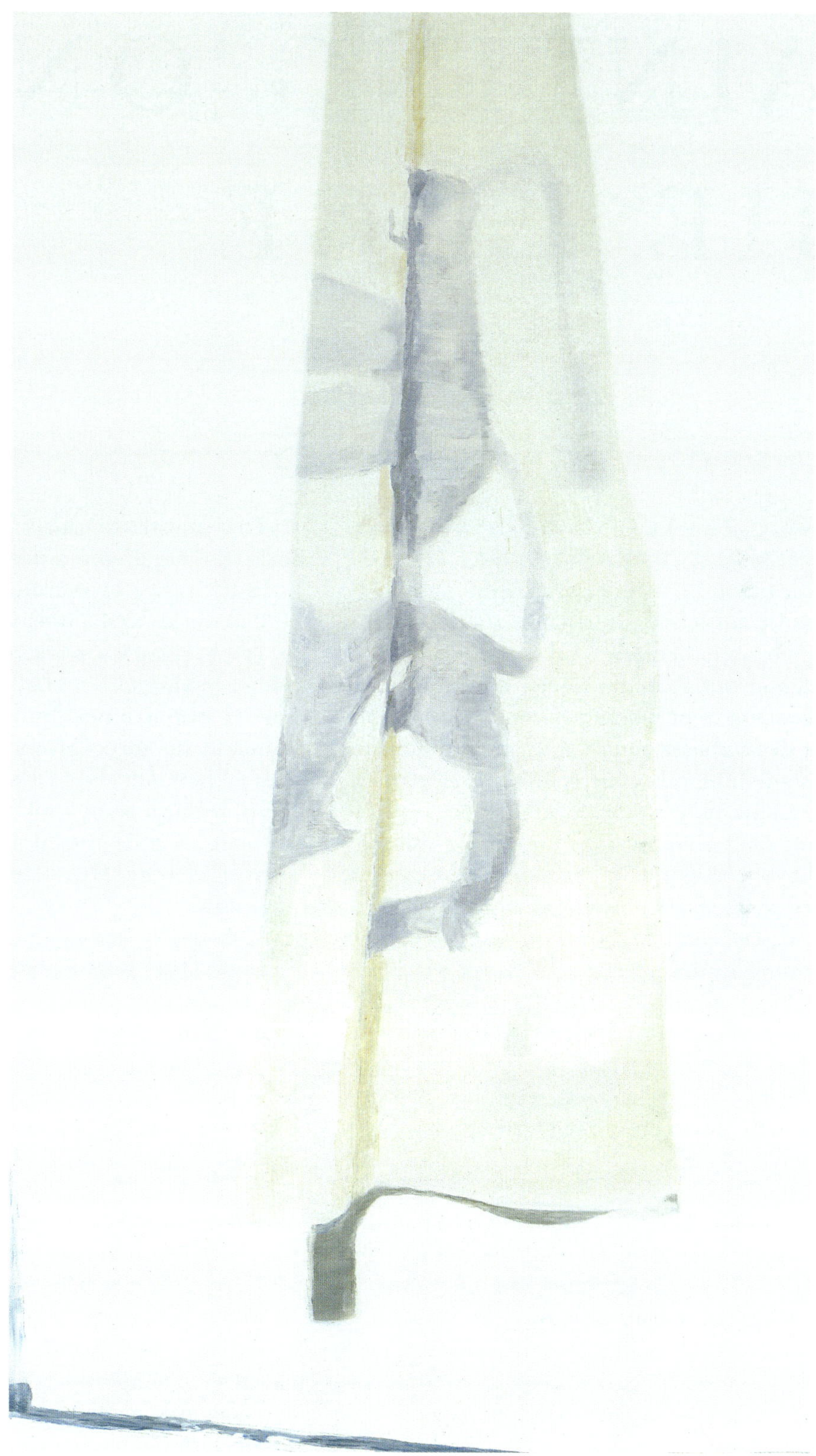

PAINTING ON THE EDGE

GERARDO MOSQUERA

Perhaps what allows Luc Tuymans to have a mainstream career as a "traditional" painter after the crushing criticism of illusionism in painting and its representational tricks is, precisely, that his work acts on the very frontier between representation and non-representation. It's about representing by not representing and not representing by representing. His works are diametrically opposed to abstraction: they describe something very concrete, they even narrate, and they always have a story behind them that the artist is not at all reluctant to tell in words. Although the describable content of the paintings is often clear and direct, there is always a will to blur, to conceal, to de-emphasize, and to use the non-figurative capacity of painting in order, in a certain sense, to hide what has been presented. RESENTMENT (1995) is a predominantly abstract picture, which could be described as the painting of a face because of two psychologically human eyes painted in the style of a portrait. Opposing pictorial techniques and philosophies interact here and make each other opaque even while they collaborate in the construction of evanescent meaning. Standing before GLOBE (1998), a painting of exceptionally large format, I don't know if I see the planet Earth photographed from a satellite, a map in the form of a globe, a ball, or all three at once.

GERARDO MOSQUERA is a freelance art critic and curator who lives in Havana, and Adjunct Curator at the New Museum of Contemporary Art, New York.

This approach usually underscores an intellectual, emotional, and symbolic treatment of themes, as in the series of evocations of solitary pillows (so "full of world" as the poet César Vallejo would say) in PILLOWS (1994), a painting curiously related to the billboard photo UNTITLED (1991) by Felix Gonzalez-Torres. But at times the method constitutes an instrument for direct symbolization as in A FLEMISH INTELLECTUAL (1995), in which the face of a famous Flemish writer all but disappears, revealing Tuymans' deeply critical attitude toward the cult of Flemish identity. THE FLAG (1995) bears similar connotations.

What really matters is not the use of ambiguity, because all art is an exercise in saying by not saying, a transmutation of images and meanings. The salient factor in this oeuvre is rather the establishment of a no-man's-land in painting, a sort of zone of silence from which the pictures speak. Tuymans does not usually generalize when commenting on his art, but refers specifically to concrete works, describing their genesis and the strategies they deploy in form and meaning. His comments bespeak the search for—and fascination with—a dawning zone of images and meaning. One might also speak of twilight painting.

On the other hand, the explicit nature of the painter's commentaries belies the existential and anti-romantic mystery that emanates from his works. As he himself has said with great precision, "The

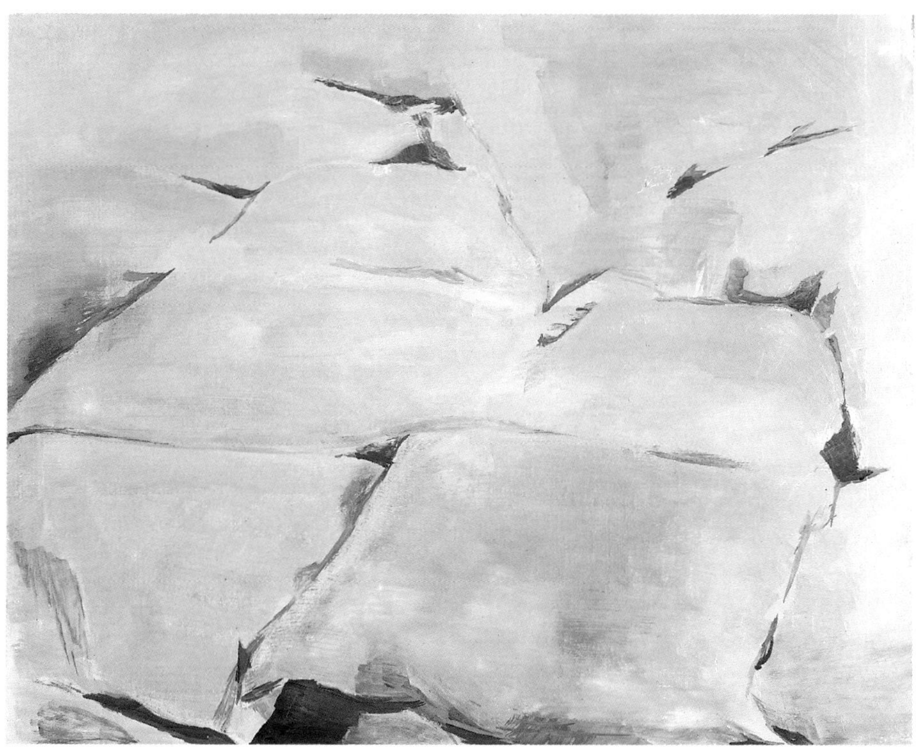

LUC TUYMANS, PILLOWS, 1994, oil on canvas, 21½ x 26⅜" / KISSEN, Öl auf Leinwand, 54,5 x 67 cm. (PHOTO: FELIX TIRRY)

FELIX GONZALEZ-TORRES, UNTITLED, 1991, billboard, installation for The Museum of Modern Art in 24 locations throughout New York City, May – June 1992 / OHNE TITEL, Plakat-Installation an 24 Orten in New York City, Mai – Juni 1992.
(PHOTO: PETER MUSCATO)

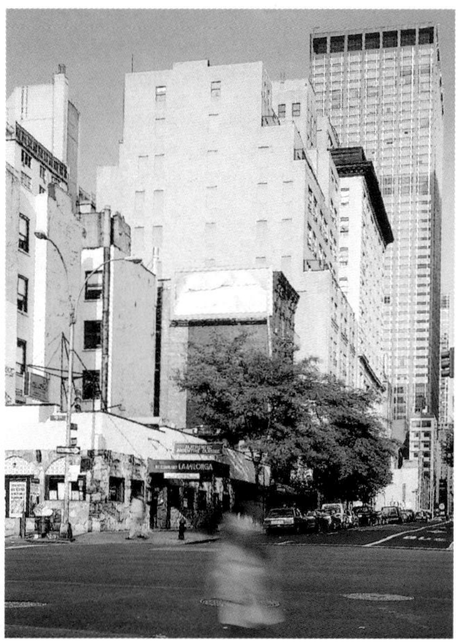

small gap between the explanation of a picture and a picture itself provides the only possible perspective on painting. My comments refer only to its ambiguity."[1]

* * *

Perhaps in no other moment in history has there been as much painting as there is today, and yet painting has never carried less weight in the circuits that legitimize art. Of course, painting commands a much wider commercial spectrum than, for example, a few flies in a glass case. Much of today's pictorial production feeds into "mid-brow" markets and thus into the aesthetic-symbolic potential of painting, into a display of professional craftsmanship, or—as occurs so often in Latin America—into the construction and reproduction of imagined spaces based on the iconographic, symbolic, and narrative functionality of painting. This applies to a sector of production that is more interested in redundancy than in the frequently faux-modernist construction of meaning, and it is fostered by the great difficulty of "saying something new" in such a deeply entrenched tradition, especially after modern experimentation. On the opposite end there exists a "high-brow" public, perhaps conservative with regard to prevailing international tendencies, that continues to view the situation from a decidedly hierarchical standpoint.

Proclaiming the death of painting has long been and in some cases still is an obsession spawned by modern art. And perhaps painting itself is infected with a suicidal hysteria that flirts with death and, as St. John of the Cross puts it "dies because it doesn't die." Not only is there a new frisson toward painting among young artists, but several of today's important artists are, in fact, painters. Some, like Gerhard Richter, are among the most radical. Painting has successfully been projected toward non-canonical developments and toward the invention of new imagery, investing it with a tension that renews its signifying power. Other artists play with the mechanisms of pictorial representation and symbolization, arguing over its social, cultural, and linguistic meanings. The resulting pictures constitute a self-deconstruction of painting. Another line carries the expansion of painting beyond itself, so that it interacts or blends with other artistic forms. But these works are valuable not only because they are self-critical, which would reinforce the condemnation of painting. They are also valuable thanks to painting's representational powers, which make it possible to elaborate new meanings beyond self-deconstruction.

However, Tuymans' paradoxically radical position takes an almost naïve attitude by moving in the opposite direction to the inside of painting itself. He has remained aloof from critical discourse about representation, and with complete spontaneity has proposed a renewed confidence in images. Such a position would seem to condemn him to marginality. His recognition and critical success are, I believe, largely due to his low profile and the personal nature of his work.

* * *

Tuymans does not like to see stereotypes imposed on Belgian art. But the country has produced a number of undeniably strange artists whose work is exceptionally idiosyncratic. There is something I feel to be very Belgian as well in Tuymans' profusion of small pictures, like collectable postcards. Could his painting be a collection of the things of this world, including the world itself transformed into a ball?

* * *

Much has been said about the "belated" nature of Tuymans' painting. As Ulrich Loock puts it, "The past perfect is the tense of his work." The traditionalism of his methods and his complete disinterest in introducing any "original" or novel component into his work have been explained by the fact that the artist rules out the possibility of creating something new. Tuymans' disenchantment may be viewed as "the suicide of authorship," and his entire output as a hypertext that refers to existing representations.

However, he does not appropriate images in the usual, deconstructive terms. Although his work undoubtedly shows a will to analysis and even a criticism of images, the artist also uses the representation of objects, landscapes, and settings to discuss their pathos and their history. The social and historical criticism implicit in such works as OUR NEW QUARTERS (1986), GAS CHAMBER (1986), or *The Heritage* series(1995) does not make them "political art" for they do not propagate; they are not extroverted but rather introverted. This is the key to Tuymans' art: it shows a personal, introspective reaction to his source materials. Be they things or preexisting images, their principal strength lies in the action of his emotions and memories.

Thus, the traditionalism of this painter is even more "serious," because his completely intuitive approach provokes an interiorized, subjective response to the act of making art, which gives shape to all his obsessions, fears, and personal demons. One is reminded more of an artist like van Gogh than of contemporary art.

Of course, it is possible to relate Tuymans to the painting of the eighties, though that painting was not exactly one of silence and personal space as in the work of Tuymans. His oeuvre might be connected to

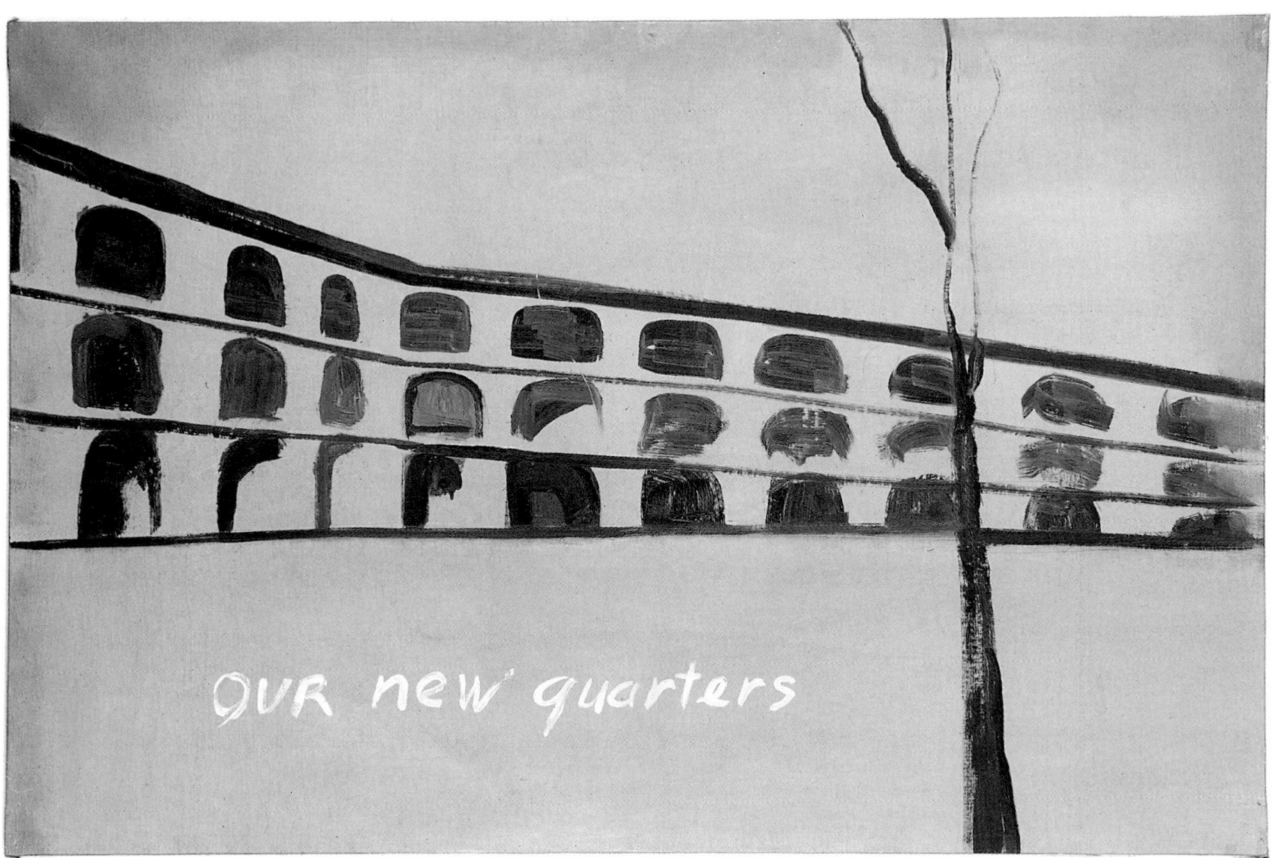

LUC TUYMANS, OUR NEW QUARTERS, 1986,
oil on canvas, 31½ x 47¼" /
UNSERE NEUE UNTERKUNFT, Öl auf Leinwand, 80 x 120 cm.
(PHOTO: RONALD STOOPS)

a greater degree with the spontaneity, the lack of interest in metier, and the marginality of "bad" painting. Moreover, his work and his attitude could be a perfect example of postmodernism. But the artist does not fit easily into any specific agenda because his intensely individualistic trajectory eludes classification. Even as a painter his work goes against the grain. His sign is solitude, both in content and position.

Now that painting seems to be rising from its ashes, Tuymans can be seen both as a survivor who has successfully exploited a traditional style to construct meaning at the end of the millennium, and as a pioneer heralding the rebirth of painting. He is a survivor in an era of monitors, internet, and elephant shit; a survivor in the sense of John Yau's remark that in our era "there are no heroes, only survivors."

The painter's anti-heroism contrasts with the penchant for spectacle that marks much contemporary art. His traditional Europeanism is at odds with the cultural and inventive diversity of an inexorably ever more globalized "international scene." But Tuymans' work is more than a curiosity in the art market of the outgoing millennium; it offers the possibility of experiencing contemporary painting the way old-style painting was felt. I am not talking about a nostalgic approach but about reactivating the introspective potential of traditional art to gain insight into our contemporary world. This refreshing possibility of mining "the past" (rather than returning to it) offers the opportunity to counteract the dominance of redundancies by (re)introducing other ways of constructing meaning.

(Translated from Spanish by A. MacAdam / G. Fittucci)

1) Luc Tuymans, "Artist's Writings," in: *Luc Tuymans* (London: Phaidon Press, 1996), p. 112.

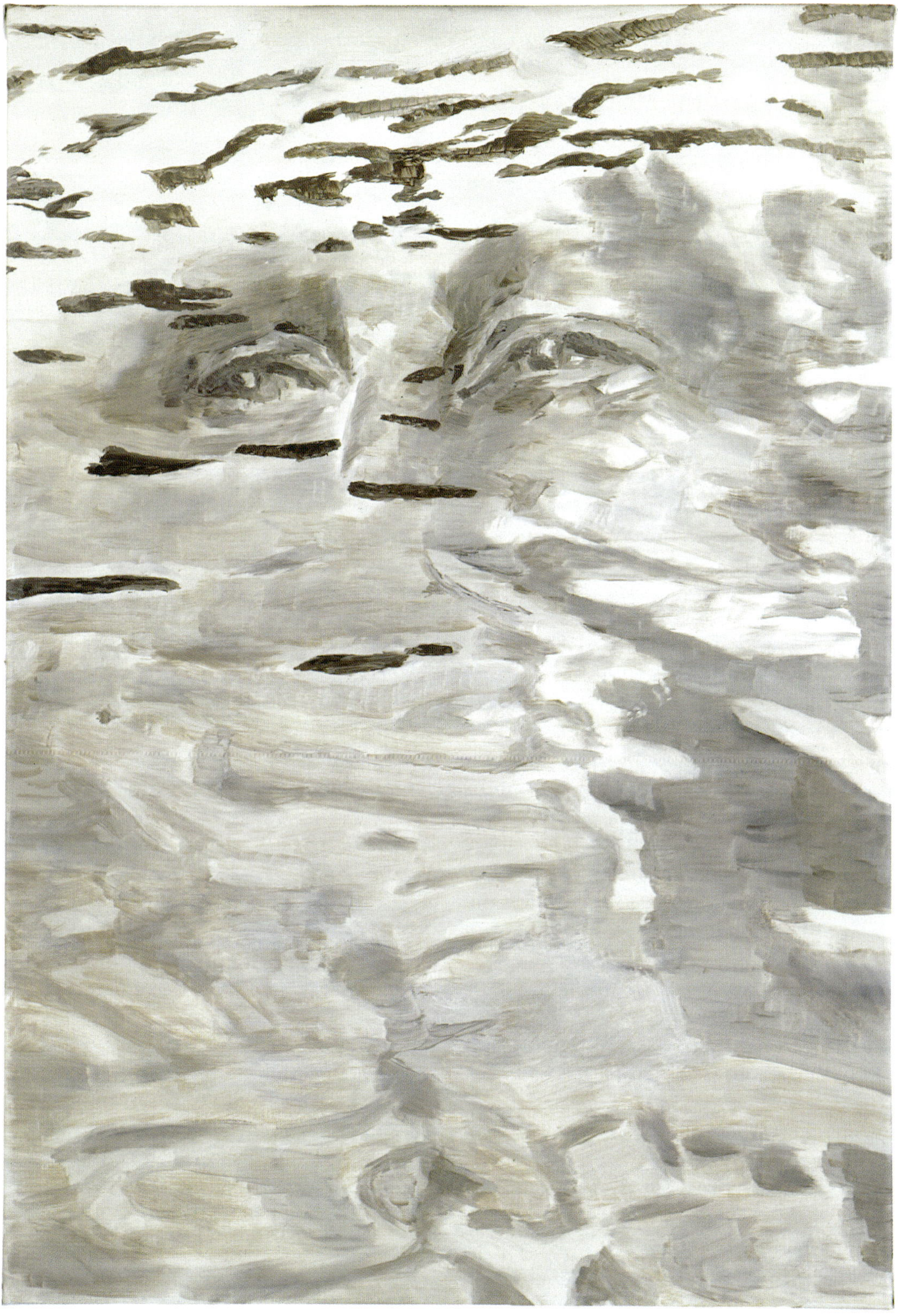

LUC TUYMANS, RESENTMENT, 1995, oil on canvas, 37¼ x 25″ / RESSENTIMENT, Öl auf Leinwand, 94,5 x 63,5 cm. (PHOTO: FELIX TIRRY)

GERARDO MOSQUERA

DIE GRENZRÄUME DER MALEREI

Was Luc Tuymans trotz der vernichtenden Kritik des Illusionismus in der Malerei eine erfolgreiche Karriere als «traditioneller» Maler ermöglicht, ist wohl die Tatsache, dass sein Werk sich genau an der Grenze zwischen darstellender und nicht darstellender Malerei bewegt. Es geht in seinen Arbeiten um das Darstellen ohne Darstellung und das Nichtdarstellen durch Darstellung. Tuymans' Werke sind alles andere als abstrakt: Sie beschreiben etwas sehr Konkretes oder erzählen sogar etwas, und immer steht dahinter eine Geschichte, die der Künstler auch ganz gern in Worte zu fassen pflegt. Der beschreibbare Inhalt der Bilder ist oft sehr klar und direkt. Dennoch ist stets auch die Absicht spürbar, etwas zu verwischen, zu verbergen oder herunterzuspielen und die nicht gegenständlichen Möglichkeiten der Malerei auszuschöpfen, um so gewissermassen wieder zu verbergen, was dargestellt ist. RESENTMENT (Ressentiment, 1995) ist ein vorwiegend abstraktes Bild, das sich als Wiedergabe eines Gesichts beschreiben liesse – da zwei ausdrucksvolle, im Stil eines Porträts gemalte menschliche Augen zu erkennen sind. Einander entgegengesetzte malerische Techniken und Philosophien treffen hier aufeinander, kommen einander in die Quere, wirken aber auch zusammen und ermöglichen dadurch erst das Aufscheinen einer ephemeren Bedeutung. Steht man etwa vor

GLOBE (Globus, 1998), einem ungewöhnlich grossformatigen Bild, so weiss man nicht, ob man die von einem Satelliten photographierte Erde, einen Globus, einen Ball oder alles zugleich vor sich hat.

Dieses Vorgehen begünstigt eine intellektuelle, emotionale und symbolische Behandlung von Themen, so auch im Fall von PILLOWS (Kissen, 1994), wo verlassene Kissen (aber so «voll von Welt», wie César Vallejo sagen würde) ein ganzes Erinnerungsgebäude heraufbeschwören. Dieses Bild weist übrigens eine seltsame Verwandtschaft auf mit dem grossen Photoplakat UNTITLED (1991) von Felix Gonzalez-Torres. Manchmal wirkt schon die Methode selbst symbolisch, wie im Fall von A FLEMISH INTELLEC-TUAL (Ein flämischer Intellektueller, 1995), wo das Gesicht eines berühmten flämischen Schriftstellers beinah bis zum Verschwinden reduziert dargestellt ist, ein Ausdruck von Tuymans' kritischer Haltung gegenüber dem flämischen Identitätskult. In eine ähnliche Richtung weist THE FLAG (1995).

Zentral ist jedoch nicht das Erzeugen von Vieldeutigkeit, denn schliesslich geht es in der Kunst immer darum, etwas zu sagen ohne es zu sagen, und um die Transformation von Bildern und Bedeutungen. Das entscheidende Merkmal dieser Kunst ist, dass sie eine Art Niemandsland innerhalb der Malerei erzeugt, eine Ruhezone, aus der heraus die Bilder sprechen. Tuymans äussert sich kaum je allgemein über sein Werk, sondern bezieht sich immer auf ganz konkrete Arbeiten und beschreibt ihre Entstehung sowie die ihnen zugrunde liegenden formalen und

---

GERARDO MOSQUERA ist freier Kunstkritiker und Kurator sowie Adjunct Curator am New Museum of Contemporary Art in New York. Er lebt in Havanna.

inhaltlichen Strategien. Seine Kommentare zeugen von seinem Interesse und seiner Vorliebe für jenen Moment, in dem Bilder und Bedeutungen gerade mal zu erahnen sind. Man könnte deshalb auch von einer Malerei der Dämmerung oder des Zwielichts sprechen.

Andrerseits stehen die ausführlichen Kommentare des Künstlers im Widerspruch zu einem existenziellen, ganz und gar unromantischen Geheimnis, das alle seine Werke umgibt. Wie er selbst mit grosser Präzision sagt: «Im schmalen Raum zwischen der Erklärung eines Bildes und dem Bild selbst eröffnet sich der einzig mögliche Blick auf die Malerei. Meine Äusserungen beziehen sich lediglich auf diese Mehrdeutigkeit.»[1]

* * *

Vielleicht ist in der Geschichte der Menschheit noch nie so viel gemalt worden wie heute, aber noch nie hat die Malerei gleichzeitig so wenig zur Legitimation der Kunst beigetragen. Selbstverständlich besitzt die Malerei ein sehr viel weiteres kommerzielles Spektrum als, sagen wir, ein paar Fliegen in einem Glas. Ein enormer Anteil der aktuellen malerischen Produktion bedient sogenannte «Mid-brow»-Märkte, die sich mehr für das ästhetisch-symbolische Potenzial der Malerei in Verbindung mit der Demonstration handwerklichen Könnens interessieren, oder – wie so oft in Lateinamerika – für die Erfindung und Darstellung imaginärer Orte unter Zuhilfenahme aller ikonographischen, symbolischen und erzählerischen Möglichkeiten der Malerei. Das bedingt einen Bereich der Produktion, der stärker am Wiederholen des Altbekannten als an einer wenigstens epigonal modernen Sinnerzeugung interessiert ist. Diese Tendenz wird durch die Schwierigkeit begünstigt, im Gefolge einer langen Tradition und angesichts der Experimente der Moderne überhaupt noch etwas Neues zu sagen. Am anderen Ende der Skala steht ein «High-brow»-Publikum, das sich gegenüber den vorherrschenden internationalen Strömungen eher konservativ verhält und künstlerischen Rang weiterhin hierarchisch versteht.

Die Behauptung, die Malerei sei tot, ist bis in unsere Tage eine Obsession der modernen Kunst. Und vielleicht leidet die Malerei selbst an dieser selbst-

mörderischen, mit dem Tod liebäugelnden Hysterie, die – mit den Worten des Johannes vom Kreuz – «stirbt, weil sie nicht stirbt». Tatsächlich ist nicht nur bei vielen jungen Künstlern das Interesse für die Malerei neu erwacht: Einige der bedeutendsten zeitgenössischen Künstler sind Maler. Einige, etwa Gerhard Richter, gehören sogar zu den radikalsten Vorreitern. Diese Malerei ist erfolgreich zu neuen Ufern aufgebrochen, hat den alten Kanon abgestreift und eine neue Bildsprache entwickelt, die ihr wieder Spannung verleiht und ihr Bedeutungspotenzial erneuert. Andere bringen die Mechanismen der bildlichen Darstellung und Symbolisierung selbst ins Spiel und diskutieren deren soziale, kulturelle und sprachliche Bedeutung. Die Bilder, die dabei entstehen, laufen auf eine Selbst-Dekonstruktion der Malerei hinaus. Eine weitere, expansivere Tendenz wiederum führt die Malerei über sich selbst hinaus und bringt sie mit anderen Kunstformen in Berührung, wobei Durchmischungen und Verwandlungen stattfinden. Wertvoll sind diese Werke aber nicht nur, weil sie «selbstkritisch» sind, was ja die Hinfälligkeit der Malerei nur bestätigen würde. Sie sind es auch dank der darstellenden Kraft der Malerei, die über ihre Selbstzerstörung hinaus das Auffinden neuer Bedeutungen ermöglicht.

Luc Tuymans' paradoxe Radikalität besteht dagegen darin, sich mit einer nahezu naiven Haltung ins Innere der Malerei selbst zu begeben. Abseits aller Debatten um Darstellung und Darstellbarkeit postuliert er mit grosser Spontaneität ein neues Vertrauen ins Bild. Eigentlich, sollte man denken, müsste ihn diese Haltung zu einer Randexistenz verurteilen. Dass er erfolgreich ist und auch von Seiten der Kritik allgemein Anerkennung geniesst, liegt wohl zu einem guten Teil am eher leisen und betont persönlichen Charakter seiner Kunst.

* * *

Tuymans mag keine stereotypen Äusserungen über belgische Kunst. Dennoch gibt es in diesem Land viele seltsame, eigenwillige Künstler, deren Werke eine sehr individuelle Bildsprache aufweisen. Etwas sehr Belgisches glaube ich auch in Tuymans' Unzahl kleiner Bilder zu erkennen, die beinah wie Ansichtskarten zum Sammeln wirken. Ist seine Malerei vielleicht eine Sammlung der Dinge dieser Welt, einschliesslich der in einen Ball verwandelten Erde selbst?

* * *

Über das «Verspätete» von Tuymans' Malerei ist schon viel gesagt worden. Laut Urich Loock ist das Plusquamperfekt die Zeitform dieses Werks. Das Traditionelle von Tuymans' Vorgehen und sein fehlendes Interesse daran, «originelle» oder neuartige Komponenten in seine Arbeit einfliessen zu lassen, lassen sich damit erklären, dass er es für unmöglich hält, etwas Neues zu schaffen. Die Nüchternheit dieses Künstlers führt zum Selbstmord der schöpferischen Gebärde und sein ganzes Werk wird zu einem Hypertext, der auf bereits bestehende Darstellungen und Ausdrucksformen verweist.

Aber Tuymans betreibt keine Appropriation im üblichen dekonstruktiven Sinn. Der analytisch-kritische Impetus seines Werks ist zwar unübersehbar, aber der Künstler verwendet die Darstellung von Gegenständen, Landschaften und Innenräumen auch dazu, um deren Pathos und Geschichte zur Sprache zu bringen. Bilder wie OUR NEW QUARTERS (Unser neues Quartier, 1986), GASKAMMER (1986) oder die Serie THE HERITAGE (Das Erbe, 1995) sind Ausdruck einer Gesellschafts- und Geschichtskritik, ohne dass es sich dabei um «politische Kunst» im eigentlichen Sinn handelt, denn diese Bilder schreien nichts nach aussen, sondern sind eher in sich gekehrt. Und darin liegt der Schlüssel zu diesem Werk, denn was Tuymans interessiert, ist die persönliche, introspektive Reaktion auf seine Motive: Seien es Gegenstände oder bereits existierende Bilder, ihre Kraft kommt in erster Linie aus den Emotionen und Erinnerungen, die sie auslösen.

Also ist der Traditionalismus dieses Künstlers noch viel «schwerwiegender», insofern er auf die Intuition vertraut und sein Schaffen als verinnerlichten, subjektiven Akt praktiziert, in dem seine persönlichen Obsessionen, Ängste und Grillen ihren Niederschlag finden. Man denkt dabei eher an einen Künstler wie Van Gogh als an zeitgenössische Kunst.

Natürlich lässt sich Tuymans durchaus mit der Malerei der 80er Jahre in Verbindung bringen, auch wenn diese nicht gerade als eine Malerei der Stille

und des privaten Raumes gelten kann. Schon eher könnte eine Verwandtschaft mit der Spontaneität, dem Desinteresse für das Handwerkliche und der Marginalität des «bad painting» vorhanden sein. Ja, sein Werk und seine Haltung könnten als Musterbeispiel der Postmoderne dienen. Aber Tuymans passt nicht wirklich in eine dieser Schubladen, zu individuell ist sein Werdegang und entzieht sich jeder Etikettierung. In malerischer und programmatischer Hinsicht ist sein Werk gleichermassen widerborstig. Sein eigentliches Zeichen ist die Einsamkeit.

Nun, da die Malerei sich wie Phönix aus der Asche zu erheben scheint, wird Tuymans als Überlebender und Pionier erkennbar: als Überlebender, der es am Ende des Jahrtausends noch einmal schaffte, aus der Überlieferung Kraft zu schöpfen, sowie als Pionier und Herold einer Wiedergeburt der Malerei. Er ist ein Überlebender in einer Zeit der Bildschirme, des Internets und des Elefantendrecks, ein Überlebender im Sinne einer Bemerkung von John Yau, der meinte, dass es in unserer Zeit «keine Helden gibt, nur Überlebende».

Das Antiheldentum dieses Künstlers kontrastiert mit dem Hang zum Spektakulären, der einen grossen Teil der zeitgenössischen Kunst auszeichnet. Seine traditionell europäische Haltung steht quer zur kulturellen Vielfalt der Einfälle und Einflüsse einer zunehmend global orientierten «internationalen Szene». Dennoch ist das Werk von Tuymans mehr als eine Kuriosität im Kunstmarkt dieses zu Ende gehenden Jahrtausends; es eröffnet uns nämlich die Möglichkeit, zeitgenössische Malerei wieder so zu erfahren, wie die alte Malerei erlebt wurde. Die Rede ist nicht von Nostalgie, sondern von der Wiederbelebung der alten introspektiven Möglichkeiten der Kunst zum besseren Verständnis der heutigen Welt. Diese erfrischende Möglichkeit, die Vergangenheit anzuzapfen (und nicht: zu ihr zurückkehren zu wollen), ist ein Mittel gegen das Erstickende der toten Wiederholung und eröffnet neue Wege der Sinnfindung.

(Übersetzung aus dem Spanischen: A. Müller, UGZ / G. Fittucci)

---

1) *Luc Tuymans*, Phaidon Press, London 1996, S. 112.

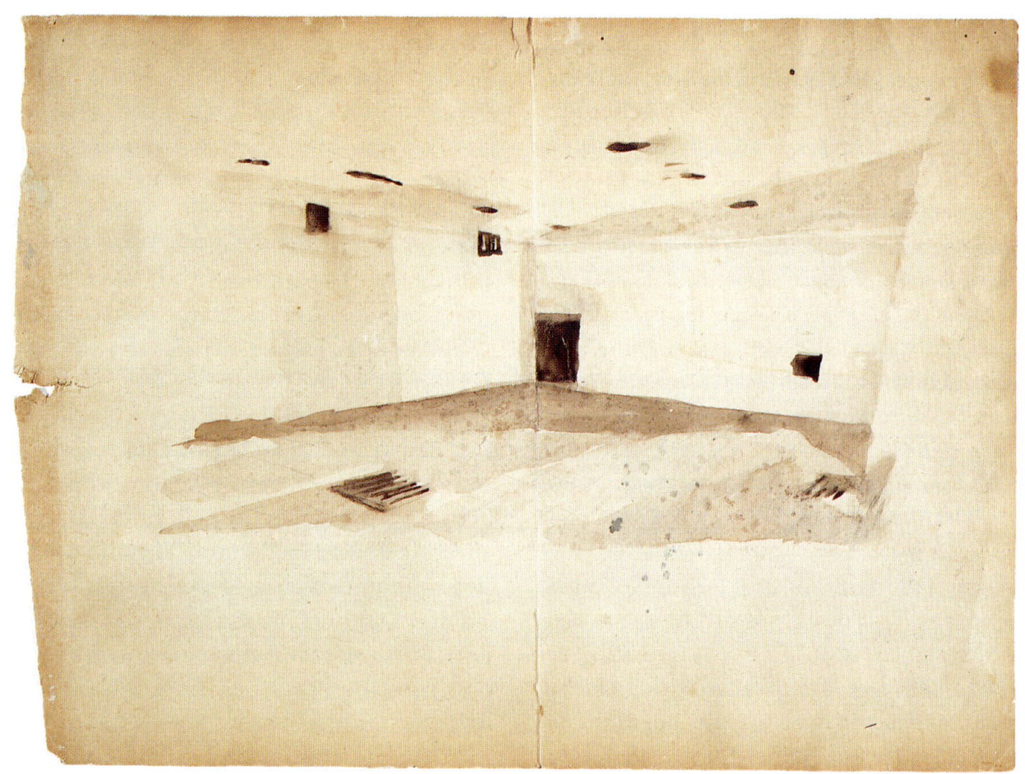

LUC TUYMANS, GAS CHAMBER, 1981,
water color and pencil on paper on cardboard, 12 x 15⅝" /
GASKAMMER, Aquarell und Bleistift auf Papier auf Karton, 30,4 x 39,8 cm.
(PHOTO: PETER HAURI, KUNSTMUSEUM BERN)

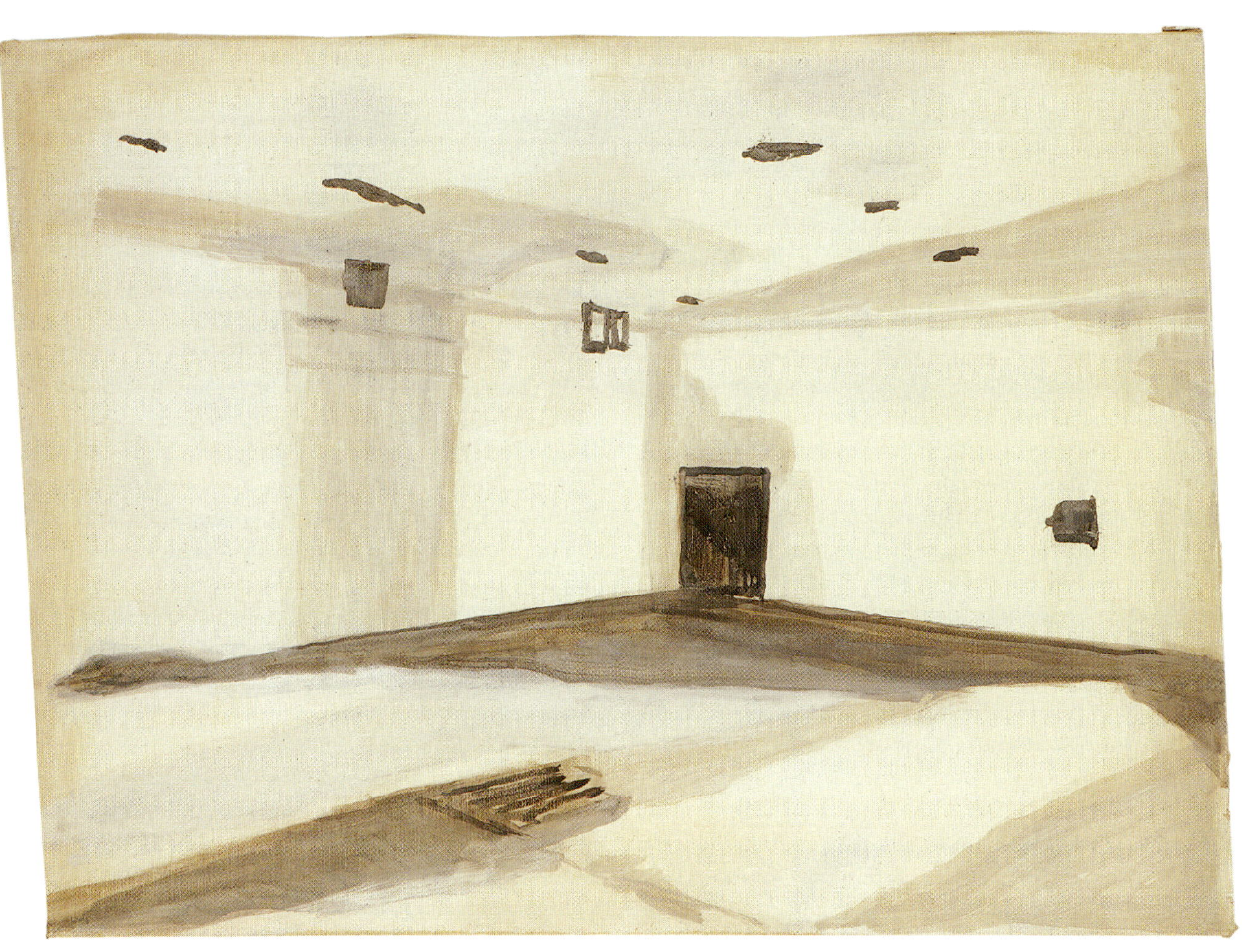

LUC TUYMANS, GAS CHAMBER, 1986,
oil on canvas, 19⅞ x 27½" / GASKAMMER, Öl auf Leinwand, 50 x 70 cm.
(PHOTO: RONALD STOOPS)

HANS RUDOLF REUST

Im dunklen Weltteil

I.

«Mwana Kitoko, The beautiful White Man.» So nannten die Völker Kongos ihr Staatsoberhaupt, König Baudouin von Belgien. Luc Tuymans hat ihn gemalt, wie er Mitte der 50er Jahre in blendend weisser Marineuniform die kleine Treppe eines Flugzeugs herabsteigt, ein klein wenig zu steif für seine elegante, schlanke Gestalt, die Hand fest um den Degen geklammert, die Augen durch eine Sonnenbrille geschützt und versteckt, zudringlichen Blicken entzogen. Das Bild Baudouins, MWANA KITOKO (2000), zeigt einen grossen Auftritt in grosser Helle, der zwischen medial inszenierter Blendung und tropischem Licht oszilliert. Die dunklen Brillenaugen geben der Figur etwas Insektenhaftes. Damit erfährt die klassische Form des Monarchenporträts eine subtile Brechung, ähnlich den Darstellungen der spanischen Granden bei Goya. Der Aufteilung des Hintergrunds folgend, wird Baudouins langer Körper in kleine, wie Kuben gemalte Segmente geteilt, als könnte sich jede Partie dieser Malerei auch gegen die anderen verselbständigen. Die Einheit der Gestalt steht in Spannung zu ihrer Auflösung in eine malerische Gliederung.

In Tuymans' Werk erschliessen sich weitere Bedeutungsschichten eines Bildes oft durch den genau konzipierten Kontext der ersten Ausstellung. Vielfach sind es die räumlichen Bedingungen, die eine bestimmte Anzahl und Konstellation von Werken verlangen. Schon beim Malen besteht eine präzise Vorstellung davon, wie die einzelnen Bilder allein, untereinander und im Raum ihrer ersten Präsentation operieren werden. Im jüngsten Zyklus für die Galerie David Zwirner in New York steht dem ganzfigurigen Porträt des Monarchen unter anderem das leicht kleinere Dreiviertelporträt eines schwarzen Mannes gegenüber. Ein wenig von der Seite in das schmale, hohe Bildfenster gewendet, tritt dieser nur mit Lendentuch und Turban bekleidete, dunkel glänzende, muskulöse Körper unerwartet aus der Finsternis auf, wie ungebeten: «In der Ferne waren undeutlich die schwarzen Schatten von Menschen zu sehen, die dem dunklen Waldrand entlanghuschten, und nahe am Fluss, in der Sonne, standen zwei Bronzefiguren mit riesigen Speeren in den Händen und phantastischen Kopfbedeckungen aus gefleckten Fellstücken, kriegerisch und bewegungslos wie Statuen.»[2] Etwas beklemmend Fremdes liegt auch über Tuymans' Figur, als wäre sie nicht ganz lebendig. Das Bild trägt den Titel STATUE (2000) und wurde tatsächlich nach einer Dekorstatue gemalt, die mitten im Serviceteil eines Antwerpener Restaurants steht. Die Gipsfigur ist etwas kleiner als lebensgross. In ihrer lackierten Oberfläche glänzt das verhaltene Raumlicht. Erst die Malerei verleiht dieser Statue

---

HANS RUDOLF REUST ist Kunstkritiker und lebt in Bern.

ZU LUC TUYMANS' NEUSTEN BILDERN

Mein Projekt ist ein Bemühen darum, den kritischen Blick vom rassischen Objekt zum rassischen Subjekt zu wenden; von den Beschriebenen und Imaginierten zu den Beschreibenden und Imaginierenden; von den Dienenden zu den Bedienten. – Toni Morrison[1]

jenen Körper, der sich beunruhigend zwischen Erstarrung und Belebung bewegt. Lebendig wird er schliesslich durch die Projektionen eines weissen Publikums. Animiert durch Sport-Erfolge oder Hip-Hop schwankt seine Verklärung des schwarzen Körpers zwischen Erotisierung und Dämonisierung.

Auch in der künstlerischen Wahrnehmung von Weissen bleiben schwarze Menschen meist anonym, wie die Gestalten, die in der angeführten Passage von Joseph Conrad namenlos aus dem Dunkel auftreten und wieder im Dunkel verschwinden. Die Lippen in der Grösse überhöht, der Blick «wilder» gemalt, und schon werden Phantasien wach. Luc Tuymans geht mit seinem Bild direkt auf diese Stereotype ein. Er geht aber auch einen Schritt weiter, indem er die Figur nicht als passive Projektionsfläche malt, sondern sie aktiv werden lässt. Während der König durch die Malerei anonymisiert wird, erhält der namenlose schwarze Mann eine Identität: Er wirft einen forschend fordernden Blick zurück auf die Voyeure.

II.

Die Gegenüberstellung dieser beiden Porträts schafft einen unmittelbaren Bezug zur belgischen Kolonialgeschichte im Kongo, die durch jüngste Publikationen in Belgien selber aus dem Dunkel ihrer

Verdrängung geholt wurde.[3] Zwischen den Berliner Afrika-Konferenzen von 1885 und 1906 wurde im Kongo-Freistaat ein Genozid verübt, dem gegen zehn Millionen Menschen durch Mord, Hunger und Krankheiten zum Opfer fielen. Es gehört zu den zynischen Lehrstücken staatlicher Medienarbeit, dass Leopold II. unter dem Vorwand geographischer Forschung und der philanthropischen Behauptung, den Sklavenhandel zu unterbinden, eines der brutalsten Systeme von Zwangsarbeit einrichten und über Jahrzehnte aufrechterhalten konnte. Durch Folter, Geiselnahme von Frauen und Kindern und durch gezielte Massenmorde wurden die einheimischen Völker zu einer exzessiven Suche nach Elfenbein, später nach Kautschuk – für die Reifen der einsetzenden Autoindustrie – gezwungen.

Ein Leopardenfell breitet sich als eine Textur dunkler Punkte über die Leinwand aus. In den rhythmisch sich versammelnden und auseinander driftenden Pinselspuren präsentiert die Malerei ihre eigene Haut, und allein das rasch lesbare Motiv deutet an, dass es hier nicht um tachistische Malerei, sondern um gemalte Flecken geht. Der Blick zerstreut sich entlang der bemalten Oberfläche von LEOPARD (2000), um sich über das Motiv unvermittelt in einen Illusionsraum zu wenden. Fasziniert bleiben wir an einzelnen Punkten hängen, driften ab, um doch nicht loszukommen. Tiefe Schatten und wärmendes

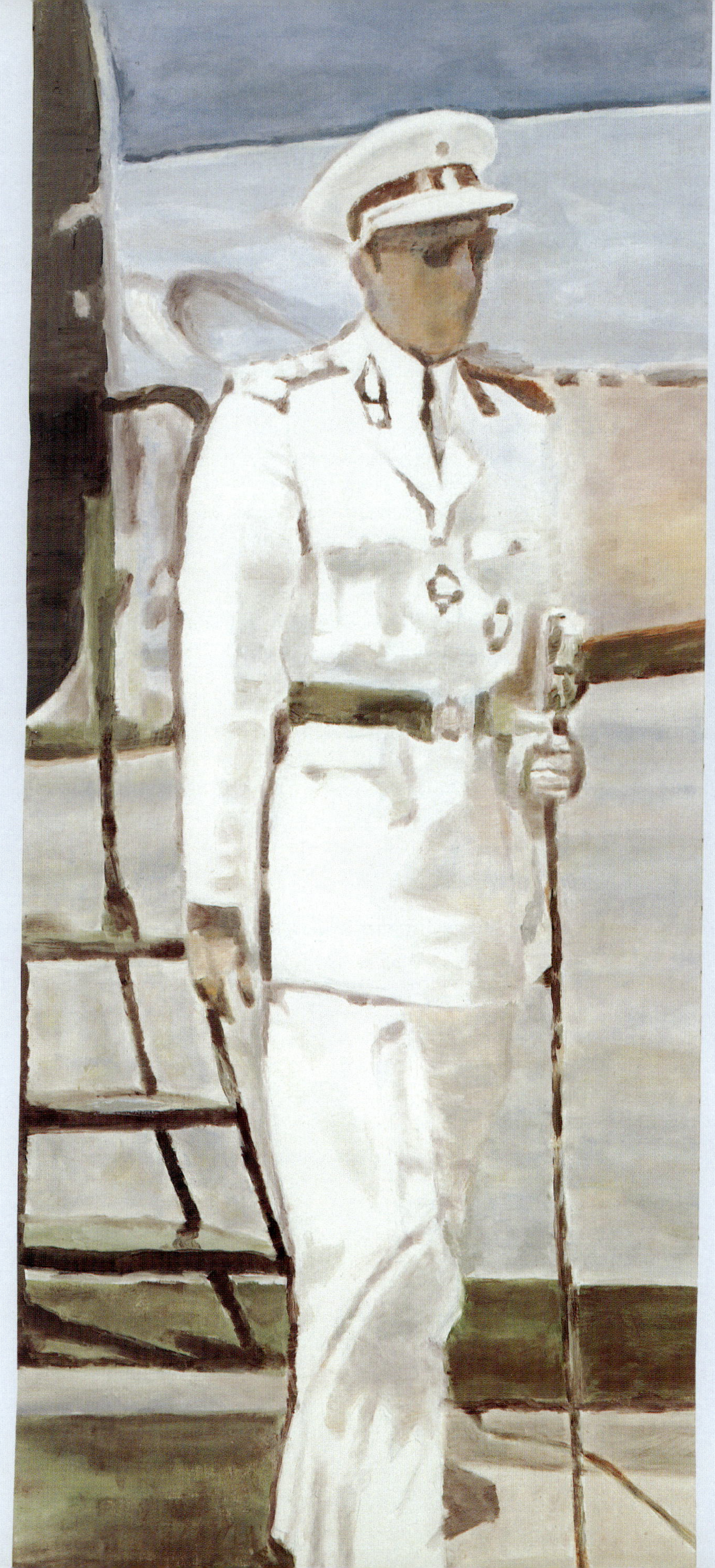

LUC TUYMANS,
MWANA KITOKO, 2000,
oil on canvas, 81⅞ x 37⁷⁄₁₆" /
Öl auf Leinwand, 208 x 90 cm.
(PHOTO: FELIX TIRRY)

Licht liegen über dem ausgebreiteten Fell, dabei scheint es sich der Wahrnehmung zu entziehen, als wäre es nur der eingezoomte Bereich einer umfassenderen Szenerie, die wir nicht überblicken, nie kontrollieren können. Im scharfen Ausschnitt von Tuymans' Bild wird das Fell von zwei schwarzen Händen, die oben links eben noch zu sehen sind, vor einem wartenden König ausgelegt, dessen Füsse knapp in die rechte obere Bildecke hineinragen. Afrikanische Herrscher trugen Leopardenfell als Machtsymbol an der Mütze. Baudouin lässt sich das Fell mit der Anspielung auf einen roten Teppich auslegen, um sich als König über zwei Kulturen zu legitimieren. Der Völkermord, der seine Macht begründet hat, lässt das kolonialisierte Herrschaftssymbol zum Indiz für westlichen Kannibalismus werden. Das abgezogene Tierfell erinnert daran, dass die «Zivilisierung» des «dunklen Weltteils» zu den dunkelsten Seiten einer aufgeklärten Zivilisation gehört.

Die Werkgruppe zum Kongo schliesst bei Tuymans' Auseinandersetzung mit dem Holocaust an und damit bei der Darstellung des Unvorstellbaren. So wenig wie der leere Raum von GASKAMMER (1986) das Geschehene fasst, so wenig zeigt ein Fell oder das Porträt einer Statue die verdrängte Geschichte. Erst mit dem Bewusstsein dessen, was das Bild nicht zeigt, werden Dimensionen des Grauens spürbar. Die Malerei kommt, wie jedes Gedächtnis, stets zu spät und zu früh. Sie vermittelt zwischen dem uneinholbaren Moment der Vergangenheit und einer Reflexion, die ihr erst entspringt. Luc Tuymans' Bilder zeigen diese Medialität, indem sie Elemente der medialen Vorlagen aufnehmen, nach denen sie gemalt wurden: die Flüchtigkeit und das Licht von Photopapieren, Film- oder Videostills. Mehrere Werke aus dem aktuellen Kontext sind in der Tat nach ausgewählten Standaufnahmen aus einem Film über Baudouins Staatsbesuch im Kongo entstanden. Unschärfen, Unkenntlichkeiten, Auslöschungen und ein filmischer Fokus öffnen jene Lücken im Bild, bei denen die Erinnerung der Betrachtenden einsetzt.

Luc Tuymans' Werk gilt bis heute als vorwiegend «psychologisch», von Schock ist die Rede, von Terror. Dabei wird seine konzeptuelle Arbeit übersehen, die auf einem spezifisch europäischen Bewusst-sein über die historische Bedingtheit psychischer Vorgänge beruht. Bereits in früheren Werkgruppen hat er sich offen mit politischen Verhältnissen auseinander gesetzt: in «Heimat» (1995), einer Ausstellung in der Galerie ZENO X in Antwerpen, welche direkt auf die wachsende Präsenz des rechtsradikalen Vlaams Blok in Antwerpen einging; oder mit «Heritage» (Erbe, 1996) bei David Zwirner in New York, einer Beschäftigung mit der amerikanischen Geschichtskonstruktion aus europäischer Perspektive. Die historisch-politische Dimension der jüngsten Arbeiten wird offensichtlich mit LUMUMBA (2000), dem Porträt Patrice Emery Lumumbas (1925–1961), des ersten frei gewählten Ministerpräsidenten der unabhängigen Republik Kongo, der nach wenigen Monaten im Amt von einer durch den Westen unterstützten Bewegung um Mobutu ermordet wurde. Tuymans schliesst damit an eine aktuelle Diskussion in Belgien an, die durch jüngste Studien über die Verwicklung des belgischen Staates, der CIA und der Vereinten Nationen in die Ermordung Lumumbas ausgelöst wurde.[4]

Zu erinnern wäre in diesem Zusammenhang an den fünfzehnteiligen Zyklus der RAF-Bilder von Gerhard Richter: 18. OKTOBER 1977 (1988). Während Richter mit seinen Bildern explizit eine kathartische Wirkung der Malerei erreichen wollte – «Trauer und Mitleid» anstelle des «Entsetzens»[5] –, sucht Tuymans die Blossstellung des Unausgesprochenen, den ideologieskeptischen Schnitt ins Bewusstsein, der die Fragen an die Geschichte wie an die Malerei ohne Distanzierung durch Trauerarbeit offen hält.

Drei Tage nach Lumumbas Ermordung haben belgische Söldner seine Leiche ausgegraben und in einem Säurebad aufgelöst, wobei einer von ihnen später gestand, drei Zähne seines Opfers persönlich aufbewahrt zu haben. Die weissen Handschuhe mit den Zähnen werden in Luc Tuymans' Malerei zum Punktum eines traumatisierten Gedächtnisses. Der Genozid bleibt undarstellbar. Tuymans versucht sich denn auch nicht an den Bergen von abgehackten Händen, die in der weltweiten Kampagne gegen die belgische Kolonialherrschaft um 1900 zum Symbol für das Menschheitsverbrechen geworden waren. Er malt kleinste, scheinbar nebensächliche Momente, die das individuelle Gedächtnis unvorbereitet treffen und sich darin festsetzen. Die Paranoia der Mörder, die zur Auslöschung von Lumumbas Leiche geführt hat, erfasst die Malerei.

III.

Politisch sind die Kongo-Bilder nicht zuletzt, weil sie in den aktuellen Diskurs um Kunst aus Afrika in den internationalen Grossausstellungen eingreifen. Dieser Diskurs spielt sich im Kontext der neusten ökonomischen Globalisierungswelle ab und spiegelt ihre Widersprüche. Der Fokussierung auf das Verschwinden aller traditionellen Differenzen durch Migration und globale Kommunikation steht die Forderung nach neuen, an den ökonomischen Differenzen kritisch geschärften kulturellen Identitäten gegenüber.

Luc Tuymans führt mit seiner jüngsten Werkreihe eine Differenz in der westlichen Wahrnehmung ein. Seine Bilder geben nicht vor, über oder stellvertretend für Afrika zu sprechen. Indem er sich ausschliesslich seiner eigenen belgischen Geschichte zuwendet, entgeht er der Gefahr einer Romantisierung des dunklen Unbekannten, wie sie die Kunst aufgeklärter Weisser durchzieht. Unter dem Titel «Romancing the Shadow» hat Toni Morrison die amerikanische Literatur des neunzehnten Jahrhunderts untersucht. Sie zeigt auf, wie weisse Autoren ihre eigenen Identitätskonflikte und Befreiungsphantasien auf eine spezifische Konstruktion von «Schwarzsein» übertragen haben: «Die schwarze Sklaverei bereicherte die kreativen Möglichkeiten des Landes. Denn in jener Konstruktion von schwarzer Hautfarbe und Sklaverei liess sich nicht nur das Nicht-frei-Sein finden, sondern auch, in der dramatischen Polarität, die durch die Hautfarbe entsteht, die Projektion des Nicht-Ichs. Das Ergebnis war eine Spielwiese für die Phantasie. Aus dem kollektiven Bedürfnis, innere Ängste zu verbinden und äussere Ausbeutung zu rationalisieren, entstand ein amerikanischer Afrikanismus – ein künstliches Gemisch aus Dunkelheit, Anderssein, Beunruhigung und Begehren, das ausschliesslich amerikanisch ist. (Natürlich gibt es auch einen europäischen Afrikanismus mit einem Gegenstück in der Kolonialliteratur.)»[6]

Luc Tuymans betreibt mit seiner Malerei die Demystifizierung dunkler Stellen in der eigenen Wahr-

nehmung. Die Überhelle, die sich in vielen seiner Bilder bis zur verletzenden Blendung steigert, erweist sich hier als eine Absage an das verklärende Pathos des Schattens. Undarstellbar ist nicht, was der Erhellung entzogen bleibt, sondern was sich einer übergreifenden Konstruktion von «Geschichte» verweigert. Kunst dient nicht der globalen Erhärtung von Fakten; eher stellt sie sich einem partikularen «Gedächtnis», das nicht zur Ruhe kommt. Die höchste Statik des Bildes ist in Tuymans' Malerei keine Festlegung von Inhalten, vielmehr eine Fixierung des Denkens auf virulente Punkte. Zwischen den einzelnen Werken in der Konstellation der Kongo-Bilder beginnt die Erhellung eines «dunklen Weltteils» in Europa.

1) Toni Morrison, «Beunruhigende Krankenschwestern und die Freundlichkeit der Haie», in: Toni Morrison, *Im Dunkeln spielen: Weisse Literatur und literarische Imagination*, Rowohlt, Reinbek bei Hamburg 1994, S. 125.
2) Joseph Conrad, *Herz der Finsternis*, Haffmans Verlag, Zürich 1992, S. 117.
3) Vgl. Adam Hochschild, *Schatten über dem Kongo. Die Geschichte eines der grossen, fast vergessenen Menscheitsverbrechen*, Klett-Cotta, Stuttgart 2000.
4) Ludo de Witte, *De moord op Lumumba*, Van Halewyck, Leuven 1999. Französische Fassung: *L'assassinat de Lumumba*, Karthala, Paris 2000.
5) Gerhard Richter im Gespräch mit Jan Thorn-Prikker, in: *Parkett* Nr. 19, 1989, S. 129ff.
6) Toni Morrison, «Vom Schatten schwärmen», in: Toni Morrison, op. cit., S. 65.

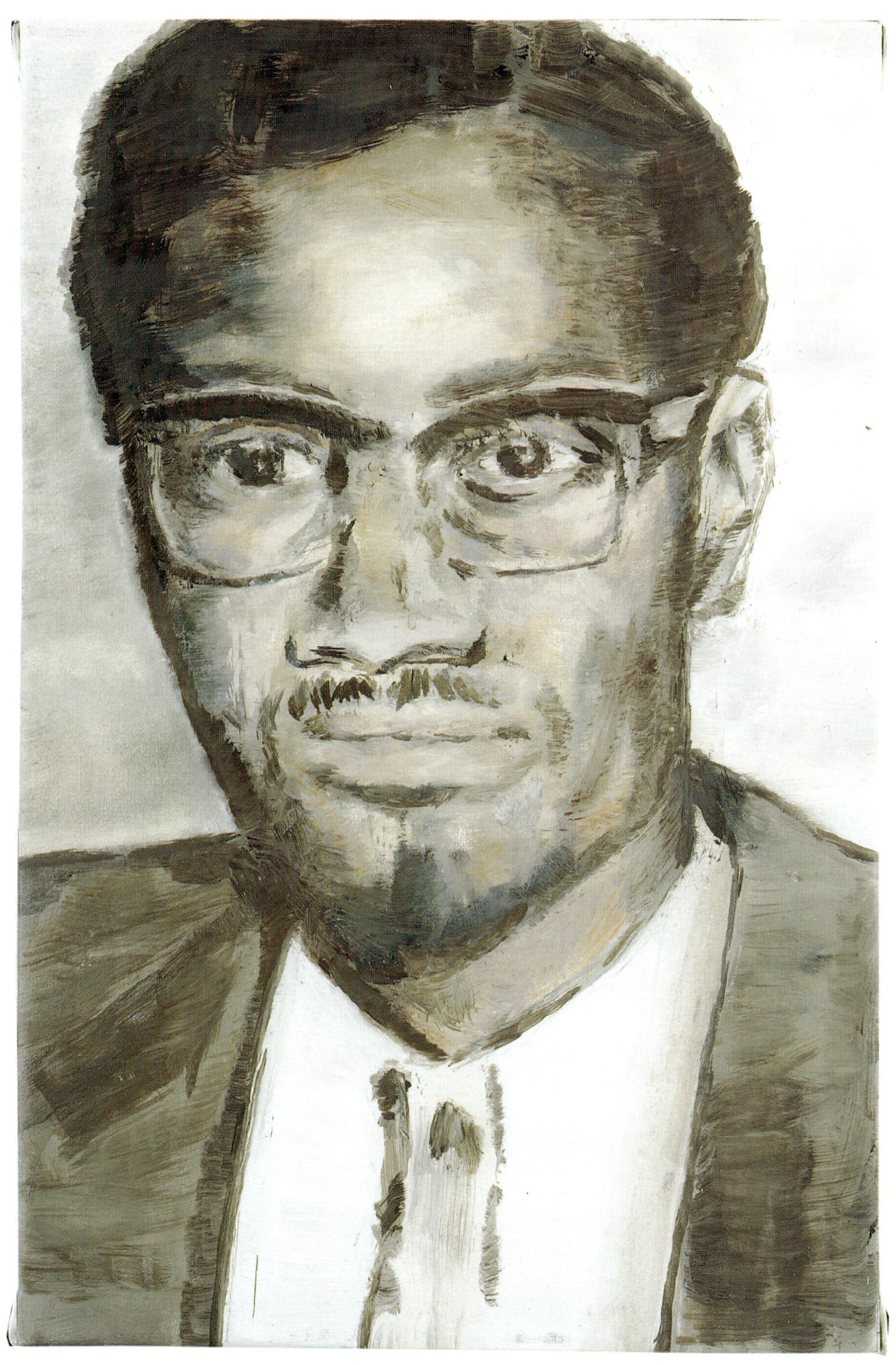

LUC TUYMANS, LUMUMBA, 2000, oil on canvas, 24½ x 18⅛" / Öl auf Leinwand, 62 x 46 cm.

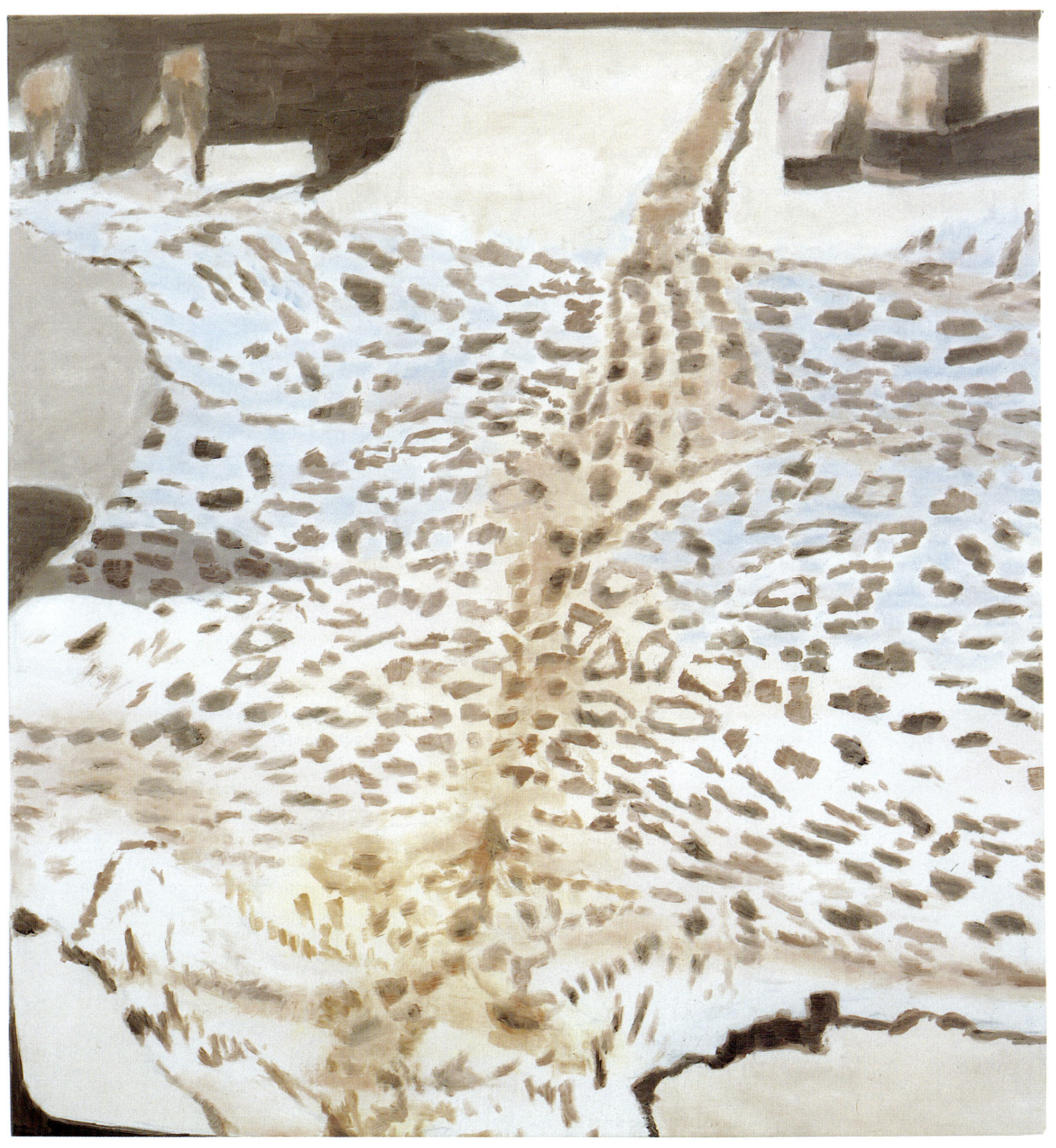

LUC TUYMANS, LEOPARD, 2000, oil on canvas, 56 x 50¾" / Öl auf Leinwand, 142 x 129 cm. (PHOTOS: FELIX TIRRY)

In the Dark Regions of the World

My project is an effort to avert the critical gaze from the racial object to the racial subject; from the described and the imagined to the describers and imaginers; from the serving to the served.
        – Toni Morrison[1]

I.

"Mwana Kitoko, The beautiful White Man." Thus did the people of the Congo address their sovereign, Baudouin, king of the Belgians. Luc Tuymans painted him descending the narrow stairs of his airplane in the mid-fifties, wearing an immaculate white Navy uniform, looking just a little too stiff for the elegance of his slim figure, one hand firmly grasping his sword, his eyes hidden behind sunglasses to protect them from the sun and the intrusive gaze of others. The painting of Baudouin, MWANA KITOKO (2000), shows a grand entrance in bright light that oscillates between the dazzling effect of a media event and the light of the tropics. The dark lens gives the figure an insect-like appearance. The classical portrait of royalty is thus subtly undermined, like Goya's paintings of Spanish grandees. Following the composition of the background, Baudouin's tall figure is divided into small segments, painted like cubes, as if each part of this painting could become independent of all the others. The unity of design is played off against this disintegration into painterly segments.

HANS RUDOLF REUST is an art critic and lives in Bern.

In Tuymans' oeuvre, a painting often acquires additional layers of meaning through the precisely devised context of its first exhibition, frequently involving spaces that require a certain number and combination of works. Even while painting, Tuymans often has a precise notion of how the picture is to operate alone, together with others, and in the room where it is first to be presented. In his most recent cycle for the David Zwirner Gallery in New York, the full-length portrait of the monarch is placed— among others—opposite a slightly smaller three-quarter portrait of a black man titled STATUE (2000). The dark, shiny muscular body, clothed only in a loincloth and a turban, suddenly emerges from the darkness at a slight angle in the narrow, tall window of the picture, as if unbidden: "Dark human shapes could be made out in the distance, flitting indistinctly against the gloomy border of the forest, and near the river two bronze figures, leaning on tall spears, stood in the sunlight under fantastic headdresses of spotted skins, war-like and still in statuesque repose."[2] Something oppressively alien also overlays Tuymans' figure, as if it were not quite alive. The subject was in fact painted from a mannequin

LUC TUYMANS' RECENT PAINTINGS

HANS RUDOLF REUST

standing in the middle of a restaurant in Antwerp. The plaster statue is not quite life-size; the subdued lighting bounces off its high-gloss surface. Only through the painting does the statue acquire a body that moves between disturbing rigidity and animation. It finally comes to life through the projections of a white viewing public. Animated by athletic successes or hip-hop, the transfiguration of the black body communicates a mood of both erotic and demonic effect.

Even in the artistic perception of whites, black people generally remain anonymous, like Joseph Conrad's nameless shapes that rise out of the darkness and sink back into it again. The lips exaggerated in size, the gaze painted to look even more "savage," and already our imaginations run wild. Luc Tuymans aims directly at these stereotypes in his picture. But he also goes a step further by not painting the figure as a passive surface of projection but rather making it active. While the king has been made anonymous through the painting, the nameless black man acquires an identity: he casts a scrutinizing and challenging look back at the voyeurs.

II.

These two portraits in juxtaposition allude directly to the colonial history of the Belgian Congo, which recent publications have drawn out of the darkness of its long suppression.[3] Between the Berlin West Africa Conference of 1885 and the year 1906, genocide, perpetrated in the Congo Free State, cost the lives of some ten million people through murder, famine, and illness. It is one of the most cynical lessons of governmental media control that Leopold II succeeded in establishing and maintaining for decades an inconceivably brutal system of forced labor under the pretext of geographical exploration and the philanthropic claim of putting an end to the slave trade. The native population was coerced into excessive exploitation of ivory and later of rubber for the tires of a nascent automobile industry by means of torture, taking women and children hostage, and deliberate mass murders.

A leopard skin spreads out across the canvas of LEOPARD (2000) as a texture of dark dots. As the brushstrokes rhythmically converge and drift apart, the painting acquires a skin of its own, and the legible motif is already enough to indicate that the painting is not tachist in nature but consists of painted spots. The gaze strays along the painted surface, but is then abruptly diverted into spatial illusion through the motif. Fascinated, the gaze is arrested by single spots, begins to drift away but cannot escape. Deep shadows and warming light quicken the flat skin but it seems to elude perception, as if the canvas were only a detail in close-up of a much larger scene that we will never see in its entirety and much less control. In Tuymans' distinctly cropped painting, two black hands that can just be seen at the upper left edge of the painting are spreading out the skin in front of the waiting king, whose feet barely reach into the upper right corner of the picture plane. African potentates once wore leopard skin caps as a symbol of power. Baudouin has the skin laid out like a red carpet, in order to legitimize his position as the king of two cultures. The genocide upon which his rule is based transforms the colonial symbol of domination into an index of the cannibalism of the West. The skinned animal reminds us that "civilizing the dark regions of the world" belongs to the darkest moments of enlightened civilization.

The group of works on the Congo leads into Tuymans' treatment of the Holocaust and therefore into the representation of the unthinkable. The empty room in GAS CHAMBER (1986) does as little to capture the event as the animal skin or the portrait of a statue does to capture suppressed history. Only when we realize what the pictures do not show, do the dimensions of the horror become palpable. Painting, like any memory, always comes too late and too soon. It mediates between the uncatchable moment of the past and a thought that springs from it. Luc Tuymans' pictures show this mediating relationship by including elements of the medial source after which they were painted: the fleetingness and the light of photographic paper, film or video stills. Several works in the current context were actually painted after selected stills from a film on Baudouin's state visit to the Congo. Fuzzy, indiscernible, or deleted areas and a cinematic focus create those gaps in a picture that activate viewers' memory.

Luc Tuymans' oeuvre is still considered largely "psychological," with criticism making use of such words as "shock" and "terror." This attitude overlooks his conceptual work, which is based on a specifically European consciousness of the historical determination of mental processes. His earlier work already openly explored political issues. "Heimat" (1995), an exhibition at ZENO X Gallery in Antwerp, explicitly addressed the growing presence of Antwerp's far right party, Vlaams Blok; and "Heritage" (1996) at David Zwirner Gallery in New York examined the American construction of history from a European perspective. The historical and political bias of recent works is unmistakable, as in the portrait LUMUMBA (2000) of Patrice Emery Lumumba (1925–1961), the first freely elected prime minister of the independent Congo Republic, who was murdered a few months after taking office by a group associated with Mobutu, which was supported by the West. Here Tuymans contributes to the current debate initiated in Belgium by the latest studies on the involvement of the Belgian government, the CIA, and the United Nations in the assassination of Lumumba.[4]

Worth remembering in this connection is the fifteen-part cycle of RAF paintings by Gerhard Richter: 18. OKTOBER 1977 (1988). While Richter explicitly wanted to achieve a cathartic effect in his series—"sorrow and compassion" instead of "horror"[5]—Tuymans wants to expose what has been left unspoken, making a skeptically ideological incision in the conscious, which keeps both historical and painterly questions open without the distancing of sorrow.

Three days after Lumumba's assassination, Belgian soldiers exhumed his body and dissolved it in an acid bath. One of the soldiers later admitted to having personally saved three of his victim's teeth. The white gloves with the teeth in Luc Tuymans' painting become the *punktum* of a traumatized memory. Genocide is still beyond representation. Thus, Tuymans does not attempt to render the mountains of chopped off hands, which became the symbol of the crimes against humanity in the world-wide campaign against the colonial oppression of the Belgians around 1900. He paints the tiniest, seemingly irrelevant moments that unexpectedly appear and take root in individual memory. The paranoia of the murderers, which led to the annihilation of Lumumba's corpse, has spilled over into the painting.

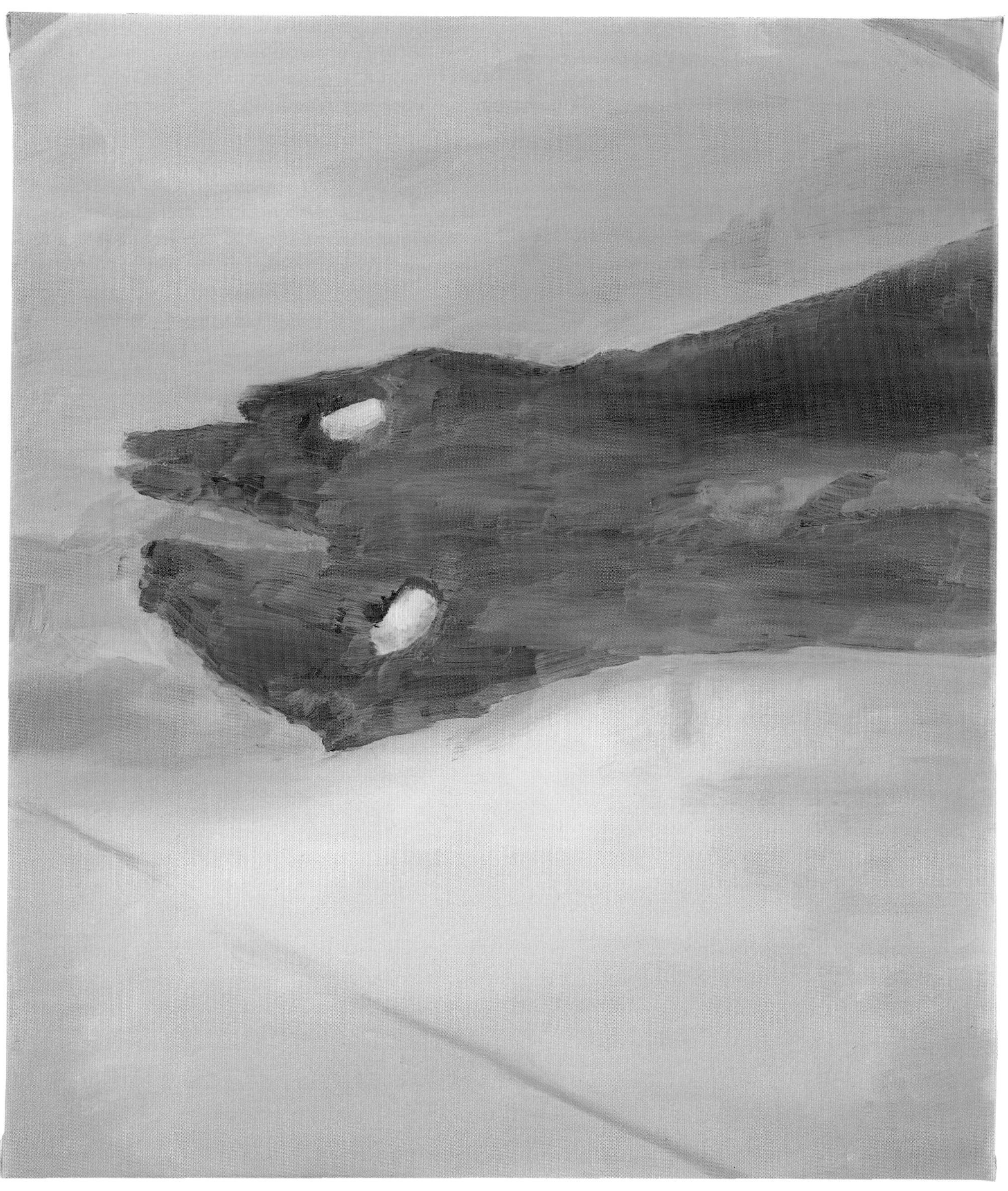

LUC TUYMANS, CHALK, 2000, oil on canvas, 28½ x 24¼" / KREIDE, Öl auf Leinwand, 72,5 x 61,5 cm. (PHOTO: FELIX TIRRY)

III.

The political impact of the Congo pictures also lies in the fact that they intervene in the current debate on art from Africa at major international exhibitions. This debate is unfolding in the context of the recent wave of economic globalization and mirrors its contradictions. The focus on the decline of traditional differences through migration and global communication is juxtaposed with the demand for new cultural identities, critically sharpened by economic inequality.

Luc Tuymans' recent series of works indicates a modification in Western perception. His paintings do not pretend to speak about or on behalf of Africa. By concentrating exclusively on his own Belgian history, he escapes the danger of romanticizing the dark unknown, which typifies the art of enlightened whites. In her essay "Romancing the Shadow" on nineteenth-century American literature, Toni Morrison shows how white writers have imposed their own conflicts of identity and fantasies of liberation on a specific construction of blackness: "Black slavery enriched the country's creative possibilities. For in that construction of blackness and enslavement could be found not only the not-free but also, with the dramatic polarity created by skin color, the projection of not-me. The result was a playground for the imagination. What rose up out of collective needs to allay internal fears and to rationalize external exploitation was an American Africanism—a fabricated brew of darkness, otherness, alarm, and desire that is uniquely American. (There also exists, of course, a European Africanism with a counterpart in colonial literature.)"[6] In his painting Luc Tuymans demystifies the dark regions of his own perception. The brightness, extreme to the point of painful blinding, that characterizes many of his pictures, proves to be a rejection of the purifying pathos of the shadow. Unrepresentable is not that which remains outside the realm of brightness, but rather that which eludes an overarching construction of "history." Art does not serve to underscore the global evidence of the facts, but instead addresses a particular "memory" that cannot find rest. The great impact of Tuymans' pictures does not lie in determining content but rather in focusing thought on virulent points. Between the individual works in the constellation of Congo paintings begins the process of illuminating another "dark region of the world": Europe.

(Translation: Catherine Schelbert)

1) Toni Morrison, "Disturbing Nurses and the Kindness of Sharks," in: Toni Morrison, *Playing in the Dark: Whiteness and the Literary Imagination* (New York: Vintage Books, 1993), p. 90.
2) Joseph Conrad, *Youth and Heart of Darkness* (London: J. M. Dent and Sons Ltd, 1965), p. 148.
3) Cf. Adam Hochschild, *King Leopold's Ghost: A Story of Greed, Terror and Heroism in Colonial Africa* (Boston/New York: Houghton Mifflin, 1998).
4) Ludo de Witte, *De moord op Lumumba* (Leuven: Van Halewyck, 1999). French version: *L'assassinat de Lumumba* (Paris: Karthala, 2000).
5) Gerhard Richter in conversation with Jan Thorn-Prikker, in: *Parkett* No.19, 1989, p. 145.
6) Toni Morrison, "Romancing the Shadow," in: Toni Morrison, op. cit., p. 38.

LUC TUYMANS, STATUE, 2000,

oil on canvas, 61 x 25 1/5" / Öl auf Leinwand, 155 x 64 cm.

(PHOTO: FELIX TIRRY)

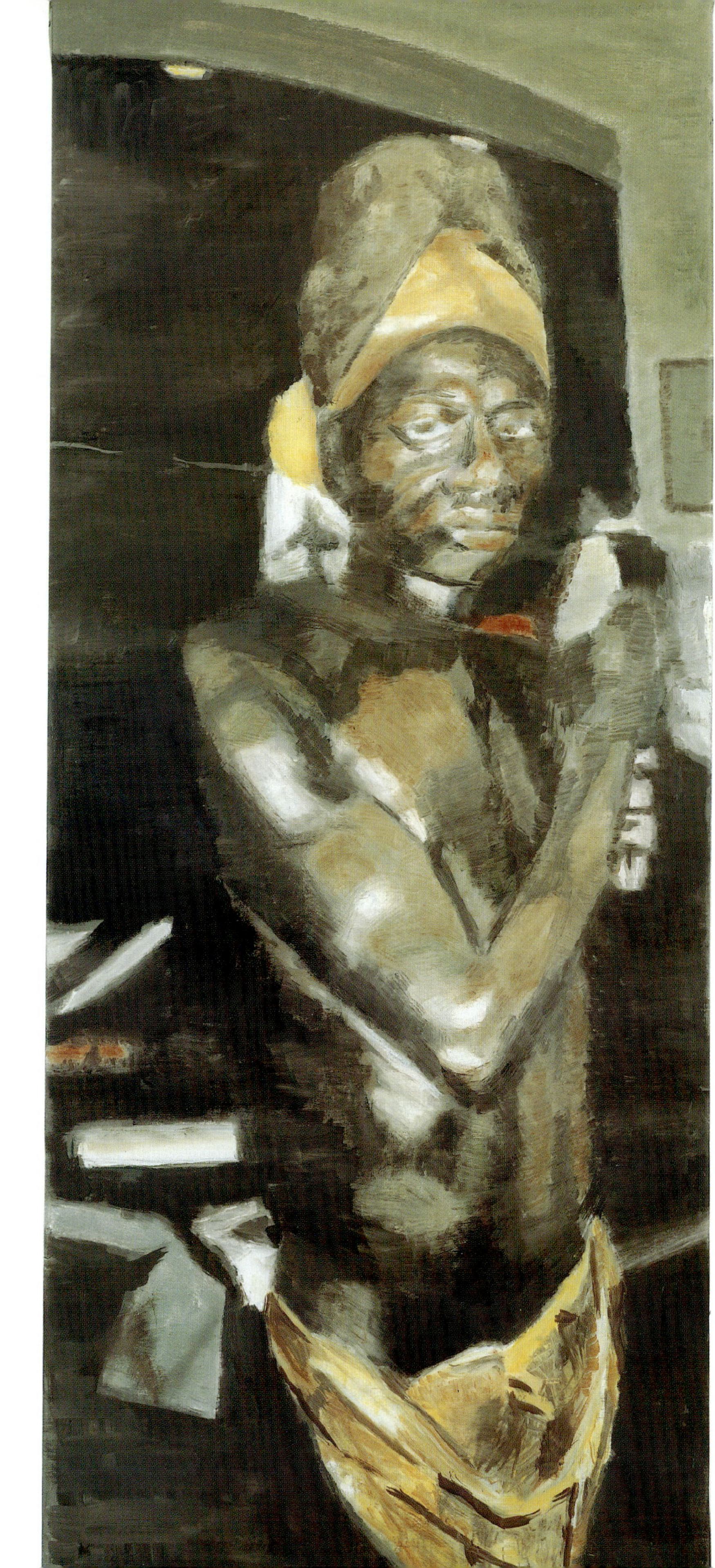

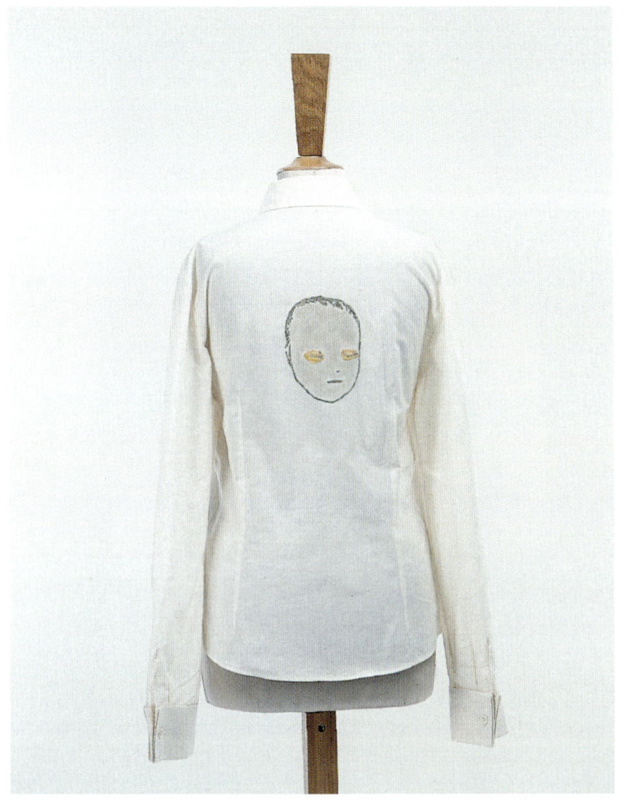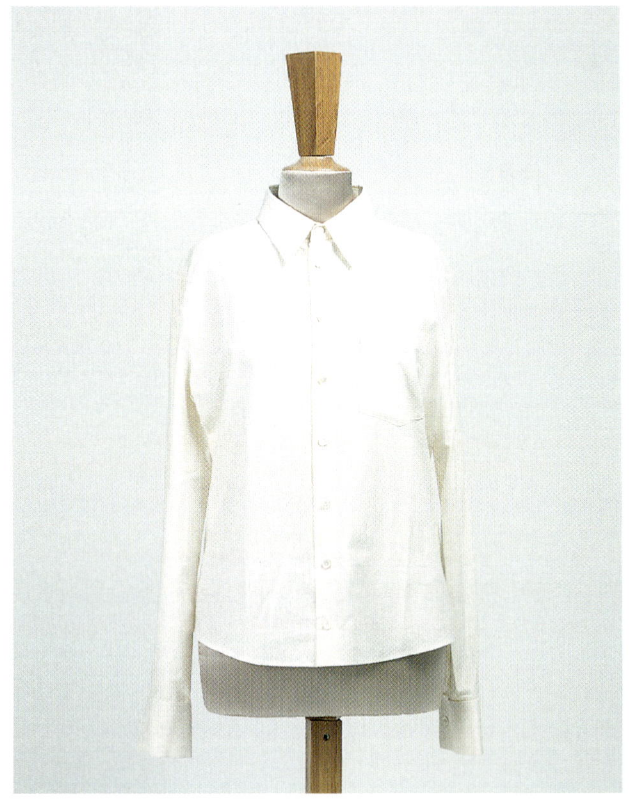

Edition for Parkett LUC TUYMANS

Silence, 1990–2000

Men's cotton shirt with reproduction of the artist's painting SILENCE, 1991.

Shirt design by Walter van Beirendonck, 3 sizes (S, M, L).

Hand-stitched version made by Trois Quarts, Antwerp.

Edition of 20, signed and numbered.

Silkscreen version printed by Lorenz Boegli, Zurich.

Edition of 99, signed and numbered.

Stille, 1990–2000

Baumwoll-Herrenhemd mit Reproduktion des Bildes SILENCE, 1991.

Hemddesign Walter van Beirendonck, 3 Grössen (S, M, L).

Handgestickte Version durch Trois Quarts, Antwerpen.

Auflage: 20, signiert und nummeriert.

Siebdruck-Version gedruckt bei Lorenz Boegli, Zürich.

Auflage: 99, signiert und nummeriert.

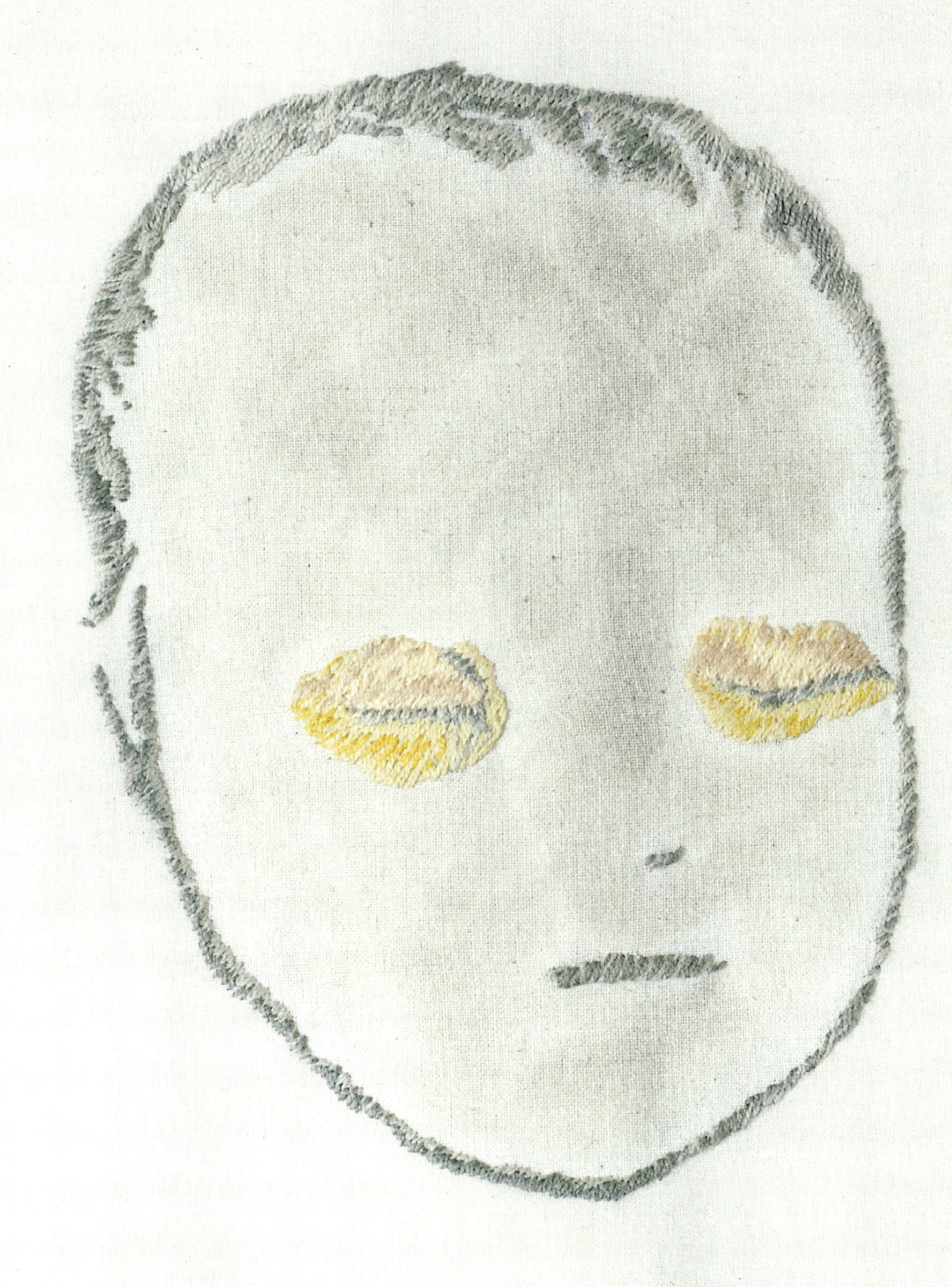

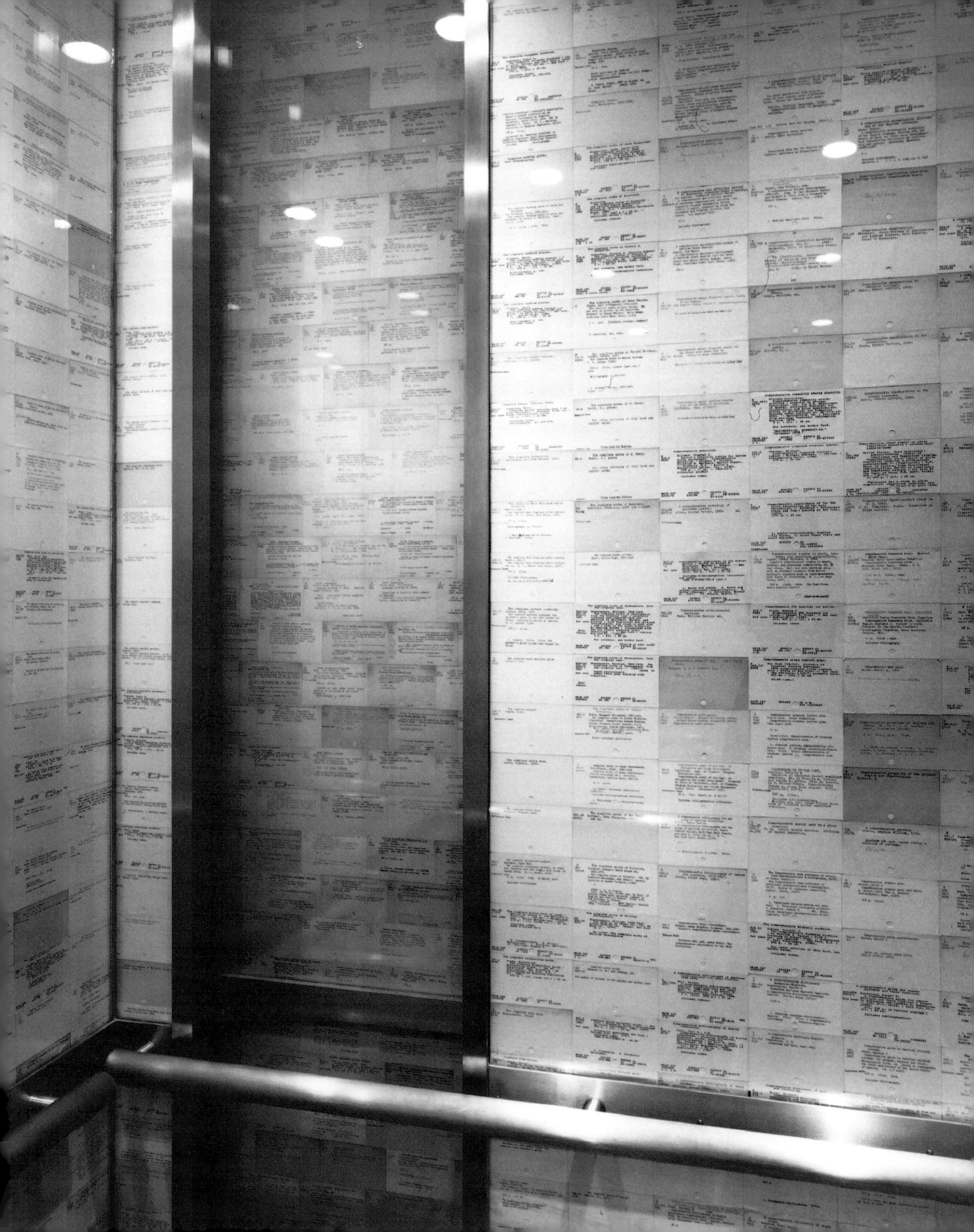

HOWARD SINGERMAN

THE BODY IN THE LIBRARY

Since 1993, David Bunn has worked inside the library, literally at first, now only virtually, but it is in the later works that the library's enclosure is most strongly felt. Before then, particularly in three large and wryly erudite installations realized in Los Angeles area museums between 1988 and 1991, Bunn's work had taken as its subject the conjunction of knowledge and power in the field of vision, Foucault's "unimpeded empire of the gaze." The library must have seemed a fitting place to continue that investigation; it gathers together all of the material he had worked on: the map and the atlas, tales of discovery and the disciplinary wisdom of ethnography. More than that, it orders them: The library is not just a collection of texts, it is a system of knowledge. According to the Dewey Decimal System, the classification system employed by most American public

libraries, our world of knowledge—and our knowledge of the world—is divided into ten categories, each of which is designated by a hundred-number span. The first class, 000–099, includes general works, such as encyclopedias; 100–199, is used for philosophy and psychology; 200–299, religion and mythology; and so on through the nine hundreds, history, geography, and travel. Whatever we write, whatever we will write, is already expected; there's always a place for it, somewhere between two other books on the shelf and in the catalogue. The library knows the field and content of each of its books, its extension and its implications: the numbers on the spine designate the address of the book and to whom—to the edges of which other texts, that is—it is addressed.

Bunn's first library work, fittingly titled A PLACE FOR EVERYTHING AND EVERYTHING IN ITS PLACE (1993), is a permanent installation at the Los Angeles Central Library, realized in two of the building's passenger elevators and in the hoist shafts that carry them. As part of a library renovation in the early

HOWARD SINGERMAN teaches art history at the University of Virginia and is the author of *Art Subjects: Making Artists in the American University* (Berkeley/London: University of California Press, 1999).

nineties, the card catalogue was replaced by a new computerized system; A PLACE FOR EVERYTHING is a souvenir of the old catalogue and a map of the library's organization. On the back wall of each shaft, and visible through a floor-to-ceiling window in the cab, a column of cards, eight stories tall, is arranged to match the subject matter of the books on each of the library's floors. Inside the cab, lining its walls, are more library cards, each of which lists a book whose title begins with either "Complete" or "Comprehensive." Sampling the library's subjects, crossing through its organizing system, the elevators are allegorical—or maybe material—search engines. The cards that line the hoist shafts are smart; they are organized by content, arranged to echo the order of the shelves and the categorical organization of knowledge. They are metaphors for the library's own metaphoric totality, the wholeness and unity of what is known. The cards inside the cabs are arranged not by call number but alphabetically; they are dumber, continually surprised. They pass without noticing from *Comprehensive Approaches to the Burned Person* to *Comprehensive Architectural Services* to *Comprehensive Atlas of the World*. Their connection is accidental, contingent, and purely metonymic.

A PLACE FOR EVERYTHING used 9506 cards; Bunn inherited the remainder of the catalogue, some two million cards, boxed for disposal by library staff in alphabetical order in 514 cardboard boxes. Since 1996, he has used that sheer, dumb order—an order without depth or internal knowledge, like Donald Judd's "one thing after another"—assembling runs of cards, of book titles and subject headings, in response to a word or phrase posed to the remains. Titles and subject headings tend not to be full sentences, certainly not complex ones, and Bunn's product is a series of usually short, minimally punctuated, and often evocative lines that seem, thanks to the alphabet, to return to a theme, or at least to a word, as though to a refrain: They look, and come to read, like poems. All the cards in the L.A. catalogue that begin with the words "after you," to take an obviously self-referential example, form a poem that seems quite close to the project of Bunn's earlier installations: "After you, Columbus/After you, Magellan/After you, Marco Polo/After you with a pis-

tol." The poem hangs on the last line; it seems to take into account each preceding line, placing each in just the right, stepped relation to the next. It unifies them, at least momentarily, under the sign of metaphor rather than the list of metonymy, opening them up to an organizing, seemingly intentional theme. It's hard to imagine that it is only the last card in a series, not an ending but merely a stop. "Take a number/Take a number/Take a number/Take a number/Take a number/Take a number, darling."

Bunn's earlier installations had travestied the gaze, that invidious, distancing vision that produces the world as an object for the viewing subject. Irony as the figure of knowing better was their primary trope. The library works turn out to be different: Their structuring division is not I (self) and other but inside and out, and their trope is metonymy. They figure not the wholeness of knowledge, the fullness and unity of the library—those aren't the cards he uses—but touch, contiguity, and enclosure. The confines of the library are inscribed most insistently in the fifty-foot-long wall of storage boxes that Bunn inherited, that he exhibited with the first card poems in Los Angeles in 1996, and that continues to live in his studio—a barricade, perhaps, certainly a kind of burden. All of the books Bunn produces, an ongoing compendium of the poems included in each exhibition, assembled by project and arranged by genre, open with an image of that wall. The books themselves trace a circular, metonymic path around, but never quite out, of the library. The first number of each edition of books is given to the L.A. Central Library; the physical catalogue that the library cut loose, deactivated and boxed, in 1986, is coming back, slowly and in a very different order than it left.

Bunn's most recent project, DOUBLE MONSTER (2000), might be read as an attempt to escape the confines of the library and the circularity his project inscribes. He has paired the L.A. cards with another catalogue, one that records a collection not of books, but of very real things. Among the things in the collection of the Mütter Museum, a museum of medical curiosities founded in 1849 and housed at the College of Physicians in Philadelphia, are the skeleton of a giant and the cast of a murderer's head, along with an assortment of needles and pins "removed from the body of an hysterical female" and a muff worn to protect the hands of an American revolutionary war surgeon at Valley Forge. Each of these things is catalogued, stood for by a large yellowing card—sometimes two or three—and in each of the works in DOUBLE MONSTER, the Mütter's card draws out and is answered by a run of cards from the L.A. catalogue. Bunn takes it as a reference, as if it said "see also," but the relationship between the Mütter card and the L.A. catalogue is slender, if specific—a repeated word, a small thought. It is, one could say, the site of subjectivity in Bunn's project, the place of the researcher as he continues his search, displacing it from one citation, one thing, to the next. Insisting on the reality, the material presence of the new work, Bunn has titled one of his poems "The Thing," a twenty-three line composition, from G. K. Chesterton's *The Thing* to Geoffrey Household's *Thing to Love*. But the Mütter card that spawned the poem implies yet other things: "Destroyed, January 24, 1941, by authority of the Mütter Committee, as specimen could not be identified." Here, the researcher learns a rather poststructural lesson, it is not the real that language covers over and hides from us, but its absence.

Like much recent art, DOUBLE MONSTER most often summons the real through the body in its opacity and its monstrousness; certainly there are monstrous bodies at the Mütter: the bodies of a famous Viennese prostitute and "a fat woman changed to adipocere," as well as a set of penis and testicles "amputated by a man in an attack of mania a potu." The body as an ordered system of parts was once a privileged trope for the organization of knowledge, for its surfaces and depth. As monstrous as it is now, the Mütter's "body of knowledge" was assembled as a testament to the medical gaze that Foucault wrote of, that opened up and catalogued the body. The bodies at the Mütter are neither quite the bright, transparent bodies of the classical encyclopedists nor the dark, oozing body of the abject in recent art and theory; rather, they are somewhere in between, in chiaroscuro. Generated by the subject cards for "Body Snatching," Bunn's search for bodies finds, among the other titles, multiple copies of Agatha Christie's *The Body in the Library*: "in the library/in

the library/in the library/in the library." There, the bodies are more often gothic, literary and, in a poem that follows from the collection's "cast of the head of A. Horn – murderer of two wives. 1844," even literate ones. One of the Mütter's most monstrous characters, Horn seems only to have wanted to do what Bunn has done, to live within the library, and to write. In answer to the card, Bunn imagined a set of chains, a confinement that was too much, marriage or prison, and then, of course, eventually, the library: "I wanted out!/I wanted to be an actress/I wanted to murder/I wanted to see/I wanted to travel/I wanted to write/I wanted to write a poem."

The body and its trace do return in DOUBLE MONSTER. But the real they offer is paper-thin; the trace is only that, a smudge or a fingerprint; and the body present only in memory, a somatic tug. Each of the found poems is exhibited with its cards hung one below the next as they came out of the drawer, proof of their authenticity, their accidental, metonymic order. The cards for longer poems can reach to the floor; they require us to bend over, even to squat, as we might have done once, some years ago, working on an essay, a dissertation, to open one of the catalogue's lower drawers. There, stooped over or getting up, we feel the materiality of the catalogue. We're getting too old, and the cards are, too. They are too material, too bodily; they require too much upkeep—that was the librarians' problem. Certainly they bear traces of other bodies on their own: stains, smears, cracked corners, and worn edges, handwritten addenda; those indexical traces that are metonymy's material equivalents. Bunn insists on one last and quite eerily beautiful link between the card and the body. Unlike the castoff cards of the L.A. catalogue, the Mütter's original cards are still safe at home in Philadelphia. What Bunn has included in his frames, the evidence that is answered and explained by the L.A. cards, are painstaking, actual size illustrations by Madena Asbell, a Los Angeles artist trained as a medical illustrator. She has taken them, with all their tatters and crossings out, their manual typewriting and copperplate script, as though they were organs and tissues, as though they were bodies, bodies of knowledge, perhaps, or just bodies in the library.

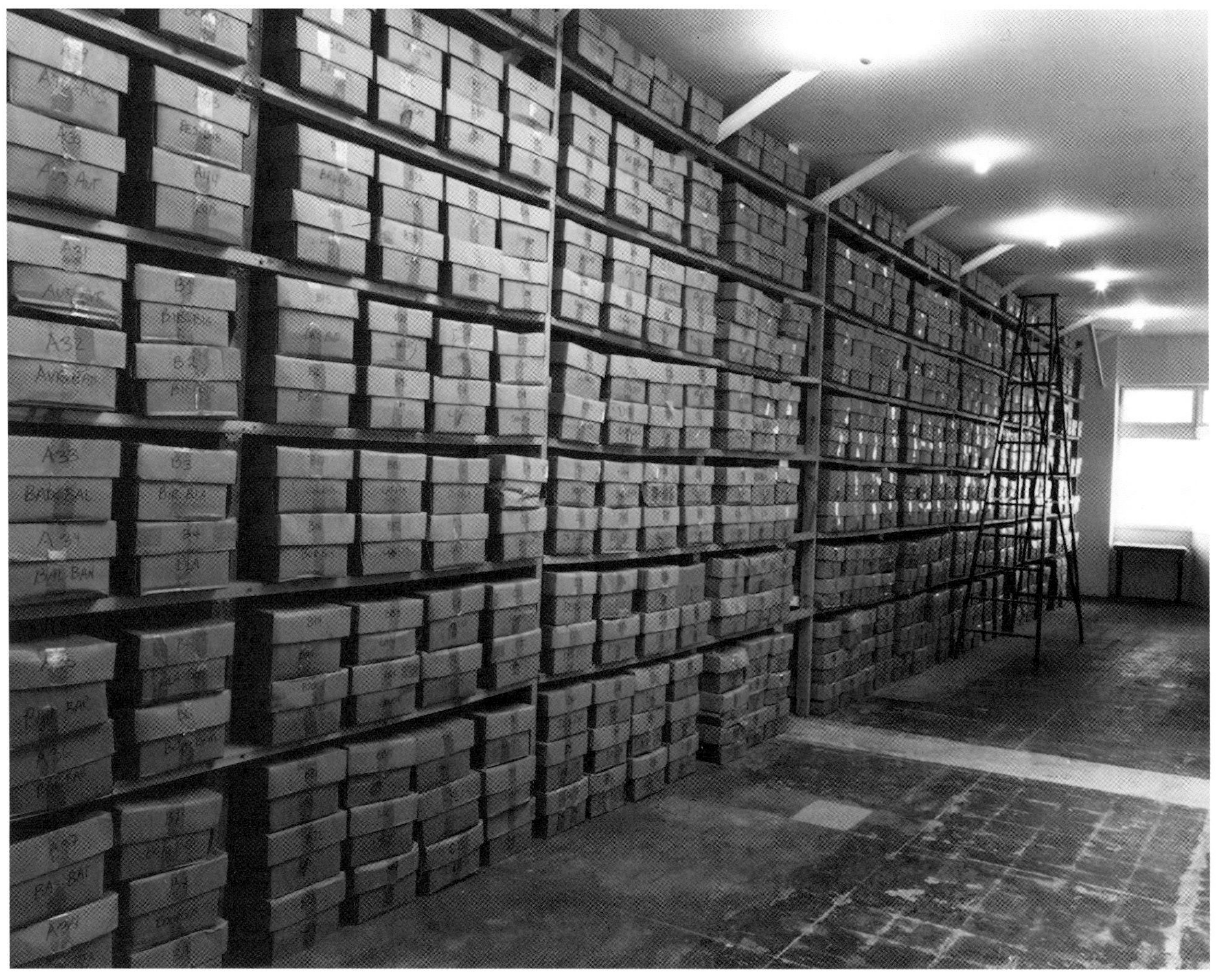

Remains of the discarded card catalogue from the Los Angeles Central Library in the studio of David Bunn. 514 original cardboard storage boxes, numbered and alphabetized, wood shelves, 12 x 50 x 2' / Reste des ehemaligen Zentralkatalogs aus der Los Angeles Central Library im Atelier von David Bunn. 514 Original-Archivschachteln, nummeriert und alphabetisch, Holzgestell, 3,66 x 15,24 x 0,61 m.

DAVID BUNN, DESTROYED, 2000, detail, acrylic, pencil, and pen and ink on paper, Mütter Museum catalogue card, medical illustration by Madena Asbell / ZERSTÖRT, Detail, Acryl, Bleistift und Feder und Tusche auf Papier, Katalogkarte aus dem Mütter-Museum, wissenschaftliche Zeichnung von Madena Asbell.

DIE LEICHE IN DER BIBLIOTHEK

HOWARD SINGERMAN

Seit 1993 hat David Bunn in der Bibliothek gearbeitet, zunächst buchstäblich, jetzt nur noch virtuell, doch es sind die späteren Arbeiten, in denen man die Abgeschiedenheit der Bibliothek am stärksten spürt. Davor hatte Bunn – vor allem in drei grossen und ironisch «gescheiten» Installationen, die er zwischen 1988 und 1991 in verschiedenen Museen im Grossraum Los Angeles realisierte – die Verbindung von Wissen und Macht auf dem Gebiet des Sehens thematisiert, Foucaults «hemmungsloses Reich des Blicks». Die Bibliothek muss ihm als idealer Ort erschienen sein, um diese Untersuchung fortzusetzen. Sie versammelt unter ihrem Dach alles Material, mit dem er sich in seinen Arbeiten auseinander gesetzt hat – die Landkarte und den Atlas, Berichte von Entdeckungen und die disziplinierte Weisheit der Ethnographie. Und mehr als das, sie ordnet dieses Material – die Bibliothek ist nicht bloss eine Sammlung von Texten, sie ist ein Wissenssystem. Im Dewey-Dezimalsystem, dem von den meisten öffentlichen Bibliotheken in Amerika verwendeten Klassifikationsschema, ist unsere Welt des Wissens – und unser Wissen über die Welt – in zehn Kategorien unterteilt, deren jede durch eine Spanne von hundert Ziffern bezeichnet wird. Die erste Klasse, 000–099, enthält allgemeine Werke wie etwa Enzyklopädien, 100–199 umfasst Philosophie und Psychologie, 200–299 Religion und Mythologie und so weiter bis zu den Neunhundertern, Geschichte, Geographie und Reisen.

HOWARD SINGERMAN unterrichtet Kunstgeschichte an der University of Virginia und ist der Verfasser von *Art Subjects: Making Artists in the American University* (University of California Press, Berkeley/London 1999).

Was immer wir schreiben, was immer wir schreiben werden, es wird bereits erwartet, und es gibt immer einen Ort dafür, irgendwo zwischen zwei anderen Büchern auf dem Regal und im Katalog. Die Bibliothek kennt das Gebiet und den Inhalt jedes ihrer Bücher, seinen Umfang und seine Hintergründe: Die Nummer auf dem Buchrücken ist quasi die Adresse des Buches und gibt an, an welche anderen Texte es gerichtet ist beziehungsweise angrenzt.

Bunns erste Bibliotheksarbeit mit dem passenden Titel A PLACE FOR EVERYTHING AND EVERYTHING IN ITS PLACE (Ein Ort für alles und alles an seinem Ort, 1993) ist eine permanente Installation in der Los Angeles Central Library, und zwar in den beiden Personenliften des Gebäudes sowie in den dazu gehörigen Liftschächten. Im Zuge der Renovierung der Bibliothek in den frühen 90er Jahren wurde der Karteikatalog durch ein Computersystem ersetzt: A PLACE FOR EVERYTHING ist eine Erinnerung an den alten Katalog und zugleich ein Organigramm der Bibliothek. An der hinteren Wand jedes Liftschachtes ist ein acht Stockwerke hoher und durch ein vom Boden bis zur Decke reichendes Fenster in der Fahrstuhlkabine sichtbarer Streifen aus Karteikarten angebracht, derart, dass die Karten thematisch den Sachgebieten der einzelnen Stockwerke entsprechen. In den Liftkabinen befinden sich entlang der Wände weitere Karteikarten, die jeweils ein Buch aufführen, dessen Titel entweder mit «Complete» (Vollständige/r) oder mit «Comprehensive» (Umfassende/r) beginnt. Indem sie alle Sachgebiete der Bibliothek versammeln und ihr Organisationssystem durchkreuzen, werden die Fahrstühle zu allegorischen – vielleicht auch materiellen – Suchmaschinen. Die Karten entlang der Liftschächte sind «clever»: nach Inhalten sortiert und so arrangiert, dass sich in ihnen die Ordnung der Regale und die kategoriale Organisation des Wissens spiegelt. Sie sind Metaphern für die metaphorische Totalität der Bibliothek selbst, für die Gesamtheit und Einheit des bestehenden Wissens. Die Karten innerhalb der Liftkabinen sind nicht nach ihren Ordnungsnummern aneinander gereiht, sondern alphabetisch. Sie sind «dümmer», ständigen Überraschungen ausgesetzt. Ohne es zu bemerken, springen sie von *Comprehensive Approaches to the Burned Person* über *Comprehensive Architectural Services* zum *Comprehensive Atlas of the World.* Ihr Zusammentreffen ist zufällig, nicht zwingend, und nur vom Wortlaut bestimmt.

A PLACE FOR EVERYTHING besteht aus 9506 Karten: Bunn erbte den Rest des Katalogs, etwa zwei Millionen Karten, die von den Bibliotheksangestellten zur Entsorgung in 514 Kartons verstaut worden waren. Seit 1996 hat Bunn diese reine, «dumme» Ordnung benützt – eine Ordnung ohne Tiefe oder inneres Wissen, wie Donald Judds «Eins nach dem anderen» – um Serien von Karten, Buchtiteln und Stichwörtern zu erstellen, wobei er jeweils ein Wort oder einen Ausdruck als Herausforderung an die verbliebenen Karten auffasste und sich so von Karte zu Karte leiten liess. Bei den Titeln und Überschriften handelt es sich in der Regel nicht um vollständige Sätze und ganz sicher nicht um komplexe. Das Resultat von Bunns Arbeit besteht also aus einer Reihe von normalerweise kurzen, beinah interpunktionsfreien Zeilen, die aber zahlreiche Assoziationen auslösen und dank der alphabetischen Ordnung immer wieder zu einem bestimmten Thema oder Wort wie zu einem Refrain zurückkehren. Sie sehen aus wie Gedichte und lesen sich auch wie solche. Um ein offenkundig selbstreflexives Beispiel zu nennen: Alle Karten im Katalog der Bibliothek von Los Angeles, die mit den Worten «After you» beginnen, bilden ein Gedicht, das stark an Bunns frühere Installationen erinnert: «After you, Columbus/After you, Magellan/After you, Marco Polo/After you with a pistol (Nach dir, Kolumbus/Nach dir, Magellan, Nach dir, Marco Polo/Dir nach mit einer Pistole)». Die letzte Zeile ist der Dreh- und Angelpunkt des Gedichtes; sie scheint jede vorangegangene Zeile zu berücksich-

tigen und jede von ihnen Schritt für Schritt ins richtige Verhältnis zur folgenden zu setzen. Sie vereinigt alle und bringt sie, mindestens vorübergehend, in einen eher metaphorischen als metonymischen Zusammenhang und bewirkt ihre Öffnung auf ein übergeordnetes, scheinbar beabsichtigtes Thema hin. Es ist schwer vorstellbar, dass es nur die letzte Karte einer fortlaufenden Reihe ist, kein Schluss, sondern einfach nur ein Innehalten. «Take a number/Take a number/Take a number/Take a number/Take a number, darling (Zieh eine Zahl…).»

Bunns frühere Installationen hatten sich über unsere Sehweise lustig gemacht, über die unfaire, distanzierende Betrachtung der Welt, die diese zum Objekt des schauenden Subjekts macht. Ironie, die rhetorische Figur des Besserwissens, war dabei ihr Hauptinstrument. Die Bibliotheksarbeiten hingegen funktionieren anders: Sie unterscheiden nicht zwischen dem Ich (Selbst) und dem Anderen, sondern zwischen Innen und Aussen, und ihr rhetorisches Instrument ist die Metonymie. Sie handeln nicht von der Gesamtheit des Wissens oder der Fülle und Einheit der Bibliothek – das sind nicht die Karten, die Bunn verwendet –, sondern von Berührung, Nachbarschaft und Abgrenzung. Das eindrücklichste Bild der die Bibliothek umschliessenden Mauer gibt die von Bunn ererbte fünfzehn Meter lange Mauer aus Archivschachteln ab, die er 1996 mit den ersten Karteikartengedichten in Los Angeles ausstellte und die in seinem Atelier weiter existiert – ein Hindernis

DAVID BUNN, HEAD OF A MURDERER, 2000,
detail of typed poem / KOPF EINES MÖRDERS, Auszug aus dem maschinengeschriebenen Gedicht.

David Bunn, HEAD OF A MURDERER, 2000, acrylic, pencil, and pen and ink on paper, typewriter on paper and discarded L.A. catalogue cards, framed in nine parts, 38¼ x 60¼" overall (Caldic Collection, Rotterdam) / KOPF EINES MÖRDERS, Acryl, Bleistift und Feder und Tinte auf Papier, Schreibmaschine auf Papier und ausgeschiedenen Katalogkarten der L.A. Central Library), gerahmt, neunteilig, insgesamt 97,2 x 153 cm.

vielleicht, aber mit Sicherheit eine Bürde. Alle Bücher, die Bunn produziert – ein fortlaufendes, nach Projekten und Genres geordnetes Kompendium aller Gedichte aus seinen Ausstellungen –, beginnen mit einer Abbildung jener Mauer. Die Bücher selbst folgen einer kreisförmigen metonymischen Spur um die Bibliothek herum, doch niemals wirklich aus ihr hinaus. Das erste Exemplar jeder Auflage erhält die Los Angeles Central Library: Der physisch greifbare Katalog, den die Bibliothek 1986 ausgeschieden, ausser Kraft gesetzt und in Schachteln verstaut hat, kehrt allmählich zurück, und zwar in einer völlig anderen Ordnung als beim Verlassen der Bibliothek.

Bunns jüngstes Projekt, DOUBLE MONSTER (Doppeltes Monster, 2000), kann als Versuch verstanden werden, den Grenzen der Bibliothek und der Zirkularität seines Projekts zu entfliehen. Die Karteikarten aus Los Angeles werden nun mit einem anderen Katalog kombiniert, einem, der nicht Bücher, sondern ganz reale Dinge verzeichnet. Unter den Beständen des Mütter-Museums, eines 1849 gegründeten Museums medizinischer Kuriositäten, das im College of Physicians in Philadelphia untergebracht ist, befinden sich ausser dem Skelett eines Riesen und dem Abguss eines Mörderhauptes ein ganzes Sortiment von Nadeln aus dem Körper einer Hysterikerin und ein Muff, der im Revolutionskrieg bei Valley Forge die Hände eines amerikanischen Feldschers schützte. All diese Dinge sind katalogisiert und durch eine oder mehrere vergilbende Karteikarten vertreten. Und bei jeder Arbeit in DOUBLE MONSTER ruft die «Mütter»-Karte eine Serie von Karten aus dem Los-Angeles-Katalog auf und wird von diesen beantwortet. Bunn benutzt sie als Verweis, so, als ob darauf stünde: «siehe auch», aber die Verbindung zwischen der «Mütter»-Karte und dem Katalog aus Los Angeles ist minimal, wenngleich spezifisch – ein Wort, das sich wiederholt, ein kleiner Gedanke. Es ist, so könnte man sagen, der Ort der Subjektivität in Bunns Projekt, das Feld des Forschers, der seine Suche fortsetzt, indem er sie von einem Zitat zum nächsten, von einer Sache zur nächsten verlagert. Bunn insistiert auf der Realität, der materiellen Präsenz seines neuen Werks und nennt eines seiner Gedichte «The Thing (Das Ding)», eine dreiundzwanzig Zeilen umfassende Komposition, von G. K. Chestertons *The Thing* bis zu Geoffrey Households *Thing to Love*. Doch die «Mütter»-Karte, die das Ganze ausgelöst hat, impliziert noch ganz andere Dinge: «Zerstört am 24. Januar 1941, mit amtlicher Genehmigung des Mütter-Komitees, da der Gegenstand nicht identifiziert werden konnte.» Dem Forscher wird hier die recht poststrukturalistische Lektion zuteil, dass die Sprache nicht das Reale verdeckt und vor uns verbirgt, sondern dessen Absenz.

Wie so oft in der zeitgenössischen Kunst beschwört auch DOUBLE MONSTER das Reale mithilfe des Körpers in seiner ganzen Undurchschaubarkeit und Ungeheuerlichkeit. Und natürlich gibt es monströse Körper im Mütter-Museum: etwa die Leiche einer berühmten Wiener Prostituierten oder die «einer dicken, in Leichenwachs verwandelten Frau» sowie ein Penis samt Hoden, die sich «ein Mann im Zustand schwerer Trunkenheit amputierte». Der Körper als geordnetes System von Teilen war einst ein beliebter Gemeinplatz der Organisation des Wissens, seiner Oberflächen und seiner Tiefe. So ungeheuerlich es uns heute vorkommen mag, das «Wissenskorpus» des Mütter-Museums ist ein Zeugnis jenes medizinischen Blicks, der den Körper öffnete und katalogisierte und über den auch Foucault schrieb. Die Körper im Mütter-Museum entsprechen weder ganz den leuchtenden, durchscheinenden Leichen der klassischen Enzyklopädisten, noch dem düsteren, klebrigen, Ekel erregenden Körper in der zeitgenössischen Kunst und Theorie des Abscheulichen, sondern sie befinden sich irgendwo im Halbdunkel dazwischen. Ausgehend von den Stichwortkarten zu «Body Snatching (Leichenraub)» fördert Bunns Suche nach Körpern bzw. Leichen neben anderen Titeln mehrere Exemplare von Agatha Christies *The Body in the Library (Der Tote in der Bibliothek)* zutage: «in the library/in the library/in the library/in the library». Die Toten sind hier zumeist schauerromantische, literarische oder aber, wie in dem Gedicht, das sich aus dem «Abguss des Hauptes von A. Horn, dem Mörder zweier Ehefrauen, 1844» ergibt, sogar echte. Horn, eine der erschreckendsten Gestalten des Mütter-Museums, hat anscheinend nichts anderes gewollt als Bunn, nämlich in der Bibliothek leben und schreiben. Als Reaktion auf seine Karte stellte sich Bunn eine Reihe von Verkettungen vor, eine zu starke Einschränkung, die Ehe oder das Gefängnis, und schliesslich, was denn sonst, die Bibliothek: «I wanted out!/I wanted to be an actress/I wanted to murder/I wanted to see/I wanted to travel/I wanted to write/I wanted to write a poem (Ich wollte raus!/Ich wollte Schauspielerin sein/Ich wollte morden/Ich wollte sehen/Ich wollte reisen/Ich wollte schreiben/Ich wollte ein Gedicht schreiben).»

Der Körper und seine Spur kommen in DOUBLE MONSTER wiederholt vor. Aber ihre Realität ist hauchdünn: Die Spur ist wirklich nur eine Spur – ein Fleck oder ein Fingerabdruck, und der Körper existiert nur in der Erinnerung, ein somatisches Zucken. Jedes der gefundenen Gedichte ist mit den dazu gehörigen Karten ausgestellt, die nacheinander von oben nach unten aufgehängt sind, in der Reihenfolge, in der sie aus der Karteischublade kamen, ein Beweis ihrer Authentizität, ihrer zufälligen, metonymischen Ordnung. Die Karten der längeren Gedichte reichen bis auf den Boden, sodass man sich zum Entziffern bücken, ja hinkauern muss, wie man das vielleicht vor Jahren gemacht hat, während der Arbeit an einem Essay, einer Dissertation, um eine der unteren Katalogschubladen herauszuziehen. Im Moment, in dem wir uns bücken oder wieder aufstehen, spüren wir die Materialität des Katalogs. Wir werden allmählich alt, und die Karten auch. Sie sind zu materiell, zu körperlich; sie verlangen zu viel Pflege – das war auch das Problem der Bibliothekare. Mit Sicherheit weisen sie Spuren anderer Körper auf: Flecken, Abdrücke, geknickte Ecken und ausgefranste Ränder, handschriftliche Ergänzungen; lauter Hinweise und Spuren, sozusagen materielle Entsprechungen der Metonymie. Bunn insistiert auf dieser letzten und unheimlich schönen Verbindung zwischen Karte und Körper. Anders als die ausgemusterten Karten des Los-Angeles-Katalogs befinden sich die Originalkarten des Mütter-Museums noch sicher daheim in Philadelphia. Was Bunn davon in seine Arbeiten aufgenommen hat, die Beweisstücke, auf welche die Los-Angeles-Karten erklärend antworten, sind peinlich genaue, originalgrosse Wiedergaben von Madena Asbell, einer Künstlerin aus Los Angeles, die über eine Ausbildung als medizinwissenschaftliche Zeichnerin verfügt. Sie hat sie nachempfunden mit all ihren Makeln und Korrekturen, mit ihrer Schreibmaschinenschrift und den gestochen scharfen handschriftlichen Einträgen, als handle es sich dabei um Organe und Gewebe, als wären es tote Körper, Körper des Wissens oder auch einfach nur Tote in der Bibliothek.

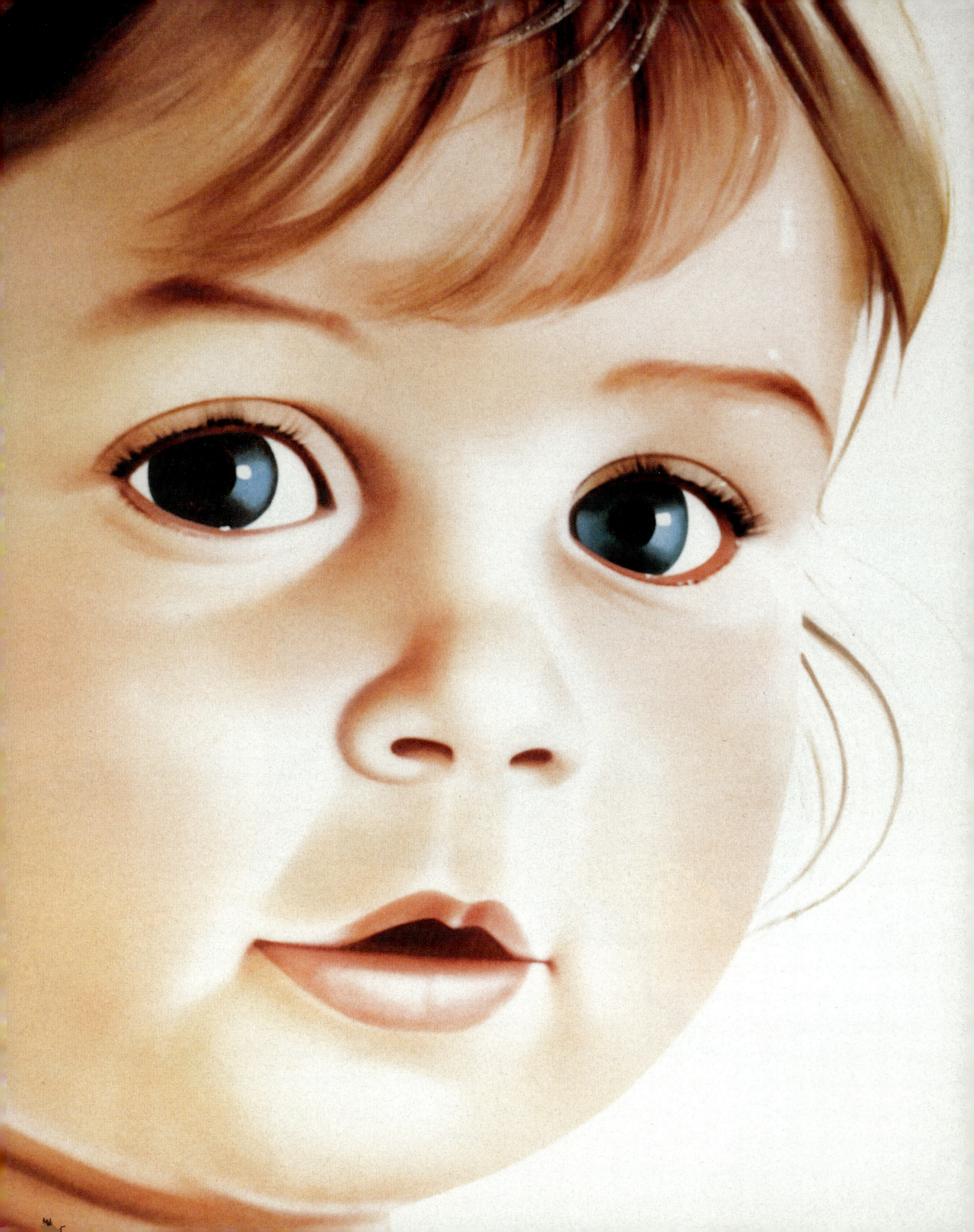

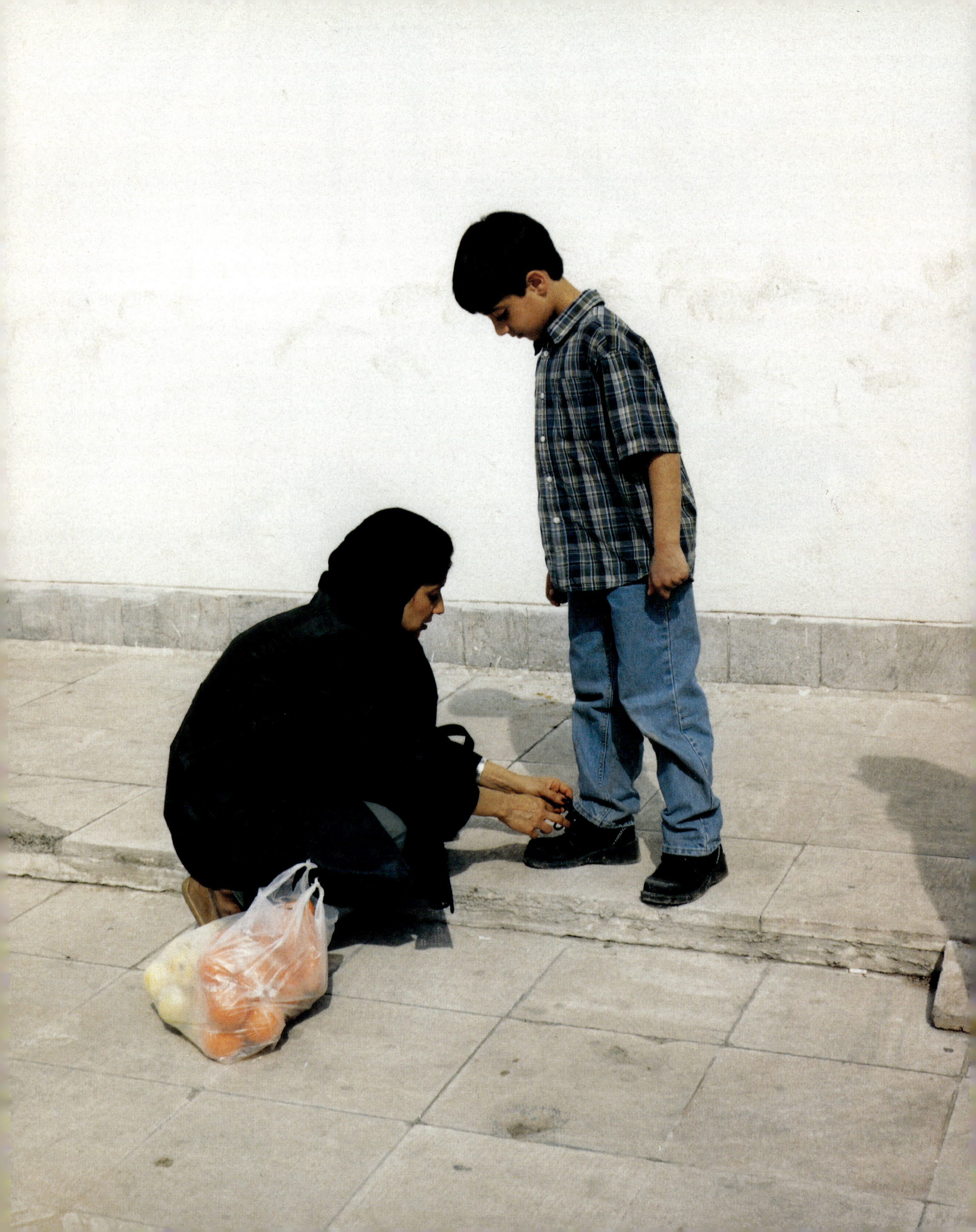

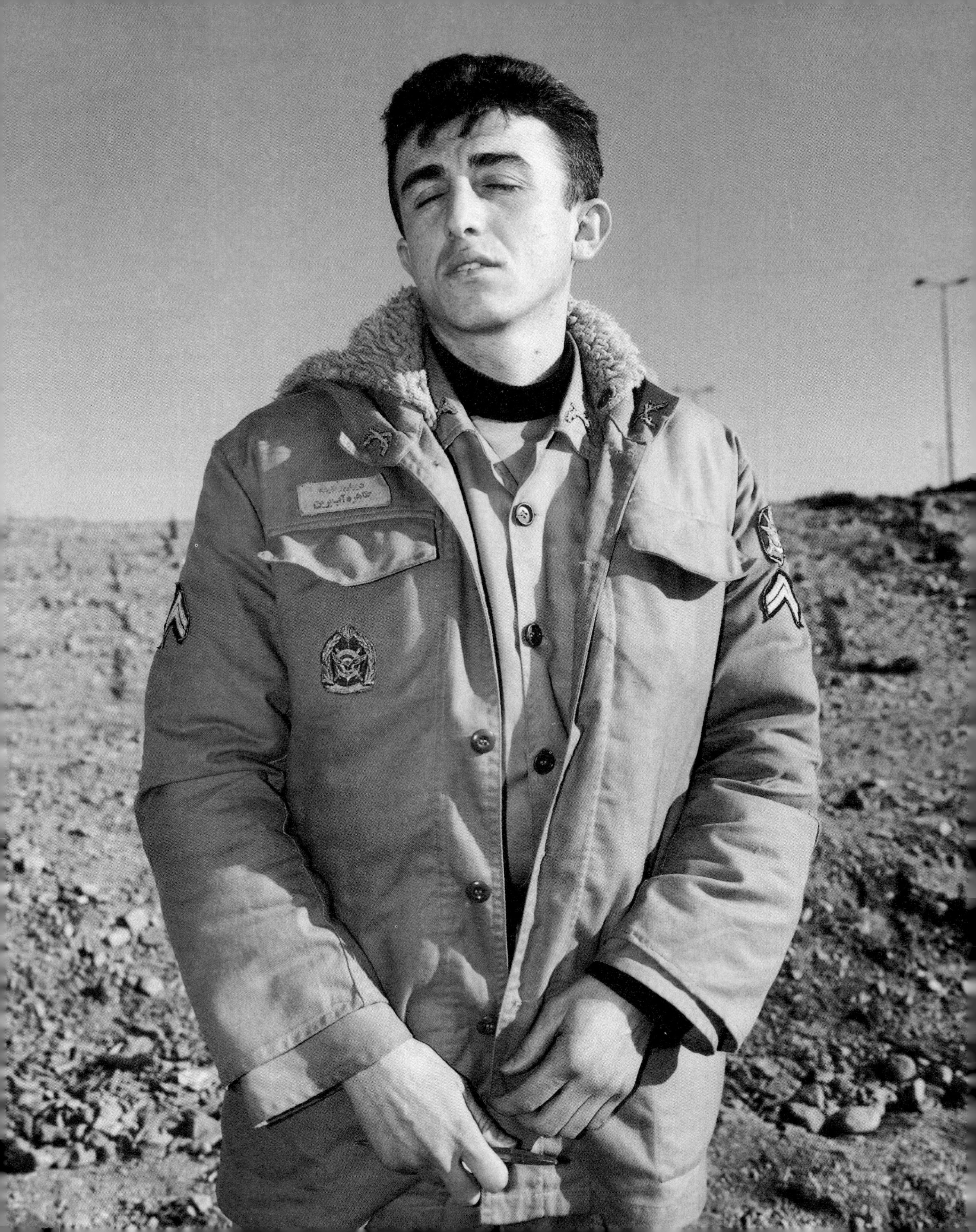

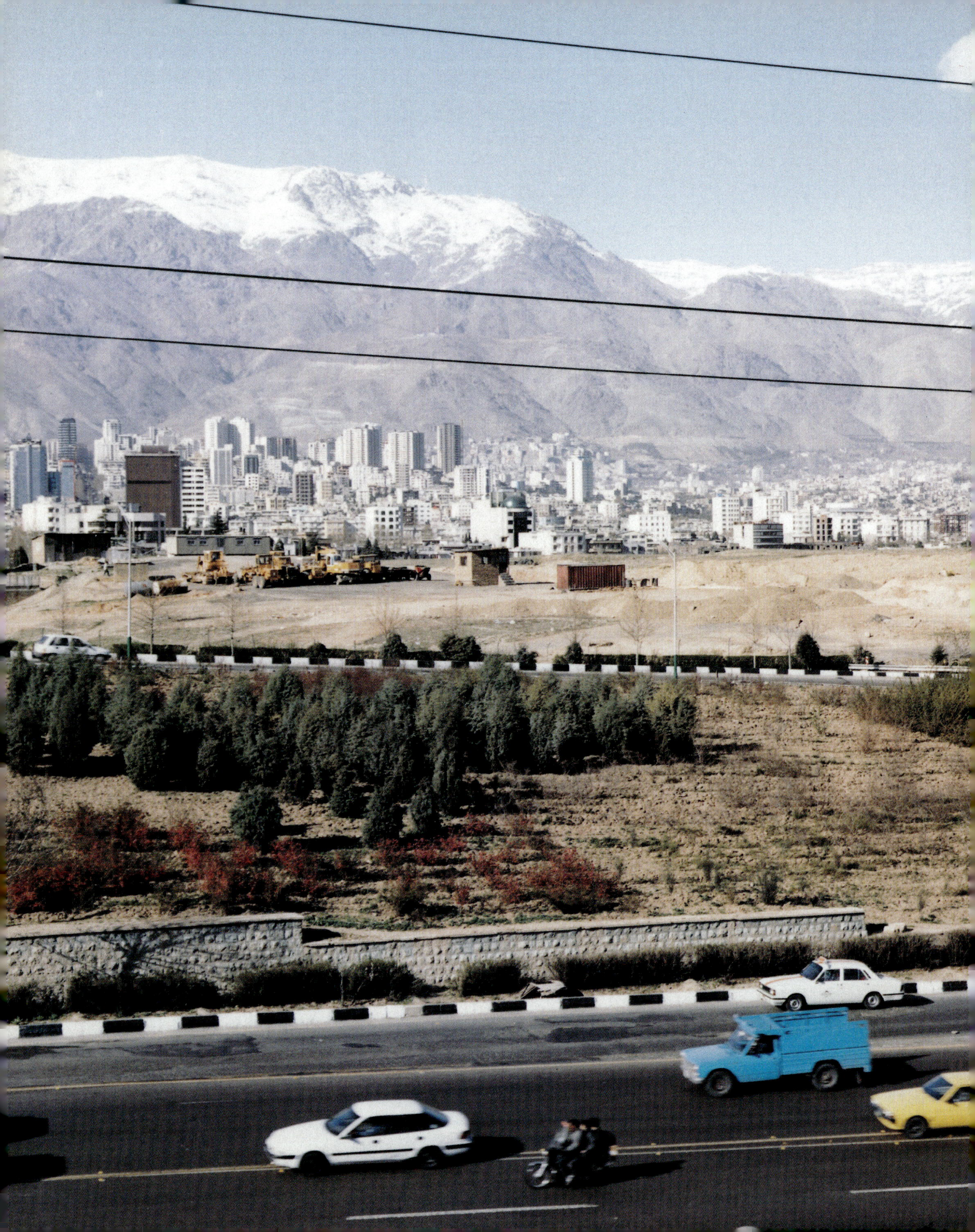

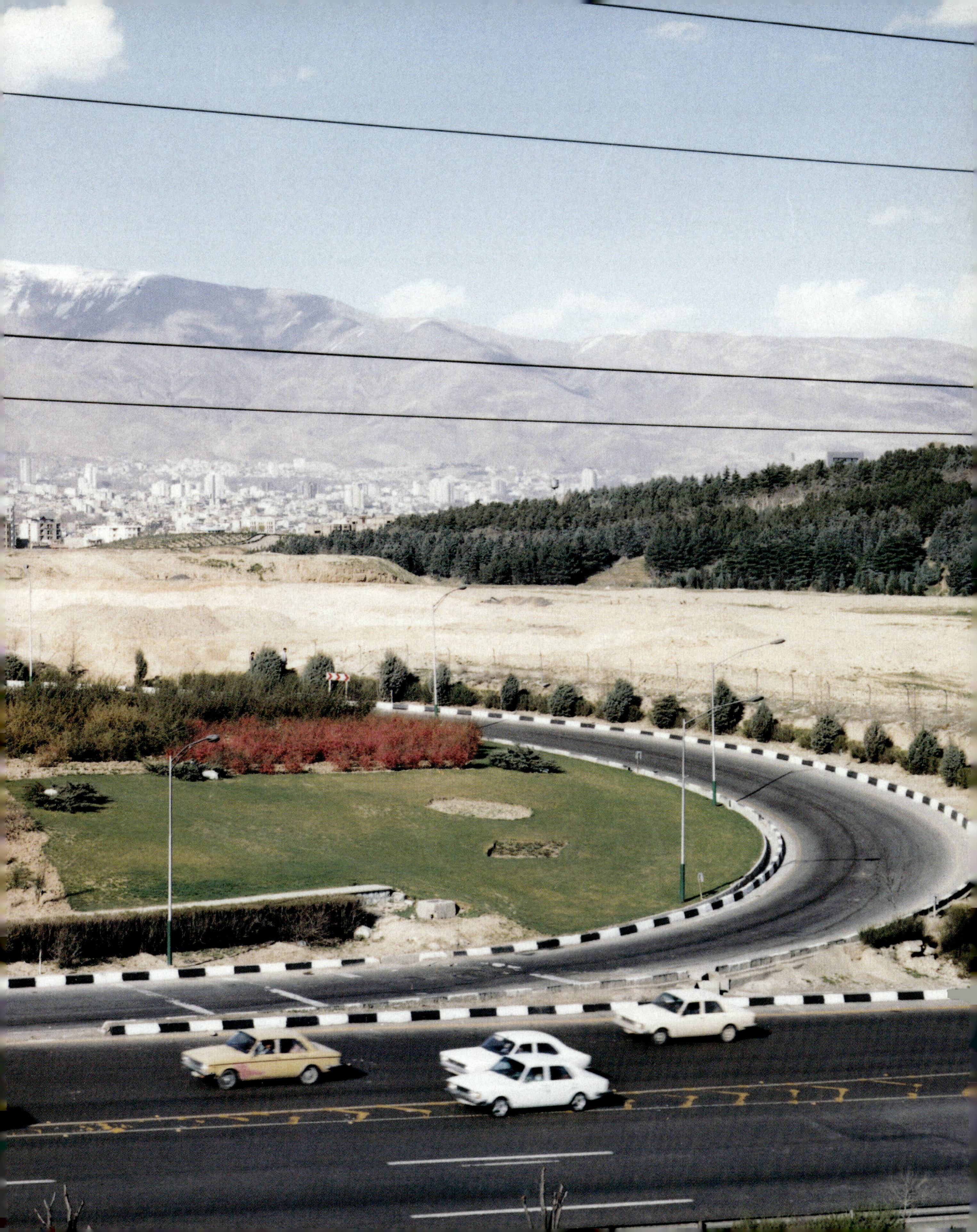

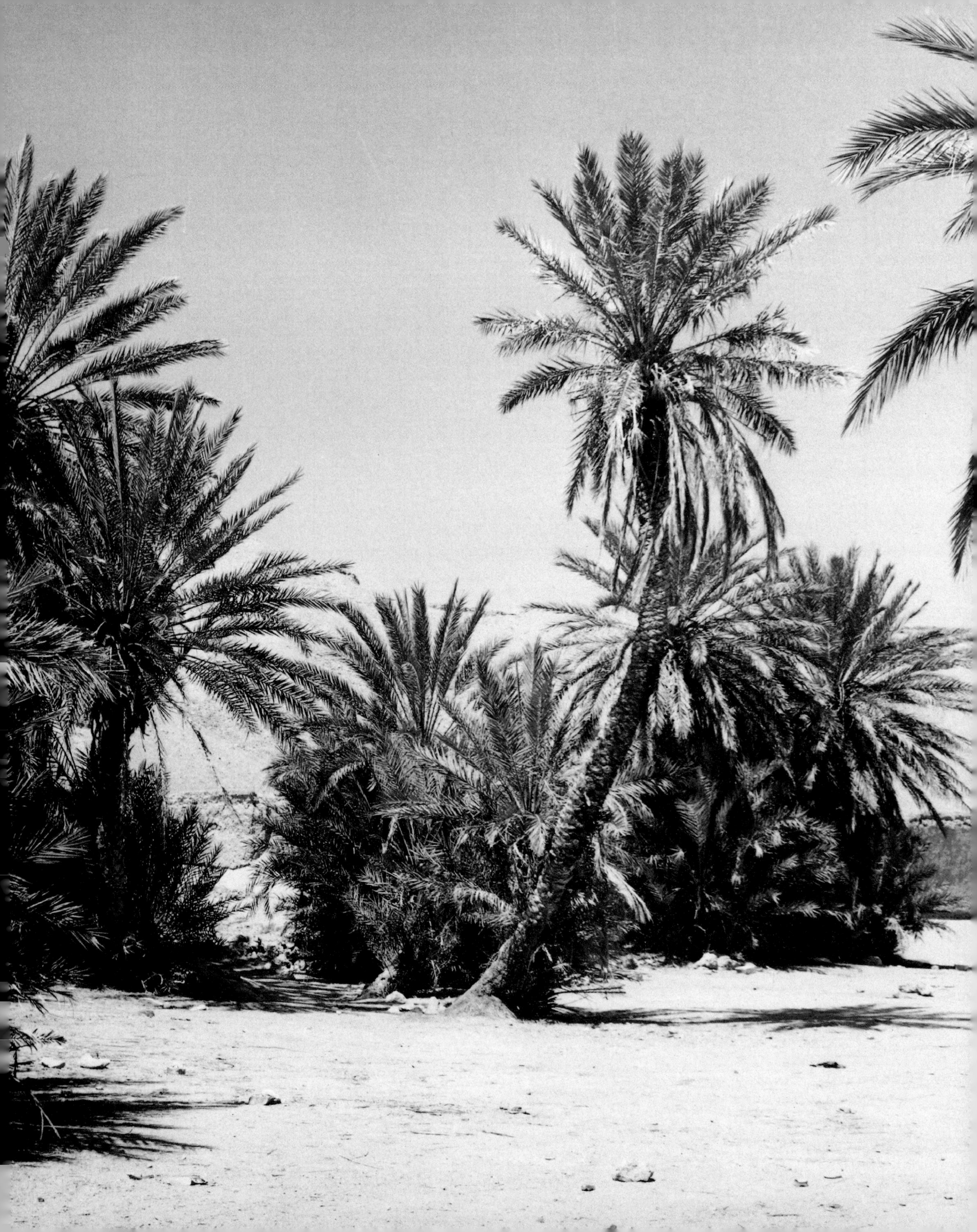

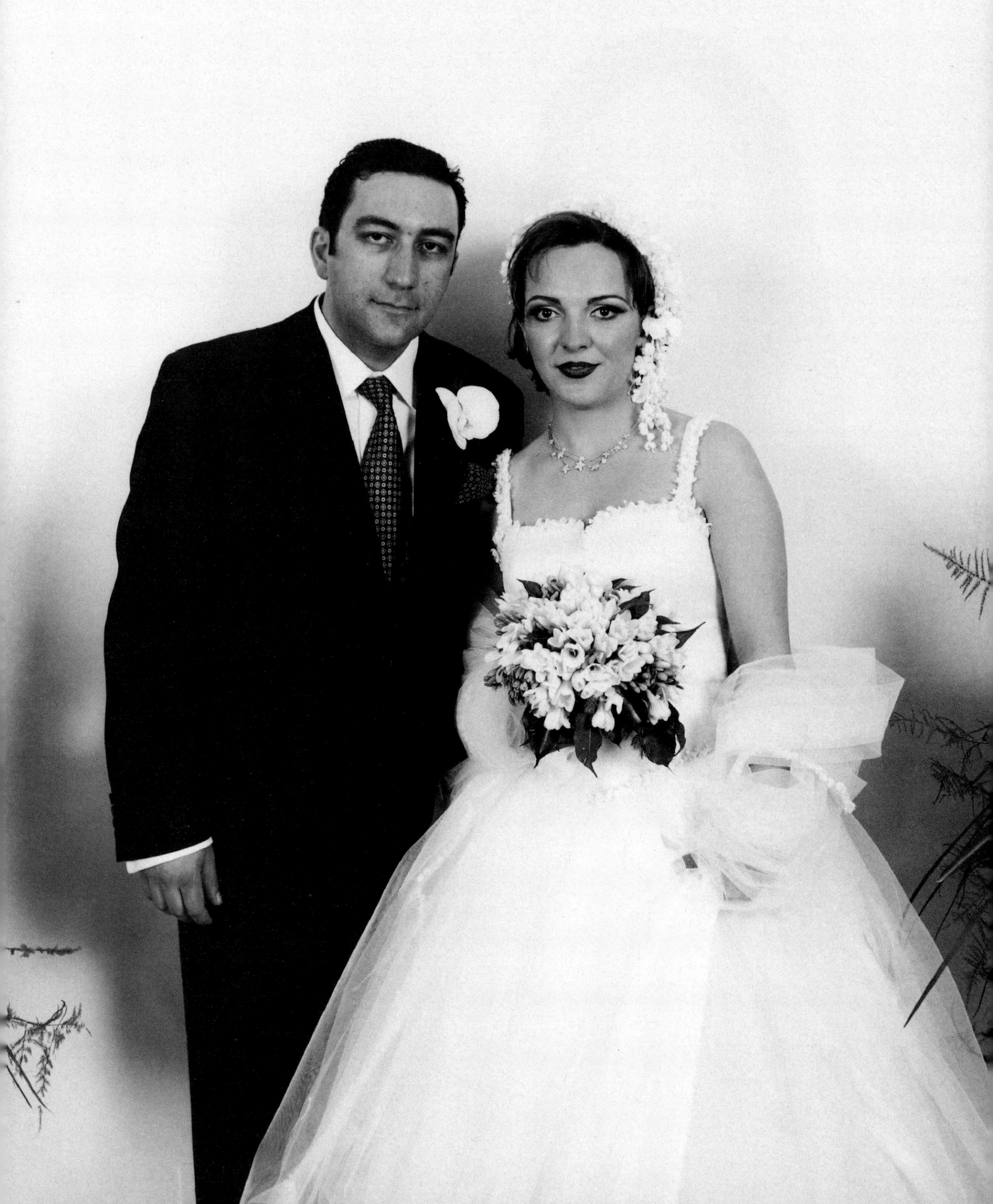

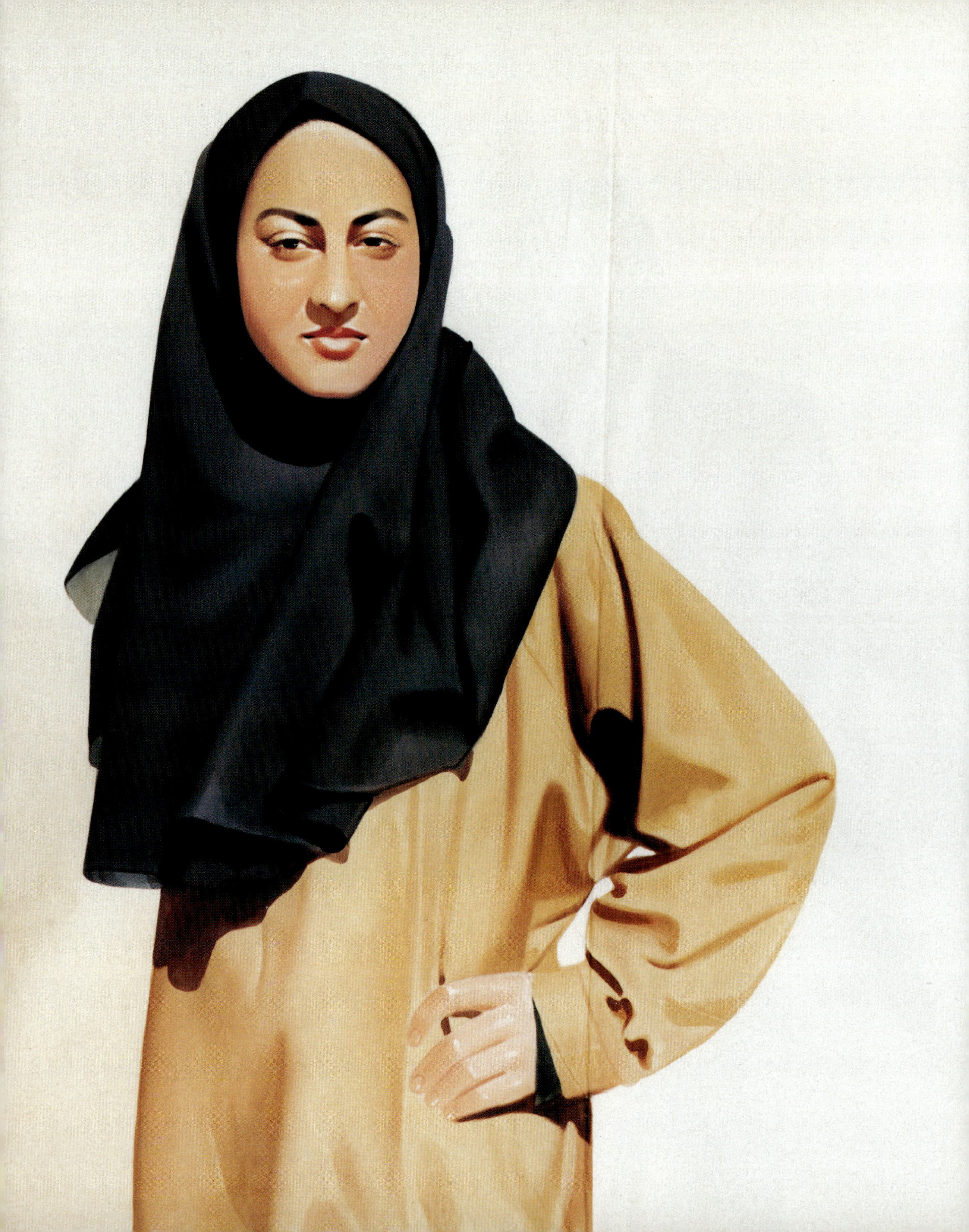

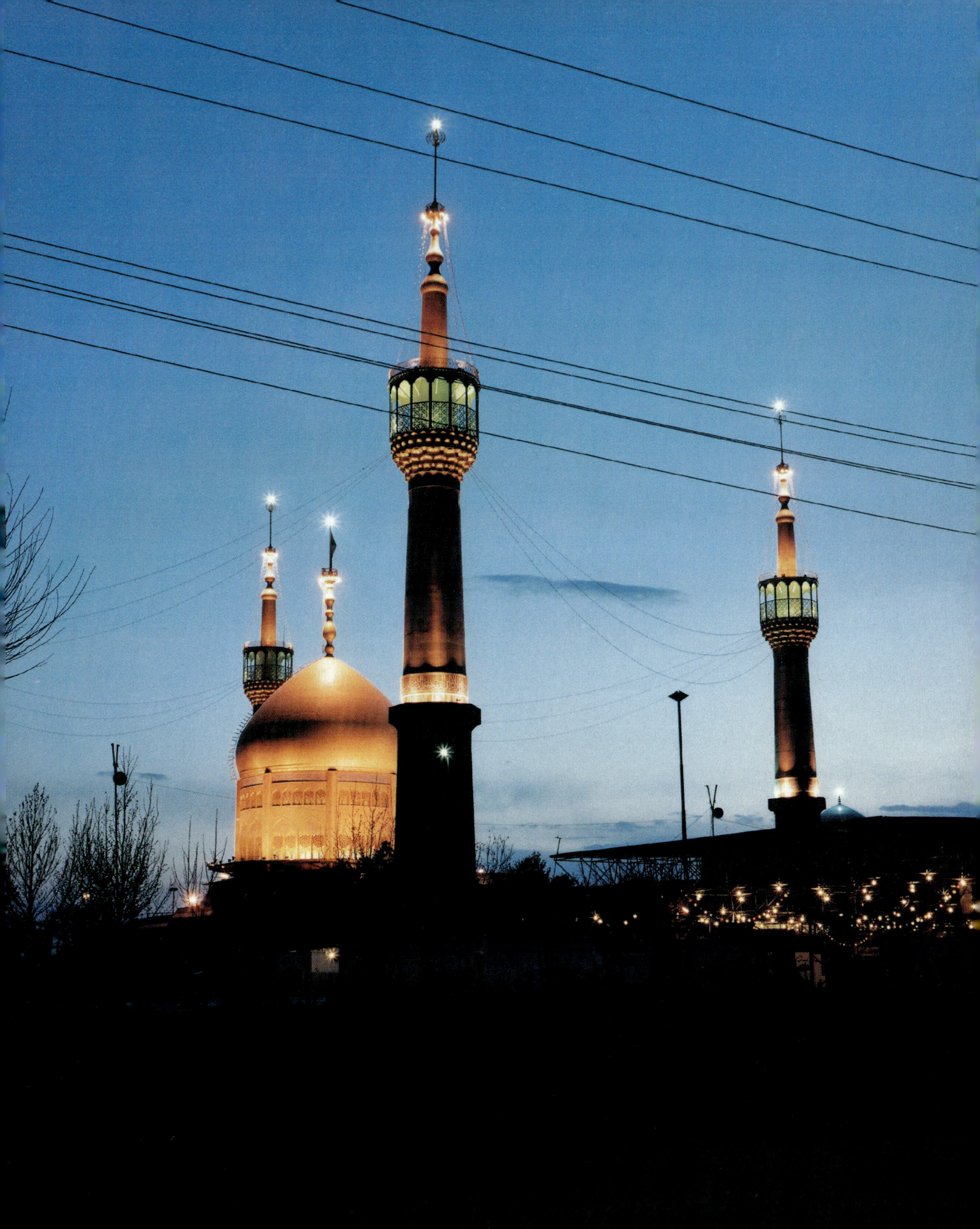

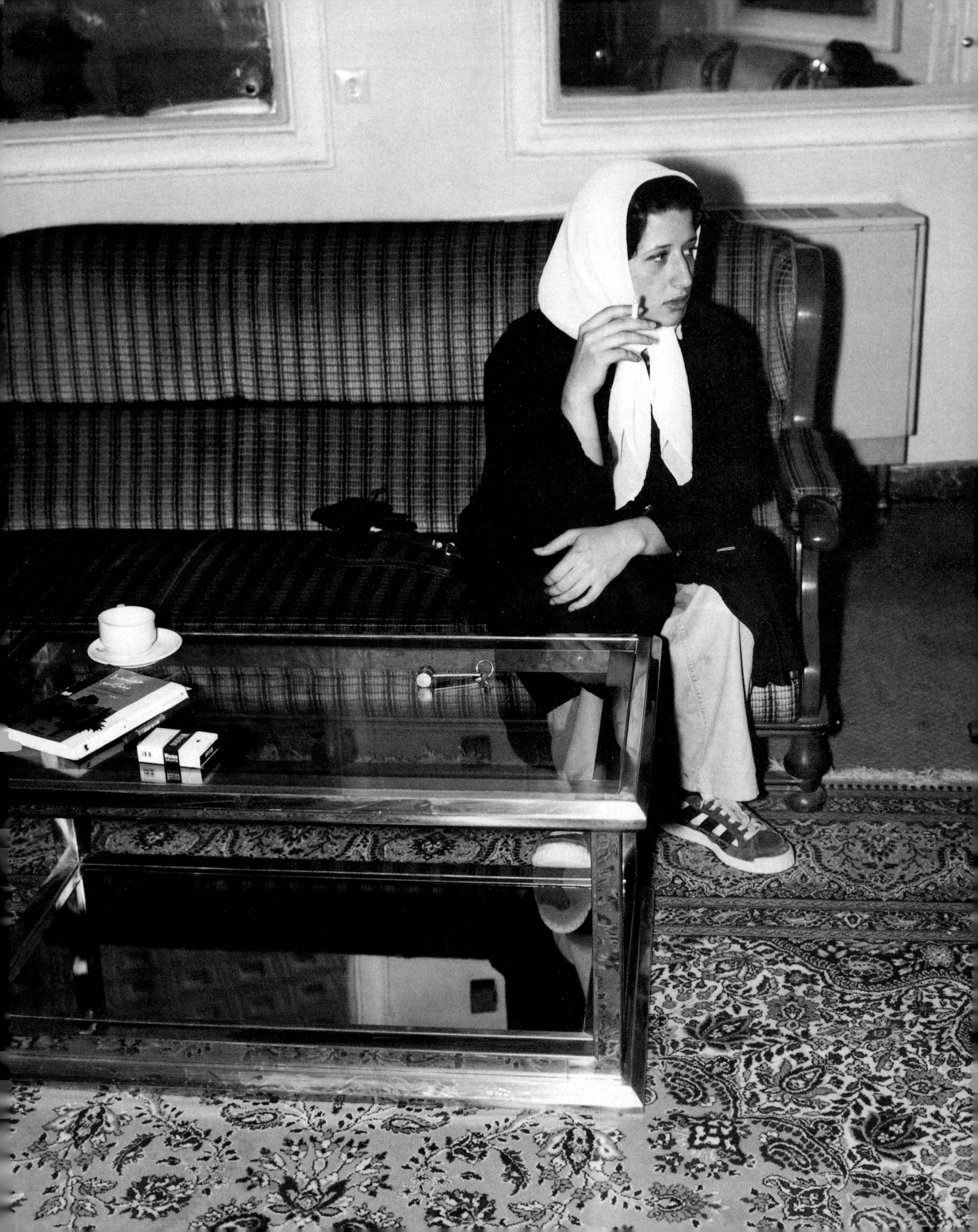

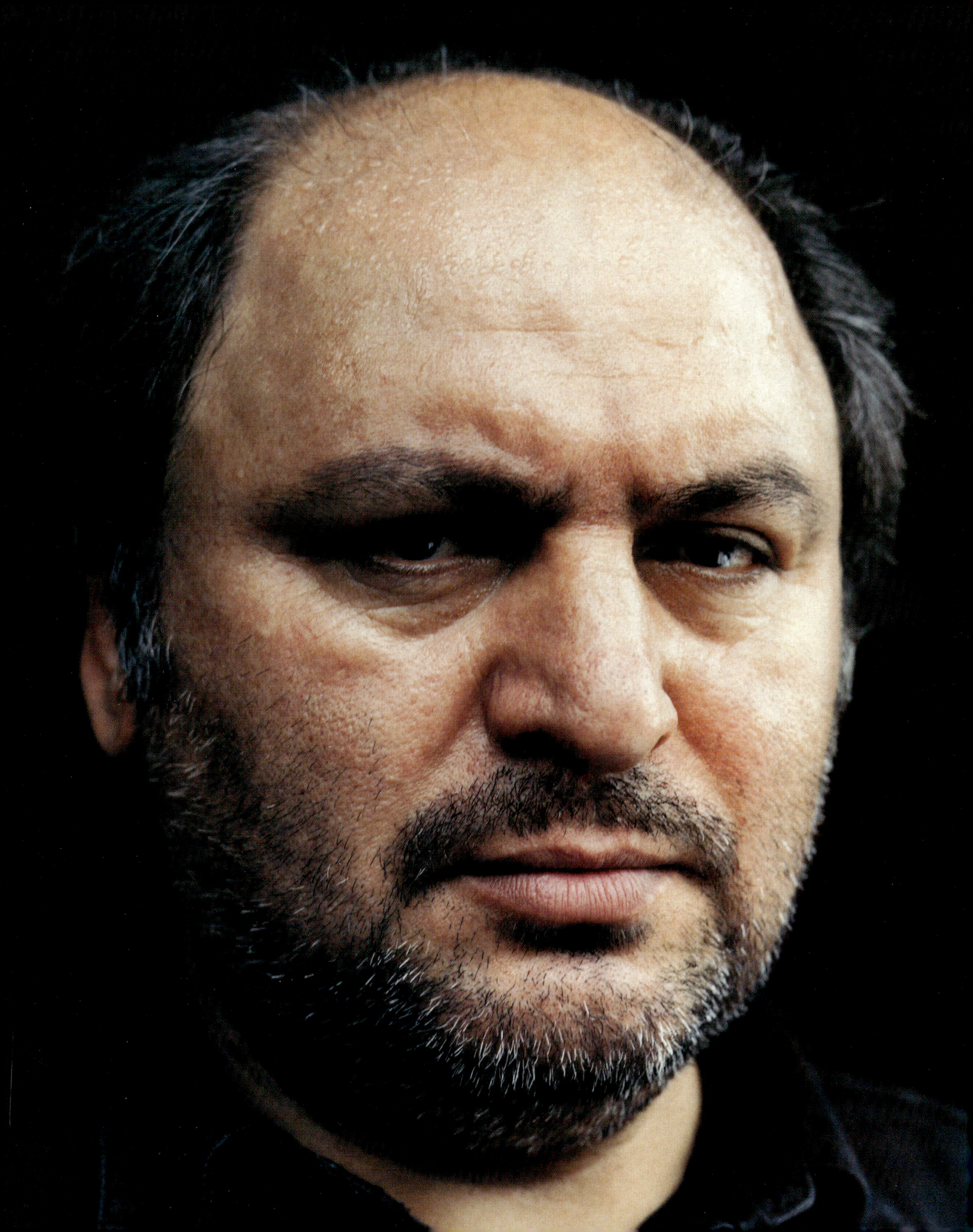

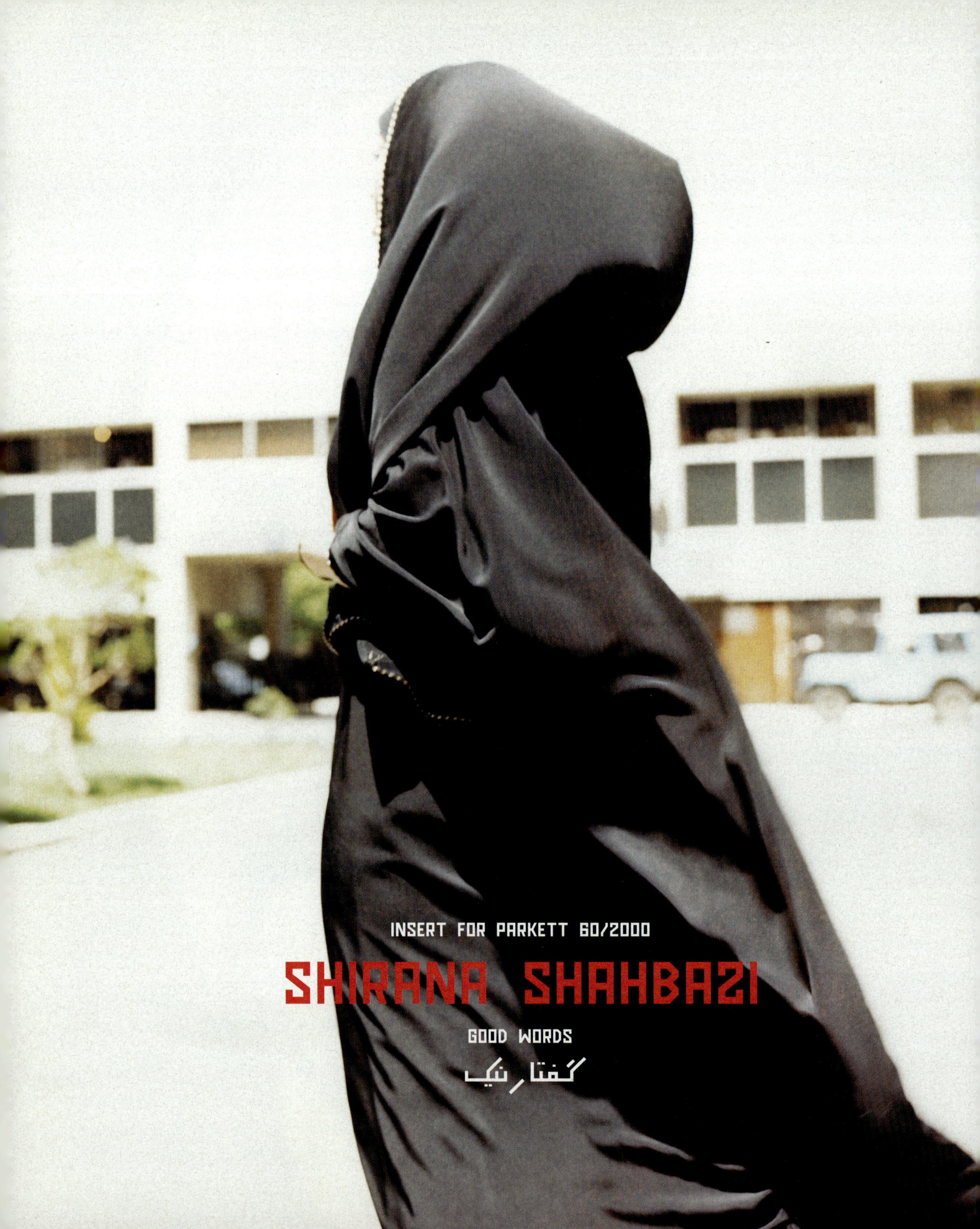

INSERT FOR PARKETT 60/2000
SHIRANA SHAHBAZI
GOOD WORDS
گفتار نیک

Thierry de Duve

Interviewed by

Cay Sophie Rabinowitz

Brussels, April 3, 2000

The following discussion has been crafted from informal meetings and one taped interview with Thierry de Duve, who is known for essays and books, such as *Kant After Duchamp,* that mingle art history with philosophy. For the millennial celebrations in Brussels, de Duve has curated an exhibition titled "Voici: 100 Years of Contemporary Art" at the Palais des Beaux Arts in Brussels, on view through January 2001.

De Duve navigates within and between disciplines. Though the exhibition includes a few works predating 1900, it is an exhibition of contemporary art based on de Duve's conception of what makes an artwork contemporary. With Manet and Gauguin integrated with Broodthaers and Michael Snow, this exhibition eschews the common expectation that periods of artistic development can be defined by calendar years and the decisive scrutiny of trained experts. Instead, de Duve invites the general public to experience and evaluate works of art selected and configured according to grammatical structures rather than historical themes.

An idiosyncratic point of departure is established, first and foremost, by the title "Voici." *Voici,* by itself, does not refer to anything unless the speaker points at something while uttering the word "voici." As if to say "this" while pointing to indicate: "this is," or "see this." Also, uttering "this" implies that the speaker is addressing someone.

The subtitle: "100 Years of Contemporary Art," recalls a 1958 show in Belgium, "Fifty Years of Modern Art," where de Duve says he first saw Seurat's LA GRANDE JATTE (1884–86).

Initially as we discussed this part of the title, "100 Years of Contemporary Art," de Duve admitted lightheartedly "of course, it's a pun, a little joke." But when asked, "How is it contemporary?" or "Why not modern or postmodern, for that matter?" he replied in earnest, "Basically, that's where the joke becomes serious. …That is to say, art, when it is any good, is always our contemporary. Even if the work is 2000 years old, it can speak to us in the present tense."

Cay Sophie Rabinowitz:
You have spent most of your life theorizing about art, looking at art, writing about art. Why are you now doing an exhibition of art?

Thierry de Duve:
I am first and foremost an art lover, and I want to share that pleasure. This may seem ironic because as a theorist I wrote on and around a work of art that you don't need to see to ponder, namely, Duchamp's readymade. Indeed, the concept seems more important than the object itself in that particular case. Not so when it comes to a painting by Matisse or Mondrian or a Bruce Nauman installation, for example. Curating is first an egotistic pleasure. The opportunity to put together works that I simply long to see together is a great thrill. To do it not just for myself but for other people is an even greater thrill.

CR: But is it also a matter of theorizing? Is this exhibition in some way also a kind of essay?

TD: The show is structured along a certain number of questions, which are of course not displayed as such in the show. Works of art that are answers to questions, which have not yet been raised, are the newest.

CR: Can you explain what you mean by "the newest"?

TD: I have seen too much art that looks like an answer to an existing question, in which case the answer seems to be illustrating the theory. Good art, from both the art lover's and the theoretician's point of view, is art that mysteriously seems to hold in itself an answer to a question which we don't know yet. My role is, then, to seek the right question to address the work with.

CR: So, it's not the answer you don't know; it's the question that you don't know yet.

TD: We have the answer, yet not the question. Works of art are affirmative gestures, even though modern art negated many things, starting with figuration. And yet all artists put into the world something that was not there before. That's why we speak of creation when it comes to art.

CR: And perhaps that might also explain the title that you chose.

TD: The title of the show, "Voici," is untranslatable as such. (For commercial reasons, we had to settle for "Look" as the English title of the catalogue.) Etymologically speaking, the French word *voici* is a contraction of *vois ceci*, which itself is a contraction of *vois ce, ici* (see this here). As opposed to *voilà* (see that there). There is a proximity of the act of looking implied in the word *voici*. It's also a presentational device. You use the word *voici* to present something to someone, whereas *voilà* is mostly used to bring an end to a conversation. *Voilà* is demonstrative, *voici* is presentational.

CR: Could you explain the three parts of the exhibition?

TD: The first part is "Me Voici" (Here I Am): the work introduces itself. Then comes "Vous Voici" (Here You Are):

the work addresses the viewer and introduces the viewer to him- or herself, making the presence of the viewer sort of self-conscious. In part three, the works collectively start speaking of us: "Nous Voici" (Here We Are).

CR: About works speaking: when the work speaks in the present tense, is it alive?

TD: To endow a mere object with the capacity to speak and to present itself is easier when the work resembles us. As long as art was figurative, it was relatively easy to consider art capable of mediating between the realm of objects and the realm of human beings, and sort of being "alive." Call it a belief system, or at least a system of conventions based on suspension of disbelief. Abstract art, clearly, made that suspension of disbelief a lot more difficult. Better put, when the belief system could no longer be upheld, art turned abstract. At the root of modernism lies the heaviest crisis of faith.

CR: Is the "Me Voici" theme a kind of strategy meant to recover the human figure? Or humanism?

TD: For an object to start speaking and introducing itself to the beholder, it takes an act of faith on our part. We're not ready for that anymore. Today's challenge is to invent a new kind of humanism. Needless to say, this is something the show cannot even graze, though I'm convinced some artists are showing the way.

CR: The "Me Voici" section is then the first part, where one enters and is confronted with art objects. But what is it about the way they are presented? And the artists themselves, why are they in this "Me Voici" category?

TD: Let me just make a few concrete comparisons of works of art, some in the show and some not. (I want the

readers to enjoy surprise if they come to the show.) Let's take Rodin's AGE OF BRONZE (1875–76). Let's now take one of Giacometti's GRANDES FEMMES (1960) which is an elongated and taller than life-size eroded bronze (cast from plaster). There is something tragic emanating from those figures in which the only resemblance to a human figure is the hieratic upright position. One big clod of clay anchors the figure to its base. Then, let's take Barnett Newman's HERE III (1966), which is a vertical slab of stainless steel planted into a small pyramid of rusted steel. The pyramid itself rests on a heavy metal plate that has been cut irregularly with a welding torch. In comparison to the Giacometti and the Rodin, it is obvious that the human figure has totally disappeared. Standing before it, you might be puzzled and say, "What does this mean? It represents nothing." Simultaneously, when you move from Rodin to Giacometti to Newman, the emphasis shifts from the statue to the base. In the Newman, virtually all the attention goes to the presentational device, as if to say: in the process we artists lost the human figure, and we were driven to acknowledge that an object standing upright needs a prop. "Voici's" presentational strategies emphasize this shift, by way of juxtapositions and comparisons. I want to address the people who do not regularly come to museums and try to show (not explain) that there is something for them in the more "difficult" Newman work as well as in the Giacometti or the Rodin. When you get to a Duchamp readymade, all reference to the human figure has vanished and you're left with a plain, ordinary object. Yet Duchamp's BICYCLE WHEEL (1913) is obviously also a base on which an object has been planted. Everybody speaks of the bicycle wheel, but we often forget the stool.

CR: I would just say it's not obviously an object placed on top of a base. In Duchamp's case, the stool is not just a base; it's the other part of the readymade. The readymade can only exist as the codependence or coexistence of these two objects.

TD: True. Just as the lady's feet belong to the Giacometti or the base to the Newman. Now, consider Manzoni's MAGIC BASE of 1961. Manzoni certainly took his lesson from Duchamp, except it's not a thing that's put on the base this time; it's a human being. Anybody who steps on the base instantly becomes a work of art. We have come full circle from Rodin, and the figure is now truly alive. To be art and to be alive are equated. Yet the irony is there for all to savor. Obviously, I have not been turned into a work of art just by stepping on the base.

CR: Except in that very moment when we see the Manzoni piece and imagine it to be so.

TD: Exactly. By an act of imagination—or to stretch things a little further, by an act of faith. Now, in what should we have faith? Art is a human institution that is subject to struggle and debate like all human institutions. Which is why "Me Voici" gives an important place to Marcel Broodthaers, who is probably the only artist in his generation to understand the post-Duchamp tragedy, that is, when the definition of art has become "anything and everything the art institution calls art."

CR: At this point we are no longer in "Me Voici."

TD: That's right. We are ready to enter "Vous Voici." And to start all over again from the viewer's point of view and judgment. A work of art doesn't exist without its beholder. Mere objects do not address people. My car in the street does not address me with a demand. It is simply an object to be used. But works of art seem to address us and to demand something of us. So the theme of the second part is the address to the beholder. What kind of object is capable of doing that—presenting the beholder to him- or herself? A mirror. Several artists have used mirrors, or representations of mirrors, for example, Gerhard Richter or Michelangelo Pistoletto, in whose work the figure mostly turns its back to us, finding itself in the mirror the way we find ourselves in front of the mirror. The "Vous Voici" section opens with a room of mirrors meant to introduce the notion of a face-to-face between beholder and object.

CR: Does that lead us into painting?

TD: Yes, and abstract painting in particular, with an emphasis on monochrome painting. Face-to-face reduced to face-to-surface. It strikes me that when painting turned abstract, some painters went straight to two extremes: a surface that reflects all light (i.e. a mirror or something close) and a surface that absorbs all light. Malevich painted his BLACK SQUARE ON A WHITE GROUND in 1913, then his WHITE SQUARE ON A WHITE GROUND in 1917. This tension has repeated itself: in 1951, Rauschenberg painted his black and his white monochrome paintings at the same time; and in 1959, Stella did his famous black paintings, and six months later painted his aluminum paintings. Aluminum, though not quite as shiny, comes very close to a mirror. The fact that repeatedly painting tackled absorptive surfaces painted black or reflective surfaces painted white is the pretext to introduce the viewer to a room of abstract art with Mondrian, Miró, Rothko, Mangold, Manzoni, Yves Klein, others, and amidst all of them one figurative portrait of a man who is looking at you, straight into your eyes (I'm not saying by whom). This is to convey with simple means the sense that although the human figure has disappeared from abstract painting—the way it has disappeared from Barnett Newman's HERE III—the human content is there. At which point I can afford to introduce the comeback of figuration in recent art without it being a return to the past or a betrayal of modernism. Gary Hill's video installation, VIEWER (1996), is a frieze of some twenty life-size people standing quasi-immobile and looking at us. The title, VIEWER, in the singular, establishes a one-to-one relationship with each of these people, who happen to be immigrants dressed in work clothes—precisely those people marginalized in Western society and whom we tend not to see. This work has a lot to say about us politically. "Vous Voici" starts with the address to the individual other and ends in the acknowledgement of otherness.

CR: I suppose we are ready to move into the "Nous Voici" section of the show. And I can sense what makes the exhibition contemporary: otherness, face-to-face, aesthetic clashes and affinities, historical dissonance?

TD: Sure. And the minute we deal with clashes and affinities, we deal with us. "Nous Voici," (Here We Are). I was talking earlier about the need for a new kind of humanism. No one can wish it into existence, of course, and certainly not merely with an art exhibition. But it's a matter of drawing the horizon line, so to speak. We are all concerned with birth, life, death, love, work, and human relationships at large—this is the stuff of our lives (the old humanist themes). To say "Nous Voici" collectively is to say we were all born once. But remember, the works of art speak and now they speak of the collective in at least three senses: the couple work-beholder, now firmly established; the works of art among themselves, what we call a collection; and us, the human community or society.

CR: So the question of the human, of what is human and what binds us all together is there.

TD: Yes. What binds us together? Sex and language, perhaps. And what tears us apart? Sex and language, again. Or love and hate, peace and war, religion, politics, the economy, and so on. A huge and hilarious Bruce Nauman neon piece speaks of sex. An extraordinary painting by Basquiat that speaks of death will enter into a quite risqué dialogue with a huge and magnificent and very joyful Matisse full of life. A splendid Manet, with lovers at a café table watched over by the waiter, theoretically echoes Sylvie Blocher's latest *Living Pictures* dealing with family relationships. There are other such dialogues.

CR: But there's also still something you're saying here in this "Nous Voici" section about address.

TD: The "Vous Voici" section, which is about address, actually paves the way for the "Nous Voici" section. The pronoun "we" has basically three characteristics and the third one will address your question, which is one for the theorist in me. The first is quantity. You don't say "we" to refer to yourself alone. "We" goes from "the two of us" to "all of us," from couple to humanity. The second is that "we" gets pronounced by one person on behalf of a group. By what right? With what legitimacy? Are artists mandated only by themselves? By their own tradition? By today's art world? By society at large? An artist speaks or ought to speak on behalf of humankind at large. And not on behalf of the art world only. This would be my position on the issue of universality in art, reality notwithstanding, multiculturalism notwithstanding, and so on. I know I'm going against the grain. For artists are not formally mandated by humanity at large. Humanism might postulate such a mandate, but humanism has been shattered and needs to be reinvented. To exclude part of humanity from art is like excluding part of humanity from reality. This is where, I believe, the third characteristic of the pronoun "we" teaches us something. While referring to the same people (say: Cay Sophie and Thierry), and uttered by one of them (say: Thierry) the pronoun "we" can be broken into two very different things: "you and I," or "she and I." In the first case the addressee is inside the "we," in the second case the addressee is outside. There is never any proof that an artist is speaking on behalf of a universal "we." Yet we can be sure of this: in order to be universal, the "we" must be a "you and I" otherwise at least one person remains outside: the person the "we" addresses. This person is then excluded from the community on behalf of which one claims to be speaking. Thus, you can't be speaking on behalf of the whole of humankind unless you address the whole of humankind. The test (not the proof) of universality in matters of art rests on universal address. And the test's test rests on whether or not you, as a viewer, feel addressed by the work in your humanity.

CR: Then the exhibition "Voici: One Hundred Years of Contemporary Art" is about the simultaneous presence of all these works in one place and the person being right there. Can you say something about how you envision the show not being "historical," in that it is not about the century at large or history?

TD: But it is about the century at large, and it is about history. It's just not about art history. The show is not an explanation of how Impressionism led to Cubism and how Cubism led to abstract art, and so on. I think it is an insult to the public to want to teach them art history against their will. One should be able to appreciate art with or without art history. The works are mingled on purpose to provoke clashes, but also to raise issues of quality and of meaning. Some canonical works of modern art have become so familiar that they are kind of dead. In a new context they can be rejuvenated and reinterpreted. Hopefully.

CR: Hopefully? I'd say inevitably.

TD: Now, one word about this century, and the dreadful fin-de-siècle mood we struggle to get out of. This century was not happy; we went through two world wars, through the Holocaust, genocide, Chechnya, and it goes on. We had to endure Nazism, and the betrayal of the modernist utopia, Communism. Though there is very little so-called "political art" in the show, because I don't endorse that as a category, "Voici" testifies in a discreet way to the tragedies of this century. The memory of the twentieth century should not be erased, and at the same time we should not enter a new century engulfed in guilt and in melancholia. It's about regaining optimism.

Thierry de Duve im Gespräch mit *Cay Sophie Rabinowitz*
Brüssel, 3. April 2000

Die folgende Diskussion ist das Ergebnis mehrerer zwangloser Treffen und eines auf Band aufgenommenen Interviews mit Thierry de Duve, Autor von Essays und Büchern wie *Kant nach Duchamp*, die Kunstgeschichte und Philosophie miteinander verbinden. Zu den Millenniumfeiern in Brüssel hat de Duve eine Ausstellung mit dem Titel «Voici: 100 Jahre zeitgenössischer Kunst» kuratiert, die bis Ende Januar 2001 im Palais des Beaux Arts in Brüssel zu sehen ist.

De Duve bewegt sich in und zwischen den Disziplinen. Auch wenn sich in dieser Ausstellung ein paar Arbeiten finden, die vor 1900 entstanden sind, so ist es doch – ausgehend von de Duves Vorstellung von «zeitgenössisch» – eine Ausstellung zeitgenössischer Kunst. Eine Show, die Manet und Gauguin Seite an Seite mit Broodthaers und Michael Snow zeigt, muss die allgemeine Erwartung enttäuschen, dass Perioden künstlerischer Entwicklung durch Kalenderjahre und Analysen erfahrener Experten bestimmt werden können. Stattdessen lädt de Duve das Publikum ein, Kunstwerke zu erfahren und zu beurteilen, deren Auswahl und Anordnung eher von grammatikalischen als kunsthistorischen Themen bestimmt ist.

Der idiosynkratische Ausgangspunkt kommt bereits im Titel zum Ausdruck: *Voici* heisst gar nichts, solange der Sprecher, der das Wort benutzt, nicht gleichzeitig auf einen Gegenstand zeigt. So als würde er «das» sagen und damit «dies da» oder «da, schau» sagen wollen. *Voici* zu sagen bedeutet auch, dass der Sprecher mit jemandem spricht.

Der Untertitel «100 Jahre zeitgenössischer Kunst» erinnert an eine 1958 in Belgien gezeigte Ausstellung: «Fünfzig Jahre moderne Kunst», in der de Duve zum ersten Mal Seurats LA GRANDE JATTE (1884–1886) gesehen hat.

Zu Beginn unseres Gesprächs, als wir uns über den Untertitel «100 Jahre zeitgenössischer Kunst» unterhielten, meinte de Duve amüsiert: «Es ist natürlich ein Wortspiel, ein kleiner Spass.» Doch auf die Frage: «Wieso zeitgenössisch?» oder «Warum nicht modern oder postmodern?», antwortete er: «Also da wird die Sache ernst... ich will damit sagen, dass Kunst, die etwas taugt, immer zeitgenössisch ist. Auch wenn eine Arbeit 2000 Jahre alt ist, hat sie uns heute noch etwas zu sagen.»

Cay Sophie Rabinowitz:
Man kennt eigentlich nur deine Theorien, deine Essays und Betrachtungen über Kunst. Warum machst du jetzt eine Ausstellung?

Thierry de Duve:
Zuallererst bin ich Kunstliebhaber und möchte das Vergnügen, das mir die Kunst bereitet, teilen. Es entbehrt vielleicht nicht einer gewissen Ironie, dass ich mich als Theoretiker mit einem Werk befasste, das man nicht gesehen haben muss, um sich darüber Gedanken zu machen, nämlich Duchamps Readymade. Tatsächlich erscheint in diesem Fall das Konzept wichtiger als der Gegenstand. Nicht so bei einem Bild von Matisse oder Mondrian oder einer Installation von Bruce Nauman. Eine Ausstellung zu kuratieren ist zunächst einmal ein selbstsüchtiges Vergnügen. Und Arbeiten zusammenzubringen, die ich schon immer zusammen sehen wollte, eine äusserst spannende Sache. Aber noch spannender ist es, dies nicht nur für mich, sondern auch für andere zu tun.

CR: Aber die Theorie spielt immer noch eine grosse Rolle? Ist diese Ausstellung nicht auch eine Art Essay?

TD: Die Ausstellung ist um ein paar Fragen herum strukturiert, die natürlich in der Schau nicht als solche sichtbar sind. Kunstwerke sind Antworten auf Fragen, die noch nicht gestellt wurden, die ganz neu sind.

CR: Was meinst du mit «ganz neu»?

TD: Ich habe schon zu viel Kunst gesehen, die sich den Anschein gibt, die Antwort auf eine bereits existierende

Frage zu sein, wobei diese Antwort jeweils nur die Illustration einer bestimmten Theorie ist. Sowohl vom Standpunkt des Kritikers wie auch des Liebhabers birgt gute Kunst auf geheimnisvolle Art und Weise die Antwort auf eine noch unbekannte Frage. Und meine Aufgabe ist es, die richtige Frage an das jeweilige Werk zu suchen.

CR: Es ist also nicht die Antwort, die du noch nicht kennst, sondern die Frage?

TD: Die Antwort liegt uns vor, aber nicht die Frage. Kunstwerke sind affirmative Gesten, auch wenn die moderne Kunst viele Dinge ablehnt, wie etwa das Figurative. Dennoch beschert jeder Künstler der Welt etwas, was es vorher noch nicht gab. Deshalb spricht man auch von Schöpfung im Zusammenhang mit Kunst.

CR: Und so erklärt sich vielleicht auch der Titel, für den du dich entschieden hast?

TD: Der Titel der Ausstellung «Voici» lässt sich eigentlich nicht übersetzen. (Aus kommerziellen Gründen mussten wir für den englischen Katalog «Look» akzeptieren.) Etymologisch gesehen ist das französische Wort *voici* eine Kurzform von *vois ceci*, das sich wiederum aus *vois ce, ici* (schau das hier) herleitet. Im Gegensatz zu *voilà* (schau das dort) impliziert *voici* eine unmittelbare Nähe. Und es ist auch ein Mittel der Präsentation. Man benutzt *voici*, um jemanden auf etwas aufmerksam zu machen, während *voilà* gewöhnlich eine Unterhaltung abschliesst. *Voilà* ist hinweisend, *voici* darlegend.

CR: Kannst du zu den drei Teilen der Ausstellung etwas sagen?

TD: Der erste Teil trägt den Titel «Me Voici» (Hier bin ich): Das Werk stellt sich vor. Danach kommt «Vous Voici» (Hier sind Sie): Das Werk wendet sich an den Betrachter und stellt den Besucher sich selbst vor, macht ihm seine Gegenwart bewusster. Im dritten Teil schliesslich sprechen die Arbeiten in ihrer Gesamtheit zu uns: «Nous Voici» (Hier sind wir).

CR: Eine Frage zum Sprechen der Arbeiten: Wenn ein Werk in der Gegenwart spricht, heisst das: es lebt?

TD: Es ist einfacher, einen Gegenstand zum Sprechen und zur Selbstdarstellung zu bringen, wenn das Werk uns gleicht. Solange Kunst noch figurativ war, konnte man sie relativ einfach als Vermittlerin zwischen der Welt der Gegenstände und der Welt menschlicher Wesen betrachten. Nennen wir es ein Glaubenssystem oder zumindest ein System von Übereinkünften, das auf der Aufhebung des Unglaubens beruht. Oder einfacher: als das Glaubenssystem nicht mehr länger aufrechterhalten werden konnte, wurde die Kunst abstrakt. Am Anfang der Moderne steht eine schwere Glaubenskrise.

CR: Ist das «Me Voici»-Thema eine Strategie, um die menschliche Gestalt wieder zurückzugewinnen? Oder einen neuen Humanismus?

TD: Dass ein Gegenstand spricht und sich dem Betrachter vorstellt, setzt auf unserer Seite einen Akt des Glaubens voraus. Und dazu sind wir nicht mehr bereit. Die Herausforderung für unsere Zeit besteht in der Erfindung eines neuen Humanismus. Natürlich kann die Ausstellung das nicht einmal ansatzweise leisten, obwohl ich überzeugt bin, dass ein paar Künstler den Weg aufzeigen.

CR: Man betrit den «Me Voici»-Teil als ersten und ist mit all dieser Kunst konfrontiert. Was hat es mit dieser Art der Präsentation auf sich? Und warum sind gerade diese Künstler in der «Me Voici»-Kategorie vertreten?

TD: Lass mich das anhand von ein paar konkreten Vergleichen von Kunstwerken erklären, manche davon sind in der Ausstellung zu sehen, andere nicht. (Ich möchte meinen Lesern nicht die Überraschung nehmen, wenn sie sich die Ausstellung anschauen.) Nehmen wir zum Beispiel Rodins BRONZEZEITALTER (1875–1876), ferner eine von Giacomettis GRANDES FEMMES (1960), eine langgestreckte und überlebensgrosse erodierte Bronze. Von den Figuren, die nur durch ihre aufrechte hieratische Haltung einer menschlichen Gestalt ähneln, geht etwas Tragisches aus. Ein dicker Lehmklumpen verbindet die Figur mit ihrer Basis. Und schliesslich Barnett Newmans HERE III (1966), eine vertikale, in eine kleine Pyramide aus rostigem Stahl eingesetzte Chromstahlplatte. Die Pyramide selbst ruht auf einer schweren, mit einem Schweissbrenner unregelmässig bearbeiteten Metallplatte. Im Vergleich zu Giacometti und Rodin fällt auf, dass von der menschlichen Gestalt nichts mehr übrig geblieben ist. Wenn man davor steht, fragt man sich vielleicht etwas ratlos: «Was bedeutet das? Es stellt nichts dar.» Gleichzeitig wird von Rodin über Giacometti zu Newman der Sockel immer wichtiger. Bei Newman wird dann die ganze Aufmerksamkeit auf die Präsentation gelenkt, als wollte das Werk sagen: Uns Künstlern ist in dem Prozess die menschliche Gestalt verloren gegangen, und wir sind gezwungen, zuzugeben, dass ein aufrecht stehender Gegenstand eine Stütze braucht. Die Präsentationsweise von «Voici» macht durch ein Nebeneinander und Vergleiche auf diesen Wandel aufmerksam. Ich möchte Leute ansprechen, die nicht regelmässig Museen besichtigen, und ihnen zeigen (nicht erklären), dass sie wie bei der Giacometti-Figur und bei Rodin auch beim «schwierigeren» Newman etwas entdecken können. Kommt man dann zu einem Readymade von Duchamp, gibt es überhaupt keinen Bezug zur menschlichen Gestalt mehr, und man hat nur noch einen einfachen Gebrauchsgegenstand vor sich. Doch Duchamps FAHRRAD-RAD (1913) hat offensichtlich noch einen Sockel, auf dem es steht. Wir sprechen nur vom Rad und vergessen dabei meist den Hocker.

CR: Ich denke, in Duchamps Fall ist der Hocker nicht nur Unterlage, sondern der andere Teil des Readymade. Dieses besteht in der Abhängigkeit der beiden Teile voneinander oder in ihrem Nebeneinander.

TD: Genau. So wie die Frauenfüsse zur Giacometti-Skulptur oder der Sockel zu Newmans Werk gehört. Aber schauen wir uns doch Manzonis MAGIC BASE (Magischer Sockel, 1961) an. Manzoni hat offensichtlich von Duchamp gelernt, nur wird hier kein Gegenstand auf den Sockel gestellt, sondern ein menschliches Wesen. Jeder, der sich drauf stellt, wird zum Kunstwerk. Damit schliesst sich der mit Rodin begonnene Kreis und die Figur ist wieder zum Leben erwacht. Kunst wird mit Leben gleichgesetzt. Doch die Ironie ist augenfällig. Denn es reicht nicht, sich auf einen Sockel zu stellen, um zum Kunstwerk zu werden.

CR: Nur in dem Augenblick, in dem wir Manzonis Arbeit sehen und uns vorstellen, es sei so.

TD: Das ist der Punkt. Durch einen Akt der Phantasie oder, noch pointierter, durch einen Akt des Glaubens. Aber woran sollen wir glauben? Kunst ist eine von Menschen geschaffene Institution, die wie alle Institutionen Kämp-

fen und Diskussionen ausgesetzt ist. Deshalb nimmt Marcel Broodthaers auch einen so wichtigen Platz in «Me Voici» ein, denn er ist wahrscheinlich der einzige Künstler seiner Generation, der die post-Duchamp'sche Tragödie versteht, das heisst, was es bedeutet, wenn die Definition von Kunst «alles umfasst, was eine Kunstinstitution als Kunst bezeichnet».

CR: Damit verlassen wir den «Me Voici»-Teil.

TD: Ja. Wir sind jetzt reif für «Vous Voici». Und wir beginnen wieder von vorne, vom Standpunkt des Betrachters und seinem Urteil ausgehend. Ohne Betrachter gibt es kein Kunstwerk. Gewöhnliche Gegenstände wenden sich nicht an uns. Mein Auto auf der Strasse stellt mir keine Frage. Es ist nur ein Gebrauchsgegenstand. Kunstwerke hingegen scheinen sich an uns zu wenden und etwas von uns zu wollen. Das Thema des zweiten Teils ist also das Ansprechen des Betrachters. Welche Art von Gegenstand ist dazu in der Lage, den Betrachter mit sich selbst zu konfrontieren? Ein Spiegel? Mehrere Künstler haben Spiegel oder Darstellungen von Spiegeln benutzt, wie etwa Gerhard Richter oder Michelangelo Pistoletto, bei dem uns die Figur meist den Rücken zuwendet und sich im Spiegel sieht, so wie wir uns vor dem Spiegel. Der «Vous Voici»-Teil beginnt mit einem Raum voller Spiegel, um das Konzept einer Konfrontation von Betrachter und Gegenstand einzuführen.

CR: Führt uns das zur Malerei?

TD: Zur abstrakten Malerei vor allem, mit Schwerpunkt auf monochromen Bildern. Aus «von Angesicht zu Angesicht» wurde «von Angesicht zu Oberfläche». Mir ist aufgefallen, dass manche Maler sich für zwei Extreme entschieden, als die Malerei abstrakt

wurde: eine Oberfläche, die das Licht vollständig reflektiert (ein Spiegel oder etwas Ähnliches) oder aber eine Oberfläche, die das Licht vollständig absorbiert. Malewitsch malte 1913 sein SCHWARZES QUADRAT AUF WEISSEM GRUND und 1917 sein WEISSES QUADRAT AUF WEISSEM GRUND. Diese Spannung wiederholte sich. 1951 malte Rauschenberg gleichzeitig seine monochromen schwarzen und weissen Bilder, und 1959 machte Frank Stella seine berühmten schwarzen Bilder, auf die ein halbes Jahr später die Aluminiumbilder folgten. Aluminium ist zwar weniger glänzend, kommt einem Spiegel aber sehr nahe. Die Tatsache, dass die Malerei sich des öfteren mit schwarz bemalten, absorbierenden Oberflächen oder weiss bemalten, reflektierenden Oberflächen beschäftigte, dient als Vorwand, um den Betrachter in einen Raum mit abstrakter Kunst zu führen, in dem Mondrian, Miró, Rothko, Mangold, Manzoni, Yves Klein und andere vertreten sind. Unter ihnen befindet sich das gegenständliche Porträt eines Mannes, der einem direkt in die Augen blickt (ich verrate nicht, von wem). Damit soll auf einfache Art und Weise demonstriert werden, dass es den menschlichen Inhalt immer noch gibt, auch wenn die menschliche Gestalt aus der abstrakten Malerei verschwunden ist – wie in Barnett Newmans HERE III. An diesem Punkt kann ich mir auch erlauben, die Rückkehr des Gegenständlichen in der jüngsten Kunst zu zeigen, ohne dass das ein Rückschritt oder ein Verrat an der Moderne wäre. Gary Hills Videoinstallation VIEWER (Betrachter, 1969) ist eine Art Fries mit ungefähr zwanzig Personen in Lebensgrösse, die mehr oder weniger unbeweglich dastehen und uns anschauen. Der Titel VIEWER

(Betrachter, im Singular) stellt zu jeder dieser Personen eine direkte Beziehung her, also zu Leuten, die sich als Immigranten in Arbeitskleidung entpuppen – genau jene Menschen, die in westlichen Gesellschaften gewöhnlich an den Rand gedrängt und vergessen werden. Eine Arbeit mit einer politischen Aussage. In «Vous Voici» wurde zuerst der einzelne Andere angeredet, um schliesslich zu einer Akzeptanz des Andersartigen überhaupt zu gelangen.

CR: Ich glaube, wir können jetzt den «Nous Voici»-Teil der Ausstellung in Angriff nehmen. Ich ahne auch, was die Ausstellung zeitgenössisch macht: das Andere, die Gegenüberstellung, ästhetische Widersprüche und Affinitäten, historische Dissonanzen?

TD: Ja, genau. In dem Augenblick, in dem wir uns mit Widersprüchen und Affinitäten auseinander setzen, setzen wir uns mit uns selbst auseinander. «Nous Voici» (Hier sind wir). Ich habe von der Notwendigkeit eines neuen Humanismus gesprochen. Natürlich kann ihn niemand herbeizaubern, vor allem nicht mit einer Ausstellung. Er ist sozusagen der Silberstreifen am Horizont. Wir beschäftigen uns alle mit Themen wie Geburt, Leben, Tod, Liebe, Arbeit und menschlichen Beziehungen. – Das ist der Stoff, der das Leben ausmacht (die alten humanistischen Themen). «Nous Voici» gemeinsam zu sagen bedeutet, dass wir alle einmal geboren wurden. Aber vergessen wir nicht, die Kunstwerke sprechen, und wenn sie von einem Kollektiv sprechen, kann das mindestens drei verschiedene Dinge meinen: das inzwischen fest etablierte Paar Kunstwerk und Betrachter; die Kunstwerke unter sich (die Sammlung), oder schliesslich uns, die menschliche Gemeinschaft oder Gesellschaft.

CR: Es ist also die Frage nach dem Menschlichen, nach dem, was uns alle verbindet.

TD: Ja. Was verbindet uns? Sex und Sprache vielleicht. Und was trennt uns? Wieder Sex und Sprache. Oder Liebe, Hass, Krieg, Frieden, Religion, Politik, die Wirtschaft und so weiter. Eine riesige und amüsante Neon-Arbeit von Bruce Nauman spricht von Sex. Ein aussergewöhnliches Bild von Basquiat, das vom Tod handelt, beginnt einen ziemlich gewagten Dialog mit einem grossen und sehr optimistischen Matisse voller Lebensfreude. Ein grossartiger Manet mit einem Liebespaar am Kaffeehaustischchen, bedient von einem Kellner, reflektiert theoretisch Sylvie Blochers letzte *Lebende Bilder*, in denen Familienbeziehungen im Mittelpunkt stehen. Es gibt noch mehr solche Dialoge.

CR: Aber du setzt dich im «Nous Voici»-Teil auch wieder mit dem «Ansprechen» auseinander.

TD: Der «Vous Voici»-Teil, in dem das Ansprechen zentrales Thema ist, ebnet den Weg für den «Nous Voici»-Teil. Das Pronomen «wir» hat drei wesentliche Merkmale; das dritte wird auf deine Frage eingehen, eine Frage, die sich an mich als Theoretiker wendet. Das erste Merkmal ist der Plural. Man sagt nicht «wir», wenn man sich selbst meint. «Wir» reicht von «wir beide» bis «wir alle», also vom Paar zur Menschheit. Das zweite Merkmal ist, dass «wir» von einer Person benutzt wird, wenn sie von einer Gruppe spricht, der sie angehört. Mit welchem Recht? In welcher Eigenschaft? Arbeiten Künstler nur im eigenen Auftrag? Im Namen ihrer eigenen Tradition? In dem der Kunstwelt von heute? Der Gesellschaft im Allgemeinen? Ein Künstler spricht, oder sollte zumindest, im Namen der gan-

zen Menschheit sprechen. Nicht nur im Namen der Kunstwelt. Diesen Standpunkt vertrete ich, wenn von der Universalität der Kunst die Rede ist, wie auch immer die Realität aussehen mag und unabhängig von Multikulturalismus und so weiter. Ich weiss, ich schwimme gegen den Strom. Denn Künstler arbeiten offiziell nicht im Auftrag der Menschheit. Der Humanismus fordert vielleicht einen solchen Auftrag, aber er ist in seinen Grundfesten erschüttert und muss neu erfunden werden. Wenn man einen Teil der Menschheit von der Kunst ausschliesst, so ist das, als würde man einen Teil der Menschheit von der Realität ausschliessen. Da, glaube ich, kann uns das dritte Merkmal des Pronomens «wir» weiterhelfen. Auch wenn es sich nur auf zwei Personen bezieht (sagen wir: Cay Sophie und Thierry) und von einer der beiden Personen ausgesprochen wird (sagen wir Thierry), kann das Pronomen «wir» zwei sehr verschiedene Dinge beinhalten: «du und ich» oder «sie und ich». Im ersten Fall bleibt die angeredete Person innerhalb des «wir», im zweiten befindet sie sich draussen. Es lässt sich nie mit Sicherheit sagen, ob ein Künstler im Namen eines universalen Wir spricht. Doch eines ist gewiss: Wenn es Allgemeingültigkeit besitzen will, muss das Wir ein «du und ich» sein, sonst bleibt zumindest eine Person ausgeschlossen: die Person, an die sich das «wir» wendet. Diese Person ist dann aus der Gemeinschaft, in deren Namen jemand zu sprechen vorgibt, ausgeschlossen. Man kann nur im Namen der Menschheit sprechen, wenn man auch die ganze Menschheit anspricht. Der Test (nicht Beweis) der Universalität in der Kunst ist die alles einschliessende Anrede. Und der Test des Tests beruht darauf, ob du als Betrachter dich vom Werk als Mensch angesprochen fühlst.

CR: In der Ausstellung «Voici: 100 Jahre zeitgenössischer Kunst» geht es also um die gleichzeitige Gegenwart all dieser Werke und des Betrachters an einem Ort. Kannst du erklären, weshalb du die Ausstellung nicht als «historisch» betrachtest und sie sich somit auch nicht mit dem Jahrhundert oder mit Geschichte befasst?

TD: Sie befasst sich schon mit dem Jahrhundert und mit Geschichte. Nur nicht mit Kunstgeschichte. Die Ausstellung erklärt nicht, wie sich aus dem Impressionismus der Kubismus und aus dem Kubismus die abstrakte Kunst usw. entwickelte. Ich betrachte es als eine Beleidigung des Publikums, es gegen seinen Willen mit Kunstgeschichte bedrängen zu wollen. Es sollte möglich sein, Kunst mit oder ohne Kunstgeschichte zu schätzen. Die Arbeiten sind absichtlich durcheinander gewürfelt, um Konflikte zu provozieren, aber auch um Fragen nach Qualität und Bedeutung stellen zu können. Manche kanonischen Werke der modernen Kunst sind uns so vertraut, dass sie mehr oder weniger tot sind. In einem neuen Kontext können sie verjüngt und neu interpretiert werden. Hoffe ich.

CR: Du hoffst? Ich würde sagen, es ist unausweichlich.

TD: Noch ein Wort zu diesem Jahrhundert und der grässlichen Fin-de-Siècle-Stimmung, aus der wir herauszukommen versuchen. Es war kein glückliches Jahrhundert; es gab zwei Weltkriege, den Holocaust, unzählige weitere Kriege, Völkermord und so weiter. Wir erlebten den Naziterror und den Verrat an einer modernen Utopie, dem Kommunismus. Trotzdem gibt es kaum «politische Kunst» in dieser Ausstellung, weil ich sie nicht als Kategorie für sich betrachte. «Voici» verweist auf diskrete Weise auf die Tragödien dieses Jahrhunderts. Die Erinnerung an das zwanzigste Jahrhundert sollte nicht ausgelöscht werden, gleichzeitig sollten wir aber auch nicht schuldbeladen und melancholisch ins neue Jahrhundert treten. Es geht darum, den verlorenen Optimismus wiederzufinden. *(Übersetzung: Uta Goridis)*

CUMULUS

IN EVERY EDITION OF PARKETT, TWO CUMULUS CLOUDS, ONE FROM AMERICA, THE OTHER FROM EUROPE, FLOAT OUT TO AN INTERESTED PUBLIC. THEY CONVEY INDIVIDUAL OPINIONS, ASSESSMENTS, AND MEMORABLE ENCOUNTERS—AS ENTIRELY PERSONAL PRESENTATIONS OF PROFESSIONAL ISSUES.

OUR CONTRIBUTORS TO THIS ISSUE ARE FRAZER WARD, WHO TEACHES ART HISTORY AT THE MARYLAND INSTITUTE, COLLEGE OF ART, BALTIMORE, AND HANS ULRICH RECK, PROFESSOR AT THE KUNSTHOCHSCHULE FÜR MEDIEN, COLOGNE.

FRAZER WARD

The Technology We Deserve

The evidentiary value of photographs was in question long before Photoshop had made its presence quite as keenly felt in the art world as it is now, and in broader contexts. The Rodney King beating incident and its aftermath provide one familiar touchstone. How often have you heard someone say, "Well, since Rodney King, you can't believe what you see"? Such statements are a little wide off the mark, though: people took to the streets, after the first King jury acquitted the police, because they did believe what they had seen in the famous video. And, of course, there are vast realms in which photography's claim to truth has ever been suspect: the fantasy scenarios of advertising have had to become increasingly ironic (if none the less successful, for that), as consumers have become less likely to accept the suggestion that they will get more girls/be more beautiful/have more freedom if they buy this or that product. Nowadays, though, the idea seems to be afoot that digital imagery renders any such investigations moot. Just as Rodney King is referenced only to reiterate that the evidentiary value of photographs has always been contextual and contested (despite their "indexicality"), so the claim that digital technology has brought about a fundamental change is anachronistic. Even though we might like the imagined security of photography as a guarantee of truth, photographs, like any other images, have always been up for interpretive grabs.

More insidiously, claims for digitization-as-revolution rest on the progressivist—I'm tempted to say dotcom—assumption that technology drives culture. On the contrary, to put it simply, everything is not different now because there are images that are a function of technology, only residually reliant on nature. To draw this out, I want to make what is perhaps initially a counter-intuitive connection, between the (pre-digital) photographic mediation of the body in performance art by Chris Burden, and the digital account of relations between bodies and technology in recent work by Aziz + Cucher. The points of contact between these moments, nearly thirty years apart, suggest that while technology may at any given time allow for new forms of expression, far broader cultural trajectories determine what can be expressed.

Chris Burden is one of a number of artists whose performances of the sev-

"

enties (despite their apparent physical extremity) clearly anticipated and integrated into their production, their doubleness in terms of audiences. That is, these artists took into account both the immediate, live audiences for their work, and the majority of people who would necessarily experience the work as it was distributed in photographic form. A number of Burden's performances were done in the presence of very small audiences or no audiences at all, except a photographer and other assistants, so that the entry of these radically embodied acts into public circulation as photographs, accompanied by texts, gave them a somewhat virtual quality, before the fact. And some of the photographs that do not picture Burden himself, such as the image of the lockers used to illustrate FIVE DAY LOCKER PIECE (April 26–30, 1971), or the image of the platform in WHITE LIGHT/WHITE HEAT (February 8–March 1, 1975), cannot strictly be said to verify the experience described in the texts (although we may choose to believe them). In the crucial instance of DOORWAY TO HEAVEN (November 15, 1973), at least, the photograph that "documents" the performance is an image of something that no one could have seen; it is a function of the technology of photography, just as digital images rest on computer technology. The characteristically blank description that accompanies the image reads as follows:

At 6 p.m. I stood in the doorway of my studio facing the Venice boardwalk. A few spectators watched as I pushed two live electric wires into my chest. The wires crossed and exploded, burning me but saving me from electrocution.[1]

DOORWAY TO HEAVEN provided for one of the most striking photographs generated by Burden's work. Burden's head, bare torso, and hands appear as if emerging from darkness. His hands, at waist level in an almost supplicatory gesture, each hold one of the wires that meet at his chest in a spectacular cascade of long, arcing sparks. The small explosion almost looks as though it emanates from Burden's chest, which is lit by the same flash that casts a somewhat unearthly light upwards, causing the dramatic shadowing of his face. His eyes, looking down, might be closed; his expression is impassive. It is not clear whether the "spectators" the description refers to were invited or incidental, and in this case the photograph suggests that it makes no difference. The instant "documented" was invisible in any case. As Johannes Lothar Schröder has observed: *A split second later, the sensation of burning would already have reached his brain and his face would have been distorted with pain. The simultaneity of calm composure and life-threatening short-circuit would have escaped the gaze of the naked eye blinded by the flash.*[2] And, in this case, the simultaneity of composure and short-circuit that makes the image so striking must also have been invisible to the photographer. So DOORWAY TO HEAVEN provides a photograph of something that in one crucial regard no one saw. Burden is sometimes denigrated as an artist whose apparent risk-taking involves a romanticization of the artist. I think he is rather cannier than that. I take the title, DOORWAY TO HEAVEN, to be somewhat ironic. His heaven seems to be a kind of abyss, suspended somewhere between act and photograph. The doorway to his studio, in this instance, serves as the entry through which his body passes, as photograph, into the circuits of representation.

This might suggest exactly the somewhat abyssal structure of the digital world, full of images of things that people have not quite seen, arrangements that don't quite meet expectations (though that is to imply their engagement with preexisting conventions). Burden's persistent interest in relations between the body and machines of different kinds is an avatar of this world. For instance, a recent series of photographic images by Aziz + Cucher, *Interiors* (1999–2000), treated, or generated—though it no longer makes a difference—by computer, envisages architectural spaces and details that are covered in, or made of, skin. A freckled corridor recedes into indistinct space; a cornice seems to breathe. The body—at least putatively at risk in its interface with technology, in Burden's work, and then dissipated into the world as representation—is in these images rendered even more diffuse, gothic, as organic and inorganic, flesh and space, become one. But although these spaces do not exist anywhere else than in the photographs, this is not a realm of pure imagining, conjured by technology, we have seen skin, we have seen rooms, corridors, corners. And we have seen Surrealism. This is not to suggest that Aziz + Cucher's work is a retooled version of collage, but at the same time, neither is their combinatory of images generated by the technology itself. The seamlessness with which skin becomes wall becomes representation may be new, so that the technology may be said to enable a different-than-before form of visual metaphor. Aziz + Cucher's photographs, however, are metaphors for the abandon and the terror of the collapse of distinctions between human and non-human, the attraction and the re-

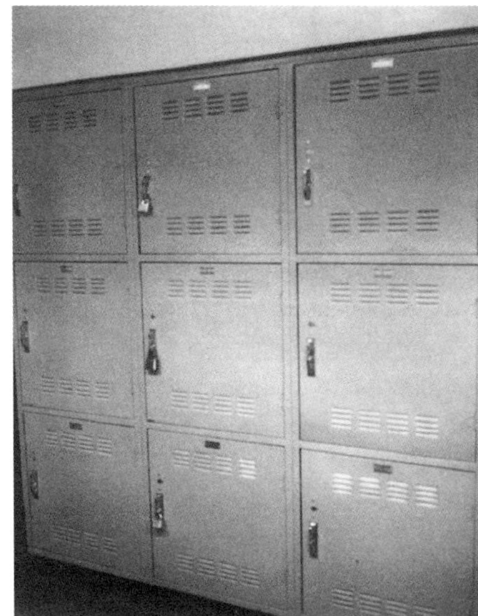

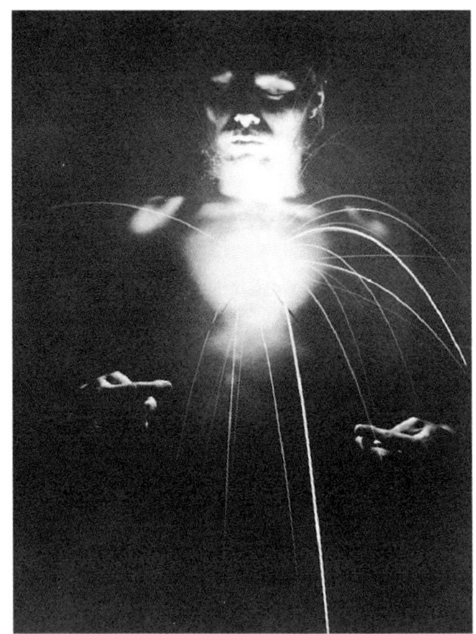

pulsion of the dissolution of limits. That is, as much as they are bound to the digital, they are also bound to a preexisting—and longstanding (think of Frankenstein)—set of cultural anxieties.

In Burden's perhaps inadvertent, sly reflection on photography's claim to truth, heaven (and, in a broader sense, representation) was constitutively bound to photographic technol-ogy, to the speed of the camera's vision that outstripped the human. Aziz + Cucher's photographic images are a function of a different technology, per-haps, or at least in their hands, more inclined toward forms of self-reflec-tion. Their digitized skin-architecture dispenses with any always-dubious pho-tographic claim to empirical truth, and represents, not heaven, but an every-where-and-nowhere that asks us to think about the effects of technology in relation to the culture from which it emerges.

1) Chris Burden, "Chris Burden: Original Texts 1971–1995" in: *Chris Burden* (Paris: Blocnotes, 1995).
2) Johannes Lothar Schröder, "Science, Heat and Time: Minimalism and Body Art in the Work of Chris Burden" in: *Chris Burden: Beyond the Limits*, ed. Peter Noever (Vienna: Austrian Museum of Applied Arts, 1996), p. 205.

AZIZ + CUCHER, INTERIOR NO. 1, 1999, C-Print, 72 x 50" / INNENRAUM NR. 1, 182,9 x 127 cm.

AZIZ + CUCHER, INTERIOR NOS. 2 & 3, 1999, C-Prints, 40 x 30" each / INNENRÄUME NR. 2 & 3, je 101,6 x 76,2 cm.

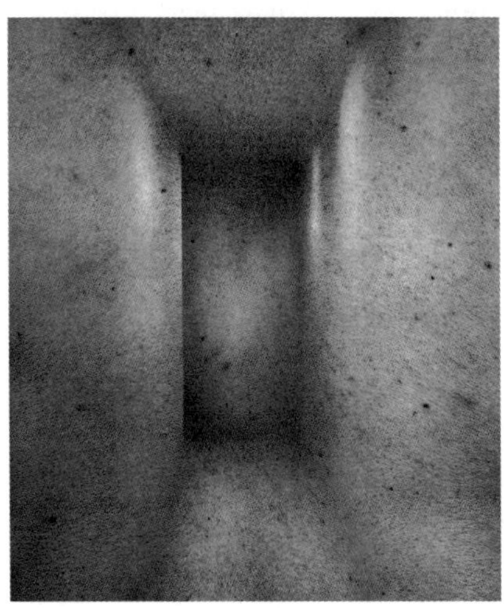

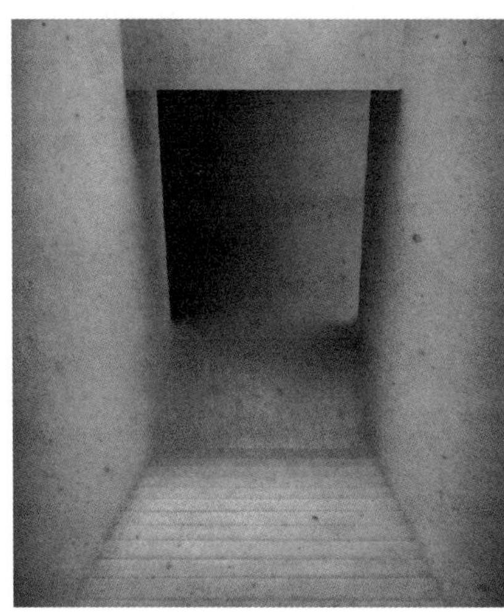

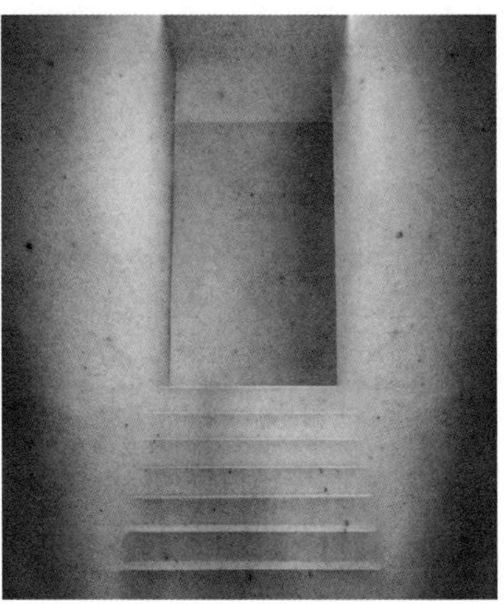

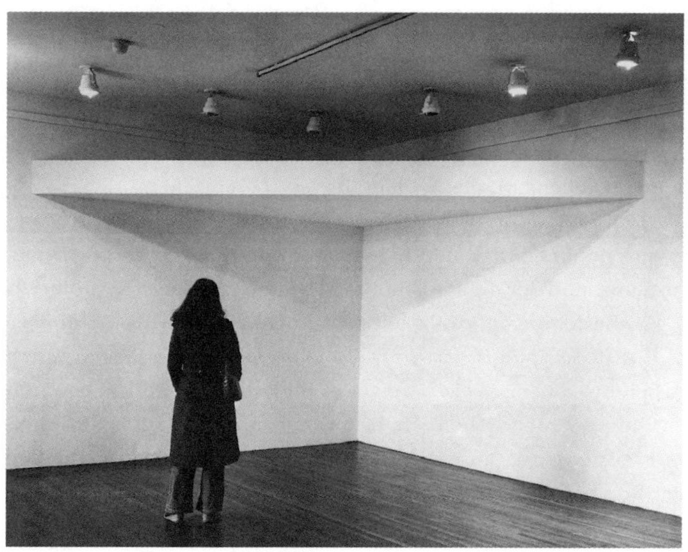

FRAZER WARD

Die Technologie, die wir verdienen

Der Wahrheitswert von Photographien wurde schon lange bevor Photoshop sich in der Kunstwelt die Geltung verschaffte, die es heute hat, in Frage gestellt, und zwar in einem viel umfassenderen Sinn. Der Fall des von der Polizei zusammengeschlagenen Rodney King ist ein vertrautes Beispiel dafür. Wie oft hat man nicht gehört: «Seit Rodney King kann man ja nicht mehr glauben, was man sieht.»? Solche Bemerkungen treffen jedoch nicht den Kern der Sache: Als die erste Rodney-King-Jury die Polizisten freisprach, gingen die Leute ja gerade auf die Strasse, weil sie glaubten, was sie in dem berühmten Video gesehen hatten. Ferner gibt es natürlich grosse Berei-che, in denen der Wahrheitsanspruch der Photographie schon immer fragwürdig war: Die Phantasiewelt der Werbung etwa wurde zusehends ironischer (ohne deshalb an Wirkung zu verlieren), je weniger die Konsumenten zu glauben bereit waren, dass sie durch das angepriesene Produkt in den Genuss von mehr Frauen/Schönheit/Freiheit kommen würden. Heutzutage scheint jedoch die Vorstellung zu herrschen, dass solche Fragestellungen in einer digitalen Bilderwelt ohnehin sinnlos seien. Rodney King anzuführen, um zum x-ten Mal darauf hinzuweisen, dass der Wahrheitswert von Photographien (trotz ihres Indiziencharakters) schon immer kontextab-hängig und damit fragwürdig gewesen sei, ist ebenso anachronistisch wie zu behaupten, die digitale Technologie habe einen grundlegenden Wandel bewirkt. Obwohl wir die scheinbare Zuverlässigkeit der Photographie gern als Wahrheitsgarantie betrachten, sind Photographien – genau wie alle anderen Bilder auch – schon immer Gegenstand der Interpretation gewesen.

Noch perfider: Jene, die die Digitalisierung als Revolution preisen, stützen sich auf den Fortschrittsglauben – am liebsten würde ich sagen: *dot.com*-Glauben –, dass die Kultur von der Technologie bestimmt wird. Das Gegenteil ist der Fall, da, einfach ausgedrückt, sich nicht alles verändert hat, nur weil es ein paar Bilder gibt, die künstlich generiert sind und sich kaum noch auf die Natur berufen. Um das etwas auszuführen, möchte ich eine zuerst vielleicht eher konstruiert wirkende Verbindung herstellen zwischen der (prä-digitalen) photographischen Vermittlung des Körpers in Chris Burdens Performancekunst und der digitalen Umsetzung von Beziehungen zwischen Körpern und Technologie in den jüngsten Arbeiten von Aziz + Cucher. Die Berührungspunkte zwischen diesen beinahe dreissig Jahre auseinander liegenden Beispielen lassen erkennen, dass es sehr viel umfassendere kulturelle Strömungen sind, die bestimmen, w a s ausgedrückt werden kann, auch wenn die Technologie immer wieder neue Ausdrucks f o r m e n ermöglicht.

Chris Burden gehört zu einer Gruppe von Künstlern, deren Performances in den 70er Jahren (auch wenn sie körperlich an die äusserste Grenze gingen) ihrer Zwiespältigkeit in Bezug auf das Publikum vollkommen bewusst waren. Will heissen, diese Künstler wandten sich sowohl an das unmittelbar gegenwärtige Publikum wie auch an die Mehrheit jener Leute, die der Arbeit erst in ihrer photographisch dokumentierten Form begegnen würden. Vom Photographen und anderen Mitarbeitern einmal abgesehen, fanden viele von Burdens Performances vor ganz wenigen Zuschauern oder ganz ohne Publikum statt. Also hatte die Verbreitung dieser radikalen Aktionen in Form von Photographien und Begleittexten von vornherein eher virtuelle Qualität. Und von einigen der Photos, auf denen Burden selbst gar nicht zu sehen ist, wie etwa das Schliessfachbild zu FIVE DAY LOCKER PIECE (Fünf Tage im Schliessfach,

26.–30. April 1971) oder das Bild der Plattform zu WHITE LIGHT / WHITE HEAT (Weisses Licht / Weisse Glut, 8. Februar – 1. März 1975), kann man eigentlich nicht sagen, dass sie die in den Texten beschriebene Erfahrung belegen (selbst wenn wir ihnen Glauben schenken). Das Photo-«Dokument» des entscheidenden Moments von DOORWAY TO HEAVEN (Himmelstor, 15. November 1973) schliesslich zeigt ein Bild, das niemand so gesehen haben kann; es ist ein reines Produkt der Phototechnik, genau wie digitale Bilder Produkte der Computertechnologie sind. Die lakonische Beschreibung des Bildes lautet: Um sechs Uhr abends stand ich an der Uferpromenade von Venice unter der Tür zu meinem Atelier. Ein paar Zuschauer beobachteten, wie ich mir zwei unter Strom stehende Elektrodrähte in die Brust stiess. Die Drähte berührten sich und bewirkten einen Kurzschluss, was zwar Verbrennungen hinterliess, mich jedoch vor dem tödlichen elektrischen Schlag bewahrte.[1]

DOORWAY TO HEAVEN lieferte eines der sensationellsten Photos im Rahmen von Burdens Werk. Der Kopf des Künstlers, sein nackter Oberkörper und seine Hände scheinen aus dem Dunkel hervorzutreten. Die Hände in Taillenhöhe halten mit beinah flehender Geste je ein Stück Elektrodraht, die auf seiner Brust aufeinander treffen und eine spektakuläre Funkenkaskade auslösen. Es sieht aus, als käme die kleine Explosion direkt aus seiner Brust, die von einem Blitz erleuchtet wird, der gleichzeitig ein geradezu überirdisches Licht nach oben wirft und dramatische Schatten auf Burdens Gesicht zeichnet. Die gesenkten Augen scheinen geschlossen; die Miene unbewegt. Ob die im Text erwähnten

Zuschauer eingeladen oder zufällig anwesend waren, ist unklar; nach dem Photo zu schliessen ist das auch nicht so wichtig. Der «dokumentierte» Augenblick war so für niemanden wahrnehmbar. Wie Johannes Lothar Schröder bemerkte: «Sekundenbruchteile später hätten die Nerven den Verbrennungsschmerz bereits ans Gehirn weitergeleitet und das Gesicht wäre schmerzverzerrt gewesen. Die Gleichzeitigkeit von ruhigem Gefasstsein und lebensgefährlichem Kurzschluss wären dem blossen, vom Blitz geblendeten Auge entgangen.[2] Also kann die Simultaneität, die das Bild so aussergewöhnlich macht, auch für den Photographen nicht sichtbar gewesen sein. DOORWAY TO HEAVEN ist ein Photo von etwas, das im entscheidenden Augenblick niemand gesehen hat. Man wirft Burden manchmal vor, seine offensichtliche Risikofreudigkeit laufe auf eine romantische Verklärung des Künstlers hinaus. Meiner Meinung nach ist er jedoch viel raffinierter. Ich verstehe den Titel DOORWAY TO HEAVEN eher ironisch. Sein Himmel scheint eine Art Abgrund zu sein, irgendwo zwischen der Aktion und dem Photo. Der Eingang zum Atelier ist in diesem Fall das Tor, durch das sein Körper als Photographie in Umlauf kommt.

Das könnte ein Hinweis auf die abgründige Struktur der digitalen Welt sein, die voller Bilder von Dingen ist, die eigentlich keiner gesehen hat, voller Kombinationen, die nicht wirklich den Erwartungen entsprechen (obwohl dies auch schon eine Verknüpfung mit bestehenden Konventionen impliziert). Burdens unvermindertes Interesse an den Beziehungen zwischen dem Körper und verschiedenen Maschinen ist ein Ausdruck dieser

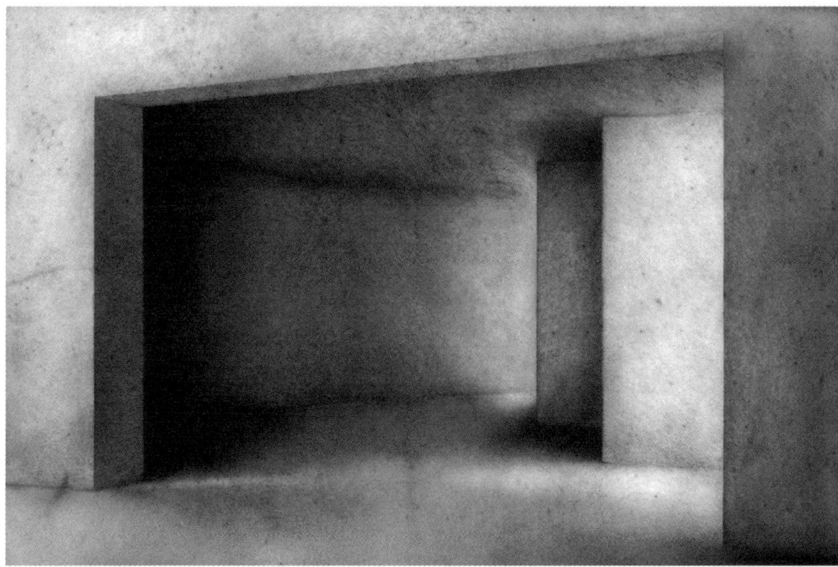

Welt. So zeigt zum Beispiel die kürzlich entstandene, computerbearbeitete bzw. -erzeugte (das lässt sich mittlerweile nicht mehr unterscheiden) Photoserie *Interiors* (Innenräume, 1999–2000) von Aziz + Cucher architektonische Räume und Details, die von einer Haut überzogen sind oder aus Haut bestehen: Ein sommersprossiger Korridor verliert sich in der Ferne; ein Gesims scheint zu atmen. Während der Körper beim Aufeinandertreffen mit der Technologie in Burdens Werk noch auf eine gefährliche Probe gestellt und später als bildliche Darstellung verbreitet wurde, ist er in diesen Bildern sehr viel diffuser und gruseliger wiedergegeben, da Organisches und Anorganisches, Fleisch und Raum eins werden.

Selbst wenn diese Räume nur auf Photos existieren, so sind sie doch keine puren, mit technologischen Mitteln erzeugten Phantasiegebilde, denn schliesslich haben wir alle schon Haut, Räume, Korridore und Ecken gesehen. Und wir sind mit dem Surrealismus vertraut. Das soll nicht heissen, dass Aziz + Cuchers Arbeit eine Art Collage mit anderen Mitteln ist, aber die Kombinationen ihrer computergenerierten Bilder ist nicht das Produkt dieser Technologie. Die Nahtlosigkeit, mit welcher Haut zu Wand und schliesslich zur bildlichen Darstellung gerinnt, mag neu sein, so dass man sagen könnte, dass wir der Technologie eine neue, früher noch nicht mögliche Form der visuellen Metapher verdan-

ken. Aziz + Cuchers Photos sind allerdings Metaphern für die Hilflosigkeit und den Schrecken, welche die Aufhebung der Grenzen zwischen Menschlichem und Nichtmenschlichem auslösen, aber auch für die Faszination und den Horror, die mit jedem Fallen von Grenzen verbunden sind. Mindestens genauso stark wie der digitalen Technologie sind Aziz + Cucher also einer langen Reihe bereits bestehender, alles andere als neuer Ängste unserer Zivilisation verpflichtet – man denke nur an *Frankenstein*.

In Burdens vielleicht unbeabsichtigt hinterhältiger Reflexion über den Wahrheitsanspruch der Photographie blieb der Himmel (und in einem weiteren Sinn auch jede Darstellung überhaupt) notwendig an die Technik der Photographie gebunden, an die Geschwindigkeit der Kameraoptik, die das menschliche Auge austrickste. Aziz + Cuchers photographische Bilder sind Produkte einer anderen Technologie, die – zumindest in ihren Händen – eher zur Selbstreflexion tendiert. Ihre digitalisierte Hautarchitektur verzichtet auf den schon immer fragwürdigen, empirischen Wahrheitsanspruch der Photographie und zeigt nicht den Himmel, sondern ein Überall-und-Nirgendwo, das uns dazu auffordert, über die Einflüsse der Technologie auf die Kultur, aus der sie entspringt, nachzudenken.

(Übersetzung: Uta Goridis)

1) Chris Burden, «Chris Burden: Original Texts 1971–1995», in: *Chris Burden*, Blocnotes, Paris 1995.
2) Johannes Lothar Schröder, «Wissenschaft, Hitze und Zeit: Minimalismus und Body Art in Chris Burdens Werk», in: *Chris Burden, Beyond the Limits*, hrsg. von Peter Noever, Österreichisches Museum für Angewandte Kunst, Wien 1996, S. 205.

CUMULUS

Aus Europa

IN JEDER AUSGABE VON PARKETT PEILT EINE CUMULUS-WOLKE AUS AMERIKA UND EINE AUS EUROPA DIE INTERESSIERTEN KUNSTFREUNDE AN. SIE TRÄGT PERSÖNLICHE RÜCKBLICKE, BEURTEILUNGEN UND DENKWÜRDIGE BEGEGNUNGEN MIT SICH – ALS JEWEILS GANZ EIGENE DARSTELLUNG EINER BERUFSMÄSSIGEN AUSEINANDERSETZUNG.

IN DIESEM BAND ÄUSSERN SICH HANS ULRICH RECK, PROFESSOR AN DER KUNSTHOCHSCHULE FÜR MEDIEN IN KÖLN, SOWIE FRAZER WARD, DOZENT FÜR KUNSTGESCHICHTE AM MARYLAND INSTITUTE, COLLEGE OF ART, IN BALTIMORE.

HANS ULRICH RECK

Die Kunst, die Utopie, die Medien

Betrachtungen zum *Jahrbuch für Künste und Apparate*

Medien gibt es, seit die Erfahrung der Fremdheit der Welt zusammen mit der Vermutung der Selbstfremdheit des Menschen auftritt. Medien vermitteln die Welt, weil die Welt nicht unmittelbar vorliegt. Sie wird als eine konstruierte Erfahrungswelt zugänglich, ist also durchaus artifiziell. Medien sind demnach nicht nur geschichtlich und technisch, sondern auch anthropologisch basiert. Sie gehören zu den von Natur aus notwendigen Artefakten. Für die symbolische Ausgestaltung dieser welthaft bedeutsamen Artefakte spielt seit je die Kunst eine besondere Rolle. Sie betrachtet die Medien als poetische Werkzeuge. Gerade das führt aktuell zu einem Problem, besetzen doch die Medien heute ein Feld hochtechnisierter Apparate und sind der Kunst nicht ohne weiteres zugänglich. Der Kunst bleibt nur übrig, so zu tun, als ob die poetische Konstruktion der Medien immer im Sinne von Werkzeugen nach ihren eigenen Zwecken gelingen könnte. Und dies auch dort, wo die Medien keine Werkzeuge mehr sind, sondern komplexe Apparate- oder Medienverbände, Maschinen, die Maschinen steuern, operative Zeichenketten, die maschinelle Kooperationen und Vernetzungen dirigieren. Deshalb ist die anthropologische Betrachtung der Artefakte nicht banal. Weil Kunst niemals nur die banale Bearbeitung von Artefakten darstellt. Ihre ausdrückliche

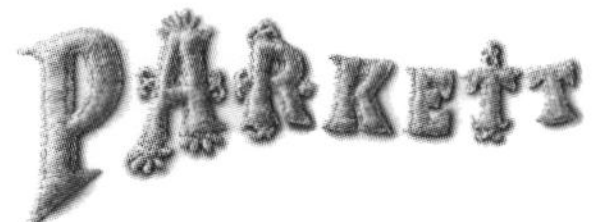

The PARKETT Series is created in collaboration with artists, who contribute an original work available exclusively to the subscribers in the form of a signed limited SPECIAL EDITION. The available works are also reproduced in each PARKETT issue.

Each SPECIAL EDITION is available by order from any one of our offices in New York or Zurich. Just fill in the details below and send this card to the office nearest you. Once your order has been processed, you will be issued with an invoice and your personal edition number. Upon receipt of payment, you will receive the SPECIAL EDITION. (Please note that supply is subject to availability. PARKETT does not assume responsibility for any delays in production of SPECIAL EDITIONS. Postage is not included.)

☐ As a subscriber to PARKETT, I would like to order the following Special Edition(s), signed and numbered by the artist.

PARKETT No.	ARTIST		
PARKETT No.	ARTIST	NAME:	
PARKETT No.	ARTIST	ADDRESS:	
PARKETT No.	ARTIST	CITY:	
PARKETT No.	ARTIST	STATE/ZIP:	
PARKETT No.	ARTIST	COUNTRY:	
PARKETT No.	ARTIST	PHONE:	

☐ I have indicated my way of payment on the reverse side of this form.

Send this form to the PARKETT office nearest you:

PARKETT PUBLISHERS   155 AV. OF THE AMERICAS   NEW YORK, NY 10013   PHONE (212) 673-2660   FAX (212) 271-0704

PARKETT VERLAG   QUELLENSTRASSE 27   CH-8031 ZÜRICH   TELEFON +41-1-271 81 40   FAX +41-1-272 43 01

PARKETT VERLAG   TANNENWALDALLEE 17   D-61348 BAD HOMBURG   FAX 06172-937 444   www.parkettart.com

---

KÜNSTLEREDITIONEN FÜR PARKETT-ABONNENTEN — 60

Die PARKETT-Buchreihe entsteht in Zusammenarbeit mit Künstlern, die eigens für die Abonnenten einen Originalbeitrag in Form einer limitierten und signierten EDITION gestalten. Diese Editionen sind auch in der Zeitschrift abgebildet und können mit dieser Bestellkarte in jedem unserer Büros in Zürich, Frankfurt oder New York bestellt werden. Sie erhalten dann Ihre persönliche Editionsnummer und eine Rechnung. Sobald wir Ihre Zahlung erhalten haben, schicken wir Ihnen Ihre Edition(en). (Lieferung nur solange vorrätig. PARKETT übernimmt keine Verantwortung für allfällige Verzögerungen bei der Herstellung der Vorzugsausgaben. Versandkosten zuzüglich.)

☐ Ich bin PARKETT-Abonnent(in) und bestelle folgende EDITION(EN), numeriert und vom Künstler signiert:

PARKETT Nr.	KÜNSTLER/IN		
PARKETT Nr.	KÜNSTLER/IN	NAME:	
PARKETT Nr.	KÜNSTLER/IN	STRASSE:	
PARKETT Nr.	KÜNSTLER/IN	PLZ/STADT:	
PARKETT Nr.	KÜNSTLER/IN	LAND:	
PARKETT Nr.	KÜNSTLER/IN	TEL.:	

☐ Meine Zahlungsweise habe ich auf der Rückseite angegeben.

Senden Sie die Bestellkarte an das PARKETT-Büro in Ihrer Nähe:

PARKETT VERLAG   QUELLENSTRASSE 27   CH-8031 ZÜRICH   TELEFON +41-1-271 81 40   FAX +41-1-272 43 01

PARKETT VERLAG   TANNENWALDALLEE 17   D-61348 BAD HOMBURG   FAX 06172-937 444   www.parkettart.com

PARKETT PUBLISHERS   155 AV. OF THE AMERICAS   NEW YORK, NY 10013   PHONE (212) 673-2660   FAX (212) 271-0704

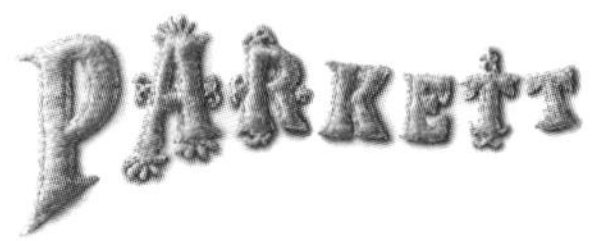

SUBSCRIBE, COMPLETE OR SEND A GIFT SUBSCRIPTION TO THE BEST BOOK SERIES ON CONTEMPORARY ARTISTS

I subscribe to the PARKETT series, starting with issue no. _______

☐ for 1 year (3 issues) at US$ 80 (USA/Canada), SFr. 118.– (Europe), SFr. 140.– (Rest of the world).

☐ for 2 years (6 issues) at US$ 145 (USA/Canada), SFr. 215.– (Europe), SFr. 265.– (Rest of the world).

☐ for 1 year (3 issues) at a 20% student discount (US$ 65 for USA/ Canada, SFr. 95.– for Europe). A copy of my student ID is enclosed.

Send a gift subscription in my name, starting with issue no. _______

☐ for 1 year (3 issues) at US$ 80 (USA/Canada), SFr. 118.– (Europe), SFr. 140.– (Rest of the world).

☐ for 2 years (6 issues) at US$ 145 (USA/Canada), SFr. 215.– (Europe), SFr. 265.– (Rest of the world). A gift card in my name will be sent to the recipient.

Postage included. All prices subject to change.

☐ I wish to complete my PARKETT collection and order the following issue no(s):

at SFr. 43.– each (up to no 43: SFr. 30.–; no. 44–48: SFr. 39.–), postage not included. Within the USA & Canada $ 32 (up to no. 43: $ 22.50; no. 44–48: $ 29), add postage: $ 5 (USA), $ 10 (Canada). (Sold out: No. 1–10, 13, 16, 19, 27, 29–31, 35)

☐ I wish to order the catalog raisonné of all PARKETT Artists' Editions from 1984–98 (60 pages, 120 color ill., published for the show at the Ludwig Museum, Cologne), for SFr. 15.– (USA: $ 12), excl. postage.

☐ I wish to order _______ copies of the new set of 101 postcards featuring PARKETT Artists' Editions for SFr. 48.– (USA: $ 32) per set, excl. postage.

NAME:

ADDRESS:

CITY:

STATE/ZIP:

COUNTRY:

TEL.:   FAX:

GIFT RECIPIENT:

ADDRESS:

CITY:

STATE/ZIP:

COUNTRY:

☐ Charge my Visa Card   ☐ Mastercard   ☐ AMEX

Card No. |___|___|___|___|___|___|___|___|___| Expiration date _______

☐ Payment enclosed (US check or money order)   ☐ Bill me

DATE

SIGNATURE

Send this form to the PARKETT office nearest you:

PARKETT PUBLISHERS   155 AV. OF THE AMERICAS   NEW YORK, NY 10013   PHONE (212) 673-2660   FAX (212) 271-0704

PARKETT VERLAG   QUELLENSTRASSE 27   CH-8031 ZÜRICH   TELEFON +41-1-271 81 40   FAX +41-1-272 43 01

PARKETT VERLAG   TANNENWALDALLEE 17   D-61348 BAD HOMBURG   FAX 06172-937 444   www.parkettart.com

ABONNIEREN, VERVOLLSTÄNDIGEN ODER VERSCHENKEN SIE DIE UMFASSENDSTE BUCHREIHE ÜBER GEGENWARTSKÜNSTLER

Ich abonniere die PARKETT-Reihe ab Nr. _______

☐ für 1 Jahr (3 Ausgaben) zu: DM 130.– (BRD), SFr. 108.– (Schweiz), SFr. 118.– (übriges Europa).

☐ für 2 Jahre (6 Ausgaben) zu: DM 238.– (BRD), SFr. 190.– (Schweiz), SFr. 215.– (übriges Europa).

☐ für 1 Jahr (3 Ausgaben) mit 20% Studentenermässigung (BRD: DM 104.–/Schweiz: SFr. 87.–/Europa: SFr. 95.–). Eine Kopie meines Studentenausweises lege ich bei.

Ich verschenke ein PARKETT-Abonnement ab Nr. _______

☐ für 1 Jahr (3 Ausgaben) zu: DM 130.– (BRD), SFr. 108.– (Schweiz), SFr. 118.– (übriges Europa).

☐ für 2 Jahre (6 Ausgaben) zu: DM 238.– (BRD), SFr. 190.– (Schweiz), SFr. 215.– (übriges Europa). Das Geschenk-Abo mit einer Geschenkkarte wird in meinem Namen versandt.

Preise einschliesslich Versandkosten. Preisänderungen vorbehalten.

☐ Ich möchte meine PARKETT-Sammlung vervollständigen und bestelle die folgende(n) noch erhältliche(n) Ausgabe(n) Nr. ____________________ zu je DM 49.–/SFr. 43.– (bis Nr. 43: DM 35.–/SFr. 30.–; Nr. 44–48: DM 45.–/ SFr. 39.–, zzgl. Versandkosten (vergriffen: Nr. 1–10, 13, 16, 19, 27, 29–31, 35)

☐ Ich bestelle das Werkverzeichnis der PARKETT-Künstlereditionen von 1984–98 (60 S., 120 Farbabb., erschienen zur Ausstellung im Museum Ludwig, Köln) für DM 18.–/SFr. 15.– zzgl. Versandkosten.

☐ Ich bestelle _______ Ex. des neuen Postkarten-Sets mit 101 PARKETT-Künstlereditionen zum Preis von DM 55.–/SFr. 48.– pro Set, zzgl. Versandkosten.

NAME:

STRASSE:

PLZ/STADT:

LAND:

TEL.:   FAX:

BESCHENKTE(R):

STRASSE:

PLZ/STADT:

LAND:

☐ Ich zahle mit Visa   ☐ Eurocard/Mastercard   ☐ AMEX

Karten Nr. |___|___|___|___|___|___|___|___|___| Gültig bis _______

☐ Mein Scheck über SFr./DM _______________________ liegt bei.

☐ Bitte senden Sie mir eine Rechnung.

DATUM

UNTERSCHRIFT

Senden Sie die Bestellkarte an das PARKETT-Büro in Ihrer Nähe:

PARKETT VERLAG   QUELLENSTRASSE 27   CH-8031 ZÜRICH   TELEFON +41-1-271 81 40   FAX +41-1-272 43 01

PARKETT VERLAG   TANNENWALDALLEE 17   D-61348 BAD HOMBURG   FAX 06172-937 444   www.parkettart.com

PARKETT PUBLISHERS   155 AV. OF THE AMERICAS   NEW YORK, NY 10013   PHONE (212) 673-2660   FAX (212) 271-0704

Tätigkeit ist es, Überschüsse der Imagination zu ermöglichen, eine Verausgabung von Reichtum, die sich nicht im Wahn der Produktion erschöpft.

Mit der so gerne – intermedial, synthetisch, simulativ, organisch usw. – herbeigeredeten Kraft der Kunst zur Integration von Sinnen und Apparaten, Technologien und Wissenschaften in einem Feld des Gesamtkunstwerks ist es heute jedenfalls nicht weit her. Und kann es auch nicht sein: Zu komplex sind die Technologien, zu ausdifferenziert ein Technosystem, das nur noch seinen eigenen Vorgaben und Zwängen folgt und von aussen kaum mehr steuerbar erscheint – weder durch Politik noch durch Ethik noch durch Ästhetik und Kunst. In den wenigsten Fällen waren Künstler am Zustandekommen aktuell bedeutsamer technischer Erfindungen beteiligt.

Die Einheit der Künste und Wissenschaften ist also ebenso Utopie geblieben wie die Synthese von technischer Lebenswelt und funktionaler Gleichheit. Der ästhetisch befreite, technisch kompetente Mensch, der selber Medium einer stetigen Anverwandlung von Technologien ist, muss als emphatische Vorstellung verstanden werden, die rhetorisch gerade dadurch zu bewegen vermag, dass ihr keine empirische Wahrscheinlichkeit zukommt. Daraus beziehen die Künste eine wesentliche Kraft: Sie markieren die Differenz, sie artikulieren einen Widerstand, insistieren auf gehaltvollen Vorstellungen eines poetischen und freiheitlichen Gebrauchs der Apparate, ohne dies durch polytechnisch wirksame Verbesserungen sofort unter Beweis stellen zu müssen. Wenn Utopie eine kritische Funktion geblieben ist, so gilt für sie, was schon Lichtenberg dem Kritiker zugestand: das Privileg, schonungslos zu

kritisieren, ohne beweisen zu müssen, dass er es besser zu machen verstünde.

Kunst hat ein wesentliches Potenzial in der Chaosfähigkeit, dank der die hierarchische Zähmung der Medien und die Reduktion ihrer Vielfalt auf standardisierte Operationen auffällig werden kann. Das erklärt, weshalb es zur poetologischen Praktik der Ortsfindung mittels einer «Kunst durch Medien» gehört, auf die Fiktion eines Mastermediums, einer Leitstelle, eines verbindlichen Organons, eines diktierenden Ablaufplans, überhaupt auf die Stelle einer zentrierenden Macht zu verzichten. Ganz ohne Zweifel steht die Telematik, das heisst die Anwendung des Computers zur elektronischen Datenverarbeitung in allergrösstem Stil, im Dienste der Optimierung.

In einer Zeit, in der um nahezu jeden Preis nahezu alles mit allem nach einheitlichen Vorgaben synchronisiert werden soll, in einer Sphäre massenmedial organisierter Weltgleichzeitigkeit und einer hierarchisch verwerteten Kommunikationsgesellschaft, in der man unter Kommunikation den Transport einheitlich standardisierter Signalketten versteht, in einer solchen Welt ist jede Anstrengung künstlerischer Praktik ein Kampf um Differenzen. Es geht der Kunst demnach nicht nur um Gestaltung, sondern auch um die Formung von Eigenzeit, um eine Sinnesorganisation, die nicht nach subjektiven Mustern des Gefälligen und nicht nach objektiven Bedingungen der minuziös getakteten Welt, des formierten Tausches standardisierter Zeichen und Dinge, Gebräuche und Findungen ausgerichtet ist. Deshalb kümmern sich künstlerische Praktiken im Zeitalter des Techno-Imaginären nicht mehr in erster Linie um die Erzeugung von Werken, sondern um die

Etablierung von Handlungen und die Erprobung von Methoden. Von der Manifestation der Repräsentationen zum Ort der vernetzenden Handlungen – das ist ein durchaus berechtigtes Leitmotiv der «Künste durch digitale Medien», quer zu den Apparaten, durch die Steuerungsimpulse der maschinisierten Vernetzungen der Befehle, Hierarchien und Operationen hindurch. Es geht der Kunst um die poetische Einrichtung eines sozialen Ortes, an dem sie Bedeutung hat: Kunst ist kritische Reflexion ihres Ortes geworden. Deshalb zwingen neue Technologien und Medien zu einer ständigen Reflexion der Ausbildungsgrundlagen von Kunstakademien und Medienhochschulen.

Mit der radikalen Autonomie der Kunst – ausgebildet von der Romantik bis zu den Innovationen am Beginn des zwanzigsten Jahrhunderts – und einer entsprechenden Schwächung der bis dahin gültigen polytechnischen und akademischen Kunstausbildung stellt sich das Verhältnis von Kunst, Wissenschaft, Technologie und Lebenswelt in einem grundsätzlich neuen Bezugsfeld dar. Gemeinhin geht man heute davon aus, dass «Kunst als solche» nicht erlernt werden kann, dass aber gerade deshalb eine technische Fähigkeit an Geräten, Materialien und Apparaten intensiv und extensiv erarbeitet werden muss.

Vor Jahrzehnten schon postulierte der Kunsthistoriker und langjährige Bürgermeister Roms, Giulio Carlo Argan, der zeitgenössische Künstler solle sich als Bildoperateur, also vermehrt technisch-kommunikativ und nicht mehr nur expressiv-ästhetisch, als isoliertes Künstlersubjekt definieren. Diese damals auch im Hinblick auf das Programm des Bauhauses formulierte

Maxime für eine aktuelle Künstlerausbildung hat im Zeitalter der digitalen Technologien eine gesteigerte Aktualität erhalten. Damit untrennbar verbunden ist die Aufgabe der Neubestimmung des Verhältnisses von «freier» und «angewandter» Kunst, von Kunst und Zivilisation, «hoher / ernsthafter» und «unterhaltender / trivialer» Kultur (E- und U-Codes). Solche Bestimmungen folgen nicht mehr länger dem ästhetischen Geschmack, sondern den künstlerischen Möglichkeiten fortgeschrittener Werkzeugnutzung und -entwicklung.

Zahlreiche Initiativen haben versucht, diese Kluft zwischen Kunst, Technik und Lebenswelt wieder zu schliessen und die «angewandte» mit der «freien» Kunst zu versöhnen. Vom Werkbund über Bauhaus und new bauhaus bis zur Hochschule für Gestaltung, Ulm, reicht die eindrucksvolle Palette von Versuchen, freie und angewandte Kunst mit den fortschrittlichsten technischen Mitteln herzustellen und mit den avancierten Wissenschaften zu verbinden. Bezogen auf die hohe Komplexität von Wissenschafts- und Technologie-Entwicklung kann kein Zweifel bestehen an der Notwendigkeit, künstlerische Methoden der Erkenntnisvermittlung und Technikanwendung in Permanenz zu erfinden. Solche Methoden haben einen für die Kunst spezifischen Zuschnitt. Die eng an Kunst und Gestaltung angelehnte Theoriebildung ist unauflöslich ein wesentlicher Bestandteil der Projektentwicklung und -umsetzung. Theorie ist selber zu einer wesentlichen Organisationsform der künstlerischen Praxis geworden.

Die Ausbildung an der Kunsthochschule für Medien in Köln (KHM) konzentriert sich demnach seit Anbeginn, das heisst seit Aufnahme des Lehrbetriebs im Oktober 1990, auf anspruchsvolle Methoden und Praktiken für künstlerische Tätigkeiten in und mit den fortgeschrittenen Medien, und zwar im Dienste einer Vielfalt der Konzepte: Der Bogen reicht vom experimentellen Installationsprojekt eines avantgardistischen Kunstgebrauchs bis zur Massenwirkung von Mediendesign, Fernsehen und Film. Aber auch umgekehrt: Vom filmischen Experiment, erneuernden TV-Versuchen, subtilen Designexperimenten bis zum Kunstwerk, das sich als massenkulturell wirksame Inszenierung einer ästhetisch gehobenen Lüge artikuliert, ist alles möglich. Die Codes sind polar und aufgespannt bis in die möglichen Extreme hinein. Was sonst säuberlich geschieden wird, Massenkultur und elitäre Kunst, hohe und niedrige Codes, subtiler und brachialer Geschmack, freie und angewandte Kunst, hohe Kunst und massenkulturelle Verwertbarkeiten, Intellektualität und Banalität, Reflexion und Popularität, Denken und Vergnügen: Hier prallt es aufeinander, reibt sich, transformiert sich im besten Falle und bewirkt Erneuerungen. Immer von Fall zu Fall, entschieden, aber bereit zur Revision, gar zur Verwerfung.

Die Fragen an künstlerische Fähigkeiten im Umgang mit digitalen Maschinen sind radikal und delikat. Nicht wenige ernsthafte Stimmen sagen, ein wirkliches Verstehen der Apparate durch die Kunst sei nicht mehr möglich. Wenn das stimmt, dann betreiben die Kunstwerke auf elektronischer Steuerungsbasis und inmitten der digital verborgenen Komponenten nichts anderes als eine schwer erträgliche, verlogene Oberflächengestaltung. Was sich heute «Medienkunst» nennt, sieht nicht selten auch so aus. Das Dekorum verkommt zur schieren, abgewerteten Dekoration. Denn zu einer bewussten Lüge wären Einstellungen nötig, die gerade nicht gegeben sind. Man sieht, dass in diesem Gedankengang gerade der Kunst ein maximales Verstehen, ein Eindringen in die sonst nur funktional prozessierenden, instrumentellen Dimensionen des Lebens abverlangt wird. Dekorum ist ja leider missverstanden und zum Vorwurf der Oberflächlichkeit verhunzt worden. Der wiederum ist nur möglich in einer Kultur systematischer Oberflächenabwertung. Und diese setzt eine gedoppelte Ontologie voraus: Eine wahre Wirklichkeit steht gegen eine scheinbare. Die von Nietzsche liquidierte, im Namen einer Artistik der Lüge und des Genusses zurückgewiesene Doppelung von Wirklichkeit und deren Karikatur im Schein, wären in diesem Argument, wenn auch verstellt, immer noch wirksam. Kein Zufall, dass das Modell des Baumeisters in der Kunst als Reservoir der Resistenz gegen beliebige und beliebig schnelle Zeichenmanipulationen überlebt.

Man könne nur verstehen, was man selber zu bauen in der Lage sei, ar-

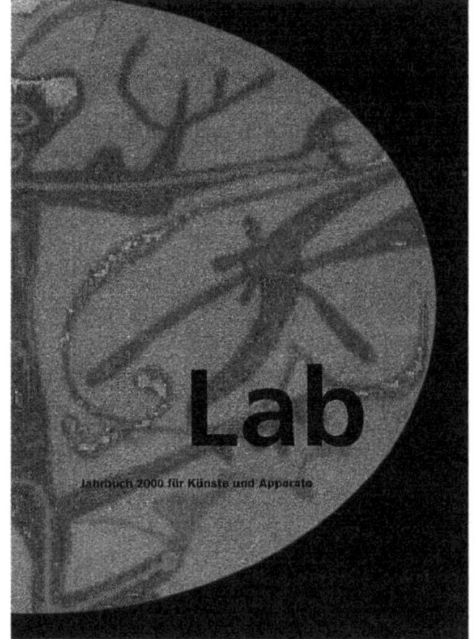

gumentierte der Geschichtsphilosoph Giambattista Vico im achtzehnten Jahrhundert. Von da bis Hegel hat man Kunst als sinnliche Erscheinung der Idee immer in den Zusammenhang kontrollierter Fabrikation gebracht. Die Werke der Kunst belegten die Entäusserung einer Idee, die in der Materialität, den Stofflichkeiten – später den Mediatisierungen – eingeschrieben sei. Kunst müsse konstruktives Verstehen ermöglichen – das ist die maximale Anforderung. Das bedingt, dass Künstler als Kunststudenten vom ersten Tag an beginnen, sich in den Stand und die Lage zu versetzen, alle von ihnen benötigten Instrumente – *tools,* wie man neudeutsch sagt – selber zu bauen. Die maximal dagegen opponierende Haltung ist, dass der Künstler nur ein Logistiker des Arrangements, der Verbindungen und Kooperationen, Konnexionen und Vermittlungen sei. Also ein Stratege letztlich semiotischer Inszenierungen, ein Taktiker der lokalen und punktuellen Verknüpfungen. Und als solcher ein Meister der Oberfläche, der Fixierung haltloser und immaterieller, flottierender und prozessierender Zeichen. Selbstverständlich findet man an der KHM beide und auch weitere Haltungen, die zwischen diesen Polen angesiedelt sind.

Kein Programm, und wenn doch, dann mehrere. Eine Theorie ist nicht genug, ein Programm zu wenig, eine einzige Welt nicht ausreichend. Kein Programm also, aber vielleicht doch eine Maxime: Sich den vielen Versuchen zu entziehen, die entstehenden Begehrlichkeiten auszunützen, um sie von Zentren medialer Macht her zu kontrollieren. Spannbreite und Kraft dieses Anspruchs können natürlich an keiner blossen Programmatik, nur an den Produkten abgelesen werden. Seit

1996 ist ein angemessener Einblick in eine Ökonomie der Intensitäten, ein Geflecht der Nachbarschaften, intellektuellen Freundschaften, ein Netz von Netzen, von singulären Insistenzen und eigenwilligen Verbindungen möglich, auch dank der Publikation *Lab. Jahrbuch für Künste und Apparate.*

Die Konzeption dieses Jahrbuchs schliesst Selbstdarstellungen aus. Seine Beiträge stammen mehrheitlich von externen Autoren, wobei diese Abgrenzung, im Unterschied zum Bestehen auf dem Blick nach aussen, keine wesentliche ist. Man kann das auch als Darbietung eines Forums für Gäste und Freunde seitens der KHM verstehen, die sich wegen ihrer Offenheit und der Vielgestaltigkeit des Programmatischen nicht abzuschliessen trachtet. Es wird keine Rezeptur vermittelt, nichts erklärt, sondern ein Panorama dargeboten, das den Interessenhorizont der KHM eröffnet, eine Fülle dessen, woran abzuarbeiten sich lohnt. Das Spektrum reicht von den intrikaten Philosophien eines Giordano Bruno, den hermetischen Verwerfungen eines Antonin Artaud, den eigensinnigen Maschinen Raymond Roussels über informatische Begründungen intuitiver Schnittstellen bis hin zu Physik und Architektur neuer Interfaces und einer Kritik der Künste. Zahlreiche *Cartes blanches* sind durch Künstlerinnen und Künstler genutzt und gestaltet worden. Ob Bild oder Text, Bildsequenz oder Bild-Text-Montage, lyrischer oder hermeneutischer Beitrag, fachwissenschaftliche Erörterung oder philosophische Kritik: Disperse Möglichkeiten des Nachdenkens, diverse Rhetoriken und Codes erscheinen hier gleich bedeutsam für die Entwicklung der Künste. Und das umfasst ihre diskursive Praxis ebenso wie ihre Poetik.

Der Diskurs der Künste, die Einheit von Theorien und Methoden, die Verflechtungen zwischen Experimenten und Apparaten, die Entwicklung neuer Modelle von Sinnlichkeit und Zeit, Technologie und Gehalt – dies alles gehört zur aktuellen Praxis der Künste. Die Trennung von Theorie und Praxis, diese alte und müde, allzu oft und selbstgefällig wiederholte Fixierung, Ausdruck der zünftischen Gängelung der Künste sowie die im Namen einer Handwerks-Religion geforderte und dann meist auch rücksichtslos umgesetzte Theorie-Feindlichkeit von Kunst und Design: Sie sind heute hoffnungslos reaktionär und unfähig, an der Entwicklung der «Künste durch Medien» sinnvoll teilzunehmen. In dieser geht es vermehrt um subtile Kompositionen, das Herstellen von produktiven Reibungsflächen und Energiefeldern, um möglichst magisch wirkende Zusammenhänge. – Als eine zeigende Kunst der Orchestrierung solcher Abläufe und Kräfte, Reibungen und Kohärenzen, Supplemente und Widersprüche versteht sich *Lab. Jahrbuch für Künste und Apparate* seit 1996.

Lab. Jahrbuch für Künste und Apparate erscheint im Verlag der Buchhandlung Walther König in Köln. Herausgegeben von der Kunsthochschule für Medien, Köln, und ihrem Freundeskreis wird es konzipiert und redigiert von Hans Ulrich Reck und Siegfried Zielinski, bisher in wechselnder Zusammenarbeit mit Wolfgang Ernst, Thomas Hensel und Nils Röller. Es präsentiert jeweils einige dutzend Text- und Bildbeiträge, analytische und poetische, künstlerische und wissenschaftliche, literarische und philosophische Beiträge auf gut 200 bis 400 Seiten mit zahlreichen, meist schwarzweissen Abbildungen.

Art, Utopia and the Media

HANS ULRICH RECK

Thoughts on the *Jahrbuch für Künste und Apparate*

The media have existed ever since a sense of self-alienation has compounded the human awareness of the alien nature of the world. We need them to mediate the world because our world often seems to be once removed. They give us access to a world that is constructed out of experiences and hence entirely artificial. Thus the media not only have their roots in history and technology but also in anthropology. As artefacts, they are intrinsically necessary. Art has always played a special part in the symbolic elaboration of these mundanely significant artefacts. It views the media as poetic tools, but lately this has become problematic because the media today operate in the context of highly advanced technology. They are not always readily accessible to art. All that art can do is to act as though the poetic constructions in which it uses the media as the tools of its trade will continue to succeed—even in those situations where the media are no longer tools but have become complicated conglomerations of equipment and media, machines controlling other machines, chains of operational signals creating other automated links and networks. Thus it is not banal to take an anthropological view of these artefacts. Because art is never satisfied with a banal presentation of artefacts. Its specific task is to encourage the imagination to flights of fancy, to be profligate with any wealth that comes its way by going beyond production for its own sake.

But these days when it comes to the much vaunted power of art—be it intermedial, synthetic, simulative or organic—to integrate the human senses and mechanical devices, science and technology into one vast *Gesamtkunstwerk*, we cannot expect too much. And rightly so: technology has become far too complex, there is far too high a level of sophistication in a techno-system that exclusively follows its own commands and compulsions and which scarcely seems controllable from outside any more—neither by politics nor ethics nor aesthetics nor art. There have only been a handful of cases where artists were involved in the development of currently significant technological advances.

Thus the union of art and science has remained as much a utopia as any hoped-for convergence of a technology-based world and social equality. The aesthetically liberated, technologically literate person, who is constantly absorbing new technologies, has to be understood as a self-contained being that surely derives the rhetorical power to move others from his/her own lack of empirical probability. This is a notable source of strength to the arts: for the arts mark differences, they articulate resistance, they insist on meaningful notions of a poetic, unconstrained deployment of technological means without these instantly having to be validated by polytechnically effective improvements. If utopia still has a critical function, then it may claim the same privilege that Lichtenberg allows critics: the right to be mercilessly critical without having to prove superior ability in that field.

Art has considerable potential for chaos, as distinct from the hierarchical taming of the media and their reduction to standardized operations. This explains why a crucial element in the poetological practice of orientation by means of "art through media" is the rejection of the fiction of a master medium, a control point, a binding organ, a mandatory schedule, in other words the rejection of some central power. It is all too clear, for instance, that telematics (the use of computers for electronic data processing in the grand style) are as a rule merely used to optimize work situations.

In an age in which almost everything is supposed—at almost any cost—to be synchronized with everything else on a regularized basis, in a world of mass-media-led, global simultaneity and in a hierarchically structured communication society in which communication means the transmission of uniformly standardized chains of signals—in a world of this kind, any striving for artistic praxis is a battle to do something different. Thus art is not just about forming but also about creating an independent time-frame, a sensual system that is neither beholden to subjective indulgence nor to the objective demands made by a metronomic world, nor to some well-established exchange of signs and things, customs and inventions. In an age of techno-imagination, artistic practices are no longer directed first and foremost towards producing works, but towards establishing work processes and exploring methods. The path from manifestations of representational imagery to the point where art is about interlinking actions is a thoroughly justified leitmotif in "art through digital media," leading as it does to the matter of equipment and on through the control signals of mechanized networks of commands, hierarchies and operations. Art is concerned with the poetic constitution of a social locus where art matters: art has become a critical reflection of its own locus. Thus new technologies and media force art

academies and media institutes to constantly review the basis of the training they are providing.

With the radical autonomy of art—that evolved during the period between the Romantic era and the innovations at the outset of the twentieth century—and a corresponding weakening in the hitherto recognized art training in polytechnics and academies, the relationship between art, science, technology, and daily life has taken on completely new dimensions. The widespread supposition nowadays is that "art as such" cannot be learnt, and that—precisely because of this—proficiency in the use of technical equipment, materials and apparatuses must be practiced all the more intensely and extensively.

Decades ago the art historian and long-time Mayor of Rome, Giulio Carlo Argan, suggested that contemporary artists should redefine themselves as image operators, that is to say, emphasizing the technical communicative side of their work and no longer presenting themselves as isolated artist-figures focused solely on expression and aesthetics. This implied plea for more up-to-date art training, which was made partly in response to the program at the Bauhaus, has acquired a new relevance in the age of digital technology. Inextricably linked with this is the need to redefine the relationship between the "fine" and the "applied" arts, between art and civilization, "high / serious" and "low / popular" culture. These definitions are no longer dependent on aesthetic taste but on the possibilities opened up by the advanced use and development of the artist's tools.

Numerous attempts have been made to close the gap between art, technology and the world we live in,

and to reconcile "applied" art and "fine" art. From the Werkbund to the Bauhaus and new bauhaus to the Hochschule für Gestaltung Ulm there has been an impressive range of initiatives to produce "fine" and "applied" art by means of the most advanced technological means and to create links with the advanced sciences. In view of the immense complexity of developments in science and technology there can be no doubt as to the necessity of finding new long-term methods for art to mediate content and to apply technology. Such methods as exist are specially adapted to art. The theories that have emerged directly from art and design play an intrinsic part in project development and implementation. Theory as such has taken on a significant role in the organization of artistic praxis.

The training at the Kunsthochschule für Medien (KHM) in Cologne has thus concentrated right from the outset—that is to say since teaching began in October 1990—on the use of progressive methods and practices for artistic undertakings in and with advanced media, to the benefit of a multiplicity of concepts: from experimental, avant-garde installations to the mass-impact of media design, television and film. But also the other way around: from filmic experiment, from innovative ventures in television and subtle designer experiments to art that hits home at all levels by means of a conscious aesthetic "deception"—anything is possible. The different levels take in polar opposites and extend outwards to their own extremes. What used to be cleanly separated as mass culture or elite art, high or low, subtle or brutish, fine or applied art, highbrow or lowbrow, intellectual or banal, reflective or popular, deliberation or pleasure: all of these now meet head-on, chafing against each other, at best transforming and arriving at new configurations. Ever different from case to case, decisively so, but always open to review, even to rejection.

The demands made of an artist's skills when s/he is dealing with digital equipment are radical and delicate. Nowadays a number of serious players in the field maintain that a true understanding of technical equipment—through art—is no longer possible. If that is so, then the works of art controlled by electronics and drawing on digitally concealed components are doing no more than perpetrating a scarcely tolerable, fake superficiality. And indeed what is known today as "media art" not infrequently looks exactly like this. *Decorum* sinks to the level of mere decoration. For the conscious deceptiveness of highly evolved art demands certain attitudes which do not pertain at present. It is clear where this line of argument is leading: that art is expected to be capable both of comprehending at the highest level and of

penetrating the otherwise purely functional, instrumental dimensions of life. *Decorum* has unfortunately been misunderstood and has been tainted with the reproach of superficiality. But by definition a reproach of this kind is only conceivable in a culture where "surfaces" are systematically despised. And this in turn implies a dual ontology: true reality as opposed to simulated reality. Nietzsche rejected the doubling of reality and its caricature in simulation—in the name of an artistry of lies and pleasure. Although in a distorted form, this notion of doubling still makes itself felt in the above reproach. It is no coincidence that the model of the building master in art has survived as a

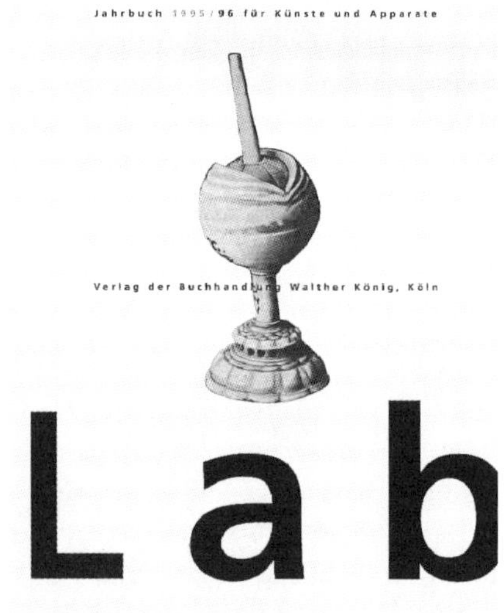

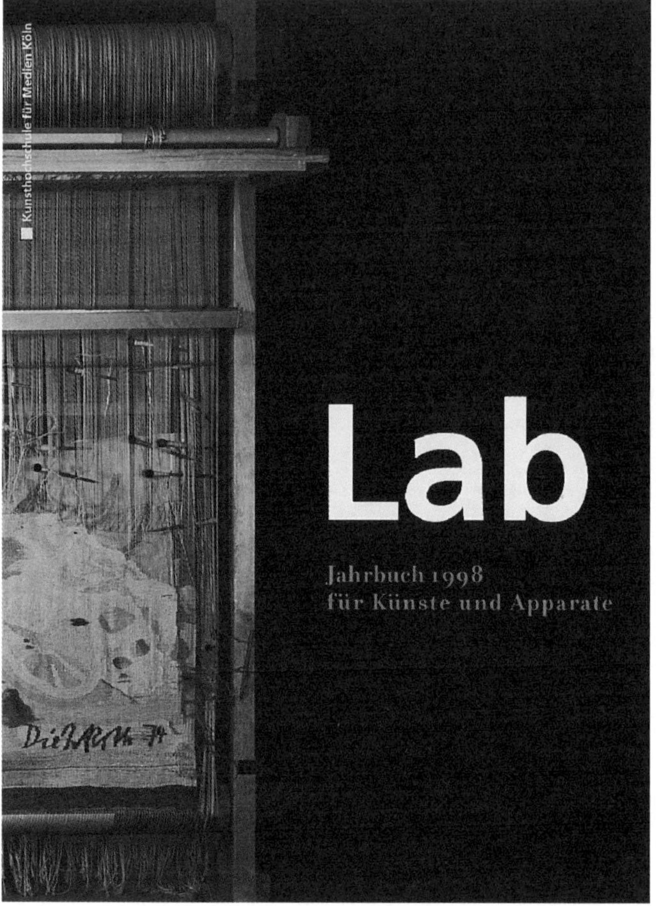

reservoir of resistance against the manipulation of signs in a random manner and at random speeds.

In the eighteenth century the philosopher Giambattista Vico wrote that one could only understand that which one was capable of constructing oneself. From that point onwards—until Hegel—art as the sensual manifestation of an idea was always seen in the context of controlled fabrication. Works of art were the exteriorization of an idea which then took shape in materials, fabrics, and later in modern media. Art is meant to facilitate constructive comprehension—that is its highest aspiration. This means that from their very first day as art students, artists try to put themselves in a position to build by their own efforts all the tools they need. The diametrically opposed attitude to this is that the artist is merely an expert in logistics, setting up arrangements, links and collaborations, connections and mediations. In other words a strategist of ultimately semiotic scenarios, a tactician making localized, punctuated links: a master of the superficial capturing signs that are restless and immaterial, floating and processual. Of course both of these attitudes will be found at the KHM along with many more situated somewhere between these two poles.

No program, or if at all, then a whole array. One theory is not sufficient, one program is too few, one single world is not enough. No program then, but perhaps a maxim: to resist the many attempts to exploit the at times concomitant desire to exert control from centers of medial power. The breadth and power of this aspiration cannot properly be understood from a program alone, the proof is in the products. In 1996, the publication *Lab.*

Jahrbuch für Künste und Apparate was set up to offer an insight into the current interchange of intensities, into a web of affinities and intellectual alliances, into a net of nets, of singular convictions and headstrong liaisons.

This yearbook has not been conceived for the purpose of self-presentation. The majority of the contributions come from external authors although this stipulation is not as important as the insistence that the focus should be on the outside world. The aim is also to provide a forum for guests and friends run by the KHM, which sets store by its openness and the varied nature of its program. The yearbook is neither prescriptive nor explicative, instead it presents a panorama that opens up the horizon of interests at the KHM, covering a wealth of topics deserving of attention. And the spectrum can range from the intricate philosophy of Giordano Bruno, the hermetic rejections of Antonin Artaud, Raymond Roussel's wayward machines to the computer background to certain intuitive interfaces, the physics and architecture of others, and a critique of the arts today. Artists have taken advantage of and shaped numerous *cartes blanches.* Whether in pictures or text, in visual sequences or in montages of words and images, whether a contribution is lyrical or hermeneutic, an academic exposé or a philosophical critique: disparate considerations, diverse rhetorics and different levels are seen here to be equally significant in the development of the arts with regard to discursive praxis and poetics alike.

The discourse of the arts, the unity of theories and methods, the interconnections between experiments and equipment, the evolution of new models of sensuality and time, of technol-

ogy and content—all of these play an intrinsic part in the arts today. There is no longer any room for the separation of theory and praxis—that tired old fixation, too often and too complacently repeated, a leftover of the stranglehold that different practitioners once had on the arts—nor for the relentless antitheory stance taken by art and design for the sake of the religion of craft skills: today such attitudes can only seem hopelessly reactionary and unfit to play a meaningful part in the development of "art through media," which is much more a matter of subtle composition, the creation of productive points of friction and energy fields, the discovery of magically interacting parameters.—Since 1996, the *Lab. Jahrbuch für Künste und Apparate* has done its utmost to demonstrate the orchestration of such processes and powers, resistances and coherences, complements and contradictions.

(Translation: Fiona Elliott)

The *Lab. Jahrbuch für Künste und Apparate* appears under the imprint of the Buchhandlung Walther König in Cologne. Published by the Kunsthochschule für Medien in Cologne and friends of the KHM, it is conceived and edited by Hans Ulrich Reck and Siegfried Zielinski, hitherto in alternating collaboration with Wolfgang Ernst, Thomas Hensel and Nils Röller. Each issue contains some dozens of texts and picture essays—analytical and poetic, artistic and scientific, literary and philosophical. Individual volumes range between 200 and 400 pages and contain numerous, mainly black-and-white illustrations. While the *Lab. Jahrbuch für Künste und Apparate* is mainly a German language publication, all contributions originally written in English are published in English.

<h1 align="center">COMPLETE YOUR PARKETT LIBRARY
VERVOLLSTÄNDIGEN SIE IHRE PARKETT-BIBLIOTHEK</h1>

OUT OF PRINT / VERGRIFFEN: **NO. 1** ENZO CUCCHI, **2** SIGMAR POLKE, **3** MARTIN DISLER, **4** MERET OPPENHEIM, **5** ERIC FISCHL, **6** JANNIS KOUNELLIS, **7** BRICE MARDEN, **8** MARKUS RAETZ, **9** FRANCESCO CLEMENTE, **10** BRUCE NAUMAN, **12** ANDY WARHOL, **13** REBECCA HORN, **16** ROBERT WILSON, **17** FISCHLI/WEISS, **19** JEFF KOONS, MARTIN KIPPENBERGER, **22** CHRISTIAN BOLTANSKI, JEFF WALL, **25** KATHARINA FRITSCH, **26** GÜNTHER FÖRG, PHILIP TAAFFE, JAMES TURRELL, **27** LOUISE BOURGEOIS, ROBERT GOBER, **29** CINDY SHERMAN, JOHN BALDESSARI, **30** SIGMAR POLKE, **31** DAVID HAMMONS, MIKE KELLEY, **35** GERHARD RICHTER, **38** ROSS BLECKNER, MARLENE DUMAS

For out-of-print issues you can register your name and address with Parkett and you will be notified, if your issue(s) become(s) available on the secondary market / Für vergriffene Bände nimmt der Verlag gerne Ihren Suchauftrag entgegen und macht Ihnen bei allfälliger Verfügbarkeit im Handel ein Angebot.

<h2 align="center">COLLABORATIONS</h2>

CHUCK CLOSE
DIANA THATER
LUC TUYMANS
PROSE, CLOSE/PEYTON, SHIFF, CLOSE/CURIGER,
ARRHENIUS, HASLINGER, GILBERT-ROLFE,
HOPTMAN, MOSQUERA, REUST
INSERT: **SHIRANA SHAHBAZI**
GREG HILTY: **JEREMY DELLER**
HOWARD SINGERMAN: **DAVID BUNN**
LES INFOS: THIERRY DE DUVE—INTERVIEW
CUMULUS: FRAZER WARD, HANS ULRICH RECK

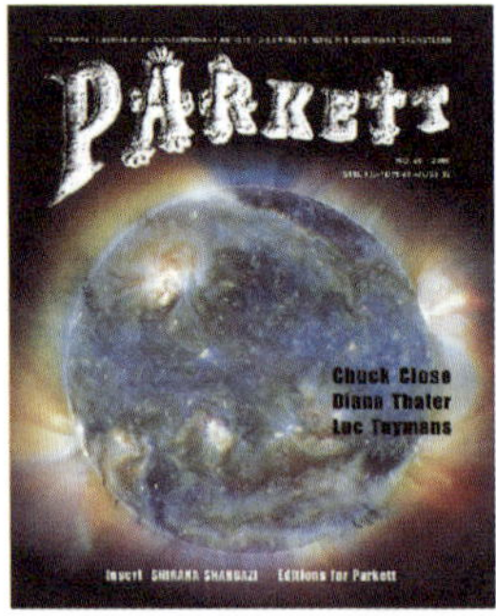

No. 60 - ISBN 3-907582-10-1

MAURIZIO CATTELAN
YASOI KUSAMA
KARA WALKER
BOURRIAUD, GINGERAS, BONAMI
PANHANS-BÜHLER, MATSUI, POLLOCK
DUBOIS SHAW, JANUS, WALKER
INSERT: **ANDREAS ZÜST**
VINCENT KATZ,
ELISABETH BRONFEN: **ANNETTE MESSAGER**
JAN AVGIKOS: **ANNA GASKELL**
LES INFOS: ALI SUBOTNICK
CUMULUS: MARGIT ROWELL, LASZLO FÖLDE
BALKON: MICHELLE NICOL

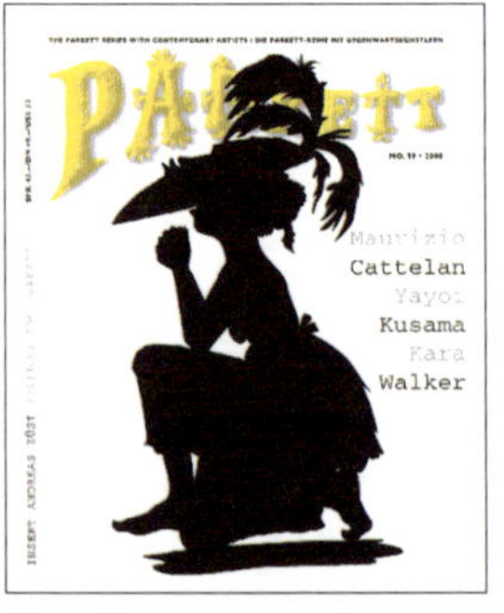

No. 59 - ISBN 3-907582-09-8

JAMES ROSENQUIST
SYLVIE FLEURY
JASON RHOADES
RUSSELL, KOONS/ROSENQUIST, HULTEN, FELIX
GLENN, LOBEL, DANNATT, RUF, KOETHER
FERGUSON, ORTH, SCHEIDEMANN/HERMANN
INSERT: **HENRY BOND**
GILDA WILLIAMS: **JANE & LOUISE WILSON**
SLAVOJ ZIZEK, PAUL D. MILLER & CHRIS OFILI
LES INFOS: ANNA HELWING
CUMULUS: DAVID ROBBINS, HILDE TEERLINCK
BALKON: KNUT EBELING

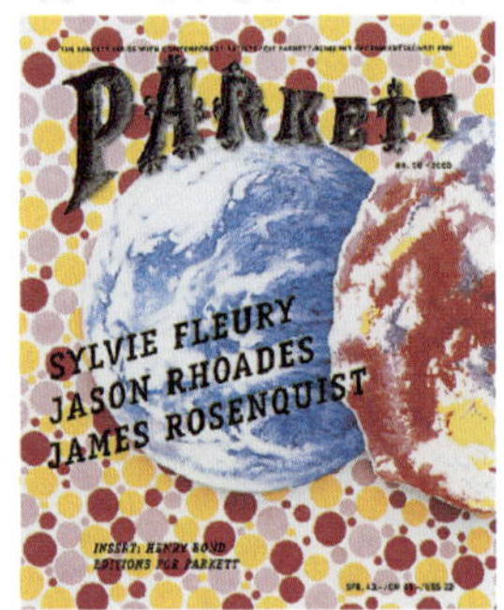

No. 58 - ISBN 3-907582-08-X

DOUG AITKEN
NAN GOLDIN
THOMAS HIRSCHHORN
ROBERTS, BONAMI, VAN ASSCHE, LEBOVICI
DANTO, LIEBMANN, FRIIS-HANSEN, HAKERT
EISENBERG, FLECK, GINGERAS, VERGNE, STEIN
DAVID GREENBERG: **DONALD BAECHLER**
ANDREA KROKSNES: **LOUISE LAWLER**
LIONEL BOVIER: **JOHN MILLER**
LES INFOS: RUDOLF SCHMITZ
CUMULUS: H.U. OBRIST, CONNIE BUTLER
BALKON: JURI STEINER & ANNELISE COSTE

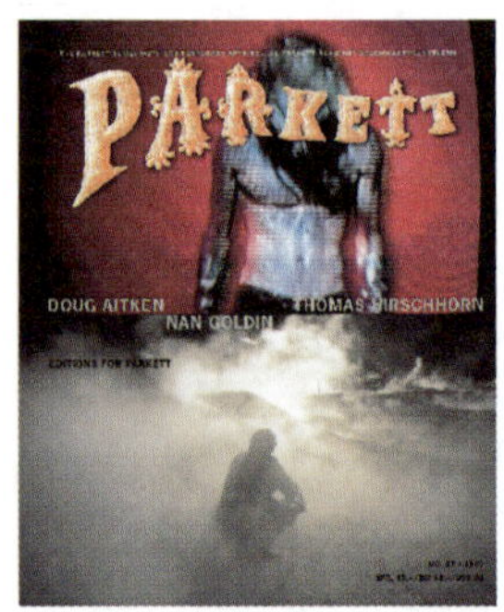

No. 57 - ISBN 3-907582-07-1

ELLSWORTH KELLY
VANESSA BEECROFT
JORGE PARDO
KELLEIN, FER, MAURER, RIMANELLI
BRYSON, TAZZI, SEWARD, AVGIKOS
FERGUSON, VÉGH, VAN WINKEL
FRANGENBERG, BUSH
GREG HILTY: **CERITH WYN EVANS**
THOMAS Y. LEVIN: **CHRISTIAN MARCLAY**
LYNNE COOKE: **DIANA THATER**
LES INFOS: DIANE LEWIS
CUMULUS: ADRIAN DANNATT, PETR NEDOMA

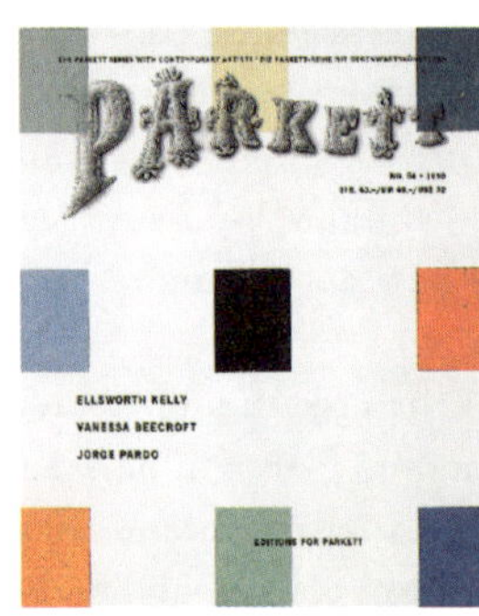

No. 56 - ISBN 3-907582-06-3

EDWARD RUSCHA
ANDREAS SLOMINSKI
SAM TAYLOR-WOOD
PERRONE, HIGGIE, SINGERMAN, SCHENKER
SCANLAN, SPECTOR, FREY, HEYNEN
GROYS/FUNCKE/HOFFMANN, BRONFEN
BONAMI, LAJER-BURCHARTH
INSERT: **KARA WALKER**
BORIS GROYS: **PAVEL PEPPERSTEIN**
RUDOLF SCHMITZ: **ALEXANDER KLUGE**
BEATRIX RUF: **EIJA-LIISA AHTILA**
CUMULUS: MICHELLE NICOL, SUELY ROLNIK

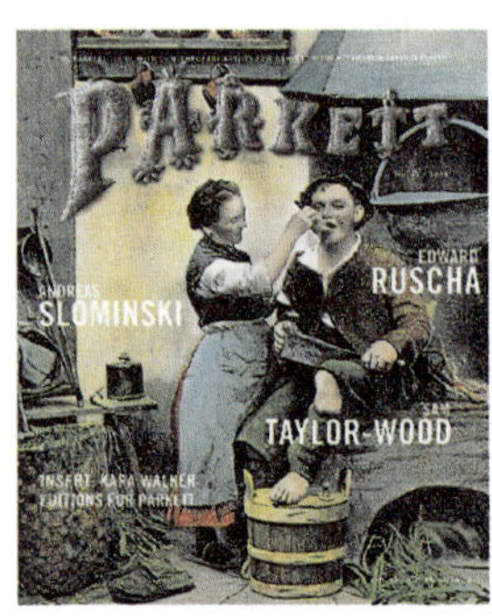

No. 55 - ISBN 3-907582-05-5

RONI HORN
MARIKO MORI
BEAT STREULI
SCHORR, GUNNARSSON, GOROVOY, LEWIS
SPECTOR, BRYSON, NAKAZAWA, NICHOLS
GOODEVE, STALS, DANTO, AMANO, SMITH
INSERT: **MATTHEW RITCHIE**
VINCENT KATZ: **ALEX KATZ**
HORST BREDEKAMP: **STEPHAN VON HUENE**
PAUL D. MILLER: **SHIRIN NESHAT**
LES INFOS:
OKWUI ENWEZOR & WILLIAM KENTRIDGE
CUMULUS: VALÉRIA PICCOLI, MARIA LIND

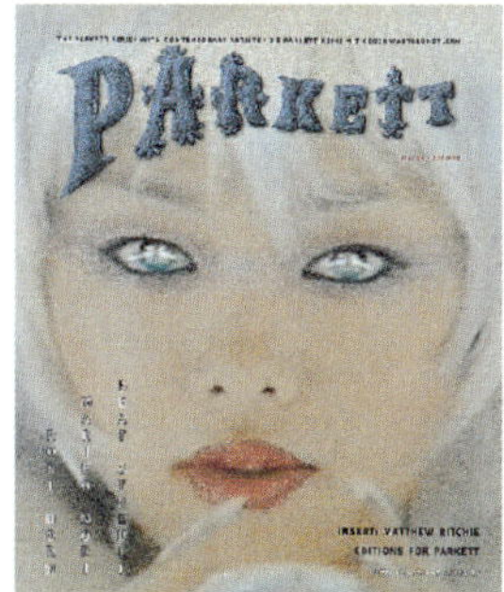

No. 54 - ISBN 3-907582-04-7

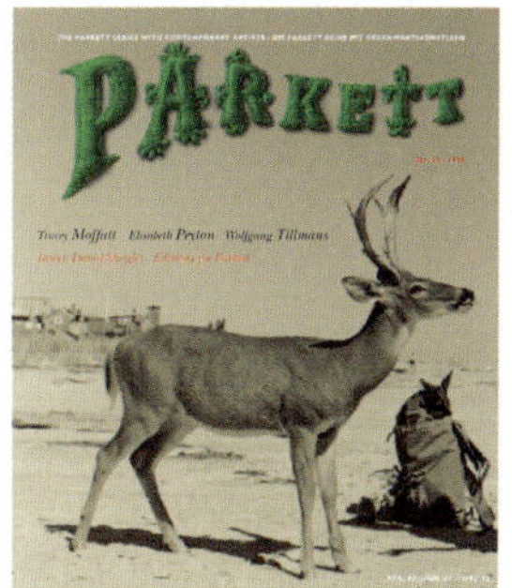

No. 53 - ISBN 3-907582-03-9

TRACEY MOFFATT
ELIZABETH PEYTON
WOLFGANG TILLMANS
MARTIN, LAJER-BURCHARTH, RIMANELLI
PILGRIM, URSPRUNG, LIEBMANN, MATSUI
WAKEFIELD, BUDNEY, NESBITT, ZIEGLER
INSERT: **DAVID SHRIGLEY**
CATHERINE BERNARD: **JOHAN GRIMONPREZ**
BERNARD MARCADÉ: **ROBERT GOBER**
LES INFOS DE L'ENFER: VALERIA LIEBERMANN
CUMULUS: BLESSING, AUPETITALLOT
BALKON: STEINER/MAGNAGUAGNO

KAREN KILIMNIK
MALCOLM MORLEY
UGO RONDINONE
SCHORR, BÜRGI, JUNCOSA, MORLEY,
EBENSZTEJN, BONAMI, VERWOERT, HOPTMAN,
INSERT: **THOMAS BAYRLE**
ED WHITE: **JEAN MICHEL OTHONIEL**
NEVILLE WAKEFIELD: **RICHARD SERRA**
GILDA WILLIAMS: **GILLIAN WEARING**
ROBERT GRESKOVIC: **MERCE CUNNINGHAM**
CUMULUS: WALKER, KURZMEYER
BALKON: CECILIA VICUÑA

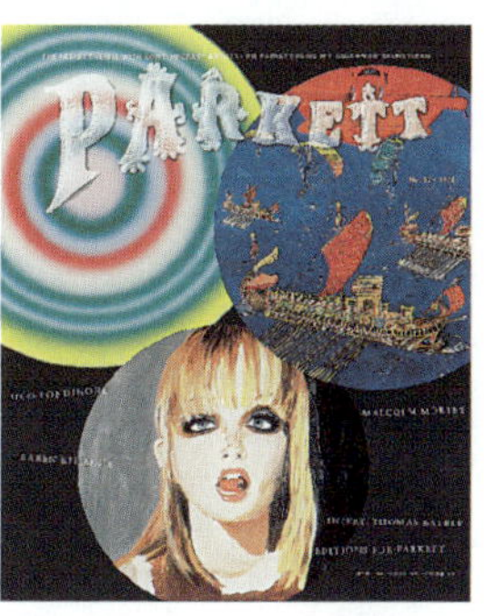

No. 52 - ISBN 3-907582-02-0

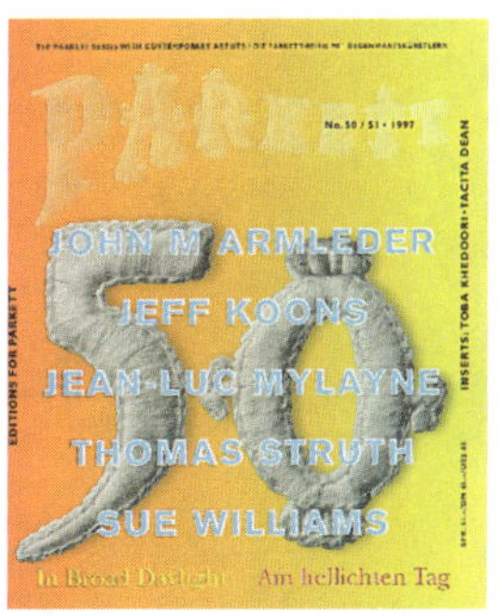

50/51 - ISBN 3-907582-00-4

JOHN M ARMLEDER, JEFF KOONS
JEAN-LUC MYLAYNE
THOMAS STRUTH, SUE WILLIAMS
DI PIETRANTONIO, BOVIER, MUNIZ,
SEWARD, LOERS, NICHOLS GOODEVE,
COOKE, DION, ARNAUDET, MYLAYNE,
CURIGER, LINGWOOD, OKUTSU, BRYSON,
SCHJELDAHL, NESBIT, DANNATT, CAMHI
INSERTS: **TOBA KHEDOORI, TACITA DEAN**
ONFRAY: **HYACINTHE RIGAUD**, NICOL: **SAM SAMORE**
MURPHY, VAN DER WALLE, STEINER,
KURT W. FORSTER: **FRANK GEHRY**
CUMULUS: COLEMAN, BIRNBAUM

LAURIE ANDERSON
DOUGLAS GORDON
JEFF WALL
FLOOD, BEZZOLA, FERGUSON
GILLICK/GORDON, BRYSON, PONTBRIAND
SCHORR, ANDERSON, BURCKHARDT, BUDNEY
INSERT: **SILVIA BÄCHLI**
COLIN DE LAND: **JOHN WATERS**
ROBERT STORR: **SEYDOU KEITA**
DANIELA SALVIONI: **CLEGG & GUTTMANN**
CUMULUS: KITTELMANN, MEYER

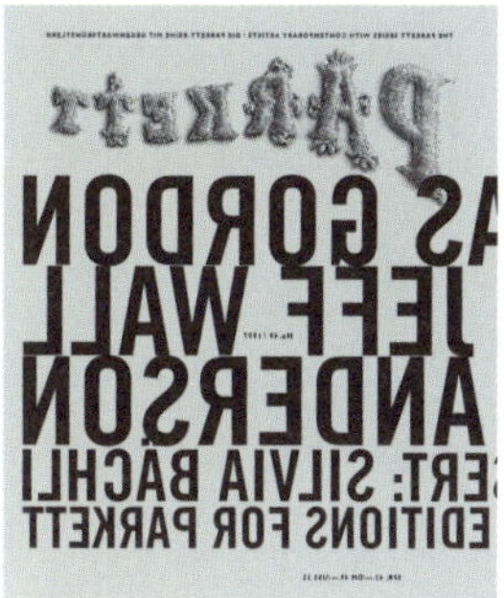

No. 49 - ISBN 3-907509-99-4

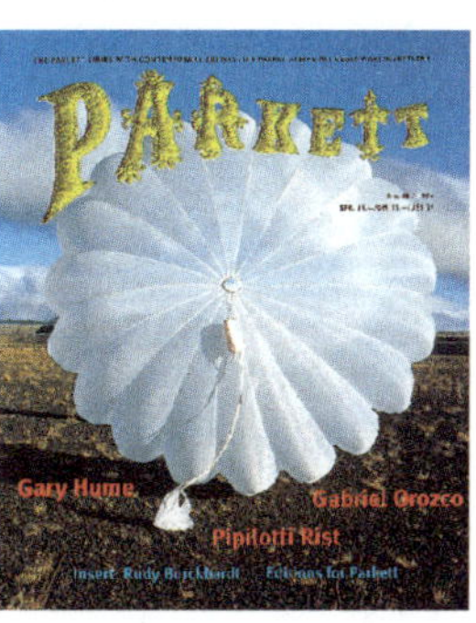

No. 48 - ISBN 3-907509-98-6

GARY HUME
GABRIEL OROZCO
PIPILOTTI RIST
BOVIER, MUIR, FOGLE, BONAMI
DE ZEGHER, SPECTOR, URSPRUNG
BABIAS, COLOMBO, ANDERSON
INSERT: **RUDY BURCKHARDT**
VINCENT KATZ: **RUDY BURCKHARDT**
VAN DER WALLE: **CHARLES LONG
& STEREOLAB**
FAYE HIRSCH: **BRUCE CONNER**
CHRISTOPH DOSWALD: **IAN ANÜLL**
CUMULUS: LEGGAT, SCHNEIDER

TONY OURSLER
RAYMOND PETTIBON
THOMAS SCHÜTTE
COOKE, RICHARD, NERI,
LEWIS, GROYS, ALS, RUGOFF,
GOODEVE, SEARLE, MARI, REUST,
WAKEFIELD, LOOCK, JANUS
INSERT: **ZOE LEONARD & CHERYL DUNYE**
JURI STEINER: **EMMA KUNZ**
MAX WECHSLER: **CHRISTOPH RÜTIMANN**
SUSAN MORGAN: **DIANE ARBUS**
CUMULUS: PRINCENTHAL, BOVIER/CHERIX

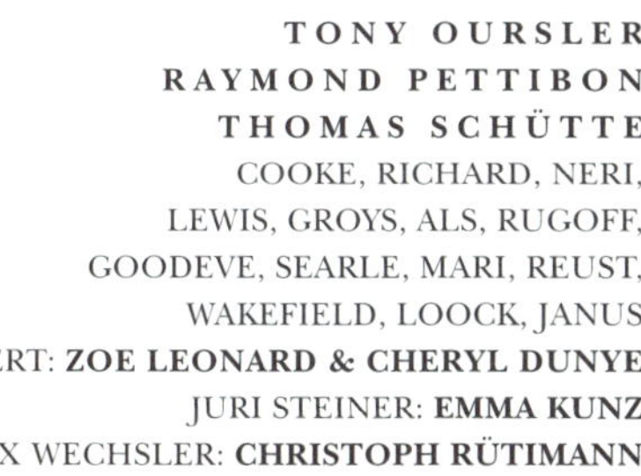

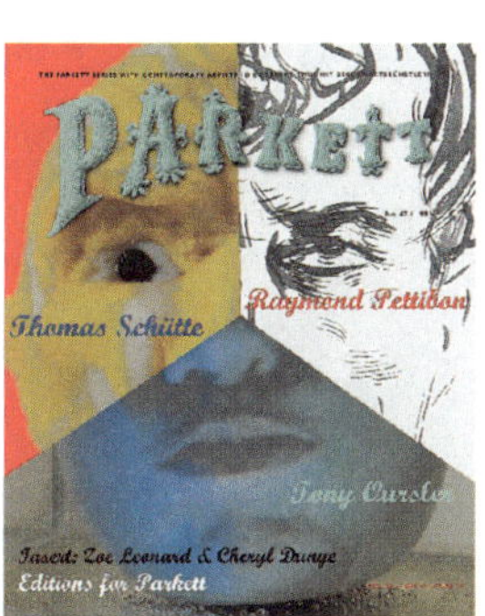

No. 47 - ISBN 3-907509-97-8

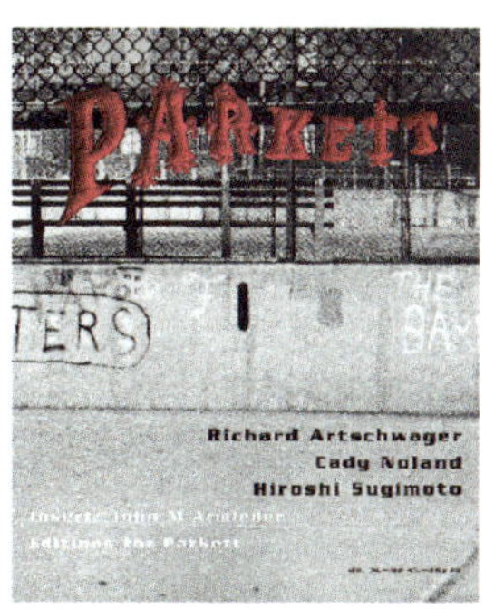

No. 46 - ISBN 3-907509-96-X

RICHARD ARTSCHWAGER
CADY NOLAND
HIROSHI SUGIMOTO
DEITCHER, SCHAFFNER, FORSTER, MUNIZ
ARMSTRONG, RELYEA, BOGDAN, GOODEVE
NICKAS, BRYSON, RUGOFF, DENSON
INSERT: **JOHN M ARMLEDER**
ROLAND WÄSPE: **ERWIN WURM**
DANIEL BIRNBAUM: **ÖYVIND FAHLSTRÖM**
LES INFOS DU PARADIS: ROBERT FLECK
CUMULUS: MILLER, VETTESE
BALKON: MARTIN HELLER

MATTHEW BARNEY
SARAH LUCAS
ROMAN SIGNER
BRYSON, ONFRAY, SEWARD, GOODEVE,
SALTZ, VAN ADRICHEM, SCHORR, FREEDMAN,
JOUANNAIS, BITTERLI, DOSWALD,
VIEWING, WECHSLER, DELAND
INSERT: **ELLIOTT PUCKETTE**
HEIDI GILPIN: **WILLIAM FORSYTHE**
ROBYN McKENZIE: **GEOFF LOWE**
MICHAEL TARANTINO: **CHANTAL AKERMAN**
CUMULUS: McEVILLEY, WAKEFIELD

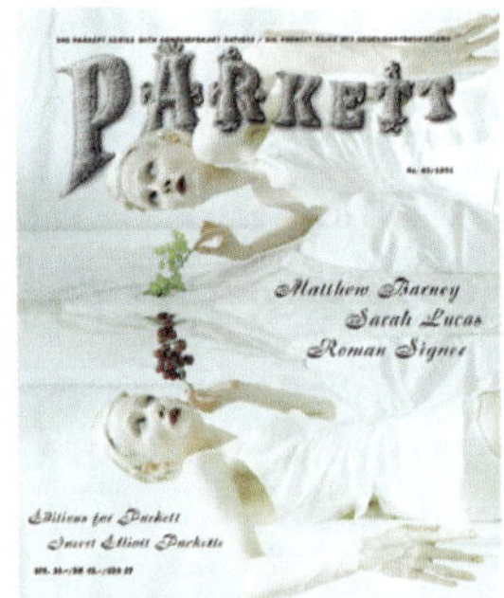

No. 45 - ISBN 3-907509-95-1

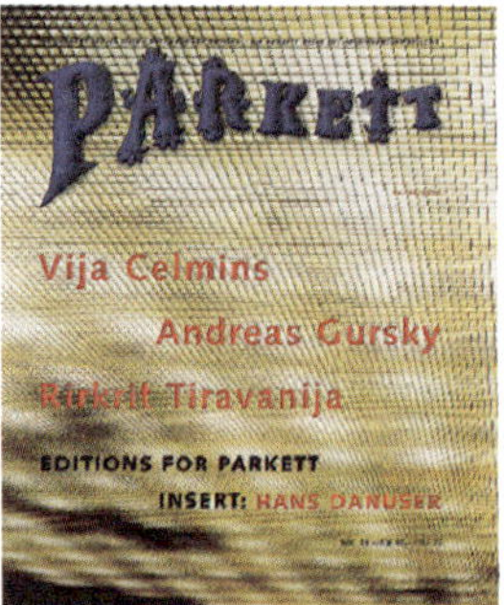

No. 44 - ISBN 3-907509-94-3

VIJA CELMINS
ANDREAS GURSKY
RIRKRIT TIRAVANIJA
PRINCENTHAL, LEWIS, SILVERTHORNE
SHIFF, CRIQUI, BURCKHARDT, WAKEFIELD
SCHORR, MELO, GILLICK, FLOOD, STEINER
INSERT: **HANS DANUSER**
LES INFOS: LIAM GILLICK & DOUGLAS GORDON
LYNNE COOKE, DAVID DEITCHER
DANIEL KURJAKOVIC: **MARIE JOSÉ BURKI**
NAN GOLDIN: **PETER HUJAR**
NOEMI SMOLIK: **ANDREAS SLOMINSKI**
JASON SIMON: **MARK DION**
LUK LAMBRECHT: **MARK LUYTEN**

JUAN MUÑOZ
SUSAN ROTHENBERG
LYNNE COOKE, ALEXANDRE MELO
JAMES LINGWOOD, GAVIN BRYARS
ROBERT CREELEY, INGRID SCHAFFNER
JEAN-CHRISTOPHE AMMANN
MARK STEVENS, JOAN SIMON
INSERT: **ROBERT SMITHSON**
NEVILLE WAKEFIELD
MICHELLE NICOL: **CARSTEN HÖLLER**
HANS-ULRICH OBRIST: **FABRICE HYBERT**

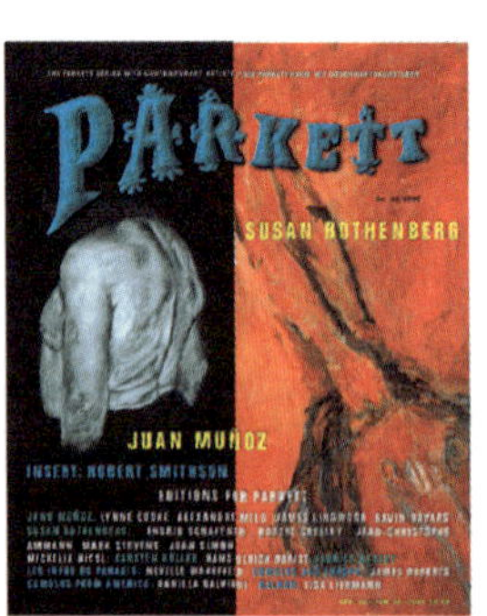

No. 43 - ISBN 3-907509-93-5

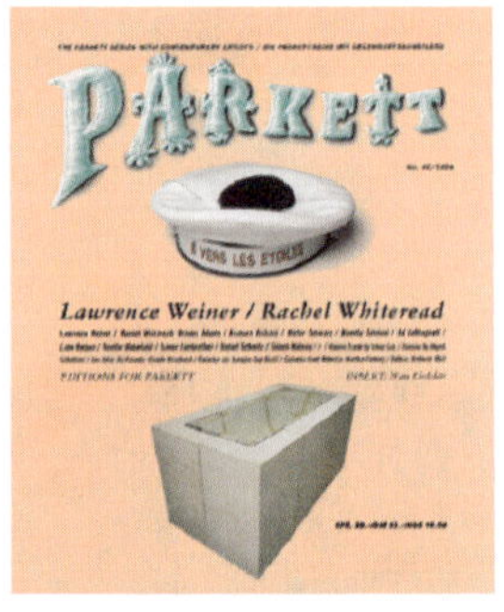

No. 42 - ISBN 3-907509-92-7

LAWRENCE WEINER
RACHEL WHITEREAD
BROOKS ADAMS, FRANCES RICHARD
DIETER SCHWARZ, DANIELA SALVIONI
ED LEFFINGWELL, LANE RELYEA
NEVILLE WAKEFIELD, RUDOLF SCHMITZ
TREVOR FAIRBROTHER, SIMON WATNEY
INSERT: **NAN GOLDIN**
VINCE LEO: **ROBERT FRANK**
CLAUDE RITSCHARD: **MARKUS RAETZ**

FRANCESCO CLEMENTE
GÜNTHER FÖRG
PETER FISCHLI / DAVID WEISS
DAMIEN HIRST
JENNY HOLZER
REBECCA HORN
SIGMAR POLKE
HOLLAND COTTER, BORIS GROYS
MAX WECHSLER, DAVID RIMANELLI
JOAN SIMON, GORDON BURN
GILBERT LASCAULT, WERNER SPIES
BICE CURIGER, JEFF PERRONE
G. ROGER DENSON, VIK MUNIZ
DAVE HICKEY

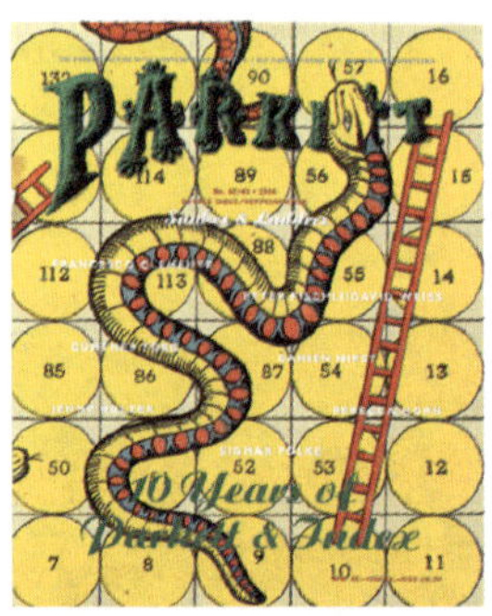

40/41 - ISBN 3-907509-90-0

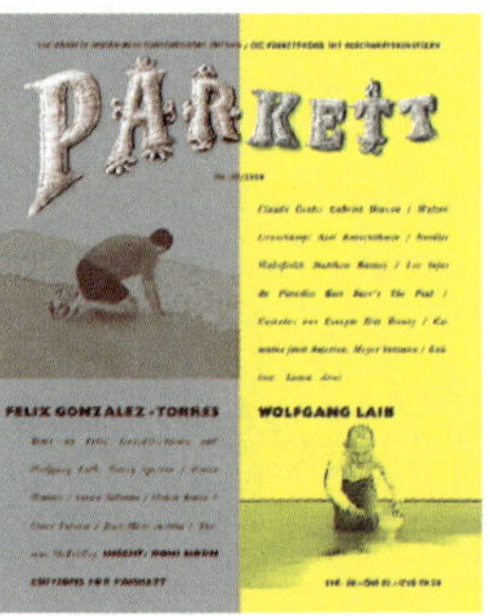

No. 39 - ISBN 3-907509-89-7

FELIX GONZALEZ-TORRES
WOLFGANG LAIB
NANCY SPECTOR, SIMON WATNEY,
SUSAN TALLMAN, DIDIER SEMIN,
CLARE FARROW, JEAN-MARC AVRILLA,
THOMAS McEVILLEY
CLAUDE GINTZ: **GABRIEL OROZCO**
WALTER GRASSKAMP: **AXEL KASSEBÖHMER**
NEVILLE WAKEFIELD: **MATTHEW BARNEY**
INSERT: **RONI HORN**
LES INFOS DU PARADIS: **BURT BARR**
CUMULUS: **MEYER VAISMAN**

CHARLES RAY
FRANZ WEST
KLAUS KERTESS, CHRISTOPHER KNIGHT
PETER SCHJELDAHL, ROBERT STORR
JAN AVGIKOS, AXEL HUBER
MARTIN PRINZHORN, ELISABETH
SCHLEBRÜGGE, HARALD SZEEMANN,
DENYS ZACHAROPOULOS
INSERT: **PIPILOTTI RIST**
JEAN BAUDRILLARD
HANS RUDOLF REUST: **LUC TUYMANS**
PARKETT INQUIRY:
CHERCHEZ LA FEMME PEINTRE!

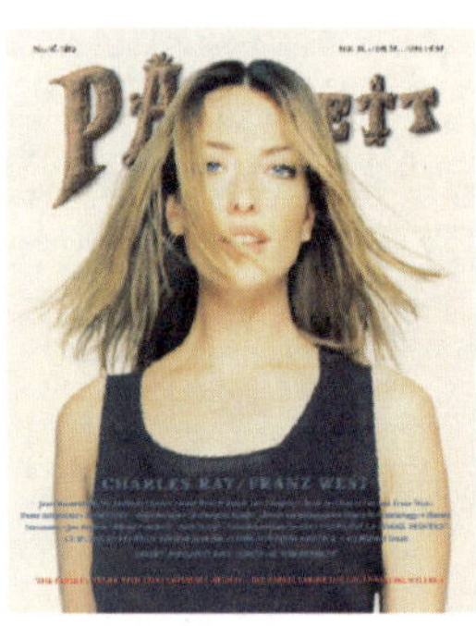

No. 37 - ISBN 3-907509-87-0

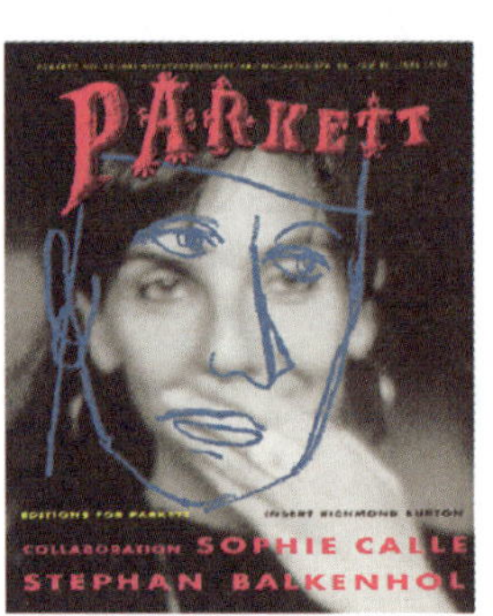

No. 36 - ISBN 3-907509-86-2

STEPHAN BALKENHOL
SOPHIE CALLE
NEAL BENEZRA, VIK MUNIZ, MAX KATZ
JEAN-CHRISTOPHE AMMANN
LUC SANTE, JOSEPH GRIGELY
PATRICK FREY, ROBERT BECK
INSERT: **RICHMOND BURTON**
URSULA PANHANS-BÜHLER: **EVA HESSE**
DOUGLAS BLAU: **JON KESSLER**
KIRBY GOOKIN: **LIZ LARNER**
LÁSZLÓ FÖLDÉNYI:
RUDOLF SCHWARZKOGLER

ILYA KABAKOV
RICHARD PRINCE
BORIS GROYS, ROBERT STORR
JAN THORN-PRIKKER
CLAUDIA JOLLES, EDMUND WHITE
SUSAN TALLMAN, DANIELA
SALVIONI, KATHY ACKER
INSERT: **TATSUO MIYAJIMA**
GUDRUN INBODEN: **ASTA GRÖTING**
LYNNE COOKE: **GARY HILL**
PATRICK McGRATH: **STEPHEN ELLIS**

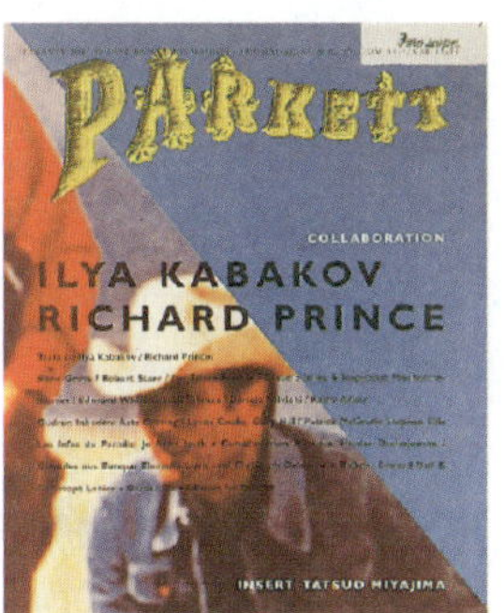

No. 34 - ISBN 3-907509-84-6

PARKETT

WOOL

TROCKEL

33

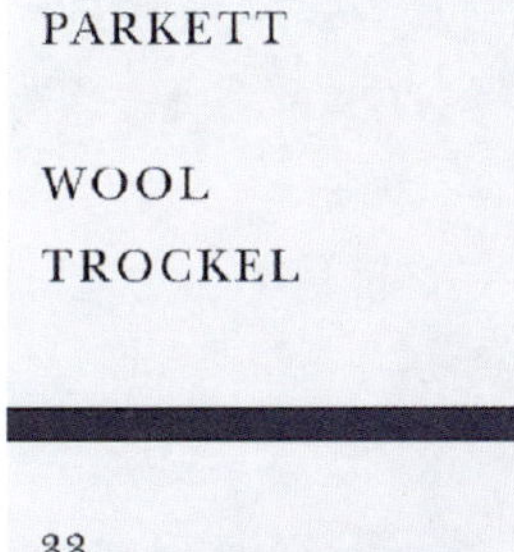

No. 33 - ISBN 3-907509-83-3

ROSEMARIE TROCKEL
CHRISTOPHER WOOL
VERONIQUE BACCHETTA,
BARRETT WATTEN,
ANNE WAGNER, JIM LEWIS,
GREIL MARCUS, JEFF PERRONE,
DIEDRICH DIEDERICHSEN
INSERT: **ADRIAN SCHIESS**
MARINA WARNER: **PENIS PLENTY**
G. ROGER DENSON:
DENNIS OPPENHEIM
CAMIEL VAN WINKEL

IMI KNOEBEL
SHERRIE LEVINE
RUDOLF BUMILLER
RAINER CRONE/DAVID MOOS
LISA LIEBMANN, DANIELA SALVIONI
ERICH FRANZ, HOWARD SINGERMANN
INSERT: **DAMIEN HIRST**
SHEENA WAGSTAFF: **VIJA CELMINS**
JIM LEWIS: **LARRY CLARK**
LIAM GILLICK: **BETHAN HUWS**
THOMAS KELLEIN: **WALTER DE MARIA**

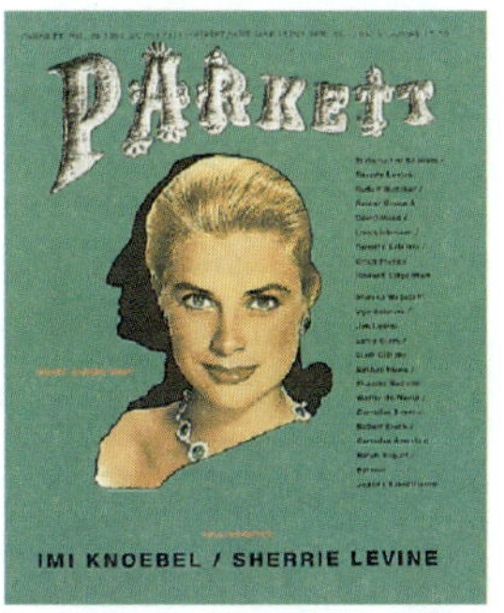

No. 32 - ISBN 3-907509-82-X

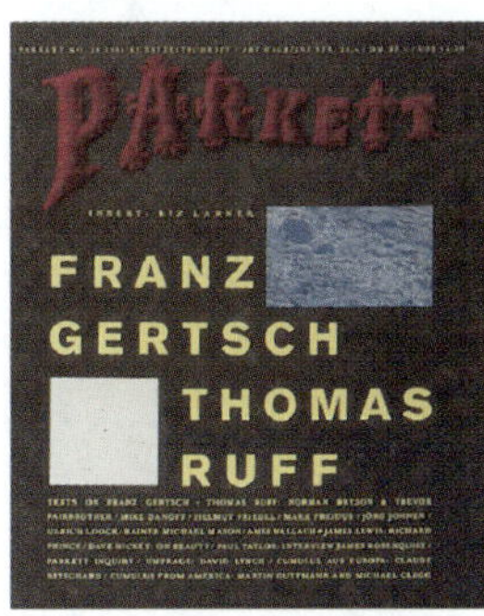

No. 28 - ISBN 3-907509-78-1

FRANZ GERTSCH
THOMAS RUFF
HELMUT FRIEDEL, ULRICH LOOCK
I. MICHAEL DANOFF, AMEI WALLACH
RAINER MICHAEL MASON
MARC FREIDUS, JÖRG JOHNEN
TREVOR FAIRBROTHER/NORMAN BRYSON
INSERT: **LIZ LARNER**
JAMES LEWIS: **RICHARD PRINCE**
DAVID HICKEY:
**THE INVISIBLE DRAGON/
DER UNSICHTBARE DRACHEN**
PAUL TAYLOR: **JAMES ROSENQUIST**

ALIGHIERO E BOETTI
JEAN-CHRISTOPHE AMMANN
GIOVAN BATTISTA SALERNO
RAINER CRONE & DAVID MOOS
FRIEDEMANN MALSCH
JEAN-PIERRE BORDAZ
ALAIN CUEFF
INSERT: **CINDY SHERMAN**
SHEENA WAGSTAFF:
SOPHIE CALLE
HERBERT LACHMEYER/
BRIGITTE FELDERER: **FRANZ WEST**
JUTTA KOETHER: **MIKE KELLEY**

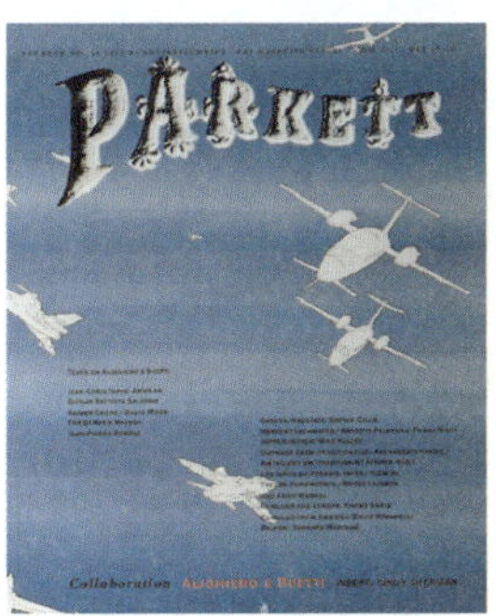

No. 24 - ISBN 3-907509-74-9

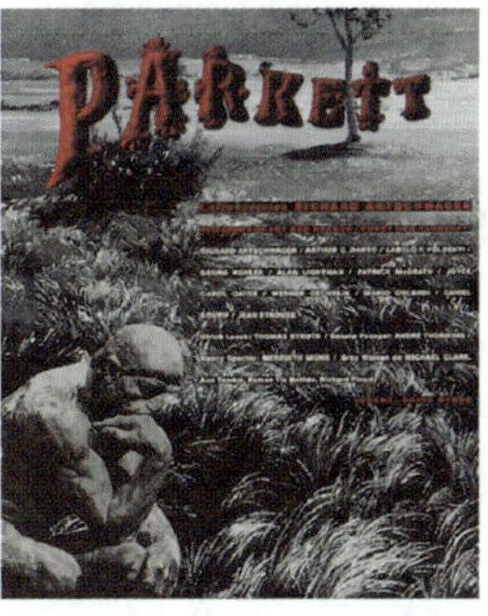

No. 23 - ISBN 3-907509-73-0

RICHARD ARTSCHWAGER
ARTHUR C. DANTO, GEORG KOHLER,
MARIO A. ORLANDO, JOYCE
CAROL OATES, WERNER OECHSLIN,
ALAN LIGHTMAN, PATRICK
McGRATH, DANIEL SOUTIF,
LASZLO F. FÖLDENYI, JEAN STROUSE
INSERT: **DAVID BYRNE**
RENATE PUVOGEL: **ANDRÉ THOMKINS**
ULRICH LOOCK: **THOMAS STRUTH**
NANCY SPECTOR: **MEREDITH MONK**

ALEX KATZ
JOHN RUSSELL, BROOKS ADAMS,
DAVID RIMANELLI, FRANCESCO
CLEMENTE, MICHAEL KRÜGER,
RICHARD FLOOD, PATRICK FREY,
CARL STIGLIANO, BICE CURIGER,
GLENN O'BRIEN
INSERT: **WILLIAM WEGMAN**
LISA LIEBMAN: **ROBERT GOBER**
JACQUELINE BURCKHARDT:
GIULIO ROMANO

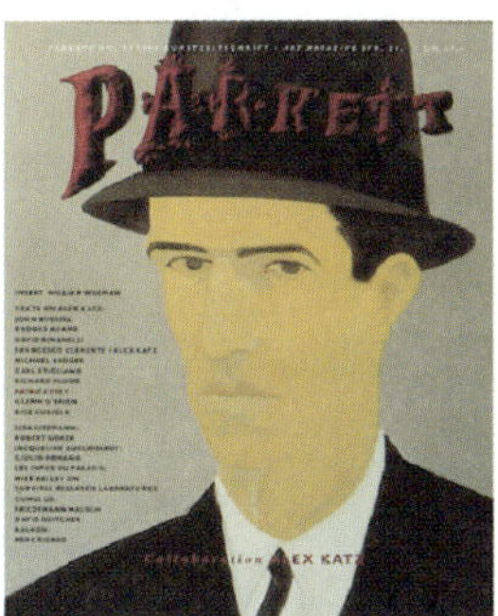

No. 21 - ISBN 3-907509-71-4

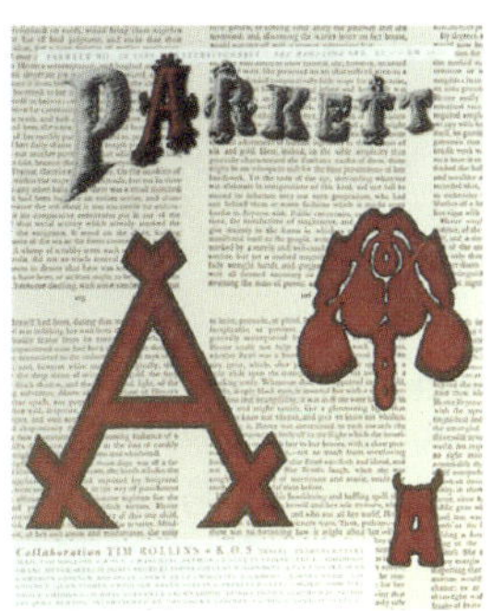

No. 20 - ISBN 3-907509-70-6

TIM ROLLINS + K.O.S.
MARSHALL BERMAN
TREVOR FAIRBROTHER
STATEMENTS, DIALOGUE 5
INSERT: **ANDREAS GURSKY**
MICHAEL NASH: **BILL VIOLA**
STEPHEN ELLIS: **ROSS BLECKNER**
KLAUS KERTESS: **TRISHA BROWN**

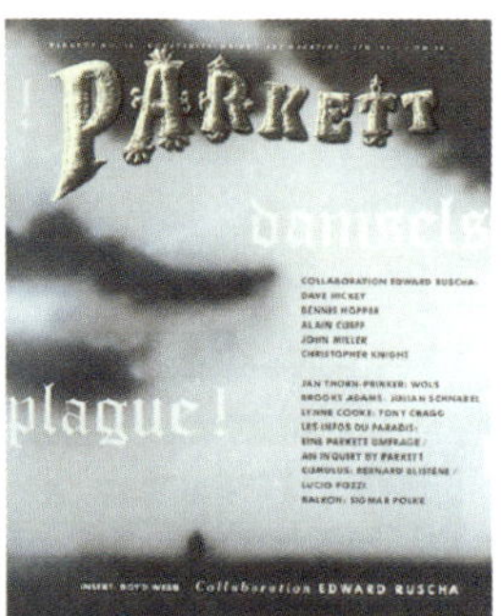

EDWARD RUSCHA
DAVE HICKEY, DENNIS HOPPER
ALAIN CUEFF, JOHN MILLER
CHRISTOPHER KNIGHT
INSERT: **BOYD WEBB**
JAN THORN-PRIKKER: **WOLS**
LYNNE COOKE: **TONY CRAGG**
BROOKE ADAMS: **JULIAN SCHNABEL**
DER KÜNSTLER ALS EXEM-
PLARISCH LEIDENDER?
EINE UMFRAGE / THE ARTIST AS A
MODEL SUFFERER? AN INQUIRY

No. 18 - ISBN 3-907509-68-4

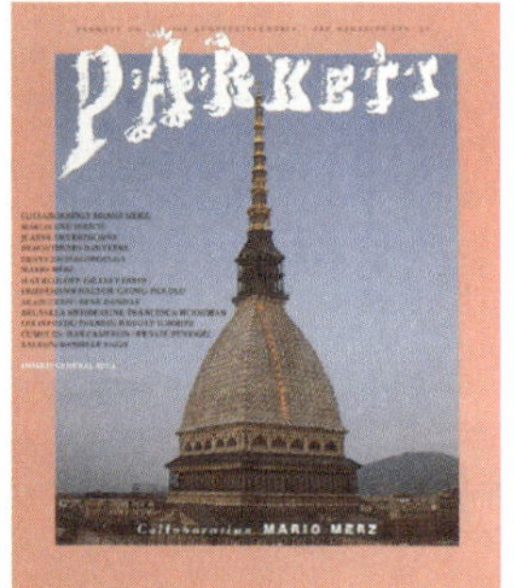

MARIO MERZ
MARLIS GRÜTERICH, JEANNE
SILVERTHORNE, DEMOSTHENES
DAVVETAS, HARALD SZEEMANN,
DENYS ZACHAROPOULOS
INSERT: **GENERAL IDEA**
MAX KOZLOFF: **GILLES PERESS**
FRIEDEMANN MALSCH:
GEORG HEROLD
BRUNELLA ANTOMARINI:
FRANCESCA WOODMAN

No. 15 - ISBN 3-907509-65-X

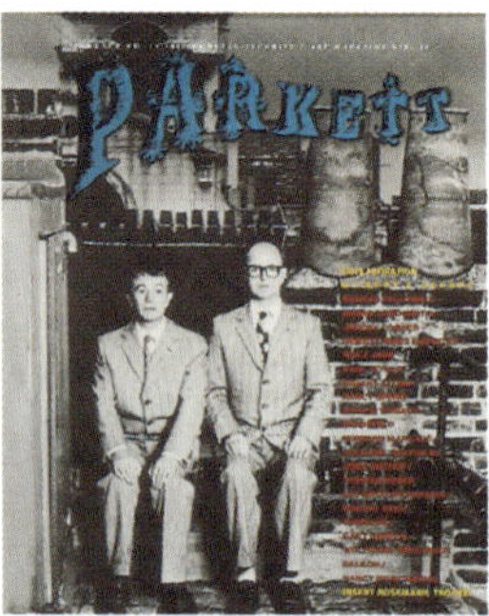

GILBERT & GEORGE
DUNCAN FALLOWELL, MARIO
CODOGNATO, JEREMY COOPER,
DEMOSTHENES DAVVETAS,
WOLF JAHN
INSERT: **ROSEMARIE TROCKEL**
ROBERT STORR: **NANCY SPERO**
HAIM STEINBACH: **MANIFESTO**
JÖRG ZUTTER: **THOMAS HUBER**

No. 14 - ISBN 3-907509-64-1

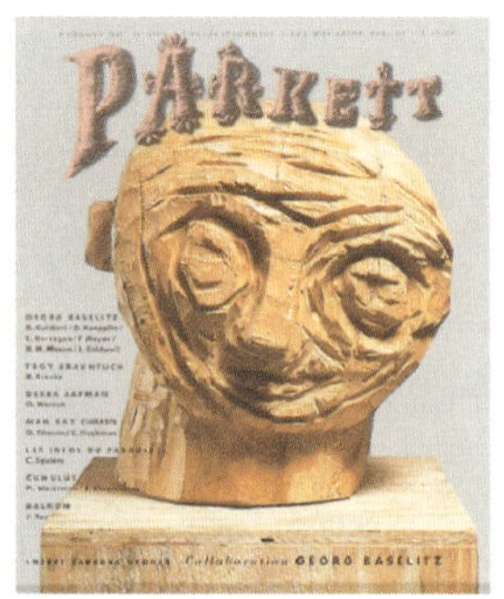

GEORG BASELITZ
REMO GUIDIERI, DIETER
KOEPPLIN, ERIC DARRAGON,
RAINER MICHAEL MASON, FRANZ
MEYER, JOHN CALDWELL
INSERT: **BARBARA KRUGER**
GRAY WATSON: **DEREK JARMAN**
CAROL SQUIERS:
PHOTO OPPORTUNITY
ROSETTA BROOKS:
TROY BRAUNTUCH

No. 11 - ISBN 3-907509-61-7

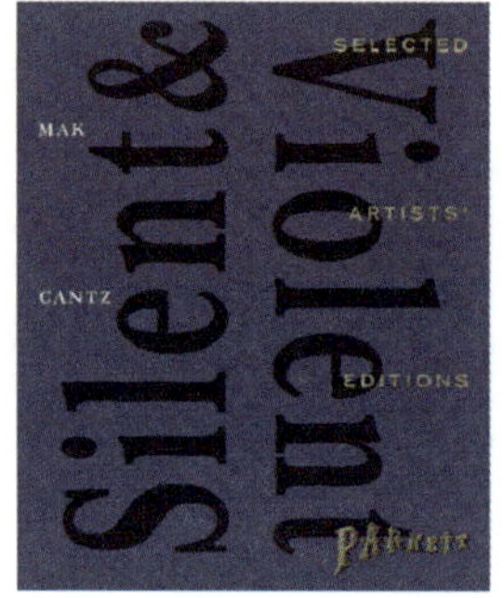

SILENT & VIOLENT
CATALOG RAISONNÉ OF ALL PARKETT ARTISTS' EDITIONS
from No. 1–44, 183 pages, 144 in color
text by Susan Tallmann, short biographies of all artists

WERKVERZEICHNIS ALLER PARKETT-KÜNSTLER-EDITIONEN
von Nr. 1–44, 183 Seiten, davon 144 in Farbe
Text von Susan Tallmann, Kurzbiographien der Künstler

sFr. 49.– / $ 39

ISBN 3-89322-796-3 (engl.), ISBN 3-89322-787-3 (dt.)

NEW PARKETT-POSTCARD SET
featuring 101 artists' editions made for Parkett

DAS NEUE PARKETT-POSTKARTEN-SET
mit 101 Editionen, die von Künstlern für
Parkett geschaffen wurden.

sFr. 48.– / $ 32

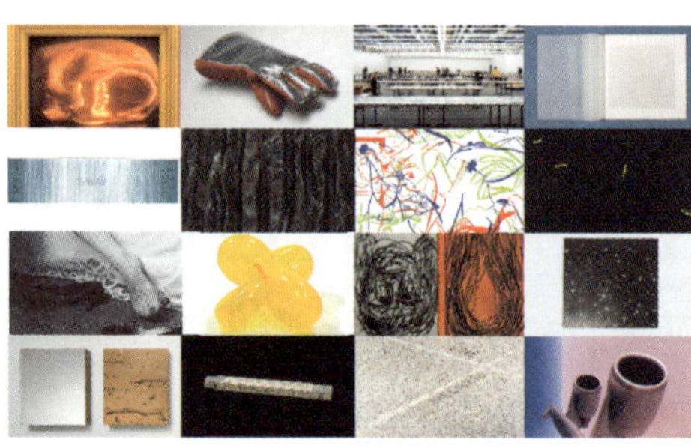

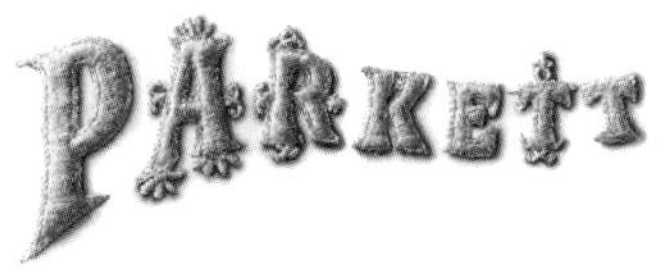

Doug Aitken, vol. 57
Laurie Anderson, vol. 49
John Armleder, vol. 50/51
Richard Artschwager, vol. 23, vol. 46
John Baldessari, vol. 29
Stephan Balkenhol, vol. 36
Matthew Barney, vol. 45
Georg Baselitz, vol. 11
Vanessa Beecroft, vol. 56
Ross Bleckner, vol. 38
Alighiero e Boetti, vol. 24
Christian Boltanski, vol. 22
Louise Bourgeois, vol. 27
Sophie Calle, vol. 36
Maurizio Cattelan, vol. 59
Vija Celmins, vol. 44
Francesco Clemente, vol. 9 & 40/41
Chuck Close, vol. 60
Enzo Cucchi, vol. 1
Martin Disler, vol. 3
Marlene Dumas, vol. 38
Eric Fischl, vol. 5
Peter Fischli/David Weiss, vol.17, 40/41
Sylvie Fleury, vol. 58
Günther Förg, vol. 26 & 40/41
Katharina Fritsch, vol. 25
Franz Gertsch, vol. 28
Gilbert & George, vol. 14
Robert Gober, vol. 27
Nan Goldin, vol. 57
Felix Gonzalez-Torres, vol. 39
Douglas Gordon, vol. 49
Andreas Gursky, vol. 44
David Hammons, vol. 31
Thomas Hirschhorn, vol. 57
Damien Hirst, vol. 40/41
Jenny Holzer, vol. 40/41
Rebecca Horn, vol. 13 & 40/41
Roni Horn, vol. 54

Gary Hume, vol. 48
Ilya Kabakov, vol. 34
Alex Katz, vol. 21
Mike Kelley, vol. 31
Ellsworth Kelly, vol. 56
Karen Kilimnik, vol. 52
Martin Kippenberger, vol. 19
Imi Knoebel, vol. 32
Jeff Koons, vol. 19, 50/51
Jannis Kounellis, vol. 6
Yayoi Kusama, vol. 59
Wolfgang Laib, vol. 39
Sherrie Levine, vol. 32
Sarah Lucas, vol. 45
Brice Marden, vol. 7
Mario Merz, vol. 15
Tracey Moffatt, vol. 53
Mariko Mori, vol. 54
Malcolm Morley, vol. 52
Juan Muñoz, vol. 43
Jean-Luc Mylayne, vol. 50/51
Bruce Nauman, vol. 10
Cady Noland, vol. 46
Meret Oppenheim, vol. 4
Gabriel Orozco, vol. 48
Tony Oursler, vol. 47
Jorge Pardo, vol. 56
Raymond Pettibon, vol. 47
Elizabeth Peyton, vol. 53
Sigmar Polke, vol. 2, 30 & 40/41
Richard Prince, vol. 34
Markus Raetz, vol. 8
Charles Ray, vol. 37
Jason Rhoades, vol. 58
Gerhard Richter, vol. 35
Pipilotti Rist, vol. 48
Tim Rollins & K.O.S., vol. 20
Ugo Rondinone, vol. 52
James Rosenquist, vol. 58

Susan Rothenberg, vol. 43
Thomas Ruff, vol. 28
Edward Ruscha, vol. 18 & 55
Thomas Schütte, vol. 47
Cindy Sherman, vol. 29
Roman Signer, vol. 45
Andreas Slominski, vol. 55
Beat Streuli, vol. 54
Thomas Struth, vol. 50/51
Hiroshi Sugimoto, vol. 46
Philip Taaffe, vol. 26
Sam Taylor-Wood, vol. 55
Diana Thater, vol. 60
Wolfgang Tillmans, vol. 53
Rirkrit Tiravanija, vol. 44
Rosemarie Trockel, vol. 33
James Turrell, vol. 25
Luc Tuymans, vol. 60
Kara Walker, vol. 59
Jeff Wall, vol. 22 & 49
Andy Warhol, vol. 12
Lawrence Weiner, vol. 42
Franz West, vol. 37
Rachel Whiteread, vol. 42
Sue Williams, vol 50/51
Robert Wilson, vol. 16
Christopher Wool, vol. 33

vol.	Collaboration			vol.	Collaboration			vol.	Collaboration		
60	Chuck Close	m	e	44	Vija Celmins	m		20	Tim Rollins + K.O.S.	m	
	Diana Thater	m	e		Andreas Gursky	m		19	Martin Kippenberger		
	Luc Tuymans	m	e		Rirkrit Tiravanija	m	e		Jeff Koons		
59	Maurizio Cattelan	m		43	Juan Muñoz	m	e	18	Ed Ruscha	m	
	Yayoi Kusama	m	e		Susan Rothenberg	m	e	17	Fischli/Weiss		
	Kara Walker	m	e	42	Lawrence Weiner	m	e	16	Robert Wilson		
58	Sylvie Fleury	m	e		Rachel Whiteread	m		15	Mario Merz	m	
	Jason Rhoades	m	e	40/41	Francesco Clemente	m	e	14	Gilbert & George	m	
	James Rosenquist	m	e		Fischli/Weiss	m		13	Rebecca Horn		
57	Doug Aitken	m	e		Günther Förg	m		12	Andy Warhol		
	Nan Goldin	m			Damien Hirst	m		11	Georg Baselitz	m	
	Thomas Hirschhorn	m			Jenny Holzer	m		10	Bruce Nauman		
56	Vanessa Beecroft	m			Rebecca Horn	m		9	Francesco Clemente		
	Ellsworth Kelly	m			Sigmar Polke	m	e	8	Markus Raetz		
	Jorge Pardo	m	e	39	Felix Gonzalez-Torres	m		7	Brice Marden		
55	Edward Ruscha	m			Wolfgang Laib	m	e	6	Jannis Kounellis		
	Andreas Slominski	m	e	38	Ross Bleckner	m		5	Eric Fischl		
	Sam Taylor-Wood	m			Marlene Dumas	m		4	Meret Oppenheim		
54	Roni Horn	m	e	37	Charles Ray	m		3	Martin Disler		
	Mariko Mori	m			Franz West	m	e	2	Sigmar Polke		
	Beat Streuli	m	e	36	Stephan Balkenhol	m		1	Enzo Cucchi		
53	Tracey Moffatt	m		36	Sophie Calle	m					
	Elizabeth Peyton	m		35	Gerhard Richter						
	Wolfgang Tillmans	m		34	Ilya Kabakov	m					
52	Karen Kilimnik	m	e		Richard Prince	m	e				
	Malcolm Morley	m	e	33	Rosemarie Trockel	m					
	Ugo Rondinone	m	e		Christopher Wool	m					
50/51	John Armleder	m		32	Imi Knoebel						
	Jeff Koons	m	e		Sherrie Levine						
	Jean-Luc Mylayne	m		31	David Hammons						
	Thomas Struth	m			Mike Kelley						
	Sue Williams	m		30	Sigmar Polke						
49	Laurie Anderson	m	e	29	John Baldessari						
	Douglas Gordon	m			Cindy Sherman						
	Jeff Wall	m		28	Franz Gertsch	m	e				
48	Gary Hume	m			Thomas Ruff	m					
	Gabriel Orozco	m		27	Louise Bourgeois						
	Pipilotti Rist	m			Robert Gober						
47	Tony Oursler	m		26	Günther Förg	m					
	Raymond Pettibon	m			Philip Taaffe	m					
	Thomas Schütte	m	e	25	Katharina Fritsch	m	e				
46	Richard Artschwager	m			James Turrell	m	e				
	Cady Noland	m		24	Alighiero e Boetti	m	e				
	Hiroshi Sugimoto	m		23	Richard Artschwager	m					
45	Matthew Barney	m		22	Christian Boltanski	m					
	Sarah Lucas	m			Jeff Wall	m					
	Roman Signer	m	e	21	Alex Katz	m	e				

m = available monograph / erhältliche Monographie, e = available edition / erhältliche Edition
Delivery subject to availability at time of order / Lieferung solange Vorrat

EDITIONS FOR PARKETT

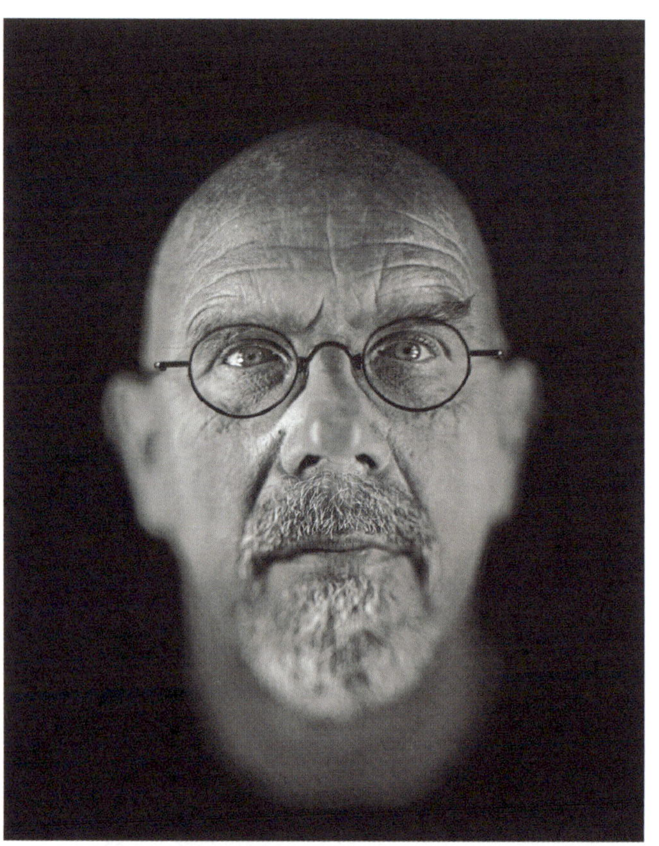

PARKETT 60

CHUCK CLOSE
SELF-PORTRAIT, 2000
Digital ink-jet print of a daguerreotype original
on Crane Muséo paper.
Printed by Adamson Editions, Washington D. C.
22 x 17" (image size 15½ x 12")
Edition of 70, signed and numbered, **$ 1400 / € 1600**

SELBSTPORTRÄT, 2000
Digitaler Ink-Jet-Print einer Daguerreotypie
auf Crane-Muséo-Papier.
Gedruckt bei Adamson Editions, Washington D.C.
56 x 43,2 cm (Bild 39,4 x 30,5 cm).
Auflage: 70, signiert und nummeriert, **sFr. 2450.–**

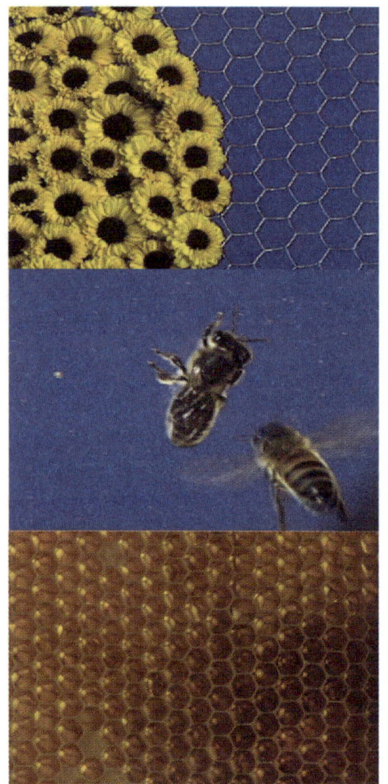

PARKETT 60

DIANA THATER
UNTITLED, 2000
DVD (Digital Video Disc)
with endless loop.
Edition of 150,
signed and numbered, **$ 350 / € 390**

OHNE TITEL, 2000
DVD (Digital Video Disc),
Endlos-Schlaufe.
Auflage: 150,
signiert und nummeriert, **sFr. 600.–**

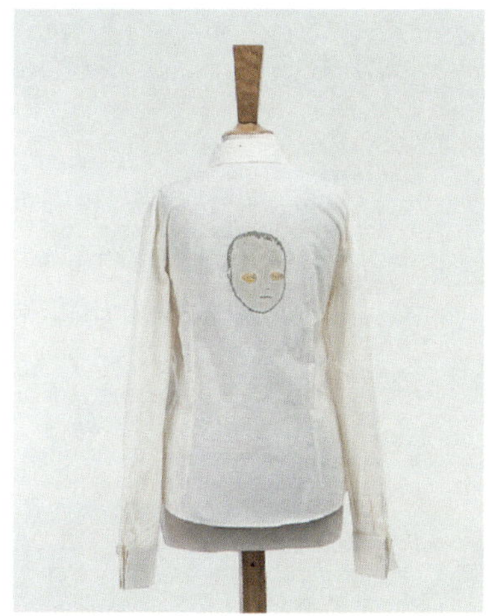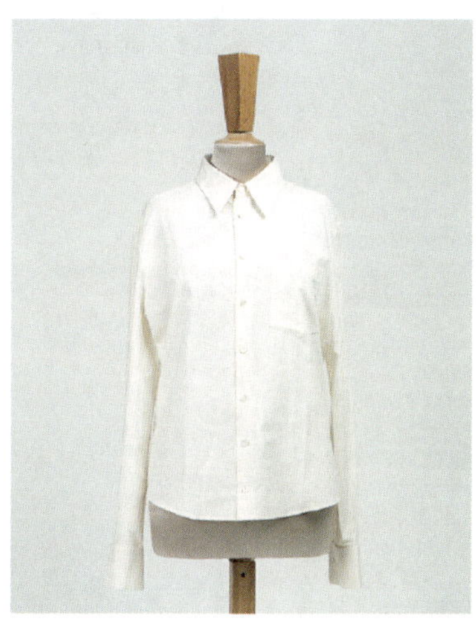

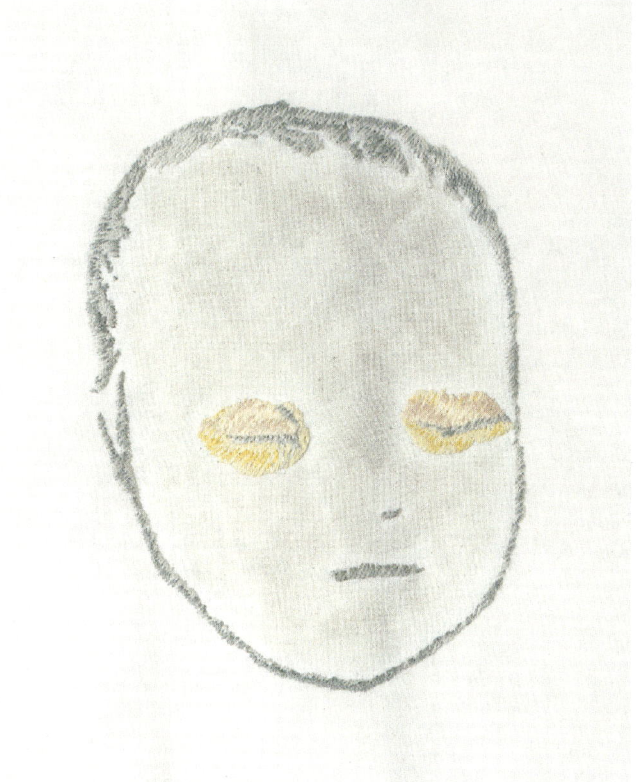

PARKETT 60

LUC TUYMANS
SILENCE, 1990–2000

Men's cotton shirt with reproduction of the artist's
painting SILENCE, 1991.
Shirt design by Walter van Beirendonck, 3 sizes (S, M, L).
Hand-stitched version made by Trois Quarts, Antwerp.
Edition of 20, signed and numbered, **$ 1900 / € 2160**
Silkscreen version printed by Lorenz Boegli, Zurich.
Edition of 99, signed and numbered, **$ 450 / € 530**

STILLE, 1990–2000

Baumwoll-Herrenhemd mit Reproduktion
des Bildes SILENCE, 1991.
Hemddesign Walter van Beirendonck,
3 Grössen (S, M, L).
Handgestickte Version durch Trois Quarts, Antwerpen.
Auflage: 20, signiert und nummeriert, **sFr. 3300.–**
Siebdruck-Version gedruckt bei Lorenz Boegli, Zürich.
Auflage: 99, signiert und nummeriert, **sFr. 800.–**

BORDERS BOOKSHOP
203–207 OXFORD STREET
CAMDEN ARTS CENTRE
ARKWRIGHT ROAD
HAYWARD GALLERY
SOUTH BANK
IAN SHIPLEY BOOKSHOP
70 CHARING CROSS ROAD
INSTITUTE OF CONTEMPORARY ARTS
12 CARLTON HOUSE TERRACE
THE MALL
SERPENTINE GALLERY
KENSINGTON GARDENS
TATE MODERN
BANKSIDE
ZWEMMER LTD. ART BOOKS
24 LITCHFIELD STREET

IRELAND / IRLAND
DUBLIN
DOUGLAS HYDE GALLERY
TRINITY COLLEGE

GERMANY / DEUTSCHLAND
DISTRIBUTOR / VERTRIEB
GVA VERLAGSSERVICE GÖTTINGEN
ANNA-VANDENHOECK-RING 36
D-37081 GÖTTINGEN
BERLIN
BÜCHERBOGEN AM SAVIGNYPLATZ
STADTBAHNBOGEN 593
GALERIE 2000 KUNSTBUCHHANDLUNG
KNESEBECKSTRASSE 56/58
WALTHER KÖNIG BUCHHANDLUNG, MUSEUM FÜR
GEGENWARTSKUNST
INVALIDENSTRASSE 50–51 IM HAMBURGER BAHNHOF
BREMEN
KUNST UND BUCH, AM NEUEN MUSEUM
WESERBURG, TEERHOF 20
BREMERHAVEN
KABINETT FÜR AKTUELLE KUNST
KARLSBURG 4
DÜSSELDORF
LITERATUR BEI RUDOLF MÖLLER
NEUSTRASSE 38
WALTHER KÖNIG BUCHHANDLUNG
HEINRICH-HEINE-ALLEE 15
FRANKFURT
KUNSTHALLE SCHIRN, KUNST-BUCH
RÖMERBERG 7
PETER NAACHER BUCHHANDLUNG
ZIEGELHÜTTENWEG 27–31
SCHUMANN & COBET BUCHHANDLUNG
BÖRSENSTRASSE 2–4
WALTHER KÖNIG BUCHHANDLUNG
DOMSTRASSE 6
HAMBURG
HELMUT VON DER HÖH BUCHHANDLUNG
GROSSE BLEICHEN 21
SAUTTER + LACKMANN BUCHHANDLUNG
ADMIRALITÄTSTRASSE 71/72
HANNOVER
MERZ KUNSTBUCHHANDLUNG
KURT-SCHWITTERS-PLATZ
KARLSRUHE
HANS MENDE BUCHHANDLUNG
KARLSTRASSE 76
KÖLN
SCHADEN.COM BUCHHANDEL
BURGMAUER 10
WALTHER KÖNIG BUCHHANDLUNG
EHRENSTRASSE 4
MÜNCHEN
HANS GOLTZ BUCHHANDLUNG
FÜR BILDENDE KUNST
TÜRKENSTRASSE 54
ILKA KÖNIG BUCHHANDLUNG
MAXIMILIANSTRASSE 35

L. WERNER BUCHHANDLUNG
TÜRKENSTRASSE 30
NÜRNBERG
HUGENDUBEL BUCHHANDLUNG
LUDWIGSPLATZ 1
STUTTGART
GALERIE VALENTIEN
KÖNIGSBAU
LIMACHER BUCHHANDLUNG
KÖNIGSTRASSE 28 / KÖNIGSBAU
WIESBADEN
OTTO HARRASSOWITZ BUCHHANDLUNG
TAUNUSSTRASSE 5

SPAIN / SPANIEN
BARCELONA
1+1 LLIBRES D'ART-ART BOOKS
PASSEIG DE SANT JOAN, 108
LAIETANA DE LLIBRETERIA
PAU CLARIS 85
MADRID
MUSEO NACIONAL REINA SOFIA
C/ SANTA ISABEL, 52

FRANCE / FRANKREICH
PARIS
COLETTE
213, RUE SAINT-HONORÉ
CENTRE POMPIDOU, FLAMMARION 4
26, RUE JACOB
GALERIE NATIONALE DU JEU DE PAUME
1, PLACE DE LA CONCORDE
LIBRAIRIE DU MUSÉE D'ART MODERNE
9, RUE GASTON DE SAINT-PAUL

ITALY / ITALIEN
MILANO
A&M BOOKSTORE
30, VIA TADINO
ROMA
GALLERIA NAZIONALE D'ARTE MODERNA
131, VIA DELLE BELLE ARTI
GALLERIA PRIMO PIANO
203, VIA PANISPERNA

NORWAY / NORWEGEN
OSLO
THE NATIONAL MUSEUM OF CONTEMPORARY ART
BANKPLASSEN 4 / SKATTEFOG

PORTUGAL
LISBOA
MODULO CENTRO DIFUSOR DE ARTE
CALÇADA DOS MESTRES 34 A–B
PORTO
MODULO CENTRO DIFUSOR DE ARTE
AV. BOAVISTA 854

SWEDEN / SCHWEDEN
STOCKHOLM
KULTURHUSET KONSTIG
MEDIA & KONSTBOKHANDEL
SERGELS TORG 3
MODERNA MUSEET
SKEPPSHOLMEN

TURKEY / TÜRKEI
ISTANBUL
ROBINSON CRUSOE BOOKS PUSULA PRODUCTIONS
389 ISTIKAL CADDESI BEYOGLU

**NETHERLANDS, BELGIUM
AND LUXEMBURG**
DISTRIBUTOR / VERTRIEB
IDEA BOOKS
NIEUWE HERENGRACHT 11
NL-1011 RK AMSTERDAM

NETHERLANDS / NIEDERLANDE
AMSTERDAM
ART BOOK
VAN BAERLESTRAAT 126

ATHENAEUM NIEUWSCENTRUM
SPUI 14–16
ROBERT PREMSELA BOOKSHOP
VAN BAERLESTRAAT 78
GRONINGEN
SCHOLTENS / WRISTERS BOOKSHOP
FULDENSTRAAT 20
ROTTERDAM
DONNER BOOKSHOP
LIJNBAAN 150

BELGIUM / BELGIEN
ANTWERPEN
F.N.A.C.
GROENPLAATS
BRUXELLES
TROPISMES LIBRAIRIES
GALERIE DES PRINCES 11
GENT
COPYRIGHT BOOKSHOP
JACOBIJNENSTRAAT 8

LUXEMBOURG / LUXEMBURG
LUXEMBOURG
CASINO LUXEMBOURG
41, RUE NOTRE-DAME

SWITZERLAND / SCHWEIZ
DISTRIBUTOR / VERTRIEB
B+I BUCH + INFORMATION
OBERFELDERSTRASSE 35
CH-8910 AFFOLTERN A. A.
BASEL
FONDATION BEYELER
BASELSTRASSE 77, RIEHEN
GALERIE STAMPA
SPALENBERG 2
JÄGGI BUCHHANDLUNG
FREIE STRASSE 32
KUNSTHALLE BASEL
KLOSTERGASSE 5
BERN
HANS HUBER AG BUCHHANDLUNG
MARKTGASSE 59
STAUFFACHER BUCHHANDLUNG
IM KUNSTMUSEUM
HODLERSTRASSE 12
LUZERN
RÄBER BÜCHER AG
FRANKENSTRASSE 7-9
GENÈVE
LIBRAIRIE PAYOT
5, RUE DE CHANTEPOULET
MENDRISIO
GABRIELE CAPELLI LIBRERIA ARCHITETTURA
4, VIA NOBILI BOSIA
ST. GALLEN
RÖSSLITOR BÜCHER
WEBERGASSE 5
ZÜRICH
CALLIGRAMME BUCHHANDLUNG
HÄRINGSTRASSE 4
HOWEG BUCHHANDLUNG
WAFFENPLATZ 1
KRAUTHAMMER BUCHHANDLUNG
OBERE ZÄUNE 24
KUNSTGRIFF BUCHHANDLUNG
LIMMATSTRASSE 270
KUNSTHAUS ZÜRICH
HEIMPLATZ 1
KUNSTKIOSK
LIMMATQUAI 31
ORELL FÜSSLI BUCHHANDLUNG
FÜSSLISTRASSE 4
SCALO BOOKS & LOOKS
WEINBERGSTRASSE 22 A
SEC 52 BUCHHANDLUNG
JOSEFSTRASSE 52

E X H I B I T I O N S

ZÜRICH

ACP **VIVIANE EHRLI**	Klingenstrasse 42 8005 Zürich Tel. 01 271 61 61	Selected Works on Paper – S. AMREIN H. ANTES, N. BHAVSAR, T. CLARKE, P. DORAZIO, I. HAASZ, J. JUSZCZYK, B. U. KORNETZKY, M. NOËL, GR. THOMSON, C. VALVERDE	**18.1.–24.3.2001**
ARS FUTURA	Bleicherweg 45 8002 Zürich Tel. 01 201 88 10	MARTIN PARR – Think of England DANIELE BUETTI – Birth of Karma	**25.11.00–20.1.2001** **2.2.–24.3.2001**
BOB VAN ORSOUW	Limmatstrasse 270 8005 Zürich Tel. 01 273 11 00	DAVID REED Weihnachten / Neujahr geschlossen SIOBHAN LIDDELL	**25.11.00–13.1.2001** **23.12.00–8.1.2001** **20.1.–24.2.2001**
BOB GYSIN	Ausstellungsstrasse 24 8005 Zürich Tel. 01 278 40 60	KLAUS BORN NIKLAUS RÜEGG	**8.12.00–27.1.2001** **2.2.–10.3.2001**
MAI 36 GALERIE	Rämistrasse 37 8001 Zürich Tel. 01 261 68 80	REMY ZAUGG THOMAS RUFF RITA McBRIDE	**19.1.–10.2.2001** **16.2.–31.3.2001** **6.4.–26.5.2001**
MARK MÜLLER	Gessnerallee 36 8001 Zürich Tel. 01 211 81 55	FRANCIS BAUDEVIN – La lettre de l'amour im Guestroom: RENÉ ZÄCH CHRISTOPH HAERLE – Neue Arbeiten DUANE ZALOUDEK – Paintings SABINA BAUMANN – Neue Arbeiten im Guestroom: SURPRISE	**13.1.–24.2.2001** **3.3.–14.4.2001** **21.4.–2.6.2001**
SEMINA RERUM **IRÈNE PREISWERK**	Cäcilienstrasse 3 8032 Zürich Tel. 01 251 26 39	SILVIA GERTSCH / XERXES ACH NIVES WIDAUER DAGMAR VARADY	**25.11.00–13.1.2001** **20.1.–10.3.2001** **17.3.–5.5.2001**
GALERIE SCHEDLER	Josefstrasse 53 8005 Zürich Tel. 01 440 61 20	DIETER HALL – Paintings WALTER PFEIFFER – Photography JOSEPH BEUYS, 50 Multiples from a Private Collection	**12.1.–24.2.2001** **3.3.–14.4.2001** **bis 25.3.2001**

E X H I B I T I O N S

ANNEMARIE VERNA	Neptunstrasse 45	ROBERT WILSON – Three Installations &	
	8032 Zürich	"Rheingold"-Drawings	**24.11.00 – 27.1.2001**
	Tel. 01 262 38 20	Weihnachten / Neujahr geschlossen	**26.12.00 – 8.1.2001**
		JERRY ZENJUK – New Paintings &	
		Watercolours	**6.2. – 24.3.2001**
		RITA McBRIDE	
		(in collaboration with Mai 36 Gallery)	**5.4. – 19.5.2001**

JAMILEH WEBER	Waldmannstrasse 6	MARKUS LÜPERTZ –	
	8001 Zürich	Paintings Sculptures	**24.11.00 – 27.1.2001**
	Tel. 01 252 10 66	CATHERINE LEE – Bronze	**24.2. – 7.4.2001**

BRIGITTE WEISS	Müllerstrasse 67	BOETSCHI, GANZ, JAFFE, LAVATER,	
	8004 Zürich	NIEDERER, RÜTHI, TODD, ZURFLUH	**12.1. – 24.2.2001**
	Tel. 01 241 83 35	CARO NIEDERER	**2.3. – 28.4.2001**
		CHARLES BOETSCHI	**4.5. – 18.6.2001**

BERN

GALERIE	Lorrainestrasse 19	ILONA RUEGG	**bis 13.1.2001**
FRIEDRICH	3013 Bern	SILVIA BÄCHLI	**26.1. – 17.3.2001**
	Tel. 031 331 33 30	CHRISTOPH SCHREIBER	**23.3. – 11.5.2001**

GENÈVE

DANIEL VARENNE	8, rue Toepffer	PAINTINGS AND DRAWINGS	
	1206 Genève	19TH AND 20TH CENTURY	
	Tel. 022 789 16 75		

ST. GALLEN

WILMA LOCK	Schmiedgasse 15	Weihnachten / Neujahr geschlossen	**23.12.00. – 10.1.2001**
	9001 St. Gallen	JÜRGEN PARTENHEIMER – New Works	**27.1. – 31.3.2001**
	Tel. 071 222 62 52		

ZUG

KUNSTHAUS ZUG	Dorfstrasse 27	HOMMAGE À JOSEF HERZOG	**bis 21.1. 2001**
	6300 Zug	BACKSTAGE – Die Sammlung	**3.2. – 18.3.2001**
	Tel. 041 725 33 44		

ART-GARAGE	Gotthardstrasse 25	DOMINIQUE ANNE SCHUETZ (DASCH)	
	6300 Zug	"Signs"-Paintings and Drawings	**20.1. – 28.4.2001**
	Tel. 041 720 45 20		

ROBERT WILSON

THROUGH JANUARY 6

ADRIAN PIPER

THROUGH JANUARY 6

SOL LeWITT

THROUGH JANUARY 13

CHRISTIAN MARCLAY

JANUARY – FEBRUARY

SOPHIE CALLE

FEBRUARY – MARCH

CÉLESTE
BOURSIER-MOUGENOT

MARCH – APRIL

SHERRIE LEVINE

MARCH – APRIL

PAULA COOPER GALLERY

521/534 WEST 21ST STREET NEW YORK 10011 TEL 212.255.1105 FAX 212.255.5156

Diana Thater and Luc Tuymans

represented by **David Zwirner**

43 Greene Street
New York, NY 10013
Fax 212-966-4952

Telephone 212-966-9074
dzwirner@davidzwirner.com
www.davidzwirner.com

JOHN McCRACKEN

STAINLESS STEEL
SCULPTURES

November 9, 2000 - January 6, 2001

ZWIRNER & WIRTH

32 E 69 St NewYork NY 10021
212.517.8677 telephone
212.517.8959 fax
www.zwirnerandwirth.com

MAI 36 GALERIE

VITO ACCONCI
FRANZ ACKERMANN
IAN ANÜLL
JOHN BALDESSARI
STEPHAN BALKENHOL
TROY BRAUNTUCH
ANKE DOBERAUER
PIA FRIES
ANDREAS GURSKY
ANDREA KNOBLOCH
RITA MCBRIDE
HARALD F. MÜLLER
MATT MULLICAN
MANFRED PERNICE
CHRISTOPH RÜTIMANN
THOMAS RUFF
JÖRG SASSE
PAUL THEK
LAWRENCE WEINER
RÉMY ZAUGG

RÉMY ZAUGG
January 19 – February 10, 2001

THOMAS RUFF
February 16 – March 31, 2001

RITA McBRIDE
April 6 – May 26, 2001

Rämistrasse 37, CH-8001 Zürich, Tel. 01 261 68 80, Fax 01 261 68 81

LUC TUYMANS

Belgian Pavilion Venice Biennial 2001

S.M.A.K. Stedelijk Museum voor Actuele Kunst Gent
3 February - 25 March 2001

Hamburger Bahnhof Berlin
May - June 2001

RAOUL DE KEYSER

S.M.A.K. Stedelijk Museum voor Actuele Kunst Gent
3 February - 25 March 2001

Renaissance Society Chicago
11 March - 22 April 2001

PATRICK VAN CAECKENBERGH

Bonnefantenmuseum Maastricht
16 September 2001 - 14 January 2002

Dirk Braeckman - Michaël Borremans -   Raoul De Keyser - Carl De Keyzer - Stan Douglas
Marlene Dumas - Jeroen Eisinga - Noritoshi Hirakawa - Johannes Kahrs - John Körmeling - Mark
Manders - Avery Preesman - Gert Robijns - Maria Serebriakova - Luc Tuymans - Patrick Van
Caeckenbergh - Maarten Vanden Abeele - Anne-Mie Van Kerckhoven - Cristof Yvoré

ZENO X GALLERY

Frank Demaegd ° Leopold De Waelplaats 16 ° 2000 Antwerp ° Belgium
Tel . 32 (0)3 216 16 26   Fax. 32 (0)3 216 09 92   E-Mail: ZENO-X @VILLAGE.UUNET.BE

Malcolm Morley
Recent Paintings

7 DECEMBER 2000 – 28 JANUARY 2001

Group show

1 FEBRUARY – 24 MARCH 2001

TEFAF Maastricht

10 – 18 MARCH 2001

Jan Vercruysse

29 MARCH – 5 MAY 2001

ART Brussels

20 – 24 APRIL 2001

Xavier Hufkens

Sint-Jorisstraat 6–8 rue Saint-Georges

Brussel 1050 Bruxelles

TEL. 32 (0)2 646 63 30 – FAX 32 (0)2 646 93 42

info@xavierhufkens.com
http://www.xavierhufkens.com

Open Tuesday to Saturday, noon to 6 pm

TONY CRAGG

DECEMBER

GIOVANNI ANSELMO
PIERRE HUYGHE

JANUARY

MARIAN GOODMAN GALLERY

24 WEST 57TH STREET   NEW YORK, NY 10019   TEL 212 977-7160

FAX 212 581-5187   GOODMAN@MARIANGOODMAN.COM

GALERIA ▪ HELGA DE ALVEAR

DR. FOURQUET 12, 28012 MADRID.TEL:(34) 91 468 05 06 FAX:(34) 91 467 51 34
e-mail:galeria@helgadealvear.net   www.helgadealvear.net

January 18 - March 2

JEFF WALL

ESTUDIO ♠ HELGA DE ALVEAR

TERESITA FERNÁNDEZ

February 14 -19

ARCO 2001

PROJECT ROOM

JAVIER VALLHONRAT

ROBERT MAPPLETHORPE

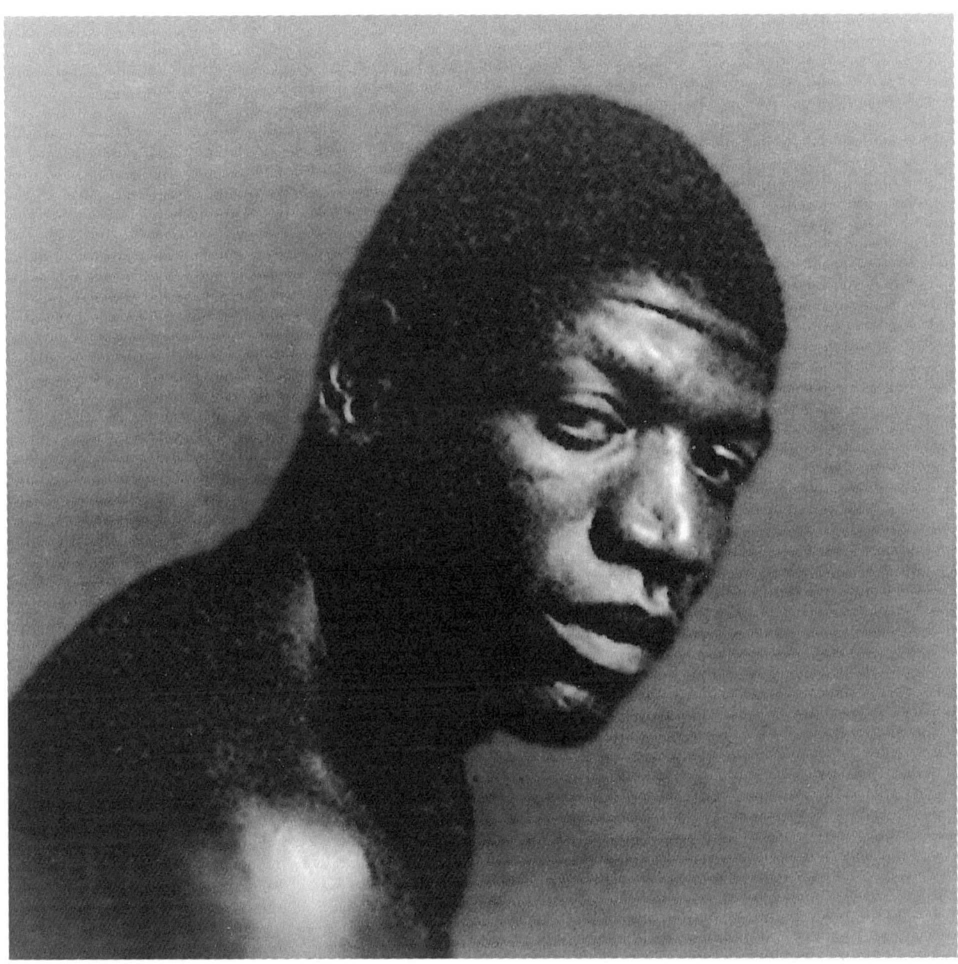

A SURVEY EXHIBITION FROM THE ESTATE
DECEMBER 2000 TO JANUARY 2001

GALERIE THADDAEUS ROPAC
AUSTRIA MIRABELLPLATZ 2, 5020 SALZBURG TEL : 43 662 881 393 FAX : 43 662 881 3939 www.ropac.net

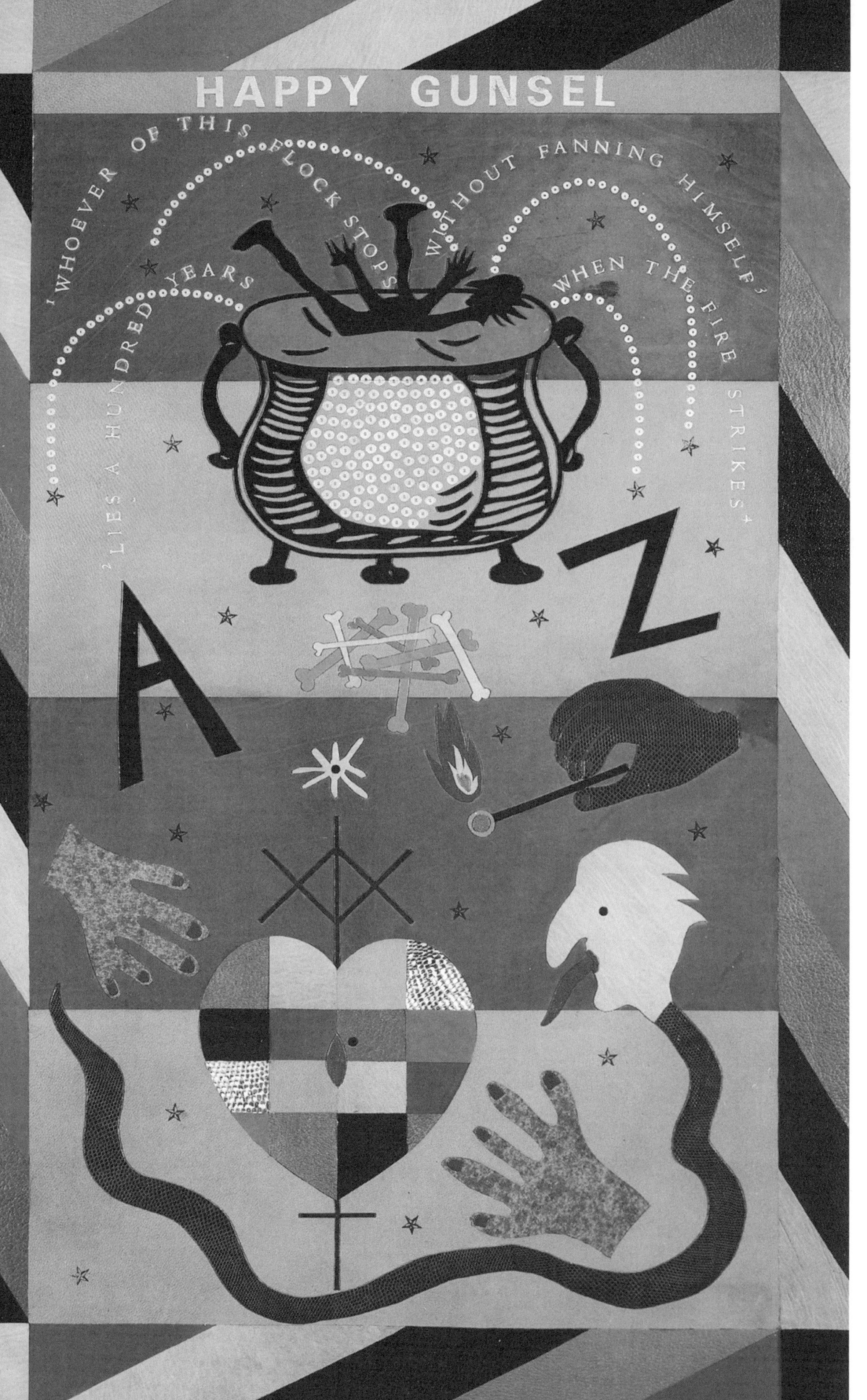

Winter 2000
Nan Goldin
Jonathan Hammer
Gary Hume
Terry Winters

Matthew Marks Gallery
523 West 24 Street
522 West 22 Street
New York NY 10011
2 1 2 - 2 4 3 - 0 2 0 0
gallery@mmarks.com

Jonathan Hammer, *Happy Gunsel*
26 3/4 x 38 1/2. Snake, box calf,
goat, lizard, sting-ray skin, and
gold leaf mounted on board

MIGUEL PALMA
GALERIA ANDRE VIANA
Rua Miguel Bombarda, 410 > 4050 - 379 > Porto - Portugal > Tel.: +351 2 339 5090 > Fax.: +351 2 339 5099 > galeria-andreviana@clix.pt

Donald Baechler
Alighiero Boetti
Greg Bogin
Maurizio Cannavacciuolo
Francesco Clemente
Greg Colson
Wim Delvoye
Nicola De Maria
Kim Dingle
Graham Gillmore
Peter Halley
Guillermo Kuitca
Milan Kunc
Wolfgang Laib
Richard Long
Aldo Mondino
Malcom Morley
Vik Muniz
Mimmo Paladino
Jennifer Reeves
Tom Sachs
Julian Schnabel
Gianni Stefanon
Richard Tuttle
Not Vital
Andy Warhol
William Wegman
Jan Worst

Galleria Cardi & Co.

opening new space
February 2001
C.so di P.ta Nuova, 38 I-20121 Milano
in collaboration with
Gian Enzo Sperone New York

Galleria Cardi

Piazza S.Erasmo,3 I-20121 Milano
tel +39 02 29003235 fax +39 02 29003382
cardi.galleria@all.it www.galleriacardi.com

G A L E R I E M E E R T R I H O U X

CARLA ACCARDI
ROBERT ADAMS
JOHN BALDESSARI
ROBERT BARRY
ENRICO CASTELLANI
HANNE DARBOVEN
MARIA ANNA DEWES
PAUL DRISSEN
SYLVIE EYBERG
ISA GENZKEN
JEF GEYS
MIMMO JODICE
PETER JOSEPH
DONALD JUDD
BRANDT JUNCEAU
LOUISE LAWLER
SOL LEWITT
KEN LUM
ROBERT MANGOLD
LILIANA MORO   JANVIER - FEVRIER
FRED SANDBACK
THOMAS STRUTH
GRAZIA TODERI   DECEMBRE - JANVIER
RICHARD TUTTLE
MICHAEL VENEZIA
IAN WALLACE
JEFF WALL

RUE DU CANAL 13
1000 BRUXELLES
VAARTSTRAAT 13
1000 BRUSSEL
TEL 02/219 14 22
FAX 02/219 37 21
greta.meert@skynet.be

20.21

Galerie Edition Kunsthandel GmbH
Meisenburgstraße 169 – 173
45133 Essen
Tel. +49 (2 01) 8 71 00 - 0
Fax +49 (2 01) 8 71 00 - 10
Email INFO@2021ART.COM
http://www.2021ART.COM

Mi – Fr 14 – 19 · Sa 11 – 16
und nach Vereinbarung:
Sprechen Sie mit Irmgard Schnell.

VA WÖLFL
9 | 12 | 2000 – 2 | 2 | 2001

VA WÖLFL: XYZ, 1996, Silbergelatine auf Barytpapier, 19,8 × 31 cm

12-01-04/2001

GALERIEN IN DÜSSELDORF

Art Galerie Leuchter + Peltzer Hermann-Josef Kuhna Malerei / KunstKöln 2001 / **Gerhard Mantz** «Virtuelle und reale Objekte»
20.1.-24.2.01 / 29.3.-1.4.01 / 17.3.-21.4.01 / Ratingerstr. 23 PLZ 40213 / Tel. +49(0)211 32 97 91 Fax 13 20 91 / art-leuchter@t-online.de / Mo.-Fr. 9-18.30, Sa. 11-14

Galerie Beck & Eggeling Mimmo Paladino / Balthus / Lyonel Feininger
bis 7.2.01 / 8.2.-28.3.01 / 3.4.-16.5.01 / Bilker Str.5 PLZ 40213 / Tel. +49(0)211-49 15 890 Fax 49 15 899 / Beck-Eggeling@t-online.de www.dobefineart.com / Di.-Fr. 11-19, Sa. 10-16

Galerie Bugdahn und Kaimer Zwischenraum # 4 «Arbeiten mit Fotografie» / **Ingolf Timpner** Fotografie / **Leslie Wayne** Malerei
12.1. - 10.2.01 / 16. 2.-31.3.01 / 6.4.-19.5.01 / Mühlengasse 3 PLZ 40213 / Tel. +49(0)211-32 91 40 Fax 32 91 47 / bugdahn.kaimer@t-online.de www.artnet.com / Di.-Fr. 10-13+14-18, Sa. 11-14 u.n.V.

Galerie Karin Fesel Mathias Kanter Farbmalerei / Lingener Kunstpreisträger 2000
17.2.-30.3.01 / Prinz-Georg-Str. 47 PLZ 40477 / Tel. +49(0)211-46 02 01 Fax 48 05 30 Mobil 0173-29 76 708 / Di-Fr. 12-18 u.n.V. Schwarze Str. 144 47665 Sonsbeck

Konrad Fischer Galerie GmbH Richard Long / Jim Lambie
bis Ende Januar / bis Ende Januar / Platanenstr. 7 PLZ 40233 / Tel. +49(0)211-68 59 08 Fax 68 97 80 / office@konradfischergalerie.de www.konradfischergalerie.de / Di.-Fr. 11-18, Sa. 11-13

Galerie M. + R. Fricke Düsseldorf-Berlin «THROUGH THE LOOKING GLASS» **u.a. Kiki Smith, Hermann Pitz, Anatolij Shuravlev, Beate Daniel, Katharina Schmidt, Martin Schwenk, Jordan Tinker...,**
26.1.-17.3.01 / Poststr. 3 PLZ 40213 / Tel. +49(0)211-32 32 34 Fax 32 95 69 / MandRFricke@compuserve.com

Galerie Wolfgang Gmyrek Galerie Wolfgang Gmyrek 1980-2000 / **Dieter Krieg**
9.1.-24.2.01 / 3.3.-21.4.01 / Mühlengasse 5 PLZ 40213 / Tel. +49(0)211-32 77 70 Fax 13 39 93 / Di.-Fr. 11-18, Sa. 11-14 u.n.V.

Galerie Cora Hölzl Neun Zeichner - von Auberger bis Tuttle / **Joachim Bandau** - Eine Gegenüberstellung
26.1.-17.3.01 / 23.3.-12.5.01 / Citadellstr. 11 PLZ 40213 / Tel. +49(0)211-32 64 12 Fax 13 12 35 / cora.hoelzl@t-online.de / Di.-Fr. 11-18.30, Sa. 12-16 u.n.V.

Galerie Gaby Kraushaar Robin Merkisch photographische Arbeiten / **Chris Newman** paintings, drawings, music
26.1.-16.3.01 / 23.3.-12.5.01 / Orangeriestr. 6 PLZ 40213 / Tel. +49(0)211 13 16 66 Fax 13 16 66 / Mi.-Fr. 13-19, Sa. 12-15

Galerie Hans Mayer GmbH Accrochage / Fritz Schwegler «Skulpturen»
bis 10.2.01 / 12.2.-30.4.01 / Grabbeplatz 2 PLZ 40213 / Tel. +49(0)211-13 21 35 Fax 13 29 48 / art.mayer@t-online.de www.artnet.com/hmayer.html / Mo.-Fr. 10-18, Sa. 10-14 + Kaistr. 10 PLZ 40221 n.V.

Galerie Ute Parduhn BIS DAHIN..., **20 Jahre Galerie Ute Parduhn / Stefan Kürten** Neue Arbeiten
bis 31.1.01 / Feb.-Apr. / Kaiserwerther Markt 6a PLZ 40489 / Tel. +49(0)211-40 06 55 Fax 40 67 0 /Mi.-Fr. 14-18 u.n.V.

Galerie Clara Maria Sels GmbH Jan Fabre und Felix Wunderlich / Natacha Lesueur
20.1.- 20.2.01 / März- April / Poststr. 3 PLZ 40213 / Tel. +49(0)211-32 80 20 Fax 32 80 26 / Di.-Fr. 14-19, Sa. 11-15 / cmsels@mail.isis.de

Galerie Christa Schübbe Heribert Haindle Raumprojekt
Januar-April / Hasseler Str. 85 PLZ 40822 Mettmann / Tel. 02104-5 33 48 Fax 5 15 80 / Di.-Fr. 15-18 + Neubrückstr. 6 Tel. 0211-32 89 85 Mi.-Do. 14-18.30 u.n.V.

Sies + Höke Galerie Cornelius Völker / Frank Darius / Sonja Alhäuser / Arco Madrid
Januar / März / April / 14-19.2.01 / Poststr. 7 PLZ 40213 / Tel. +49(0)211-13 56 67 Fax 13 56 68 / sies-hoeke@t-online.de / Di.-Fr. 12-18.30, Sa. 12-14.30

Galerie Hans Strelow Vier Positionen abstrakter Kunst – **Stella, Knoebel, Partenheimer, Münch**
19.1.-24.3.01 / Luegplatz 3 PLZ 40545 / Tel. +49(0)211-55 55 03 Fax 57 63 08 / Di.-Fr. 10-18.30, Sa. 10-13.30

Galerie Thomas Taubert Gisela Kleinlein / Leni Hoffmann / Ingrid Weber
bis 27.1.01 / 16.2.-14.4.01 / 27.4.-16.6.01 / Mühlengasse 3 PLZ 40213 / Tel.+49(0)211-46 28 49 Fax 48 49 491 Mobil 0172-91 33 999 / galerie@taubert.net www.taubert.net / Di.-Fr. 10-18, Sa. 12-16 u.n.V.

Galerie Peter Tedden M. Meyer – F. D. Schlemme / Peter Rusam Malerei / **Alireza Varzandeh**
12.1.-25.2.01 / 2.3.-21.4.00 / 27.4.-31-5.01 / Bilker Str. 6 PLZ 40213 / Tel. +49(0)211-13 35 28 Fax 13 35 28 / Di.-Fr. 13-19, Sa. 10-16

Galerie Vömel GmbH Hans Tisdall Gouachen auf Papier / **Graphik des XX. Jahrhunderts**
Januar / Februar- April / Orangeriestr. 6 PLZ 40213 / Tel. +49(0)211 32 74 22 Fax 13 52 67 / Dorothee.Vömel@t-omline.de www.galerie-vömel.de / Mo.-Fr. 10-18, Sa. 10-13

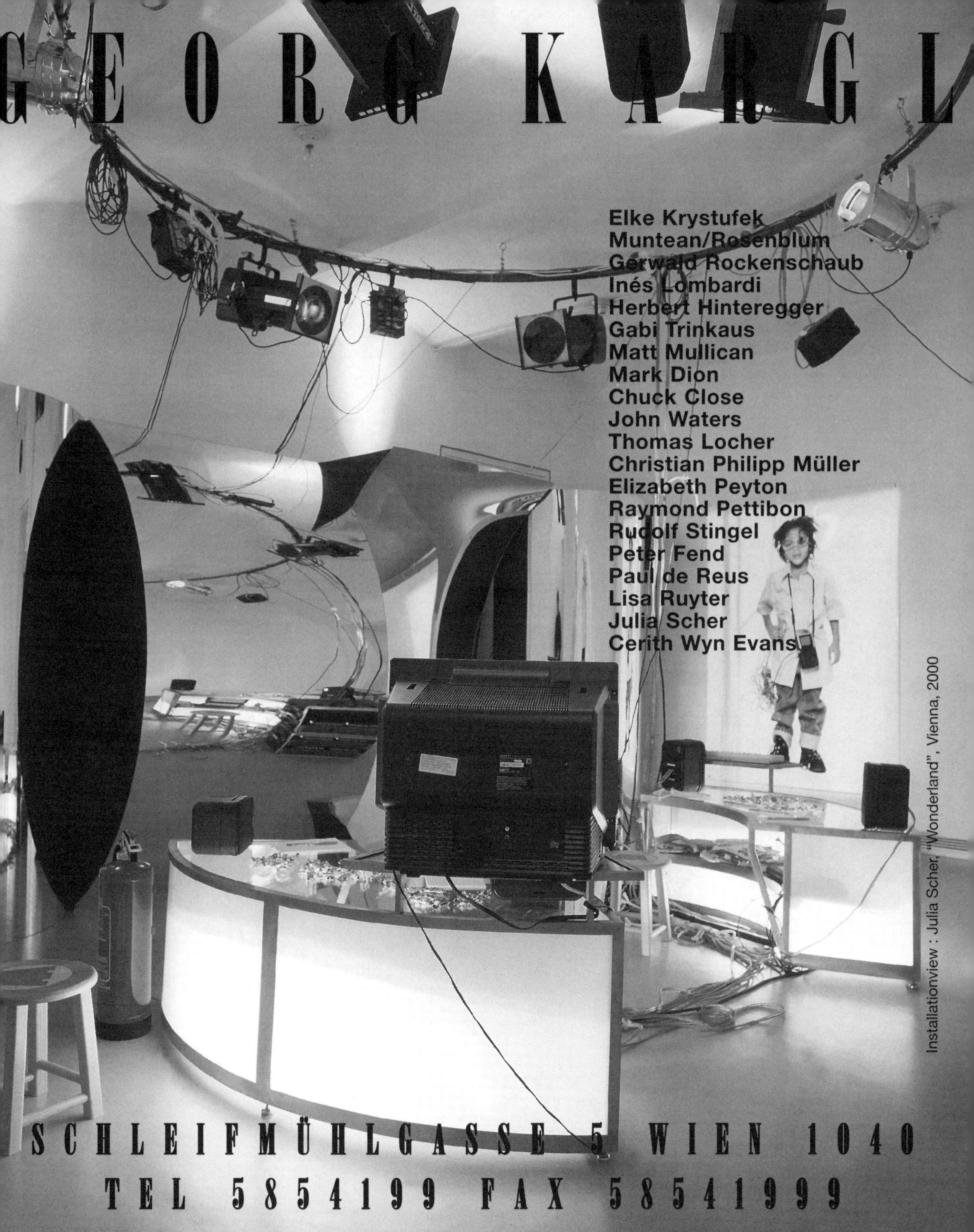

GEORG KARGL

Elke Krystufek
Muntean/Rosenblum
Gerwald Rockenschaub
Inés Lombardi
Herbert Hinteregger
Gabi Trinkaus
Matt Mullican
Mark Dion
Chuck Close
John Waters
Thomas Locher
Christian Philipp Müller
Elizabeth Peyton
Raymond Pettibon
Rudolf Stingel
Peter Fend
Paul de Reus
Lisa Ruyter
Julia Scher
Cerith Wyn Evans

Installationview : Julia Scher, "Wonderland", Vienna, 2000

SCHLEIFMÜHLGASSE 5 WIEN 1040
TEL 5854199 FAX 58541999

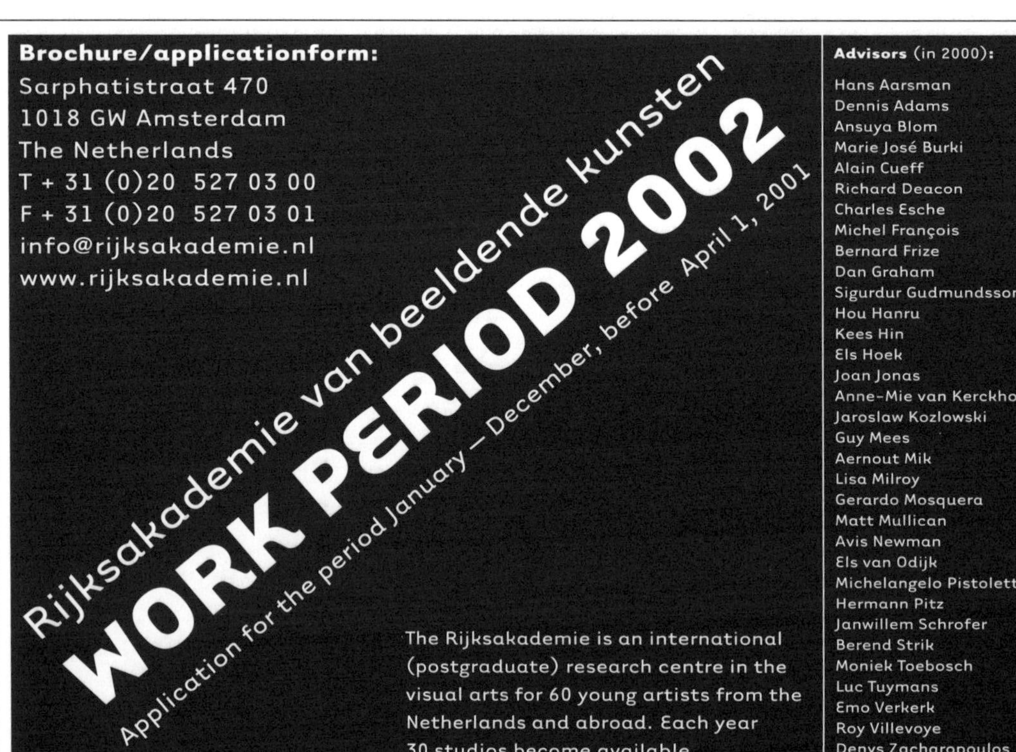

Brochure/applicationform:
Sarphatistraat 470
1018 GW Amsterdam
The Netherlands
T + 31 (0)20 527 03 00
F + 31 (0)20 527 03 01
info@rijksakademie.nl
www.rijksakademie.nl

Rijksakademie van beeldende kunsten
WORK PERIOD 2002
Application for the period January – December, before April 1, 2001

The Rijksakademie is an international
(postgraduate) research centre in the
visual arts for 60 young artists from the
Netherlands and abroad. Each year
30 studios become available.

Advisors (in 2000):

Hans Aarsman
Dennis Adams
Ansuya Blom
Marie José Burki
Alain Cueff
Richard Deacon
Charles Esche
Michel François
Bernard Frize
Dan Graham
Sigurdur Gudmundsson
Hou Hanru
Kees Hin
Els Hoek
Joan Jonas
Anne–Mie van Kerckhoven
Jaroslaw Kozlowski
Guy Mees
Aernout Mik
Lisa Milroy
Gerardo Mosquera
Matt Mullican
Avis Newman
Els van Odijk
Michelangelo Pistoletto
Hermann Pitz
Janwillem Schrofer
Berend Strik
Moniek Toebosch
Luc Tuymans
Emo Verkerk
Roy Villevoye
Denys Zacharopoulos

Technical facilities:

metal
stone
ceramics
glass
woodwork
wax/plaster
plastics
paint
graphics
computer
and electronic
technology
sound, video/film
and photography

Other facilities:

library
collections
artists
documentation

Erlenstrasse 15
CH-4058 Basel
www.nk-ed.com

Fon (061) 683 3265
Fax (061) 683 3266
mail@nk-ed.com

Gianni MOTTI	plant
Christoph BÜCHEL	baut
Eric HATTAN	räumt
Nicolas KRUPP	verkauft

Vorsicht: LKW-Verkehr, Betreten des NT-Areals auf eigenes Risiko

D o m i n i q u e   A n n e   S c h u e t z
[D A S C H]

20. Januar bis 28. April 2001

« S I G N S »

Acrylbilder und Zeichnungen

art·garage

	Gotthardstrasse 25	Tel. +41 41 720 45 20
	CH–6300 Zug	Fax +41 41 720 45 21
	www.artgarage.ch	E-Mail artgarage@datazug.ch
Öffnungszeiten:	Di bis Fr 10 bis 19 Uhr	Sa 10 bis 17 Uhr

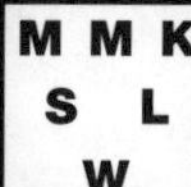

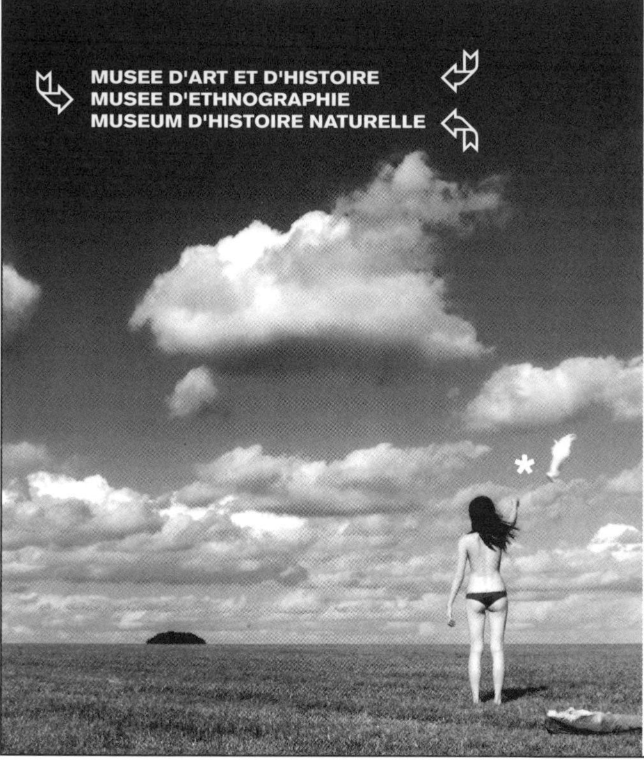

Musée d'art et d'histoire • Esplanade Léopold-Robert 1 — CH-2000 Neuchâtel
Tél. 032 717 79 20 - Fax 032 717 79 29 • http://www.ne.ch/neuchatel/mahn
Musée d'ethnographie • 4, rue Saint-Nicolas - CH-2000 Neuchâtel
Tél. 032 718 1960 - Fax 032 718 1969 • http://www.ne.ch/neuchatel/men
Muséum d'histoire naturelle • 14, rue des Terreaux - CH-2000 Neuchâtel
Tél. 032 717 79 60 - Fax 032 717 79 69 • http://www.ne.ch/neuchatel/mhn

> mardi-dimanche 10 -18h • mercredi entrée libre
Concept & design: F. Cordey, Neuchâtel - www.fcordey.ch • Photo: Kent Baker, New York

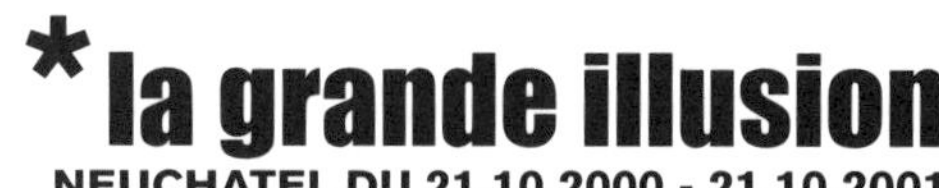

ARCHITETTOLOGIA URBANA / URBAN ARCHITECTOLOGY

grafica con trasferimento a caldo/heat transfer prints

PHYLLIS SELTZER

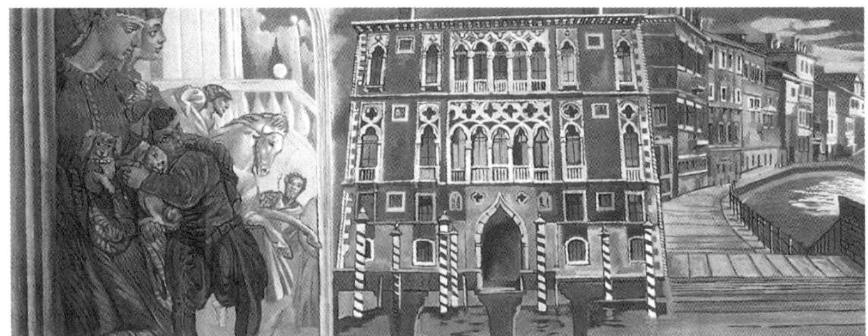

DAL 1 AL 15 MARZO • MARCH 1–15, 2001

Artecultura Via Ciovasso

19–20121 Milano • 864.64.093 • FAX: 860.833

Ricevimento con l' Artista
Il 1° Marzo 2001 alle 18,00

Artist's reception
March 1, 2001 6:00pm

Aura Ed. 2
Grafica con trasferimento a caldo
cm. 40,5 x cm. 101,5
non sbiadisce
Aura Ed. 2
Heat Transfer Print
19" x 50" 1999

Open: Wed - Sun 10 - 17
Tuesday 10 - 19

Kim Soo Ja

February 3 - March 18, 2001

A. K. Dolven

April 7 - May 20, 2001

Projekt raum

Sous la terre, il y a le ciel
Curated by
Evelyne Jouanno

Kunsthalle Bern
Helvetiaplatz 1
CH-3005 Bern
Phone +41 31. 351 00 31
Fax   +41 31. 352 53 85
E-mail: kunsthalle@bluewin.ch
www.kunsthallebern.ch

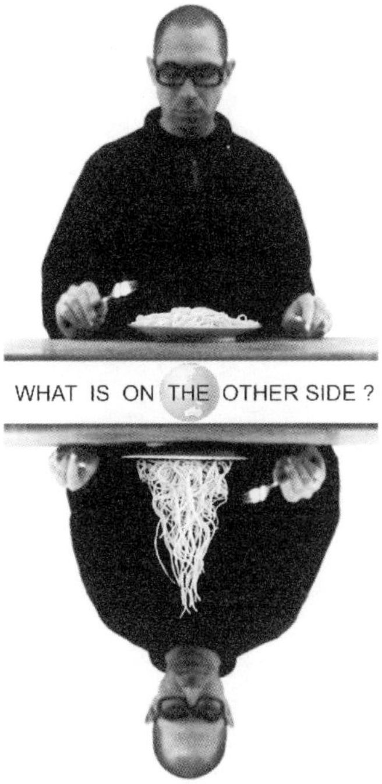

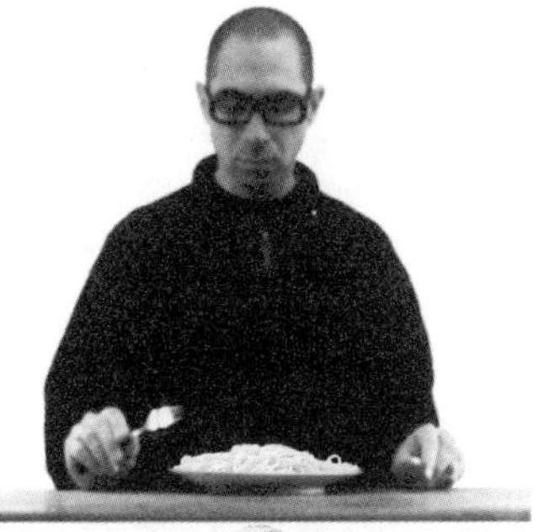

ISKUSSTWO 2000

Neue Kunst aus Moskau, St. Petersburg und Kiew
12.1.-25.2.2001
KUNSTVEREIN ROSENHEIM - STÄDT. GALERIE

Max Bram Pl. 2, D-83022 Rosenheim, Tel. 08031-361447 / 81421
Fax 08031-81896, e-mail: itruebswetter@altavista.net

Curators:Natalia Filonenko, Alexander Yakimovich, Iris Trübswetter
Catalogue: 180 p., in the exhibition DM 39.-,when forwarded DM 49.

artists from St. Petersburg
O. UND A. FLORENSKY
VLADISLAV MAMYSHEV
OLGA TOBRELUTS
artists from Moscow
AES
GLEB ALEYNIKOV
TANYA ANTOSHINA
VLADIMIR ARCHIPOV
ALEXANDER BRENER
GOR CHAHAL
VADIM FISHKIN
DMITRIJ GUTOV
PAQITO INFANTE - ARANA
NINA KOTEL

OLEG KULIK
YURI LEJDERMAN
TANYA LIEBERMAN
VLADIMIR SALNIKOV
YEVGENY SEMYONOV
YEFIMOV / CHERNISHEV
artists from Kiev
SERHIY BRADKOV
ILYA CHICHKAN
OLEXANDER HNILITSKY
MAXIM MAMSIKOV
KIRILL PROTSENKO
VASYL TSAHOLOV
OLEXANDER VERESHAK
MARGARITA ZINETS

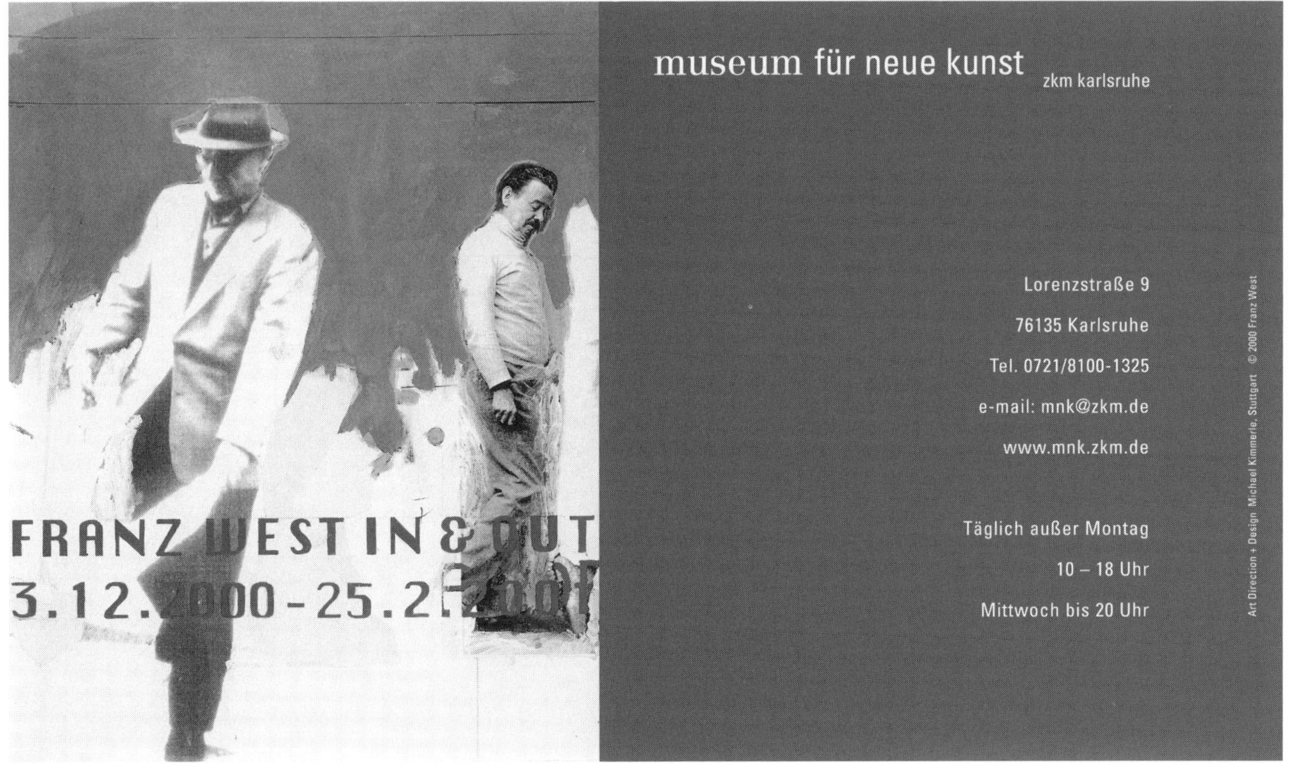

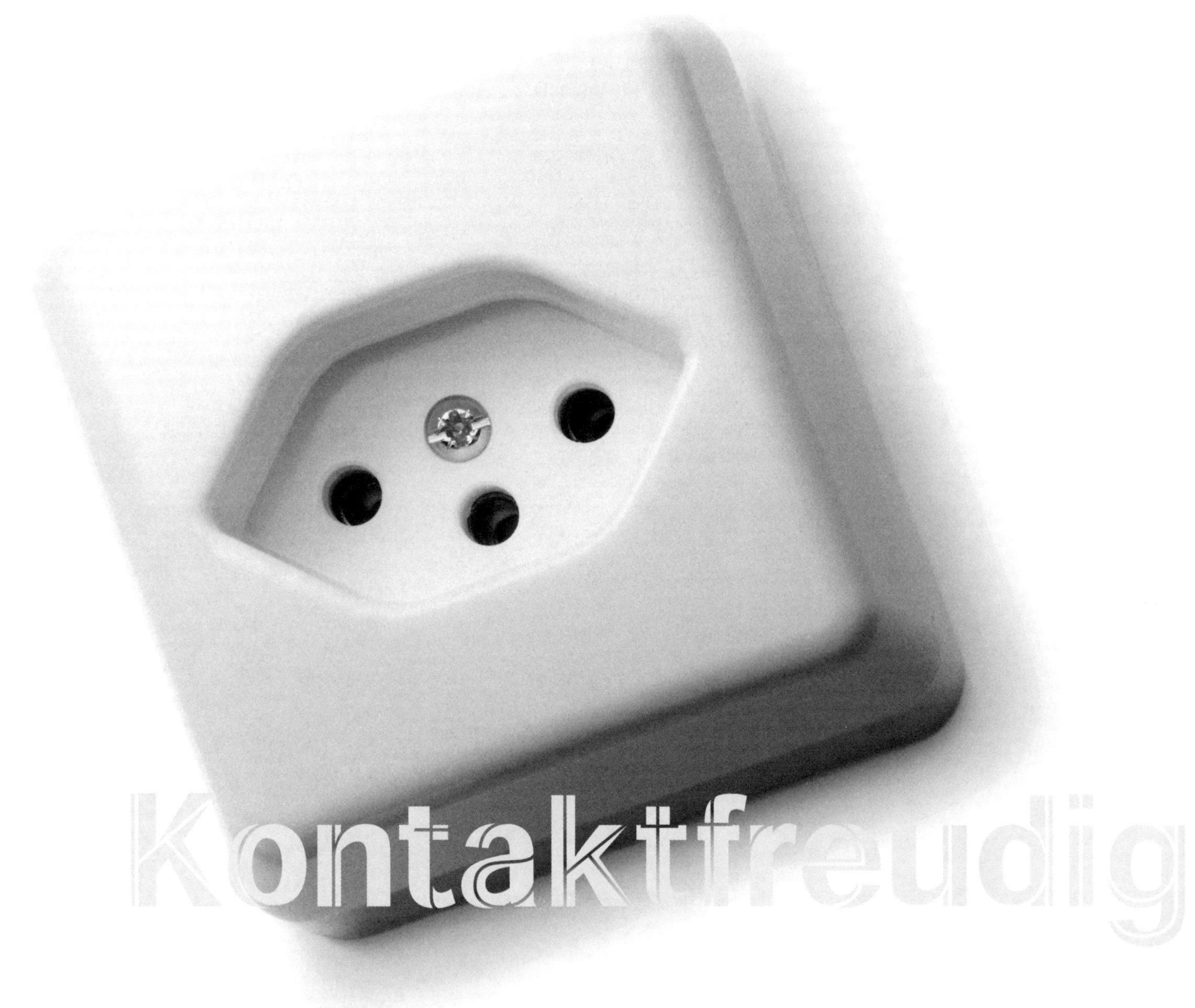

Zürichsee Druckereien AG • Seestrasse 86 • Postfach • 8712 Stäfa • Telefon 01 928 53 03 • Telefax 01 928 53 10 • Internet http://www.zsd.ch

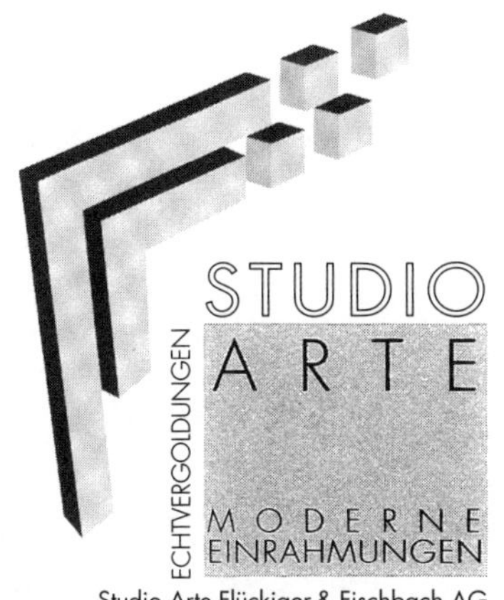

Studio Arte Flückiger & Fischbach AG
Stauffacherquai 46, 8004 Zürich
Telefon 01-245 86 00
Telefax 01-241 35 85

FINE ART FRAMING

FRAMERS OF ALL THE PARKETT EDITIONS

ON VIEW AT THE NEW YORK MUSEUM OF MODERN

ART FROM MARCH 21ST TO JUNE 12TH, 2001.

"Run, the old world is behind you   "

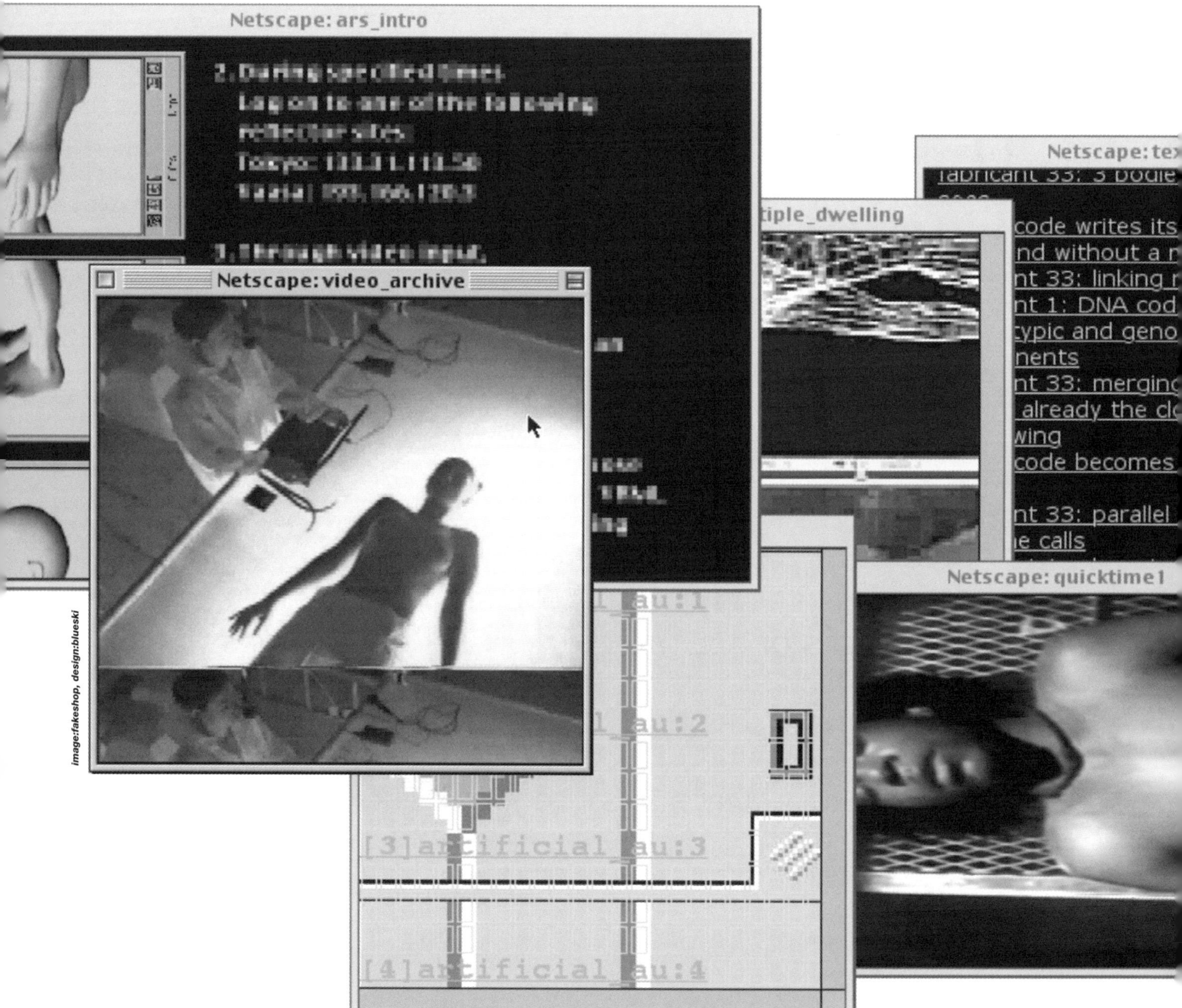

Netscape: ars_intro

2. During specified times:
Log on to one of the following
reflector sites:
Tokyo:
Osaka:

1. Through video input.

Netscape: video_archive

image:fakeshop, design:blueski

tiple_dwelling

Netscape: tex

fabricant 33: 3 bodie

code writes its
nd without a r
nt 33: linking r
nt 1: DNA cod
typic and geno
nents
nt 33: merging
already the cl
wing
code becomes

nt 33: parallel
e calls

Netscape: quicktime1

[3]artificial_au:3

[4]artificial_au:4

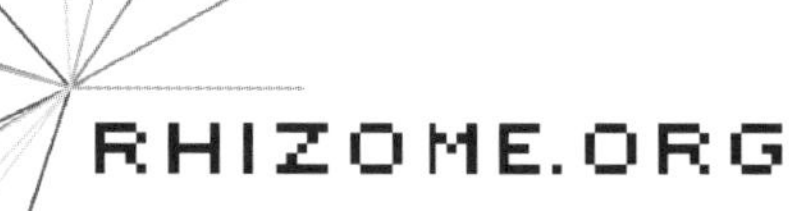

RHIZOME.ORG

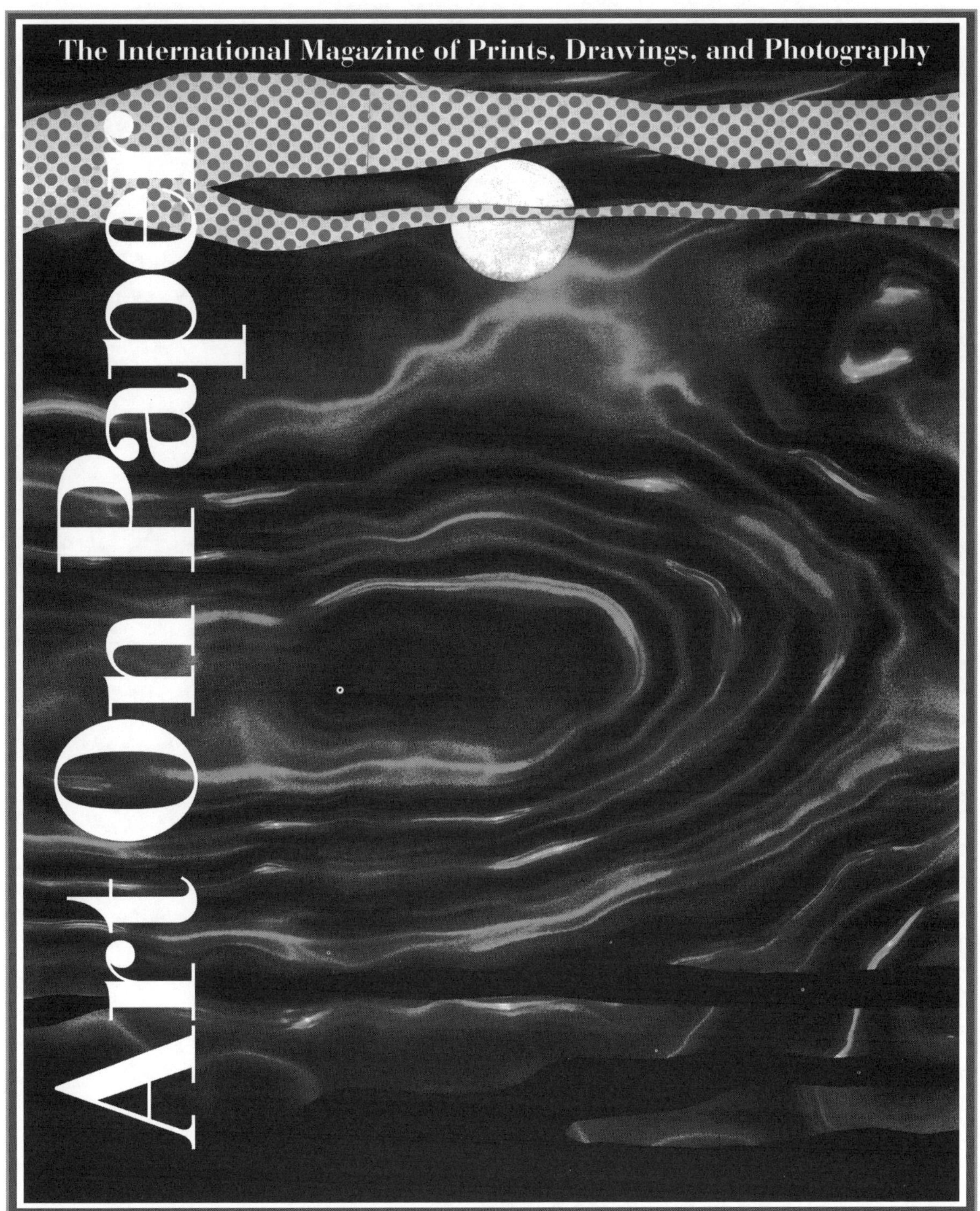
The International Magazine of Prints, Drawings, and Photography
Art On Paper

BLIND SPOT

ISSUE SIXTEEN $14

DOUG AITKEN

DAVID ARMSTRONG

JITKA HANSLOVA

DAMIEN HIRST

MIRIAM LAPLANTE

ENRIQUE MARTY

GEORGES ROUSSE

This Issue Comes to Life

BLIND SPOT EXHIBITION

with support from eyestorm

December 14 - January 27

Robert Mann Gallery
210 Eleventh Avenue
New York, NY 10001

WWW.BG-GALERIE.CH

AUSSTELLUNGSSTRASSE 24, 8005 ZÜRICH
T 01 278 40 60—F 01 278 40 50—INFO@BG-GALERIE.CH

Klaus Born
8. Dezember–27. Januar—Eröffnung 7. Dezember 2000—18–21 Uhr

Niklaus Rüegg
2. Februar–10. März—Eröffnung 1. Februar 2001—18–21 Uhr

DI–FR 12–18—SA 11–16

C = K + E*

Switzerland's top class strategic consultancy for corporations, industrial leaders and other artists.

Please ask for further details:

Klaus J. Stöhlker AG
Zollikerstrasse 114
CH-8702 Zollikon-Zürich
Tel. ++41-1-396 48 88
Fax ++41-1-396 48 80
klaus.stohlker@stohlker.ch
www.stohlker.ch

Stöhlker & Partner GmbH
Alt-Stralau 19
D-10245 Berlin
Tel. ++49-30-216 40 54
Fax ++49-30-216 20 36
mail@stoehlker.de
www.stoehlker.com

*** Communication = Knowledge + Energy**

29. MÄRZ – 1. APRIL 2001

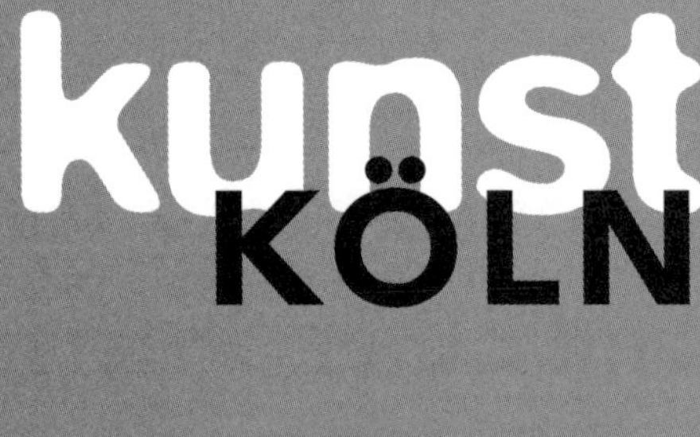

kunst
KÖLN
2001

Internationale Messe
für Editionen, Art Brut,
Kunst nach 1960

weitere Informationen:
KölnMesse GmbH
Messeplatz 1, D-50679 Köln
tel. (0)221/821-3215, fax (0)221/821-3734
www.kunst-koeln.de

KölnMesse

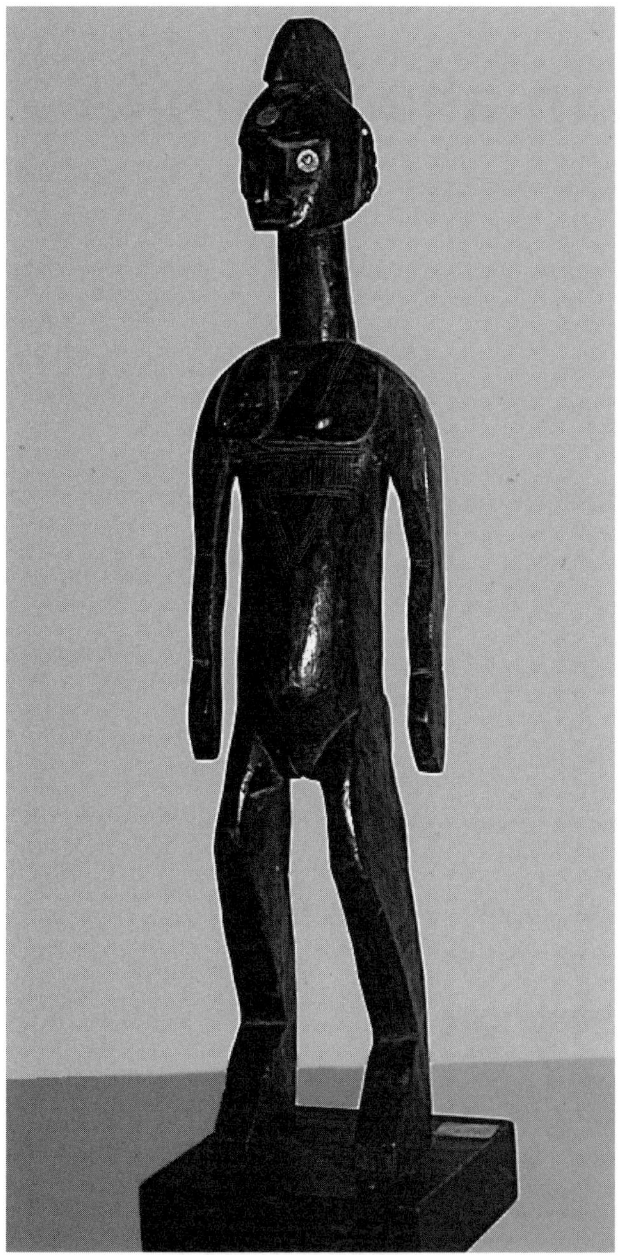

AFRIKANISCHE UND OZEANISCHE KUNST

24. NOVEMBER - 23. DEZEMBER 2000

GALERIE PATRIK FRÖHLICH

DIENERSTRASSE 21, 8004 ZÜRICH, FON+FAX: 01 242 89 00
email:patrikfroehlich@access.ch, www.artnet.com/pfroehlich.html

Mittwoch bis Freitag  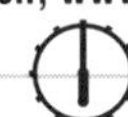 **Samstag**  

John M Armleder

Sylvie Fleury

Gaylen Gerber

Peter Z. Herzog

Thomas Hirschhorn

Jean-Luc Manz

Thom Merrick

Olivier Mosset

Gerwald Rockenschaub

Muntean/Rosenblum

Adrian Schiess

Galerie Susanna Kulli

Davidstrasse 40

CH-9000 St. Gallen

Tel. 071 223 59 58

Fax 071 223 59 35

www.susannakulli.ch

Offen:

Di bis Fr 14–18, Sa 10–17

Kunst

2001

Zürich

International Contemporary Art Fair

23–26 November

ABB Hall 550

Zurich-Oerlikon

Phone +41 1 381 00 52

www.kunstzuerich.ch

Combined Ticket for city art museums

of Zurich and Winterthur

Tourist Service

Phone +41 1 215 40 00

Open Gallery Weekend

24–25 November

28. April–1. Mai 2001
art frankfurt
Die europäische Messe für junge Kunst: New Attitudes, Kunst ab den
60er Jahren, Editions District, ArtKino. Für Fachbesucher und Publikum.
11–20 Uhr. Messe Frankfurt, Halle 1, Eingang City. Infoline +49 (0)69 7575 6694
www.artfrankfurt.de

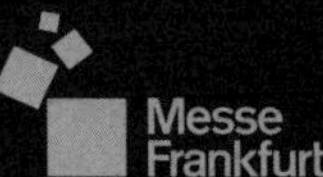
Messe
Frankfurt

Art | 32 | Basel | 13–18 | June | 2001
The Art Fair

Art 32 Basel, P.O. Box, CH-4021 Basel
Tel. +41 61 686 20 20, Fax +41 61 686 26 86, E-Mail: Info@ArtBasel.com, www.ArtBasel.com

Messe Basel.

sponsored by UBS

FOCUS: VIENNA

JOHANES ZECHNER + ERWIN BOHATSCH

24. November 2000 – 27. Januar 2001

GALERIE LELONG ZÜRICH

Utoquai 31 · 8008 Zürich · Telefon 01/251 11 20 · Fax 01/262 52 85

Öffnungszeiten: DI–FR 11–18 Uhr, SA 11–16 Uhr

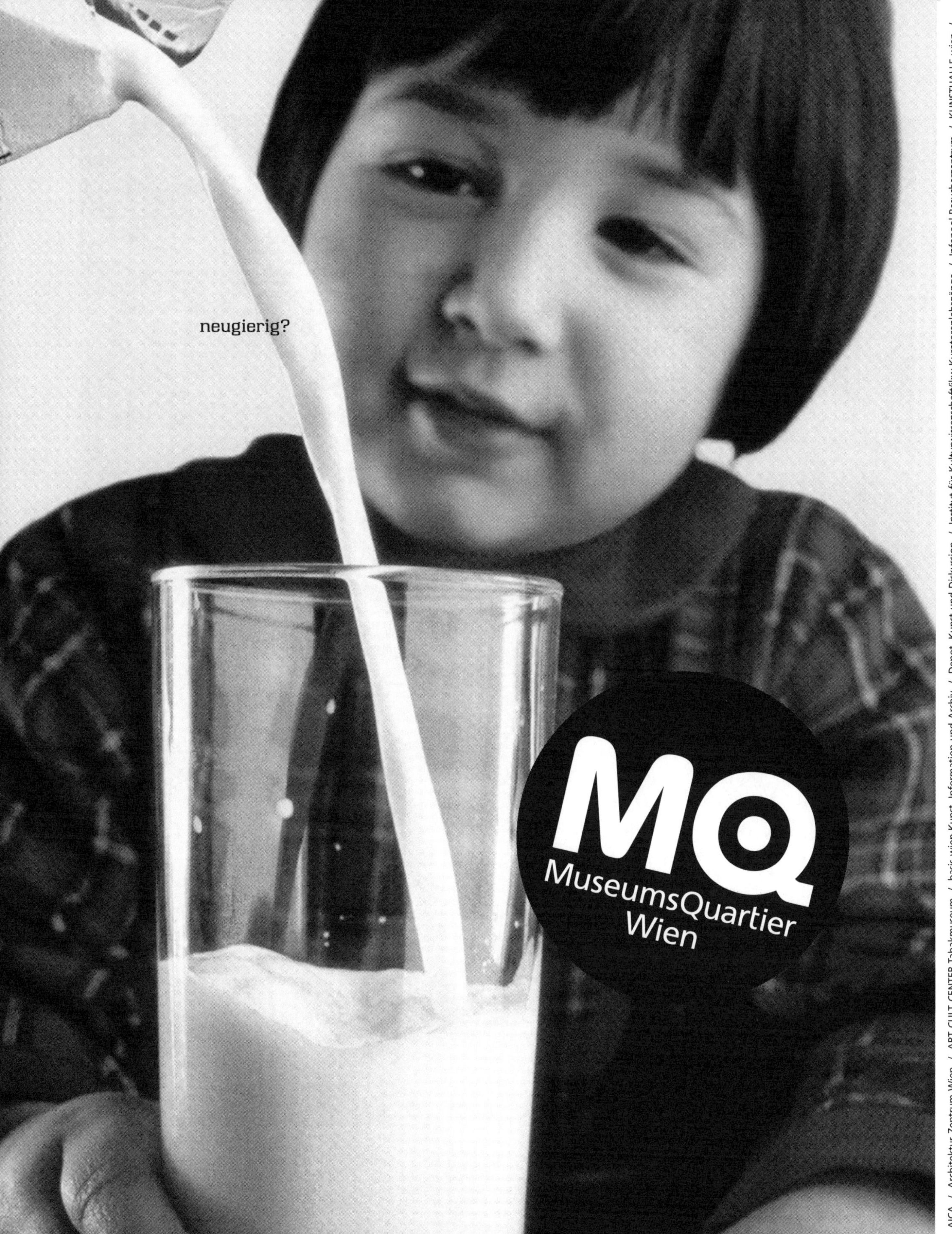

neugierig?
MQ
MuseumsQuartier Wien
AICA / Architektur Zentrum Wien / ART CULT CENTER-Tabakmuseum / basis wien-Kunst, Information und Archiv / Depot. Kunst und Diskussion / Institut für Kulturwissenschaft/ikw-Kuratorenlehrgänge / Infopool-Besucherzentrum /
Leopold Museum / Museum moderner Kunst Stiftung Ludwig Wien / Public Netbase t0/Media-Space! / Quartier 21 / springerin-Hefte für Gegenwartskunst / Tanzquartier Wien / Theaterhaus für Kinder / Verband österreichischer Galerien
moderner Kunst / Wiener Festwochen / wienXtra-kinderinfo / ZOOM Kindermuseum / MuseumsQuartier Wien, Museumsplatz 1, A-1070 Wien, Tel.: +43/1/523 58 81, www.mqw.at / Eröffnung ab Juni 2001

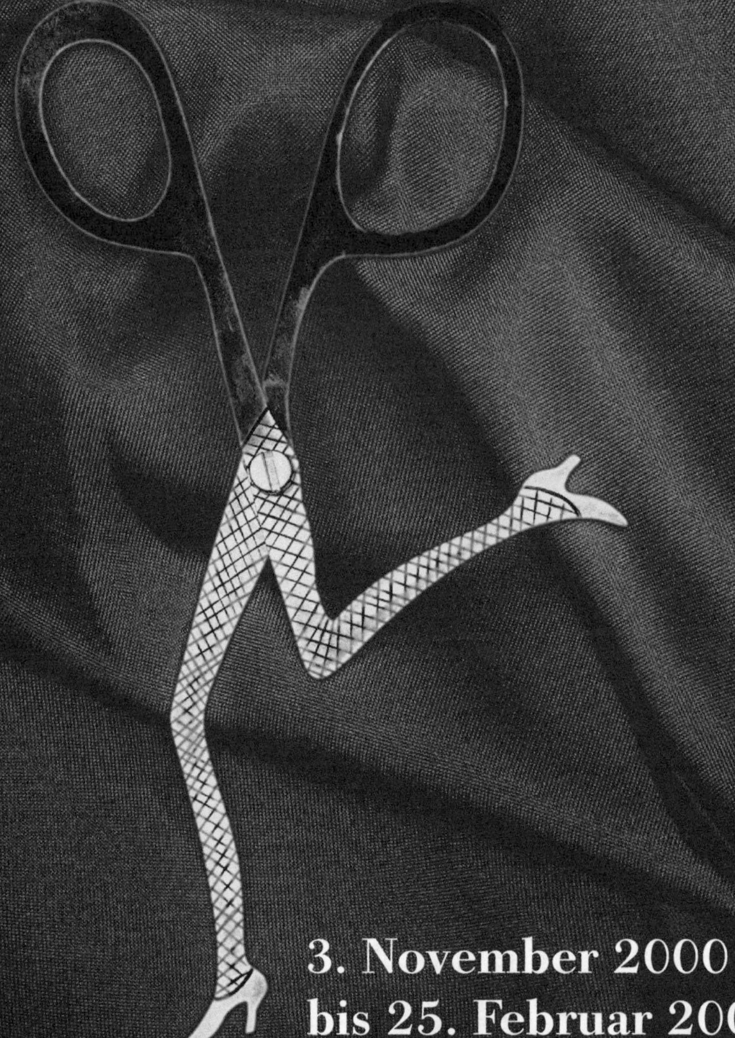
Leidenschaft ist unser Antrieb
Sigmar Polke – Die gesamten Editionen (1963–2000)
3. November 2000
bis 25. Februar 2001
Kunst- und Ausstellungshalle der Bundesrepublik Deutschland
Museumsmeile Bonn · Friedrich-Ebert-Allee 4 · 53113 Bonn ·
Telefon 0228/ 9171-200 · www.bundeskunsthalle.de
Dienstag – Mittwoch 10 – 21 Uhr, Donnerstag bis Sonntag 10 – 19 Uhr, Freitag kostenloser Eintritt
für Schulklassen, Montag sowie 24. und 31. Dezember geschlossen

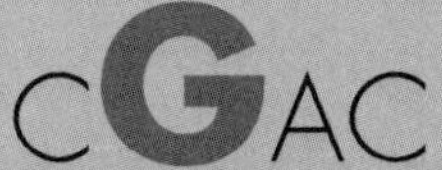

Rúa Ramón del Valle Inclán s/n
15704 Santiago de Compostela
Tel. + 34 981 546 619
Fax + 34 981 546 605
cgac@xunta.es
www.cgac.org

Exhibition Programme
December 2000 - May 2001

Georges Rousse. Interventions
Closing December 10

French and Italian Artists in ARCO
Foundation and CGAC Collections
Closing January 7

Sarah Dobai
Closing January 7

Florence Paradeis
Closing January 7

Mondophrenetic™
Closing January 14

Stephan Balkenhol
January - April

Garage
January - February

Marine Hugonnier
February - April

Vari Caramés
February - April

Juan Navarro Baldeweg
Mars - May

Peter Wüthrich
April - July

Efraín Almeida
April - July

Pamen Pereira
April - July

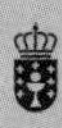

XUNTA DE GALICIA
CONSELLERÍA DE CULTURA,
COMUNICACIÓN SOCIAL E TURISMO

karyn lovegrove gallery

Polly Apfelbaum
Ingrid Calame
Floyd Claypool
Francesca Gabbiani
Bill Henson
Candida Höfer
Axel Hütte
Paul Morrison
Callum Morton
Simon Periton
Annelies Strba
Ricky Swallow

Karyn Lovegrove Gallery
6150 Wilshire Boulevard #8
Los Angeles CA 90048 USA
Telephone: 323 525 1755
Facsimile: 323 525 1245
Email: lovegrovek@aol.com
www.karynlovegrovegallery.com

SEAN KELLY GALLERY

43 MERCER STREET
NEW YORK NY 10013
TELEPHONE 212 343-2405
FAX 212 343-2604
www.skny.com

Callum Innes

DECEMBER 1 2000 - JANUARY 13 2001

Thomas Joshua Cooper

JANUARY 18 2001 - MARCH 3 2001

The Armory Show 2001

FEBRUARY 23 2001 - FEBRUARY 26 2001

Pier 88 Booth #100
The Show Piers on the Hudson

THOMAS AMMANN FINE ART AG ZURICH

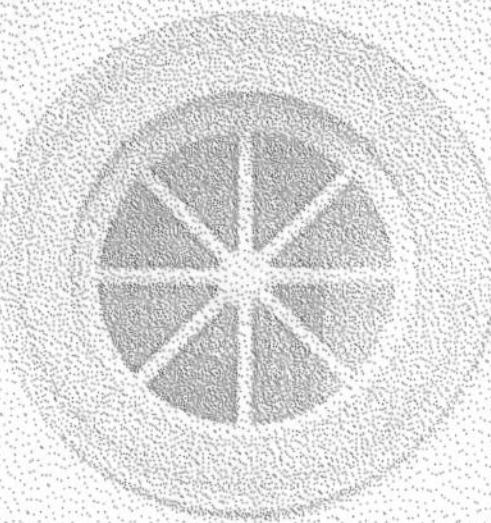

IMPRESSIONIST & 20TH CENTURY MASTERS

SELECTED WORKS BY MAJOR ARTISTS

BACON
BALTHUS
BEUYS
BRAQUE
CALDER
CHAGALL
ERNST
GIACOMETTI
KANDINSKY
KIRCHNER
KLEE
DE KOONING
LEGER
LICHTENSTEIN
MARDEN
MATISSE
MIRO
PICASSO
RYMAN
ROTHKO
TAAFFE
TWOMBLY
WARHOL

RESTELBERGSTRASSE 97   CH-8044 ZÜRICH   TEL. (411) 360 51 60   FAX (411) 360 51 61

www.ammann-fineart.ch

markus**lüpertz**

paintingssculptures

24 november 2000 – 17 january 2001

catherine**lee**

bronze

24 february – 7 april 2001

galerie jamileh weber

waldmannstrasse 6
ch–8001 zurich
telefon +41 1 252 10 66
telefax +41 1 252 11 32
www.jamilehweber.com
jamilehweber@access.ch
tu-fr 11–18h, sa 10–16h
and by appointment